EVERYMAN, I will go with thee,
and be thy guide,
In thy most need to go by thy side

for George and Jane Bornstein

Πρόσωπα τῆς ἀγάπης, ὅπως τἄθελεν ἡ ποίησίς μου

C. A. Patrides is G. B. Harrison Professor of English Literature in the University of Michigan at Ann Arbor. An Honored Scholar of the Milton Society and twice Guggenheim Fellow, he is the author and editor of well over twenty works on the literature of the Renaissance, including the companion Everyman volume of *The English Poems of George Herbert* (1974).

The Complete English Poems of John Donne

Edited by C. A. PATRIDES

G. B. Harrison Professor of English Literature
University of Michigan at Ann Arbor

Dent: London and Melbourne
EVERYMAN'S LIBRARY

Phototypeset in 10/11pt VIP Bembo by
D. P. Media Limited, Hitchin, Hertfordshire
Printed and bound in Great Britain by
Richard Clay (The Chaucer Press) plc, Bungay, for
J. M. Dent & Sons Ltd
Aldine House, 33 Welbeck Street, London W1M 8LX
First published in Everyman Paperback, 1985

British Library Cataloguing in Publication Data

Donne, John
   The complete English poems of John Donne.—
   (Everyman's library)
   I. Title   II. Patrides, C.A.
   821'.3   PR2245

   ISBN 0-460-10091-2
   ISBN 0-460-11091-8 Pbk

Contents

To the Reader

My primary responsibility in this edition has been to provide a reliable text; my secondary, to resist an excess of annotation; and my third, to avoid the impertinence of mere paraphrases, save where explication was self-evidently required.

A Note on Abbreviations

References in parentheses involving letters (e.g., *JRR*, *TS*, etc.) are expanded in the list of abbreviations, below, p. 510. References in parentheses involving numbers preceded by the symbol § (e.g., §79, §341, etc.) are to the numbered entries in the bibliography, below, pp. 510–556.

Readings from various editions and manuscripts are identified in the notes with a formula. For example, 'acc. to 1635–69 and several MSS' means that the reading given is 'according to the editions published from 1635 to 1669 as well as several of the reported manuscripts'.

Biblical quotations are from the King James ('Authorized') Version of 1611, unless otherwise stated. The place of publication is given only if it is other than London or New York.

The Text

The text of Donne's poetry can vex an editor into nightmares. The only substantial poems published during his lifetime are the two *Anniversaries* and the related 'Funerall Elegie'; nearly everything else appeared posthumously, principally though not entirely in the *Poems* of 1633 and 1635. Additionally, however, we have numerous manuscripts – detailed in §§158, 163, and 168, but especially in Peter Beal's remarkably inclusive *Index of English Literary Manuscripts*, Vol. I: *1450–1625*

(1980), pp. 243–555 – which are notable for their variable authority, variable contents, and variable readings. The present edition rests on the following principles:

1. The basic text is of the *Poems* of 1633, as supplemented by the *Poems* of 1635 and such later editions through and beyond the last in the seventeenth century (1669) as appeared to be relevant. The authority of the printed versions has been defended by Donne's most formidable editor, Sir Herbert Grierson (§158), and by constructive textual critics like George Williamson (§188). The further reason I had for accepting that authority is deceptively simple: save for Donne's lifetime, his reputation to our own century is based on the printed versions, not on the manuscripts.

2. The authority of the printed versions is itself variable, however. In particular, poems first published in the 1669 edition are here approached with great caution and amended liberally in the light of the manuscripts. After all, only the 1669 edition managed so to misread a line in 'The Extasie' (l. 4) as to displace 'Sat we two, one anothers best' by 'Sate we on one anothers breasts'!

3. The various *general* subdivisions of Donne's poetry (e.g. *Songs and Sonets*, *Letters to Severall Personages*, etc.) are duplicated from their strict arrangement in the *Poems* of 1635. The *individual* poems within each subdivision (e.g. 'The Extasie' in *Songs and Sonets*, 'The Calme' in *Letters to Severall Personages*, etc.) are here arranged according to their sequence in 1635 (cf. the different arrangement in the *Poems* of 1633, below, Appendix I), and thereafter as they happen to appear in all other editions (irrelevant poems that often interrupt the sequence – that is to say, commendatory poems on Donne and poems erroneously ascribed to him – are of course bypassed). Thus, the subdivision *Songs and Sonets* begins with 'A Flea' (34th in 1633, but first in 1635) and 'The good-morrow' (8th in 1633, but second in 1635); there follow, as in both 1633 and 1635, the twenty-five poems up to and including 'Loves Alchymie'; and so on through the other poems as first published in 1633, next in 1635 ('Farewell to love' and 'A Lecture upon the Shadow'), then in 1649 ('Sonnet. The Token'), and finally in 1650 ('Selfe Love').

4. Readings provided by the reported manuscripts have been adopted only where the early printed versions are self-evidently inadequate; but even then I was mindful of (a) the relative authority of the various manuscripts, (b) the extent to which they agree among themselves, and (c) the respect they must command often – but not, I would insist, always – in verbal matters. I have certainly not presumed to offer my own emendations when the printed versions and the principal reported manuscripts opposed me.

5. Variants within different 'states' of any single edition – that is to say, the occasional provision of different readings in one and the same edition – are mentioned in the footnotes only if they are of substantial importance.

6. Important readings in the reported manuscripts and the various early editions that happen to differ from the readings in my text are incorporated in the footnotes. Such readings, like the variants (see #5), provide opportunities for each reader to construct his own text or, at the very least, to observe how others read – or, indeed, misread – a line, a phrase, or a word. The restriction of the textual apparatus to matters of self-evident importance, however, has had an unfortunate consequence: I was obliged to bypass several hilarious misreadings, such as a manuscript's transmutation of our 'sin-burd'ned soules' ('The Storme', l. 47) into 'Sun-burnt soules'!

7. The punctuation adheres most closely to the original sources (see #1 and #4): unwarranted editorial emendations have been generally avoided, on the principle that 'the old punctuation is a better guide' (§188). Sometimes in disagreement with every other modern editor, I have retained the 1633 punctuation even in cases such as the following two:

> Women, are like the Arts, forc'd unto none,
> Open to'all searchers, unpriz'd, if unknowne.
> (Elegy III, ll. 5–6)

> By thee the seely Amorous sucks his death
> By drawing in a leprous harlots breath,
> By thee, the greatest staine to mans estate
> Falls on us, to be call'd effeminate;
> (Elegy IV, ll. 59–62)

In the former example, all modern editors have removed the 1633 comma after 'Women'; and in the latter, displaced the 1633–39 comma after 'breath' with the 1650–69 semicolon. The emendations make excellent grammatical sense; but, I would argue, they impair the *dramatic* sense, in the first case by depriving it of its telling staccato rhythm, and in the second of its equally meaningful torrential explosiveness.

8. The wording and the punctuation have been emended whenever an emendation was obviously required; nor did I provide a footnote to that effect in each case since I wanted to reduce pedantry to an absolute minimum. My silent emendations include, for example, my displacement of the basic 1633 text in 'Twicknam garden', l. 24, where 'womans' (acc. to many MSS) corrects 'womens' (acc. to 1633–69 and some MSS); in 'The Baite', l. 18, where 'with' (acc. to all MSS) corrects 'which' (acc. to 1633); in 'Loves diet', l. 25, where 'reclaim'd' (acc. to 1635–69 and most MSS) corrects 'redeem'd' (acc. to 1633); or in 'Loves growth', ll. 6–7, where I have removed the 1633 break between the lines since it destroys the form evidently intended. Thus, too, in punctuation: my comma, for example, in 'A Lecture upon the Shadow', l. 4, silently corrects both the semicolon of 1635–39 and the colon of 1650–69.

9. As different editions approach Donne's text differently, a study of their diverse principles is instructive in itself. The committed reader would doubtless wish to ponder the reasons for the provision by A. J. Smith of a modernized text (§166), and by Helen Gardner of one heavily dependent on select manuscripts (§§168–69, also §170). The present effort has benefited vastly from three other editions in particular: Grierson's, which is indispensable by virtue as much of the answers it supplies as of the questions it raises (§158); John Hayward's, which may compromise much but does so, I think, in order to remain editorially self-effacing (§159); and John T. Shawcross's, which may at times be adventurous in its annotation but, in textual matters, confirms one's belief that common sense should always reign supreme (§163).

10. For particular reasons, the text of two poems deviates from the principles stated above: 'A Letter to the Lady Carey, and Mrs Essex Riche', which is here reproduced from the

unique copy in Donne's hand (p. 303), and 'Henrico Wottoni in Hibernia belligeranti', which is transcribed from the Burley manuscript (p. 321).

11. The text of the two *Anniversaries* is basically that of the first editions of 1611 and 1612 respectively, as edited by Frank Manley in 1963 (§167). It is reprinted here with the permission of The Johns Hopkins University Press.

12. No attempt has been made to theorize on dates of composition. As I indicate on two occasions (below, pp. 46 and 135), we lack the information needed in order firmly to determine the dates of most poems.

The textual principles once established, however, the editor of Donne's poetry would be well advised to approach them with scepticism. One should ever hold in mind that the single poem we possess in Donne's own handwriting (see below, p. 303) would not have been admitted as reliable textual witness had we not known that it is by Donne himself! More to the point, we may not presume that a 'definitive' or 'final' text is even possible, not only because the witnesses to such a text are far too variable, but especially because Donne would have provided one had he cared half as much about the state of his poems as did either Jonson or Milton.

For some reflections on the various editorial practices evident in the preparation of Donne's text, the interested reader may wish to consult my essay 'John Donne Methodized: or, How to improve Donne's impossible text with the assistance of his several editors', *MP*, 83 (1985).

A Note on the Symbol '

In the text, the symbol ' indicates that the two words flanking it – for example, *make'it* (below, p. 79, l. 6) – should be pronounced with hardly any break between them.

The Annotation

Traditionally, the textual apparatus and the annotation are kept apart; but here they are merged, to enable the reader to possess all relevant information at a glance.

The annotation is generally restrained: unfamiliar words are explained, obscure references clarified, grammatical complexities refined, and some unfamiliar constructions reconstituted. But to the extent that Donne's expansive sense depends on the linguistic and grammatical structures he favours, I demonstrate throughout this edition my conviction that ponderous annotation of his poetry would in fact severely restrict his meaning.

Acknowledgements

Over the nine years it has taken me to prepare this edition, different versions of my Introduction were delivered as lectures in universities and colleges ranging from those at Tel-Aviv, Florence, and Aberdeen, to those at Williamstown in Massachusetts, Kingston in Ontario, and Riverside in California. I am grateful to my patient audiences for having guided my efforts to understand Donne better than I did before they lent me their ears and habitually their counsel.

The preparation of this edition has involved any number of other pleasures, among them my re-reading of Donne's poetry in the most ideal context imaginable, the home of Messrs Iain Miller and Donald Matthews on the island of Lesbos. I have also been assisted greatly, and often crucially, by friends and colleagues who responded with alacrity to my pleas for help. For generous advice on my Introduction, the text, the annotation, and the bibliography, I am grateful to Professors Albert C. Labriola of Duquesne University, Marvin Murillo of Tulane University, and John R. Roberts of the University of Missouri at Columbia. For particularly indispensable advice, I am especially grateful to Professor John T. Shawcross of the University of Kentucky at Lexington and Raymond B. Waddington of the University of California at Davis.

Ever since I joined the Advisory Board of the proposed Variorum Edition of Donne's poetry, I benefited greatly by the assistance extended to me on a number of occasions by the Board's members. Characteristically, Professor Ernest W. Sullivan of Texas Tech University imparted to me his discovery of the partial text of Elegy XX published as early as 1654 (see below, p. 186), while Professor Ted-Larry Pebworth of the University of Michigan at Dearborn supplied me with essential materials inclusive of his transcription of the verse letter to Wotton in the Burley manuscript (p. 321).

The preparation of this edition was substantially affected by several sustained studies of Donne (notably those by Charles M. Coffin in 1937, J. B. Leishman in 1951, Clay Hunt in 1954, Arnold Stein in 1962, N. J. C. Andreasen in 1967, and John Carey in 1981), the labours of editors who preceded me in annotating Donne's poetry (notably Herbert Grierson in 1912, Helen Gardner in 1952–78, Theodore Redpath in 1956, A. L. Clements in 1966, W. Milgate in 1967–78, John T. Shawcross in 1967, Frank J. Warnke in 1967, and A. J. Smith in 1971), the often crucial explications of Donne's meaning by the scholars I mention in my notes and bibliography, and the Gordian resolutions of textual problems by first-rate textual critics like George Williamson (§188). But when all is said I remain, as I must, primarily indebted to the *OED*.

My previous university at York, and my present one at Ann Arbor, have supported this edition with subsidies in the form of clerical help, supplies provided, and grants awarded as a matter of course. But I am equally grateful to the staffs of their respective libraries, and to the staffs of the British Library, the Bodleian Library, the Cambridge University Library, and the New York Public Library, who assisted me vitally at every turn.

I am finally grateful to The Johns Hopkins University Press for permission to reprint the text of Frank Manley's edition of *The Anniversaries* (§167); The Bodley Head for permission to make such use as I needed of John Hayward's edition (§159); Doubleday & Company Inc. for permission to lean on the text of John T. Shawcross's edition (§163); Methuen & Company Ltd for permission to reprint the Twickenham text of Pope's 'versifications' of two Donne satires, from the one-volume *Poems of Alexander Pope*, edited by John Butt (1963); and Faber & Faber Ltd and Harcourt Brace Jovanovitch Inc. for permission to reprint the extract from T. S. Eliot's 'Whispers of Immortality'.

Ann Arbor, December 1984   C. A. P.

An Outline of Donne's Life
within the context of contemporary events

[The most authoritative modern biography of Donne is by R. C. Bald (§196); but Izaak Walton's *Life* (§313) remains the one literary masterpiece within the canon of Donne's critical heritage. For more detailed chronologies of Donne's life, see Bald (§196: pp. 537–46), Shawcross (§163: pp. xiii–xvi), and A. J. Smith (§166: pp. 17–25); for a chronology of events, consult Patrides & Waddington (§109: pp. 365–69).]

1572　Donne born (sometime between 24 January and 19 June) in London, the third of six children of John and Elizabeth Donne. Ben Jonson born. Massacre of St Bartholomew.

1574　Joseph Hall born.

1575　Tasso's *Gerusalemme liberata* published.

1576　Donne's father died; his mother married Dr John Syminges.

1577　Donne's sister Elizabeth died. Drake's circumnavigation of the globe begins. Holinshed's *Chronicle* published.

1578　Donne's sisters Mary and Katherine died.

1579　Spenser's *Shepherds' Calendar* and North's translation of Plutarch published.

1580　Camoës died; John Webster born (?). Montaigne's *Essais* (I–II) published.

1584　Donne matriculated at Hart Hall (later absorbed into Hertford College), Oxford. William of Orange assassinated. Francis Beaumont born. Ralegh's colonization of Virginia fails.

1585　Ronsard died.

1587　Mary Queen of Scots executed. Marlowe's *Tamburlaine* (I–II) acted.

1588   Defeat of the Spanish Armada. Donne's stepfather died.
        Donne at Cambridge (?). Hobbes born.

1589   Donne possibly abroad to 1591 (?). Marlowe's *Dr Faustus* first (?) acted.

1590   Donne's mother married to Richard Rainford (1591?).
        Spenser's *Faerie Queene* (I–III) published. Du Bartas died.

1591   Herrick born. Harington's translation of Ariosto's *Orlando furioso* published.

1592   Donne admitted to Lincoln's Inn; Master of the Revels (1593). Montaigne died.

1593   Donne's brother Henry died. George Herbert, Izaak
        Walton born. Marlowe died. Hooker's *Of the Laws of Ecclesiastical Polity* (I–IV) published.

1594   Swan Theatre built (1596?). Tintoretto died.

1595   Sidney's *Apologie for Poetrie* and Spenser's *Amoretti* and
        Epithalamion published. *Midsummer Night's Dream*
        first (?) acted; also *Richard II*. War in Ulster. Ralegh's
        voyage to Guiana. Tasso died. Thomas Carew born.

1596   Donne takes part in the expedition to Cadiz. Spenser's
        Faerie Queene (IV–VI) published; also his *Four
        Hymns*. *The Merchant of Venice* first (?) acted. The
        Edict of Nantes. Descartes born.

1597   Donne takes part in the expedition to the Azores;
        becomes secretary to Sir Thomas Egerton, the Lord
        Keeper. Bacon's first ten *Essays*, Kepler's *Mysterium
        cosmographicum* published.

1598   Burghley died; also Philip II of Spain.

1599   Globe Theatre opened. Oliver Cromwell born. Spenser
        died. *Julius Caesar* and *Henry V* first acted.

1600   Fortune Theatre opened. Calderón born; also the future
        Charles I. Hooker died; Giordano Bruno burnt in
        Rome. *Hamlet* first (?) acted. William Gilbert's *De
        magnete* published.

1601   Donne Member of Parliament for Brackley, North-
        ampton; married secretly to Egerton's niece Anne
        More. Essex executed. *Twelfth Night* first (?) acted.

1602   Donne's marriage made public; dismissed from
        Egerton's service. Bodleian Library in Oxford opened.

1603   Peace in Ireland. Death of Elizabeth I; accession of James I. The Millenary Petition. Donne's daughter Constance born.

1604   Donne's son John born. The Hampton Court Conference. *Othello* first acted.

1605   Donne travels to France and possibly Italy (?); his third child George born. Bacon's *Advancement of Learning* published. The Gunpowder Plot. Sir Thomas Browne born. *King Lear* first (?) acted. Cervantes' *Don Quixote*, Part I, published (Part II in 1615).

1606   Donne moves to Mitcham. *Macbeth*, Jonson's *Volpone* and Tourneur's *Revenger's Tragedy* first (?) acted. Rembrandt, Corneille born.

1607   Donne takes lodgings in the Strand, London; his fourth child Francis born; Latin verses on *Volpone* published. *Antony and Cleopatra* first acted (1606?); also *Coriolanus* (1608?). First successful English colony founded, in Virginia.

1608   Donne's fifth child Lucy born. Robert Cecil created Earl of Salisbury, appointed Lord Treasurer. Milton born. Sylvester's translation of Du Bartas: 1st complete edition.

1609   Donne's sixth child Bridget born; 'The Expiration' published in Ferrabosco's *Ayres*. Spenser's *Faerie Queene*: 1st folio edition. Shakespeare's *Sonnets* published.

1610   Donne obtains honorary M.A. from Oxford; incorporated at Cambridge; his *Pseudo-Martyr* published. Jonson's *Alchemist* first acted; also Shakespeare's *Winter's Tale* (1611?). Galileo reports on his telescopic view of the heavens. Henry IV of France assassinated; accession of Louis XIII (Marie de' Medici regent).

1611   Donne's seventh child Mary born; *Ignatius his Conclave* and *The First Anniversary* published; with Sir Robert Drury on the Continent (to 1612). The King James ('Authorized') Version of the Bible published. *The Tempest* first (?) acted. Chapman's *Iliad* completed, followed by *The Odyssey* (1614–15). Charles IX of

Sweden died; accession of Gustavus Adolphus (to 1632).

1612 Donne's two *Anniversaries* published; also 'Breake of day' in Corkine's *Second Booke of Ayres*; his eighth child stillborn. Prince Henry, the heir apparent, died; also Salisbury. Robert Carr, later Earl of Somerset, in favour. Last burning of a heretic in England.

1613 Donne's ninth child Nicholas born, died within the year; his elegy on Prince Henry published in *Lachrymae lachrymarum* (3rd ed.). Princess Elizabeth married to Frederick Elector Palatine. Sir Thomas Overbury murdered. Cleveland, Crashaw born.

1614 Donne Member of Parliament for Taunton, Somerset; his children Mary and Francis died. Ralegh's *History of the World* published. Webster's *Duchess of Malfi* first (?) acted. El Greco died.

1615 Donne ordained deacon and priest at St Paul's Cathedral; appointed a royal chaplain; made honorary D.D. at Cambridge; his tenth child Margaret born. George Villiers, later Duke of Buckingham, in favour.

1616 Donne chosen Divinity Reader at Lincoln's Inn; his eleventh child Elizabeth born. Shakespeare died. Jonson's *Works* published.

1617 Donne delivers his first sermon at Paul's Cross, preaches thereafter widely; his twelfth child stillborn (surviving by now: seven); death of his wife Anne.

1618 The Synod of Dort. The Thirty Years War (to 1648). Ralegh executed. Bacon appointed Lord Chancellor. Cowley born.

1619 Donne with Viscount Doncaster's embassy to Germany (to early 1620). Kepler's *De harmonice mundi* published. Inigo Jones begins the Whitehall Banqueting House (completed 1622).

1620 The Pilgrim Fathers sail in the *Mayflower* and found Plymouth Colony in New England. Bacon's *Novum organum* published.

1621 Donne appointed Dean of St Paul's. Bacon impeached. Burton's *Anatomy of Melancholy* published. Marvell,

La Fontaine born. Philip III of Spain died; accession of Philip IV (to 1665)

1622 Two of Donne's sermons published, followed by others (1623 ff.); Henry Vaughan, Molière born.

1623 Donne seriously ill. The 1st Shakespeare Folio published. Pascal born.

1624 Donne's *Devotions upon Emergent Occasions* published. Cardinal Richelieu chief minister in France.

1625 Death of James I; accession of Charles I who married Henrietta Maria of France. Outbreak of the plague. Nicholas Ferrar settles at Little Gidding in Huntingdonshire. Milton admitted to Christ's College, Cambridge. Webster died.

1626 Lancelot Andrewes, Bacon died. John Aubrey born.

1627 Donne's daughter Lucy died; also Sir Henry Goodyer, the Countess of Bedford, and Magdalen Lady Danvers (Herbert's mother). War with France (to 1629).

1628 The Petition of Right. Buckingham assassinated. William Harvey's discovery of the circulation of the blood published. Bunyan born. Malherbe died.

1630 Donne's final illness began. Prince Charles (later Charles II) born. The Great Migration to Massachusetts begins; Boston founded.

1631 Donne died 31 March, survived by six of his twelve children. Dryden born.

[Published posthumously: *Poems* (1633, reissued and often augmented thereafter to 1669); *Juvenilia* (1633); *Biathanatos* (c. 1646); *Paradoxes* etc. (1652); *Essays in Divinity* (1651); *Death's Duell* [his last sermon] (1632), *LXXX Sermons* (1640), *Fifty Sermons* (1649), *XXVI Sermons* (1660), as well as other sermons published individually and in shorter collections; *Letters to Severall Persons of Honour* (1651) as well as other letters in a number of collections including Gosse's (below, p. 522); and other editions of *Ignatius his Conclave* (1634), *Devotions* (1634), etc. For details, consult Keynes (§153).]

'Extreme, and scattring bright': The Poetry of John Donne

> With Donne, whose muse on dromedary trots,
> Wreathe iron pokers into true-love knots;
> Rhyme's sturdy cripple, fancy's maze and clue,
> Wit's forge and fire-blast, meaning's press and screw.
>
> Coleridge, 'On Donne's Poetry' (1818?)

> Donne, I suppose, was such another
> Who found no substitute for sense,
> To seize and clutch and penetrate;
> Expert beyond experience,
>
> He knew the anguish of the marrow
> The ague of the skeleton;
> No contact possible to flesh
> Allayed the fever of the bone.
>
> T.S.Eliot, 'Whispers of Immortality' (1920)

I

Donne is in the first instance coarse. The judgement is ventured in earnest, and meant not in denigration but in praise. In extreme reaction to the mellifluous verses of his immediate predecessors and contemporaries, he deployed extreme means in order to focus attention on neglected dimensions of human experience. We may with Ben Jonson sever the means deployed from the experience illumined, offended by the one ('Done for not keeping of accent deserved hanging') yet appreciative of the other ('Done [is] the first poet in the World in some things').* We may also, with Henry Hallam, scan only the means, and thereby conclude – as conclude we must – that 'Donne is the most inharmonious of our versifiers, if he can be

---

* As reported by William Drummond of Hawthornden (*Ben Jonson*, ed. C. H. Herford and Percy Simpson [Oxford, 1925], I, 133 and 135). The abbreviations in use throughout are explained above, p. 1.

said to have deserved such a name by lines too rugged to seem metre'.[1] On the face of it, certainly, Donne's violation of 'accent' – 'the chiefe Lord and grave Governour of Numbers' or metre, according to Samuel Daniel[2] – appears very nearly to have wrecked poetry, much as Joyce's deviant tactics seem to have dismantled the novel. But in Donne as in Joyce manner aspires to an engagement with matter, and the mode of articulation with that which is articulated. The risks taken were manifestly grave; but we may consider that English poetry since Donne could not – and, demonstrably, did not – confine itself to the range that obtained before his advent. His patterns of thought were, as patterns of thought, not unique; but the frequent harshness surrounding those patterns, the intentionally *bent* sounds, pierced realms no poet had yet ventured to explore. In this respect it is an understatement even to claim as I claimed, that Donne is in the first instance coarse.

II

Francis Thompson in 1899 commended Donne as 'pungent, clever, with metre like a rope all hanks and knots'.[3] Thompson is in the direct line of descent from Thomas Carew who in his elegy on Donne – itself the seventeenth century's most perceptive exercise in literary criticism (below, p. 496) – praised the 'masculine expression', the robust metrical and linguistic calisthenics:

> Our stubborne language bends, made only fit
> With her tough-thick-rib'd hoopes to gird about
> Thy Giant phansie
>
> (ll. 50–2)

Yet this is precisely what Dryden disapproved when he wished that Donne 'had taken care of his words, and of his numbers',

1. In his *Introduction to the Literature of Europe* (1837–9), quoted in §756: p. 316.
2. *A Defence of Rhyme* (1603?), in *Elizabethan Critical Essays*, ed. G. Gregory Smith (Oxford, 1904), II, 379.
3. *Literary Criticism*, ed. Terence L. Connolly (1948), p. 251.

eschewing in particular his habitual 'rough cadence'.[4] Those antagonistic to Donne, in other words, condemn precisely what his partisans approve. What does the practice of Donne suggest?

Two widely loved poems point the way. The first is the song beginning 'Sweetest love, I do not goe'; the other, 'A Valediction forbidding mourning'. The song expresses a single mood in very simple terms. Its tone is quintessentially melodious, gentle, serene:

> Sweetest love, I do not goe,
>   For wearinesse of thee,
> Nor in hope the world can show
>   A fitter Love for mee . . .

– and so on for some thirty-five more lines in perfectly modulated iambic rhythm. It is of course obvious that the song is utterly different from the poems usually regarded as characteristically Donne's.[5] Did he write it to proclaim his competence in a mode the other poems reject? But I submit that it was also meant as a norm – a metrical norm – we should recall whenever the slightest deviation is detected elsewhere. In 'A Valediction forbidding mourning', for instance, the nominal argument is that lovers may without alarm be parted physically since they are joined spiritually; yet the comforting thought is phrased rather oddly:

> Dull sublunary lovers love
>   (Whose soule is sense) cannot admit
> Absence, because it doth remove
>   Those things which elemented it.

4. *A Discourse concerning the Original and Progress of Satire* (1693) and *An Essay of Dramatic Poesy* (1668), respectively; in *Essays of John Dryden*, ed. W. P. Ker (Oxford, 1900), I, 52, and II, 102.
5. For a different reading of the poem, the emphasis on its 'disjunction of argument' however muted, consult Murray Roston (§287: Ch. II).

But we by a love, so much refin'd,
    That our selves know not what it is,
Inter-assured of the mind,
    Care lesse, eyes, lips, hands to misse.
                    (ll. 13–20)

The oddity is in the last line, which in accordance with the
norm should have had only four stresses but has six:

    Cáre lésse, eýes, líps, hánds to mísse.

In traditionally idealistic versions, we may remind ourselves,
the rhythm adheres to the basic iambic pattern. Shakespeare,
for instance, wrote of

                    sweet beauty's best,
    Of hánd, of fo'ot, of líp, of eýe, of brów,
                    (Sonnet CVI, ll. 5–6)

Donne could be just as regular when the occasion demanded:

        the great soule which here amongst us now
Doth dwell, and moves that hánd, and tóngue, and brów,
                    (*Metempsycosis*, ll. 61–2)

Where he wished to be emphatic, however, he deviated from
the norm as in the arrangement of the crucial words in a
strongly-accented sequence:

  Hath my náme, wórds, hánd, fe'et, he'art, mínde and wít;
                ('To Mr R. W.: If, as mine is', l. 6)

or, much more relevant thematically:

        I never stoop'd so low, as they
        Which on an eýe, che'eke, líp, can prey,
                    ('Negative Love', ll. 1–2)

By the same token, the departure from the iambic pattern in
the line already quoted –

Cáre lésse, eýes, líps, hánds to mísse

– joins the intentionally reduced syllables[6] to affirm through the disturbed rhythm what the sense expressly denies. In short, the 'Valediction' may scarcely be regarded as 'perhaps the most consistently spiritual' of Donne's secular poems (§195: p. 225). Its nominal argument is nominal only so far as the narrator is concerned, for its actual argument – consciously on the part of the poet, 'unconsciously' on the part of the narrator – is that the physical separation of the lovers will matter very much, as matter very much it must. The detail may or may not persuade. But if we care to lavish on Donne's poetry the close study it demands, even a mere detail will alert us to the presence of a 'counter-movement' which, present in his best poems, is here confirmed through the expressly sexual orientation of his celebrated analogy of the two souls to 'stiffe' compasses:

> Thy soule the fixt foot, makes no show
>   To move, but doth, if the'other doe.
>
> And though it in the center sit,
>   Yet when the other far doth rome,
> It leanes, and hearkens after it,
>   And growes erect, as that comes home.
>
> (ll. 26–32)

The conflation of the spiritual and the physical in the 'Valediction' is commensurate to a like emphasis in the poems we are to examine later. In advance, however, it is well to understand in what sense Donne had – *pace* Dryden – 'taken care of his words, and of his numbers'. The generalization of that elegant poet and critic, John Crowe Ransom, still obtains: 'Donne's skill is of the highest technical expertness in English poetry' (§277: p. 286).

The skill is disclosed variously and, at its best, in direct

---

6. To seven, if one follows the text of 1633 as I do, in opposition to the increased regularity of eight syllables provided by the MSS (see below, p. 98, note on 20).

relation to the unfolding sense. True, where the skill coincides with the sense only fitfully, the weaknesses of Donne are displayed with impressive clarity. Lines often hesitate between prose and poetry, for instance:

> Let us love nobly, and live, and adde againe
> Yeares and yeares unto yeares,
>
> ('The Anniversarie', ll. 28–9)

or:

> For ill is ill, and good good still,
>
> ('Communitie', l. 2)

and again:

> If we love things long sought, *Age* is a thing
> Which we are fifty yeares in compassing.
>
> (Elegy IX, ll. 33–4)

Equally, we expect a poet to improve on the vapid supposition that 'some man, unworthy to be possessor of old or new love, himself being false or weak, thought his pain and shame would be lesser if on womankind he might his anger wreak'; and we are distressed when we read precisely that:

> Some man unworthy to be possessor
> Of old or new love, himselfe being false or weake,
> Thought his paine and shame would be lesser,
> If on womankind he might his anger wreake,
>
> ('Confined Love', ll. 1–4)

Where the skill is commensurate to the sense, however, Donne persuades utterly. The grammar and the punctuation are on such occasions wont to be tortuous in the extreme, broken in order forcefully to make a point as in 'The Canonization':

> And wee in us finde the'Eagle and the dove,
> The Phœnix ridle hath more wit
> By us, we two being one, are it.
>
> (ll. 22–4)

or syncopated in order to suggest the lover's agony as in 'The Legacie':

> When I dyed last, and Deare, I dye
>   As often as from thee I goe,
>   Though it be but an houre agoe,
> And Lovers houres be full eternity,
> I can remember yet, that I . . .
>
> (ll. 1 ff.)

– and so on. But the lines are also likely to respond to the demands of the sense, expanding in one instance, contracting in the next, and sometimes compacted within two monosyllables which herald the imminent change in the argument:

> Though shee were true, when you met her,
> And last, till you write your letter,
>   Yet shee
>   Will bee
> False, ere I come, to two, or three.
>
> ('Song: Goe, and catche', ll. 23–7)

or:

>   when thou
>   Art in anguish
>   And dost languish
>   For some one
>   That will none,
> Or prove as false as thou art now.
>
> ('The Message', ll. 19–24)

It may also be that the external form of Donne's poems is not casually conceived since four-fifths of the poems he cast in stanzas appear to employ patterns he did not repeat. But to what extent there is a conjunction of the form without and the argument within, must be left to the judgement – and possibly to the ingenuity – of the given reader.

My emphasis on Donne's attention to 'accent' is meant to balance the praise commonly bestowed on his language. Donne's originality does not reside in his linguistic pyrotechnics, however 'colloquial' their nature and surprising their effects. It resides in his manipulation of metre – 'metre like a rope all hanks and knots' – which alone is capable of conveying his stupendous range of tone. Granted that the satirists of the late sixteenth century deployed an equally 'astonishing roughness';[7] granted also that the Elizabethan dramatists provided him with numerous instances of variable cadences;[8] and granted, too, that non-dramatic poets at home and abroad had already exploited some of his more celebrated images, even the image of the compasses in the 'Valediction'.[9] These contexts are indispensable for a full cognizance of 'the moment', and could profitably be amplified by studies of the dramatic dimension inherent in 'dialogues' Platonic as well as Neoplatonic (Bembo, Leone Ebreo, Castiglione, *et al.*) no less than Augustinian (in the *Confessions*) and eventually scientific too (in Galileo's *Dialogues on the Two Great Systems of the World*, 1632). But details appertaining to the background do not necessarily clarify Donne's achievement in the immediate foreground, *id est*, his introduction into lyric poetry of elements innate to dramatic literature, his boldness in adjusting those elements to his immediate purposes, his use of variable cadences to evoke diverse emotional states. Within English poetry Donne's metrical innovations are comparable only to those of Gerard Manley Hopkins, save that the influence of Hopkins was limited while Donne's was extensive. Mindful but of Donne's striking opening lines, we identify readily the progeny of the equally dramatic starting points in Pope or Browning:

7. George Saintsbury, in *HG*, p. 15.
8. It is reported that Donne was 'a great frequenter of Playes' (Sir Richard Baker, *A Chronicle of the Kings of England* [1643], p. 156). But Donne's modern biographer, R. C. Bald, oddly counters that 'the drama seems to have left surprisingly few traces on Donne's work' (§196: p. 72). Surely the *dramatic* nature of that work is trace enough?
9. Its use by Guarini in Italy and Joseph Hall in England is noted by Mario Praz and F. P. Wilson, both cited in §250: p. 231. But see also the pertinent studies by Rosemary Freeman and Josef Lederer (§§39, 249).

> Shut, shut the door, good John! fatigu'd I said,
> Tye up the knocker, say I'm sick, I'm dead . . .
> (Epistle to Dr Arbuthnot)

> Now, don't, sir! Don't expose me! Just this once!
> This was the first and only time, I'll swear . . .
> (Mr Sludge, 'the Medium')

Donne's 'rough cadence' taught generations of poets to look with their ears.

III

We accept that Donne's poems are dramatic, and more specifically dramatic monologues presupposing a listener. Each has in consequence its particular 'voice', its distinct narrator; and each, its own 'theatrical' language.

The theatrical language encompasses the conceits, that is to say elaborate comparisons, extended analogies, or (in T. S. Eliot's phrase) 'distended metaphors and similes'.[10] The operative words here are not the nouns but the adjectives ('elaborate', 'extended', 'distended') which suggest dimensions beyond mere similitudes. As Eliot further explained, a conceit is 'the elaboration (contrasted with the condensation) of a figure of speech to the farthest stage to which ingenuity can carry it'.[11] Not designed for dull sublunary minds, it was often abused during the Renaissance; and aspiring writers were therefore often warned that conceits, and even the less hazardous similitudes, 'are not to be taken from things altogether different'.[12] One might after all leap over the decorous into the risible, as did the preacher heard by Du Perron: 'Lord, wipe my beak clean with the napkin of thy love'. In Donne's case, of course, there is always 'The Flea'.

10. 'Andrew Marvell' (1921), in §220: p. 262.
11. 'The Metaphysical Poets' (1921), *ibid.*, p. 242.
12. John Weemes, *The Christian Synagogue* (1623), p. 281.

'The Flea' was a very popular poem, and surprisingly tradi-
tional; for many poets had already pined to be fleas, hoping to
land on the bosom of their beloved and even (the ultimate
felicity this) to be slapped to death.[13] Donne's version is cer-
tainly erotic, possibly to the point of vulgarity; but it is also
highly ingenious, certainly to the point of exhilaration. The
argument, such as it is, involves the transmutation of the
amorous insect into a symbol of the desired union.[14] But it is
the technique that impresses, involving as it does a conceit
elaborated 'to the farthest stage to which ingenuity can carry
it'. Dr Johnson would not have approved, and did not; yet he
might have said of 'The Flea' what he remarked of another
whimsical work, Sir Thomas Browne's *Garden of Cyrus*, that it
is 'a perpetual triumph of fancy to expand a scanty theme'.[15]
And 'The Flea' is of the scantiest.

Conceits elaborated through an entire poem are most
unusual in Donne. So far, 'The Flea' is an exception; and so is
'The good-morrow':

> I wonder by my troth, what thou, and I
> Did, till we lov'd? were we not wean'd till then?
> But suck'd on countrey pleasures, childishly?
> Or snorted we in the seaven sleepers den?
> T'was so; But this, all pleasures fancies bee
> If ever any beauty I did see,
> Which I desir'd, and got, t'was but a dreame of thee.

13. The tradition, centred on the late mediaeval *Carmen de pulice*
    ascribed to Ovid (translated in §335: pp. 148–9), issued in a
    collection of over fifty poems in several languages gathered for
    Etienne Pasquier's *La Puce de Madame des Roches* (1582; see §§169,
    335, 361).
14. As Helen Gardner notes in §169: p. 174. Murray Roston detects
    in the poem 'an intellectual and emotional energy that belies its
    apparently casual tone' (§287: Ch. II).
15. 'The Life of Sir Thomas Browne' (1756), in Browne, *The Major
    Works*, ed. C. A. Patrides (1977), p. 494.

And now good morrow to our waking soules,
Which watch not one another out of feare;
For love, all love of other sights controules,
And makes one little roome an every where.
Let sea-discoverers to new worlds have gone,
Let Maps to other, worlds on worlds have showne,
Let us possesse one world, each hath one, and is one.

My face in thine eye, thine in mine appeares,
And true plaine hearts doe in the faces rest,
Where can we finde two better hemispheares
Without sharpe North, without declining West?
What ever dyes, was not mixt equally;
If our two loves be one, or, thou and I
Love so alike, that none doe slacken, none can die.

The conceit in 'The good-morrow', initiated in the wide-ranging allusions of the first stanza, surfaces in the reference to newly discovered lands in the second, advances promptly to new maps superimposed upon the old, links them with the hemispheric faces of the two lovers, suggests that the hemispheres of the world are to those of the faces as both are to the eyeballs, and proclaims at last the assimilation of the external globe by the self-sufficient lovers, their hemispheric entities now fused into one perfect sphere. The idealistic vision charms; but realistic as Donne was, he could not utterly forego the past when the lovers 'suck'd on countrey pleasures, childishly'. 'The good-morrow' delineates an aspiration, not an accomplished fact. The imperative is clear enough: '*Let* us possesse our world . . .' So is 'the modest tentativeness' of the concluding lines where two propositions are alike based upon an *if*:[16]

If our two loves be one, or, though and I
Love so alike, that none doe slacken, none can die.

16. As Arnold Stein observed in §449: p. 73. Louis L. Martz also argued, in a lecture, that Donne frequently resorted to 'the conditional *if*' in order to qualify his apparently unqualified claims.

Donne's poetry, it is clear, endures an expansion.

The expansion is also evident in Donne's use of several distinct narrators who not only include more than one woman but represent diverse and often conflicting attitudes. These attitudes do not cohere into a vision of 'the softness of love', as Dryden wished they might have done.[17] They cohere in terms of reality that encompasses not only softness but violent passion, tenderness as well as cynicism, restraint and frenzy, joy and unqualified hate. In Donne's words,

> To Love, and Griefe tribute of Verse belongs,
> But not of such as pleases when 'tis read,
>> ('The Triple Foole', ll. 17–18)

Extreme emotions, passionately felt, are conveyed in appropriately extreme terms. Love – '*all* love' – is 'fever'. It involves 'fire of Passion, sighes of ayre, / Water of teares, and earthly sad despaire'. It induces misery, for it is a 'spider . . . which transubstantiates all, / And can convert Manna to gall'.[18] Rebuffed, love can lead to hate; and indulged in strictly for sexual gratification – 'the tillage of a harsh rough man' – it can yield chillingly clinical epigrams on the male animal ('Men leave behinde them that which their sin showes, / And are, as theeves trac'd, which rob when it snows') or repulsive lines on the bestiality of woman:

> Thine's like the dread mouth of a fired gunne,
> Or like the hot liquid metalls newly runne
> Into clay moulds, or like to that Ætna
> Where round about the grasse is burnt away.
> Are not your kisses then as filthy, and more,
> As a worme sucking an invenom'd sore?[19]

17. Donne, said Dryden, 'perplexes the minds of the fair sex with nice speculations of philosophy, when he should engage their hearts, and entertain them with the softness of love' (*A Discourse* etc.: as above, note 5 [II, 19]).

18. *Seriatim*: 'To the Countess of Huntingdon: That ripe side of earth', l. 31; 'The Dissolution', ll. 9–10; and 'Twicknam Garden', ll. 6–7.

19. *Sapho to Philænis*, ll. 39–40, and Elegy VIII, ll. 39–44; respectively.

Lines of this order, it must be emphasized, are not only directed outwardly in furious denunciation of their recipient. Given the omnipresent dramatic context, they are also directed inwardly against the speaker in oblique condemnation of his obsessions.

The point is of some moment since we might be tempted to attribute to Donne attitudes characteristic of his narrators. We may certainly not deny the frequent cynicism of the *Songs and Sonets*, and especially the ultimate cynicism in 'Communitie':

> Chang'd loves are but chang'd sorts of meat,
> And when hee hath the kernell eate,
> 　Who doth not fling away the shell?
>
> 　　　　　　　　　　(ll. 22–4)

Nor may we deny the explicit endorsement of promiscuity in several poems, whether in 'The Indifferent' ('I can love both faire and browne') or in one of the elegies:

> 　all beasts change when they please,
> Shall women, more hot, wily, wild then these,
> Be bound to one man . . . ?
>
> 　　　　　　　　　　(Elegy III, ll. 11–13)

The ascription of such attitudes to Donne could lead us – and has led us – to reproach him as a 'lascivious prig' (§214: p. 81). Granted, the women who flap their wings about his narrators appear to be there only in order to flap. Granted also that the contempt is consequently total:

> Women are all like Angels; the faire be
> Like those which fell to worse;
>
> 　　　　　　　　　　(Elegy II, ll. 29–30)

or:

> Hope not for minde in women; at their best,
> Sweetnesse, and wit they'are, but, *Mummy*, possest.
>
> 　　　　　　　　　　('Loves Alchymie', ll. 23–4)

Women's constant inconstancy, moreover, appears to elicit Donne's approval in line with the categorical manner of another poet:

> We had need to goe borrow that fantastique glasse
> Invented by *Galileo* the Florentine,
> To view another spacious world i' th' Moone,
> And looke to find a constant woman there.

But this sentiment, voiced by the Cardinal in *The Duchess of Malfi* (II, iv, 24–7), can hardly be said to reflect Webster's own convictions. Can it be said to reflect Donne's, the dramatic nature of his poems notwithstanding?

'Passion', says D. H. Lawrence's Ursula, 'is only part of love. And it seems so much because it can't last. That is why passion is never happy' (*The Rainbow*, Ch. XIII). The dimension she seeks, and eventually secures, does not negate passion but places it within an apocalyptic reality – itself passionately apprehended – which stands on earth yet is fitted to the overarching heaven. Donne's experience inclined him to a parallel balance. The fever of love is not love itself. It is but the passion of love: the spider that converts manna to gall, the self-centred gratification of the senses, the promiscuity, the lasciviousness. True, most of Donne's narrators are, even at the best of times, egocentric. But are not lovers by definition egocentric, self-regarding and self-sufficient, turned inwardly upon themselves? As 'The Sunne Rising' proclaims,

> She'is all States, and all Princes, I,
>   Nothing else is.
>
>   (ll. 21–2)

'Nothing else is' because love – not the raging fever but the sustained joy – can possess a world where time and place are annihilated:

> Love, all alike, no season knowes, nor clyme,
> Nor houres, dayes, moneths, which are the rags of time.
>   (*ibid.*, ll. 9–10)

> our love hath no decay;
> This, no to morrow hath, nor yesterday,
> ('The Anniversarie', ll. 7–8)

> though thy heart depart,
> It stayes at home,
> ('Loves infinitenesse', ll. 29–30)

or, more expansively, from the memorable peroration in one of the elegies (XII: 'His parting from her'):

> when I change my Love, I'll change my heart;
> Nay, if I wax but cold in my desire,
> Think, heaven hath motion lost, and the world, fire:
> Much more I could, but many words have made
> That, oft, suspected which men would perswade;
> Take therefore all in this: I love so true,
> As I will never look for less in you.

Such affirmations persuade not only experientially. They persuade aesthetically too, because in accordance with the norm – the metrical norm as before stated – their rhythm confirms what their sense expressly claims.

Love in Donne's poetry is not etherealized out of existence. As he once wrote to Sir Henry Wotton, 'You (I think) and I am much of one sect in the Philosophy of love; which though it be directed upon the minde, doth inhere in the body, and find piety entertainment there' (§179: p. 121). Some poems, 'The Canonization' for example, scale upwardly: 'Beg from above / A patterne of our love!' But the common preference is for the middle regions mapped in 'Aire and Angels': 'Love must not be, but take a body too' (l. 10). As the second of the verse letters to the Countess of Huntingdon likewise maintains, 'The soule with body, is a heaven combin'd / With earth, and for mans ease, but nearer joyn'd' (ll. 97–8). Affirmations of this order echo not the nominal but the actual argument of 'A Valediction forbidding mourning' (as above), itself linked to the emphatic statement in the elegy already quoted:

Rend us in sunder, thou canst not divide
Our bodies so, but that our souls are ty'd,
(Elegy XII, ll. 69–70)

'Loves growth' assents, all the more because it provides a context for the reference in the 'Valediction' to earth-bound, 'elemented' love:

Love's not so pure, and abstract, as they use
To say, which have no Mistresse but their Muse,
But as all else, being elemented too,
Love sometimes would contemplate, sometimes do.
(ll. 11–14)

Love is not *agape* or *eros*; it is both. Nor is it monomaniacally Platonic or exclusively Petrarchan since it qualifies the one tradition in the light of the other, and both in terms of experience. According to a reiterated word, love is a 'mixture'; and according to a recurring image, a circle ('perfect motions are all circular' ['To the Lady Bedford', l. 31]). It involves when all is said the invitation extended by the narrator of 'The undertaking': 'forget the Hee and Shee' (l. 20).

'The Extasie' tries to forget, and fails brilliantly. The title raises expectations of the suspension of the physical in a riotous display of religious masochism, or (if we are cognizant of primitive pathology) any of the morbid states of unconsciousness inclusive of catalepsy. But Donne would not have been Donne had he met our expectations. The first surprise generated by 'The Extasie' is its external appearance. It should have been promiscuous in its deviation from the norm, the stanzas disordered and the lines disarrayed; but it is in fact temperate, the stanzas ordered and the lines highly controlled. Within, the argument advances with a serenity to the point of detachment. The basic premise, we have been assured, occurs also in Giordano Bruno:

Fascination by love takes place when owing to very frequent looking or to an intense, though instantaneous, look, one eye meets another, and two eye-beams reciprocally encounter, and light couples together with light. Then spirit joins with spirit; and

> the superior light informing the inferior one, they
> come to sparkle through the eyes, rushing to, and
> penetrating, the inner spirit which is rooted in the
> heart; and in this manner they kindle erotic fire.[20]

But the 'erotic fire' in Donne's poem is not particularly erotic,
or even a fire. The act of consummation may be presumed to
have already taken place when the poem begins; if so, the
ensuing reflections are about the implications of that act. There
are no surprises: the 'mixture' here as elsewhere involves an
upward aspiration as well as the acceptance of the 'elemented'
nature of love. But the complexities are infinite, aimed as they
are at validating the incomprehensible mystery succinctly
stated in another poem: 'All love is wonder' (Elegy II, l. 25).
The brilliance is palpable. It depends on the use of metrically
significant words which call attention to themselves, as in the
case of the etymologically pregnant 'interinanimates' (l. 42),
and also highly sophisticated adjustments to the syntax in
order to qualify the nominal argument:

> But O alas, so long, so farre
> 　　Our bodies why doe wee forbeare?
> They'are ours, though not wee, Wee are
> 　　The intelligences, they the spheares.
> We owe them thankes, because they thus,
> 　　Did us, to us, at first convay,
> Yeelded their senses force to us,
> 　　Nor are drosse to us, but allay.
>
> 　　　　　　　　　　　　(ll. 49–56)

'I should never find fault with metaphysical poems', said
Coleridge, 'were they all like this, or but half as excellent'
(§210: p. 524).

IV

Donne's concern with love is so ample that before it all else
appears to buckle. But Donne is in fact the foremost English
poet – as well as greatest English prose-writer – of death.

20. *Candelaio*, I, 10; quoted by Mario Praz in *HG*, p. 70.

Death was for Donne an obsession. While his love of love was mutable though all-pervasive, and ephemeral though spacious, his love of death was undeviating, constant, permanent, fixed. He did not maintain death only metaphorically, in the sense that the separation of lovers is a type of the dissolution to come. He maintained it literally, as a dissolution at once expected and presently present. Confined to a body prone to illness – 'an infirme and valetudinary body' he called it on one occasion (§179: p. 174) – he reported to his friend Sir Henry Goodyer in about 1608:

> I have contracted a sicknesse which I cannot name nor describe. For it hath so much of a continual Cramp, that it wrests the sinews, so much of a Tetane, that it withdraws and puls the mouth, and so much of the Gout, (which they whose counsell I use, say it is) that it is not like to be cured . . . (§179: pp. 31–2)

Another letter of the same period exhibits the consequences:

> The pleasantnesse of the season displeases me. Every thing refreshes and I wither, and I grow older and not better, my strength diminishes, and my load growes, and being to passe more and more stormes, I finde that I have not only cast out all my ballast which nature and time gives, Reason and discretion, and so am as empty and light as Vanity can make me; but I have over fraught my self with Vice . . . (*ibid.*, pp. 78–9)

More than twenty years later, at the apex of his fame but deprived of his beloved wife and ever tormented by ill health, he told his sister, 'I have never good temper, nor good pulse, nor good appetite, nor good sleep'. He added:

> I am afraid that Death will play with me so long, as he will forget to kill me; and suffer me to live in a languishing and uselesse age. A life, that is rather a forgetting that I am dead, then of living.[21]

21. §179: p. 316, and *A Collection of Letters, made by Sir Tobie Mathews* (1660), p. 351; respectively.

The burden of the letters is borne even more compulsively by the poems. The infrequently read elegiac tribute to Cecilia Bulstrode, for instance, explicitly demonstrates how a conventional lament in conventional clichés is transformed as Donne foregoes the occasion and the departed lady in favour of a paean to death:

> Th'earths face is but thy Table; there are set
>   Plants, cattell, men, dishes for Death to eate.
> In a rude hunger now hee millions drawes
>   Into his bloody, or plaguy, or sterv'd jawes.
> Now hee will seeme to spare, and doth more wast,
>   Eating the best first, well preserv'd to last.
> Now wantonly he spoiles, and eates us not,
>   But breakes off friends, and lets us peecemeale rot . . .
> How could I thinke thee nothing, that see now
>   In all this All, nothing else is, but thou . . .
> And though thou beest, O mighty bird of prey,
>   So much reclaim'd by God, that thou must lay
> All that thou kill'st at his feet, yet doth hee
>   Reserve but few, and leaves the most to thee.
>   ('Elegie on Mistris Boulstred', ll. 5–34)

Death – 'the whirle-poole death' – is present not only in elegiac poems, however. Death is also present where he appears to have been virtually stilled into extinction. One of the most famous of the *Holy Sonnets*, for instance, nominally advances from the loftiness of the octave's sweeping movement to the meekness of the sestet's threnodic rhythms:

> At the round earths imagin'd corners, blow
> Your trumpets, Angells, and arise, arise
> From death, you numberlesse infinities
> Of soules, and to your scattred bodies goe,
> All whom the flood did, and fire shall o'erthrow,
> All whom warre, dearth, age, agues, tyrannies,
> Despaire, law, chance, hath slaine, and you whose eyes,
> Shall behold God, and never tast deaths woe,
> But let them sleepe, O Lord, and mee mourne a space,

For, if above all these, my sinnes abound,
'Tis late to aske abundance of thy grace,
When wee are there; here on this lowly ground,
Teach mee how to repent; for that's as good
As if thou'hadst seal'd my pardon, with thy blood.

But to invoke the metrical norm as before is to realize that the departure from the basic iambic beat in the octave induces a counter-movement, affirming through the disturbed rhythm what the sweeping movement endeavours to bypass:

Áll whóm the flo'od díd, and fíre shall o'erthrów,
All whóm wárre, de'arth, áge, águes, týrannies,
Despaíre, láw, chánce . . .

The same pattern surfaces in another celebrated sonnet, 'Death be not proud', where the congregation of three strongly-accented words – 'Fate, Chance, kings' (l. 9) – calls attention to the masters not of death but of ourselves.

Multiform death also provided Donne with a vocabulary to reinforce his canescent vision of the world and man's state within it. The lines

Whilst in our soules sinne bred and pamper'd is,
Our soules become wormeaten carkases[22]

are not at all exceptional. The imagery of decay, decomposition, dissolution, pervades the secular and the sacred poems alike, sustaining *inter alia* the survey of the universe in a verse letter of 1614:

all is withered, shrunke, and dri'd,
All Vertues ebb'd out to a dead low tyde,
All the worlds frame being crumbled into sand,
Where every man thinks by himselfe to stand,
Integritie, friendship, and confidence,
(Ciments of greatnes) being vapor'd hence . . .
('To the Countesse of Salisbury', ll. 9–14)

22. 'On himself', ll. 15–16. See also John Carey's chapter on Death, in his brilliant study of Donne's 'life, mind, and art' (§207).

Donne's fear of death was probably minimal; but his fear of that fear was all-encompassing.

V

The *Songs and Sonets* are commonly read to the exclusion of Donne's other poems: the verse letters, the satires, the elegies, the two *Anniversaries*. The verse letters to his friends and patrons were dismissed by Donne himself as 'the sallads and onions of *Micham*',[23] yet he must have known they were not necessarily the one, and much less the other. In their nature essentially dramatic, they are based on the principle that 'more then kisses, letters mingle Soules';[24] and they include poems in which the syntax may often be impossible but the diction is quite agreeable, the rhymes are generally certain, and the numbers painless. Of the many which may be commended, the several letters addressed to the Countess of Bedford are particularly noteworthy in that their poetic quality is sustained and their thematic concerns jointly disclose 'the Idea of a Woman' as claimed on behalf of the two *Anniversaries* (see below). The second of these letters ('You have refin'd mee') is a provident achievement which redeems even the uncertainties spasmodically evident elsewhere.

Donne's satires – five in number[25] – were like his elegies written periodically from the early 1590s. Their tone and argument are summarily indicated in the claim of one speaker in particular: 'I do hate / Perfectly all this towne' (II, 1–2). But the hate is Swiftian, and rises to the level of great art. The first satire is concerned with the abuses of opportunists and lechers; the second, of lawyers; the fourth, of courtiers; the fifth, of officers and suitors; while the third satire – 'central in both

23. §179: p. 63. Mitcham in Surrey was Donne's residence for some five years.

24. From the opening line of 'To Sir Henry Wotton: Sir, more then kisses' etc.

25. 'The Progresse of the Soule' – not to be confused with the similar title of *The Second Anniversarie* – also partakes of the spirit of the satires. So do still other poems, for example the verse letter to Wotton cited in the previous note.

position and theme' – is an idealistic soliloquy on the spiritual values which the narrator sees everywhere perverted (§506). Eminently moral, the five satires aim in the direction pointed by Izaak Walton's rhetorical question:

> Was every sinne,
> Character'd in his *Satyres*? made so foule
> That some have fear'd their shapes, and kept their soule
> Freer by reading verse?[26]

The poems are attended by the triumvirate of Roman satirists, bearing the mark of the stinging mockery of Horace, the premeditated roughness of Persius, and the intentional hyperboles of Juvenal. They are 'satirique fyres', as Donne said, 'writt / In skorne of all'.[27] Their language, images, syntax, metre, are violent, tortuous, contorted, brilliantly conveying the scorching indignation, the burning hatred. But towering above the negative tableaux stands the positive image of truth:

> on a huge hill,
> Cragg'd, and steep, Truth stands, and hee that will
> Reach her, about must, and about must goe . . .
> (Satire III, ll. 79 ff.)

Donne does not pretend that the ascent is easy. The pilgrim's progress – a 'progress of self-discovery', it has been accurately said (§519: p. 120) – is along a narrow path fraught with obstacles, witness the laborious punctuation and the repetition of 'about must, and about must goe'. One is reminded of Satan's ascent toward light in *Paradise Lost*:

> So hee with difficulty and labour hard
> Moved on, with difficulty and labour hee.
> (II, 1021–2)

Individually, Donne's satires are among his most successful productions; and jointly, his most perfectly orchestrated

26. 'An Elegie upon Dr Donne', in the 1633 edition of Donne's *Poems*; in §753: p. 92.

27. 'To Mr R. W.: Kindly I envy', ll. 7–8.

cluster of poems. In time they were to impress themselves upon a greater poet, Pope, who versified two of them, the second and the fourth (reprinted below, Appendix IV). Donne, wrote Pope in 1706, 'has infinitely more wit than he wanted versification; for the great dealers in wit, like those in trade, take least pains to set off their goods, while the haberdashers of small wit spare for no decorations or ornaments'.[28] The validity of Donne's versification, we observe, is not denied; and though Pope moulded it to his purposes, he remained fully aware of Donne's brilliant use of the dramatic voice and his impressive correlation of sense and rhythm. The awareness is apparent not in the juvenile pompousness of *An Essay on Man* or the sparkling frivolities of *The Rape of the Lock* but in the consummate discriminations of *The Dunciad* generally, and of the epistles in particular. The line of descent, I am suggesting, leads from Donne's merciless portrait of the parasitic courtier – the 'thing' of his fourth satire (ll. 18 ff.) – through Pope's version of it (ll. 24 ff.) to the crushing portrait of Sporus in the *Epistle to Dr Arbuthnot* (ll. 305 ff.).

Donne's elegies borrow their general designation from Ovid's *Amores* which the Elizabethans commonly termed 'elegies'. Strikingly uneven, they have irritated so many readers so much that one of them renounced even one of the best, the ninth elegy known as 'The Autumnall' ('The poem is a mess' [§386: p. 104]). More charitably it might be claimed that the elegies provoke what a novelist is said to have said of the productions of a fellow craftsman, 'inconceivable boredom associated with the most extreme ecstasy which it is possible to imagine'.[29] In part at least, the boredom sets in especially when Donne tries to impress us with his originality as a thinker. For his ideas are on the whole simple; and though they dazzle if phrased vigorously, they only embarrass if not. The following

28. Letter to Wycherley, 10 April 1706; in *Literary Criticism of Alexander Pope*, ed. Bertrand A. Goldgar (Lincoln, Nebr., 1955), p. 29.

29. The source is no longer within my ken. I used to think that the remark was made by Henry James about Proust; but it appears I was far too optimistic! Professor Leon Edel assures me that the attribution of the remark to James is inaccurate.

lines are a fair measure of political astuteness misplaced intel-
lectually if not dramatically too:

> Sick Ireland is with a strange warr possest
> Like to an Ague; now raging, now at rest;
> Which time will cure: yet it must doe her good
> If she were purg'd, and her head vayne let blood.
>
> (Elegy XX, ll. 13–16)

We need not passionately anathematize Donne's
'convulvulus-growth of intellectual whim-whams'.[30] Suffice
it that on occasions such as the one cited, the schism between
the matter and the manner, or the sense and its poetic articula-
tion, terminates in what may fairly be described as obscenity.
The judgement is not moral in that the elegies are preoccupied
'with fairly irrelevant nastiness' (§483: p. 57): it is, rather,
aesthetic – or, better still, it is moral *because* it is aesthetic. 'The
Perfume' (IV), for instance, is obscene because its basic idea
and the supporting language are vicious to excess, unredeemed
even by the dramatic context (ll. 57 ff.):

> Base excrement of earth, which dost confound
> Sense, from distinguishing the sicke from sound;
> By thee the seely Amorous sucks his death
> By drawing in a leprous harlots breath;
> By thee, the greatest staine to mans estate
> Falls on us, to be call'd effeminate;

– and the like. Also aesthetically obscene is 'The Comparison'
(VIII) because it multiplies a few powerful lines (ll. 39–44)[31]
without any sense of economy; 'Julia' (XIII), because it re-
visits the obsessive interest in vomit; the so-called 'Variety'
(XVII), because it admits embarrassing clichés and perfunctory
rhymes; and 'Loves Progress' (XVIII), because a promising

---

30. J. E. V. Crofts, in *HG*, p. 89. 'Though interested in thought',
Mario Praz has more accurately observed, Donne 'was no origi-
nal thinker himself . . . He was like a lawyer choosing the fittest
arguments for a case in hand, not like a searcher after universally
valid truth' (in *HG*, p. 68).

31. Quoted earlier, p. 25.

journey across the female body founders in risibly excessive analogies:

> The Nose (like to the first Meridian) runs
> Not 'twixt an East and West, but 'twixt two suns;
> It leaves a Cheek, a rosie Hemisphere
> On either side, and then directs us where
> Upon the Islands fortunate we fall,
> Not faynte *Canaries* but *Ambrosiall*,
> Her swelling lips . . .
> These, and the glorious Promontory, her Chin
> Ore past; and the streight *Hellespont* between
> The *Sestos* and *Abydos* of her breasts . . .
>
> (ll. 47 ff.)

– and so on. Against these failures in judgement, however, is 'the most extreme ecstasy which it is possible to imagine'. Such ecstasy centres on 'The Dreame' (X), where an uncommon serenity is reflected in the exceptional stanzaic form; 'The Bracelet' (XI) – so much admired by Ben Jonson that he had it 'by heart' – where an inauspicious subject is transmuted by a superbly dramatic tone; 'His parting from her' (XII), where sense coincides with skill 'of the highest technical expertness'; 'The Expostulation' (XV) – also attributed to Jonson (*Underwood*, No. 41) – where the rampant antifeminism is dexterously related to the narrator's oscillating emotions ('Now have I curst, let us our love revive'); and 'On his Mistris' (XVI), where the Miltonic sweep of the first sentence heralds a dramatic situation sustained with passionate energy to the very end. Donne's elegies often ascend to greatness; yet it is telling that they also descend to aesthetic grossness.

The two *Anniversaries* are the only substantial poems published in Donne's lifetime. Their given subject, the fourteen-year-old Elizabeth Drury who died in 1610, was not intimately known to Donne ('I never saw the Gentlewoman' [§179: p. 239]). A funeral elegy he wrote at the time claimed that 'shee / Being spent, the world must needes decrepit bee' (ll. 29–30) – a notion judged sufficiently attractive to have been multiplied by nearly five hundred lines on the first anniversary of her death (*An Anatomy of the World*, 1611), and by as many on the second (*Of the Progres of the Soule*, 1612). Approached theoretically, the two *Anniversaries* have provided numerous opportunities for the display of scholarly expertise. They have been seen to manifest the direct or indirect influence of the meditative tradition associated with St Ignatius Loyola on the one hand (§577) and of the tradition of the mixed genre – instruction, meditation, and praise – developed by Protestants on the other (§573). They have also been seen to belong to a qualified tradition of the funeral elegy, else to the traditions variously centred on *sapientia creata*, St Lucy, and Petrarch's *Trionfi*; yet because their 'oppositions and contradictions' linger stubbornly, they have also been triumphantly proclaimed to be 'paradoxical poems'.[32] As regards their structure, the two poems are on occasion said to be 'a single poem' (§587: p. 375); but if indeed two, then they are companion pieces closely related through a series of antitheses. The 'anatomy' in the first anniversary is largely negative, but in the second positive. The first is a descent into sin, but the second an ascent to virtue. The setting of the one is time, earth, the sublunar world of nature; but that of the second is space, heaven, the supernatural regions. The *Anniversaries* oppose 'doubt and faith, despair and hope, death and the triumph of immortality'.[33]

Not everyone will confuse the background with the foreground, however. It could be argued that, regarded as poems, the two *Anniversaries* have their great moments – but they are only moments. It could even be maintained that the first poem is bombastic in tone and opaque in aim, while the second is no less marred in phraseology than it is precarious in orientation. True, Donne himself is reported to have said of the first what is also applicable to the second, that 'he described the Idea of a Woman and not as she was'. But the remark does not answer

32. *Seriatim*: W. M. Lebans (§572); Frank Manley (§167); Richard E. Hughes (§570); Silvia Ruffo-Fiore (§288: p. 81); and Rosalie Colie (§563).

33. Marjorie H. Nicolson, in §581: p. 82. Patrick Mahony (§576) quotes Nicolson's antitheses and cites the others mentioned from Louis L. Martz, George Williamson, *et al.*, as well as from his own storehouse. See also Carol M. Sicherman (§587).

Jonson's strictures of the *style*, namely, that as the poems were
not written in celebration of the Virgin Mary, they are 'profane
and full of Blasphemies'.[34] At issue, in other words, is Donne's
lack of economy, made worse by his inability to feel Elizabeth
Drury's death upon his pulses (as Keats would have said). The
result is a fabricated hysteria which impels Donne to several
infelicities, for instance the elevation of the girl at the expense
of hapless Eve *and* the sum of her descendants:

> One woman at one blow, then kill'd us all,
> And singly, one by one, they kill us now.
>   (I, 106–7)

The lack of moderation disconcerts. Donne was perfectly free
to associate the girl's death with the widespread belief in the
decline of man's stature, but he was not at liberty to do so in
casual lines such as:

>   in length is man
> Contracted to an inch, who was a span.
> For had a man at first, in Forrests stray'd,
> Or shipwrack'd in the Sea, one would have laid
> A wager that an Elephant, or Whale
> That met him, would not hastily assaile
> A thing so equall to him:
>   (I, 135–41)

The exaggerations mar even the much-praised second *Anniversary*. The hysteria continues, attended as usual by immoderate
claims about 'this deluge, grosse and generall', 'this rotten
world', and the like; by the questionable realism of 'the putrid
stuffe, which thou dost spit' (l. 273); and by the linguistic
crudity in the description of the effects of sin:

> The poyson'is gone through all, poysons affect
> Chiefly the cheefest parts, but some effect
> In Nails, and Haires, yea excrements, will show;
>   (II, 335–7)

34. Donne's remark and Jonson's stricture are alike in *Ben Jonson*, ed.
    C. H. Herford and Percy Simpson (Oxford, 1925), I, 133. Elsewhere Donne wrote of Elizabeth Drury, 'I took such a person, as
    might be capable of all that I could say' (§179: p. 239).

Hyperbole also generates at times unintended amusement, as in the earnest plea to the 'immortall' girl:

> though thou wouldst refuse
> The name of Mother, be unto my Muse,
> A Father
>
> (II, 33–5)

There is only slight evidence that the Father responded.

Positively, the *Anniversaries* are useful in that they confirm Donne's obsession with multiform death; and negatively, in that they delineate the limits of his originality as a thinker and evince the perils attendant upon his flirtation with hyperbole. The poems are, like a particular category of sins, splendid.

VI

In 1619, some ten years after he composed his prose extravaganza *Biathanatos*, Donne remarked that it was 'a Book written by *Jack Donne*, and not by D[octor] *Donne*' (§179: p. 22). The claim that his life was neatly divided into two periods, the secular and the sacred, may or may not be credited; but that his poetry was likewise divided, is not open to question. For one, several of his divine poems – *The Litanie* for instance, but also some of the *Holy Sonnets* – were written before his ordination; and for another, his secular poems frequently partake of the sacred dimension, and indeed vice-versa. The interpenetration of the two realms has disconcerted a number of readers, one of whom marks 'the drastic impropriety of the theological conceits' in 'The Canonization' and protests because Donne is 'impertinently confounding mere carnality with a prime mystery of religion' (§290: pp. 22, 51). But are not lovers wont to describe their experiences in language borrowed from theology? And have not some of the most moving expressions of divine love been set forth in explicitly secular terms? Love, as I said earlier, is both *agape* and *eros*. The formidable tradition centred on the Song of Solomon is otherwise an impertinence; and so, among other testaments, is the stunning summary of Christian experience by St Ignatius of Antioch: 'my love (*eros*) is crucified'.[35]

Donne's divine poems include 'To Mr Tilman after he had taken orders', which is less than divine, and hardly a poem; 'The Crosse', which is so ingenious that its stated aims are misplaced en route; and the seven interlocking 'holy sonnets' comprising *La Corona*, which in offering a 'crown of prayer and praise' invite comparison with Herbert's brilliantly economic 'A Wreath'. But the divine poems also include 'Goodfriday, 1613. Riding Westward', whose cosmic sweep involves an eschatological journey toward the Last Judgement in the West, correlated with Christ's first advent in the East (§617); 'A Hymne to God the Father', whose lyrical complexity depends on the impressive coincidence of the form without and the argument within, impacted to assert the endless restlessness of man; and *The Litanie*, where the underestimated argument encompasses touchstone lines such as:

> Oh, to some
> Not to be Martyrs, is a martyrdome.
>
> (ll. 89–90)

The *Holy Sonnets* designated 'Divine Meditations' (pp. 434 ff.) reflect the varieties of religious experience in the Psalms, re-enacted in the light of the cosmic patterns of the Christian view of history (§682). The influence of the Psalms – 'formes of joy and art'[36] – can scarcely be denied. But the pressure exerted by the Book of Lamentations was even more decisive. Its characteristic mood of black despair could not have escaped Donne, especially once he versified its passionate cries of agony:

35. ὁ ἐμός ἔρως ἐσταύρωται (*Epistola ad Romanos*, VII, 2; quoted by 'Dionysius the Areopagite', *De divinis nominibus*, IV, 12). On the tradition centred on the Song of Solomon, see Stanley Stewart, *The Enclosed Garden* (Madison, 1966). In fact, as Donne reminds us, the Scriptures 'abound with the notions of *Love*, of *Spouse*, and *Husband*, and *Marriadge Songs*, and *Marriadge Supper*, and *Marriadge-Bedde*' (*Sermons*, VII, 87).

36. 'Upon the Translation of the Psalmes', l. 34.

I am the man which hath affliction seene,
    Under the rod of Gods wrath having beene,
He hath led mee to darknesse, not to light,
    And against mee all day, his hand doth fight . . .

His hand hath of my sinnes framed a yoake
    Which wreath'd, and cast upon my neck, hath broke
My strength . . .

. . . oughtest thou, O Lord, despise us thus
    And to be utterly enrag'd at us?
        (*The Lamentations of Jeremy*, ll. 177–9, 53–5, 389–90)

The violent imagery here as in the *Holy Sonnets* proclaims how intermittent the sense of God's favour is, and how impossible readily to attain 'the peace that passeth understanding'. On the other hand, Donne controlled the potential hysteria by resorting in his version of the Lamentations to rhyme, and in the *Holy Sonnets* to the mould of the sonnet.

The sonnet as form tempers, moderates, restrains. So far, it may even be said to intimate a terminal Order which the *Holy Sonnets* never directly assert, and sometimes even question. As an organizational principle, the sonnet afforded Donne opportunities to provide for a nominal division after the Shakespearean model (three quatrains and a couplet), yet an actual one after the Italian pattern (an octave and a sestet). But the most impressive aspect of Donne's use of the sonnet is that he appears not to use the form at all. So swift is the flow of the given movement, and so overpowering are the punctuation and the imagery, that the rhymed lines are submerged until we are, abruptly, stopped. Always excepting Hopkins, I am not aware of any English poet who has so thoroughly obliterated the sonnet form even as he was demonstrating its immense powers.

The *Holy Sonnets* share with other poems Donne's obsession with death. They also share his obsession with love, often explicitly physical love, as in the imagery of the sonnets beginning 'Batter my heart' and 'As due by many titles', but also in the audacious plea that Christ's spouse may be 'open to most men' (in 'Show me deare Christ'). The tonal range is immense.

As the opening lines of several sonnets indicate, it encompasses the moving acceptance of

> Since she whom I lov'd hath payd her last debt . . .

the reflective amazement of

> I am a little world made cunningly . . .

the passionate anxiety of

> Show me deare Christ, thy Spouse, so bright and
>   clear . . .

the triumphant vision of

> At the round earths imagin'd corners, blow
> Your trumpets, Angells . . .

or the sheer terror of

> What if this present were the worlds last night?

Donne mounts in the dramatically variable *Songs and Sonets*, the perfectly orchestrated satires, the fitfully great elegies, and even the amiable verse letters. But the summit of his art is in the *Holy Sonnets*.

VII

Donne was much praised in his lifetime, under-praised thereafter, and over-praised earlier this century. The lowest point of his reputation was during the eighteenth century, in spite – and doubtless because – of the revision of his satires by Pope. At the outset of the nineteenth century, however, Donne was inching forward; by the end of it, he was rising meteorically; and three decades later he was stepping gingerly into the throne said to have been vacated by Milton. T. S. Eliot's judgement was crucial. Donne, he proclaimed in 1921, is distinguished by 'a direct sensuous apprehension of thought or a recreation of thought into feeling', whereas poets like Milton and Dryden are merely responsible for a 'dissociation of sensibility' (§220: pp. 246, 247). In retrospect, it is not easy to decide which was admired more, Donne's poetry or Eliot's apocalyptic theory. In time, of course, the theory was challenged with some zest

(§737); yet it was already undercut by Eliot himself when he proposed as an afterthought that Donne displays 'a manifest fissure between thought and sensibility'. 'His learning', added Eliot rather unkindly, 'is just information suffused with emotion, or combined with emotion not essentially relevant to it' (§727: p. 8).

Donne would have had a wry comment or two to make about his undulating fortunes, possibly borrowing a parallel from a familiar field: 'the Astronomers of the world are not so much exercised, about all the Constellations, and their motions, formerly apprehended and beleeved, as when there arises a new, and irregular meteor' (§162: p. 392). Donne's irregularity persists. But indispensable as it was to his patterns of thought, it sounds his uniqueness; and inimitable, it thunders his greatness. Carew rightly recognized that

> thy strict lawes will be
> Too hard for Libertines in Poetrie
> ('An Elegie upon . . . Donne', ll. 61–2)

Donne founded no 'school' because he was, like all major poets, unrepeatable. Some minor talents waited on him, as minor talents do; but those who are often said to constitute 'the school of Donne' – Herbert, Vaughan, Crashaw, Marvell – absorbed the example and rejected the overpowering voice. They would have said of Donne much as Keats was later to say of Milton: 'Life to him would be death to me'.[37] For Donne entices the most unsympathetic, captures the most hostile, subdues the most antagonistic; and by tomorrow we may think so too.

37. Letter to George and Georgiana Keats, 21 September 1819.

Songs and Sonets

Songs and Sonets was first specified as a category in the 1635 edition of Donne's *Poems*. Literally, however, the category will scarcely serve, since most of the poems it includes are by no means 'songs', much less sonnets in the strict sense of that term; indeed, the one poem expressly designated a 'sonnet' – *if* it is Donne's (below, p. 124) – is precisely the one that is not a sonnet. In fact, the category is intended to call attention to the essentially lyrical dimension of Donne's poems in the same general way that the 'sorts of Poetry' enumerated by Sir Philip Sidney in his *Apologie for Poetrie* (1583) had included 'that Lyricall kind of Songs and Sonnets'. Within such a generalized context, 'sonnet' should be seen as connected with 'sonata' and denoting any short poem – particularly a short love poem – such as might conceivably be set to music (§§90, 229).

Songs and Sonets encompasses fifty-five poems, always provided that the last two (pp. 124–26) may confidently be attributed to Donne. Some editors have added to the category by transferring into it still other poems. Gardner, for instance, has so treated Elegie X ('The Dreame'), while Shawcross has done as much with the same poem as well as with Elegie IX ('The Autumnall') and the untitled poem beginning 'When my harte was mine owne'. In the absence of fully persuasive reasons for transferring poems from category to category, however, the present edition confines itself to the traditional fifty-five.

Of these poems, only two were published in full in Donne's lifetime, 'Breake of day' (p. 68) and 'The Expiration' (p. 119). Even so, the dates of composition are not known either generally about the poems at large or particularly about most individual poems. Attempts to arrange the *Songs and Sonets* in accordance with their presumed dates of composition must be approached with extreme scepticism.

On the text of the poems and their arrangement in the ensuing pages, see 'The Text', above, pp. 1–5; and on the abbreviations used throughout: above, p. 1, and below, pp. 511–13.

The Flea.

Marke but this flea, and marke in this,
How little that which thou deny'st me is;
It suck'd me first, and now sucks thee,
And in this flea, our two bloods mingled bee;
Thou know'st that this cannot be said   5
A sinne, nor shame, nor loss of maidenhead,
   Yet this enjoyes before it wooe,
     And pamper'd swells with one blood made of two
    And this, alas, is more then wee would doe.

Oh stay, three lives in one flea spare,   10
Where wee almost, yea more then maryed are.
This flea is you and I, and this
Our mariage bed, and mariage temple is;
Though parents grudge, and you, w'are met,
And cloystered in these living walls of Jet.   15

The Flea. Printed 34th in the sequence of *Songs and Sonets* in the *Poems* of 1633, but shifted to first place from 1635. Sometimes said to have been quite popular in its time, the poem partakes of an extensive tradition of erotic poems centred on fleas (see above, p. 23). Donne may be reworking a French model which had, with parallel explicitness, punned on 'puce' (flea) and 'pucelage' (maidenhead) [§469].
1. Perhaps a parody of a preacher's *exemplum* (§385).
3. *It suck'd me first*: 'Mee it suck'd first' (acc. to 1669 and some MSS).
4. Sexual intercourse was thought literally to involve the mingling of bodies, making one of two (l. 8).
5. *Thou know'st that this*: 'Confess it. This' (acc. to 1669 and some MSS).
6. *nor shame, nor losse*: 'or shame, or loss' (ditto).
9 (also 11). *then*: than.
9. *would*: 'could' (acc. to 1669).
11. *yea*: 'nay' (acc. to 1669 and some MSS).
15. *use*: habit.

Though use make you apt to kill mee,
 Let not to that, selfe murder added bee,
 And sacrilege, three sinnes in killing three.

Cruell and sodaine, hast thou since
Purpled thy naile, in blood of innocence?   20
Wherein could this flea guilty bee,
Except in that drop which it suckt from thee?
Yet thou triumph'st, and saist that thou
Find'st not thy selfe, nor mee the weaker now;
 'Tis true, then learne how false, feares bee;   25
 Just so much honor, when thou yeeld'st to mee,
 Will wast, as this flea's death tooke life from thee.

The good-morrow.

I wonder by my troth, what thou, and I
Did, till we lov'd? were we not wean'd till then?
But suck'd on countrey pleasures, childishly?
Or snorted we in the seaven sleepers den?
T'was so; But this, all pleasures fancies bee   5
If ever any beauty I did see,
Which I desir'd, and got, t'was but a dreame of thee.

The Flea.
16. *kill* – like *die* – was in Renaissance slang often (though by no means
     always) equated with sexual intercourse; the act was believed to reduce
     one's lifespan (see below, p. 122, ll. 24–5).
21. *Wherein*: 'In what' (acc. to some MSS).

The good-morrow. Printed 8th in the sequence of *Songs and Sonets* in 1633 but
     shifted to second place from 1635; there follow, in both editions, the
     twenty-five poems up to and including 'Loves Alchymie' (below,
     p. 86). The poem – discussed above, p. 24 – is a variation of the
     traditional *aubade* or piece of music played or sung at dawn.
 3. *countrey*: rustic; hence unrefined (§169).
     countrey pleasures, childishly: 'childish pleasures seelily' (acc. to 1669 and
     some MSS).
 4. *snorted*: snored; 'slumbred' (ditto). *the seaven sleepers den*: the cave in
     which seven Christian youths, fleeing the persecution of Decius
     (A.D. 249), slept for nearly two centuries.
 5. *But this*: except for this.

And now good morrow to our waking soules,
Which watch not one another out of feare;
For love, all love of other sights controules,   10
And makes one little roome, an every where.
Let sea-discoverers to new worlds have gone,
Let Maps to other, worlds on worlds have showne,
Let us possesse onc world, each hath one, and is one.

My face in thine eye, thine in mine appeares,   15
And true plaine hearts doe in the faces rest,
Where can we finde two better hemispheares
Without sharpe North, without declining West?
What ever dyes, was not mixt equally;
If our two loves be one, or, thou and I   20
Love so alike, that none doe slacken, none can die.

10. *For*: 'But' (acc. to many MSS).
13. *Maps*: possibly of the heavens, showing newly discovered celestial *worlds*; or of the earth – the period's cordiform or heart-shaped maps – showing two hemispheres (§440).
    to other, worlds on: 'to other worlds our' (acc. to 1669) or 'to others, worlds on' (acc. to several MSS). *other*: other people.
14. *possesse*: implies absolute mastery; in Donne's time the word still retained its metaphoric connection with demonic possession (§383).
    one world: 'our world' (acc. to many MSS).
15. For the converse, see below, p. 74, l. 23.
17. *better*: 'fitter' (acc. to 1635–69 and most later MSS).
18. *sharpe*: bitterly cold; *declining*: where the sun descends (§163). *North* was associated with evil; *West*, with death (see below, p. 494, note on 11–15).
19–21. 'Too good for mere wit', said Coleridge of this triplet. 'It contains a deep practical truth' (§210).
19. *was not*: 'is not' (acc. to 1669).
20. *thou and I*: i.e. *if* thou and I.
20–21. *or, thou and I . . . can die*: 'both thou and I / Love just alike in all, none of these loves can die' (acc. to 1635–69 and some MSS).

Song.

Goe, and catche a falling starre,
　Get with child a mandrake roote,
Tell me, where all past yeares are,
　Or who cleft the Divels foot,
Teach me to heare Mermaides singing,　　　　　　5
Or to keep off envies stinging,
　　　　And finde
　　　　What winde
Serves to advance an honest minde.

If thou beest borne to strange sights,　　　　　　10
　Things invisible to see,
Ride ten thousand daies and nights,
　Till age snow white haires on thee,
Thou, when thou retorn'st, wilt tell mee
All strange wonders that befell thee,　　　　　　15
　　　　And sweare
　　　　No where
Lives a woman true, and faire.

If thou findst one, let mee know,
　Such a Pilgrimage were sweet,　　　　　　　20
Yet doe not, I would not goe,
　Though at next doore wee might meet,

Song. For an anonymous musical setting of the poem, see §§163, 169, 190.
　2.　*mandrake*: 'a narcotic herb with a forked root, thought to resemble the
　　　human form. It supposedly shrieked when pulled out of the ground, its
　　　cry killing all humans who heard it; hence the impossibility of getting it
　　　with child. Ironically, its fruit when eaten by women was supposed to be
　　　an aide in conception' (§162; see §325).
　3.　*past yeares*: 'times past' (acc. to 1669).
　4.　The devil's foot was considered cleft because of identification with goats
　　　and Pan (§163).
　5.　*Mermaides*: the common designation of the Sirens (§281).
　11.　*to see*: 'see' (acc. to some MSS) or 'goe see' (ditto).
　14.　*when thou retorn'st:* 'at thy returne' (ditto).
　19–20.　The lines appear to admit the possibility of a faithful woman (§391).
　20.　*sweet*: 'sweet;' (acc. to 1669).

Though shee were true, when you met her,
And last, till you write your letter,
   Yet shee   25
   Will bee
False, ere I come, to two, or three.

Womans constancy.

Now thou hast lov'd me one whole day,
To morrow when thou leav'st, what wilt thou say?
Wilt thou then Antedate some new made vow?
   Or say that now
We are not just those persons, which we were?   5
Or, that oathes made in reverentiall feare
Of Love, and his wrath, any may forsweare?
Or, as true deaths, true maryages untie,
So lovers contracts, images of those,
Binde but till sleep, deaths image, them unloose?   10
   Or, your owne end to Justifie,
For having purpos'd change, and falsehood; you
Can have no way but falsehood to be true?
Vaine lunatique, against these scapes I could
   Dispute, and conquer, if I would,   15
   Which I abstaine to doe,
For by to morrow, I may thinke so too.

Song.
27. *I*: 'she' (acc. to 1669).

Womans constancy. 'A misnomer', said Coleridge. 'The title ought to be –
  Mutual Inconstancy' (§210).
 8. *Or*: 'For' (acc. to 1635–54).
  true: real.
14. *lunatique*: under the moon's sway, therefore changeable, inconstant, as
  well as madly foolish (*ALC*).
  scapes: subterfuges.

The undertaking.

I have done one braver thing
    Then all the *Worthies* did,
And yet a braver thence doth spring,
    Which is, to keepe that hid.

It were but madnes now t'impart   5
    The skill of specular stone,
When he which can have learn'd the art,
    To cut it can finde none.

So, if I now should utter this,
    Others (because no more   10
Such stuffe to worke upon, there is,)
    Would love but as before.

But he who lovelinesse within
    Hath found, all outward loathes,
For he who colour loves, and skinne,   15
    Loves but their oldest clothes.

If, as I have, you also doe
    Vertue'attir'd in woman see,
And dare love that, and say so too,
    And forget the Hee and Shee;   20

The undertaking. Untitled in 1633; first entitled from 1635; also entitled in
     several MSS *Platonique Love*.
  1.   *braver*: more courageous; also more showy (§449).
  2. (also 26). *Then*: than.
  2.   The traditional nine *Worthies* were often noted for their boasting (§356).
  3.   *And*: omitted in several MSS.
  6.   *specular stone*: old selenite, an ancient building material 'transparent as
     glasse, or crystall' (*Sermons*, VII, 397), believed by Donne to be 'a thing
     unknowne/To our late times' (below, p. 300, ll. 28–9; §§172, 282, 315,
     324; cf. §409).
7–8. Also punctuated, 'When he, which can have learn't the art / To cut, can
     finde none' (acc. to 1669).
 18. On the symbol ', see above, p. 5.
     attir'd: omitted from 1635–69.
 20. See above, p. 29.

And if this love, though placed so,
  From prophane men you hide,
Which will no faith on this bestow,
  Or, if they doe, deride:

Then you have done a braver thing   25
  Then all the *Worthies* did.
And a braver thence will spring
  Which is, to keepe that hid.

The Sunne Rising.

    Busie old foole, unruly Sunne,
     Why dost thou thus,
Through windowes, and through curtaines call on us?
Must to thy motions lovers seasons run?
     Sawcy pedantique wretch, goe chide   5
     Late schoole boyes and sowre prentices,
  Goe tell Court-huntsmen, that the King will ride,
  Call countrey ants to harvest offices;
Love, all alike, no season knowes, nor clyme,
Nor houres, dayes, moneths, which are the rags of time. 10

     Thy beames, so reverend, and strong
     Why shouldst thou thinke?
I could eclipse and cloud them with a winke,
But that I would not lose her sight so long:

The Sunne Rising. Entitled in some MSS *Ad Solem*; in others, *To the Sunne.*
  1–14. 'Fine vigorous exultation', exclaimed Coleridge, 'both soul and body
     in full puissance!' (§210).
  3. *call*: 'look' (acc. to 1669).
  6. *and*: 'or' (ditto).
     sowre: 'slowe' (acc. to some MSS).
  7. *the King will ride*: James I was an enthusiastic hunter.
  9. *all alike*: always the same (§169).
  12. *Why shouldst thou*: 'Dost thou not' (acc. to 1635–69).

If her eyes have not blinded thine,   15
    Looke, and to morrow late, tell mee,
Whether both the'India's of spice and Myne
  Be where thou leftst them, or lie here with mee.
Aske for those Kings whom thou saw'st yesterday,
And thou shalt heare, All here in one bed lay.   20

She'is all States, and all Princes, I,
    Nothing else is.
Princes doe but play us, compar'd to this,
All honor's mimique; All wealth alchimie;
    Thou sunne art halfe as happy'as wee,   25
    In that the world's contracted thus.
  Thine age askes ease, and since thy duties bee
  To warme the world, that's done in warming us.
Shine here to us, and thou art every where;
This bed thy center is, these walls, thy spheare.   30

The Indifferent.

I can love both faire and browne,
Her whom abundance melts, and her whom want betraies,
Her who loves lonenesse best, and her who maskes and
        plaies,
Her whom the country form'd, and whom the town,

The Sunne Rising.
17 (also 21 and 25). On the symbol ', see above, p. 5.
17.   *both th'India's*: i.e. the East Indies, 'the land of Perfumes and Spices', and
        the West Indies, 'the land of Gold, and of Mynes' (as Donne described
        them in a letter: §§158, 169).
        Myne: 'This use of the word specifically for mines of gold, silver, or
        precious stones is, I believe, peculiar to Donne' (Coleridge: §210).
21–22. See above, p. 27.
24.   *alchimie*: here in the sense of imposture, 'glittering dross' (*OED*: §158).
27.   *askes*: requires (*ALC*).
30.   *spheare*: the sun's orbit around the earth (*center*) in the Ptolemaic system
        (§163).

The Indifferent. Entitled in some MSS *A Songe*. Cf. Ovid, *Amores*, Book II
        (Elegy 4).
  3. *lonenesse*: 'lovers' (acc. to 1669).
        maskes: 'sports' (ditto).

Her who beleeves, and her who tries,   5
Her who still weepes with spungie eyes,
And her who is dry corke, and never cries;
I can love her, and her, and you and you,
I can love any, so she be not true.

Will no other vice content you?   10
Wil it not serve your turn to do, as did your mothers?
Or have you all old vices spent, and now would finde
      out others?
Or doth a feare, that men are true, torment you?
Oh we are not, be not you so,
Let mee, and doe you, twenty know.   15
Rob mee, but binde me not, and let me goe.
Must I, who came to travaile thorow you,
Grow your fixt subject, because you are true?

Venus heard me sigh this song,
And by Loves sweetest Part, Variety, she swore,   20
She heard not this till now; and that it should be so no
      more.
She went, examin'd, and return'd ere long,
And said, alas, Some two or three
Poore Heretiques in love there bee,
Which thinke to stablish dangerous constancie.   25
But I have told them, since you will be true,
You shall be true to them, who'are false to you.

5.   *beleeves*: trusts her lover.
     tries: tests him (§172).
7.   *corke*: a favourite metaphor for what was dry and withered (§158).
12. *Or have you all old*: 'Have you old' (acc. to some MSS).
13. *feare*: 'shame' (ditto).
15. *know*: in a sexual sense (§163).
17. *travaile*: hardship or labour, with a pun on 'travell' as verb (the actual
     reading of 1635–69). *thorow*: through.
19. *Venus*: represented here as a goddess of inconstancy (§195).
     sigh: 'sing' (acc. to 1669).
20. *Part*: 'sweet' (acc. to 1669 and some MSS).
     Variety: cf. Elegie XVII, below, p. 175.
21. *and that it*: 'it' (acc. to 1635–69) or 'and it' (acc. to several MSS).
25. *dangerous*: the dangerous doctrine of.
27. On the symbol ', see above, p. 5.

Loves Usury.

For every houre that thou wilt spare mee now,
        I will allow,
Usurious God of Love, twenty to thee,
When with my browne, my gray haires equall bee;
Till then, Love, let my body raigne, and let   5
Mee travell, sojourne, snatch, plot, have, forget,
Resume my last yeares relict: thinke that yet
        We'had never met.

Let mee thinke any rivalls letter mine,
        And at next nine   10
Keepe midnights promise; mistake by the way
The maid, and tell the Lady of that delay;
Onely let mee love none, no, not the sport
From country grasse, to comfitures of Court,
Or cities quelque choses, let report   15
        My minde transport.

This bargaine's good; if when I'am old, I bee
        Inflam'd by thee,
If thine owne honour, or my shame, or paine,
Thou covet most, at that age thou shalt gaine.   20

Loves Usury.
  2.   *twenty*: the *bargaine* (17) involves a twenty-fold rate of interest (§166).
  5.   *raigne*: 'range' (acc. to 1635–69 and some MSS).
  6.   *snatch*: 'match' (acc. to 1635–54).
  7.   *relict*: the one loved, now discarded.
  8 (also 17). On the symbol ', see above, p. 5.
  10. *at next nine*: at 9 a.m. after the assignation at midnight.
  13. *sport*: i.e. the game of love; the word is followed by a comma (acc. to
       most MSS) or a semicolon (acc. to 1669).
  14. *comfitures*: confections.
  15. *quelque choses*: literally dainties, fancy trifles (§172).
       let: 'let not' (acc. to 1635–54 and some MSS).
  16. *transport*: i.e. range freely across the various possibilities for love
       reported to be available in country, court, and city.
  20. The comma is given after 'most' in the 1633 edition but after 'covet' in
       several MSS.

Doe thy will then, then subject and degree,
And fruit of love, Love I submit to thee,
Spare mee till then, I'll beare it, though she bee
   One that loves mee.

The Canonization.

For Godsake hold your tongue, and let me love,
 Or chide my palsie, or my gout,
My five gray haires, or ruin'd fortune flout,
 With wealth your state, your minde with Arts improve,
  Take you a course, get you a place,   5
  Observe his honour, or his grace,
Or the King's reall, or his stamped face
 Contemplate, what you will, approve,
 So you will let me love.

Alas, alas, who's injur'd by my love?   10
 What merchants ships have my sighs drown'd?
Who saies my teares have overflow'd his ground?
 When did my colds a forward spring remove?
  When did the heats which my veines fill
  Adde one more to the plaguie Bill?   15
Soldiers finde warres, and Lawyers finde out still
 Litigious men, which quarrels move,
 Though she and I do love.

Loves Usury.
21. *subject*: the person loved; *degree*: the intensity of the love involved.

The Canonization. Boldly conflating the secular and the sacred, the poem
  probably draws even on the Roman Catholic procedures governing
  canonization (§339).
 3. *five*: 'true' (acc. to 1635–54).
 6. i.e. pay court to some Lord or Bishop (§166).
 7. *stamped face*: i.e. on coins; *reall* also means 'royal', a Spanish coin (§163).
 8. *approve*: experience, try (*OED*: §172).
13. *forward*: early.
15. *more*: 'man' (acc. to 1669 and most MSS).
  plaguie Bill: weekly list of those dead of the plague (§164).
18. *Though*: 'While' (acc. to 1669).

Call us what you will, wee are made such by love;
   Call her one, mee another flye,   20
We'are Tapers too, and at our owne cost die,
    And wee in us finde the'Eagle and the dove,
      The Phœnix ridle hath more wit
     By us, we two being one, are it.
So, to one neutrall thing both sexes fit,   25
    Wee dye and rise the same, and prove
    Mysterious by this love.

Wee can dye by it, if not live by love,
    And if unfit for tombes and hearse
Our legend bee, it will be fit for verse;   30
    And if no peece of Chronicle wee prove,
      We'll build in sonnets pretty roomes;
     As well a well wrought urne becomes
The greatest ashes, as half-acre tombes,
    And by these hymnes, all shall approve   35
    Us *Canoniz'd* for Love.

20.   *fly*: a common example of both ephemerality and unbridled sexuality (§383; cf. §461), said to be hermaphroditic and resurrectable (§337).

21 (also 22). On the symbol ', see above, p. 5.

21.   *Tapers*: candles, self-killed in that they consume themselves; with phallic connotations (§195).
    die (also 26, 28); often equated with sexual intercourse (as above, p. 48, note on 16); the *cost* is the reduction in one's lifespan (*ibid.*).

22–23. The *Eagle* is symbolic of strength (and masculinity); the *dove*, of gentleness (and femininity). The *Phoenix* is the fabled Arabian bird, self-killed once every millennium but promptly resurrected from its own ashes. The allusions are secular because indubitably Petrarchan (§288) but also sacred because the three birds jointly and severally represent the Trinity (§388). Alchemical implications may also be present (§218).

29.   *hearse*: the ornate canopy over any elaborate Renaissance tomb (§383).

30.   *legend*: the word also meant 'the life of a saint' (§332).

31.   *peece*: fragment; also masterpiece and even fortress (§404).

32.   *sonnets*: in the generalized sense of 'love poems', as in the title *Songs and Sonets* (§383: see above, p. 46).
    roomes: the Italian word for 'room' is stanza.

33.   *becomes*: suits, befits (§172).

35.   *approve*: confirm (§172).

And thus invoke us; You whom reverend love
  Made one anothers hermitage;
You, to whom love was peace, that now is rage,
  Who did the whole worlds soule contract, and drove 40
    Into the glasses of your eyes
    So made such mirrors, and such spies,
That they did all to you epitomize,
  Countries, Townes, Courts: Beg from above
  A patterne of our love. 45

The triple Foole.

  I am two fooles, I know,
For loving, and for saying so
  In whining Poëtry;
But where's that wiseman, that would not be I,
  If she would not deny? 5
Then as th'earths inward narrow crooked lanes
Do purge sea waters fretfull salt away,
  I thought, if I could draw my paines,
Through Rimes vexation, I should them allay,
Griefe brought to numbers cannot be so fierce, 10
For, he tames it, that fetters it in verse.

  But when I have done so,
Some man, his art and voice to show,
  Doth Set and sing my paine,
And, by delighting many, frees againe 15
  Griefe, which verse did restraine.

The Canonization.
40. *contract*: 'extract' (acc. to several MSS), in an alchemical sense.
45. *patterne*: a technical term in Neoplatonic thought for Ideas in the mind of
    God (§383).
    our: 'your' (acc. to 1669 and several MSS).

The triple Foole. Entitled in some MSS *Song.*
6–7. Seawater was thought to be filtered by its passage through the earth (§169).
 9. *allay*: followed by a comma in 1633–39 but by a full stop in 1650–69.
10. *numbers*: poetic metre.
13. *and*: 'or' (acc. to 1669).
14. *Set*: i.e. to music.

To Love, and Griefe tribute of Verse belongs,
But not of such as pleases when'tis read,
   Both are increased by such songs:
For both their triumphs so are published,   20
And I, which was two fooles, do so grow three;
Who are a little wise, the best fooles bee.

Lovers infinitenesse.

If yet I have not all thy love,
Deare, I shall never have it all,
I cannot breath one other sigh, to move;
Nor can intreat one other teare to fall.
And all my treasure, which should purchase thee,   5
Sighs, teares, and oathes, and letters I have spent,
Yet no more can be due to mee,
Then at the bargaine made was ment,
If then thy gift of love were partiall,
That some to mee, some should to others fall,   10
   Deare, I shall never have Thee All.

The triple Foole.
18.   On the symbol ', see above, p. 5.
20.   *triumphs*: 'trialls' (acc. to several MSS).

Lovers infinitenesse. The 1633 title is not confirmed by any MS; possibly it
     should be *Loves infinitenesse* (§158; but see §172). Most MSS provide no
     title; some give *Mon Tout* (My Everything). The punctuation raises some
     questions, as the notes indicate. For a musical setting of a modified
     version of this poem in John Dowland's *A Pilgrim's Solace* (1612), see
     §169.
  1.   *if*: on 'the conditional *if*', here and throughout, see above, p. 24, note
     16.
     all: the poem's most pervasive word (§374).
  4. *fall*: followed by a full stop in 1633 but a semicolon in 1635–69.
  5. *And all*: 'All' (acc. to all MSS).
  8 (also 32). *Then*: than; 'That' (acc. to 1639–45).
  9. *partiall*: 'generall' (acc. to some MSS).
 11. *Thee*: 'It' (acc. to 1635–69).

Or if then thou gavest mee all,
All was but All, which thou hadst then,
But if in thy heart, since, there be or shall,
New love created bee, by other men,   15
Which have their stocks intire, and can in teares,
In sighs, in oathes, and letters outbid mee,
This new love may beget new feares,
For, this love was not vowed by thee,
And yet it was, thy gift being generall,   20
The ground, thy heart is mine, what ever shall
  Grow there, deare, I should have it all.

Yet I would not have all yet,
Hee that hath all can have no more,
And since my love doth every day admit   25
New growth, thou shouldst have new rewards in store;
Thou canst not every day give me thy heart,
If thou canst give it, then thou never gavest it:
Loves riddles are, that though thy heart depart,
It stayes at home, and thou with losing savest it: 30
But wee will have a way more liberall,
Then changing hearts, to joyne them, so wee shall
  Be one, and one anothers All.

12. *gavest*: 'givest' (acc. to 1669).
13. *then*: followed by a comma in 1633 but a full stop in 1635–54.
14. *heart*: 'breast' (acc. to some MSS).
   since: since that time.
17. *and*: 'in' (acc. to 1635–69 and some MSS).
19. *thee*: followed by a comma in 1633–35 but a full stop in 1639–69.
21. *ground*: legally, in the sale of land, the crops growing on the land belonged to the new owner unless otherwise stipulated (§162).
   is: 'was' (acc. to 1635–54 and some MSS).
25. *heart*: 'love' (acc. to some MSS); *admit*: 'begett' (ditto).
26. *growth*: 'love' (acc. to some MSS); cf. *Loves growth*, below, p. 79 (§374).
27 ff. Probably a deliberate reply to Sir Philip Sidney's 'My true love hath my heart and I have his' (§229).
29–30. The lines also read: 'Except mine come when thine doth part / And in such giving it, thou savest it'; or 'Perchance mine comes, when thine doth parte, / And by such losing it, thou savest it' (acc. to individual MSS).
31. *have*: 'love' (acc. to 1669) or 'find' (acc. to some MSS).
32. *joyne*: 'coyne' (acc. to one MS) or 'winne' (acc. to others).
   them: 'us' (acc. to 1669).

Song.

Sweetest love, I do not goe,
　For wearinesse of thee,
Nor in hope the world can show
　A fitter Love for mee,
　　But since that I   5
Must dye at last, 'tis best,
To use my selfe in jest
　Thus by fain'd deaths to dye;

Yesternight the Sunne went hence,
　And yet is here to day,   10
He hath no desire nor sense,
　Nor halfe so short a way:
　　Then feare not mee,
But beleeve that I shall make
Speedier journeyes, since I take   15
　More wings and spurres than hee.

O how feeble is mans power,
　That if good fortune fall,
Cannot adde another houre,
　Nor a lost houre recall!   20
　　But come bad chance,
And wee joyne to'it our strength,
And wee teach it art and length,
　It selfe o'r us to'advance.

Song. Coleridge praised the poem's 'sweetness and tenderness of expression,
　　chastened by a religious thoughtfulness and faith' (§210). According to
　　Walton's conjecture, Donne on leaving for the Continent in 1611 wrote
　　this poem and *A Valediction forbidding mourning* (below, p. 97) for his
　　wife (§313). For an anonymous musical setting, see §§163, 169, 190.
　　Most MSS print the first four lines of each stanza as two long lines; a few
　　MSS also print the 6th and 7th lines as one long line.
6.　　'At the last must part 'tis best' (acc. to 1635–54).
7.　　*To use*: 'Thus to use' (acc. to 1635–69).
8.　　*fain'd deaths*: i.e. absences.
15.　　*Speedier*: 'Hastier' (acc. to 1669).
22.　　*joyne*: 'add' (acc. to some MSS). On the symbol ' (also l. 24), see above,
　　　p. 5.

When thou sigh'st, thou sigh'st not winde,   25
 But sigh'st my soule away,
When thou weep'st, unkindly kinde,
 My lifes blood doth decay.
  It cannot bee
That thou lov'st mee, as thou say'st,   30
If in thine my life thou waste,
 Thou art the best of mee.

Let not thy divining heart
 Forethinke me any ill,
Destiny may take thy part,   35
 And may thy feares fulfill,
  But thinke that wee
Are but turn'd aside to sleepe;
They who one another keepe
 Alive, ne'r parted bee.   40

The Legacie.

When I dyed last, and, Deare, I dye
 As often as from thee I goe,
 Though it be but an houre agoe,
And Lovers houres be full eternity,
I can remember yet, that I   5
 Something did say, and something did bestow;
Though I be dead, which sent mee, I should be
Mine owne executor and Legacie.

Song.
25–28. Every sigh or tear was supposed to shorten life a little (*ALC*).
27. *kinde*: means both natural and affectionate (§167).
32. *Thou*: 'That' (acc. to 1635–54 and some MSS) or 'Which' (acc. to 1669).
  best: 'life' (ditto).
33. *divining*: prophetic.
36. *may*: 'make' (acc. to 1639–54).
38. *turn'd*: 'laid' (acc. to 1669).

The Legacie. Entitled in some MSS *Song*.
 3. *but*: omitted in some MSS.
 7. *sent*: 'meant' (acc. to 1635–54).
  should: 'might' (acc. to 1669).

I heard mee say, Tell her anon,
   That my selfe, (that's you, not I,)   10
   Did kill me, and when I felt mee dye,
I bid mee send my heart, when I was gone,
But I alas could there finde none,
   When I had ripp'd me, 'and search'd where hearts
      did lye,
It kill'd mee againe, that I who still was true,   15
In life, in my last Will should cozen you.

Yet I found something like a heart,
   But colours it, and corners had,
   It was not good, it was not bad,
It was intire to none, and few had part.   20
As good as could be made by art
   It seem'd, and therefore for our losses sad,
I meant to send this heart in stead of mine,
But oh, no man could hold it, for twas thine.

A Feaver.

Oh doe not die, for I shall hate
   All women so, when thou art gone,
That thee I shall not celebrate,
   When I remember, thou wast one.

10.   *that's*: 'that is' (acc. to 1635–69).
14.   On the symbol ', see above, p. 5. The line also reads: 'When I had ripp'd, and search'd where hearts should lye' (acc. to 1635–69 and some MSS).
16.   *cozen*: cheat.
18.   *But*: 'For' (acc. to 1650–69).
      colours it: i.e. it was painted, hypocritical; *and corners had*: unlike the perfect form of the circle (§172).
20.   *intire to*: given to, possessed by.
      part: i.e. any part of it.
23.   *meant*: 'thought' (acc. to several MSS).
      this: 'that' (acc. to 1635–69 and several MSS).

But yet thou canst not die, I know,   5
    To leave this world behinde, is death,
But when thou from this world wilt goe,
    The whole world vapors with thy breath.

Or if, when thou, the worlds soule, goest,
    It stay, tis but thy carkasse then,   10
The fairest woman, but thy ghost,
    But corrupt wormes, the worthyest men.

O wrangling schooles, that search what fire
    Shall burne this world, had none the wit
Unto this knowledge to aspire,   15
    That this her feaver might be it?

And yet she cannot wast by this,
    Nor long beare this torturing wrong,
For much corruption needfull is
    To fuell such a feaver long.   20

These burning fits but meteors bee,
    Whose matter in thee is soone spent.
Thy beauty,'and all parts, which are thee,
    Are unchangeable firmament.

A Feaver.
  8. *vapors*: evaporates.
      with: 'in' (acc. to 1669).
  9. *the worlds soule*: this Neoplatonic concept, here Petrarchan in its hyper-
      bole, is especially relevant to the two *Anniversaries* (below, pp. 325 ff.).
 13. *schooles*: scholastic philosophers generally (here inclusive of Stoics) and
      medieval ones particularly, who debated the nature of the *fire* at history's
      terminal conflagration.
 18. *beare*: 'endure' (acc. to 1669).
      torturing: 'tormenting' (acc. to some MSS).
 19. *For much*: 'For more' (acc. to several MSS) or 'Far more' (acc. to several
      MSS).
 23. On the symbol ', see above, p. 5.
 24. *firmament*: according to the Ptolemaic astronomy – increasingly obsoles-
      cent in Donne's time – the regions above the moon were regarded as
      unchangeable because incorruptible, unlike our sublunar world with its
      ephemeral *meteors* (21).

Yet 'twas of my minde, seising thee,   25
   Though it in thee cannot persever.
For I had rather owner bee
   Of thee one houre, than all else ever.

Aire and Angels.

Twice or thrice had I loved thee,
Before I knew thy face or name;
So in a voice, so in a shapelesse flame,
Angells affect us oft, and worship'd bee,
   Still when, to where thou wert, I came   5
Some lovely glorious nothing I did see,
   But since, my soule, whose child love is,
Takes limmes of flesh, and else could nothing doe,
   More subtile than the parent is,
Love must not be, but take a body too,   10
   And therefore what thou wert, and who
      I did Love aske, and now
That it assume thy body, I allow,
And fixe it selfe in thy lip, eye, and brow.

A Feaver.
25. *Yet 'twas of*: 'And here as' (acc. to 1669).
    seising: in the legal sense of taking possession; cf. *owner* in l. 27 (§172).
27. *For*: 'Yet' (acc. to 1669).
27–28. Coleridge admired these lines ('Just and affecting') but thought the
     preceding ones 'detestable' (§210).

Aire and Angels. Intolerant of doctrinaire interpretations, the poem invites
     readers to decide several questions for themselves (see notes on ll. 24 and
     26–28). Even the poem's stanza is inverted: it is apparently a free varia-
     tion of the sonnet, the sestet preceding the octave (§449, also §466).
 1–2. Cf. *The good-morrow*, ll. 6–7: 'If ever any beauty I did see, / . . . t'was but
     a dream of thee'.
  4. *affect*: influence; also, have affection for (§466).
  5. *Still*: always.
  6. *nothing*: see *Negative Love*, below, p. 117.
  9. *subtile*: rarefied, more delicate (*OED*).
 10. See above, p. 28.
 13. *assume*: also in a theological sense; cf. *inhere* (22).

Whilst thus to ballast love, I thought,   15
And so more steddily to have gone,
With wares which would sinke admiration,
I saw, I had loves pinnace overfraught,
   Ev'ry thy haire for love to worke upon
Is much too much, some fitter must be sought;   20
   For, nor in nothing, nor in things
Extreme, and scattring bright, can love inhere;
   Then as an Angell, face, and wings
Of aire, not pure as it, yet pure doth weare,
   So thy love may be my loves spheare;   25
     Just such disparitie
As is twixt Aire and Angells puritie,
T'wixt womens love, and mens will ever bee.

18.   *pinnace*: a small light vessel; also, a woman and – most unexpectedly – a prostitute (*OED*: §§405, 426); with a possible pun? (*ALC*, §405).

22.   *Extreme*: extremely.
    scattring: 'scattering' (acc. to 1639–69).
    inhere: abide in; remain in mystical union with (*OED*). Cf. above, p. 28: 'love . . . doth inhere in the body'.

23–24. In order to become visible to us, angels 'assume' a body, much as the soul and love do (cf. 7–13). But in a comparative sense their very natures are, as Donne thought, 'but grosse bodies' (*Sermons*, VII, 344). Increasingly through his time it was held that 'in comparison of God [angels] are bodies, in comparison of us they are pure and mighty spirits' (thus Henry Lawrence in 1646; see §107).

24.   Does *it* refer to *Angell* (23) or to *aire* (24) – or, conceivably, to both?

25.   *spheare*: as above, p. 54, note on 30.

26–28. Do the lines assert that (1) women's love is purer than men's, (2) men's is purer than women's, (3) both, (4) neither? Cf. §466.

27.   *Aire*: 'Airs' (acc. to 1669).

Breake of day.

'Tis true, 'tis day, what though it be?
O wilt thou therefore rise from me?
Why should we rise, because 'tis light?
Did we lie downe, because t'was night?
Love which in spight of darknesse brought us hether,   5
Should in despight of light keepe us together.

Light hath no tongue, but is all eye;
If it could speake as well as spie,
This were the worst, that it could say,
That being well, I faine would stay,   10
And that I lov'd my heart and honor so
That I would not from him, that had them, goe.

Must businesse thee from hence remove?
Oh, that's the worst disease of love,
The poore, the foule, the false, love can   15
Admit, but not the busied man.
He which hath businesse, and makes love, doth doe
Such wrong, as when a maryed man doth wooe.

The Anniversarie.

All Kings, and all their favorites,
All glory of honors, beauties, wits,
The Sun it selfe, which makes times, as they passe,
Is elder by a yeare, now, then it was

Breake of day. One of only two of the *Songs and Sonets* to be published in
    Donne's lifetime, the poem first appeared in William Corkine's *Second
    Booke of Ayres* in 1612 (§229); for its musical setting, see §§163, 169, 190.
  1 ff. The speaker is a woman, as in *Confined Love* and *Selfe Love*.
  6. *in despight*: 'in dispight' (acc. to 1650–54 and several MSS).
     keepe: 'holde' (acc. to some MSS).
 15. *foule*: 'foole' (acc. to a MS).
 18. *as when*: 'as if' (acc. to several MSS).
     doth: 'should' (ditto).

The Anniversarie.
  3. *they*: the *times* or the *Kings* or both; changed to 'these' (in 1635–54).
  4 (also 22). *then*: than.

When thou and I first one another saw: 5
All other things, to their destruction draw,
   Only our love hath no decay;
This, no to morrow hath, nor yesterday,
Running it never runs from us away,
But truly keepes his first, last, everlasting day.   10
   Two graves must hide thine and my coarse,
   If one might, death were no divorce,
Alas, as well as other Princes, wee,
(Who Prince enough in one another bee,)
Must leave at last in death, these eyes, and eares,   15
Oft fed with true oathes, and with sweet salt teares;
   But soules where nothing dwells but love
(All other thoughts being inmates) then shall prove
This, or a love increased there above,
When bodies to their graves, soules from their graves
      remove.   20

   And then wee shall be throughly blest,
   But wee no more, then all the rest.
Here upon earth, we'are Kings, and none but wee
Can be such Kings, nor of such subjects bee;
Who is so safe as wee? where none can doe   25
Treason to us, except one of us two.
   True and false feares let us refraine,
Let us love nobly, and live, and adde againe
Yeares and yeares unto yeares, till we attaine
To write threescore, this is the second of our raigne.   30

10. *his*: i.e. its; 'the' (acc. to some MSS).
11. *coarse*: corpse.
12. Most modern editors end the line with a full stop.
17. In 1633–69 the line ends with a semicolon.
18. *inmates*: temporary lodgers.
     prove: experience.
19. *there above*: in heaven.
21. *throughly*: thoroughly.
22. *wee* (acc. to most MSS): 'now' (acc. to 1633–69).
23. On the symbol ', see above, p. 5.
23–24. *and none but wee / Can be such Kings*: 'and but wee / None are such Kings'
     (acc. to 1669 and several MSS).
24. *of such*: i.e. kings.
27. *refrain*: curb.
30. *threescore*: sixty, the Biblical full span of life.

A Valediction of my name, in the window.

I.

My name engrav'd herein,
Doth contribute my firmnesse to this glasse,
    Which, ever since that charme, hath beene
    As hard, as that which grav'd it, was,
Thine eye will give it price enough, to mock   5
    The diamonds of either rock.

II.

'Tis much that glasse should bee
As all confessing, and through-shine as I,
    'Tis more, that it shewes thee to thee,
    And cleare reflects thee to thine eye.   10
But all such rules, loves magique can undoe,
    Here you see mee, and I am you.

III.

As no one point, nor dash,
Which are but accessaries to this name,
    The showers and tempests can outwash,   15
    So shall all times finde mee the same;
You this intirenesse better may fulfill,
    Who have the patterne with you still.

A Valediction of [i.e. on] *my name*. One MS helpfully adds, 'Upon the ingravinge
of his name with a Diamonde in his mistris windowe when he was to
travel'. Valediction is the general designation of any poem bidding
farewell (§158).

4. *that which* (en)*grav'd it*: a diamond.
5. *eye*: 'eyes' (acc. to several MSS).
6. Diamonds either from old rock – considered the best kind – or new rock
    (§356).
8. *through-shine*: transparent.
12. *am you*: 'see you' (acc. to 1669).
14. *accessaries*: 'accessarie' (acc. to many MSS).
17. *intirenesse*: 'settled constancy, of which the engraved name is the type'
    (§166).

IV.

    Or if too hard and deepe
This learning be, for a scratch'd name to teach,   20
  It, as a given deaths head keepe,
  Lovers mortalitie to preach,
Or thinke this ragged bony name to bee
    My ruinous Anatomie.

V.

    Then, as all my soules bee,   25
Emparadis'd in you, (in whom alone
  I understand, and grow and see,)
  The rafters of my body, bone
Being still with you, the Muscle, Sinew, and Veine,
    Which tile this house, will come againe.   30

VI.

    Till my returne, repaire
And recompact my scattered body so.
  As all the vertuous powers which are
  Fix'd in the starres, are said to flow,
Into such characters, as graved bee   35
    When these starres have supremacie:

VII.

    So since this name was cut
When love and griefe their exaltation had,
  No doore 'gainst this names influence shut,
  As much more loving, as more sad,   40
'Twill make thee; and thou shouldst, till I returne,
    Since I die daily, daily mourne.

---

21. *a given deaths head*: a representation of a skull, often on a ring, given as a
    reminder of mortality.
24. *ruinous Anatomie:* tattered skeleton (§207).
25. *all my soules*: the traditional three – intellectual, vegetative, sensitive – that
    help us respectively to *understand*, *grow*, *see* (27); see further below,
    p. 300, note on 34–35.
28. *rafters*: bones which are the 'Beames, and Timbers, and Rafters of . . .
    these bodies of ours' (*Sermons*, V, 352: §158).
36. *have supremacie*: are in the ascendant.
42. *die daily*: as lovers do when they are apart (see above, p. 63, ll. 1 ff.).

VIII.

When thy inconsiderate hand
Flings ope this casement, with my trembling name,
  To looke on one, whose wit or land,   45
  New battry to thy heart may frame,
Then thinke this name alive, and that thou thus
      In it offendst my Genius.

IX.

And when thy melted maid,
Corrupted by thy Lover's gold, and page,   50
  His letter at thy pillow'hath laid,
  Disputed it, and tam'd thy rage,
And thou begin'st to thaw towards him, for this,
      May my name step in, and hide his.

X.

And if this treason goe   55
To an overt act, and that thou write againe;
  In superscribing, this name flow
  Into thy fancy, from the pane.
So, in forgetting thou remembrest right,
      And unaware to mee shalt write.   60

44. *ope*: 'out' (acc. to most MSS).
46. *battry*: amorous assault (§163).
48. *Genius*: guardian spirit.
49. *melted*: softened into supporting the lover's cause (§172).
50. *and*: 'or' (acc. to 1669 and some MSS).
    page: male servant.
51. On the symbol ', see above, p. 5.
52. *Disputed it*: argued in its favour.
52–53. The lines also read, 'Disputed thou it, and tame thy rage. / If thou to
    him begin'st to thaw for this,' (acc. to 1669).
55. *goe*: 'growe' (acc. to some MSS).
55–56. The allusion is to the legal distinction between treasonable intent and
    treason manifested in an overt act (§172).
57. *In superscribing, this name* . . . : i.e. in addressing the letter, may this
    name . . . (OED: §169).
    this: 'my' (acc. to 1669).
58. *pane*: 'Pen' (acc. to 1635–69 and some MSS).

XI.

But glasse, and lines must bee,
No meanes our firme substantiall love to keepe;
  Neere death inflicts this lethargie,
  And this I murmure in my sleepe;
Impute this idle talke, to that I goe,   65
  For dying men talke often so.

Twicknam garden.

Blasted with sighs, and surrounded with teares,
  Hither I come to seeke the spring,
  And at mine eyes, and at mine eares,
Receive such balmes, as else cure every thing,
  But O, selfe traytor, I do bring   5
The spider love, which transubstantiates all,
  And can convert Manna to gall,
And that this place may thoroughly be thought
  True Paradise, I have the serpent brought.

A Valediction of my name.
63. *lethargie*: coma (§166).
64. *this*: 'thus' (acc. to 1635–69 and some MSS).
65. *goe*: depart, tantamount for a lover to *dying* (see note on 42).

Twicknam garden. Twickenham Park was the residence of Donne's friend and
    patroness Lucy, Countess of Bedford, from 1608 to 1618 (cf. below,
    p. 266). But the relevance of the estate to the poem is a matter of dispute.
1. *surrounded*: overflowing (§158).
3. *eares*: 'years' (acc. to 1669).
3–4. The metaphor is that of the Catholic sacrament of extreme unction
    (§195).
6. The *spider* was said to turn 'all into excrement and poison' (§169);
    anciently classified as a worm, it was believed to germinate without
    sexual intercourse, here representing the narrator's unfulfilled sexuality
    (§288).
    transubstantiates: alters the substance of; with an obvious reference to its
    theological application to the Eucharist.
7. *Manna*: the food of the Israelites in the desert (Exodus 16.14–15); also
    typologically representative of the Eucharist.
9. *serpent*: Satan specifically, evil generally.

'Twere wholsomer for mee, that winter did   10
  Benight the glory of this place,
  And that a grave frost did forbid
These trees to laugh and mocke mee to my face;
  But that I may not this disgrace
Indure, nor yet leave loving, Love let mee   15
  Some senslesse peece of this place bee;
Make me a mandrake, so I may grow here,
  Or a stone fountaine weeping out my yeare.

Hither with christall vyals, lovers come,
  And take my teares, which are loves wine,   20
  And try your mistresse Teares at home,
For all are false, that tast not just like mine;
  Alas, hearts do not in eyes shine,
Nor can you more judge womans thoughts by teares,
  Then by her shadow, what she weares.   25
O perverse sexe, where none is true but shee,
  Who's therefore true, because her truth kills mee.

10. *that*: if.
12. *grave*: heavy.
    did: 'would' (acc. to some MSS).
14. *that I may not*: 'since I cannot' (acc. to 1669).
15. *nor yet leave loving*: 'nor leave this garden' (acc. to 1635–69 and many
    MSS).
16. *Senslesse*: insensible.
    peece: 'part' (acc. to some MSS).
17. *mandrake*: for its lore, see above, p. 50, note on 2.
    grow: 'groane' (acc. to some MSS), which is what the mandrake is said to
    do when uprooted; but *grow* (acc. to 1633–69 and several MSS) fits the
    meaning well enough (§188).
18. The line ends in a comma in some MSS and editions (1633, 1669) but a
    full stop in others (1635–54).
19. *christall vyalls*: the small vessels in ancient tombs, believed in Donne's
    time to have been tear-bottles to collect mourners' tears (§169).
20. *loves*: 'lovers' (acc. to 1639).
23. The converse is stated in *The good-morrow*, l. 16: 'true plaine hearts doe in
    the faces rest' (§195).
21. *try*: test.
25. *Then*: than.
26. *true*: i.e. faithful to her present lover, which makes her perverse in the
    narrator's eyes.

Valediction to his booke.

I'll tell thee now (deare Love) what thou shalt doe
   To anger destiny, as she doth us,
   How I shall stay, though she Esloygne me thus
And how posterity shall know it too;
     How thine may out-endure   5
       Sybills glory, and obscure
       Her who from Pindar could allure,
  And her, through whose helpe *Lucan* is not lame,
And her, whose booke (they say) *Homer* did finde, and
      name.

Study our manuscripts, those Myriades   10
   Of letters, which have past twixt thee and mee,
   Thence write our Annals, and in them will bee
To all whom loves subliming fire invades,
     Rule and example found;
       There, the faith of any ground   15
       No schismatique will dare to wound,
  That sees, how Love this grace to us affords,
To make, to keep, to use, to be these his Records,

This Booke, as long-liv'd as the elements,
   Or as the worlds forme, this all-graved tome   20
   In cypher writ, or new made Idiome;
Wee for loves clergie only'are instruments,

Valediction to ['of' in several MSS] *his booke.* Cf. above, p. 70.
  3. *Esloygne*: eloin, remove far off (*OED*).
  6–9. The traditions cited are to the Cumaean *Sibyl*, a legendary prophetess;
    the poetess Corinna, who defeated the great *Pindar* in poetic competi-
    tions; Polla Argentaria, who assisted her husband *Lucan* with his poetry;
    and the mythical Egyptian prophetess Phantasia, who is reputed to have
    been *Homer*'s source.
 13. *subliming*: purifying.
 15. *the faith of any ground*: the orthodoxy of any fundamental doctrine (§169).
 16. *schismatique*: one who has separated from a Church (cf. p. 106, l. 20).
 17. *That sees*: if he sees.
 20. *tome* (i.e. heavy book): 'to me' (acc. to 1639–54) or 'Tomb' (acc. to 1669
    and some MSS).
 22. On the symbol ', see above, p. 5.

When this booke is made thus,
Should againe the ravenous
Vandals and Goths invade us,   25
Learning were safe; in this our Universe
Schooles might learne Sciences, Spheares Musick, Angels
      Verse.

Here Loves Divines, (since all Divinity
Is love or wonder) may finde all they seeke,
Whether abstract spirituall love they like.   30
Their Soules exhal'd with what they do not see,
      Or, loth so to amuze,
      Faiths infirmitie, they chuse
      Something which they may see and use;
For, though minde be the heaven, where love doth sit, 35
Beauty a convenient type may be to figure it.

Here more than in their bookes may Lawyers finde,
Both by what titles, Mistresses are ours,
And how prerogative these states devours,
Transferr'd from Love himselfe, to womankinde,   40
      Who though from heart, and eyes,
      They exact great subsidies,
      Forsake him who on them relies
And for the cause, honour, or conscience give,
Chimeraes, vaine as they, or their prerogative.   45

25. *invade*: 'inundate' (acc. to many MSS and most modern editors); but
     'invade' (acc. to 1633–69 and several MSS) fits the meaning well enough,
     as does the 1633 punctuation so often tampered with (see §188).
27. *Schooles*: scholastic philosophers, esp. medieval.
     Spheares: celestial bodies, said to emit *Musick*.
     Verse: presumably angelic hymns.
30. *abstract*: 'abstracted' (acc. to 1669).
31. *exhal'd*: drawn out.
32. *amuze*: bemuse, puzzle (§250).
36. *type*: an earthly reflection of the celestial original.
     figure: represent.
38–39. *titles*, *states*: legal rights or entitlements to the possession of property
     (§166). *these states*: 'those rites' (acc. to some MSS).

Here Statesmen, (or of them, they which can reade,)
  May of their occupation finde the grounds,
  Love and their art alike it deadly wounds,
If to consider what 'tis, one proceed,
    In both they doe excell   50
      Who the present governe well,
      Whose weaknesse none doth, or dares tell;
  In this thy booke, such will their nothing see,
As in the Bible some can finde out Alchimy.

Thus vent thy thoughts; abroad I'll studie thee,   55
  As he removes farre off, that great heights takes;
  How great love is, presence best tryall makes,
But absence tryes how long this love will bee;
    To take a latitude
      Sun, or starres, are fitliest view'd   60
      At their brightest, but to conclude
  Of longitudes, what other way have wee,
But to marke when, and where the darke eclipses bee?

47. *grounds*: basic principles (cf. l. 15).
53. *such*: such people.
     their nothing: their nothingness.
55. *vent*: 'went' (acc. to 1635–54).
56. *takes*: measures (§166).
58. *tryes*: tests.
59–63. Strictly imagined, the comparison rests on 'a purely verbal basis'
     (§158). *Latitude* means breadth, *longitude* length; but one may *conclude of*
     (determine) longitude by comparing the times at which an eclipse is
     observed from different points (§164).
61. *At their brightest*: at their actual or apparent highest point in relation to the
     observer (§351).

Communitie.

Good wee must love, and must hate ill,
For ill is ill, and good good still,
 But there are things indifferent,
Which wee may neither hate, nor love,
But one, and then another prove,   5
 As wee shall finde our fancy bent.

If then at first wise Nature had
Made women either good or bad,
 Then some wee might hate, and some chuse,
But since shee did them so create,   10
That we may neither love, nor hate,
 Onely this rests, All, all may use.

If they were good it would be seene,
Good is as visible as greene,
 And to all eyes it selfe betrayes,   15
If they were bad, they could not last,
Bad doth it selfe, and others wast,
 So, they deserve nor blame, nor praise.

But they are ours as fruits are ours,
He that but tasts, he that devours,   20
 And he that leaves all, doth as well,
Chang'd loves are but chang'd sorts of meat,
And when hee hath the kernell eate,
 Who doth not fling away the shell?

Communitie. Untitled in 1633 and most MSS; first entitled from 1635. On the
 poem see §400.
 2. *still*: always.
 3. *indifferent*: see above, p. 54.
 5. *prove*: try.
 12. *rests*: remains.
   All, all may use: all men may use all women (hence the title: women are
   common property).
 21. *that*: 'which' (acc. to several MSS).

Loves growth.

I scarce beleeve my love to be so pure
  As I had thought it was,
  Because it doth endure
Vicissitude, and season, as the grasse;
Me thinkes I lyed all winter, when I swore,   5
My love was infinite, if spring make'it more.
But if this medicine, love, which cures all sorrow
With more, not onely bee no quintessence,
But mixt of all stuffes, paining soule, or sense,
And of the Sunne his working vigour borrow,   10
Love's not so pure, and abstract, as they use
To say, which have no Mistresse but their Muse,
But as all else, being elemented too,
Love sometimes would contemplate, sometimes do.

And yet no greater, but more eminent,   15
  Love by the Spring is growne;
  As, in the firmament,
Starres by the Sunne are not inlarg'd, but showne,
Gentle love deeds, as blossomes on a bough,
From loves awakened root do bud out now.   20

Loves growth. Entitled in several MSS *Spring*. The poem is perhaps a companion piece to *Aire and Angels* (above, p. 66), partly because both are variations of the sonnet, the sestet preceding the octave (§449).

1. *pure*: simple and unmixed, therefore not subject to change (§169).
4. *grasse*: cf. 'All flesh is grass' (Isaiah 40.6: §273).
6. On the symbol ', see above, p. 5.
  more: the poem's most pervasive word (§374).
8. *quintessence*: the reputed fifth element of life beyond the sublunar four (air, earth, fire, and water); in its pure state it was expected to cure all ills (cf. below, p. 86, note on 7).
9. *paining*: 'vexing' (acc. to 1635–69 and some MSS).
10. *working*: 'active' (ditto).
13. *elemented*: compounded of all the elements, *mixt of all stuffes* (9); cf. above, p. 29, and below, p. 114, ll. 1–4.
18–19. One MS reads, 'Stars are not by the sunne enlarg'd; but showne / Greater; Loves deeds' etc. In the text above, 'so' is presupposed before *Gentle* (§188). The lines probably argue that stars inclusive of the planets are *not inlarg'd* but only *showne* by virtue of the light from the sun which they reflect; so, too, love is only shown to be *more eminent* (15) by spring's influence which causes it to reveal itself (§395; cf. §334).

If, as in water stir'd more circles bee
Produc'd by one, love such additions take,
Those like so many spheares, but one heaven make,
For, they are all concentrique unto thee,
And though each spring doe adde to love new heate,   25
As princes doe in times of action get
New taxes, and remit them not in peace,
No winter shall abate the springs encrease.

Loves exchange.

Love, any devill else but you,
Would for a given Soule give something too.
At Court your fellowes every day,
Give th'art of Riming, Huntsmanship, or play,
For them which were their owne before;   5
Onely I have nothing which gave more,
But am, alas, be being lowly, lower.

I aske no dispensation now
To falsifie a teare, or sigh, or vow,
I do not sue from thee to draw   10
A *non obstante* on natures law,
These are prerogatives, they inhere
In thee and thine; none should forsweare
Except that hee *Loves* minion were.

Loves growth.
23. *spheares*: the transparent, 'pure' spheres in which the planets were
     thought to be embedded; they were of course *concentrique* (24) to the
     earth.
27. *New taxes*: so, too, growing love levies its own taxes, involving several
     obligations (§457).
28. *the*: 'this' (acc. to 1635–69 and some MSS).

Loves exchange.
 4. *or*: 'and' (acc. to most MSS).
     Play: gambling.
 9. *or . . . or*: 'a . . . a' (acc. to 1669).
11. *A non obstante*: a waiving of any law in favour of an individual (§158).
14. *minion*: one specially favoured or beloved; not used in a contemptuous
     sense (*OED*: §158).

Give mee thy weaknesse, make mee blinde,   15
Both wayes, as thou and thine, in eies and minde;
Love, let me never know that this
Is love, or, that love childish is.
Let me not know that others know
That she knowes my paines, lest that so   20
A tender shame make me mine owne new woe.

If thou give nothing, yet thou'art just,
Because I would not thy first motions trust;
Small townes which stand stiffe, till great shot
Enforce them, by warres law *condition* not.   25
Such in loves warfare is my case,
I may not article for grace,
Having put love at last to shew this face.

This face, by which he could command
And change the Idolatric of any land,   30
This face, which wheresoe'r it comes,
Can call vow'd men from cloisters, dead from tombes,
And melt both Poles at once, and store
Deserts with cities, and make more
Mynes in the earth, than Quarries were before.   35

For this, love is enrag'd with mee,
Yet kills not; if I must example bee
To future Rebells; If th'unborne
Must learne, by my being cut up, and torne:

22.   On the symbol ', see above, p. 5.
23.   *motions*: impulses.
24–25. By the law of war, small towns which hold out against siege until
       heavy attack subdues them cannot set conditions of surrender (§163).
27.   *article*: make stipulations (§169).
28.   *this*: 'his' (acc. to 1669).
29–33. Coleridge thought these lines an 'Extravaganza truly *Donnesque*'
       (§210).
35.   *Mynes*: see above, p. 54, note on 17.
36.   *For, this love* (acc. to 1633–69): most modern editors punctuate 'For this ,
       love'.

Kill, and dissect me, Love; for this   40
Torture against thine owne end is,
Rack't carcasses make ill Anatomies.

Confined Love.

Some man unworthy to be possessor
Of old or new love, himselfe being false or weake,
   Thought his paine and shame would be lesser,
If on womankind he might his anger wreake,
      And thence a law did grow,   5
      One might but one man know;
      But are other creatures so?

   Are Sunne, Moone, or Starres by law forbidden,
To smile where they list, or lend away their light?
   Are birds divorc'd, or are they chidden   10
If they leave their mate, or lie abroad a night?
      Beasts doe no joyntures lose
      Though they new lovers choose,
      But we are made worse than those.

Loves exchange.
42.   Anatomists avoided using the carcasses of men who died of torturing,
     wounds, illnesses, or beheading (§192).

Confined Love. Untitled in 1633 and most MSS; first entitled from 1635.
     Headed in one MS, 'To the worthiest of all my Lovers'; in another, 'To
     the worthiest of all my lov my virtuous Mrs P'.
1 ff. The speaker is a woman, as in *Breake of day* and *Selfe Love*: note esp. l. 6.
3.   *lesser*: 'the lesser' (acc. to some MSS).
6.   *might*: 'should' (acc. to many MSS).
9.   *lend*: 'bend' (acc. to 1669).
11. *mate* (acc. to 1633–39): 'meate' (acc. to 1650–69).
     a night: i.e. a-night; 'all night' (acc. to 1669).
12. *jointures*: joining, union; also joint holding of an estate by husband and
     wife for life (*OED: ALC*).

Who e'r rigg'd faire ship to lie in harbors,   15
And not to seeke new lands, or not to deale withall?
    Or built faire houses, set trees, and arbors,
Only to lock up, or else to let them fall?
            Good is not good, unlesse
            A thousand it possesse,   20
            But doth wast with greedinesse.

The Dreame.

Deare love, for nothing lesse then thee
Would I have broke this happy dreame,
            It was a theame
For reason, much too strong for phantasie,
Therefore thou wakd'st me wisely; yet   5
My Dreame thou brok'st not, but continued'st it,
Thou art so truth, that thoughts of thee suffice,
To make dreames truths; and fables histories;
Enter these armes, for since thou thoughtst it best,
Not to dreame all my dreame, let's act the rest.   10

As lightning, or a Tapers light,
Thine eyes, and not thy noise wak'd mee;
            Yet I thought thee
(For thou lovest truth) an Angell, at first sight,

Confined Love.
16. *seeke new lands*: 'seeke lands' (acc. to 1639–69).
     deale withall: trade with.
     withall: 'with all' (acc. to 1635–69).
17. *built* (acc. to 1633–35): 'build' (acc. to 1639–69).
20. *it possesse*: possess it.
21. *wast*: waste away.

The Dreame. Cf. Elegy X, below, p. 154.
 1. *then*: than.
 7. *so*: such.
     truth (acc. to 1633 and many MSS): 'true' (acc. to 1635–69 and several
     MSS).
10. *act*: 'doe' (acc. to many MSS).
11–12. Cf. 'A Candle wakes some men, as well as a noyse' (*Sermons*, IX, 366:
     §158).
14. *an Angell*: 'but an Angell' (acc. to many MSS).

But when I saw thou sawest my heart,   15
And knew'st my thoughts, beyond an Angels art,
When thou knew'st what I dreamt, when thou knew'st
        when
Excess of joy would wake me, and cam'st then,
I must confesse, it could not chuse but bee
Prophane, to thinke thee any thing but thee.   20

Comming and staying show'd thee, thee,
But rising makes me doubt, that now,
        Thou art not thou.
That love is weake, where feare's as strong as hee;
'Tis not all spirit, pure, and brave,   25
If mixture it of *Feare*, *Shame*, *Honor*, have;
Perchance as torches which must ready bee,
Men light and put out, so thou deal'st with mee,
Thou cam'st to kindle, goest to come; Then I
Will dreame that hope againe, but else would die.   30

A Valediction of weeping.

        Let me powre forth
My teares before thy face, whil'st I stay here,
For thy face coines them, and thy stampe they beare,
And by this Mintage they are something worth,

The Dreame.
16.   One's *thoughts* are hidden from *Angels* and known solely to God.
17.   The second *when*: 'then' (acc. to 1669).
19.   *must*: 'doe' (acc. to most MSS).
20.   *Prophane*: 'Profaness' (ditto).
21.   *show'd thee, thee*: showed you to be yourself.
22.   *doubt*: fear.
24.   *feare's as strong* (acc. to 1633–54 and many MSS): 'feares are strong' (acc.
      to 1669 and several MSS).
25.   *pure*: simple, 'unmixed'.
27–28.   Cf. 'a *Torch* that hath been lighted, and used *before*, is easier lighted then
      a *new torch*' (*Sermons*, II, 131: §169).
29.   *Then I*: 'Thus I' (acc. to several MSS).

A Valediction of [i.e. on] *weeping*. Entitled in some MSS *A Valediction of Teares*;
      in others, simply *A Valediction*. Cf. above, p. 70.
  3.   *coines*: produces; also, gives value.

                For thus they bee   5
                Pregnant of thee,
Fruits of much griefe they are, emblemes of more,
When a teare falls, that thou falst which it bore,
So thou and I are nothing then, when on a divers shore.

                On a round ball   10
A workeman that hath copies by, can lay
An Europe, Afrique, and an Asia,
And quickly make that, which was nothing, *All*,
                So doth each teare,
                Which thee doth weare,   15
A globe, yea world by that impression grow,
Till thy teares mixt with mine doe overflow
This world, by waters sent from thee, my heaven
      dissolved so.

                O more then Moone,
Draw not up seas to drowne me in thy spheare,   20
Weepe me not dead, in thine armes, but forbeare
To teach the sea, what it may doe too soone,
                Let not the winde
                Example finde,
To doe me more harme, then it purposeth,   25
Since thou and I sigh one anothers breath,
Who e'r sighes most, is cruellest, and hastes the others
      death.

  8. 'His tear, signed by her image, falls to the ground: her reflection in it falls
      too' (§229).
      falst (acc. to 1633–69): 'falls' (acc. to most MSS).
  9. *diverse shore*: different countries.
10–13. Cf. 'if a flat Map be but pasted upon a round Globe, the farthest East,
      and the Farthest West meet, and are all one' (Donne, in a letter: §169).
 15. i.e. which bears your image.
 16. *world*: 'would' (acc. to 1669).
 19. *more then Moone*: not just a satellite of the world but the world itself
      (§163).
 20. *up*: 'thy' (acc. to 1669).
26–27. As above, p. 63, note on 25–28.

Loves Alchymie.

Some that have deeper digg'd loves Myne then I,
Say, where his centrique happinesse doth lie:
      I have lov'd, and got, and told,
But should I love, get, tell, till I were old,
I should not finde that hidden mysterie;   5
      Oh, 'tis imposture all:
And as no chymique yet th'Elixar got,
      But glorifies his pregnant pot,
      If by the way to him befall
Some odoriferous thing, or medicinall,   10
  So, lovers dreame a rich and long delight,
  But get a winter-seeming summers night.

Our ease, our thrift, our honor, and our day,
Shall we, for this vaine Bubles shadow pay?
      Ends love in this, that my man,   15
Can be as happy'as I can; If he can
Endure the short scorne of a Bridegroomes play?
      That loving wretch that sweares,
'Tis not the bodies marry, but the mindes,
      Which he in her Angelique findes,   20

Loves Alchymie. Entitled in several MSS *Mummye* (see l. 24).
2. *centrique*: central, essential.
3. *told*: counted (i.e. the successful love affairs: §172).
7. *chymique*: alchemist.
    Elixar: the alchemists' Elixir Vitae, supposed to heal all diseases; some-
    times identified with the Philosopher's Stone, expected to transmute
    metals into gold (§158).
8. *pregnant pot*: a common alchemical analogy between the preparation of
    the Philosopher's Stone and human generation (§218).
10. i.e. some of the byproducts discovered by alchemists searching for the
    elixir (§127).
12. *winter-seeming summers night*: i.e. cold and short.
15. *man*: servant.
16 (also 24). On the symbol ', see above, p. 5.
17. i.e. 'endure the soon-past indignity of the role of a Bridegroom'? (§169).

> Would sweare as justly, that he heares,
> In that dayes rude hoarse minstralsey, the spheares.
> Hope not for minde in women; at their best,
> Sweetnesse, and wit they'are, but, *Mummy*, possest.

The Curse.

> Who ever guesses, thinks, or dreames he knowes—
> Who is my mistris, wither by this curse;
>   His only, and only his purse
>   May some dull heart to love dispose,
> And shee yeeld then to all that are his foes;   5
>   May he be scorn'd by one, whom all clse scorne,
>   Forsweare to others, what to her he'hath sworne,
>   With feare of missing, shame of getting torne;
>
> Madnesse his sorrow, gout his cramp, may hee
> Make, by but thinking, who hath made him such: 10

Loves Alchymie.
21–22. No mortal ever *heares* the music emitted by the celestial *spheares*, see
           The Merchant of Venice, V, i, 60–65.
22.   *dayes*: i.e. wedding day's.
24.   Punctuated by some modern editors, 'Sweetnesse and wit, they're but
           Mummy, possest' (§§158, 159, 169); but the punctuation of 1633–54,
           given here, is defensible (see §§188, 383).
           Mummy: body without mind; also a reputed panacea prepared from a
           mummified body, most bitter to the taste (see the detailed account in Dr
           Samuel Johnson's *Dictionary*).
           possest: as above, p. 49, note on 14.

The Curse. Printed 35th in the sequence of *Songs and Sonets* in 1633, immedi-
           ately after *The Flea*, itself shifted to first place from 1635 (see above,
           p. 47). The poem is entitled in some MSS *Dirae* (i.e. The Furies). Its
           antecedents are classical: 'A certaine auncient form of poesie by which
           men did use to reproach their enemies' (George Puttenham, in 1589:
           §169).
  3.   'Him, only for his purse' (acc. to 1669).
  4.   *heart*: 'whore' (ditto).
  5.   *And she yeeld then to*: 'And then yield unto' (ditto).
  7.   On the symbol ', see above, p. 5.
  8.   Torn between fear of not winning her and shame of winning her (§163).
  9.   *cramp*: 'cramps' (acc. to 1669 and many MSS).
10.   *him*: 'them' (acc. to 1669).

And may he feele no touch
Of conscience, but of fame, and bee
Anguish'd, not that'twas sinne, but that'twas shee:
   In early and long scarcenesse may he rot,
   For land which had been his, if he had not   15
   Himselfe incestuously an heire begot:

May he dreame Treason, and beleeve, that hee
Meant to performe it, and confesse, and die,
         And no record tell why:
         His sonnes, which none of his may bee,   20
Inherite nothing but his infamie:
   Or may he so long Parasites have fed,
   That he would faine be theirs, whom he hath bred,
   And at the last be circumcis'd for bread:

The venom of all stepdames, gamsters gall,   25
What Tyrans, and their subjects interwish,
         What Plants, Myne, Beasts, Foule, Fish,
         Can contribute, all ill, which all
Prophets, or Poets spake; And all which shall
   Be annex'd in schedules unto this by mee,   30
   Fall on that man; For if it be a shee
   Nature beforehand hath out-cursed mee.

12. *fame*: public opinion, public reputation (§250); 'shame' (acc. to several
     MSS).
14. *scarcenesse*: poverty.
14–16. The lines also read, 'Or may he for her vertue reverence / One that
     hates him onely for impotence, / And equall Traitors be she and his sense'
     (acc. to 1635–69 and many MSS).
18. *Meant*: 'Went' (acc. to some MSS).
24. i.e. may he become a Jew in order either 'to benefit from the mutual
     assistance customary in the Jewish community' (§164) or 'to obtain
     sustenance, since proverbially Jews, the moneylenders of London, were
     miserly'? (§163).
26. *Tyrans*: the common variant of 'Tyrants' (acc. to 1639–69).
     interwish: the word is representative of Donne's fondness for recip-
     rocities, commonly averred through verbs with the prefix 'inter-' (§207).
30. *schedules*: appended supplementary papers (*ALC*).

The Message.

Send home my long strayd eyes to mee,
Which (Oh) too long have dwelt on thee,
Yet since there they have learn'd such ill,
    Such forc'd fashions,
    And false passions,   5
      That they be
      Made by thee
Fit for no good sight, keep them still.

Send home my harmlesse heart againe,
Which no unworthy thought could staine,   10
Which if it be taught by thine
    To make jestings
    Of protestings,
      And breake both
      Word and oath,   15
Keepe it, for then 'tis none of mine.

Yet send me back my heart and eyes,
That I may know, and see thy lyes,
And may laugh and joy, when thou
    Art in anguish   20
    And dost languish
      For some one
      That will none,
Or prove as false as thou art now.

The Message. The seven poems up to and including *A Valediction forbidding
   mourning* (below, p. 97), placed at the outset of *Songs and Sonets* in 1633.
   were shifted to their present position from 1635. The sequence of the
   seven poems is the same in all editions. *The Message*, untitled in 1633, was
   first entitled from 1635; some MSS entitle it *Song*. For Giovanni
   Coperario's musical setting, see §§163, 169, 190.
  3. *yet since*: 'But if they' (acc. to 1669).
 11. *Which* (acc. to 1633 and many MSS): 'But' (acc. to 1635–69).
 14. *breake* (acc. to 1633–69): 'crosse' (acc. to most MSS and all modern
    editors).
 16. *Keepe it, for then*: 'Keep it still' (acc. to 1669).
 19. The line also reads, 'And may laugh, when that Thou' (acc. to some
    MSS).
 23. i.e. that will have none of you.
 24. *art*: 'dost' (acc. to 1669).

A nocturnall upon S. *Lucies* day,
Being the shortest day.

Tis the yeares midnight, and it is the dayes,
Lucies, who scarce seaven houres herself unmaskes,
　The Sunne is spent, and now his flasks
　Send forth light squibs, no constant rayes;
　　The worlds whole sap is sunke:　　　　　　　　5
The generall balme th'hydroptique earth hath drunk,
Whither, as to the beds-feet life is shrunke,
Dead and enterr'd, yet all these seeme to laugh,
Compar'd with mee, who am their Epitaph.

Study me then, you who shall lovers bee　　　　　10
At the next world, that is, at the next Spring:
　For I am every dead thing,
　In whom love wrought new Alchimie.
　　For his art did expresse
A quintessence even from nothingnesse,　　　　　15

A nocturnall upon S. Lucies day. The nocturns or night offices of the Roman
　Catholic Church are set services or, as here, night prayers ('vigils') held
　in the primitive church at midnight. This particular nocturnal is held on
　the night of December 12th which, as the shortest day of the year
　(according to the old calendar in use in Donne's time), marks the onset of
　the winter solstice as the sun enters the sign of the Goat (Capricorn). But
　it also marks the ensuing day's festival of St Lucy, the virgin martyr and
　patron saint of sight, who is ever associated by way of her name with
　light (*luce*: §195).
3.　*flasks*: powder-flasks, i.e. stars, thought to store up light from the sun;
　also, mocking remarks (§195).
4.　*squibs*: firecrackers.
6.　*balme*: the vital substance held to pervade all organic bodies.
　hydroptique: dropsical, immoderately thirsty.
　On the symbol ', see above, p. 5.
7.　*to the beds-feet*: it was believed that, at the moment of death, the departing
　soul retreated to the foot of the bed (§198).
12.　*every* (acc. to 1633 and some MSS): 'a very' (acc. to 1635–69).
14.　*expresse*: extract (an alchemical term).
15.　*quintessence*: as above, p. 79, note on 8. In fact, the *new Alchimie* (13) is an
　inversion of all alchemical aspirations (§218; but cf. §350).

From dull privations, and leane emptinesse
He ruin'd mee, and I am re-begot
Of absence, darknesse, death; things which are not.

All others, from all things, draw all that's good,
Life, soule, forme, spirit, whence they beeing have,   20
  I, by loves limbecke, am the grave
   Of all, that's nothing. Oft a flood
     Have wee two wept, and so
Drownd the whole world, us two; oft did we grow
To be two Chaosses, when we did show   25
Care to ought else; and often absences
Withdrew our soules, and made us carcasses.

But I am by her death, (which word wrongs her)
Of the first nothing, the Elixer grown;
  Were I a man, that I were one,   30
  I needs must know, I should preferre,
   If I were any beast,
Some ends, some means; Yea plants, yea stones detest,
And love, all, all some properties invest,
If I an ordinary nothing were,   35
As shadow, a light, and body must be here.

16. The semicolon supplied at line's end by some modern editors (§§158, 163, 169) is not defensible (see §§188, 414).
17. *ruin'd*: destroyed; also, broken down into elements (§162).
21. *Limbecke*: alembic, an apparatus used in alchemical distillation.
25. *two Chaosses*: i.e. whenever they parted; cf. *Othello*: 'when I love thee not, / Chaos is come again' (III, iii, 91–92).
29. *the first nothing*: the 'nothing' out of which God created the world. *Elixer*: as above, p. 86, note on 7.
33. *Stones*, as Donne said, 'may have life' (*Sermons*, IX, 147: §158).
34. *all some properties invest*: all existing things have some distinguishing qualities (§164).
36. *As*: such as.
   must be: must exist (in order to produce the *ordinary nothing*).

But I am None; nor will my Sunne renew.
You lovers, for whose sake, the lesser Sunne
  At this time to the Goat is runne
    To fetch new lust, and give it you,   40
      Enjoy your summer all,
Since shee enjoyes her long nights festivall,
Let mee prepare towards her, and let mee call
This houre her Vigill, and her eve, since this
Both the yeares, and the dayes deep midnight is.   45

Witchcraft by a picture.

I fixe mine eye on thine, and there
  Pitty my picture burning in thine eye,
My picture drown'd in a transparent teare,
  When I looke lower I espie,
    Hadst thou the wicked skill   5
By pictures made and mard, to kill,
How many wayes mightst thou performe thy will?

But now I have drunke thy sweet salt teares,
  And though thou poure more I'll depart;
My picture vanish'd, vanish feares,   10
  That I can be endamag'd by that art;
    Though thou retaine of mee
One picture more, yet that will bee,
Being in thine owne heart, from all malice free.

A nocturnall upon S.Lucies day.
 37. *None*: i.e. nothing.
 38. *the lesser Sunne*: the real sun.
 39. *Goat*: see headnote, above; goats were traditionally associated with
      lechery (cf. above, p. 50, note on 4).
 44. *Vigill*: see headnote, above.

Witchcraft by a picture. Entitled in some MSS *The Picture.*
  6. Witches were said to kill their victims by making and then destroying
      their pictures.
  8. *sweet salt*: 'sweetest' (acc. to several MSS).
 10. *feares*: 'all feares' (acc. to 1635–54).
 11. *that*: 'thy' (acc. to some MSS).
 14. *from all*: 'from' (ditto) or 'from thy' (ditto).

The Baite.

Come live with mee, and bee my love,
And wee will some new pleasures prove
Of golden sands, and christall brookes:
With silken lines, and silver hookes.

There will the river whispering runne   5
Warm'd by thy eyes, more than the Sunne.
And there the'inamor'd fish will stay,
Begging themselves they may betray.

When thou wilt swimme in that live bath,
Each fish, which every channell hath,   10
Will amorously to thee swimme,
Gladder to catch thee, than thou him.

If thou, to be so seene, beest loath,
By Sunne, or Moone, thou darknest both,
And if my selfe have leave to see,   15
I need not their light, having thee.

Let others freeze with angling reeds,
And cut their legges, with shells and weeds,
Or treacherously poore fish beset,
With strangling snare, or windowie net: 20

The Baite. First partially published in William Corkine's *Second Booke of Ayres*
(1612); untitled in 1633 and some MSS; entitled from 1635; also quoted –
in a slightly different version – in Izaak Walton's *The Compleat Angler*
(1653), where it is claimed that the poem was 'made to shew the world
that [Donne] could make soft and smooth Verses'. The poem varies
Christopher Marlowe's 'The Passionate Shepherd to his Love' and Sir
Walter Ralegh's 'The Nymph's Reply'.
6. *thy*: 'thine' (acc. to 1669 and some MSS).
7. *stay*: 'play' (acc. to 1669).
8. *Begging*: begging that.
11. *to*: 'unto' (acc. to some MSS).
15. *my selfe*: 'my heart' (ditto).
17. *reeds*: rods made from reeds.
20. *windowie*: 'winding' (acc. to 1669).

Let coarse bold hands, from slimy nest
The bedded fish in banks out-wrest,
Or curious traitors, sleavesilke flies
Bewitch poore fishes wandring eyes.

For thee, thou needst no such deceit,　　　　　　　　25
For thou thy selfe art thine owne bait,
That fish, that is not catch'd thereby,
Alas, is wiser farre than I.

The Apparition.

When by thy scorne, O murdresse, I am dead,
And that thou thinkst thee free
From all solicitation from mee,
Then shall my ghost come to thy bed,
And thee, fain'd vestall in worse armes shall see;　　　5
Then thy sicke taper will begin to winke,
And he, whose thou art then, being tyr'd before,
Will, if thou stirre, or pinch to wake him, thinke
　　　　Thou call'st for more,
And in false sleepe will from thee shrinke,　　　　　10

The Baite.
23.　*sleavesilke flies*: lures made of untwisted silk.
25.　*thou needst*: 'there needs' (acc. to some MSS).
27.　*catch'd*: 'caught' (acc. to several MSS).

The Apparition. The title includes theological implications of a manifestation,
　　an epiphany, an advent (§341). For William Lawes's musical setting of
　　the poem, see §163.
2.　*that thou thinkst*: 'thou shalt think' (acc. to 1669).
5.　*fain'd*: wished for; also, 'feigned' or pretended (§424).
　　vestall: virgin consecrated to the Roman goddess Vesta.
6.　*winke*: flicker.
7.　*Art then*: 'art' (acc. to 1669).
10.　*in false sleepe will from*: 'in false sleepe from' (acc. to 1635–54) or 'in a false
　　sleep even from' (acc. to 1669 and some MSS).

And then poore Aspen wretch, neglected thou
Bath'd in a cold quicksilver sweat wilt lye
     A veryer ghost than I,
What I will say, I will not tell thee now,
Lest that preserve thee'; and since my love is spent,   15
I'had rather thou shouldst painfully repent,
Then by my threatnings rest still innocent.

The broken heart.

He is starke mad, who ever sayes,
   That he hath been in love an houre,
Yet not that love so soone decayes,
   But that it can tenne in lesse space devour;
Who will beleeve mee, if I sweare   5
That I have had the plague a yeare?
   Who would not laugh at mee, if I should say,
   I saw a flaske of *powder burne a day?*

Ah, what a trifle is a heart,
   If once into loves hands it come!   10
All other griefes allow a part
   To other griefes, and aske themselves but some,
They come to us, but us Love draws,
Hee swallows us, and never chawes:

The Apparition.
11. *Aspen*: trembling.
12. The quicksilver sweat bath was the commonest treatment for syphilis
    (§407).
13. *veryer*: truer.
15 (also 16). On the symbol ', see above, p. 5.
17. *rest still*: 'keep thee' (acc. to several MSS).

The broken heart. Entitled in some MSS *Song.*
 8. *flaske*: powder-flask; 'flash' (acc. to 1635–69 and some MSS).
14. *chawes*: chews.

By him, as by chain'd shot, whole rankes doe dye,   15
He is the tyran Pike, our hearts the Frye.

If 'twere not so, what did become
   Of my heart, when I first saw thee?
I brought a heart into the roome,
   But from the roome, I carried none with mee;   20
If it had gone to thee, I know
Mine would have taught thine heart to show
    More pitty unto mee: but Love, alas
    At one first blow did shiver it as glasse.

Yet nothing can to nothing fall,   25
   Nor any place be empty quite,
Therefore I thinke my breast hath all
   Those peeces still, though they be not unite;
And now as broken glasses show
A hundred lesser faces, so   30
    My ragges of heart can like, wish, and adore,
    But after one such love, can love no more.

15. *chain'd shot*: 'chain-shott' (acc. to several MSS), i.e. cannon balls so
    chained as to cut down whole ranks of men.
16. *tyran*: a common variant of 'Tyrant' (acc. to 1669).
    our hearts: 'and we' (ditto).
    Frye: small fish, devoured by the *Pike*.
17. *did*: 'could' (acc. to several MSS) or 'would' (ditto).
24. *first*: 'fierce' (ditto).
25–26. Matter can never be totally annihilated, nor can there be a complete
    vacuum (§166).
29. *glasses*: mirrors.
30. *hundred*: 'thousand' (acc. to many MSS).

A Valediction forbidding mourning.

As virtuous men passe mildly away,
  And whisper to their soules, to goe,
Whilst some of their sad friends doe say,
  The breath goes now, and some say, no.

So let us melt, and make no noise,   5
  No teare-floods, nor sigh-tempests move,
T'were prophanation of our joyes
  To tell the layetie our love.

Moving of th'earth brings harmes and feares,
  Men reckon what it did and meant,   10
But trepidation of the spheares,
  Though greater farre, is innocent.

Dull sublunary lovers love
  (Whose soule is sense) cannot admit
Absence, because it doth remove   15
  Those things which elemented it.

A Valediction forbidding mourning. Subtitled in some MSS 'To his love upon his departure from her' or 'Upon the partinge from his Mistris'. According to Walton's conjecture, Donne on leaving for the Continent in 1611 wrote this poem and the Song 'Sweetest love' (above, p. 62) for his wife (§313); but it is by no means certain that this was in fact so. The poem's rich texture compresses imagery drawn from as far afield as hermetic alchemy (§344). Coleridge thought it an 'admirable poem which none but Donne could have written' (§210). See above, pp. 16 ff., cf. p. 70.

3. *Whilst*: 'And' (acc. to several MSS).
5. *So*: the word serves notice that an analogy is intended; cf. *As* (1).
6. *move*: stir up.
8. *our*: 'of our' (acc. to many MSS).
9. *Moving of th'earth*: earthquakes; or perhaps the Copernican view of the earth's movement about the sun, argued in Donne's time as a theory (*ALC*). *brings*: causes.
11. *trepidation*: 'trembling' or fearful agitation, a condition observed in the perturbations in the supposedly regular motions of the celestial *spheares* (§162); cf. above, p. 80, note on 23.
13. *sublunary*: earthly and changeable (literally, 'below the moon').
14. *sense*: either sensuality or simply an undue reliance on the senses (§164).
15. *Absence*: a pun.
16. *Those things*: 'The thing' (acc. to 1669).
     elemented: as above, p. 79, note on 13.

But we by a love, so much refin'd,
    That our selves know not what it is,
Inter-assured of the mind,
    Care lesse, eyes, lips, hands to misse.   20

Our two soules therefore, which are one,
    Though I must goe, endure not yet
A breach, but an expansion,
    Like gold to ayery thinnesse beate.

If they be two, they are two so   25
    As stiffe twin compasses are two,
Thy soule the fixt foot, makes no show
    To move, but doth, if the'other doe.

And though it in the center sit,
    Yet when the other far doth rome,   30
It leanes, and hearkens after it,
    And growes erect, as that comes home.

Such wilt thou be to mee, who must
    Like th'other foot, obliquely runne.
Thy firmnes makes my circle just,   35
    And makes me end, where I begunne.

19. *Inter-assured*: see above, p. 88, note on 26.
20. *lips, hands* (acc. to 1633): 'lips, and hands' (acc. to 1669 and all MSS); see above, pp. 17–18.
24. *gold*: its chemical symbol ☉ may be anticipatory of the compass image (§418); both images appear to draw on language traditionally descriptive of man's relation with God (§215).
25. *If*: on 'the conditional *if*', see above, p. 24, note 16.
25 ff. It was questioned in Donne's time whether a man and a woman 'fitly may to compasses compare' (see §438); yet the image, scarcely original with Donne, had already become an accepted emblem of constancy (§39: see esp. above, p. 21, note 9). Later, Dr Samuel Johnson said of it that 'it may be doubted whether absurdity or ingenuity has the better claim' (§240); but Coleridge was equally persuaded that 'Nothing was ever more admirably made out' (§210).
26. *twin compasses*: i.e. the two legs of a compass.
32. *erect*: also in the sexual sense; cf. *stiffe* (24).
34. *obliquely*: diverging from the straight line or course.
35. *makes*: 'drawes' (acc. to some MSS).
     circle: 'circles' (acc. to 1639–54).

The Extasie.

Where, like a pillow on a bed,
  A Pregnant banke swel'd up, to rest
The violets reclining head,
  Sat we two, one anothers best;
Our hands were firmely cimented   5
  With a fast balme, which thence did spring,
Our eye-beames twisted, and did thred
  Our eyes, upon one double string,
So to'entergraft our hands, as yet
  Was all the meanes to make us one,   10
And pictures in our eyes to get
  Was all our propagation.
As 'twixt two equall Armies, Fate
  Suspends uncertaine victorie,
Our soules, (which to advance their state,   15
  Were gone out,) hung 'twixt her, and mee.

The Extasie. The fifteen poems up to and including *The Computation* (below,
    p. 120) form the same sequence in both 1633 and 1635. The longest of the
    Song and Sonets, the present poem was highly praised by Coleridge (see
    above, p. 30) and said by Ezra Pound to be 'Platonism believed. The
    decadence of trying to make pretty speeches and of hunting for some-
    thing to say temporarily checked . . .' (§169).
3 (also 37). *violet*: an emblem of faithful love and truth (§166); but also, in its
    physical nature, self-evidently sensuous.
3.   *reclining*: 'decling' (acc. to 1669).
5.   *cimented*: 'cementation' was according to Paracelsus a chemical process
    involving the penetration of one solid by another at high temperature
    (§207).
6.   *With*: (acc. to 1633 and most MSS): 'By' (acc. to 1635–69).
    a fast balme: a steadfast or fastening warm moisture (§169), or a fragrant
    garden herb (*OED*: §436), or – literally and euphemistically – sweat, part
    of the usual jokes about 'oily palms' (§342) and thus suggestive of
    lustfulness (§195).
9.   *entergraft*: 'engraft' (acc. to 1635–69 and some MSS).
9 (also 69 and 77). On the symbol ', see above, p. 5.
11.   *in*: 'on' (acc. to most MSS).
    get: beget.
15.   *their*: 'our' (acc. to 1635–69 and some MSS).

And whil'st our soules negotiate there,
   Wee like sepulchrall statues lay,
All day, the same our postures were,
   And wee said nothing, all the day.   20
If any, so by love refin'd,
   That he soules language understood,
And by good love were growen all minde,
   Within convenient distance stood,
He (though he knowes not which soul spake,   25
   Because both meant, both spake the same)
Might thence a new concotion take,
   And part farre purer then he came.
This Extasie doth unperplex
   (We said) and tell us what we love,   30
Wee see by this, it was not sexe
   Wee see, we saw not what did move:
But as all severall soules containe
   Mixture of things, they know not what,
Love, these mixt soules, doth mixe againe,   35
   And makes both one, each this and that.
A single violet transplant,
   The strength, the colour, and the size,
(All which before was poore, and scant,)
   Redoubles still, and multiplies.   40
When love, with one another so
   Interinanimates two soules,
That abler soule, which thence doth flow,
   Defects of loneliness controules.

---

25. *knowes*: 'knew' (acc. to 1635–69 and most MSS).
27. *concotion*: in the alchemical sense of sublimation or purification.
28. *then*: than.
29. *Extasie*: described by Donne in a letter as 'a departing, and secession, and
     suspension of the soul' (§158).
33. *severall*: separate.
34. *Mixture of things*: i.e. 'elemented' (as above, p. 79, note on 13).
36. *this and that*: i.e. both he and she.
42. *Interinanimates* (acc. to most MSS): 'Interanimates' (acc. to 1633–69 and
     some MSS); in both cases intimating *anima* (the vital principle, hence
     'soul') as much as 'animal'. Cf. above, p. 88, note on 26.

Wee then, who are this new soule, know,   45
   Of what we are compos'd, and made,
For, th'Atomies of which we grow,
   Are soules, whom no change can invade.
But O alas, so long, so farre
   Our bodies why doe wee forbeare?   50
They are ours, though not wee, Wee are
   The intelligences, they the spheares.
We owe them thankes, because they thus,
   Did us, to us, at first convay,
Yeelded their senses force to us,   55
   Nor are drosse to us, but allay.
On man heavens influence workes not so,
   But that it first imprints the ayre,
For soule into the soule may flow,
   Though it to body first repaire.   60
As our blood labours to beget
   Spirits, as like soules as it can,
Because such fingers need to knit
   That subtile knot, which makes us man:
So must pure lovers soules descend   65
   T'affections, and to faculties,
Which sense may reach and apprehend,
   Else a great Prince in prison lies.

---

47. *Atomies*: 'Atomes' (acc. to 1669), i.e. components.
51. *though not*: 'though they are not' (acc. to most MSS).
52. *intelligences*: the angels supposed to govern the celestial spheres. *spheares* (acc. to 1633–69, see §188): 'spheare' (acc. to most MSS, see §421). In the latter reading, souls = intelligences, bodies = one sphere (§402); but the former reading appears to be faithful to the ongoing enquiry.
55. *senses force*: 'forces, sense,' (acc. to most MSS).
56. *drosse*: the impurity discarded during the process of *concoction* (27). *allay*: alloy.
57–58. The stars were believed to exert their influence on *man* by first influencing the *ayre*.
59. *For*: 'Soe' (acc. to most MSS).
60. *repair*: goes to.
61–64. Medical opinion held that the three types of spirits (animal, vital, natural) were subtile substances of an aerial nature made of the lightest part of the blood, which governed the body and all its parts (§192).
64. *makes*: 'make' (acc. to 1635–39).
64–67. See above, p. 66, ll. 7–10.
68. *great Prince*: the 'abler soule' (43)? soul *and* body?

To'our bodies turne wee then, that so
 Weake men on love reveal'd may looke;   70
Loves mysteries in soules doe grow,
 But yet the body is his booke.
And if some lover, such as wee,
 Have heard this dialogue of one,
Let him still marke us, he shall see   75
 Small change, when we'are to bodies gone.

Loves Deitie.

I long to talke with some old lovers ghost,
 Who dyed before the god of Love was borne:
I cannot thinke that hee, who then lov'd most,
 Sunke so low, as to love one which did scorne.
But since this god produc'd a destinie,   5
And that vice-nature, custome, lets it be;
 I must love her, that loves not mee.

Sure, they which made him god, meant not so much:
 Nor he, in his young godhead practis'd it.
But when an even flame two hearts did touch,   10
 His office was indulgently to fit
Actives to passives. Correspondencie
Only his subject was; It cannot bee
 Love, till I love her, that loves mee.

The Extasie.
71. *revealed*: a pun on 'revelation' as both epiphany and nudity (§290).
72. *his*: 'the' (acc. to 1669).
76. *gone*: 'growne' (acc. to 1635–69 and some MSS).

Loves Deitie.
 6. *vice-nature*: substitute for nature (*ALC*).
 9. *his young godhead*: Cupid's early days as god.
10. *even*: equal.
12. *Actives to passives*: male lovers to female ones.
14. The line also reads, 'Love, if I love, who loves not me' (acc. to 1635–54).

But every moderne god will now extend   15
  His vast prerogative, as far as Jove.
To rage, to lust, to write to, to commend,
  All is the purlewe of the God of Love.
Oh were wee wak'ned by this Tyrannie
To ungod this child againe, it could not bee   20
  I should love her, who loves not mee.

Rebell and Atheist too, why murmure I,
  As though I felt the worst that love could doe?
Love may make me leave loving, or might trie
  A deeper plague, to make her love mee too,   25
Which since she loves before, I'am loth to see;
Falshood is worse than hate; and that must bee
  If shee whom I love, should love mee.

Loves diet.

To what a combersome unwieldinesse
And burdenous corpulence my love had growne,
  But that I did, to make it lesse,
  And keepe it in proportion,
Give it a diet, made it feed upon   5
That which love worst endures, *discretion*.

15. *will*: wants to.
18. *purlewe* (purlieu): disafforested outskirts of a forest, subject to royal
    authority; hence, any sphere of authority or influence (§164).
19. *Oh were wee wak'ned*: 'Were we not weak'ned' (acc. to 1669).
21. The line also reads, 'That I should love, who loves not me' (acc. to most
    MSS).
22. *Rebell*: because he rebelled against *destinie* (5).
    Atheist: because he disbelieves in Cupid.
24. *may*: 'might' (acc. to most MSS).
26. *loves before*: has a lover already.

Above one sigh a day I'allow'd him not,
Of which my fortune, and my faults had part;
  And if sometimes by stealth he got
  A she sigh from my mistresse heart,   10
And thought to feast on that, I let him see
'Twas neither very sound, nor meant to mee;

If he wroung from mee'a teare, I brin'd it so
With scorne or shame, that him it nourish'd not;
  If he suck'd hers, I let him know   15
  'Twas not a teare, which hee had got,
His drinke was counterfeit, as was his meat;
For, eyes which rowle towards all, weepe not, but
    sweat.

What ever he would dictate, I writ that,
But burnt my letters; When she writ to me,   20
  And that that favour made him fat,
  I said, if any title bee
Convey'd by this, Ah, what doth it availe,
To be the fortieth name in an entaile?

Loves diet.
  7 (also 13). On the symbol ', see above, p. 5.
  7. *him*: i.e. love.
11. *feast*: 'feede' (acc. to some MSS).
12. *sound*: genuine.
     to: for (?).
13. *brin'd*: salted.
17. *meat*: i.e. her nourishing sighs (7 ff.).
18. *For*: 'Her' (acc. to 1669).
19. The line also reads, 'Whate'er might him distast I still writ that' (acc. to
     1650–54) or 'Whatsoever hee would distast I writt that' (acc. to some
     MSS).
20. The semicolon is removed in one edition (1635) and transferred to line's
     end in others (1639–54).
21. *that that*: 'if that' (acc. to 1635–69).
24. i.e. the fortieth person named in an order of succession for inheriting an
     estate (§166).
     name: 'man' (acc. to 1669).

Thus I reclaim'd my buzard love, to flye   25
At what, and when, and how, and where I chuse;
   Now negligent of sports I lye,
   And now as other Fawkners use,
I spring a mistresse, sweare, write, sigh and weepe:
And the game kill'd, or lost, goe talke, and sleepe.   30

The Will.

   Before I sigh my last gaspe, let me breath,
   Great love, some Legacies; Here I bequeath
   Mine eyes to *Argus*, if mine eyes can see,
   If they be blinde, then Love, I give them thee;
   My tongue to Fame; to'Embassadours mine eares;   5
     To women or the sea, my teares;
   Thou, Love, hast taught mee heretofore
By making mee serve her who'had twenty more,
That I should give to none, but such, as had too much
    before.

   My constancie I to the plancts give,   10
   My truth to them, who at the Court doe live;
   Mine ingenuity and opennesse,
   To Jesuites; to Buffones my pensivenesse;

Loves diet.
25. *buzard*: a rapacious but sluggish species of hawk; also, a blockhead (§172).
29. *spring a mistresse*: as a falconer springs or starts up a bird for the hawk to chase (§169).
30. *and*: 'or (acc. to 1635–69 and some MSS).

The Will. Entitled in one MS *His Last Will and Testament*; in another, *Loves Will*; and in still others, *Loves Legacies*.
3. *Argus*: the hundred-eyed monster of Greek mythology.
5. *Fame*: rumour, commonly represented with many mouths.
5 (also 8, 14, 54). On the symbol ', see above, p. 5.
8. *serve*: 'love' (acc. to 1669).
10. *planets*: etymologically, 'wanderers'; hence inconstant.
12. *ingenuity*: ingenuousness.
13. *Jesuites*: widely regarded in Donne's time as prime exemplars of dissimulation.

My silence to'any, who abroad hath beene;
  My mony to a Capuchin.   15
Thou Love taught'st me, by appointing mee
To love there, where no love receiv'd can be,
Onely to give to such as have an incapacitie.

My faith I give to Roman Catholiques;
All my goods works unto the Schismaticks   20
Of Amsterdam: my best civility
And Courtship, to an Universitie;
My modesty I give to souldiers bare;
  My patience let gamesters share.
Thou Love taughtst mee, by making mee   25
Love her that holds my love disparity,
Onely to give to those that count my gifts indignity.

I give my reputation to those
Which were my friends; Mine industrie to foes;
To Schoolemen I bequeath my doubtfulnesse; 30
My sicknesse to Physitians, or excesse;
To Nature, all that I in Ryme have writ;
  And to my company my wit;
Thou love, by making mee adore
Her, who begot this love in mee before,   35
Taughtst me to make, as though I gave, when I did but
  restore.

---

15. *Capuchin*: a Franciscan monk, vowed to total poverty.
18. *an incapacitie*: 'no good Capacitie' (acc. to 1669).
19–27. The stanza is omitted in most MSS.
19–21. Anglicans like Donne regarded *faith* and *good works* as alike indispens-
  able to man's salvation; but, they claimed, Catholics down-played the
  former, and Calvinists like the extreme ones of Amsterdam the latter.
22. *Courtship*: courtliness, courtesy (§166).
23. *bare*: immodest in their manner of dress and mode of behaviour.
26. *disparity*: i.e. beneath her.
30. *Schoolemen*: medieval scholastic philosophers.
31. *excesse*: intemperance, regarded as a cause of sickness.
36. *did*: 'do' (acc. to 1635–69).

To him for whom the passing bell next tolls,
I give my physick bookes; my writen rowles
Of Morall counsels, I to Bedlam give;
My brazen medals, unto them which live   40
In want of bread; To them which passe among
    All forrainers, mine English tongue.
  Thou, Love, by making mee love one
Who thinkes her friendship a fit portion
For yonger lovers, dost my gifts thus disproportion.   45

Therefore I'll give no more; But I'll undoe
The world by dying; because love dies too.
Then all your beauties will be no more worth
Then gold in Mines, where none doth draw it forth.
And all your graces no more use shall have   50
    Then a Sun dyall in a grave,
  Thou Love taughtst mee, by making mee
Love her, who doth neglect both mee and thee,
To'invent, and practise this one way, to'annihilate all
    three.

The Funerall.

Who ever comes to shroud me, do not harme
    Nor question much
That subtile wreath of haire, which crowns my arme;
The mystery, the signe you must not touch,

The Will.
38. *physick*: medical.
39. *Bedlam*: London's insane asylum of St Mary of Bethlehem.
40. *brazen medals*: Roman bronze coins, useless to the starving (§169).
45. *disproportion*: mismatch (§163).
49 (also 51). *Then*: than.
52. *making*: 'appointing' (acc. to some MSS).
54. *all three*: 'thee' (acc. to 1669).

The Funerall.
 3. *subtile*: as above, p. 66, note on 9.
    which crowns my arme: 'about mine arm' (acc. to 1669).

For'tis my outward Soule,   5
Viceroy to that, which unto heaven being gone,
    Will leave this to controule,
And keep these limbes, her Provinces, from dissolution.

For if the sinewie thread my braine lets fall
    Through every part,   10
Can tye those parts, and make mee one of all;
Those haires which upward grew, and strength and art
    Have from a better braine,
Can better do'it; Except she meant that I
    By this should know my pain,   15
As prisoners then are manacled, when they'are
    condemn'd to die.

What ere shee meant by'it, bury it by me,
    For since I am
Loves martyr, it might breed idolatrie,
If into others hands these Reliques came;   20
    As'twas humility
To afford to it all that a Soule can doe,
    So,'tis some bravery,
That since you would have none of mee, I bury some of
    you.

6.   *unto*: 'then to' (acc. to most MSS).
9.   *sinewie thread*: the spinal cord and nervous system.
12.   *those*: 'These' (acc. to most MSS).
14 (also 16, 17). On the symbol ', see above, p. 5.
14.   *Except*: unless.
17.   *by*: 'with' (acc. to 1635–69 and most MSS).
18–20. Cf. *The Relique*, 2nd stanza (below, p. 112).
23.   *bravery*: bravado.
24.   *have*: in a sexual sense (acc. to 1633–69 and some MSS, see §188): 'save' (acc. to most MSS).
    bury: both the burial of the bracelet of hair with the lover's body and a symbolic sexual conquest of the beloved (§195).

The Blossome.

Little think'st thou, poore flower,
  Whom I have watch'd sixe or seaven dayes,
And seene thy birth, and seene what every houre
Gave to thy growth, thee to this height to raise,
And now dost laugh and triumph on this bough,   5
        Little think'st thou
That it will freeze anon, and that I shall
To morrow finde thee falne, or not at all.

Little think'st thou poore heart
  That labour'st yet to nestle thee,   10
And think'st by hovering here to get a part
In a forbidden or forbidding tree,
And hop'st her stiffenesse by long siege to bow:
        Little think'st thou,
That thou to morrow, ere that Sunne doth wake,   15
Must with this Sunne, and mee a journey take.

But thou which lov'st to bee
  Subtile to plague thy selfe, wilt say,
Alas, if you must goe, what's that to mee?
Here lyes my businesse, and here I will stay: 20
You goe to friends, whose love and meanes present
        Various content
To your eyes, eares, and tast, and every part.
If then your body goe, what need your heart?

Well then, stay here; but know,   25
  When thou hast stayd and done thy most;
A naked thinking heart, that makes no show,
Is to a woman, but a kinde of Ghost;

The Blossome.
12. *forbidden* because the affair is illicit; *forbidding* because she repels his advances.
15. *that Sunne*: his beloved, as against *this Sunne* (16) which is the real sun.
18. *Subtile*: subtle.
22. *content*: satisfaction.
23. *tast* (acc. to 1633–69, see §188): 'tongue' (acc. to most MSS).
24. *your*: 'you have a' (acc. to many MSS).

How shall shee know my heart; or having none,
      Know thee for one?   30
Practise may make her know some other part,
But take my word, shee doth not know a Heart.

      Meet mee at London, then,
      Twenty dayes hence, and thou shalt see
Mee fresher, and more fat, by being with men,   35
Then if I had staid still with her and thee.
For Gods sake, if you can, be you so too;
      I will give you
There, to another friend, whom wee shall finde
As glad to have my body, as my minde.   40

The Primrose.

      Upon this Primrose hill,
      Where, if Heav'n would distill
A shoure of raine, each severall drop might goe
To his owne primrose, and grow Manna so;
And where their forme, and their infinitie   5
      Make a terrestriall Galaxie,
      As the small starres doe in the skie:

The Blossome.
35. *fat*: prosperous (§166).
36. *Then*: than.
38. *will*: 'would' (acc. to many MSS).

The Primrose. Subtitled in 1635–69, 'being at Montgomery Castle, upon the
    hill, on which it is situate'. The estate was the seat of the Herbert family
    and the home of Sir Richard Herbert, the poet's brother; but its relevance
    to the poem is a matter of dispute (cf. headnote to *Twicknam Garden*,
    above, p. 73).
 3. *severall*: separate.
 4. *Manna*: annotated by a botanist of Donne's time as 'Honydew, cleaving
    to the leaves before the rising of the Sunne as it were Snow, or rather
    Candied Sugar' (§422); on the primary meaning, see above, p. 73, note
    on 7; cf. §451.
 7. i.e. in the Milky Way (§162).

I walke to finde a true Love; and I see
That'tis not a mere woman, that is shee,
But must, or more, or lesse then woman bee.   10

    Yet know I not, which flower
      I wish; a sixe, or foure;
For should my true-Love lesse than woman bee,
She were scarce any thing; and then, should she
Be more then woman, shee would get above   15
    All thought of sexe, and thinke to move
    My heart to study her, and not to love;
Both these were monsters; Since there must reside
Falshood in woman, I could more abide,
She were by art, then Nature falsify'd.   20

    Live Primrose then, and thrive
    With thy true number five;
And women, whom this flower doth represent,
With this mysterious number be content;
Ten is the farthest number, if halfe ten   25
    Belongs unto each woman, then
    Each woman may take halfe us men,
Or if this will not serve their turne, Since all
Numbers are odde, or even, and they fall
First into this five, women may take us all.   30

10 (also 15, 20). *then*: than.
12. *a six, or foure*: a six- or a four-petalled flower.
16. *sexe*: cited by the *OED* as the earliest example of this use of the word; but
    see also above, p. 100, l. 31 (§250).
17. *and*: omitted in 1635–39 and some MSS.
18. *monsters*: freaks.
22. *five*: the usual number of a primrose's petals.
23–30. 'since ten is the *farthest* [i.e. highest] *number* and woman's number,
    five, is half ten, a woman may *take* half the male population as sexual
    partners. On the other hand, since *all / Numbers are odde, or even* and since
    woman's number is the first to comprise one from each category, five
    may be said to contain all numbers and, correspondingly, woman to be
    licensed to take *all* men' (§451).
26. *Belongs*: 'Belonge' (acc. to most MSS).
29. *and*: 'Since' (acc. to 1635–69).

The Relique.

When my grave is broke up againe
Some second ghest to entertaine,
(For graves have learn'd that woman-head
To be to more then one a Bed)
    And he that digs it, spies   5
A bracelet of bright haire about the bone,
    Will he not let'us alone,
And thinke that there a loving couple lies,
Who thought that this device might be some way
To make their soules, at the last busie day,   10
Meet at this grave, and make a little stay?

    If this fall in a time, or land,
    Where mis-devotion doth command,
Then, he that digges us up, will bring
Us, to the Bishop, and the King,   15
    To make us Reliques; then
Thou shalt be a Mary Magdalen, and I
    A something else thereby;
All women shall adore us, and some men;
And since at such time, miracles are sought,   20
I would have that age by this paper taught
What miracles wee harmlesse lovers wrought.

The Relique.
1–2. Old graves were often dug up to make room for new tenants (§229).
3.   *that*: the word must be fully sounded (§229).
4 (also 26). *then*: than.
7.   On the symbol ', see above, p. 5.
9.   *thought*: 'hop'd' (acc. to some MSS).
    some: 'a' (ditto).
10. *last busie day*: the Day of Judgement, when the scattered parts of each risen body will be united with their soul.
13. *mis-devotion*: devotion to a false ideal (§415).
14. *Then, he that digges us up*: 'He that doth digge yt up' (acc. to several MSS).
17. *Mary Magdalen*: Christ's devoted follower.
18. *something else*: possibly Christ?
21. *this paper*: this poem.

First, we lov'd well and faithfully,
Yet knew not what wee lov'd, nor why,
Difference of sex no more wee knew,   25
Then our Guardian Angells doe,
    Comming and going, wee,
Perchance might kisse, but not between those meales.
    Our hands ne'r toucht the seales,
Which nature, injur'd by late law, sets free,   30
These miracles wee did; but now alas,
All measure, and all language, I should passe,
Should I tell what a miracle shee was.

The Dampe.

When I am dead, and Doctors know not why,
    And my friends curiositie
Will have me cut up to survay each part,
When they shall finde your Picture in my heart,
    You thinke a sodaine dampe of love   5
    Will through all their senses move,
And worke on them as mee, and so preferre
Your murder, to the name of Massacre.

The Relique.
24.   *what*: what in each other.
25–26. The lines also read, 'Difference of Sex we never knew, / No more then
      Guardian Angells do' (acc. to 1635–69).
26.   Angels were usually thought to be discarnate spirits; but see above,
      p. 67, note on 23–24.
27–28. Kissing in salutation and on leave-taking.
28.   *not*: 'yet' (acc. to 1669).
      meales: the love feast (*agape*) of the early Christians (§432).
29.   *seales*: colloquially, the sexual organs (§164).
32.   *passe*: surpass, transcend.

The Dampe.
4.   *When*: 'And' (acc. to 1669).
    my: 'mine' (acc. to 1650–69).
5.   *dampe*: noxious vapour; also, a sort of stupor or trance (*OED*: §229). The
    word may also refer to the stifling gas in a mine which snuffs out both the
    lamps and the lives of the miners (§340).
6.   *through*: 'thorough' (acc. to some MSS).
7.   *preferre*: promote.

Poore victories; But if you dare be brave,
　　　　And pleasure in your conquest have,　　　　　10
First kill th'enormous Gyant, your *Disdaine*,
And let th'enchantresse *Honor*, next be slaine,
　　　　And like a Goth and Vandall rize,
　　　　Deface Records, and Histories
Of your owne arts and triumphs over men,　　　　15
And without such advantage kill me then.

For I could muster up as well as you
　　　　My Gyants, and my Witches too,
Which are vast *Constancy*, and *Secretnesse*,
But these I neyther looke for, nor professe,　　　　20
　　　　Kill mee as Woman, let mee die
　　　　As a meere man; doe you but try
Your passive valor, and you shall finde than,
In that you'have odds enough of any man.

The Dissolution.

Shee'is dead; And all which die
　　To their first Elements resolve;
And wee were mutuall Elements to us,
　　　　And made of one another.

The Dampe.
10.　*your*: 'the' (acc. to 1669).
13–14.　The barbarian hordes that overwhelmed the declining Roman Empire
　　threatened to abrogate its civilization too.
15.　*arts*: 'acts' (acc. to 1669).
21.　*kill . . . die*: as above, p. 48, note on 16.
22.　*try*: test.
23.　*than*: then.
24.　*In that*: 'Naked' (acc. to 1635–69 and several MSS).
　　On the symbol ', see above, p. 5.

The Dissolution. The poem, often read as a funeral elegy, has also been seen as
　primarily erotic (§392).
1.　On the symbol ', see above, p. 5.
1–4.　The lines are a fuller commentary on the nature of 'elemented' life and
　love (cf. above, p. 79, note on 13).

My body then doth hers involve, 5
And those things whereof I consist, hereby
In me abundant grow, and burdenous,
    And nourish not, but smother.
  My fire of Passion, sighes of ayre,
Water of teares, and earthly sad despaire, . 10
    Which my materialls bee,
But ne'r worne out by loves securitie,
Shee, to my losse, doth by her death repaire,
    And I might live long wretched so
But that my fire doth with my fuell grow. 15
    Now as those Active Kings
  Whose foraine conquest treasure brings,
Receive more, and spend more, and soonest breake:
This (which I am amaz'd that I can speake)
    This death, hath with my store 20
      My use encreas'd.
And so my soule more earnestly releas'd,
Will outstrip hers; As bullets flowen before
A latter bullet may o'rtake, the pouder being more.

9–10. The analogy is to the four constituent elements of the physical world:
    fire, air, water, earth.
10. *earthly*: 'earthy' (acc. to 1635–69).
12. *ne'r*: 'neere' (acc. to 1635–69), in both cases meaning nearly.
    securitie: recklessness (§169).
13. *repaire*: restore.
15. *fire*: i.e. passion.
18. *breake*: break down financially.
19. *speak*: speak of.
21. *use*: expenditure.
22. *earnestly*: eagerly.
23. *flowen*: shot.
24. *latter*: 'later' (acc. to 1669).

A Jeat Ring sent.

> Thou art not so black, as my heart,
>   Nor halfe so brittle, as her heart, thou art;
> What would'st thou say? shall both our properties by thee
>   bee spoke,
>   Nothing more endlesse, nothing sooner broke?
>
>   Marriage rings are not of this stuffe;   5
>   Oh, why should ought lesse precious, or less tough
> Figure our loves? Except in thy name thou have bid it say
>   I'am cheap, and nought but fashion, fling me'away.
>
>   Yet stay with mee since thou art come,
>   Circle this fingers top, which did'st her thombe.   10
> Be justly proud, and gladly safe, that thou dost dwell with
>   me,
>   She that, Oh, broke her faith, would soon breake thee.

A Jeat Ring sent. Entitled in one MS *To a Jeat Ring sent to me* (i.e. by a lady).
  1.   *Thou*: the poem is an address to the ring.
       black: constant.
  3.   *spoke*: symbolized.
  6.   i.e. than the gold of marriage rings.
  7.   *Figure*: represent.
       Except: unless.
  8.   *fling*: a pun on 'jet' and the French *jette* or throw away (§159).
       On the symbol ', see above, p. 5.
 10.   Thumb-rings were not uncommon in Donne's time.

Negative love.

I never stoop'd so low, as they
Which on an eye, cheeke, lip, can prey,
   Seldome to them, which soare no higher
   Then vertue or the minde to'admire,
For sense, and understanding may   5
   Know, what gives fuell to their fire:
My love, though silly, is more brave,
For may I misse, when ere I crave,
If I know yet, what I would have.

If that be simply perfectest   10
Which can by no way be exprest
   But *Negatives*, my love is so.
   To All, which all love, I say no.
If any who deciphers best,
   What we know not, our selves, can know,   15
Let him teach mee that nothing; This
As yet my ease, and comfort is,
Though I speed not, I cannot misse.

Negative love. In a few MSS entitled *The Nothing*; in others, given both titles.
3.   *to them*: i.e. *stoop'd* to them.
4.   *than*: then.
     On the symbol ', see above, p. 5.
5.   *For*: 'Both' (acc. to some MSS).
7.   *silly*: plain.
     brave: courageous.
8.   *misse*: fail to obtain what I want.
     crave: i.e. a woman.
11. *way*: 'means' (acc. to 1669).
12. *Negatives*: alluding to the *via negativa*, the Christian tradition of defining God negatively, rather by what He is not than by what He is.
15. As Donne once said, Adam named all the creatures but not himself because 'he understood himselfe lesse' (*Sermons*, IX, 256: §158).
16. *nothing*: cf. 'lovely glorious nothing', above, p. 66, l. 6.
17. *As yet*: until then.
18. i.e. though I succeed not, I cannot fail (*ALC*).

The Prohibition.

      Take heed of loving mee,
At least remember, I forbade it thee;
Not that I shall repaire my'unthrifty wast
Of Breath and Blood, upon thy sighes, and teares,
By being to mee then that which thou wast;   5
But, so great Joy, our life at once outweares,
Then, least thy love, by my death, frustrate bee,
If thou love mee, take heed of loving mee.

      Take heed of hating mee,
Or too much triumph in the Victorie.   10
Not that I shall be mine owne officer,
And hate with hate againe retaliate;
But thou wilt lose the stile of conquerour,
If I, thy conquest, perish by thy hate.
Then, least my being nothing lessen thee,   15
If thou hate mee, take heed of hating mee.

      Yet, love and hate mee too,
So, these extreames shall ne'r their office doe;
Love mee, that I may die the gentler way;
Hate mee, because thy love is too great for mee;   20
Or let these two, themselves, not me decay;

The Prohibition. Untitled in some MSS; the last stanza is omitted in others.
1.   *Take heed*: beware.
3.   *repaire my'unthrifty wast*: 'repay in unthrifty a wast' (acc. to 1669).
     On the symbol ', see above, p. 5.
4.   *upon*: by drawing upon.
5.   *mee then that which* (acc. to 1633, see §188): 'thee then what to me' (acc. to
     1635–69, several MSS, and most modern editors) or 'mee then what to
     me' (acc. to two MSS). The line is omitted in some MSS.
7 (also 15). *least*: lest.
11. *officer*: agent of revenge.
15. *lessen thee*: diminish your glory (§172).
18. *ne'r their* (acc. to 1633–69, §188): 'neythers' or 'neyther' or 'neyther their'
     (acc. to various MSS).
19. *die*: as above, p. 48, note on 16.
20. *thy* (acc. to 1635–69 and some copies of 1633): 'my' (acc. to most copies of
     1633).

So shall I live thy stay, not triumph bee;
Lest thou thy love and hate and mee undoe,
To let mee live, Oh love and hate mee too.

The Expiration.

So, so, breake off this last lamenting kisse,
   Which sucks two soules, and vapors Both away,
Turne thou ghost that way, and let mee turne this,
   And let our selves benight our happiest day,
We aske none leave to love; nor will we owe   5
   Any, so cheape a death, as saying, Goe;

Goe; and if that word have not quite kil'd thee,
   Ease mee with death, by bidding mee goe too.
Oh, if it have, let my word worke on mee,
   And a just office on a murderer doe.   10
Except it be too late, to kill me so,
   Being double dead, going, and bidding, goe.

The Prohibition.
22.   *stay* (acc. to 1633 and several MSS, see §188): 'Stage' (acc. to 1635–69 and
     several MSS).
23–24. The lines also read, 'Then lest thou thy love hate, and mee thou undoe /
     O let me live, yet love and hate me too' (acc. to 1635–54 and several MSS).

The Expiration. Entitled in some MSS *Valediction*. The first of Donne's poems
    to be published even if in a different form, it appeared with a musical
    setting in Alfonso Ferrabosco's *Book of Ayres* (1609); for the setting, see
    §§163, 169, 190.
1.   *So, so*: 'So, go' (acc. to 1669).
    breake: 'leave' (acc. to some MSS).
2.   *vapors*: evaporates.
4.   *selves*: 'soules' (acc. to some MSS).
    benight: to cloud (*OED*).
5.   *aske*: 'ask'd' (acc. to many MSS).
9.   *Oh*: 'Or' (acc. to 1635–69 and several MSS).
11.   *Except*: unless.

The Computation.

For the first twenty yeares, since yesterday,
 I scarce beleev'd, thou could'st be gone away,
For fotty more, I fed on favours past,
 And forty'on hopes, that thou would'st, they might last
Teares drown'd one hundred, and sighes blew out two, 5
 A thousand, I did neither thinke, nor doe,
  Or not divide, all being one thought of you;
  Or in a thousand more, forgot that too.
Yet call not this long life; But thinke that I
Am, by being dead, Immortall; Can ghosts die? 10

The Paradox.

No Lover saith, I love, nor any other
  Can judge a perfect Lover;
Hee thinkes that that else none can or will agree,
  That any loves but hee:
I cannot say I lov'd, for who can say   5
  Hee was kill'd yesterday.
Love with excesse of heat, more yong then old,
  Death kills with too much cold;

The Computation. On the mounting hyperboles, cf. Jonson's second song to
 Celia ('Kisse me, sweet') and Marvell's *To his Coy Mistress* – and, behind
 both, the celebrated fifth song of Catullus, *Vivamus, mea Lesbia*.
1. *For*: 'From' (acc. to 1669).
 the: 'my' (acc. to 1635–69 and some MSS).
2. *could'st*: 'wouldst' or 'could' (acc. to various MSS).
3. *For*: 'And' (acc. to 1669 and some MSS).
4. On the symbol ', see above, p. 5.
6. *neither*: 'nothing' (acc. to some MSS).
7. *divide*: 'deem'd' (acc. to 1635–54 and some MSS).
9. *call*: 'thinke' (acc. to some MSS).

The Paradox. Untitled in 1633 and most MSS; entitled from 1635. In 1633 the
 poem stood apart from, and as the last of, the *Songs and Sonets*; it gained
 its present position, after *The Computation*, from 1635.
3. *can or will agree*: 'can, nor will agree' (acc. to many MSS).
6 ff. *kill'd* (also *die* etc.): as above, p. 48, note on 16.
7. *Love with*: i.e. love kills by.
 then: than.

Wee dye but once, and who lov'd last did die,
  Hee that saith twice, doth lye: 10
For though hee seeme to move, and stirre a while,
  It doth the sense beguile.
Such life is like the light which bideth yet
  When the lifes light is set,
Or like the heat, which fire in solid matter   15
  Leaves behinde, two houres after.
Once I lov'd and dyed; and am now become
  Mine Epitaph and Tombe.
Here dead men speake their last, and so do I;
  Love-slaine, loe, here I dye.   20

Farewell to love.

   Whilst yet to prove,
I thought there was some Deitie in love
 So did I reverence, and gave
Worship, as Atheists at their dying houre
Call, what they cannot name, an unknowne power, 5
 As ignorantly did I crave:
   Thus when
Things not yet knowne are coveted by men,
 Our desires give them fashion, and so
As they waxe lesser, fall, as they sise, grow.   10

The Paradox.
10. *he that saith twice*: he that says we die twice (§169).
12. *the sense beguile*: deceive one's senses (§163).
14. *lifes light* (acc. to 1633–69 and many MSS): 'lights life' (acc. to many MSS
  and all modern editors), in both cases meaning the sun.
19. *Here*: i.e. in their epitaphs.
20. *dye*: 'lye' (acc. to several MSS and all modern editors).

Farewell to love. This poem, and the next one, were first published in the 1635
  edition; they concluded the *Songs and Sonets* until the addition of *Sonnet.*
  The Token (1649) and *Selfe Love* (1650).
 1. i.e. while still inexperienced.
 9. *fashion*: form.
10. *fall*: abate.
  sise: increase in size; 'rise' (acc. to one MS). The word, like *waxe lesser*, has
  a sexual reference (§430).

But, from late faire
His highnesse sitting in a golden Chaire,
    Is not lesse cared for after three dayes
By children, then the thing which lovers so
Blindly admire, and with such worship wooe;   15
    Being had, enjoying it decayes:
                And thence,
What before pleas'd them all, takes but one sense,
    And that so lamely, as it leaves behinde
A kinde of sorrowing dulnesse to the minde.   20

        Ah cannot wee,
As well as Cocks and Lyons jocund be,
    After such pleasures, unlesse wise
Nature decreed (since each such Act, they say,
Diminisheth the length of life a day)   25
    This; as shee would man should despise
                The sport,
Because that other curse of being short,
    And onely for a minute made to be
Eager, desires to raise posterity.   30

        Since so, my minde
Shall not desire what no man else can finde,
    I'll no more dote and runne
To pursue things which had indammag'd me.

12. i.e. a gingerbread figure purchased at a recent fair.
14. *then*: than.
     the thing: love-making.
18. *all*: all the senses.
     takes: affects.
19. *as*: that.
21–30. The stanza, much amended by some editors, has been preserved by
     others in its original state, also reproduced here; for the details, see §172:
     App. IV.
22. *Cocks and Lyons*: reputed to be the only male creatures not to feel *dulnesse*
     (20) after sexual intercourse.
24–25. Lust was thought literally to destroy the body but also the soul because
     it is a mortal sin (§195).
31. *Since so*: since that is so.

And when I come where moving beauties be,   35
  As men doe when the summers Sunne
      Growes great,
Though I admire their greatnesse, shun their heat;
  Each place can afford shadowes. If all faile,
'Tis but applying worme-seed to the Taile.   40

A Lecture upon the Shadow.

Stand still, and I will read to thee
A Lecture, Love, in loves philosophy.
    These three houres that we have spent,
    Walking here, Two shadowes went
Along with us, which we our selves produc'd;   5
But, now the Sunne is just above our head,
    We doe those shadowes tread;
    And to brave clearnesse all things are reduc'd.
  So whilst our infant loves did grow,
  Disguises did, and shadowes, flow,   10
  From us, and our cares; but, now 'tis not so.

That love hath not attain'd the high'st degree,
Which is still diligent lest others see.

Farewell to love.
35. *moving beauties*: women whose beauty moves or stirs.
40. *worme-seed*: used as an aphrodisiac.
      the Taile: the penis.
39–40. The lines may mean: if, in spite of my resolution to avoid sex, I
      succumb, I could rationalize my defeat by looking on the act as merely
      therapeutic (§413).

A Lecture upon the Shadow. First published in 1635 (see headnote to the previous
      poem). Untitled in several MSS; entitled in 1635 *Song*, in one MS *Loves
      lecture*, in another *Loves Philosophy*, and in still others *The Shadowe*;
      gained its present title from 1650.
  4. *Walking*: 'In walking' (acc. to several MSS).
  6. The instant of noon is an image for the total openness of fulfilled love
      (§207).
  8. *brave*: splendid.
  9 (also 14). *loves*: 'love' (acc. to several MSS).
  12. *high'st*: 'least' (acc. to several MSS).

Except our loves at this noone stay,
We shall new shadowes make the other way.   15
    As the first were made to blinde
    Others; these which come behinde
Will worke upon our selves, and blind our eyes.
If our loves faint, and westwardly decline;
     To me thou, falsly, thine,   20
    And I to thee mine actions shall disguise.
  The morning shadowes weare away,
  But these grow longer all the day,
  But oh, loves day is short, if love decay.

Love is a growing, or full constant light;   25
And his first minute, after noone, is night.

Sonnet. The Token.

Send me some tokens, that my hope may live,
  Or that my easelesse thoughts may sleep and rest;
Send me some honey to make sweet my hive,
  That in my passions I may hope the best.
I beg noe ribbond wrought with thine owne hands,   5
  To knit our loves in the fantastick straine
Of new-toucht youth; nor Ring to shew the stands
  Of our affection, that as that's round and plaine,

Farewell to love.
14. *Except*: unless.
17. *behinde*: i.e. later.
19. *If our loves faint*: 'If once love faint' (acc. to some MSS).
    westwardly: adversely (cf. above, p. 49, note on 18).
25. *first* (acc. to all MSS): 'short' (acc. to 1635–69).

The Token. Not a sonnet in the strict sense of the term, the poem was first
    published in 1649 (see headnote, above, p. 121). Its authenticity has been
    doubted often, for it appears to be 'untypical' of Donne.
  1. *tokens*: 'token' (acc. to some MSS).
  4. *passions*: 'passion' (acc. to several MSS).
  5. *noe* (acc. to several MSS) corrects the obviously erroneous 'nor' (acc. to
    1649–69).
  6. *fantastick strain*: capricious ways.
  7. *new-toucht*: i.e. by love.
    stands: standards.

So should our loves meet in simplicity.
  No, nor the Coralls which thy wrist infold,   10
Lac'd up together in congruity,
  To shew our thoughts should rest in the same hold,
No, nor thy picture, though most gracious,
  And most desir'd 'cause 'tis like thee best;
Nor witty Lines, which are most copious,   15
  Within the Writings which thou hast addrest.

Send me nor this, nor that, t'increase my score,
But swear thou thinkst I love thee, and no more.

[Selfe Love.]

He that cannot chuse but love,
And strives against it still,
Never shall my fancy move;
For he loves agaynst his will;
Nor he which is all his own,   5
And can att pleasure chuse,
When I am caught he can be gone,
And when he list refuse.

The Token.
10. As love-charms, *Coralls* were reputed to lure or entice (§399).
12. *rest in the same hold*: be similarly harmonious; also alluding to the *hold* of the charm cast by the *Coralls*.
14. *'cause 'tis like thee best*: 'because best like the best' (acc. to several MSS).
16. *addrest*: written.
17. *score*: 'store' (acc. to several MSS).

[*Selfe Love*]. Not ever attributed to Donne with confidence, the poem was first published in 1650 (see headnote, above, p. 121). Untitled in all early editions and MSS, it owes its present title to a conjecture proposed in 1896 (§157). Equally conjectural is its occasional subdivision into quatrains (e.g. §§163, 166).
1 ff. The speaker is a woman, as in *Breake of day* and *Confined Love*.
6. The line (acc. to one MS) corrects the obviously erroneous 'And cannot pleasure chuse' (acc. to 1650–69).
8. *list*: please.

Nor he that loves none but faire,
For such by all are sought;   10
Nor he that can for foul ones care,
For his Judgement then is nought:
Nor he that hath wit, for he
Will make me his jest or slave
Nor a fool for when others, . . .   15
He can neither . . . . . .
Nor he that still his Mistresse payes,
For she is thrall'd therefore:
Nor he that payes not, for he sayes
Within shee's worth no more.   20
Is there then no kinde of men
Whom I may freely prove?
I will vent that humour then
In mine own selfe love.

11. *foul ones*: 'fouleness' (acc. to one MS).
15–16. The gaps occur in all extant versions.
17. *payes* (acc. to some MSS): 'prayes' (acc. to 1650–69).
18. *thralled*: enslaved.
22. *prove*: approve.
23. *humour*: disposition (see below, p. 336, note on 241).

Epigrams

Classical in origin, the epigram was practised with considerable expertise by many Renaissance poets. William Drummond of Hawthornden, Jonson's friend, thought that Donne 'might easily be the best Epigrammatist we have found in *English*' (below, p. 137). All but the last four of the ensuing epigrams appeared in the first edition of Donne's poems in 1633; of the remaining, one was first printed by Sir John Simeon in 1857 ('The Lier': §171), two by Sir Edmund Gosse in 1899 ('Cales and Guyana' and 'Sir John Wingefield'; below, p. 522), and one by Roger E. Bennett in 1942 ('The Jughler': §160).

Hero and *Leander*.

Both rob'd of aire, we both lye in one ground,
Both whom one fire had burnt, one water drownd.

Hero and Leander – i.e. the lovers who drowned in the Hellespont.
  1–2. *air . . . ground . . . fire . . . water*: the four elements (as above, p. 115, note on 9–10).

Pyramus and *Thisbe*.

Two, by themselves, each other, love and feare
Slaine, cruell friends, by parting have joyn'd here.

Pyramus and Thisbe – i.e. the lovers who exchanged their vows through a chink in the wall separating their two houses, and committed suicide when each assumed the other had been killed.

Niobe.

By childrens births, and death, I am become
So dry, that I am now mine owne sad tombe.

Niobe – i.e. the mother whose seven sons and seven daughters were killed by
    Apollo and Artemis, and who continued to weep even after she was
    changed into a stone.

A burnt ship.

Out of a fired ship, which, by no way
But drowning, could be rescued from the flame,
Some men leap'd forth, and ever as they came
Neere the foes ships, did by their shot decay;
So all were lost, which in the ship were found,   5
   They in the sea being burnt, they in the burnt
      ship drown'd.

A burnt ship.
  4.   *decay*: die.

Fall of a wall.

Under an undermin'd, and shot-bruis'd wall
A too-bold Captaine perish'd by the fall,
Whose brave misfortune, happiest men envi'd,
That had a towne for tombe, his bones to hide.

Fall of a wall – i.e. during a battle at Corunna in 1589, which resulted in the
    death of several English soldiers.
  4.   *towne*: 'towre' (acc. to 1635–69).
     bones: 'corps' (acc. to some MSS).

A lame begger.

I am unable, yonder begger cries,
To stand, or move; if he say true, hee *lies*.

A lame begger. Cf. the variant *On a Cripple* in one MS: 'I cannot goe sit, stand,
the cripple cries / What doth he then? if he say true he lyes' (§163).

A selfe accuser.

Your mistris, that you follow whores, still taxeth you:
'Tis strange that she should thus confesse it, though'it be true.

A selfe accuser.
 2.   *confess it*: 'confess' (acc. to several MSS).
      On the symbol ', see above, p. 5.

A licentious person.

Thy sinnes and haires may no man equall call,
For, as thy sinnes increase, thy haires doe fall.

A licentious person. Entitled in one MS *A Whorer* (§171).
 2.   *haires doe fall*: i.e. as a result of syphilis.

Antiquary.

If in his Studie he hath so much care
To'hang all old strange things, let his wife beware.

Antiquary. Entitled in one MS *Hammon*, on whom see below, p. 224, l. 87.
 2.   On the symbol ', see above, p. 5.

Disinherited.

Thy father all from thee, by his last Will,
Gave to the poore; Thou hast good title still.

Phryne.

Thy flattering picture, *Phryne*, is like thee,
Onely in this, that you both painted be.

Phryne – i.e. any latter-day emulator of the famous courtesan of ancient
      Athens.
   2. *you*: 'wee' (acc. to a MS).

An obscure writer.

Philo, with twelve yeares study, hath beene griev'd
To be understood; when will hee be beleev'd?

An obscure writer.
   1. *Philo*: no real person intended.
   2. *To'be understood*: whenever he was understood.
      On the symbol ', see above, p. 5.

Klockius.

Klockius so deeply hath sworne, ne'r more to come
In bawdie house, that hee dares not goe home.

Klockius (untitled in 1633, thus entitled in MSS). The name may derive from
      the Dutch *kloek*, 'a sly person' (§163).
   1. *sworne*: 'vowd' (acc. to several MSS).
      more (omitted in some MSS).

Raderus.

Why this man gelded *Martiall* I muse,
Except himselfe alone his tricks would use,
As *Katherine*, for the Courts sake, put downe Stewes.

Raderus – i.e. Matthew Rader, the German editor of an expurgated edition of
    Martial's works (§§158, 171).
  3. *Katherine*: not yet identified.
    Stewes: brothels.

Mercurius Gallo–Belgicus.

Like *Esops* fellow-slaves, Ꝋ *Mercury*,
Which could do all things, thy faith is; and I
Like *Esops* selfe, which nothing; I confesse
I should have had more faith, if thou hadst lesse;
Thy credit lost thy credit: 'Tis sinne to doe,   5
In this case, as thou wouldst be done unto,
To beleeve all: Change thy name: thou art like
Mercury in stealing, but lyest like a *Greeke*.

Mercurius Gallo-Belgicus – i.e. an early representative of the yellow press,
    issued in Latin at Cologne.
  1–2. Aesop was said to have been a slave, purchased once he averred he knew
    nothing while two other slaves pompously claimed to know everything
    (§171).
  5. *credit . . . credit*: credulousness . . . credulity (§171).
  8. *Mercury*: the patron of thieves.
    but: 'and' (acc. to several MSS).
    like a Greek: Greeks were habitually regarded by Western Europeans as
    very devious.

Ralphius.

Compassion in the world againe is bred:
Ralphius is sick, the broker keeps his bed.

Ralphius (untitled in 1633, thus entitled in LSS).
   2.   *broker*: pawnbroker.

The Lier.

Thou in the fields walkst out thy supping howers,
    And yet thou swearst thou hast supp'd like a king:
Like Nebuchadnezar perchance with grass and flowers,
    A sallet worse then Spanish dyeting.

The Lier.
   2.   *swearst*: 'sayst' (acc. to some MSS).
   3.   *Nebuchadnezar*: the mythical Babylonian king who was 'driven from
        men, and did eat grass as oxen' (Daniel 4.33).
   4.   *sallet*: salad; the Spanish were thought by the English to have an appalling
        diet.
        then: than.

Cales *and Guyana*.

If you from spoyle of th'old worlds farthest end
To the new world your kindled valors bend,
What brave examples then do prove it trew
That one things end doth still beginne a new.

Cales and Guyana. After the English sack of Cadiz ('Cales') in southwest Spain
        in 1596, it was planned to attack the Spaniards in Guiana in South
        America; but Guiana's 'harvest' was in fact 'nip'd in the spring' (see
        below, p. 291, l. 18).
   1.   *you*: possibly Sir Walter Ralegh (§163).
        th'old worlds farthest end: Cadiz lies west even of Gibraltar.

Sir John Wingefield.

Beyond th'old Pillers many have travailed
Towards the Suns cradle, and his throne, and bed.
A fitter Piller our Earle did bestow
In that late Iland; for he well did know
Farther then Wingefield no man dares to goe.   5

Sir John Wingefield (entitled in the MSS either *Il Cavalliere Gio: Wingef* or *On Cavallero Wingfeild*) – i.e. the heroic commander who died during the attack on Cadiz in 1596 (§ 196).
1. *Pillers*: 'the Pillars of Hercules', that is, the Straits of Gibraltar.
   travailed: travelled; also, laboured.
2. *throne, bed*: the earth's south and north (§472).
3. *our Earle*: Essex.
4. *Iland*: Cadiz is linked with the mainland by a bridge.
5. *then*: than.
   Wingefield: a pun, i.e. wing-field (§ 472).

The Jughler.

Thou call'st me effeminat, for I love womens joyes;
I call not thee manly, though thou follow boyes.

The Jughler (the title *Manliness* given by three modern editors [§§160, 166, 171] is a conjecture).
1. *joyes*: 'toyes' (acc. to a MS).

Elegies

'The original meaning of *elegia* or *elegeia*', we have been told, 'was a funeral elegy written in elegiacs (*elegi*), that is to say, in couplets consisting of an hexameter followed by a pentameter, but Ovid and other Roman poets used the word to describe a love-poem written in metre' (§250; with an account of the Latin love-elegy's conventions in §488). By Donne's time, in consequence, Ovid's *Amores* were habitually termed 'elegies'. So were Donne's own efforts, even if their Ovidian dimension is quite pronounced for some readers (§250), distinctly less so for others (§483). In the event, Donne's elegies became in his own time the most popular of his poems (§§479, 486; see also above, pp. 36–8).

As a group, Donne's elegies pose problems concerning (1) their canon, (2) their numbering and therefore their sequence, and (3) their titles. Concerning the canon, the present edition prints the twenty elegies accepted initially by Grierson (§158) and next by Hayward, Smith, and Warnke (§§159, 164, 166). But the reader should be mindful of at least two other possible strategies: Gardner's (§169), who accepted only fourteen elegies, banished five to the list of poems of doubtful authorship, added *A Funeral Elegy to L.C.* (here printed among the *Epicedes*), and transferred Elegy X to *Songs and Sonets*; and Shawcross's (§163), who accepted sixteen elegies, transferred IX and X to *Songs and Sonets*, and refused even to mention XIII and XIV. Still another poem, *Sapho to Philænis*, often printed with the elegies, is here made available in a category of its own (below, pp. 189–91).

The sequential numbering of the elegies is borrowed from Grierson since the edition of 1633 is dependable only until Elegy V, and that of 1635 only until Elegy X. The titles, finally, presented less of a problem: they are here reproduced

from 1635, which was the first edition to provide them, save
that Elegies VI and VII are untitled here as they are in all the
available sources.

The poems are often thought to have been composed in the
mid-1590s. But as they cannot in fact be dated with certainty,
the caution advised in connection with the *Songs and Sonets*
(above, p. 46) is apposite to the present occasion too.

Elegie I.
Jealosie.

Fond woman, which would'st have thy husband die,
And yet complain'st of his great jealousie;
If swolne with poyson, hee lay in'his last bed,
His body with a sere-barke covered,
Drawing his breath, as thick and short, as can   5
The nimblest crocheting Musitian,
Ready with loathsome vomiting to spue
His Soule out of one hell, into a new,
Made deafe with his poore kindreds howling cries,
Begging with few feign'd teares, great legacies,   10
Thou would'st not weepe, but jolly,'and frolicke bee,
As a slave, which to morrow should be free;
Yet weep'st thou, when thou seest him hungerly
Swallow his owne death, hearts-bane jealousie.
O give him many thanks, he'is courteous,   15
That in suspecting kindly warneth us.

Elegie I. First published and thus numbered in 1633; first entitled in 1635.
1.   *Fond:* foolish.
     die: as above, p. 48, note on 16.
3 (also 11, 15, 29, 30). On the symbol ', see above, p. 5.
4.   *sere-barke covered:* coated in scabs (§207); 'sere-cloth' (acc. to 1669 and
     some MSS).
9.   *poore:* 'pure' (acc. to some MSS).
13. *hungerly:* hungrily.
14. *hearts-bane:* poison-bearing, destructive.

Wee must not, as wee us'd, flout openly,
In scoffing ridles, his deformitie;
Nor at his boord together being satt,
With words, nor touch, scarce lookes adulterate.   20
Nor when he swolne, and pamper'd with great fare
Sits downe, and snorts, cag'd in his basket chaire,
Must wee usurpe his owne bed any more,
Nor kisse and play in his house, as before.
Now I see many dangers; for that is   25
His realme, his castle, and his diocesse.
But if, as envious men, which would revile
Their Prince, or coyne his gold, themselves exile
Into another countrie,'and doe it there,
Wee play'in another house, what should we feare?   30
There we will scorne his houshold policies,
His seely plots, and pensionary spies,
As the inhabitants of Thames right side
Do Londons Major; or Germans, the Popes pride.

18.   *deformitie*: ugliness.
19.   *boord*: table.
21.   *great*: 'high' (acc. to 1669 and several MSS).
25.   *it*: 'that' (acc. to most MSS).
30.   The line also reads, 'We into some third place retyred were' (acc. to
      several MSS).
32.   *seely*: ineffective, futile (§164).
      pensionary: paid.
33–34. Southwark, the area south of the river Thames, tended to *scorne* (31)
      the authority of London; so, ever since the Reformation, the Germans
      oppose papal authority.
34.   *Major*: an obsolete form of 'Mayor' (acc. to 1669).

Elegie II.
The Anagram.

Marry, and love thy *Flavia*, for, shee
Hath all things, whereby others beautious bee,
For, though her eyes be small, her mouth is great,
Though they be Ivory, yet her teeth be jeat,
Though they be dimme, yet she is light enough, 5
And though her harsh haire fall, her skinne is rough;
What though her cheeks be yellow, her haire's red,
Give her thine, and she hath a maydenhead.
These things are beauties elements, where these
Meet in one, that one must, as perfect, please. 10
If red and white and each good quality
Be in thy wench ne'r aske where it doth lye.
In buying things perfum'd, we aske; if there
Be muske and amber in it, but not where.
Though all her parts be not in th'usuall place, 15
She'hath yet an Anagram of a good face.

Elegie II. First published and thus numbered in 1633; first entitled in 1635. Much admired by William Drummond of Hawthornden, the poem led him to call Donne 'the best Epigrammatist we have found in *English*' (§250). Drummond also perceived that the poem belongs with Torquato Tasso's 'stanzas against beauty' ('Sopra la bellezza', in *Rime*, No. 37) in the extensive tradition 'in praise of ugliness' (§490). Popular as all of Donne's elegies were, the present one was particularly favoured by the period's anthologists (§169).

4. *they*: i.e. her lips. One of the period's anthologists revised the line thus: 'Her Lipps though Ivory, yet her Teeth are Jett' (§189); and another wrote: 'Though her lips Ivory be, her teeth be fat' (§159).

5. *they*: i.e. her eyes.

6. *haire fall*: 'hair's foul' (acc. to 1669).

8. *thine*: i.e. hair (which will fall anyway when one gets syphilis) and virginity (which will be the only sort she will ever have).

14. *amber*: ambergris.

16 (also 26, 32). On the symbol ', see above, p. 5.

16. *Anagram*: the parts of her face once rearranged – as the letters in an anagram are wont to be – the face may be *good*, always depending on one's interpretation.

If we might put the letters but one way,
In the leane dearth of words, what could wee say?
When by the Gamut some Musitions make
A perfect song, others will undertake,   20
By the same Gamut chang'd, to equall it.
Things simply good, can never be unfit;
She's faire as any, if all be like her,
And if none bee, then she is singular.
All love is wonder; if wee justly doe   25
Account her wonderfull, why'not lovely too?
Love built on beauty, soone as beauty, dies,
Chuse this face, chang'd by no deformities;
Women are all like Angels; the faire be
Like those which fell to worse; but such as thee,   30
Like to good Angels, nothing can impaire:
'Tis lesse griefe to be foule, than to'have beene faire.
For one nights revels, silke and gold we chuse,
But, in long journeyes, cloth, and leather use.
Beauty is barren oft; best husbands say,   35
There is best land, where there is foulest way.
Oh what a soveraigne Plaister will shee bee
If thy past sinnes have taught thee jealousie!
Here needs no spies, nor eunuches; her commit
Safe to thy foes; yea, to a Marmosit.   40

18.   *the*: 'that' (acc. to 1635–69 and some MSS).
      words: 'letters' (acc. to several MSS).
19.   *Gamut*: the entire musical scale.
22.   *simply good*: good by nature.
      unfit: useless; also, broken down.
29–31. Omitted in one MS; but other lines – not hereafter noted – are also
      omitted in various MSS.
30.   *those which fell*: the angels who, after the War in Heaven, were banished to
      Hell.
35.   *husbands*: husbandmen, tillers; also married men, with a sexual inuendo
      (§166).
37.   *soveraigne Plaister*: the most effective 'medicine' (to use an anthologist's
      word: §159).
40.   *Marmosit*: weasel, reputed to be very lecherous (§166).

When Belgiaes citties, the round countries drowne,
That durty foulenesse guards, and armes the towne:
So doth her face guard her; and so, for thee,
Which, forc'd by businesse, absent oft must bee,
Shee, whose face, like clouds, turnes the day to night,   45
Who, mightier then the sea, makes Moores seem white,
Who, though seaven yeares, she in the Stews had laid,
A Nunnery durst receive, and thinke a maid,
And though in childbeds labour she did lie,
Midwifes would sweare,'twere but a tympanie,   50
Whom, if shee'accuse her self, I credit lesse
Then witches, which impossibles confesse,
Whom Dildoes, Bedstaves, and her Velvet Glasse
Would be as loath to touch as Joseph was:
Onc like none, and lik'd of none, fittest were,   55
For, things in fashion every man will weare.

41. *round countries drowne*: 'foule Country drownes' (acc. to some MSS).
     drowne: by opening the dikes, as a defence against enemies from surround-
     ing *countries*.
42. *durty foulenesse*: the refuse is so formidable that it *guards* and *armes* the
     besieged cities.
47. *Stews*: brothels.
49. *childbeds*: 'childbirths' (acc. to 1669 and several MSS).
50. *tympanie*: tumour or morbid swelling (*OED*).
53–54. Omitted in 1635–54.
53. i.e. phalluses, bedboards, and her velvet-backed mirror (§163): instru-
     ments of female masturbation (§166).
54. i.e. as *Joseph* had refused to *touch* Potiphar's wife (Genesis 39.7 ff.).

Elegie III.
Change.

Although thy hand and faith, and good workes too,
Have seal'd thy love which nothing should undoe,
Yea though thou fall backe, that apostasie
Confirme thy love; yet much, much I feare thee.
Women, are like the Arts, forc'd unto none,   5
Open to'all searchers, unpriz'd, if unknowne.
If I have caught a bird, and let him flie,
Another fouler using these meanes, as I,
May catch the same bird; and, as these things bee,
Women are made for men, not him, nor mee.   10
Foxes and goats; all beasts change when they please,
Shall women, more hot, wily, wild then these,
Be bound to one man, and did Nature then
Idly make them apter to'endure then men?
They'are our clogges, not their owne; if a man bee   15
Chain'd to a galley, yet the galley'is free;
Who hath a plow-land, casts all his seed corne there,
And yet allowes his ground more corne should beare;
Though Danuby into the sea must flow,
The sea receives the Rhene, Volga, and Po.   20
By nature, which gave it, this liberty
Thou lov'st, but Oh! canst thou love it and mee?

Elegie III. First published and thus numbered in 1633; first entitled in 1635.
   1.   *faith, and good works*: religious terms (see above, p. 106, note on 19–21),
        here used in a strictly secular sense.
   3.   *apostasie*: abandonment of religious faith or principles.
   5.   *forc'd unto*: 'forbid to' (acc. to one MS).
   6 (also 14, 15, 16, 25, 27, 35). On the symbol ', see above, p. 5.
   8.   *fouler*: fowler.
        these: 'those' (acc. to 1669 and many MSS).
  11.   *Foxes*: symbolic of cunning; *and goats*: of lechery (as above, p. 92, note
        on 39).
  12 (also 14, 25, 26). *then*: than.
  13.   *did*: 'bid' (acc. to 1669).
  15.   *clogges*: impediments, encumbrances (*OED*).
        not: 'and' (acc. to some MSS).
  19–20. i.e. the rivers of southeast Europe, central Europe, Russia and north-
        ern Italy, respectively.

Likenesse glues love: and if that thou so doe,
To make us like and love, must I change too?
More then thy hate, I hate'it, rather let mee   25
Allow her change, then change as oft as shee,
And soe not teach, but force my'opinion
To love not any one, nor every one.
To live in one land, is captivitie,
To runne all countries, a wild roguery;   30
Waters stincke soone, if in one place they bide
And in the vast sea are more putrifi'd:
But when they kisse one banke, and leaving this
Never looke backe, but the next banke doe kisse,
Then are they purest; Change'is the nursery   35
Of musicke, joy, life, and eternity.

Elegie IV.
The Perfume.

Once, and but once found in thy company,
All thy suppos'd escapes are laid on mee;
And as a thiefe at barre, is question'd there
By all the men, that have been rob'd that yeare,
So am I, (by this traiterous meanes surpriz'd)   5
By thy Hydroptique father catechiz'd.

Elegie III.
23. *Likenesse glues love*: as the next line suggests, one tends to *like* (and have
     like interests, temperaments, etc.) and thereby to *love*.
     and if that thou so: 'Then if so thou' (acc. to one MS) or 'And then if so
     thou' (ditto).
32. *more* (acc. to 1633–54): 'worse' (acc. to several MSS) or 'worst' (ditto).
     putrifi'd: 'purified' (acc. to 1650–54, 1669).

Elegie IV. First published and thus numbered in 1633; first entitled in 1635.
     Also entitled in one MS *That he was betrayed by a perfume* (§187); and in
     another, *Discovered* etc. (§169).
2. *escapes*: sexual escapades.
3. *at barre*: in court.
5. One MS interestingly closes the parentheses after *meanes* (§187).
6. *Hydroptique*: see above, p. 90, note on 6.

Though he had wont to search with glazed eyes,
As though he came to kill a Cockatrice,
Though hee hath oft sworne, that hee would remove
Thy beauties beautie, and food of our love,   10
Hope of his goods, if I with thee were seene,
Yet close and secret, as our soules, we'have beene.
Though thy immortall mother which doth lye
Still buried in her bed, yet will not dye,
Takes this advantage to sleepe out day-light,   15
And watch thy entries, and returnes all night,
And, when she takes thy hand, and would seeme kind,
Doth search what rings, and armelets she can finde,
And kissing notes the colour of thy face,
And fearing least thou'art swolne, doth thee embrace;   20
And to trie if thou long, doth name strange meates,
And notes thy paleness, blushing, sighs, and sweats;
And politiquely will to thee confesse
The sinnes of her owne youths ranke lustinesse;
Yet love these Sorceries did remove, and move   25
Thee to gull thine owne mother for my love.
Thy little brethren, which like Faiery Sprights
Oft skipt into our chamber, those sweet nights,
And, kist and ingled on thy fathers knee,
Were brib'd next day, to tell what they did see,   30

7–8. The lines are omitted in 1633 and several MSS.
7. *glazed*: bleary (§483).
8. *Cockatrice*: the basilisk, 'the most venemous serpent that is' (Bullokar) and fabled to kill by its glance.
12 (also 20, 48, 66, 67, 72). On the symbol ', see above, p. 5.
15. *Takes*: 'take' (acc. to many MSS).
    to sleepe out day-light: cf. 'to out sleepe day light' (acc. to one MS: §187).
20. *swolne*: pregnant.
21. *To trie if thou long*: to test if you desire something (because of the pregnancy).
22. *blushing*: 'blushings' (acc. to some MSS).
23. *politique*: craftily.
26. *gull*: deceive.
29. *ingled*: fondled (*OED*); in various MSS or editions altered to 'nigled' or 'juggled' – both in the sense of tricked – or 'dandled'.

The grim eight-foot-high iron-bound serving-man,
That oft names God in oathes, and onely than,
He that to barre the first gate, doth as wide
As the great Rhodian Colossus stride,
Which, if in hell no other paines there were,   35
Makes mee feare hell, because he must be there:
Though by thy father he were hir'd to this,
Could never witnesse any touch or kisse;
But Oh, too common ill, I brought with mee
That, which betray'd mee to my enemie: 40
A loud perfume, which at my entrance cryed
Even at thy fathers nose, so were wee spied.
When, like a tyran King, that in his bed
Smelt gunpowder, the pale wretch shivered;
Had it beene some bad smell, he would have thought   45
That his owne feet, or breath, that smell had wrought.
But as wee in our Ile emprisoned,
Where cattell onely,'and diverse dogs are bred,
The pretious Unicornes, strange monsters, call,
So thought he good, strange, that had none at all.   50
I taught my silkes, their whistling to forbeare,
Even my opprest shoes, dumbe and speechlesse were,
Onely, thou bitter sweet, whom I had laid
Next mee, mee traiterously hast betraid,
And unsuspected hast invisibly   55
At once fled unto him, and staid with mee.

32. *than*: then.
34. *Colossus*: the huge statue of Apollo at Rhodes, one of the world's seven
      wonders.
37. *to*: 'for' (acc. to some MSS).
40. *my*: 'mine' (acc. to 1635–69 and some MSS).
43. *When*: 'Then' (acc. to some MSS).
      tyran: tyrant (as above, p. 96, l. 16).
47. *Ile*: Britain.
49. *pretious*: because the fabulous unicorn's horn was thought to be magical
      and medicinal.
50. *good*: 'sweet' (acc. to 1669).
52. *opprest*: in the sense of pressing, a torture used to make stubborn prison-
      ers talk (§166); but also in the sense of down-trodden.
54. *Next mee*: 'Next to my heart' (acc. to one MS).

Base excrement of earth, which dost confound
Sense, from distinguishing the sicke from sound;
By thee the seely Amorous sucks his death
By drawing in a leprous harlots breath,   60
By thee, the greatest staine to mans estate
Falls on us, to be call'd effeminate;
Though you be much lov'd in the Princes hall,
There, things that seeme, exceed substantiall.
Gods, when yee fum'd on altars, were pleas'd well,   65
Because you'were burnt, not that they lik'd your smell,
You'are loathsome all, being taken simply'alone,
Shall wee love ill things joyn'd, and hate each one?
If you were good, your good doth soone decay;
And you are rare, that takes the good away.   70
All my perfumes, I give most willingly
To'embalme thy fathers corse; What? will hee die?

Elegie V.
His Picture.

Here take my Picture; though I bid farewell;
Thine, in my heart, where my soule dwels, shall dwell.
'Tis like me now, but I dead, 'twill be more
When wee are shadowes both, than'twas before.

Elegie IV.
57. *Excrement*: growth (the perfume is excreted from flowers etc.).
59–60. Medical opinion held that contagion was effected by the breath (§192).
59. *seely*: 'silly' (acc. to one MS: §187), i.e. simple (lover).
64. i.e. appearances exceed reality, substantial things (*ALC*).
69. *your*: 'that' (acc. to one MS).
72. *corse*: corpse.

Elegie V. First published and thus numbered in 1633; first entitled in 1635. Also
  entitled in one MS *Travelling he leaves his Picture with his mystris* (§169).
 1. *Picture*: miniature portrait.
 3. *dead*: i.e. absent; hence *come backe* (5).
 4. *shadowes*: pictures; also ghosts (i.e. once they are absent from one
     another and thereby *dead*).
 4 (also 9, 11). On the symbol ', see above, p. 5.

When weather-beaten I come backe; my hand,   5
Perhaps with rude oares torne, or Sun beams tann'd,
My face and brest of hairecloth, and my head
With cares rash sodaine stormes, being o'rspread,
My body'a sack of bones, broken within,
And powders blew staines scatter'd on my skinne;   10
If rivall fooles taxe thee to'have lov'd a man,
So foule, and course, as, Oh, I may seeme than,
This shall say what I was: and thou shalt say,
Doe his hurts reach mee? doth my worth decay?
Or doe they reach his judging minde, that hee   15
Should now love lesse, what hee did love to see?
That which in him was faire and delicate,
Was but the milke, which in loves childish state
Did nurse it: who now is growne strong enough
To feed on that, which to disus'd tasts seemes tough.   20

6. *Perhaps*: 'Perchance' (acc. to some MSS).
7. *brest of hairecloth*: shirt of penitents or ascetics, made of hair.
8. *rash sodaine stormes, being*: 'rash sudden storms' (acc. to some MSS) or
   'rash sodaine horiness' (ditto) or 'harsh sodaine horinesse' (acc. to
   1635–69) or 'rash, cruel, sudden storms' (acc. to one MS).
   o'rspread: 'o'erprest' (acc. to some MSS).
10. *powders*: i.e. gunpowder's.
12. *course*: coarse.
    than: then.
14 (also 15). *reach*: affect.
16. *now*: 'like and' (acc. to several MSS).
17–20. Cf. 'every one that useth milk is unskilful in the word of righteous-
    ness: for he is a babe. But strong meat belongeth to them that are full of
    age, [who] have their sense exercised to discern both good and evil'
    (Hebrews 5.13–14: §163).
19. *nurse*: 'nourish' (acc. to some MSS).
20. *disus'd*: unaccustomed; 'weake' (acc. to 1650–69).

Elegie VI.

Oh, let mee not serve so, as those men serve
Whom honours smoakes at once fatten and sterve;
Poorely enrich't with great mens words or lookes;
Nor so write my name in thy loving bookes
As those Idolatrous flatterers, which still   5
Their Princes stiles, with many Realmes fulfill
Whence they no tribute have, and where no sway.
Such services I offer as shall pay
Themselves, I hate dead names: O then let mee
Favorite in Ordinary, or no favorite bee.   10
When my Soule was in her owne body sheath'd,
Nor yet by oathes betroth'd, nor kisses breath'd
Into my Purgatory, faithlesse thee,
Thy heart seem'd waxe, and steele thy constancie.
So, carelesse flowers strow'd on the waters face,   15
The curled whirlepooles suck, smack, and embrace,
Yet drowne them; so, the tapers beamie eye
Amorously twinkling, beckens the giddie flie,
Yet burnes his wings; and such the devill is,
Scarce visiting them, who are intirely his.   20
When I behold a streame, which, from the spring,
Doth with doubtfull melodious murmuring,

Elegie VI. First published in 1633; first thus numbered in 1635. Not entitled in
any early edition; the titles proposed by some editors – for example,
'Recusancy' (§169) – are but conjectures.
  2. *honours smoakes*: vain delusions of honour (*OED*: §169).
      fatten: 'flatter' (acc. to 1669 and some MSS).
      sterve: starve.
  6. *stiles*: titles.
      Realmes: 'names' (acc. to 1669).
      fulfill: fill up.
  7. *where*: 'bear' (acc. to 1669).
 10. *Favorite in Ordinary*: regular favourite; the phrase burlesques an official
title (§164).
 11. *her*: 'mine' (acc. to some MSS).
 17. *tapers*: i.e. candle's.
 18. *flie*: moth.

Or in a speechlesse slumber, calmely ride
Her wedded channels bosome, and then chide
And bend her browes, and swell if any bough   25
Do but stoop downe, or kisse her upmost brow:
Yet, if her often gnawing kisses winne
The traiterous banks to gape, and let her in,
She rusheth violently, and doth divorce
Her from her native, and her long-kept source,   30
And rores, and braves it, and in gallant scorne,
In flattering eddies promising retorne,
She flouts the channell, who thenceforth is drie;
Then say I; that is shee, and this am I.
Yet let not thy deepe bitternesse beget   35
Carelesse despaire in mee, for that will whet
My minde to scorne; and Oh, love dull'd with paine
Was ne'r so wise, nor well arm'd as disdaine.
Then with new eyes I shall survay thee,'and spie
Death in thy cheekes, and darknesse in thine eye;   40
Though hope bred faith and love; thus taught, I shall
As nations do from Rome, from thy love fall.
My hate shall outgrow thine, and utterly
I will renounce thy dalliance; and when I
Am the Recusant, in that resolute state,   45
What hurts it mee to be'excommunicate?

24. *then*: 'there' (acc. to 1635–69 and several MSS).
26. *upmost*: 'utmost' (acc. to 1635–69 and most MSS).
28. *banks*: 'banke' (acc. to several MSS).
33. *the*: 'her' (acc. to 1635–69 and some MSS).
     who: 'which' (ditto).
39 (also 46). On the symbol ', see above, p. 5.
41. *bred*: 'breed' (acc. to 1635–69 and several MSS).
42. *As nations do from Rome*: England was not the only nation to have rejected
     papal authority.
44. *dalliance*: serious conversation; also, amorous toying (*OED*: §483).
45. *Recusant*: anyone who opposed a particular authority but, at this time,
     especially any Roman Catholic in opposition to the established Church
     of England.
46. *excommunicate*: cut off from communion.

Elegie VII.

Natures lay Ideot, I taught thee to love,
And in that sophistrie, Oh, thou dost prove
Too subtile: Foole, thou didst not understand
The mystique language of the eye nor hand:
Nor couldst thou judge the difference of the aire   5
Of sighes, and say, this lies, this sounds despaire.
Nor by the'eyes water call a maladie
Desperately hot, or changing feaverously.
I had not taught thee then, the Alphabet
Of flowers, how they devisefully being set   10
And bound up, might with speechlesse secrecie
Deliver arrands mutely, and mutually.
Remember since all thy words us'd to bee
To every suitor; *I, if my friends agree.*
Since, household charmes, thy husbands name to teach,   15
Were all the love trickes, that thy wit could reach;
And since, an houres discourse could scarce have made
One answer in thee, and that ill arraid
In broken proverbs, and torne sentences.
Thou art not by so many duties his,   20
That from the worlds Common having sever'd thee,
Inlaid thee, neither to be seene, nor see,

Elegie VII. First published in 1633; first thus numbered in 1635. Not entitled in
    any early edition; the titles proposed by some editors – for example,
    Tutelage (§169) – are but conjectures.
1. *Natures lay Ideot*: ignorant simpleton by nature (§169)? ignorant uninitiate
    in the workings of nature (§166)? a dunce (§498)?
2. *sophistrie*: cunning craft.
7 (also 24). On the symbol ', see above, p. 5.
7. *eyes water*: tears.
    call: 'know' (acc. to 1635–69 and some MSS).
10–12. A reference to the arrangement of flowers in a bouquet in such a
    manner as to convey amorous messages (§164).
10. *they devisefully* (i.e. emblematically: §166): 'their device in' (acc. to some
    MSS).
13. *since*: when.
14. *I*: also in the sense of 'aye'.
19. *sentences*: common sayings, wise like *proverbs*.
22. *Inlaid*: enclosed, confined.

As mine: who have with amorous delicacies
Refin'd thee'into a blis-full paradise.
Thy graces and good words my creatures bee,   25
I planted knowledge and lifes tree in thee,
Which Oh, shall strangers taste? Must I alas
Frame and enamell Plate, and drinke in glasse?
Chafe waxe for others seales? breake a colts force
And leave him then, beeing made a ready horse?   30

Elegie VIII.
The Comparison.

As the sweet sweat of Roses in a Still,
As that which from chaf'd muskats pores doth trill,
As the Almighty Balme of th'early East,
Such are the sweat drops of my Mistris breast,
And on her necke her skin such lustre sets,   5
They seeme no sweat drops, but pearle coronets.

Elegie VII.
23. *who*: 'which' (acc. to most MSS).
25. *words*: 'workes' (acc. to 1669 and some MSS).
26. Cf. the Tree of Knowledge of Good and Evil, and the Tree of Life, in
     Eden (24: *paradise*).
28. *Frame and enamell Plate*: create gold- or silver-plated goblets adorned with
     enamel.
29. *Chafe*: heat and melt.
     seales: as in letters; but here the reference is obscene (as above, p. 113,
     note on 29).

Elegie VIII. First published in 1633; first thus numbered and entitled in 1635.
 1. *Still*: distillery.
 2. *muskats*: musk-cat's (i.e. the musk deer's secretion, used to make per-
     fume).
     trill: trickle.
 3. *Balme*: the balm of Gilead, a fragrant balsam (Jeremiah 46.11–12: §163).
 4. *sweat*: 'sweet' (acc. to some MSS).
     of: 'on' (ditto).
 4 (also 8). The full stop at line's end is changed by most modern editors to a
     comma.
 6. *coronets* (acc. to 1633–69 and several MSS), i.e. decorative bands forming
     part of a woman's head-dress: 'carcanets' (acc. to some MSS), i.e.
     necklaces.

Ranke sweaty froth thy Mistresse's brow defiles,
Like spermatique issue of ripe menstruous boiles,
Or like the skumme, which, by needs lawlesse law
Enforc'd, Sanserra's starved men did draw   10
From parboild shooes, and bootes, and all the rest
Which were with any soveraigne fatnes blest,
And like vile stones lying in saffrond tinne,
Or warts, or wheales, they hang upon her skinne.
Round as the world's her head, on every side,   15
Like to the fatall Ball which fell on Ide,
Or that whereof God had such jealousie,
As, for the ravishing thereof we die.
Thy *head* is like a rough-hewne statue of jeat,
Where marks for eyes, nose, mouth, are yet scarce set;   20
Like the first Chaos, or flat seeming face
Of Cynthia, when th'earths shadowes her embrace.
Like Proserpines white beauty-keeping chest,
Or Joves best fortunes urne, is her faire brest.

7. *thy Mistresse*: as opposed to *my Mistris* (4); the distinction, usually
    heralded by *thine* or *your*, pervades the poem.
9. *by needs lawlesse law*: by the uncustomary and profane law of necessity
    (§163).
10–12. The siege of Sancerre in 1573 occasioned famine of horrendous dimen-
    sions (§473).
12. *soveraigne*: surpassing.
13. *stones lying*: 'lying stones' (acc. to 1635 and all MSS).
    stones lying in saffrond tinne: fake jewels in a fake setting of gilded tin
    (§166).
14. *wheales*: weals, pustules (*OED*).
16. *Ball*: the golden apple of discord which, thrown among the guests at *Ide*
    (Mount Ida in Asia Minor), led to Paris' judgement and the Trojan War.
17. *that*: i.e. the apple of the Tree of Knowledge in Eden.
    jealousie: anxiety.
19. *thy head*: i.e. thy mistress' head.
20. *yet scarce*: 'scarcely' (acc. to some MSS).
21. *the first Chaos*: the disordered matter created by God out of 'nothing' (as
    above, p. 91, note on 29) and used to build the universe.
22. i.e. the moon, during its early phases.
23. *chest*: the box with the ointment of beauty that Psyche took from Proser-
    pina Queen of Hades (§166).
24. *best fortunes urne*: of the two urns of Zeus, the other was of ill fortune
    (*Iliad*, 24.527).

Thine's like worme eaten trunkes, cloth'd in seals skin,   25
Or grave, that's dust without, and stinke within.
And like that slender stalke, at whose end stands
The wood-bine quivering, are her armes and hands,
Like rough bark'd elmboughes, or the russet skin
Of men late scurg'd for madnes, or for sinne,   30
Like Sun-parch'd quarters on the citie gate,
Such is thy tann'd skins lamentable state.
And like a bunch of ragged carrets stand
The short swolne fingers of thy gouty hand,
Then like the Chymicks masculine equall fire,   35
Which in the Lymbecks warme wombe doth inspire
Into th'earths worthlesse part a soule of gold,
Such cherishing heat her best lov'd part doth hold.
Thine's like the dread mouth of a fired gunne,
Or like hot liquid metalls newly runne   40
Into clay moulds, or like to that Ætna
Where round about the grasse is burnt away.
Are not your kisses then as filthy, and more,
As a worme sucking an invenom'd sore?
Doth not thy fearfull hand in feeling quake,   45
As one which gath'ring flowers, still feares a snake?
Is not your last act harsh, and violent,
As where a Plough a stony ground doth rent?

26–29. The lines are omitted in some MSS.
26. *dust*: 'durt' (acc. to some MSS).
     stinke: 'stench' (ditto).
28 (also 34). The comma at line's end is changed by most modern editors to a
     full stop.
30. *scurg'd for madness*: the common method of expelling the 'devils' said to
     inhabit insane persons.
31. *quarters*: dilapidated houses (§163) or, possibly, quartered bodies of
     malefactors (§166).
35. *Chymicks*: i.e. alchemist's.
36. *Lymbeck*: as above, p. 91, note on 21.
37. *part*: 'durt' (acc. to 1635 and all modern editors) or 'dust' (acc. to some
     MSS).
41. *Ætna*: Sicily's active volcano.
46. *feares*: 'feard' (acc. to some MSS).
47. *act*: the sexual one.
48. *where* (acc. to 1633): 'when' (acc. to 1635).
     rent: rend.

So kisse good Turtles, so devoutly nice
Are Priests in handling reverent sacrifice,   50
And such in searching wounds the Surgeon is
As wee, when wee embrace, or touch, or kisse.
Leave her, and I will leave comparing thus,
She, and comparisons are odious.

Elegie IX.
The Autumnall.

No *Spring*, nor *Summer* Beauty hath such grace,
   As I have seen in one *Autumnall* face,
Yong *Beauties* force our love, and that's a *Rape*,
   This doth but *counsaile*, yet you cannot scape.
If t'were a *shame* to love, here t'were no *shame*,   5
   Affections here take *Reverences* name.
Were her first yeares the *Golden Age;* That's true,
   But now shee's *gold* oft tried, and ever new.

Elegie VIII.
49.   *Turtles*: turtle-doves.
51.   *such* (acc. to most MSS): 'nice' (acc. to 1633–69). The line alludes to a
         physician's probe – an instrument with a blunt end – used to explore the
         direction and depth of wounds (§207).

Elegie IX. First published and thus entitled in 1633; first numbered in 1635. A
         few MSS provide titles such as *A Paradox of an ould woman* or *Elegie
         Autumnall on the Ladie Shandoys* or – the most tradition-bound of claims –
         *An autumnall face: on the Ladie S*ʳ *Ed. Herbart mothers Ladie Danvers*, i.e.
         the mother of George Herbert. The most influential endorsement of the
         latter theory was Izaak Walton's (see *George Herbert: The Critical Heritage*,
         ed. C. A. Patrides [London, 1983], p. 95); see also below, p. 296. Mod-
         ern editors print the poem sometimes in block setting without indenta-
         tion (§169) and sometimes in quatrains (§163).
1.   The seasonal motif is important throughout (§485).
3.   *our*: 'your' (acc. to 1635–54 and many MSS).
4.   *counsaille*: counsel, recommend.
6.   *Affections*: 'Affection' (acc. to some MSS and all modern editors).
         take: 'takes' (ditto).
7.   *Were her first yeares*: her first years were.
         Golden Age: the legendary age of peace and innocence.
8.   *tried*: tested.

That was her torrid and inflaming time,
   This is her tolerable *Tropique clyme*.   10
Faire eyes, who askes more heate then comes from hence,
   He in a fever wishes pestilence.
Call not these wrinkles, *graves;* If *graves* they were,
   They were *Loves graves;* for else he is no where.
Yet lies not love *dead* here, but here doth sit   15
   Vow'd to this trench, like an *Anachorit*.
And here, till hers, which must be his *death*, come,
   He doth not digge a *Grave*, but build a *Tombe*.
Here dwells he, though he sojourne ev'ry where,
   In *Progresse*, yet his standing house is here.   20
Here, where still *Evening* is; not *noone*, nor *night;*
   Where no *voluptuousnesse*, yet all *delight*.
In all her words, unto all hearers fit,
   You may at *Revels*, you at *counsaile*, sit.
This is loves timber, youth his under-wood;   25
   There he, as wine in *June*, enrages blood,
Which then comes seasonabliest, when our tast
   And appetite to other things, is past;
Xerxes strange *Lydian* love, the *Platane* tree,
   Was lov'd for age, none being so large as shee,   30
Or else because, being yong, nature did blesse
   Her youth with ages glory, *Barrennesse*.
If we love things long sought, *Age* is a thing
   Which we are fifty yeares in compassing.

10.   *tolerable*: 'habitable' (acc. to 1635–69 and some MSS).
      tolerable Tropique: temperate.
11 (also 40, 46). *then*: than.
13.   *graves*: burial places; also trenches (cf. 16).
14.   *for*: 'or' (acc. to 1635–69 and some MSS).
16.   *Anachorit*: 'Anchorite' (acc. to some MSS), a hermit confined to a particular place.
20.   *Progresse*: as in a monarch's formal journey.
      standing house: fixed above.
24.   *you at*: 'you may at' (acc. to several MSS).
25.   *under-wood*: inflammable brushwood.
26.   *enrages*: 'bringes' (acc. to one MS) or 'breeds' (acc. to another).
29.   King Xerxes was partial to a very tall and beautiful – but also barren – plane tree he had found in Lydia.
30.   *large*: 'old' (acc. to 1635–69).

If transitory things, which soone decay,   35
 Age must be lovelyest at the latest day.
But name not *Winter-faces*, whose skin's slacke;
 Lanke, as an unthrifts purse; but a soules sacke;
Whose *Eyes* seeke light within, for all here's shade;
 Whose *mouthes* are holes, rather worne out, then made; 40
Whose every tooth to a severall place is gone,
 To vexe their soules at *Resurrection;*
Name not these living *Deaths-heads* unto mee,
 For these, not *Ancient*, but *Antique* be.
I hate extreames; yet I had rather stay   45
 With *Tombs*, then *Cradles*, to weare out a day.
Since such loves motion natural is, may still
 My love descend, and journey downe the hill,
Not panting after growing beauties, so,
 I shall ebbe out with them, who home-ward goe.   50

Elegie X.
The Dreame.

Image of her whom I love, more then she,
 Whose faire impression in my faithfull heart,

Elegie IX.
38. *soules:* 'fooles' (acc. to 1635–54).
41–42. At the Last Judgement, one's soul is expected to be joined to the
  resurrected *severall* (different) parts of the body.
43. *Deaths-heads:* as above, p. 71, note on 21.
47. *motion natural:* 'naturall lation' (acc. to some MSS) or 'naturall statyon'
  (acc. to others and 1635–69).
50. *out:* 'on' (acc. to 1635–69 and severall MSS).

Elegie X. First published in 1633; first thus numbered and entitled in 1635. The
 division into three stanzas of eight lines each and a final couplet – first
 ventured by Bennett (§160) and followed by other modern editors – is
 not warranted by any early edition or MS. See also *The Dreame*, above,
 p. 83.
 1. *Image:* not an objectively visible portrait but a mental picture and an
  abstract 'idea' (§489), perhaps a Platonic one similar to Spenser's 'fairer
  forme' (§476); But see §495.
  more: i.e. more real than her actual self.
 1 (also 11, 20, 26). *then:* than.

Makes mee her *Medall*, and makes her love mee,
  As Kings do coynes, to which their stamps impart
The value: goe, and take my heart from hence,   5
  Which now is growne too great and good for me:
Honours oppresse weake spirits, and our sense,
  Strong objects dull, the more, the lesse wee see.
When you are gone, and *Reason* gone with you,
  Then *Fantasie* is Queene and Soule, and all;   10
She can present joyes meaner then you do;
  Convenient, and more proportionall.
So, if I dreame I have you, I have you,
  For, all our joyes are but fantasticall.
And so I scape the paine, for paine is true;   15
  And sleepe which locks up sense, doth lock out all.
After a such fruition I shall wake,
  And, but the waking, nothing shall repent;
And shall to love more thankfull Sonnets make,
  Then if more *honour*, *teares*, and *paines* were spent. 20
But dearest heart, and dearer image stay;
  Alas, true joyes at best are *dreame* enough;
Though you stay here you passe too fast away:
  For even at first lifes *Taper* is a snuffe.
Fill'd with her love, may I be rather grown   25
Mad with much *heart*, then *ideott* with none.

3. *Medall*: commemorative coin or metal disk worn as a charm (§169).
8. *the more*: the stronger the image's impact.
11. *meaner*: more common (i.e. less idealized); also, more moderate (§195).
12. *Convenient*: more fitting.
14. *fantasticall*: produced by *Fantasie* (10).
15. *true*: real.
19. *Sonnets*: as above, p. 58, note on 32.
24. *snuffe*: burned wick.
26. *ideott*: one without sense (§163).

Elegie [XI].
The Bracelet.

Upon the losse of his Mistresses Chaine,
for which he made satisfaction.

Not that in colour it was like thy haire,
For Armelets of that thou maist let me weare:
Nor that thy hand it oft embrac'd and kist,
For so it had that good, which oft I mist:
Nor for that silly old moralitie,   5
That as these linkes were knit, our love should bee:
Mourne I that I thy seavenfold chaine have lost;
Nor for the luck sake; but the bitter cost.
O, shall twelve righteous Angels, which as yet
No leaven of vile soder did admit;   10
Nor yet by any way have straid or gone
From the first state of their Creation;
Angels, which heaven commanded to provide
All things to me, and be my faithfull guide;
To gaine new friends, t'appease great enemies;   15
To comfort my soule, when I lie or rise;
Shall these twelve innocents, by thy severe
Sentence (dread judge) my sins great burden beare?
Shall they be damn'd, and in the furnace throwne,
And punisht for offences not their owne?   20
They save not me, they doe not ease my paines,
When in that hell they'are burnt and tyed in chains;

Elegie [XI]. First published and thus entitled in 1635; the numbering hereafter
    adheres to Grierson's (§158). According to William Drummond of
    Hawthornden, Ben Jonson had this poem 'by heart'; it was one of the
    reasons why Jonson 'esteemeth John Donne the first poet in the world in
    some things'.
  5. *moralitie*: symbolic significance (§164).
  6. *were knit*: 'are knitt' (acc. to one MS) or 'are tyed' (acc. to others).
  9. *Angels*: here and throughout, the double reference is to the celestial
      spirits and to the English gold coins.
 10. *soder*: solder.
 11. *way*: 'fault' (acc. to one MS) or 'taint' (acc. to others).
 19. *damn'd*: 'burn'd' (acc. to one MS).
 22 (also 47). On the symbol ', see above, p. 5.

Were they but Crownes of France, I cared not,
For, most of these, their countryes naturall rot
I think possesseth, they come here to us,   25
So pale, so lame, so leane, so ruinous.
And howsoe'r French Kings most Christian be,
Their Crownes are circumcis'd most Jewishly;
Or were they Spanish Stamps, still travelling,
That are become as Catholique as their King,   30
Those unlickt beare-whelps, unfil'd pistolets
That (more than Canon shot) availes or lets;
Which negligently left unrounded, looke
Like many angled figures, in the booke
Of some great Conjurer that would enforce   35
Nature, as these doe justice, from her course.
Which, as the soule quickens head, feet and heart,
As streames like veines, run through th'earth's every part,
Visit all Countries, and have slily made
Gorgeous *France*, ruin'd, ragged and decay'd,   40
Scotland, which knew no State, proud in one day,
And mangled seventeen-headed *Belgia*:

23. *Crownes of France*: French coins, said to be *leane* etc. (26) or *circumcis'd*
    (28), i.e. trimmed, curtailed, debased.
24. *countryes naturall*: 'naturall countrys' (acc. to several MSS). The *rot* said
    to be *naturall* to France is syphilis.
26. *pale, lame, leane*: 'leane', 'pale', 'lame' (acc. to one MS) or other variants.
29. *Spanish Stamps*: Spanish coins, the effect of their use as bribery described
    thereafter (esp. 39 ff.).
30. *Catholique*: in the religious sense, but also as universal, ever-present.
31. *unlickt beare-whelps*: it was believed that new-born bears were licked into
    shape by their mothers.
    pistolets: gold coins, *unfil'd* because irregular in shape; also, small fire-
    arms (*ALC*).
32. *availes or lets*: allows or hinders.
34-36. A reference to the conjuring of spirits through the use of geometrical
    diagrams (§166).
40. *France* had been wellnigh *ruin'd* by the Wars of Religion.
41. *Scotland*, far too poor to behave as a *State*, may do so if puffed up (*proud*)
    with Spanish gold.
42. *seventeen-headed Belgia*: the provinces comprising the Netherlands and
    Belgium, then at war with Spain.

Or were it such gold as that wherewithall
Almighty *Chymiques* from each minerall,
Having by subtle fire a soule out-pull'd;   45
Are dirtely and desperately gull'd:
I would not spit to quench the fire they'are in,
For, they are guilty of much hainous Sin.
But, shall my harmlesse angels perish? Shall
I lose my guard, my ease, my food, my all?   50
Much hope which they should nourish will be dead,
Much of my able youth, and lusty head
Will vanish, if thou love let them alone,
For thou wilt love me lesse when they are gone,
And be content that some lowd squeaking Cryer   55
Well-pleas'd with one leane thred-bare groat, for hire,
May like a devill roare through every street;
And gall the finders conscience, if they meet.
Or let mee creepe to some dread Conjurer,
That with phantastique scheames fils full much paper;   60
Which hath divided heaven in tenements,
And with whores, theeves, and murderers stuft his rents
So full, that though hee passe them all in sinne,
He leaves himselfe no roome to enter in.
But if, when all his art and time is spent,   65
Hee say 'twill ne'r be found; yet be content;
Receive from him that doome ungrudgingly,
Because he is the mouth of destiny.
    Thou say'st (alas) the gold doth still remaine,
Though it be chang'd, and put into a chaine,   70

44. *Chymiques*: alchemists.
45. *a soule out-pull'd*: fire extracted the minerals' *prima materia*, called 'soul of
       mercury' (§169).
46. *gull'd*: tricked.
47. *are*: 'were' (acc. to some MSS).
52. *Cryer*: town crier.
56. *groat*: an older, silver coin.
60. *fils full*: 'fullfill' or 'fullfills' (acc. to various MSS).
61. *tenements*: 'houses' or signs of the Zodiac.
62. *his*: 'her' (acc. to some MSS).
       stuft his rents: paid his rent.

So in the first falne angels, resteth still
Wisdome and knowledge; but'tis turn'd to ill:
As these should doe good works; and should provide
Necessities; but now must nurse thy pride,
And they are still bad angels; Mine are none,   75
For, forme gives being, and their forme is gone:
Pitty these Angels yet; their dignities
Passe Vertues, Powers, and Principalities.
   But, thou art resolute; Thy will be done;
Yet with such anguish, as her onely sonne   80
The Mother in the hungry grave doth lay,
Unto the fire these Martyrs I betray.
Good soules, (for you give life to every thing)
Good Angels, (for good messages you bring)
Destin'd you might have beene to such an one,   85
As would have lov'd and worship'd you alone:
One that would suffer hunger, nakednesse,
Yea death, ere he would make your number lesse.
But, I am guilty of your sad decay;
May your few fellowes longer with me stay.   90
   But ô thou wretched finder whom I hate
So that I almost pitty thy estate:
Gold being the heaviest metal amongst all,
May my most heavy curse upon thee fall:
Here fetter'd, manacled, and hang'd in chains,   95
First mayst thou bee; then chaind to hellish paines;
Or be with forraine gold brib'd to betray
Thy Countrey, and faile both of it and thy pay.

71. *falne*: i.e. once they rebelled in Heaven.
76. *forme*: the essential determinant principle of a thing (§169).
77. The semicolon is in some MSS changed to a comma and placed after
    Angels.
78. *Vertues* etc.: orders of angels.
79–82. The lines are intended to be 'confusedly blasphemous': the mistress
    becomes God the Father (cf. *dread judge* in 18), the lover appears to share
    Christ's obedience in the Garden and the Virgin's agony at the Deposi-
    tion (§483).
92. *that*: 'much that' (acc. to many MSS) or 'much as' (acc. to others).
98. *it*: 'that' (acc. to one MS).

May the next thing thou stoop'st to reach, containe
Poyson, whose nimble fume rot thy moist braine;   100
Or libels, or some interdicted thing,
Which negligently kept, thy ruine bring.
Lust-bred diseases rot thee; and dwell with thee
Itching desire, and no abilitie.
May all the evils that gold ever wrought;   105
All mischiefe that all devils ever thought;
Want after plenty; poore and gouty age;
The plagues of travellers; love; marriage
Afflict thee, and at thy lives last moment,
May thy swolne sinnes themselves to thee present.   110
   But, I forgive; repent thee honest man:
Gold is Restorative, restore it then:
But if from it thou beest loath to depart,
Because 'tis cordiall, would 'twere at thy heart.

104. *no abilitie*: i.e. to attempt intercourse.
105. *evils that gold ever*: 'hurt which ever Gold' (acc. to one MS).
109. *last*: 'latest' (acc. to some MSS).
112. *Gold is Restorative*: i.e. medicinal, particularly for the heart; hence l. 114: *cordiall* (§164).
113. *But*: 'Or' (acc. to one MS).
     from: 'with' (acc. to others).

Elegie [XII].
His parting from her.

Since she must go, and I must mourn, come night,
Environ me with darkness, whilst I write:
Shadow that hell unto me, which alone
I am to suffer when my Love is gone.
Alas the darkest Magick cannot do it,   5
Thou and greate Hell to boot are shadows to it.
Should *Cinthia* quit thee, *Venus*, and each starre,
It would not forme one thought dark as mine are.
I could lend thee obscureness now, and say,
Out of my self, There should be no more Day,   10
Such is already my felt want of sight,
Did not the fires within me force a light.
Oh Love, that fire and darkness should be mixt,
Or to thy Triumphs soe strange torments fixt!
Is't because thou thy self art blind, that wee   15
Thy Martyrs must no more each other see?
Or tak'st thou pride to break us on the wheel,
And view old Chaos in the Pains we feel?
Or have we left undone some mutual Right,
Through holy fear, that merits thy despight?   20
No, no. The falt was mine, impute it to me,
Or rather to conspiring destinie,

Elegie [XII]. First published in a short version of forty-two lines in 1635 and in a
    full version in 1669 (hence the several amendments made in the ensuing
    text as shown in representative instances in the notes); thus entitled in
    1635; title dropped in 1669; entitled in one MS *At his Mistris departure*.
    The poem is sometimes excluded from the canon (e.g. §169).
  4.   *Love:* 'soule' (acc. to 1635–54).
  6.   *to boot are*: 'are nought but' (acc. to some MSS).
  7.   *Cinthia*: the moon.
       Venus: the evening star.
 17.   *the wheel*: a form of torture involving breaking a victim's legs.
 18.   *old Chaos*: as above, p. 150, note on 21.
 19.   *Right*: i.e. Rite.
 20.   The line also reads, 'That thus with parting thou seek'st us to spight?'
       (acc. to 1669).

Which (since I lov'd for forme before) decreed,
That I should suffer when I lov'd indeed:
And therefore now, sooner then I can say,   25
I saw the golden fruit, 'tis rapt away.
Or as I had watcht one drop in a vast stream,
And I left wealthy only in a dream.
Yet Love, thou'rt blinder then thy self in this,
To vex my Dove-like friend for my amiss: 30
And, where my own glad truth may expiate
Thy wrath, to make her fortune run my fate.
So blinded Justice doth, when Favorites fall,
Strike them, their house, their friends, their followers all.
Was't not enough that thou didst dart thy fires   35
Into our blouds, inflaming our desires,
And made'st us sigh and glow, and pant, and burn,
And then thy self into our flame did'st turn?
Was't not enough, that thou didst hazard us
To paths in love so dark, so dangerous: 40
And those so ambush'd round with household spies,
And over all thy husbands towring eyes
That flam'd with oylie sweat of jealousie,
Yet went we not still on with Constancie?
Have we not kept our guards, like spie on spie?   45
Had correspondence whilst the foe stood by?
Stoln (more to sweeten them) our many blisses
Of meetings, conference, embracements, kisses?

23.   The line also reads, 'Which (since I lov'd) for me before decreed' (acc. to
      1669 and some MSS).
      for forme: in appearance only.
25 (also 29, 92). *then*: than.
26.   *golden fruit*: which Tantalus in Hades could never reach.
30.   *amiss*: fault.
31.   *own glad* (acc. to some MSS): 'one sad' (acc. to 1669).
34.   *followers* (acc. to some MSS): 'favourites' (acc. to 1669 and some MSS).
42.   *husbands towring*: 'towred husbands' (acc. to one MS) or 'husbands
      towred' (acc. to others).
43.   *That flam'd with oylie* (acc. to some MSS): 'Inflam'd with th'ouglie' (acc.
      to 1669).

Shadow'd with negligence our most respects?
Varied our language through all dialects, 50
Of becks, winks, looks, and often under-boards
Spoak dialogues with our feet far from our words?
Have we prov'd all these secrets of our Art,
Yea, thy pale inwards, and thy panting heart?
And, after all this passed Purgatory, 55
Must sad divorce make us the vulgar story?
First let our eyes be rivited quite through
Our turning brains, and both our lips grow to:
Let our armes clasp like Ivy, and our fear
Freese us together, that we may stick here, 60
Till Fortune, that would rive us, with the deed,
Strain her eyes open, and it make them bleed.
For Love it cannot be, whom hitherto
I have accus'd, should such a mischief doe.
Oh fortune, thou'rt not worth my least exclame, 65
And plague enough thou hast in thy own shame.
Do thy great worst, my friend and I have armes,
Though not against thy strokes, against thy harmes.
Rend us in sunder, thou canst not divide
Our bodies so, but that our souls are ty'd, 70
And we can love by letters still and gifts,
And thoughts and dreams; Love never wanteth shifts.
I will not look upon the quickning Sun,
But straight her beauty to my sense shall run;

49. *Shadow'd*: obscured, covered up.
    most: 'best' (acc. to 1669).
51. *becks*: nods.
    under-boards: under the table.
54. *inwards, and thy panting*: 'colours, inward as thy' (acc. to several MSS).
56. *vulgar*: common, usual.
57. *rivited*: riveted.
61. *rive* (acc. to several MSS): rend; 'reave' (acc. to another MS) or 'ruine' (acc. to 1669).
62. *her*: 'his' (acc. to 1669).
    it: 'yet' (ditto).
65. *exclame*: complaint.
66. *shame*: 'name' (acc. to 1669).
67. *Do thy great*: 'Fortune, doe thy' (acc. to 1635–54).
69. *Rend*: 'Bend' (acc. to 1635–54).

The ayre shall note her soft, the fire most pure;   75
Water suggest her clear, and the earth sure;
Time shall not lose our passages; the Spring
How fresh our love was in the beginning;
The Summer how it ripened in the eare;
And Autumn, what our golden harvests were.   80
The Winter I'll not think on to spite thee,
But count it a lost season, so shall shee.
And dearest Friend, since we must part, drown night
With hope of Day, burthens well born are light.
Though cold and darkness longer hang somewhere,   85
Yet *Phoebus* equally lights all the Sphere.
And what he cannot in like Portions pay,
The world enjoyes in Mass, and so we may.
Be then ever your self, and let no woe
Win on your health, your youth, your beauty: so   90
Declare your self base fortunes Enemy,
No less by your contempt then constancy:
That I may grow enamoured on your mind,
When my own thoughts I there reflected find.
For this to th'comfort of my Dear I vow,   95
My Deeds shall still be what my words are now;

75–76. The four constituent elements of the physical world (as above,
    p. 115, note on 9–10).
76. *clear*: innocent.
77. *passages*: acts of love.
78. The line also reads, 'Shall tell how fresh our love was in the beginning'
    (acc. to one MS) or 'Shall tell our love was fresh in . . .' etc. (acc. to
    another).
79. *ripened*: 'inripened' (acc. to 1639–69).
    eare: 'yeare' (acc. to 1635–69).
86. *Phoebus*: the sun. *Sphere*: the universe.
87. *he*: 'we' (acc. to 1669).
89. *ever your*: 'your fayrest' (acc. to some MSS).
92. *by your contempt then constancy* (acc. to some MSS): 'be your contempt
    then her inconstancy' (acc. to 1669).
94. *there reflected* (acc. to several MSS): 'here neglected' (acc. to 1669).
96. *words* (acc. to some MSS): 'deeds' (acc. to 1635–69 and some MSS).

The Pole shall move to teach me ere I start;
And when I change my Love, I'll change my heart;
Nay, if I wax but cold in my desire,
Think, heaven hath motion lost, and the world, fire: 100
Much more I could, but many words have made
That, oft, suspected which men would perswade;
Take therefore all in this: I love so true,
As I will never look for less in you.

Elegie [XIII].
Julia.

Harke newes, ô envy, thou shalt heare descry'd
My *Julia;* who as yet was ne'r envy'd.
To vomit gall in slander, swell her vaines
With calumny, that hell it selfe disdaines,
Is her continuall practice, does her best,   5
To teare opinion even out of the brest
Of dearest friends, and (which is worse than vile)
Sticks jcalousie in wedlock, her owne childe
Scapes not the showres of envie, To repeate
The monstrous fashions, how, were, alive, to eate   10
Deare reputation. Would to God she were
But halfe so loath to act vice, as to heare

Elegie [XII].
97. *Pole* (acc. to several MSS): the pole star, the fixed point of the stellar
     system (§169); but 'Poles' (acc. to 1669 and some MSS).
     start: deviate, swerve.
100. *motion*: celestial movement; also passion.
     fire: an element (see note on 75–76); also passion.
102. *would* (acc. to one MS): 'could' (acc. to another) or 'most' (acc. to 1669).

Elegie [XIII]. First published and thus entitled in 1635; sometimes excluded
    from the canon (e.g. §§163, 169).
  7. *vile*: 'vilde' (acc. to two MSS).

My milde reproofe. Liv'd *Mantuan* now againe,
That fœmall Mastix, to limme with his penne
This she *Chymera*, that hath eyes of fire,   15
Burning with anger, anger feeds desire,
Tongued like the night-crow, whose ill boding cries
Give out for nothing but new injuries,
Her breath like to the juice in *Tenarus*
That blasts the springs, though ne'r so prosperous,   20
Her hands, I know not how, us'd more to spill
The food of others, than her selfe to fill.
But oh her minde, that *Orcus*, which includes
Legions of mischiefs, countlesse multitudes
Of formlesse curses, projects unmade up,   25
Abuses yet unfashion'd, thoughts corrupt,
Mishapen Cavils, palpable untroths,
Inevitable errours, self-accusing loathes:
These, like those Atoms swarming in the Sunne,
Throng in her bosome for creation.   30
I blush to give her halfe her due; yet say,
No poyson's halfe so bad as *Julia*.

13. *Mantuan*: the Italian poet Baptista Spagnuoli, one of whose eclogues
     entitles him to be called *fœmall Mastix*, i.e. the scourge of women (14).
14. *limme*: limn, paint.
15. *Chymera*: a mythical monster with lion's head, goat's body, and serpent's
     tail.
17. *night-crow*: a bird of ill omen (§166).
19. *the juice in Tenarus*: the excretions of a cavern in Laconia in Greece,
     believed to be a passage to Hades (§158).
23. *Orcus*: the Roman Hades.
27. *untroths*: i.e. untruths.
28. *loathes*: hatreds; 'oathes' (acc. to some MSS).
29. *Atoms*: motes in the sunbeam (*OED*).
31. *yet*: 'only this' (acc. to one MS) or 'but this' (acc. to another).

Elegie [XIV].
A Tale of a Citizen and his Wife.

I sing no harme good sooth to any wight,
To Lord or foole, Cuckold, begger or knight,
To peace-teaching Lawyer, Proctor, or brave
Reformed or reduced Captaine, Knave,
Officer, Jugler, or Justice of peace,   5
Juror or Judge; I touch no fat sowes grease,
I am no Libeller, nor will be any,
But (like a true man) say there are too many.
I feare not *ore tenus*, for my tale,
Nor Count nor Counsellour will redd or pale.   10
A citizen and his wife the other day
Both riding on one horse, upon the way
I overtooke, the wench a pretty peate,
And (by her eye) well fitting for the feate.
I saw the lecherous Citizen turne backe   15
His head, and on his wifes lip steale a smacke,
Whence apprehending that the man was kinde,
Riding before, to kisse his wife behinde,
To get acquaintance with him I began
To sort discourse fit for so fine a man: 20
I ask'd the number of the Plaguy Bill,
Ask'd if the Custome Farmers held out still,

Elegie [*XIV*]. First published and thus entitled in 1635; sometimes excluded
    from the canon (e.g. §§163, 169). The notes record only representative
    changes adopted from the MSS.
  6. *touch no fat sowes grease*: question no rich man's side-pickings (§166).
  9. *ore tenus*: in law, a sentence by word of mouth.
 10. *will redd*: 'will looke redd' (acc. to 1635–54).
 13. *peate*: merry girl.
 17. *kinde*: proper.
 21. *Plaguy*: 'Plaguing' (acc. to 1635–54). *Plaguy Bill*: as above, p. 57, note on
    15.
 22. *Custome Farmers*: collectors of customs fees on imported goods, who *held*
    out against the full amount due.

Of the Virginian plot, and whether Ward
The traffique of the Midland seas had marr'd.
Whether the Brittaine *Burse* did fill space,   25
And likely were to give th'Exchange disgrace;
Of new-built *Algate*, and the *More-field* crosses,
Of store of Bankerouts, and poore Merchants losses
I urged him to speake; But he (as mute
As an old Courtier worne to his last suite)   30
Replies with onely yeas and nayes; At last
(To fit his element) my theame I cast
On Tradesmens gaines; that set his tongue agoing,
Alas, good sir (quoth he) *There is no doing*
In Court nor City now; she smil'd and I,   35
And (in my conscience) both gave him the lie
In one met thought: but he went on apace,
And at the present time with such a face
He rail'd, as fray'd me; for he gave no praise,
To any but my Lord of *Essex* dayes;   40
Call'd those the age of action; true (quoth Hee)
There's now as great an itch of bravery,
And heat of taking up, but cold lay downe,
For, put to push of pay, away they runne;
Our onely City trades of hope now are   45
Bawd, Tavern-keeper, Whore and Scrivener;
The much of priviledg'd kingsmen, and the store
Of fresh protections make the rest all poore;

23.   *the Virginian plot*: the new effort to colonize Virginia in 1609.
23–24. *Ward*: a pirate active in the *Midland*, i.e. the Mediterranean.
25.   *the Brittaine Burse*: a stock exchange opened in 1609.
27.   *Aldgate* was *new-built* (rebuilt) in 1609; *the More-field crosses* were the new
       walks built across the Moorfield marsh (§158).
32.   *fit*: 'hit' (acc. to some MSS).
34.   *no doing* in business but, evidently, much *doing* in amorous exploits.
39.   *fray'd*: frightened.
40.   *Essex* was executed in 1601.
41.   *those . . . Hee* (acc. to some MSS): 'that . . . I' (acc. to 1635).
44.   *push of pay*: the test of action (§166).
46.   *Scrivener*: drafter of documents, notary, broker.
47.   *priviledg'd kingsmen*: men holding monopolies bestowed by the king.
48.   *protections*: privileged exemptions from being sued.

In the first state of their Creation,
Though many stoutly stand, yet proves not one   50
A righteous pay-master. Thus ranne he on
In a continued rage: so void of reason
Seem'd his harsh talke, I sweat for feare of treason.
And (troth) how could I lesse? when in the prayer
For the protection of the wise Lord Major,   55
And his wise brethrens worships, when one prayeth,
He swore that none could say Amen with faith.
To get him off from what I glowed to heare,
(In happy time) an Angel did appeare,
The bright Signe of a lov'd and wel-try'd Inne,   60
Where many Citizens with their wives have bin
Well us'd and often; here I pray'd him stay,
To take some due refreshment by the way.
Looke how hee look'd that hid the gold (his hope)
And at returne found nothing but a Rope,   65
So he on me, refus'd and made away,
Though willing she pleaded a weary day:
I found my misse, struck hands, and praid him tell
(To hold acquaintance still) where he did dwell;
He barely nam'd the street, promis'd the Wine,   70
But his kinde wife gave me the very Signe.

49. i.e. when initially granted these privileges.
55. *Major*: as above, p. 136, note on 34.
62. *used*: entertained; also, taken advantage of.
64–65. The old anecdote tells of the man who lost his gold but found a rope,
       and used the rope to hang himself. The source is a Greek epigram
       attributed to Plato (§493).
67. *day*: 'stay' (acc. to 1635).
68. *found my misse*: realized that my plan had failed.
     shook: 'struck' (acc. to some MSS).
     and: 'yet' (ditto).
71. *Signe*: the signboard of the house; also a covert invitation (§166).

Elegie [XV].
The Expostulation.

To make the doubt cleare, that no woman's true,
 Was it my fate to prove it strong in you?
Thought I, but one had breathed purest aire,
 And must she needs be false because she's faire?
Is it your beauties marke, or of your youth,   5
 Or your perfection, not to study truth?
Or thinke you heaven is deafe, or hath no eyes?
 Or those it hath, smile at your perjuries?
Are vowes so cheape with women, or the matter
 Whereof they are made, that they are writ in water, 10
And blowne away with winde? Or doth their breath
 (Both hot and cold) at once make life and death?
Who could have thought so many accents sweet
 Form'd into words, so many sighs should meete
As from our hearts, so many oathes, and teares   15
 Sprinkled among, (all sweeter by our feares
And the divine impression of stolne kisses,
 That seal'd the rest) should now prove empty blisses?
Did you draw bonds to forfet? signe to breake?
 Or must we reade you quite from what you speake, 20

Elegie [XV]. First published in 1633; first entitled in 1635. Also published in
 Ben Jonson's *Under-wood* (1640), where it joins three other poems (nos.
 38–41) alike attributed to Donne. But it would appear that only the
 present one is actually by Donne (consult §§478, 496).

2. *strong*: 'full' (acc. to *Under-wood*).
3. *purest*: 'the purer' (ditto).
8. *it*: 'she' (acc. to some MSS).
  hath, smile: 'has, winke' (acc. to *Under-wood*).
12. Some modern editors close the parentheses after *once*.
  make: 'threat' (acc. to *Under-wood*).
14. *Form'd into*: 'Tun'd to our' (ditto).
15. *As*: 'Blowne' (ditto).
16. *sweeter*: 'sweetened' (acc. to 1635–69 and some MSS).
17. *impression*: imprint.
18. *should:* 'could' (acc. to *Under-wood*).
19. *to forfet*: in order to forfeit them; *to breake*: in order to go bankrupt.

And finde the truth out the wrong way? or must
    Hee first desire you false, would wish you just?
O I prophane, though most of women be
    This kinde of beast, my thought shall except thee;
My dearest love, though froward jealousie,   25
    With circumstance might urge thy'inconstancie,
Sooner I'll thinke the Sunne will cease to cheare
    The teeming earth, and *that* forget to beare,
Sooner that rivers will runne back, or Thames
    With ribs of Ice in June would bind his streames;   30
Or Nature, by whose strength the world endures,
    Would change her course, before you alter yours;
But O that treacherous breast to whom weake you
    Did trust our Counsells, and wee both may rue,
Having his falshood found too late, 'twas hee   35
    That made me *cast* you guilty, and you mee
Whilst he, black wretch, betray'd each simple word
    Wee spake, unto the cunning of a third;
Curst may hee be, that so our love hath slaine,
    And wander on the earth, wretched as *Cain*,   40
Wretched as hee, and not deserve least pitty;
    In plaguing him, let misery be witty;
Let all eyes shunne him, and hee shunne each eye,
    Till hee be noysome as his infamie;
May he without remorse deny God thrice,   45
    And not be trusted more on his Soules price;
And after all selfe torment, when hee dyes,
    May Wolves teare out his heart, Vultures his eyes,

22. *would*: who would.
24. *This kinde of beast*: 'The common Monster' (acc. to *Under-wood*).
    my thought: 'Love' (ditto).
25. *froward*: perverse.
    though froward; 'however' (acc. to *Under-wood*).
26. *thy inconstancie*: 'constancy' (acc. to one MS) or 'the contrary' (acc. to
    Under-wood). On the symbol ', see above, p. 5.
30. *would*: 'will' (acc. to 1635–69 and some MSS).
36. *cast*: consider.
40. *Cain*: *wretched* because he had killed his brother Abel (Genesis 4.8 ff.).
45. As St Peter had denied Jesus thrice.
46. *on his Soules price*: i.e. though the fate of his soul is at stake (§166).

Swine eate his bowels, and his falser tongue
  That utter'd all, be to some Raven flung,   50
And let his carrion coarse, be a longer feast
  To the Kings dogges, then any other beast;
Now have I curst, let us our love revive;
  In mee the flame was never more alive;
I could beginne againe to court and praise,   55
  And in that pleasure lengthen the short dayes
Of my lifes lease; like Painters that do take
  Delight, not in made worke, but whiles they make;
I could renew those times, when first I saw
  Love in your eyes, that gave my tongue the law   60
To like what you lik'd; and at maskes and playes
  Commend the selfe same Actors, the same wayes;
Aske how you did, and often with intent
  Of being officious, be impertinent;
All which were such soft pastimes, as in these   65
  Love was as subtilly catch'd, as a disease;
But being got it is a treasure sweet,
  Which to defend is harder then to get:
And ought not be prophan'd on either part,
  For though 'tis got by *chance*, 'tis kept by *art*.   70

52 (also 68). *then*: than.
53. *revive*: 'receive' (acc. to *Under-wood*).
58. *Delight, not in made worke*: 'Not in made workes delight' (acc. to some MSS).
60. *the law*: i.e. the right.
61. *and*: 'or' (acc. to *Under-wood*).
64. *officious*: obliging.
     he: 'grow' (acc. to *Under-wood*).
     impertinent: presumptuous.
65. *soft*: 'lost' (acc. to *Under-wood*).

Elegie [XVI].
On his Mistris.

By our first strange and fatall interview,
By all desires which thereof did ensue,
By our long starving hopes, by that remorse
Which my words masculine perswasive force
Begot in thee, and by the memory   5
Of hurts, which spies and rivals threatned me,
I calmly beg. But by thy fathers wrath,
By all paines, which want and divorcement hath,
I conjure thee, and all the oathes which I
And thou have sworne to seale joynt constancy,   10
Here I unsweare, and overswear them thus,
Thou shalt not love by wayes so dangerous.
Temper, ô faire Love, loves impetuous rage,
Be my true Mistris still, not my faign'd Page;
I'll goe, and, by thy kinde leave, leave behinde   15
Thee, onely worthy to nurse in my minde,
Thirst to come backe; ô if thou die before,
My soule from other lands to thee shall soare.
Thy (else Almighty) beautie cannot move
Rage from the Seas, nor thy love teach them love,   20
Nor tame wilde Boreas harshnesse; Thou has reade
How roughly hee in peeces shivered
Faire Orithea, whom he swore he lov'd.
Fall ill or good, 'tis madnesse to have prov'd

Elegie [XVI]. First published and thus entitled in 1635. Entitled in two MSS *On his Mistress desire to be disguised and to goe like a Page with him*; and in another, *His wife would have gone as his Page*.

3.   *remorse*: pity.
7.   *fathers*: 'parents' (acc. to several MSS).
12. *wayes*: 'means' (acc. to 1669 and several MSS).
14. *faign'd*: disguised (see headnote).
18. The line also reads, 'From other lands my soule towards thee' (acc. to 1635–69 and some MSS).
19. *move*: take away.
21–23. The ill-natured north wind Boreas, in courting the nymph Orithyia, overcame her by resorting to brute force (§51).
24. *Fall*: 'Full' (acc. to one MS).
     prov'd: experienced.

Dangers unurg'd; Feed on this flattery,   25
That absent Lovers one in th'other be.
Dissemble nothing, not a boy, nor change
Thy bodies habite, nor mindes; bee not strange
To thy selfe onely. All will spie in thy face
A blushing womanly discovering grace;   30
Richly cloath'd Apes, are call'd Apes, and as soone
Ecclips'd as bright we call the Moone the Moone.
Men of France, changeable Camelions,
Spittles of diseases, shops of fashions,
Loves fuellers, and the rightest company   35
Of Players, which upon the worlds stage be,
Will quickly know thee, and no lesse, alas!
Th'indifferent Italian, as we passe
His warme land, well content to thinke thee Page,
Will hunt thee with such lust, and hideous rage,   40
As *Lots* faire guests were vext. But none of these
Nor spungy hydroptique Dutch shall thee displease,
If thou stay here. O stay here, for, for thee
England is onely a worthy Gallerie,
To walke in expectation, till from thence   45
Our greatest King call thee to his presence.

27.   *Dissemble*: hide; also, simulate (§169).
31.   An apposite Greek proverb had been cited by Erasmus: '*An ape is an ape, be she clothed in purple*, so a woman is a woman (that is to saie) a foole, what so ever parte she plaie' (§475).
31–32. *as soone | Ecclips'd as bright*: whether the moon is in eclipse or at its brightest.
34.   *Spittles*: hospitals, esp. for venereal diseases.
35.   *Loves*: 'Lives' (acc. to 1669 and some MSS).
37.   In 1669 and the MSS the line appears in several versions.
     know: also in the sexual sense.
     alas: possibly a pun on 'a lass' (*ALC*).
38.   *indifferent*: i.e. as ready to make love to women as to men.
40.   *hunt*: 'haunt' (acc. to severall MSS).
41.   *Lots faire guests*: the angels who, assumed to be men, were demanded by the Sodomites (Genesis 19.5).
42.   *spungy hydroptique*: soaking up drink insatiably, as if dropsical (as above, p. 141, note on 6).
44.   *Gallerie*: antechamber.
46.   *King*: i.e. God.

When I am gone, dreame me some happinesse,
Nor let thy lookes our long hid love confesse,
Nor praise, nor dispraise me, nor blesse nor curse
Openly loves force, nor in bed fright thy Nurse   50
With midnights startings, crying out, oh, oh
Nurse, ô my love is slaine, I saw him goe
O'r the white Alpes alone; I saw him I,
Assail'd, fight, taken, stabb'd, bleed, fall, and die.
Augure me better chance, except dread *Jove*   55
Thinke it enough for me to'have had thy love.

Elegie [XVII].

The heavens rejoyce in motion, why should I
Abjure my so much lov'd variety,
And not with many youth and love divide?
Pleasure is none, if not diversifi'd:
The sun that sitting in the chaire of light   5
Sheds flame into what else soever doth seem bright,
Is not contented at one Signe to Inne,
But ends his year and with a new beginnes.
All things doe willingly in change delight,
The fruitfull mother of our appetite: 10

Elegie [*XVI*].
49.   *nor blesse*: 'blesse' (acc. to some MSS).
55.   *Augure me better chance*: predict for me a better fate.
        except: unless.
56.   On the symbol ', see above, p. 5.

Elegie [*XVII*]. First published in 1650. Not entitled in any early edition; the
        titles proposed by some editors – for example, *Variety* (§158) – are but
        conjectures. The poem is sometimes excluded from the canon (e.g.
        §169).
  2.   *much lov'd*: 'beloved' (acc. to several MSS).
  3.   *love* (acc. to the MSS): 'lov'd' (acc. to 1650–69).
        divide: share.
  5.   *else soever doth seem*: 'else seems' or 'ever else seems' or 'else is not so' (acc.
        to various MSS).
  7.   *Signe*: i.e. of the Zodiac.
        to Inne: to lodge.

Rivers the clearer and more pleasing are,
Where their fair spreading streames run wide and farr;
And a dead lake that no strange bark doth greet,
Corrupts it self and what doth live in it.
Let no man tell me such a one is faire,   15
And worthy all alone my love to share.
Nature in her hath done the liberall part
Of a kinde Mistresse, and imploy'd her art
To make her loveable, and I aver
Him not humane that would turn back from her: 20
I love her well, and would, if need were, dye
To doe her service. But followes it that I
Must serve her onely, when I may have choice?
The law is hard, and shall not have my voice.
The last I saw in all extreames is faire,   25
And holds me in the Sun-beames of her haire;
Her nymph-like features such agreements have
That I could venture with her to the grave:
Another's brown, I like her not the worse,
Her tongue is soft and takes me with discourse: 30
Others, for that they well descended are,
Do in my love obtain as large a share;
And though they be not fair, 'tis much with mee
To win their love onely for their degree.
And though I faile of my required ends,   35
The attempt is glorious and it selfe commends.

12. *fair spreading*: 'broad silver' (acc. to one MS).
     farr (ditto): 'cleare' (acc. to 1650–69).
13. *bark*: 'banks' (acc. to one MS).
     strange bark: foreign vessel.
16. The line also reads, 'And only worthy to be past compare' (acc. to one
     MS).   *share*: 'inheire' (ditto).
19. *aver* (ditto): 'ever' (acc. to 1650–69).
20. In some MSS the line appears in several versions.
     humane: human, civil.
23. One MS has an additional line after 23: 'Of other beauties, and in change
     rejoice?'
27. *agreements*: agreeable qualities.
31. *are* (acc. to some MSS): 'were' (acc. to 1650–69).
34. *degree*: position in society; also amorous abilities.

How happy were our Syres in ancient times
Who held plurality of loves no crime!
With them it was accounted charity
To stirre up race of all indifferently;   40
Kindreds were not exempted from the bands:
Which with the Persian still in usage stands.
Women were then no sooner asked then won,
And what they did was honest and well done.
But since this title honour hath been us'd,   45
Our weake credulity hath been abus'd;
The golden laws of nature are repeald,
Which our first Fathers in such reverence held;
Our liberty revers'd and Charter's gone,
And we made servants to opinion,   50
A monster in no certain shape attir'd,
And whose originall is much desir'd,
Formlesse at first, but growing on it fashions,
And doth prescribe manners and laws to nations.
Here love receiv'd immedicable harmes,   55
And was dispoiled of his daring armes.
A greater want then is his daring eyes,
He lost those awfull wings with which he flies;
His sinewy bow, and those immortall darts
Wherewith he'is wont to bruise resisting hearts;   60

37.   *sires*: the polygamous patriarchs of the Old Testament.
40.   *stirre up race*: beget children (§166).
41.   *bands*: sexual unions.
43.   *asked*: 'wou'd' (acc. to one MS).
       then won: than won.
45.   *title* (acc. to several MSS): 'little' (acc. to 1650–69).
       honour: chastity (§164).
48.   *first Fathers*: 'great grandsires' (acc. to one MS).
49.   *and*: 'our' (acc. to some MSS).
50.   *we*: 'we're' (acc. to one MS).
52.   *whose originall*: 'on whose origin' (ditto).
53.   *it* (ditto): 'its' (acc. to 1650–69).
55.   *love*: Cupid.
       immedicable: incurable.
58.   *then*: than.
60.   *bruise*: 'wound' (acc. to one MS).
       On the symbol ', see above, p. 5.

Onely some few strong in themselves and free
Retain the seeds of antient liberty,
Following that part of love although deprest,
And make a throne for him within their brest,
In spight of modern censures him avowing   65
Their Soveraigne, all service him allowing.
Amongst which troop although I am the least,
Yet equall in perfection with the best,
I glory in subjection of his hand,
Nor ever did decline his least command: 70
For in whatever forme the message came
My heart did open and receive the same.
But time will in his course a point discry
When I this loved service must deny.
For our allegiance temporary is,   75
With firmer age returnes our liberties.
What time in years and judgement we repos'd,
Shall not so easily be to change dispos'd
Nor to the art of severall eyes obeying,
But beauty with true worth securely weighing,   80
Which being found assembled in some one
Wee'l leave her ever, and love her alone.

63. *part*: party or faction.
    deprest: suppressed.
72. *same*: 'flame' (acc. to one MS).
79. *eyes*: i.e. enticements.
80. *securely*: 'sincerely' (acc. to one MS) or 'unpartially' (ditto).
82. *leave*: 'love' (acc. to some MSS).

Elegie [XVIII].
Loves Progress.

Who ever loves, if he do not propose
The right true end of love, he's one that goes
To sea for nothing but to make him sick:
Love is a bear-whelp born, if we o're lick
Our love, and force it new strange shapes to take,   5
We erre, and of a lump a monster make.
Were not a Calf a monster that were grown
Face 'd like a man, though better then his own?
Perfection is in unitie: preferr
One woman first, and then one thing in her.   10
I when I value gold, may think upon
The ductilness, the application,
The wholsomness, the ingenuitie,
From rust, from soil, from fire ever free:
But if I love it, 'tis because 'tis made   15
By our new nature (Use) the soul of trade.
   All these in women we might think upon
(If women had them) and yet love but one.
Can men more injure women then to say
They love them for that, by which they're not they?   20
Makes virtue woman? must I cool my bloud
Till I both be, and find one wise and good?

Elegie [XVIII]. First published in *Wit and Drollery* (1661) and in 1669 (hence the
    necessary adjustments in the ensuing text as shown in representative
    instances in the notes). Not entitled in 1669; thus entitled in some MSS
    and, in one, *An Elegie on Loves Progresse*. 'Progress' has the particular
    sense of a journey or expedition (§254).
  4. *Love is*: 'And love is' (acc. to some MSS) or 'And Loves' (ditto).
      o're lick: cf. above, p. 157, note on 31.
  5. *strange*: 'strong' (acc. to 1669).
  8 (also 19, 27, 38, 87, 90). *then*: than.
  14. *ever*: 'forever' (acc. to several MSS).
  16. *Use*: habit, 'custome' (as above, p. 102, l. 6).
  18. *and*: 'but' (acc. to some MSS).
      one: one thing (cf. 10).

May barren Angels love so. But if we
Make love to woman; virtue is not she:
As beauty'is not nor wealth: He that strayes thus   25
From her to hers, is more adulterous,
Then if he took her maid. Search every sphear
And firmament, our *Cupid* is not there:
He's an infernal god and under ground,
With *Pluto* dwells, where gold and fire abound;   30
Men to such Gods, their sacrificing Coles
Did not on Altars lay, but pits and holes:
Although we see Celestial bodies move
Above the earth, the earth we Till and love:
So we her ayres contemplate, words and heart,   35
And virtues; but we love the Centrique part.
    Nor is the soul more worthy, or more fit
For love, then this, as infinite as it.
But in attaining this desired place
How much they erre; that set out at the face?   40
The hair a Forest is of Ambushes,
Of springes, snares, fetters and manacles:
The brow becalms us when 'tis smooth and plain,
And when 'tis wrinckled, shipwracks us again.
Smooth, 'tis a Paradice, where we would have   45
Immortal stay, but wrinkled 'tis our grave.

23. *barren*: because devoid of bodies.
25. *beauty'is not:* 'beauties no' (acc. to 1669).
     On the symbol ', see above, p. 5.
27. *if he*: 'hee that' (acc. to some MSS).
     sphear (also 87): see above, p. 80, note on 23.
28. *not there*: no celestial body is named after Cupid.
29–30. Cupid may be sought *under ground* because his service demands *gold* in
     the purse and *fire* in the heart (§169).
     Pluto: god of the underworld.
31–32. According to pagan custom, sacrifices to the infernal gods were placed
     in trenches in the earth (§164).
36. *the Centrique part*: the universe's centre, i.e. the earth.
38. *as infinite as it*: the body is no less infinite than the soul, since both will be
     resurrected (§482).
40. *erre*: 'stray' (acc. to some MSS).
42. *springes*: nooses for trapping small game (§166).
46. *but*: 'and' (acc. to some MSS).

The Nose (like to the first Meridian) runs
Not 'twixt an East and West, but 'twixt two suns;
It leaves a Cheek, a rosie Hemisphere
On either side, and then directs us where   50
Upon the Islands fortunate we fall,
Not faynte *Canaries*, but *Ambrosiall*,
Her swelling lips; To which when wee are come,
We anchor there, and think our selves at home,
For they seem all: there Syrens songs, and there   55
Wise Delphick Oracles do fill the ear;
There in a Creek where chosen pearls do swell,
The Rhemora her cleaving tongue doth dwell.
These, and the glorious Promontory, her Chin
Ore past; and the streight *Hellespont* betweene   60
The *Sestos* and *Abydos* of her breasts,
(Not of two Lovers, but two Loves the neasts)
Succeeds a boundless sea, but yet thine eye
Some Island moles may scattered there descry;
And Sailing towards her *India*, in that way   65
Shall at her fair Atlantick Navell stay;

47. *first* (acc. to all MSS): 'sweet' (acc. to 1669).
     the first Meridian was thought by Donne to run through *the Islands fortunate* (51), i.e. the Canaries.
52. *Canaries*: both the isles and their light wine.
53. The line is from the MSS; 1669 reads, 'Unto her swelling lips when we are come'.
55. *Syrens song*: the enchanting singing of the mermaids (cf. above, p. 50, note on 5) that attracted Odysseus's mariners to their doom (*Odyssey* XII).
56. *Delphick Oracles*: the ancient Greek shrine to Apollo at Delphi, noted for its oracular revelations.
57. *There*: 'Then' (acc. to 1669 and some MSS).
58. *Rhemora*: a sucking-fish, supposed able to stop ships by *cleaving* (clinging) to them by its mouth.
60. The line is from the MSS; 1669 reads, 'Being past the Straits of Hellespont between'.
61. *Sestos* and *Abydos* were cities on opposite shores of the *Hellespont*, the respective homes of the *two Lovers* Hero and Leander (62; cf. above, p. 127).
63. *yet*: 'that' (acc. to some MSS).
65. *India*: here, the still unknown yet fascinating East generally.

Though thence the Current be thy Pilot made,
Yet ere thou be where thou wouldst be embay'd,
Thou shalt upon another Forest set,
Where many Shipwrack, and no further get.   70
When thou art there, consider what this chace
Mispent by thy beginning at the face.
   Rather set out below; practice my Art,
Some Symetry the foot hath with that part
Which thou dost seek, and is thy Map for that   75
Lovely enough to stop, but not stay at:
Least subject to disguise and change it is;
Men say the Devil never can change his.
It is the Emblem that hath figured
Firmness; 'tis the first part that comes to bed.   80
Civilitie we see refin'd: the kiss
Which at the face began, transplanted is,
Since to the hand, since to the imperial knee,
Now at the Papal foot delights to be:
If Kings think that the nearer way, and do   85
Rise from the foot, Lovers may do so too.
For as free Spheres move faster far then can
Birds, whom the air resists, so may that man
Which goes this empty and Ætherial way,
Then if at beauties elements he stay.   90
Rich Nature hath in women wisely made
Two purses, and their mouths aversely laid:

67. *thence, thy* (acc. to the MSS): 'there', 'the' (acc. to 1669).
68. *wouldst* (acc. to the MSS): 'should'st' (acc. to 1669).
     embay'd: laid within a bay, shut in.
70. *many*: 'some doe' (acc. to some MSS).
74. *Symetry*: likeness.
78. *his*: his cleft foot (see above, p. 50, note on 4).
80. *Firmness*: constancy.
83–84. Kissing the emperor's *knee* betokened feudal fealty; and *the Papal foot* (toe), total submission to Rome (§166).
85. *nearer*: closest in affection.
87. *Spheres*: the celestial bodies.
90. *elements* (acc. to the MSS): 'enemies' (acc. to 1669).
92. *Two purses*: the mouth and the vulva (§166).
     aversely: lying at an angle to one another.

They then, which to the lower tribute owe,
That way which that Exchequer looks, must go:
He which doth not, his error is as great,   95
As who by Clyster gave the Stomack meat.

Elegie [XIX].
To his Mistress
Going to Bed.

Come, Madam, come, all rest my powers defie,
Until I labour, I in labour lie.
The foe oft-times having the foe in sight,
Is tir'd with standing though he never fight.
Off with that girdle, like heavens Zone glittering,   5
But a fair fairer world incompassing.
Unpin that spangled breastplate which you wear,
That th'eyes of busie fooles may be stopt there.
Unlace your self, for that harmonious chyme,
Tells me from you, that now it is bed time.   10
Off with that happy busk, which I cnvie,
That still can be, and still can stand so nigh.

Elegie [XVIII].
96.   *Clyster* [i.e. enemal] *gave* (acc. to one MS): 'glister gives' (acc. to 1669
        and some MSS).
        meat: food.

Elegie [XIX]. First published and thus entitled in 1669 (some necessary adjust-
        ments in the ensuing text are shown in representative instances in the
        notes).
2.   *in labour*: in anxious anticipation.
4.   *standing*: the speaker is drawing attention to his erection (§207); hence *up
        right* (24).
        he: 'they' (acc. to some MSS).
5.   *heavens Zone*: i.e. the Milky Way (as above, p. 110, note on 7).
        glittering: 'glistering' (acc. to several MSS).
7.   *breastplate*: bodice.
9.   *chyme*: produced by the chiming watch she wears.
11. *busk*: corset.

Your gown going off, such beautious state reveals,
As when from flowry meads th'hills shadowe steales.
Off with that wyerie Coronet and shew   15
The haiery Diademe which on you doth grow:
Now off with those shooes, and then softly tread
In this loves hallow'd temple, this soft bed.
In such white robes, heaven's Angels us'd to be
Receavd by men: thou Angel bringst with thee   20
A heaven like Mahomets Paradice, and though
Ill spirits walk in white, we easly know,
By this these Angels from an evil sprite,
Those set our hairs, but these our flesh upright.

    Licence my roaving hands, and let them go,   25
Before, behind, between, above, below.
O my America! my new-found-land,
My kingdome, safeliest when with one man man'd,
My Myne of precious stones: My Emperie,
How blest am I in this discovering thee!   30
To enter in these bonds, is to be free;
Then where my hand is set, my seal shall be.

    Full nakedness! All joyes are due to thee,
As souls unbodied, bodies uncloth'd must be,

---

14. *from* (acc. to the MSS): 'through' (acc. to 1669).
15. *that*: 'your' (acc. to some MSS).
     Coronet: as above, p. 149, note on 6.
17. *softly*: 'safely' (acc. to several MSS).
20. *Receavd by* (acc. to the MSS): 'Reveal'd to' (acc. to 1669).
21. *Mahomets Paradice* was said to be filled with carnal pleasures.
22. *Ill*: 'All' (acc. to 1669 and several MSS).
     in white: i.e. disguised, in order to deceive men.
23. *these Angels*: i.e. women.
24. *our flesh*: 'the flesh' (acc. to some MSS).
25–27. According to Juan Luis Borges, the lines demonstrate Donne's 'greatness as a poet' (*Other Inquisitions*, trans. Ruth L. C. Simms [Austin, 1964, and London, 1973], p. 89).
28. *kingdome, safeliest*: adjusted acc. to one MS.
29. *Emperie*: empire.
30. *discovering*: also in the sense of uncovering.
31. *bonds*: 'Bands' (acc. to some MSS).

To taste whole joyes. Jems which you women use   35
Are like Atlanta's balls, cast in mens views,
That when a fools eye lighteth on a Jem,
His earthly soul may covet theirs, not them:
Like pictures, or like books gay coverings made
For lay-men, are all women thus array'd.   40
Themselves are mystick books, which only wee
(Whom their imputed grace will dignifie)
Must see reveal'd. Then since that I may know;
As liberally, as to a Midwife shew
Thy self: cast all, yea, this white lynnen hence,   45
There is no pennance, much less innocence:
   To teach thee, I am naked first; why then
What needst thou have more covering then a man.

36. The allusion may be to the suitor who, in a race with Atalanta, cast
   golden apples in her way so as to delay her; but here the sexes are
   reversed. Yet *balls* could simply mean breasts (§480).
38. *covet* (acc. to one MS): 'court' (acc. to 1669).
40. *lay-men*: the laiety, outsiders generally.
41. *only* (acc. to the MSS) is placed in 1669 after *are*.
42. *imputed grace*: in Protestant theology, the bestowal of Divine Grace so as
   to direct men to salvation.
43. *see*: 'be' (acc. to some MSS).
46. *There, much less* (acc. to several MSS): 'There', 'due to' (acc. to 1669 and
   some MSS) or 'Here', 'much less' (acc. to some MSS).
   pennance, innocence: both represented by *white* (45).
47. *teach*: 'shewe' (acc. to one MS).
   then (also 48): than.

Elegie [XX].
Loves Warre.

Till I have peace with thee, warr other men,
And when I have peace, can I leave thee then?
All other Warrs are scrupulous; Only thou
O fayr free Citty, maist thyselfe allowe
To any one: In Flanders, who can tell   5
Whether the Master presse; or men rebell?
Only we know, that which all Ideots say
They beare most blows which come to part the fray.
France in her lunatique giddines did hate
Ever our men, yea and our God of late;   10
Yet she relyes upon our Angels well,
Which nere returne; no more then they which fell.
Sick Ireland is with a strange warr possest
Like to an Ague; now raging, now at rest;
Which time will cure: yet it must doe her good   15
If she were purg'd, and her head vayne let blood.

Elegie [XX]. First published from a MS, and thus entitled, in *The Shakespearean
    Miscellany*: *Miscellaneous Poetry*, ed. F. G. Waldron (London, 1802),
    pp. 1–2. Also entitled in one MS *Making of Men*; a shorter version
    comprised solely of ll. 29–46 published in *The Harmony of the Muses*
    (1654) is simply headed *To his Mistris*.
1. *warr other men*: let other men war.
3. *are scrupulous*: have precise rules.
5. *Flanders*: the Netherlands, where the *men rebell* against the Spaniards (6),
    and the Spanish *Master* rules tyranically (*presse*).
6. *presse*: 'peeres' (acc. to some MSS).
    lunatique: see above, p. 51, note on 14.
9. *giddines*: i.e. the swift changes in policy that attended the death of the
    Catholic Henri III, the accession of the Protestant Henri de Navarre, and
    the latter's conversion to Catholicism.
10. *our God*: the God of the English Protestants, renounced by the French
    Catholics *of late* (see previous note).
11. *Angels*: the coins which financed Henri de Navarre but, on his conversion
    to Catholicism, were *nere returne*[d] (12).
12. *they which fell*: the disobedient angels expelled from Heaven.
13–16. See above, p. 37.
14. *Ague*: malarial fever.

And Midas joyes our Spanish journeys give,
We touch all gold, but find no food to live.
And I should be in the hott parching clime,
To dust and ashes turn'd before my time.   20
To mew me in a Ship, is to inthrall
Mee in a prison, that weare like to fall;
Or in a Cloyster; save that there men dwell
In a calme heaven, here in a swaggering hell.
Long voyages are long consumptions,   25
And ships are carts for executions.
Yea they are Deaths; Is't not all one to flye
Into an other World, as t'is to dye?
Here let mee warr; in these armes lett mee lye;
Here lett mee parlee, batter, bleede, and dye.   30
Thy armes imprison me, and myne armes thee,
Thy hart thy ransome is: take myne for mee.
Other men war that they their rest may gayne;
But wee will rest that wee may fight agayne.
Those warrs the ignorant, these th'experienc'd love,   35
There wee are always under, here above.
There Engins farr off breed a just true feare,
Neere thrusts, pikes, stabs, yea bullets hurt not here.
There lyes are wrongs; here safe uprightly ly;

17. *Midas*: the mythical king who turned everything he touched into gold.
     our Spanish journeys: English raids on Spanish ships transporting gold and
     silver from the Americas.
19. *Should*: 'shall' (acc. to severall MSS).
     the: 'that' (ditto).
21. *mew*: enclose.
     inthrall: enslave.
22. *that weare like*: that might be about (§163).
24. *swaggering*: boasting; lurching.
25. *consumptions*: deprivations.
31. *Thy*: 'Thyne' (acc. to several MSS).
32. The line also reads, 'Thy heart my ransom is, take mine for thee:' (acc. to
     the 1654 version [see headnote]).
35. *love*: 'prove' (acc. to the 1654 version).
37. *Engins*: offensive weapons generally (§169).
37–39. The lines also read, 'There Engins a far off move a just feare, / But
     Thrusts, Pricks, Stabs; nay, bullets hurt not / There lies are wrong; here
     wee'l uprightly lie' (acc. to the 1654 version).
39. *uprightly*: flat on her back (§166).

There men kill men, we'will make one by and by.   40
Thou nothing; I not halfe so much shall do
In these Warrs, as they may which from us two
Shall spring. Thousands wee see which travaile not
To warrs; But stay swords, armes, and shott
To make at home; And shall not I do then   45
More glorious service, staying to make men?

40.   On the symbol ', see above, p. 5.
41.   *shall*: 'can' (acc. to the 1654 version).
44–45.   The lines also read, 'but stay at home, swords, guns and shot / Do make
      for others;' (acc. to the 1654 version); also, 'But stay swords, weapons
      armes and shott' etc. (acc. to one MS: §159).

Sapho to Philænis

First published in 1633, the poem is often printed with the elegies (cf. above, p. 134); and though sometimes excluded from the canon (e.g. §169), it is no less firmly reinstated as 'the first female homosexual love poem in English' (§207). The Greek poetess Sappho, who lived and wrote on the Aegean island of Lesbos about 600 B.C., appears to have been catholic in her tastes or, as Donne might have said, 'indifferent' (see above, p. 174, note on 38); here she is presented as addressing a young girl whose name literally means 'female friend' (§163). In form, the poem belongs within the tradition of wittily erotic 'letters' began in Ovid's *Heroides* or heroical epistles.

Where is that holy fire, which *Verse* is said
   To have? is that inchanting force decai'd?
Verse that drawes *Natures* workes, from *Natures* law,
   Thee, her best worke, to her worke cannot draw.
Have my teares quench'd my old *Poetique* fire;   5
   Why quench'd they not as well, that of *desire?*
Thoughts, my mindes creatures, often are with thee,
   But I, their maker, want their libertie.
Onely thine image, in my heart, doth sit,
   But that is waxe, and fires environ it.
My fires have driven, thine have drawne it hence;   10
   And I am rob'd of *Picture*, *Heart*, and *Sense*.

1. *holy*: 'hott' (acc. to some MSS).
   holy fire: because of poetry's reputed heavenly origins.
3. *drawes*: copies, imitates.
   from: in accordance with.

Dwells with me still mine irksome *Memory*,
    Which, both to keepe, and lose, grieves equally.
That tells me'how faire thou art: Thou are so faire,   15
    As *gods*, when *gods* to thee I doe compare,
Are grac'd thereby; And to make blinde men see,
    What things *gods* are, I say they'are like to thee.
For, if we justly call each silly *man*
    A *litle world*, What shall we call thee than?   20
Thou are not soft, and cleare, and strait, and faire,
    As *Down*, as *Stars*, *Cedars*, and *Lillies* are,
But thy right hand, and cheek, and eye, only
    Are like thy other hand, and cheek, and eye.
Such was my *Phao* awhile, but shall be never,   25
    As thou, wast, art, and, oh, maist be ever.
Here lovers sweare in their *Idolatrie*,
    That I am such; but *Griefe* discolors me.
And yet I grieve the lesse, least *Griefe* remove
    My beauty, and make me'unworthy of thy love.   30
Plaies some soft boy with thee, oh there wants yet
    A mutuall feeling which should sweeten it.
His chinne, a thorny hairy unevennesse
    Doth threaten, and some daily change possesse.

15–17. i.e. *Thou art so faire* that when I *compare* you to the *gods*, the *gods* are *grac'd* by the comparison.
15 (also 18, 30, 62). On the symbol ', see above, p. 5.
16. *to thee I doe*: 'I doe to thee' (acc. to one MS) or 'I doe to men' (ditto).
17. *thereby*: 'by thee' (ditto).
19. *silly*: ordinary.
20. *litle world*: the traditional belief that man's microcosm corresponds to the macrocosm of the universe.
    than (also 37): then.
22. *down*: i.e. birds' under-plumage.
    Cedars: 'as Cedars' (acc. to some MSS).
25. *Phao*: a handsome youth of Lesbos, beloved of Sappho.
26. *maist be*: 'maist thou be' (acc. to 1635–69) or 'shalt be for' (acc. to one MS).
    ever: 'forever' (acc. to some MSS).
29. *least*: lest.
31–54. The lines are omitted in some MSS.
31. *wants*: is wanting.

Thy body is a naturall *Paradise*,   35
    In whose selfe, unmanur'd, all pleasure lies,
Nor needs *perfection*; why shouldst thou than
    Admit the tillage of a harsh rough man?
Men leave behinde them that which their sin showes,
    And are, as theeves trac'd, which rob when it snowes.   40
But of our dallyance no more signes there are,
    Then *fishes* leave in streames, or *Birds* in aire.
And betweene us all sweetnesse may be had;
    All, all that *Nature* yields, or *Art* can adde.
My two lips, eyes, thighs, differ from thy two,   45
    But so, as thine from one another doe;
And, oh, no more; the likenesse being such,
    Why should they not alike in all parts touch?
Hand to strange hand, lippe to lippe none denies;
    Why should they brest to brest, or thighs to thighs?   50
Likenesse begets such strange selfe flatterie,
    That touching my selfe, all seemes done to thee.
My selfe I embrace, and mine owne hands I kisse,
    And amorously thanke my selfe for this.
Me, in my glasse, I call thee; But alas,   55
    When I would kisse, teares dimme mine *eyes*, and *glasse*.
O cure this loving madnesse, and restore
    Me to mee; thee, my *halfe*, my *all*, my *more*.
So may thy cheekes red outweare scarlet dye,
    And their white, whitenesse of the *Galaxy*,   60
So may thy mighty,'amazing beauty move
    Envy'in all *women*, and in all *men*, *love*,
And so be *change*, and *sicknesse*, farre from thee,
    As thou by comming neere, keep'st them from me.

36. *unmanur'd*: unfertilized.
42. *Then*: than.
55. *glasse*: mirror.
58. *thee*: 'shee' (acc. to 1633).
     halfe: 'hearte' (acc. to some MSS).
59–60. The lines also read, 'So may thy cheekes outweare all scarlet dye / May
     blisse and thee be one eternallye' (acc. to one MS).
60. *Galaxy*: the Milky Way (§162).
61. *mighty*: 'almighty' (acc. to one MS).

Epithalamions

The first two poems, alike written in 1613, are Donne's major endeavours to write within a genre that had recently been enriched by Spenser's polyphonic *Epithalamion* (1595). But the third of these poems, most likely dating from Donne's student days at Lincoln's Inn, raises a number of questions (see head-note on p. 209).

The erratic punctuation in all three poems has in several cases been emended discreetly.

An Epithalamion, Or mariage Song on the Lady *Elizabeth*, and *Count Palatine* being married on St. *Valentines* day.

I.

Haile Bishop Valentine, whose day this is,
  All the Aire is thy Diocis,
  And all the chirping Choristers
And other birds are thy Parishioners,

An Epithalamion etc.: occasioned by the marriage of Princess Elizabeth, the only daughter of James I, to Frederick, Elector Palatine, on 14 February 1613. The event, celebrated on a national scale, yielded several other poetic tributes too.

1–2. *Bishop Valentine*, the saint whose feast *day* was 14 February, had jurisdiction ('diocese') over flying things.

Thou marryest every yeare   5
The Lirique Larke, and the grave whispering Dove,
The Sparrow that neglects his life for love,
The household Bird, with the red stomacher,
        Thou mak'st the black bird speed as soone,
As doth the Goldfinch, or the Halcyon;   10
The husband cocke lookes out, and straight is sped,
And meets his wife, which brings her feather-bed.
This day more cheerfully than ever shine,
This day, which might enflame thy self, Old Valentine.

II.

Till now, Thou warmd'st with multiplying loves   15
        Two larkes, two sparrowes, or two Doves,
        All that is nothing unto this,
For thou this day couplest two Phœnixes;
        Thou mak'st a Taper see
What the sunne never saw, and what the Arke   20
(Which was of foules, and beasts, the cage, and park,)
Did not containe, one bed containes, through Thee,
        Two Phœnixes, whose joyned breasts
Are unto one another mutuall nests,
Where motion kindles such fires, as shall give   25
Yong Phœnixes, and yet the old shall live.
Whose love and courage never shall decline,
But make the whole year through, thy day, O Valentine.

7. The sparrow's short life was popularly attributed to its proverbial
    lechery.
8. *stomacher*: waistcoat.
9. *speed*: prosper, in spite of its blackness.
10. *Halcyon*: the kingfisher, said to induce serenity.
11. *straight*: 'soone' (acc. to some MSS).
    sped: satisfied.
18. *two Phœnixes*: in itself exceptional, since only one of the legendary birds
    could exist at any one time.
20–22. It was generally agreed that the legendary phœnix was not taken
    aboard Noah's Ark – possibly because it was legendary (§501).
21. *foules*: 'fowle' (acc. to 1635–69).
27. *courage*: sexual desire (§254).

III.

Up then faire Phœnix Bride, frustrate the Sunne,
  Thy selfe from thine affection   30
  Takest warmth enough, and from thine eye
All lesser birds will take their Jollitie.
  Up, up, faire Bride, and call,
Thy starres, from out their severall boxes, take
Thy Rubies, Pearles, and Diamonds forth, and make 35
Thy selfe a constellation, of them All,
  And by their blazing, signifie,
That a Great Princess falls, but doth not die;
Bee thou a new starre, that to us portends
Ends of much wonder; And be Thou those ends. 40
Since thou dost this day in new glory shine,
May all men date Records, from this thy Valentine.

IIII.

Come forth, come forth, and as one glorious flame
  Meeting Another, growes the same,
  So meet thy Fredericke, and so   45
To an unseparable union growe.
  Since separation
Falls not on such things as are infinite,
Nor things which are but one, can disunite,
You'are twice inseparable, great, and one; 50
  Goe then to where the Bishop staies,
To make you one, his way, which divers waies
Must be effected; and when all is past,
And that you'are one, by hearts and hands made fast,
You two have one way left, your selves to'entwine, 55
Besides this Bishops knot, or Bishop Valentine.

35. *forth*: 'out' (acc. to a MS).
37. Blazing comets were thought to portend a prince's death.
  their: 'this' (acc. to most MSS).
39. *new starre*: cf. below, p. 337, note on 259–60.
42. *date Records*: as now we date events from the appearance of the star that heralded Christ's nativity.
46. *growe* (acc. to several MSS): 'goe' (acc. to 1633–69).
52. *his way*: through the sacrament of marriage, as distinct from the other *way* (55) of sexual consummation.
56. *knot*: see previous note.
  or (acc. to most MSS): 'O' (acc. to 1633–54).

V.

But oh, what ailes the Sunne, that here he staies,
  Longer to day, then other daies?
  Staies he new light from these to get?
And finding here such store, is loth to set? 60
  And why doe you two walke
So slowly pac'd in this procession?
Is all your care but to be look'd upon,
And be to others spectacle, and talke?
  The feast, with gluttonous delaies, 65
Is eaten, and too long their meat they praise,
The masquers come too late, and'I thinke, will stay,
Like Fairies, till the Cock crow them away. ·
Alas, did not Antiquity assigne
A night, as well as day, to thee, O Valentine? 70

VI.

They did, and night is come; and yet wee see
  Formalities retarding thee.
  What meane these Ladies, which (as though
They were to take a clock in peeces,) goe
  So nicely about the Bride; 75
A Bride, before a good night could be said,
Should vanish from her cloathes, into her bed,
As Soules from bodies steale, and are not spy'd.
  But now she is laid; What though shee bee?
Yet there are more delayes, For, where is he? 80
He comes, and passes through Spheare after Spheare,
First her sheetes, then her Armes, then any where.
Let not this day, then, but this night be thine,
Thy day was but the eve to this, O Valentine.

---

58. *then*: than.
60. *store*: abundance; 'starres' (acc. to 1635–69).
65. *gluttonous*: 'glorious' (acc. to a MS).
67. *masquers*: guests taking part in the wedding-masque (§170).
  too late: 'late' (acc. to 1635–69).
  thinke: 'feare' (acc. to a MS).
75. *nicely*: delicately.
81. *Spheare*: see above, p. 80, note on 23.
83. *this day, then*: 'then this day' (acc. to some MSS).

VII.

Here lyes a shee Sunne, and a hee Moone here,   85
    She gives the best light to his Spheare,
      Or each is both, and all, and so
They unto one another nothing owe,
      And yet they doe, but are
So just and rich in that coyne which they pay,   90
That neither would, nor needs forbeare nor stay;
Neither desires to be spar'd, nor to spare,
    They quickly pay their debt, and then
Take no acquittances, but pay again;
They pay, they give, they lend, and so let fall   95
No such occasion to be liberall.
More truth, more courage in these two do shine,
Then all thy turtles have, and sparrows, Valentine.

VIII.

And by this act of these two Phenixes
    Nature againe restored is,   100
      For since these two are two no more,
Ther's but one Phenix still, as was before.
      Rest now at last, and wee
As Satyres watch the Sunnes uprise, will stay
Waiting, when your eyes opened, let out day,   105
Onely desir'd, because your face wee see;
      Others neare you shall whispering speake,
And wagers lay, at which side day will breake,

---

85. *here*: 'there' (acc. to 1650–69 and some MSS).
90. *coyne*: i.e. their own sexual pleasure.
94. *acquittances* (plural acc. to 1635–69 and several MSS, singular acc. to 1633 and some MSS): receipts for debts paid.
98. *Then*: than.
    turtles: turtle-doves, symbols of true love; *sparrows*: symbols of 'courage' (see note on 27).
100. *restored*: from the effects of the Fall of Man.
104. *Satyres*: satyrs given to revels through the dawn.
105. *Waiting*: attending the customary serenade of the newlyweds on the morning after their marriage (§170).
108. *at which side*: i.e. of their curtained four-poster bed.

And win by'observing, then, whose hand it is
That opens first a curtaine, hers or his;   110
This will be tryed to morrow after nine,
Till which houre, wee thy day enlarge, O Valentine.

ECCLOGUE.
1613. December 26.

Allophanes finding Idios *in the country in Christmas time,
reprehends his absence from court, at the mariage of the
Earle of Sommerset,* Idios *gives an account of his purpose
therein, and of his absence thence.*

Allophanes.
Unseasonable man, statue of ice,
   What could to countries solitude entice
Thee, in this yeares cold and decrepit time?
   Natures instinct drawes to the warmer clime
Even small birds, who by that courage dare,   5
   In numerous fleets, saile through their Sea, the aire.

An Epithalamion.
109. *win by*: 'wiselie' (acc. to a MS).
111. *tryed*: tested.
     after nine: ten o'clock was the usual hour for the public appearance of
     members of the fashionable world (§170); cf. below, p. 237, l. 175.
112. *wee*: 'all' (acc. to a MS).
     enlarge: prolong.

Ecclogue. Entitled in several MSS *Epithalamion at the Marriage of the Earl of
    Somerset* – i.e. Robert Carr, who as King James I's favourite had been
    created Viscount Rochester and then Earl of Somerset, and was married
    on the date specified in the title to Lady Frances Howard, herself
    recently divorced from the Earl of Essex (see note on l. 123). The
    newlyweds would soon be implicated in, and convicted for, the murder
    of Sir Thomas Overbury.
      'Idios' is probably Donne, the private citizen with no official position
    at Court; 'Allophanes' (literally, one who seems like another) is his
    friend Sir Robert Ker or Carr, who bears the same name as the bride-
    groom.
  5. *small*: 'smaller' (acc. to 1635–69).

What delicacie can in fields appeare,
   Whil'st Flora'herselfe doth a freeze jerkin weare?
Whil'st windes do all the trees and hedges strip
   Of leafes, to furnish roddes enough to whip   10
Thy madnesse from thee; and all springs by frost
   Have taken cold, and their sweet murmure lost;
If thou thy faults or fortunes would'st lament
   With just solemnity, do it in Lent;
At Court the spring already advanced is,   15
   The Sunne stayes longer up; and yet not his
The glory is, farre other, other fires.
   First, zeale to Prince and State; then loves desires
Burne in one brest, and like heavens two great lights,
   The first doth governe dayes, the other nights.   20
And then that early light, which did appeare
   Before the Sunne and Moone created were,
The Princes favour is defus'd o'r all,
   From which all Fortunes, Names, and Natures fall;
Then from those wombes of starres, the Brides bright
      eyes,   25
   At every glance, a constellation flyes,
And sowes the Court with starres, and doth prevent
   In light and power, the all-ey'd firmament;
First her eyes kindle other Ladies eyes,
   Then from their beames their jewels lusters rise,   30
And from their jewels torches do take fire,
   And all is warmth, and light, and good desire;

---

8.   *Flora*: the goddess of flowers.
     freeze: frieze, a coarse woollen fabric; 'buff' (acc. to a MS).
12. *Have*: 'Having' (acc. to 1635–69).
     murmure (singular acc. to most MSS, plural acc. to 1633–69).
21–22. Light was made on the first day of creation, but the sun and the moon
      on the fourth (Genesis 1.3–19).
23. *defus'd*: diffused.
27. *prevent*: exceed.
28. *firmament*: see above, p. 65, note on 24.

Most other Courts, alas, are like to hell,
    Where in darke plotts, fire without light doth dwell;
Or but like Stoves, for lust and envy get   35
    Continuall, but artificiall heat;
Here zeale and love growne one, all clouds disgest,
    And make our Court an everlasting East.
And can'st thou be from thence?

Idios.   No, I am there.
As heaven, to men dispos'd, is every where,   40
So are those Courts, whose Princes animate,
    Not onely all their house, but all their State.
Let no man thinke, because he is full, he hath all,
    Kings (as their patterne, God) are liberall
Not onely in fulnesse, but capacitie,   45
    Enlarging narrow men, to feele and see,
And comprehend the blessings they bestow.
    So, reclus'd hermits often times do know
More of heavens glory, then a worldling can.
    As man is of the world, the heart of man,   50
Is an epitome of Gods great booke
    Of creatures, and man need no farther looke;
So is the Country of Courts, where sweet peace doth,
    As their one common soule, give life to both,
I am not then from Court.

Allophanes.   Dreamer, thou art.   55
    Think'st thou fantastique that thou hast a part

---

34. *plotts* (acc. to 1635–39 and most MSS): 'places' (acc. to 1633 and 1669).
     fire without light: a well-known property of Hell, 'darkness visible' in
     Milton's phrase (*Par. Lost*, I, 63).
37. *disgest*: disperse.
40. *dispos'd*: open.
43. *full*: having all he wants.
49. *then*: than.
50–52. Man the 'little world' (cf. below, p. 438, l.1) epitomizes the universe
     at large, and his heart the book of creatures.
53. *of Courts*: an epitome of Courts.
54. *one*: 'own' (acc. to 1635–69 and some MSS).
55. *I am not then from Court*: 'And am I then from Court?' (acc. to 1635–69).

In the East–Indian fleet, because thou hast
  A little spice, or Amber in thy taste?
Because thou art not frozen, art thou warme?
  Seest thou all good because thou seest no harme?   60
The earth doth in her inward bowels hold
  Stuffe well dispos'd, and which would faine be gold,
But never shall, except it chance to lye,
  So upward, that heaven gild it with his eye;
As, for divine things, faith comes from above,   65
  So, for best civill use, all tinctures move
From higher powers; From God religion springs,
  Wisdome, and honour from the use of Kings.
Then unbeguile thy selfe, and know with mee,
  That Angels, though on earth employd they bee,   70
Are still in heav'n, so is hee still at home
  That doth, abroad, to honest actions come.
Chide thy selfe then, O foole, which yesterday
  Might'st have read more then all thy books bewray;
Hast thou a history, which doth present   75
  A Court, where all affections do assent
Unto the Kings, and that, that Kings are just?
  And where it is no levity to trust?
Where there is no ambition, but to'obey,
  Where men need whisper nothing, and yet may;   80

57. *East-Indian* (acc. to most MSS): 'Indian' (acc. to 1633–69); cf. above,
    p. 54, note on 17.
58. *Amber*: ambergris, often used in cooking.
61–68. Alluding to the alchemical belief that the rays of the sun (*heaven*) have
    the power to transmute certain minerals (*Stuffe well dispos'd*) into gold
    (§218).
61. *inward* (acc. to most MSS): 'inner' (acc. to 1633–69).
66. *tinctures*: the pure, quintessential principles within substances.
68. *use*: customary practice.
69. *unbeguile*: undeceive.
70. *employd*: i.e. primarily as guardian angels.
74. *then*: than.
    bewray: reveal.
75. present: 'represent' (acc. to some MSS).
77. *that, that*: 'that he' (acc. to some MSS).
78. *no levity*: not frivolous.

Where the Kings favours are so plac'd, that all
   Finde that the King therein is liberall
To them, in him, because his favours bend
   To vertue, to the which they all pretend?
Thou hast no such; yet here was this, and more,   85
   An earnest lover, wise then, and before.
Our little Cupid hath sued Livery,
   And is no more in his minority,
Hee is admitted now into that brest
   Where the Kings Counsells and his secrets rest,   90
What hast thou lost, O ignorant man?

Idios.   I knew
   All this, and onely therefore I withdrew.
To know and feele all this, and not to have
   Words to expresse it, makes a man a grave
Of his owne thoughts; I would not therefore stay   95
   At a great feast, having no grace to say.
And yet I scap'd not here; for being come
   Full of the common joy, I utter'd some;
Reade then this nuptiall song, which was not made
   Either the Court or mens hearts to invade,   100
But since I'am dead, and buried, I could frame
   No Epitaph, which might advance my fame
So much as this poor song, which testifies
   I did unto that day some sacrifice.

---

84. *pretend*: aspire.
87. *sued Livery*: sought service with a nobleman.
92. *therefore*: for this reason.
101. *dead, and buried*: the social condition of men in the country, away from
     the Court.

[Epithalamion.]

I.
The time of the Mariage.

Thou art repriv'd old yeare, thou shalt not die,   105
Though thou upon thy death bed lye,
   And should'st within five dayes expire,
Yet thou art rescu'd by a mightier fire,
   Then thy old Soule, the Sunne,
When he doth in his largest circle runne.   110
The passage of the West or East would thaw,
And open wide their easie liquid jawe
To all our ships, could a Promethean art
Either unto the Northerne Pole impart
The fire of these inflaming eyes, or of this loving heart. 115

II.
Equality of persons.

But undiscerning Muse, which heart, which eyes,
   In this new couple, dost thou prize,
    When his eye as inflaming is
As hers, and her heart loves as well as his?
    Be tryed by beauty, and than   120
The bridegroome is a maid, and not a man.

105ff.   _Epithalamion_ (the designation, acc. to most MSS, is omitted in 1633–69).
107.   _within five dayes_: the marriage was celebrated on 26 December.
108.   _by_: 'from' (acc. to 1635–69).
109.   _Then_: than.
110.   _largest circle_: the summer solstice.
111.   _the West or East_: the Northwest Passage or the Northeast one.
113.   _Promethean_: Prometheus stole fire from heaven and gave it to men.
120.   _tryed_: tested.
      than: then.

If by that manly courage they be tryed,
Which scornes unjust opinion; then the bride
Becomes a man. Should chance or envies Art
Divide these two, whom nature scarce did part?   125
Since both have both th'enflaming eyes, and both the
     loving heart.

III.
Raysing of the Bridegroome.

Though it be some divorce to thinke of you
    Singly, so much one are you two,
    Let me here contemplate thee,
First cheerfull Bridegroome, and first let mee see,   130
    How thou prevent'st the Sunne,
And his red foming horses dost outrunne,
How, having laid downe in thy Soveraignes brest
All businesses, from thence to reinvest
Them, when these triumphs cease, thou forward art   135
To shew to her, who doth the like impart,
The fire of thy inflaming eyes, and of thy loving heart.

IIII.
Raising of the Bride.

But now, to Thee, faire Bride, it is some wrong,
    To thinke thou wert in Bed so long,
    Since Soone thou lyest downe first, tis fit   140
Thou in first rising should'st allow for it.

123. *unjust opinion*: a defensive allusion to the scandal that the affair had
    caused (§207).
124. *or*: 'our' (acc. to 1669).
126. *both th'enflaming eyes* (acc. to most MSS): 'th'enflaming eye' (acc. to
    1633).
128. *Singly* (acc. to most MSS): 'Single' (acc. to 1633–69).
129. *Let* (acc. to 1633–69 and most MSS): 'Yet let' (acc. to some MSS and all
    modern editors).
131. *prevent'st*: anticipate.
134. *reinvest*: take up again.

> Pouder thy Radiant haire,
Which if without such ashes thou would'st weare,
Thou, which, to all which come to looke upon,
Art meant for Phœbus, would'st be Phaëton.   145
For our ease, give thine eyes th'unusual part
Of joy, a Teare; so quencht, thou maist impart,
To us that come, thy inflaming eyes, to him, thy loving
> heart.

V.
Her Apparrelling.

Thus thou descend'st to our infirmitie,
> Who can the Sun in water see.   150
> Soe dost thou, when in silke and gold,
Thou cloudst thy selfe; since wee which doe behold,
> Are dust, and wormes, 'tis just
Our objects be the fruits of wormes and dust;
Let every Jewell be a glorious starre,   155
Yet starres are not so pure, as their spheares are.
And though thou stoope, to'appeare to us, in part,
Still in that Picture thou intirely art,
Which thy inflaming eyes have made within his loving
> heart.

145.   *Art* (acc. to several MSS): 'Are' (acc. to 1633 and several MSS) or 'West'
       (acc. to 1635–69).
       Phaëton: son of the sun-god Helios (*Phœbus*), he was granted permission
       to drive his father's chariot and nearly scorched the world on losing
       control of the horses.
150.   *see*: see reflected.
154.   *the fruits of wormes and dust*: i.e. *silke and gold* (151).
156.   *spheares*: see above, p. 80, note on 23.

VI.
Going to the Chappell.

Now from your Easts you issue forth, and wee,   160
    As men which through a Cipres see
    The rising sun, doe thinke it two,
Soe, as you goe to Church, doe thinke of you,
    But that vaile being gone,
By the Church rites you are from thenceforth one.   165
The Church Triumphant made this match before,
And now the Militant doth strive no more;
Then, reverend Priest, who Gods Recorder art,
Doe, from his Dictates, to these two impart
All blessings, which are seene, or thought, by Angels
    eye or heart.   170

VII.
The Benediction.

Blest payre of Swans, Oh may you interbring
    Daily new joyes, and never sing;
    Live, till all grounds of wishes faile,
Till honor, yea till wisedome grow so stale,
    That, new great heights to trie,   175
It must serve your ambition, to die;
Raise heires, and may here, to the worlds end, live
Heires from this King, to take thankes, you, to give,

---

164. *vaile*: the impediment of our sight, by which we see them as two distinct beings (§166).
166–67. *Triumphant*: i.e. celestial; *Militant*: earthly.
171. *interbring*: see above, p. 88, note on 26.
172. *never sing*: cf. below, p. 343, note on 407.
173. *grounds of*: reasons for.
178. *from*: 'for' (acc. to some MSS).
    you, to give: which you are to give.

Nature and grace doe all, and nothing Art.
May never age, or error overthwart   180
With any West, these radiant eyes, with any North,
    this heart.

VIII.
Feasts and Revells.

But you are over-blest. Plenty this day
    Injures; it causeth time to stay;
      The tables groane, as though this feast
Would, as the flood, destroy all fowle and beast.   185
      And were the doctrine new
That the earth mov'd, this day would make it true;
For every part to dance and revell goes.
They tread the ayre, and fal not where they rose.
Though six houres since, the Sunne to bed did part,   190
The masks and banquets will not yet impart
As to these weary eyes, A Center to this heart.

IX.
The Brides going to bed.

What mean'st thou Bride, this companie to keep?
    To sit up, till thou faine wouldst sleep?
      Thou maist not, when thou art laid, doe so.   195
Thy selfe must to him a new banquet grow,
      And you must entertaine
And doe all this daies dances o'er againe.

180. *overthwart*: obstruct.
181. *West*: i.e. decline; *North*: coldness (cf. above, p. 49, note on 18).
185. *flood*: Noah's.
186–89. *doctrine*: the rotation of the earth about the sun, first proposed by
     Aristarchus of Samos, had formed part of Copernicus's theory (1543).
     fal not where they rose: i.e. because of the earth's rotation!
191. *masks*: i.e. for the eyes; also, entertainments (masques).

Know that if Sun and Moone together doe
Rise in one point, they doe not set so too.   200
Therefore thou maist, faire Bride, to bed depart,
Thou art not gone, being gone; where e'r thou art,
Thou leav'st in him thy watchfull eyes, in him thy loving
    heart.

X.
The Bridegroomes comming.

As he that sees a starre fall, runs apace,
    And findes a gellie in the place,   205
      So doth the Bridegroome haste as much,
Being told this starre is falne, and findes her such.
    And as friends may looke strange,
By a new fashion, or apparrells change,
Their soules, though long acquainted they had beene,   210
These clothes, their bodies, never yet had seene.
Therefore at first shee modestly might start,
But must forthwith surrender every part,
As freely, as each to each before, gave either eye or heart.

XI.
The good night.

Now as in Tullias tombe, one lampe burnt cleare,   215
    Unchang'd for fifteene hundred yeare,
      May these love-lamps we here enshrine,

200. *point*: i.e. of time (§170).
205–6. Referring to a genus of algae which appears as a jelly-like mass on dry
      soil after rain and was believed to be the remains of a fallen star or
      meteor (§207).
214. *eye*: 'hand' (acc. to 1650–69).
215–16. A popular story claimed that a lamp in the tomb of Cicero's daughter
      Tullia had burned for 1500 years.

In warmth, light, lasting, equall the divine.
    Fire ever doth aspire,
And makes all like it selfe, turnes all to fire,   220
But ends in ashes, which these cannot doe,
For none of these is fuell, but fire too.
This is joyes bonfire, then, where loves strong Arts
Make of so noble individual parts
One fire of foure inflaming eyes, and of two loving
      hearts.   225

Idios.
As I have brought this song, that I may doe   226
    A perfect sacrifice, I'll burne it too.

Allophanes.
No Sir. This paper I have justly got,
    For, in burnt incense, the perfume is not
His only that presents it, but of all;   230
    What ever celebrates this Festivall
Is common, since the joy thereof is so.
    Nor may your selfe be Priest: But let me goe,
Backe to the Court, and I will lay'it upon
    Such Altars, as prize your devotion.   235

222.   *these*: 'them' (acc. to some MSS).
223.   *where*: 'when' (acc. to a few MSS).
266 ff. The lines to the end are omitted in one MS.
231.   *Festivall*: 'nuptiall' (acc. to a MS).

Epithalamion made at Lincolnes Inne.

The Sun-beames in the East are spred,
Leave, leave, faire Bride, your solitary bed,
  No more shall you returne to it alone,
It nourseth sadnesse, and your bodies print,
Like to a grave, the yielding downe doth dint;   5
     You and your other you meet there anon;
     Put forth, put forth that warme balme-breathing thigh,
Which when next time you in these sheets wil smother,
    There it must meet another,
        Which never was, but must be, oft, more nigh; 10
Come glad from thence, goe gladder than you came,
To day put on perfection, and a womans name.

Daughters of London, you which bee
Our Golden Mines, and furnish'd Treasurie,
  You which are Angels, yet still bring with you   15
Thousands of Angels on your mariage daies,
Help with your presence, and devise to praise
    These rites, which also unto you grow due,
    Conceitedly dresse her, and be assign'd,
By you, fit place for every flower and jewell,   20
    Make her for love fit fewell
        As gay as Flora, and as rich as Inde;

Epithalamion etc. Entitled in some MSS *Epithalamion on a Citizen*, the poem
    may be a mock epithalamion in parody of Spenser's celebrated marriage
    song (§504) or an earnest effort to imitate Spenser (§505).
 5. *dint*: indent.
12. *day*: 'night' (acc. to a MS).
12 (also 24, 36, etc.). The refrain at the end of each stanza suggests that the
    bride is presently 'completed' (§502).
14. *Mines*: also in a bawdy sense.
    furnish'd: well supplied (§170).
16. *Angels*: as above, p. 156, note on 9.
17. *devise*: device, inventiveness.
19. *Conceitedly*: fancifully.
22. *Flora*: as in the previous poem, note on 8.
    Inde: India, suggestive of opulence.

So may shee faire and rich, in nothing lame,
To day put on perfection, and a womans name.

And you frolique Patricians,   25
Sonnes of these Senators wealths deep oceans,
  Ye painted courtiers, barrels of others wits,
Yee country men, who but your beasts love none,
Yee of those fellowships whereof hee's one,
  Of study and play made strange Hermaphrodits,   30
  Here shine; This Bridegroom to the Temple bring.
Loe, in yon path which store of straw'd flowers graceth,
  The sober virgin paceth;
      Except my sight faile, 'tis no other thing;
Weep not nor blush, here is no griefe nor shame,   35
To day put on perfection, and a womans name.

Thy two–leav'd gates faire Temple unfold,
And these two in thy sacred bosome hold,
  Till, mystically joyn'd, but one they bee;
Then may thy leane and hunger-starved wombe   40
Long time expect their bodies and their tombe,
  Long after their owne parents fatten thee;
  All elder claimes, and all cold barrennesse,
All yeelding to new loves bee far for ever,
    Which might these two dissever,   45
      Alwaies, all th'other may each one possesse;
For, the best Bride, best worthy of praise and fame,
To day puts on perfection, and a womans name.

23. *faire and rich, in* (acc. to 1633–69 and several MSS): 'faire, rich, glad, and
     in' (acc. to some MSS).
     lame: imperfect.
26. *Sonnes* (acc. to 1635–69): punning on 'suns'; 'Some' (acc. to 1633).
27. *painted*: ostentatious; also, not what they seem (§166).
29. *fellowships*: the Inns of Court.
30. *Hermaphrodits*: combining opposite functions in one nature, that is, study
     and play (§166).
35. *shame*: 'blame' (acc. to a MS).
37–42. 'A revolting analogy' (§504)?
43. *elder claimes*: previous claims on the love of either partner (§170).
45. *Which*: 'Never' (acc. to a MS).
46. *Alwaies* (acc. to 1633–69): 'All wayes' (acc. to one MS and some modern
     editors).
47. *praise*: 'prayer' (acc. to some MSS).

Winter dayes bring much delight,
Not for themselves, but for they soon bring night; 50
   Other sweets wait thee then these diverse meats,
Other disports than dancing jollities,
Other love tricks than glancing with the eyes,
    But that the Sun still in our halfe Spheare sweates;
      Hee flies in winter, but he now stands still. 55
Yet shadowes turne; Noone point he hath attain'd,
     His steeds will be restrain'd,
       But gallop lively downe the Westerne hill;
Thou shalt, when he hath runne the worlds half frame,
To night put on a perfection, and a womans name. 60

The amorous evening starre is rose,
Why then should not our amorous starre inclose
   Her selfe in her wish'd bed? Release your strings
Musicians, and dancers take some truce
With these your pleasing labours, for great use 65
   As much wearinesse as perfection brings;
    You, and not only you, but all toyl'd beasts
Rest duly; at night all their toyles are dispensed;
But in their beds commenced
    Are other labours, and more dainty feasts; 70
She goes a maid, who, lest she turne the same
To night puts on perfection, and a womans name.

49.   *Winter* (acc. to 1633–69 and some MSS): 'Oh winter' (acc. to several MSS and all modern editors). The wedding occurred in the summer (see note on 55).
50.   *for they*: because they.
51.   *then*: than.
55.   *flies*: i.e. hastens to the west; *stands still*: appears to dally in the summer.
56.   *shadowes turne*: i.e. after the noon hour, when they move in the opposite direction.
57.   *will* (acc. to 1633–69 and most MSS): 'nill' (acc. to a MS and §158; see §233).
59.   *runne* (acc. to 1635–69): 'come' (acc. to 1633 and several MSS).
     worlds (acc. to 1633): 'Heavens' (acc. to 1635–69).
61.   *starre*: Venus.
68.   *dispensed*: dispensed with.
71.   *turne*: return.

Thy virgins girdle now untie,
And in thy nuptiall bed (loves alter) lye
  A pleasing sacrifice; now dispossesse   75
Thee of these chaines and robes which were put on
T'adorne the day, not thee; for thou, alone,
    Like vertue'and truth, art best in nakednesse;
      This bed is onely to virginitie
A grave, but, to a better state, a cradle;   80
Till now thou wast but able
  To be what now thou art; then that by thee
No more be said, *I may bee*, but, *I am*,
To night put on perfection, and a womans name.

Even like a faithfull man content,   85
That this life for a better should be spent,
  So, shee a mothers rich stile doth preferre,
And at the Bridegroomes wish'd approach doth lye,
Like an appointed lambe, when tenderly
    The priest comes on his knees t'embowell her;   90
      Now sleep or watch with more joy; and O light
Of heaven, to morrow rise thou hot, and early;
This Sun will love so dearely
    Her rest, that long, long we shall want her sight;
Wonders are wrought, for shee which had no maime,   95
To night puts on perfection, and a womans name.

74. *alter*: altar.
86. *spent*: extinguished; also, exchanged (§166).
87. *stile*: status, title.
90. *embowell*: disembowel as in the *sacrifice* (75) of a paschal *lambe* (89); but
     also in the sense that something is to be put into the bowels (§207).
93. *This Sun*: the bride.
94. *want*: lack.
95. *maime*: cf. *in nothing lame* (l. 23), inclusive of her virginity; amended to
     'name' (acc. to 1635–69 and most MSS).

Satyres

Donne's five satires reflect one aspect of the traditional *satura* in particular, its roughness in both subject and expression. An altogether different aspect would eventually prove central to the performance of the Augustans, witness Pope's 'versification' of two of Donne's satires (reprinted below, Appendix IV, pp. 500 ff.).

Donne's roughness was not welcomed by the censors since all five satires, initially refused a licence, were permitted to appear only after some lines were removed (see notes to Satyre I, 69–70 and 74–75, as well as Satyre II, 134–36).

Like the elegies, the satires may have been written in the early 1590s, possibly beginning as early as 1593 or mainly in 1587–98 (§526); but they may also have been written periodically, the third satire possibly composed as late as 1620, after Donne took orders (§525). Whatever their actual dates of composition, however, they appear in their final form to constitute 'a unified narrative' intended to be read 'as a whole' (§512). The poem appended to the satires, 'Upon Mr Thomas Coryats Crudities', is but an appendage, representative of those poems which partake of the spirit of the five satires proper.

The uncertain punctuation has on occasion been emended discreetly.

Satyre I.

Away thou fondling motley humorist,
Leave mee, and in this standing woodden chest,
Consorted with these few bookes, let me lye
In prison, and here be coffin'd, when I dye;
Here are Gods conduits, grave Divines; and here   5
Natures Secretary, the Philosopher;
And jolly Statesmen, which teach how to tie
The sinewes of a cities mistique bodie;
Here gathering Chroniclers, and by them stand
Giddie fantastique Poëts of each land.   10
Shall I leave all this constant company,
And follow headlong, wild uncertaine thee?
First sweare by thy best love in earnest
(If thou which lov'st all, canst love any best)
Thou wilt not leave mee in the middle street,   15
Though some more spruce companion thou dost meet
Not though a Captaine do come in thy way
Bright parcell gilt, with forty dead mens pay,
Not though a briske perfum'd piert Courtier
Deigne with a nod, thy courtesie to answer.   20
Nor come a velvet Justice with a long
Great traine of blew coats, twelve, or fourteen strong,
Wilt thou grin or fawne on him, or prepare
A speech to Court his beautious sonne and heire!

Satyre I.
   1. *fondling*: foolish (§514); 'changeling' (acc. to 1635–69 and most MSS).
      motley humorist: changeable zany (§166).
   2. *chest*: chamber for study.
   5. *conduits*: channels.
   6. Referring to Aristotle.
   7. *jolly*: presumptuous; 'wily' (acc. to 1635–69 and a few MSS).
   9. *gathering*: who merely gather information.
  13. *love in earnest*: 'love, here, in earnest' (acc. to 1635–69).
  18. *parcel gilt*: partly gilded.
      dead mens pay: pay for men kept on the muster roll though dead.
  19. *piert*: pert, dapper
  22. *blew coats*: liveried servants.

For better or worse take mee, or leave mee: 25
To take, and leave mee is adultery.
Oh monstrous, superstitious puritan,
Of refin'd manners, yet ceremoniall man,
That when thou meet'st one, with enquiring eyes
Dost search, and like a needy broker prize   30
The silke, and gold he weares, and to that rate
So high or low, dost raise thy formall hat:
That wilt consort none, untill thou have knowne
What lands hee hath in hope, or of his owne,
As though all thy companions should make thee   35
Jointures, and marry thy deare company.
Why should'st thou that dost not onely approve,
But in ranke itchie lust, desire, and love
The nakednesse and barenesse to enjoy,
Of thy plumpe muddy whore, or prostitute boy   40
Hate vertue, though shee be naked, and bare?
At birth, and death, our bodies naked are;
And till our Soules be unapparrelled
Of bodies, they from blisse are banished.
Mans first blest state was naked, when by sinne   45
Hee lost that, yet hee was cloath'd but in beasts skin,
And in this course attire, which I now weare,
With God, and with the Muses I conferre.
But since thou like a contrite penitent,
Charitably warn'd of thy sinnes, dost repent   50

25. *or worse*. 'and worse' (acc. to some MSS).
27. *puritan*: purist.
30. *broker*: pawnbroker.
    prize: appraise.
32. *raise*: 'vaile', i.e. doff (acc. to several MSS).
33. *none*: 'with none' (acc. to some MSS).
36. *Jointures*: estates owned jointly by husband and wife.
38. *ranke itchie*: licentious and hankering (§171).
40. *muddy*: foul.
45. *blest*: 'best' (acc. to some MSS).
46. *yet* (omitted acc. to 1635–69 and a few MSS).
    beasts skin: as related in Genesis 3.21.
47. *course*: coarse.
50. *warn'd* (acc. to 1635): 'warm'd' (acc. to 1633).

These vanities, and giddinesse, loe
I shut my chamber doore, and come, lets goe.
But sooner may a cheape whore, who hath beene
Worne by as many severall men in sinne,
As are black feathers, or musk-colour hose,   55
Name her childs right true father, 'mongst all those:
Sooner may one guesse, who shall beare away
The infant of London, Heire to an India,
And sooner may a gulling weather-Spie
By drawing forth heavens Scheme tell certainly   60
What fashioned hats, or ruffes, or suits next yeare
Our subtile-witted antique youths will weare;
Then thou, when thou depart'st from mee, canst show
Whither, why, when, or with whom thou wouldst go.
But how shall I be pardon'd my offence   65
That thus have sinn'd against my conscience?
Now we are in the street; He first of all
Improvidently proud, creepes to the wall,
And so imprisoned, and hem'd in by mee
Sells for a little state his libertie,   70
Yet though he cannot skip forth now to greet
Every fine silken painted foole we meet,

54. *by*: 'out by' (acc. to 1650–69).
55. Both were fashionable.
58. *infant* (acc. to 1633–54 and most MSS): the 'Infante', a princess or prince
     of Spain; also read as 'Infanta' (acc. to some MSS and most modern
     editors) and even 'Infantry'! (acc. to 1669).
     Heire to an India: i.e. to vast wealth.
59. *gulling weather-Spie*: deceitful weather prophet.
62. *subtile-witted* (acc. to some MSS): 'subtile wittied' (acc. to 1633–54 and a
     few MSS) or 'supple-witted' (acc. to some MSS) or 'giddy-headed'
     (acc. to 1669).
     antique: antic, fantastic.
63. *Then*: than.
     mee: 'hence' (acc. to several MSS).
68. *creepes to the wall*: walks on the pavement's inside position, as befits a
     person of higher social rank.
70. *state*: status; 'room' (acc. to a MS).
     his (acc. to 1635–69 and all MSS): 'high' (acc. to 1633).
71. *skip forth now*: 'now step forth' (acc. to a few MSS).

He them to him with amorous smiles allures,
And grins, smacks, shrugs, and such an itch endures,
As prentises, or schoole-boyes which doe know   75
Of some gay sport abroad, yet dare not goe.
And as fidlers stop lowest, at highest sound,
So to the most brave, stoops hee nigh'st the ground.
But to a grave man, he doth move no more
Then the wise politique horse would heretofore,   80
Or thou O Elephant or Ape wilt doe,
When any names the King of Spaine to you.
Now leaps he upright, Joggs me, and cryes, Do you see
Yonder well favoured youth? Which? Oh, 'tis hee
That dances so divinely; Oh, said, I,   85
Stand still, must you dance here for company?
Hee droopt, wee went, till one (which did excell
Th'Indians, in drinking his Tobacco well)
Met us; they talk'd; I whispered, let'us goe,
'T may be you smell him not, truely I doe;   90
He heares not mee, but, on the other side
A many-coloured Peacock having spide,
Leaves him and mee; I for my lost sheep stay;
He followes, overtakes, goes on the way,
Saying, him whom I last left, all repute   95
For his device, in hansoming a sute,

73. *them* (acc. to 1635 and the MSS): 'then' (acc. to 1633).
77. Since a viol de gamba is held upright, the stops for high notes are literally positioned lowest.
78. *brave*: finely dressed.
80. *Then*: than.
    the wise politique horse: a certain Mr Banks and his performing horse Morocco had become famous c. 1595 (§507).
81–82. Omitted (not necessarily censored) in 1633, possibly because of the thrust against the Spanish monarchy.
81. *Elephant or Ape*: both exhibited in London c. 1594.
88. *Tobacco*: thought at the time to be intended for *drinking*, not smoking.
89. On the symbol ', see above, p. 5.
90. *'T may*: 'May' (acc. to many MSS).
95. *repute*: esteem.
96. *device*: invention.
    hansoming a sute: embellishing a suit.

To judge of lace, pinke, panes, print, cut, and plight,
Of all the Court, to have the best conceit;
Our dull Comedians want him, let him goe;
But Oh, God strengthen thee, why stoop'st thou so?   100
Why, he hath travayld. Long? No, but to me
Which understand none, he doth seeme to be
Perfect French, and Italian; I replyed,
So is the Poxe; He answered not, but spy'd
More men of sort, of parts, and qualities;   105
At last his Love he in a windowe spies,
And like light dew exhal'd, he flings from mee
Violently ravish'd to his lechery.
Many were there, he could command no more;
Hee quarrell'd, fought, bled; and turn'd out of dore   110
   Directly came to mee hanging the head,
   And constantly a while must keepe his bed.

97.   *pinke, panes, print*: decorative hole or eyelet, strips of cloth, crimping of
      pleats.
      plight: state of the clothes; also appearing as 'pleite' or 'pleate' (acc. to
      1635–69 and several MSS).
98.   *Court*: 'towne' (acc. to a MS).
      conceit: conception, notion.
99.   *dull Comedians*: superficial comic actors who base their art on externals
      (clothes).
100. *stoop'st*: 'stopp'st' (acc. to 1635–54).
101. The line's punctuation is erratic in both the MSS and the editions.
104. *Poxe*: syphilis, said to be partial to France and Italy.
105. *of sort, of parts*: of rank and talents (§171).
108. *lechery* (acc. to 1635–69 and all MSS): 'liberty' (acc. to 1633).
109. *were there*: 'there were' (acc. to 1650–69).
      command: possess her exclusively.

Satyre II.

Sir; though (I thanke God for it) I do hate
Perfectly all this towne, yet there's one state
In all ill things so excellently best,
That hate, toward them, breeds pitty towards the rest.
Though Poëtry indeed be such a sinne   5
As I thinke that brings dearths, and Spaniards in,
Though like the Pestilence and old fashion'd love,
Ridlingly it catch men; and doth remove
Never, till it be sterv'd out; yet their state
Is poore, disarm'd, like Papists, not worth hate.   10
One, (like a wretch, which at Barre judg'd as dead,
Yet prompts him which stands next, and cannot reade,
And saves his life) gives ideot actors meanes
(Starving himselfe) to live by his labor'd sceanes;
As in some Organ, Puppits dance above   15
And bellows pant below, which them do move.
One would move Love by rithmes; but witchcrafts charms
Bring not now their old feares, nor their old harmes:
Rammes, and slings now are seely battery,
Pistolets are the best Artillerie.   20
And they who write to Lords, rewards to get,
Are they not like singers at doores for meat?

Satyre II. Entitled in one MS *Law Satyre*.
  4.   *pitty*: cf. below, Satyre III, 1–4.
  6.   *dearths*: famine.
  7.   *Pestilence*: plague.
      and: 'or' (acc. to some MSS).
  8.   *Ridlingly it*: 'It riddlingly' (acc. to most MSS).
 10.   *Papists*: the Roman Catholics were relentlessly persecuted under Elizabeth I.
 13.   *saves his life*: criminals could on occasion escape execution by giving proof of literacy.
      ideot: ignorant; cf. above, p. 148, note on 1, and p. 155, note on 26.
 17.   *move*: cause.
      rithmes: 'rimes' (acc. to most MSS).
 19.   *Rammes*: battering rams.
      seely battery: ineffectual weapons of assault (§166).
 20.   *Pistolets*: see above, p. 157, note on 31.
 22.   *singers at doores*: 'Boyes singing at doores' (acc. to several MSS) or a similar emendation.

And they who write, because all write, have still
That excuse for writing, and for writing ill;
But hee is worst, who (beggarly) doth chaw   25
Others wits fruits, and in his ravenous maw
Rankly digested, doth those things out-spue,
As his owne things; and they are his owne, 'tis true,
For if one eate my meate, though it be knowne
The meate was mine, th'excrement is his owne: 30
But these do mee no harme, nor they which use
To out-doe Dildoes, and out-usure Jewes;
To out-drinke the sea, to out-sweare the Letanie;
Who with sinnes all kindes as familiar bee
As Confessors; and for whose sinfull sake,   35
Schoolemen new tenements in hell must make:
Whose strange sinnes, Canonists could hardly tell
In which Commandements large receit they dwell.
But these punish themselves; the insolence
Of Coscus onely breeds my just offence,   40
Whom time (which rots all, and makes botches poxe,
And plodding on, must make a calfe an oxe)
Hath made a Lawyer, which was (alas) of late
But a scarce Poët; jollier of this state,

25. *chaw*: chew.
27. *Rankly*: coarsely. *digested*: 'disgested' (acc. to some MSS); cf. above, p. 199, note on 37.
32. *out-doe* (acc. to 1633–69 and most MSS): 'out-swive' (acc. to some MSS and §159); both words mean 'out-copulate' (§171).
    Dildoes: artificial phalluses; the word was displaced in 1633 by a dash.
33. *Letanie* (displaced in 1633 by a dash; 'gallant, he' acc. to 1650–54; the word was first provided in 1669).
34. *all* (acc. to 1635–69 and most MSS): 'of all' (acc. to 1633 and a few MSS).
36. *Schoolemen*: medieval scholastic theologians subdivided Hell into as many regions as there are sins.
37. *Canonists*: experts in canon law.
38. *receit*: receptacle, region.
40. *just*: 'great' (acc. to most MSS) or 'harts' (acc. to a MS).
41. *makes botches poxe*: reveals boils to be syphilis.
44. *a scarce* (acc. to most MSS): feeble; 'scarce a' (acc. to 1633–69 and some MSS).
    jollier: prouder.
    this: 'that' (acc. to some MSS) or 'his' (ditto).

Then are new benefic'd ministers, he throwes   45
Like nets, or lime-twigs, wheresoever he goes,
His title of Barrister, on every wench,
And wooes in language of the Pleas, and Bench:
A motion, Lady; Speake Coscus; I have beene
In love, ever since *tricesimo* of the Queene,   50
Continuall claimes I have made, injunctions got
To stay my rivals suit, that hee should not
Proceed, spare mee; In Hillary terme I went,
You said, If I return'd next size in Lent,
I should be in remitter of your grace;   55
In th'interim my letters should take place
Of affidavits: words, words, which would teare
The tender labyrinth of a soft maids eare,
More, more, then ten Sclavonians scolding, more
Then when winds in our ruin'd Abbeyes rore;   60
Which sicke with Poëtrie, and possest with muse
Thou wast, and mad, I hop'd; but men which chuse
Law practise for meere gaine, bold soule, repute
Worse then imbrothel'd strumpets prostitute.

45.   *Then*: than.
      benefic'd: given ecclesiastical preference such as a rectory.
46.   *lime-twigs*: snares.
48.   *Pleas*: the Court of Common Pleas; *Bench*: the higher court of the
      Queen's Bench.
49.   *motion*: an application for a ruling.
50.   *tricesimo*: the thirtieth year of Elizabeth's reign (1588).
51.   *Continuall claimes*: claims formally repeated at intervals; *injunction*:
      orders from Chancery to stay proceedings (§166).
53.   *Hilary terme*: the English legal year's first term, 23 January to 12
      February.
54.   *next*: 'this' (acc. to several MSS).
      size: assize.
55.   *in remitter of*: retrospectively entitled to.
56–57.   *take place* / *Of affidavits*: serve as sworn statements in his absence
      (§166).
59 (also 60, 64, 73).   *then*: than.
59.   *Sclavonians scolding*: Slavs brawling in their cacophonous languages.
61.   *Which*: 'When' (acc. to 1654 and some MSS) or 'Then' (acc. to a MS).
63.   *meere*: 'more' (acc. to a MS).
      repute: should be esteemed to be.

Now like an owelike watchman, hee must walke   65
His hand still at a bill, now he must talke
Idly, like prisoners, which whole months will sweare
That onely suretiship hath brought them there,
And to every suitor lye in every thing,
Like a Kings favourite, yea like a King;   70
Like a wedge in a blocke, wring to the barre,
Bearing like Asses, and more shamelesse farre
Then carted whores, lye, to the grave Judge; for
Bastardy abounds not in Kings titles, nor
Symonie and Sodomy in Churchmens lives,   75
As these things do in him; by these he thrives.
Shortly (as the sea) hee will compasse all the land,
From Scots, to Wight; from Mount, to Dover strand.
And spying heires melting with luxurie,
Satan will not joy at their sinnes, as hee.   80
For as a thrifty wench scrapes kitching-stuffe,
And barrelling the droppings, and the snuffe,
Of wasting candles, which in thirty yeare
(Relique-like kept) perchance buyes wedding geare;
Peecemeale he gets lands, and spends as much time   85

66.   *bill*: his halberd.
68.   *suretiship*: standing surety for someone who defaults.
69–70 (also 74–75). Censored, these lines were represented in 1633 by dashes.
70.   *Like*: 'Lye like' (acc. to a MS).
        yea (acc. to most MSS): 'or' (acc. to 1635–69).
71–72. The numismatic image concerns an ingot shaped in a mould (*blocke*):
        the *wedge* is the lower die of the anvil, the *barre* the upper one; *Asses* is the
        plural of the Roman bronze coin *as* (§509; cf. §§158, 171, 188).
73.   *carted*: transported in a cart.
77.   *compasse*: encompass.
        the land (acc. to 1633–69): 'our land' (acc. to most MSS).
78.   North (Scotland), south (the Isle of *Wight*), west (St Michael's *Mount* in
        Cornwall), east (the shores of *Dover*).
79.   *luxurie*: lust; 'gluttonie' (acc. to a few MSS).
82.   *barrelling*: storing up.
        snuffe: see above, p. 155, note on 24.
84.   *Relique-like* (acc. to most MSS): 'Reliquely' (acc. to 1633–69 and a few
        MSS).
        geare: 'chear' (acc. to 1669).

Wringing each Acre, as men pulling prime.
In parchment then, large as his fields, hee drawes
Assurances, bigge, as gloss'd civill lawes,
So huge, that men (in our times forwardnesse)
Are Fathers of the Church for writing lesse.   90
These hee writes not; nor for these written payes,
Therefore spares no length; as in those first dayes
When Luther was profest, He did desire
Short *Pater nosters*, saying as a Fryer
Each day his beads, but having left those lawes,   95
Addes to Christs prayer, the Power and glory clause.
But when he sells or changes land, he'impaires
His writings, and (unwatch'd) leaves out, *ses heires*,
As slily as any Commentator goes by
Hard words, or sense; or in Divinity   100
As controverters, in vouch'd Texts, leave out
Shrewd words, which might against them cleare the doubt.
Where are those spred woods which cloth'd hertofore
Those bought lands? not built, nor burnt within dore.
Where's th'old landlords troops, and almes? In great hals 105
Carthusian fasts, and fulsome Bachanalls

86. *Wringing*: wresting.
     men: 'Maids' (acc. to 1669).
     pulling prime: drawing a winning hand in the card game of primero.
87. *drawes*: draws up.
88. *Assurances*: deeds of conveyance.
     gloss'd civill lawes: commentaries upon the civil law (§166).
89. *times forwardnesse*: advanced days.
94–96. *Pater nosters*: the prayer 'Our Father which art in heaven . . .' (Luke
     11.2–4), which Luther while a monk preferred *short* but later lengthened
     by adding the *clause* 'For thine is the Kingdom and the Power and the
     Glory'.
97. On the symbol ', see above, p. 5.
98. *ses heires*: 'his heirs', the phrase which once omitted from the deed of
     conveyance allows the lawyer to secure the land for himself.
99. *goes by*: bypasses.
101. *controverters*: controversialists.
     vouch'd: said to be authoritative.
105. The line is punctuated variously in both MSS and editions.
     troops, and almes: the old landlord's employees and beneficiaries.
106. *Carthusian*: the monastic order noted for its austerity.

Equally I hate; meanes blesse; in rich mens homes
I bid kill some beasts, but no Hecatombs,
None starve, none surfet so; But (Oh) we allow,
Good workes as good, but out of fashion now,　　　　110
Like old rich wardrops; but my words none drawes
Within the vast reach of th'huge statute lawes.

Satyre III.

Kinde pitty chokes my spleene; brave scorn forbids
Those teares to issue which swell my eye-lids;
I must not laugh, nor weepe sinnes, and be wise,
Can railing then cure these worne maladies?
Is not our Mistresse faire Religion,　　　　　　　　5
As worthy of all our Soules devotion,
As vertue was to the first blinded age?
Are not heavens joyes as valiant to asswage
Lusts, as earths honour was to them? Alas,
As wee do them in meanes, shall they surpasse　　10
Us in the end, and shall thy fathers spirit

Satyre II.
107.　*blesse*: 'blest' (acc. to 1635–69 and a few MSS).
108.　*Hecatombs*: wholesale slaughters.
110.　*Good workes*: see above, p. 106, note on 19–21.
111.　*wardrops*: wardrobes.

Satyre III. 'If you would teach a scholar in the highest form how to *read*',
　　　Coleridge advised, 'take Donne, and of Donne this satire. When he has
　　　learnt to read Donne, with all the force and meaning which are involved
　　　in the words, then send him to Milton, and he will stalk on like a master
　　　enjoying his walk' (§210).
　　　　　The satire is entitled in one MS *Of Religion*.
　1.　*chokes*: 'checks' (acc. to 1635–54).
　　　spleene: commonly regarded as the seat of both melancholy and mirth.
　4.　*Can*: 'May' (acc. to some MSS).
　　　worne: ingrained.
　7.　*to* (acc. to 1635–69 and most MSS): 'in' (acc. to 1633 and a few MSS).
　　　age: i.e. the pre-Christian era, *blinded* because it was not privy to
　　　revealed truth (see note on 9/10).
　8.　*valiant*: strong.
　9.　*honour was*: 'honours were' (acc. to some MSS).
　9 (also 10).　*them*: the ancients, whom *wee* surpass *in meanes* because of the
　　　truth revealed to us.

Meete blinde Philosophers in heaven, whose merit
Of strict life may be imputed faith, and heare
Thee, whom hee taught so easie wayes and neare
To follow, damn'd? O if thou dar'st, feare this.   15
This feare great courage, and high valour is;
Dar'st thou ayd mutinous Dutch, and dar'st thou lay
Thee in ships woodden Sepulchers, a prey
To leaders rage, to stormes, to shot, to dearth?
Dar'st thou dive seas, and dungeons of the earth?   20
Hast thou couragious fire to thaw the ice
Of frozen North discoveries? and thrise
Colder then Salamanders, like divine
Children in th'oven, fires of Spaine, and the line,
Whose countries limbecks to our bodies bee,   25
Canst thou for gaine beare? and must every hee
Which cryes not, Goddesse, to thy Mistresse, draw,
Or eat thy poysonous words? courage of straw!
O desperate coward, wilt thou seeme bold, and
To thy foes and his (who made thee to stand   30
Sentinell in his worlds garrison) thus yeeld,
And for the forbidden warres, leave th'appointed field?

13. *may be*: the caution is well advised, for the possibility of counting one's decent life ('good works') in lieu of faith would be anathema to most Protestants (cf. above, p. 106, note on 19–21).
14. *so easie wayes and neare*: 'wayes easie and neere' (acc. to several MSS).
17. *mutinous Dutch*: the Low Countries had been attempting to be freed from their Spanish conquerors since 1568, not without *ayd* from England.
    Dutch, and dar'st: 'Dutch? dar'st' (acc. to several MSS).
22. *North discoveries*: expeditions to discover the Northwest Passage.
23. *then*: than.
    Salamanders: popularly regarded as cold-blooded enough to withstand fire.
24. *Children in th'oven*: the three cast into a furnace by Nebuchadnezzar (Daniel 3.20 ff.).
    fires of Spain: the autos-da-fé of the Spanish Inquisition.
    the line: the equator.
25. *limbecks*: see above, p. 91, note on 21.
27. *draw*: i.e. his sword.
30 (also 35). *his*: God's.
31. *Sentinell*: 'Souldier' (acc. to several MSS).
    his: 'this' (acc. to 1669 and a few MSS).
32. *forbidden*: 'forbid' (acc. to 1635–69).

Know thy foe, the foule devill h'is, whom thou
Strivest to please: for hate, not love, would allow
Thee faine, his whole Realme to be quit; and as   35
The worlds all parts wither away and passe,
So the worlds selfe, thy other lov'd foe, is
In her decrepit wayne, and thou loving this,
Dost love a withered and worne strumpet; last,
Flesh (it selfes death) and joyes which flesh can taste,   40
Thou lovest; and thy faire goodly soule, which doth
Give this flesh power to taste joy, thou dost loath;
Seeke true religion. O where? Mirreus
Thinking her unhous'd here, and fled from us,
Seekes her at Rome, there, because hee doth know   45
That shee was there a thousand yeares agoe,
He loves her ragges so, as wee here obey
The statecloth where the Prince sate yesterday,
Crants to such brave Loves will not be inthrall'd,
But loves her onely, who at Geneva is call'd   50
Religion, plaine, simple, sullen, yong,
Contemptuous, yet unhansome. As among

33–34. The lines read variously in the MSS and the editions; I follow 1633.
35. *quit*: 'rid' (acc. to many MSS).
36–38. On nature's decay, more fully averred in *The First Anniversary*, see below, pp. 327 ff.
38. *wayne*: wane, decline.
40. *it selfes* (acc. to 1635–69 and most MSS): 'it selfe' (acc. to 1633 and a few MSS).
43 ff. The seekers after *true religion* are: the Catholic *Mirreus*, the Calvinist *Crants* (49), the Anglican *Graius* (55), the separatist *Phrygius* (62 and note), and the Erastian *Graccus* (65 and note). Cf. Holy Sonnet XVIII, below, p. 446.
44. *here*: in England, where Catholicism had been *unhous'd* by Henry VIII.
47. *He*: 'And' (acc. to 1635–54).
     her (acc. to most MSS): 'the' (acc. to 1633–69 and a few MSS).
     ragges: remnants of truth beneath the ceremonial trappings.
48. *statecloth*: the canopy over the chair of state.
49. *Crants*: 'Grants' (acc. to a few MSS) or 'Crantz' or 'Crates' or 'Morus' (acc. to individual MSS).
50. *Geneva*: where Calvin erected his theocracy.
51. *sullen*: dismal; 'solemne' (acc. to a few MSS).

Lecherous humors, there is one that judges
No wenches wholsome, but course country drudges.
Graius stayes still at home here, and because   55
Some Preachers, vile ambitious bauds, and lawes
Still new like fashions, bid him thinke that shee
Which dwels with us, is onely perfect, hee
Imbraceth her, whom his Godfathcrs will
Tender to him, being tender, as Wards still   60
Take such wives as their Guardians offer, or
Pay valewes. Carelesse Phrygius doth abhorre
All, because all cannot be good, as one
Knowing some women whores, dares marry none.
Graccus loves all as one, and thinkes that so   65
As women do in divers countries goe
In divers habits, yet are still one kinde;
So doth, so is Religion; and this blind-
nesse too much light breeds; but unmoved thou
Of force must one, and forc'd but one allow;   70
And the right; aske thy father which is shee,
Let him aske his; though truth and falshood bee
Neare twins, yet truth a little elder is;
Be busic to seeke her, beleeve mee this,
Hee's not of none, nor worst, that seekes the bcst.   75
To adore, or scorne an image, or protest,

53. *humors*: dispositions (see below, p. 336, note on 241).
54. *course*: coarse.
57. *bid* (acc. to the MSS): 'bids' (acc. to 1633–69).
60. *Tender to him*: present to him.
62. *valewes*: fines ('the value of the marriage') imposed upon wards who
     refused a marriage arranged by their guardians.
     Phrygius: 'careless' in that, as a separatist sectarian, he cares for no one
     else (see §515).
65. *Graccus*: an Erastian, holding that the religion of the monarch should
     determine the religion of the country (§164).
70. *Of force*: of necessity.
     forc'd: when compelled to choose.
73. *elder*: because it pre-existed the *falshood* ushered in by the Fall of Man.
75. *not of none, nor worst*: not of no faith, nor the worst faith (*ALC*).
76. *adore*: like Catholics; *scorne an image*: like all anti-Catholics; *protest*: like
     Protestants.

May all be bad; doubt wisely, in strange way
To stand inquiring right, is not to stray;
To sleepe, or runne wrong, is: on a huge hill,
Cragg'd, and steep, Truth stands, and hee that will   80
Reach her, about must, and about must goe;
And what the hills suddennes resists, winne so;
Yet strive so, that before age, deaths twilight,
Thy Soule rest, for none can worke in that night.
To will, implyes delay, therefore now doe.   85
Hard deeds, the bodies paines; hard knowledge too
The mindes indeavours reach, and mysteries
Are like the Sunne, dazzling, yet plaine to all eyes;
Keepe the truth which thou hast found; men do not stand
In so ill case here, that God hath with his hand   90
Sign'd Kings blanck-charters to kill whom they hate,
Nor are they Vicars, but hangmen to Fate.
Foole and wretch, wilt thou let thy Soule be tyed
To mans lawes, by which she shall not be tryed
At the last day? Will it then boot thee   95
To say a Philip, or a Gregory,
A Harry, or a Martin taught thee this?

---

78.   *stray*: 'stay' (acc. to some MSS).
79.   *huge*: 'high' (ditto).
80.   *Cragg'd*: 'Ragged' or 'Rugged' (ditto).
      stands: 'dwells' (ditto).
81.   *about must goe*: 'about goe' (ditto).
84.   *Soule*: 'minde' (acc. to most MSS).
      that: 'the' (acc. to 1635–54).
      that night: cf. 'the night cometh when no man can work' (John 9.4).
90.   *case*: 'case here' (acc. to several MSS).
92.   *hangmen to*: executors of any orders from.
93.   *Soule*: 'selfe' (acc. to a MS).
94.   *not* (omitted acc. to 1635–54).
95.   *the last day*: the Last Judgement.
      Will it (acc. to 1633 and some MSS): 'Or will it' (acc. to 1635–69) or 'Oh will it' (acc. to many MSS and all modern editors).
      boot: profit; 'serve' (acc. to several MSS).
96–97. The Catholic *Philip* II of Spain and Pope *Gregory* XIII or XIV, and the Protestant Henry VIII of England and *Martin* Luther: the foremost secular and religious leaders of sixteenth-century Europe.
97.   *thee*: 'me' (acc. to 1669 and a few MSS).

Is not this excuse for mere contraries,
Equally strong? cannot both sides say so?
That thou mayest rightly obey power, her bounds know;
Those past, her nature, and name is chang'd; to be
Then humble to her is idolatrie;
As streames are, Power is; those blest flowers that dwell
At the rough streames calme head, thrive and do well,
But having left their roots, and themselves given   105
To the streames tyrannous rage, alas are driven
Through mills, and rockes, and woods, and at last, almost
Consum'd in going, in the sea are lost:
So perish Soules, which more chuse mens unjust
Power from God claym'd, then God himselfe to trust.   110

Satyre IV.

Well; I may now receive, and die; My sinne
Indeed is great, but I have beene in
A Purgatorie, such as fear'd hell is
A recreation, and scant map of this.
My minde, neither with prides itch, nor yet hath been   5
Poyson'd with love to see, or to bee seene,
I had no suit there, nor new suite to shew,
Yet went to Court; But as Glaze which did goe

Satyre III.
  98. *mere*: absolute.
  99. *strong*: 'true' or 'strange' (acc. to individual MSS).
103–10. The image, it has been said, 'unites all the varying emphases of the
     five satires' (§195).
104. *do*: 'prove' (acc. to many MSS).
105. *left*: 'lost' (acc. to a few MSS).
107. *and rockes*: 'rocks' (acc. to 1635–69 and most MSS).
110. *then*: than.

Satyre IV. Entitled in one MS *Of the Courte*.
  1. *receive*: i.e. Holy Communion (§171).
  2. *I*: 'yet' (acc. to 1635–69 and a few MSS).
  4. *and scant*: 'to and scarce' (acc. to a MS and §158).
  8. *Glaze*: 'Glare' (acc. to 1635–69 and severall MSS), in either case
     fictitious.

To'a Masse in jest, catch'd, was faine to disburse
The hundred markes, which is the Statutes curse,   10
Before he scapt; So'it pleas'd my destinie
(Guilty of my sin of going), to thinke me
As prone to all ill, and of good as forget-
full, as proud, as lustfull, and as much in debt,
As vaine, as witlesse, and as false as they   15
Which dwell at Court, for once going that way.
Therefore I suffered this; Towards me did runne
A thing more strange, then on Niles slime, the Sunne
E'r bred, or all which into Noahs Arke came:
A thing, which would have pos'd Adam to name,   20
Stranger then seaven Antiquaries studies,
Then Africks Monsters, Guianaes rarities,
Stranger then strangers; One, who for a Dane,
In the Danes Massacre had sure beene slaine,
If he had liv'd then; And without helpe dies,   25
When next the Prentises 'gainst Strangers rise.
One, whom the watch at noone lets scarce goe by,
One, to whom, the examining Justice sure would cry,

9.   On the symbol ', here and throughout, see above, p. 5.
     a (omitted acc. to 1635–69 and some MSS).
10. *hundred markes*: the statutory fine for attending Catholic Mass.
12. *of*: 'in' (acc. to 1635–54).
14. The second *as* (omitted acc. to 1635–69 and many MSS).
18 (also 21, 22, 23). *then*: than.
18–19. *on Niles slime . . . bred*: the Egyptian sun was anciently believed to
     generate many strange creatures out of the Nile's mud, not unlike some
     of those included in Noah's Ark.
20. *pos'd*: puzzled even Adam, who was otherwise able to name every
     creature (Genesis 2.19–20).
21. *seaven*: i.e. several.
22. *Guianaes rarities*: as recently reported in Sir Walter Ralegh's *The Discov-
     ery of Guiana* (1596).
23. *strangers*: foreigners, so disliked in Donne's time that, if Danes, they
     would have been exterminated as in *the Danes Massacre* (24) in 1012 or in
     the riot of the apprentices (26) in 1517.
27. *the watch at noone*: i.e. even the guard at full daylight.

Sir, by your priesthood tell me what you are.
His cloths were strange, though coarse; and black,
   though bare;   30
Sleeveless his jerkin was, and it had beene
Velvet, but 'twas now (so much ground was seene)
Become Tufftaffatie; and our children shall
See it plaine Rashe awhile, then nought at all.
This thing hath travail'd, and saith, speakes all tongues   35
And only knoweth what to all States belongs.
Made of th'Accents, and best phrase of all these,
He speakes one language; If strange meats displease,
Art can deceive, or hunger force my tast,
But Pedants motley tongue, souldiers bumbast,   40
Mountebankes drugtongue, nor the termes of law
Are strong enough preparatives, to draw
Me to beare this, yet I must be content
With his tongue: in his tongue, call'd complement:
In which he can win widdowes, and pay scores,   45
Make men speake treason, cosen subtlest whores,
Out-flatter favorites, or outlie either
Jovius, or Surius, or both together.

29. *priesthood*: Jesuits and seminary priests were declared traitors in procla-
     mations from 1581 ff.
30. *bare*: threadbare.
31. *jerkin*: short coat, usually sleeved.
33. *Tufftaffatie*: tafetta or thin glossy silk, tufted.
34. *Rashe*: a smooth silk fabric.
35. *This*: 'The' (acc. to 1635–69).
38. *one* (acc. to most MSS and all editions): 'no' (acc. to some editors: §§158,
     163).
39. *Art*: the culinary one.
40. The confused jargon of the learned, and the bragging one of soldiers.
41. The jargon of quack-doctors, and that of lawyers.
43. *beare*: 'heare' (acc. to 1669).
44. *complement*: compliment, in a pejorative sense (cf. l. 148).
45. *scores*: accounts.
46. *cosen*: cheat.
47. *or*: 'and' (acc. to several MSS).
48. The Catholic historians Paolo Giovio (d. 1552) and Laurentius Surius
     (d. 1578) were regarded by Protestants as biased.

He names mee, and comes to mee; I whisper, God!
How have I sinn'd, that thy wraths furious rod,   50
This fellow chuseth me? He saith, Sir,
I love your judgement; Whom doe you prefer,
For the best linguist? And I seelily
Said, that I thought Calepines Dictionarie;
Nay, but of men, most sweet Sir. Beza then,   55
Some Jesuites, and two reverend men
Of our two Academies, I named; There
He stopt mee, and said; Nay, your Apostles were
Good pretty linguists, and so Panurge was;
Yet a poore gentleman; all these may passe   60
By travaile. Then, as if he would have sold
His tongue, he praised it, and such wonders told
That I was faine to say, If you'had liv'd, Sir,
Time enough to have beene Interpreter
To Babells bricklayers, sure the Tower had stood.   65
He adds, If of court life you knew the good,
You would leave lonenesse; I said, not alone

50.   *rod*: i.e. the courtier, ironically viewed as God's scourge.
51.   *chuseth*: 'chaseth' (acc. to several MSS).
53.   *seelily*: naively.
54.   *Calepines Dictionarie*: the much amended polyglot dictionary edited by Ambrose Calepine (d. 1511).
55.   *Beza*: the French Calvinist Théodore de Bèze, industrious author and translator of the Greek New Testament into Latin (1556).
56.   *Some*: 'Some other' or 'two other' (acc. to individual MSS).
56–57.   The two *Academies* are the universities of Oxford and Cambridge; the *two reverend men* are identified in a MS as John Reynolds, President of Corpus Christi College, Oxford, from 1598, and Lancelot Andrewes, Master of Pembroke College, Cambridge, from 1589, who alike helped with the Authorized Version of the Bible in 1611 (§527).
59.   *linguists*: because of the gift of tongues bestowed on them at Pentecost (Acts 2.4–6).
     Panurge: the multilingual friend of Rabelais's Pantagruel (II, 9).
61.   *travaile*: travel and toil.
62.   *wonders* (acc. to 1635–69 and most MSS): 'words' (acc. to 1633 and a few MSS).
65.   *Tower*: i.e. of Babel (Genesis 11.1–9).
66.   *adds*: 'answears' (acc. to a MS).
67.   *lonenesse* (acc. to 1635–69 and some MSS): 'lonelinesse' (acc. to 1633 and a few MSS).
     alone: unique.

My lonenesse is, but Spartanes fashion,
To teach by painting drunkards, doth not last
Now; Aretines pictures have made few chast;   70
No more can Princes courts, though there be few
Better pictures of vice, teach me vertue;
He, like to a high strecht lute string squeakt, O Sir,
'Tis sweet to talke of Kings. At Westminster,
Said I, The man that keepes the Abbey tombes,   75
And for his price doth with who ever comes,
Of all our Harries, and our Edwards talke,
From King to King and all their kin can walke:
Your eares shall heare nought, but Kings; your eyes meet
Kings only; The way to it, is Kingstreet.   80
He smack'd, and cry'd, He's base, Mechanique, coarse,
So are all your Englishmen in their discourse.
Are not your Frenchmen neate? Mine? as you see,
I have but one Frenchman, looke, hee followes mee.
Certes they are neatly cloth'd. I, of this minde am,   85
Your only wearing is your Grogaram.
Not so Sir, I have more. Under this pitch
He would not flie; I chaff'd him; But as Itch
Scratch'd into smart, and as blunt iron ground
Into an edge, hurts worse: So, I (foole) found,   90
Crossing hurt mee; To fit my sullennesse,

68–69. The Spartans dissuaded their young men from drunkenness by show-
     ing them drunk slaves.
69.   *last*: 'taste' (acc. to 1635–54).
70.   Pietro Aretino had in 1524 written obscene sonnets to accompany the
     erotic paintings of Giulio Romano.
80.   *Kingstreet*: the street from Charing Cross to Westminster Palace.
81.   *smack'd*: i.e. his lips.
     Mechanique: low, vulgar.
83.   *Mine?* (acc. to 1635–54 and the MSS): 'Fine,' (acc. to 1633).
84.   *Frenchman*: French servant; emended to 'Sir' (acc. to 1635–69).
85.   *Certes*: certainly.
86.   *your*: 'this' (acc. to many MSS).
     Grogaram: grosgrain, a fabric largely of silk.
87.   *pitch*: the highest point of a trained falcon's ascent.
88.   *chaff'd*: teased.

He to another key, his stile doth addresse,
And askes, what newes? I tell him of new playes.
He takes my hand, and as a Still, which staies
A Sembriefe, 'twixt each drop, he nigardly,   95
As loth to enrich mee, so tells many a lie.
More then ten Hollensheads, or Halls, or Stowes,
Of triviall houshold trash he knowes; He knowes
When the Queene frown'd, or smil'd, and he knowes what
A subtle States-man may gather of that;   100
He knowes who loves; whom; and who by poyson
Hasts to an Offices reversion;
He knowes who'hath sold his land, and now doth beg
A licence, old iron, bootes, shooes, and egge-
shels to transport; Shortly boyes shall not play   105
At span-counter, or blow-point, but they pay
Toll to some Courtier; And wiser then all us,
He knowes what Ladie is not painted; Thus
He with home-meats tries me; I belch, spue, spit,
Looke pale, and sickly, like a Patient; Yet   110
He thrusts on more; And as if he'undertooke

92.   *addresse*: 'dresse' (acc. to 1635–69).
94.   *Still*: distilling apparatus.
      staies: pauses.
95.   *Sembriefe*: semibreve, extending the length of a whole note.
97.   *then*: than.
      Hollensheads etc.: the sixteenth-century chroniclers Raphael Holinshed,
      Edward Hall, and John Stow.
98.   The line is punctuated variously in the MSS and the editions.
102. *an Offices reversion*: the succession of some important position of state
      (§166).
104. *and*: 'or' (acc. to several MSS).
105. *transport*: import and export (cf. l. 170).
106. *span-counter*, *blow-point*: children's games.
      they (acc. to most MSS): 'shall' (acc. to 1633–69).
107. *then*: than.
108. *what*: 'which' (acc. to many MSS).
      not painted: i.e. but in fact is ill.
109. *home-meats*: domestic gossip.
      tries: 'cloyes' (acc. to 1635–69).
111. *on more*: 'more' or 'me more' or 'me' (acc. to various MSS).
      he: 'hee had' (acc. to 1635–69).

To say Gallo-Belgicus without booke
Speakes of all States, and deeds, that have been since
The Spaniards came, to the losse of Amyens.
Like a bigge wife, at sight of loathed meat,   115
Readie to travaile: So I sigh, and sweat
To heare this Makeron talke in vaine: For yet,
Either my humour, or his owne to fit,
He like a priviledg'd spie, whom nothing can
Discredit, Libells now 'gainst each great man.   120
He names a price for every office paid;
He saith, our warres thrive ill, because delai'd;
That offices are entail'd, and that there are
Perpetuities of them, lasting as farre
As the last day; And that great officers,   125
Doe with the Pirates share, and Dunkirkers.
Who wasts in meat, in clothes, in horse, he notes;
Who loves Whores, who boyes, and who goats.
I more amas'd then Circes prisoners, when
They felt themselves turne beasts, felt my selfe then   130
Becomming Traytor, and mee thought I saw
One of our Giant Statutes ope his jaw

---

112. *Gallo-Belgicus*: see the relevant epigram above, p. 131.
113. *have* (acc. to 1635): 'hath' (acc. to 1633).
114. *came*: with the Armada in 1588.
      the losse of Amyens: Amiens fell to the Spaniards in March 1597 but was
      soon recaptured by the French.
115. *bigge*: pregnant.
116. *to travaile*: to go into labour.
      sigh: 'belche' (acc. to a few MSS).
117. *Makeron*: blockhead; also dandy.
118. *humor*: disposition (see below, p. 336, note on 241).
119. *priviledg'd spie*: the informer who entraps others by uttering indiscre-
      tions himself.
123–25. The offices of state have been settled (*entail'd*) in perpetuity, to the
      Last Judgement (*day*).
123. The second *that* (omitted acc. to 1635–54).
126. *Dunkirkers*: pirates headquartered in Dunkirk.
129. *then*: than.
      Circes prisoners: Odysseus and his companions (*Odyssey*, X, 203 ff.).
132. *Giant Statutes*: statutes against treason; but perhaps orders such as the
      1599 prohibition of the further printing of satires without special per-
      mission (§512).

To sucke me in; for hearing him, I found
That as burnt venome Leachers do grow sound
By giving others their soares, I might growe   135
Guilty, and he free: Therefore I did shew
All signes of loathing; But since I am in,
I must pay mine, and my forefathers sinne
To the last farthing; Therefore to my power
Toughly and stubbornly I beare this crosse; But the'houre 140
Of mercy now was come; He tries to bring
Me to pay a fine to scape his torturing,
And saies, Sir, can you spare me; I said, willingly;
Nay, Sir, can you spare me a crowne? Thankfully I
Gave it, as Ransome; But as fidlers, still,   145
Though they be paid to be gone, yet needs will
Thrust one more jigge upon you: so did hee
With his long complementall thankes vexe me.
But he is gone, thankes to his needy want,
And the prerogative of my Crowne: Scant   150
His thankes were ended, when I, (which did see
All the court fill'd with more strange things then hee)
Ran from thence with such or more haste, then one
Who feares more actions, doth haste from prison;
At home in wholesome solitarinesse   155
My precious soule began, the wretchednesse

134–36. *That . . .free*: censored, these lines are represented in 1633 by dashes.
134. *venome*: 'venom'd' (acc. to many MSS).
      Leachers: lechers afflicted with syphilis (*burnt*) were popularly expected
      to be freed of it on infecting someone else (§171).
137. *in*: involved (§171).
139. *my power*: i.e. the limits of my endurance.
141. *mercy now*: 'redemption now' or 'my redemption' (acc. to various MSS).
144. *a crowne*: a coin, five shillings.
148. *complementall*: cf. note on 44.
150. *the prerogative of my Crowne*: the rights of the sovereign, in this case the
      speaker's money (144).
      Scant: scarcely.
152 (also 153). *then*: than.
154. *actions*: lawsuits.
      haste (acc. to 1633–69 and some MSS); 'make' (acc. to most MSS and all
      modern editors).
156. *precious*: 'piteous' (acc. to 1635–69 and most MSS).

Of suiters at court to mourne, and a trance
Like his, who dreamt he saw hell, did advance
It selfe on mee, Such men as he saw there,
I saw at court, and worse, and more; Low feare   160
Becomes the guiltie, not the accuser; Then,
Shall I, nones slave, of high borne, or rais'd men
Feare frownes? And, my Mistresse Truth, betray thee
To th'huffing braggart, puft Nobility? ─
No, no, Thou which since yesterday hast beene   165
Almost about the whole world, hast thou seene,
O Sunne, in all thy journey, Vanitie,
Such as swells the bladder of our court? I
Thinke he which made your waxen garden, and
Transported it from Italy to stand   170
With us, at London, flouts our Presence, for
Just such gay painted things, which no sappe, nor
Tast have in them, ours are; And naturall
Some of the stocks are, their fruits, bastard all.
'Tis ten a clock and past; All whom the Mues,   175
Baloune, Tennis, Dyet, or the stewes,
Had all the morning held, now the second
Time made ready, that day, in flocks, are found

158. *his*: Dante's, in the *Inferno*.
159. *on*: 'o'er' (acc. to 1635–69 and several MSS).
164. *th'* (acc. to 1669 and most MSS; omitted acc. to 1633–54).
168. *swells the bladder of*: puffs up (cf. *puft* in l. 164).
169. *your*: 'yon' or 'the' (acc. to various MSS).
169–71. *waxen garden*: artificial gardens in wax had apparently been exhibited
         by Italian puppeteers.
170. *Transported*: 'Transplanted' (acc. to several MSS).
171. *flouts*: mocks.
      Presence: 'Court here' (acc. to several MSS) or 'Courtiers' (acc. to
      1635–69).
173. *naturall*: also in the sense of illegitimate.
174. *stocks*: stems; also, lines of descent.
175. *ten a clock*: see above, p. 197, note on 111.
      Mues: stables or riding schools.
176. *Baloune*: balloon, here a game much like handball.
      Dyet: eating.
      stewes: brothels.
178. *are*: 'were' (acc. to 1635–54).

In the Presence, and I, (God pardon mee.)
As fresh, and sweet their Apparrells be, as bee   180
The fields they sold to buy them; For a King
Those hose are, cry the flatterers; And bring
Them next weeke to the Theatre to sell;
Wants reach all states; Me seemes they doe as well
At stage, as court; All are players, who e'r lookes   185
(For themselves dare not goe) o'r Cheapside books,
Shall finde their wardrops Inventory; Now,
The Ladies come; As Pirats, which doe know
That there came weak ships fraught with Cutchannel,
The men board them; and praise, as they thinke, well,   190
Their beauties; they the mens wits; Both are bought.
Why good wits ne'r weare scarlet gownes, I thought
This cause, These men, mens wits for speeches buy,
And women buy all reds which scarlets die.
He call'd her beauty limetwigs, her haire net.   195
She feares her drugs ill laid, her haire loose set;
Would not Heraclitus laugh to see Macrine,
From hat, to shooe, himselfe at doore refine,
As if the Presence were a Moschite, and lift
His skirts and hose, and call his clothes to shrift,   200

179.   *Presence*: i.e. of the entire court.
       and I: I was there too.
180.   *their*: 'th'' (acc. to several MSS).
184.   *Wants reach all states*: the need for such goods affects individuals of all
       ranks.
       seemes: 'thinks' (acc. to several MSS).
186.   *Cheapside books*: the ledgers of the clothiers in the market district of
       Cheapside.
187.   *wardrops*: 'wardrobes' (acc. to 1635–69).
188.   *doe*: 'did' (acc. to several MSS).
189.   *Cutchannel*: cochineal, an expensive scarlet dye.
192.   *scarlet gownes*: ceremonial robes of the highly placed.
195.   *limetwigs* (snares: cf. above, p. 221, l. 46), *net*: here, trite compliments.
196.   *drugs ill laid*: make-up badly applied.
       loose: 'ill' (acc. to a MS).
197.   *Heraclitus*: normally described as 'the weeping philosopher' (c. 500 B.C.).
       Macrine: fictitious.
199.   *Moschite*: mosque, which one enters after removing his shoes.
200.   *skirts and hose*: 'cloake aloft' (acc. to a MS).
       shrift: confession.

Making them confesse not only mortall
Great staines and holes in them; but veniall
Feathers and dust, wherewith they fornicate:
And then by *Durers* rules survay the state
Of his each limbe, and with strings the odds trye   205
Of his neck to his legge, and wast to thighes.
So in immaculate clothes, and Symetrie
Perfect as circles, with such nicetie
As a young Preacher at his first time goes
To preach, he enters, and a Lady which owes   210
Him not so much as good will, he arrests,
And unto her protests protests protests
So much as at Rome would serve to have throwne
Ten Cardinalls into the Inquisition;
And whispered by Jesu, so often, that A   215
Pursevant would have ravish'd him away
For saying of our Ladies psalter; But 'tis fit
That they each other plague, they merit it.
But here comes Glorius that will plague them both,
Who, in the other extreme, only doth   220
Call a rough carelessenesse, good fashion;
Whose cloak his spurres teare; whom he spits on

201–3. The clothes' stains and holes are *mortall* because irreparable; their
'fornication' with feathers and dust, which can be brushed away,
amounts but to *veniall* (pardonable) sins.
204–6. *rules*: Albrecht Dürer's in his books *Of Human Proportion* and *The Art of
Measurement* (1525, 1528); Donne's lines suggest an intimate familiarity
with the painter's work (§379).
205. *odds trye*: test or measure the proportions.
211. *he*: 'straight' (acc. to several MSS).
212. *protests* (thrice): to her prótests he protésts that she should not protést; he
is – what else? – a 'Protestant'.
216. *Pursevant*: i.e. pursuivant, a public officer employed to discover Roman
Catholics, especially disguised priests and Jesuits; specified in some
MSS as Richard Topcliffe, the most feared one of all.
217. *of* (omitted acc. to several MSS).
our Ladies psalter: the Rosary (§171).
220. *the other extreme*: i.e. from Macrine (197 ff.).
221. *cloak*: long enough to be torn by spurs (§171).
222. *whom*: 'or whom' (acc. to 1635–69).

He cares not, His ill words doe no harme
To him; he rusheth in, as if arme, arme,
He meant to crie; And though his face be as ill   225
As theirs which in old hangings whip Christ, still
He strives to looke worse, he keepes all in awe;
Jeasts like a licenc'd foole, commands like law.
Tyr'd, now I leave this place, and but pleas'd so
As men which from gaoles to'execution goe,   230
Goe through the great chamber (why is it hung
With the seaven deadly sinnes?) being among
Those Askaparts, men big enough to throw
Charing Crosse for a barre, men that doe know
No token of worth, but Queenes man, and fine   235
Living, barrells of beefe, flaggons of wine;
I shooke like a spyed Spie; Preachers which are
Seas of Wits and Arts, you can, then dare,
Drowne the sinnes of this place, for, for mee
Which am but a scarce brooke, it enough shall bee   240
To wash the staines away; though I yet
With *Macchabees* modestie, the knowne merit
Of my worke lessen: yet some wise man shall,
I hope, esteeme my writs Canonicall.

223.   *not, His*: 'not hee. His' (acc. to 1635–69).
225.   *meant*: 'came' (acc. to a few MSS).
226.   *hangings*: tapestries depicting the scourging of Christ.
       still (acc. to 1635–69 and most MSS): 'yet still' (acc. to 1633 and a few
       MSS).
230.   *men which from* (acc. to the MSS): 'men from' (acc. to 1633–69).
231.   *the great chamber*: a place of assembly.
232.   *With*: with the tapestry of.
       deadly sinnes: cf. note on 201–3.
233.   *Askaparts*: like a legendary giant, thirty feet high.
234.   *Charing Crosse*: the imposing cross set up by Edward I.
235.   *Queenes*: in the Queen's service.
236.   *beefe*: hence beef-eaters; but emended to 'Beere' (acc. to a MS).
237.   *spyed*: espied, detected.
240.   *scarce*: 'scant' (acc. to 1635–69) or 'shallow' (acc. to some MSS).
242.   *Macchabees modestie*: cf. 'if I have done well, and as is fitting the story, it is
       that which I desired: but if slenderly and meanly, it is that which I could
       attain unto' (2 Maccabees 15.38). The Books of the Maccabees are
       apocryphal and, for Protestants, not *Canonicall* (244) – i.e. not part of
       the Biblical canon, authoritative.

Satyre V.

Thou shalt not laugh in this leafe, Muse, nor they
Whom any pitty warmes; He which did lay
Rules to make Courtiers, (hee being understood
May make good Courtiers, but who Courtiers good?)
Frees from the sting of jests all who in extreme   5
Are wreched or wicked: of these two a theame
Charity and liberty give me. What is hee
Who Officers rage, and Suiters misery
Can write, and jest? If all things be in all,
As I thinke, since all, which were, are, and shall   10
Bee, be made of the same elements:
Each thing, each thing implyes or represents.
Then man is a world; in which, Officers
Are the vast ravishing seas; and Suiters,
Springs; now full, now shallow, now drye; which, to   15
That which drownes them, run: These selfe reasons do
Prove the world a man, in which, officers
Are the devouring stomacke, and Suiters
The excrements, which they voyd; all men are dust;
How much worse are Suiters, who to mens lust   20
Are made preyes. O worse then dust, or wormes meat
For they do eate you now, whose selves wormes shall eate.
They are the mills which grinde you, yet you are
The winde which drives them; and a wastfull warre

Satyre V. The poem – entitled in one MS *Of the miserie of the poore suitors at Court*
   – extends Donne's concern with abuses in law first voiced in Satyre II;
   here he draws on personal experiences during his service as secretary to
   Sir Thomas Egerton, Lord Keeper of England, who in 1597 was inves-
   tigating malpractices in the legal profession.
2. *warmes*: 'warnes' (acc. to a few MSS).
    He: Castiglione, author of *The Courtier* (1528, translated by Thomas
    Hoby in 1561).
7. *Charity*: i.e. toward the wretched; *liberty*: to censure the wicked.
11. *the same elements*: the basic four (see above, p. 115, note on 9–10).
14. *ravishing*: 'ravenous' or 'ravening' (acc. to individual MSS).
16. *selfe*: same.
21 (also 29). *then*: than.

Is fought against you, and you fight it; they   25
Adulterate lawe, and you prepare their way
Like wittals, th'issue your owne ruine is;
Greatest and fairest Empresse, know you this?
Alas, no more then Thames calme head doth know
Whose meades her armes drowne, or whose corne o'rflow: 30
You Sir, whose righteousnes she loves, whom I
By having leave to serve, am most richly
For service paid, authorized, now beginne
To know and weed out this enormous sinne.
O Age of rusty iron! Some better wit   35
Call it some worse name, if ought equall it;
The iron Age *that* was, when justice was sold, now
Injustice is sold dearer farre; allow
All demands, fees, and duties; gamsters, anon
The mony which you sweat, and sweare for, is gon   40
Into other hands: So controverted lands
Scape, like Angelica, the strivers hands.
If Law be the Judges heart, and hee
Have no heart to resist letter, or fee,
Where wilt thou appeale? powre of the Courts below   45
Flow from the first maine head, and these can throw
Thee, if they sucke thee in, to misery,
To fetters, halters; But if the injury
Steele thee to dare complaine, Alas, thou goest
Against the stream, when upwards: when thou art most 50

27. *wittals*: wittols, any man who acquiesces in his wife's adultery.
28. *Empresse*: Queen Elizabeth I.
30. *meades*: meadows.
31. *Sir*: Egerton (see headnote).
35. *Age of . . . iron*: see below, p. 343, note on 426.
37–39. The lines are punctuated variously in the MSS and the editions; I
      follow 1633.
39. *demands*: 'claymed' (acc. to 1635–69).
     gamsters: gamblers.
40. *sweare for*: take oaths for.
41. *controverted*: disputed.
42. *Angelica*: the heroine of Ariosto's *Orlando Furioso* was popular with one
     suitor too many.
44. *letter*: i.e. from a person of influence; *fee*: bribe.
46. *first maine head*: Elizabeth (as above, l. 28).

Heavy and most faint; and in these labours they,
'Gainst whom thou should'st complaine, will in the way
Become great seas, o'r which, when thou shalt bee
Forc'd to make golden bridges, thou shalt see
That all thy gold was drown'd in them before;   55
All things follow their like, only who have may have more.
Judges are Gods; he who made and said them so,
Meant not that men should be forc'd to them to goe,
By meanes of Angels; When supplications
We send to God, to Dominations,   60
Powers, Cherubins, and all heavens Courts, if wee
Should pay fees as here, Daily bread would be
Scarce to Kings; so 'tis. Would it not anger
A Stoicke, a coward, yea a Martyr,
To see a Pursivant come in, and call   65
All his cloathes, Copes; Bookes, Primers; and all
His Plate, Challices; and mistake them away,
And aske a fee for comming? Oh, ne'r may
Faire lawes white reverend name be strumpeted,
To warrant thefts: she is established   70
Recorder to Destiny, on earth, and shee
Speakes Fates words, and but tells us who must bee
Rich, who poore, who in chaires, who in jayles:
Shee is all faire, but yet hath foule long nailes,

52. *the*: 'thy' (acc. to 1635–69).
57. *said*: 'stil'd' (acc. to a few MSS).
59. *Angels*: see above, p. 156, note on 9.
60–61. *Dominations* etc.: angels were thought to rise hierarchically through several orders, often – but not always – said to be nine (see §108).
61. *Courts* (plural acc. to 1635–69 and most MSS, singular acc. to 1633 and a few MSS).
65–67. *Pursivant*: pursuivants (see previous poem, note on 216) would *mistake* – i.e. mis-take, misappropriate – all evidence of Catholic loyalties, such as vestments (*Copes*), prayer books (*Primers*), and liturgical utensils (*Challices*).
68. *aske* (acc. to 1669 and most MSS): 'lack' (acc. to 1633–54).
72. *but* (omitted acc. to 1633–69).
73. *chaires*: sedan-chairs (§164) or, more generally, high officers; 'chaynes' (acc. to a MS).

With which she scracheth Suiters; In bodies 75
Of men, so in law, nailes are th'extremities,
So Officers stretch to more then Law can doe,
As our nailes reach what no else part comes to.
Why barest thou to yon Officer? Foole, Hath hee
Got those goods, for which erst men bared to thee? 80
Foole, twice, thrice, thou hast bought wrong, and now
   hungerly
Beg'st right; But that dole comes not till these dye.
Thou had'st much, and lawes Urim and Thummim trie
Thou wouldst for more; and for all hast paper
Enough to cloath all the great Carricks Pepper. 85
Sell that, and by that thou much more shalt leese,
Then Haman, when he sold his Antiquities.
O wretch that thy fortunes should moralize
Esops fables, and make tales, prophesies.
Thou art the swimming dog whom shadows cosened, 90
And div'st, neare drowning, for what vanished.

76.   *th'* (omitted acc. to 1633–69).
77 (also 87). *then*: than.
79.   *barest*: i.e. your head, take your hat off.
80.   *erst* (omitted acc. to 1633).
82.   *dole*: just share.
     these: the law-officers.
83.   *Urim and Thummim*: gems empowering their wearer to speak with divine
     authority (Exodus 28.30).
84.   *paper*: the endless documents.
85.   *the great Carricks Pepper*: 'the Great Carrack', a seven-decker Spanish ship,
     captured in 1592 replete with a substantial cargo of pepper.
86.   *leese*: lose.
87.   The Book of Esther, in detailing *Haman*'s offer to pay for the extermina-
     tion of the Jews, does not indicate that he was to have paid his agents by
     selling his treasures; he was in any case hanged.
     when: 'if' (acc. to 1635–54 and some MSS).
88.   *that*: in that.
90.   Referring to Aesop's fable of the greedy dog which, trying to grab the
     meat from the mouth of his shadow reflected in the water, lost the real
     meat he held.
91.   *And*: 'Which' (acc. to 1635–69).
     div'st: 'div'd' or 'div'dst' (acc. to various MSS).

Upon Mr Thomas Coryats Crudities

Oh to what heigh will love of greatnesse drive
Thy leaven'd spirit, *Sesqui-superlative?*
Venice vast lake thou hadst seen, and wouldst seeke than
Some vaster thing, and foundst a Curtizan.
That inland Sea having discover'd well   5
A Cellar-gulfe, where one might sayle to hell
From Heydelberg, thou longdst to see: and thou
This Booke greater then all producest now.
Infinit worke, which doth so farre extend,
That none can study it to any end.   10
T'is no one thing; it is not fruite nor roote,
Nor poorely limited with head or foote.
If man be therefore man, because he can
Reason, and laugh, thy booke doth halfe make man.
One halfe beeing made, thy modesty was such,   15
That thou on th'other halfe wouldst never touch.
When wilt thou be at full, great Lunatique?
Not till thou exceed the world? canst thou be like
A prosperous nose-borne wenne, which sometimes growes
To be farre greater then the mother-nose?   20

Upon Mr Thomas Coryats Crudities. Quite distinct from the five satires proper,
    the poem was first published – together with several mock-panegyrics by
    other poets – in Coryate's *Crudities hastily gobbled up in five months travells*
    (1611) and reprinted with the present title from 1649. Thomas Coryate
    (d. 1617) was a learned eccentric often lampooned affectionately by the
    wits of the time.
  2. *leaven'd*: puffed up; 'learned' (acc. to 1649–69).
      Sesqui-superlative: 'a superlative and a half' (§171).
  3. *lake*: the Venetian lagoon.
      than: then.
  6. *Cellar-gulfe*: the Great Tun of Heidelberg, which Coryate estimated to be
      stocked with 28,000 gallons of wine.
  8 (also 20). *then*: than.
14. *halfe make man*: since it only makes one *laugh*.
17. *Lunatique*: see above, p. 51, note on 14.
19. *prosperous*: big.
      wenne: swelling.

Go then, and as to thee, when thou didst go,
Munster did Townes, and *Gesner* Authors show,
Mount now to *Gallo-belgicus:* appeare
As deepe a States-man, as a Gazettier.
Homely and familiarly, when thou com'st backe,   25
Talke of *Will* Conquerour, and *Prester Jacke*.
Go bashfull man, lest here thou blush to looke
Upon the progresse of thy glorious booke,
To which both Indies sacrifices send;
The west sent gold, which thou didst freely spend,   30
(Meaning to see't no more) upon the presse.
The East sends hither her deliciousnesse;
And thy leaves must imbrace what comes from thence,
The Myrrhe, the Pepper, and the Frankincense.
This magnifies thy leav's; but if they stoope   35
To neighbour wares, when Merchants do unhoope
Voluminous barrels; if thy leaves do then
Convey these wares in parcels unto men;
If for vast Tomes of Currans, and of Figs,
Of medcinall, and Aromatique twigs,   40
Thy leaves a better method do provide,
Divide to pounds, and ounces subdivide;
If they stoope lower yet, and vent our wares,
Home-*manufactures*, to thicke popular Faires,

---

22. Sebastian Munster authored *The Cosmography of the Universe* (1541) as
     Konrad von Gesner did *The Library of the Universe* (1545).
23. *Gallo-belgicus*: see the epigram above, p. 131.
26. *Will*: William, who was crowned king of England in 1066.
     Prester Jacke: 'Priest' John, who was imagined to reign beyond Persia.
29. *both Indies*, as well as *west* (30) and *East* (32): see above, p. 54, note on 17.
31. *upon the presse*: on the publication of Coryate's book.
33. *leaves*: pages.
36. *neighbour*: adjacent.
36 (also 46). *wares*: the items which the book's pages are to wrap.
39. *Tomes* (acc. to 1611): 'Tons' (acc. to 1649).
43. *vent*: vend, sell.
44. *Home-manufactures*: home-made items.
     thicke: crowded.

If *omni-prægnant* ther, upon warme stals   45
They hatch all wares for which the buyer cals,
Then thus thy leaves we justly may commend,
That they all kind of matter comprehend.
Thus thou, by meanes which th'Ancients never tooke,
A Pandect makest, and Universall booke.   50
The bravest Heroes, for publike good
Scatter'd in divers lands, their lims and bloud.
Worst malefactors, to whom men are prize,
Do publike good cut in Anatomies.
So will thy booke in peeces: For a Lord   55
Which casts at Portescues, and all the board,
Provide whole bookes; each leafe enough will be
For friends to passe time, and keepe companie
Can all carouse up thee? No, thou must fit
Measures; and fill out for the half-pint wit.   60
Some shall wrap pils, and save a friends life so,
Some shall stop muskets, and so kill a fo.
Thou shalt not ease the Critiques of next age
So much, at once their hunger to asswage.
Nor shall wit-pyrates hope to finde thee lye   65
All in one bottome, in one Librarie.
Some leaves may paste strings there in other bookes,
And so one may, which on another lookes,
Pilfer, alas, a little wit from you,
But hardly much; and yet I thinke this true;   70

---

45. *omni-prægnant*: since the book's pages will in a sense *hatch* (46) the items
the people buy.
50. *Pandect*: 'A booke treating of all matters: also the Volume of the Civill
Law called *Digests*' (Bullokar).
Universall: cf. note on 22.
53. *prize*: victims.
54. *cut*: dissected for medical purposes.
56. *Portescues*: the Portuguese coins 'crusadoes'.
59. *carouse up thee*: drink deeply to your health.
fit: limit, in accordance with one's capacity to drink.
65. *wit-pyrates*: thieves of other people's wit.
67. *paste strings*: be pasted over the strings used to tie the quires of a book
(§171).
70. *hardly much*: 'I meane from one page which shall paste strings in a booke'
(Donne's marginal note).

As *Sybils* was, your booke is mysticall,
For every peece is as much worth as all.
Therefore mine impotency I confesse;
The healths which my braine beares must be farre lesse;
Thy Gyant-wit o'rethrowes me, I am gone,   75
And rather then reade all, I would reade none.

71.   *Sybils*: the book of the Cumaean Sibyl, a prophetess.
74.   *healths*: toasts honouring Coryate.
76.   *then*: than.

Letters to Severall Personages

Variably successful as they are, Donne's 'verse letters' have been slighted more than has any other cluster of his poems. It may be regarded as axiomatic, however, that the patient reader will here discover many a brilliant achievement beyond the six poems selected for commendation earlier (p. 34).

The art of the epistle in verse as well as in prose is formidably extensive. Letters in prose were composed – the word is used advisedly – as much by Cicero as by St Paul (§703); while the Renaissance witnessed a veritable explosion of such enterprises, most notably by humanists of the order of Erasmus. As part of this tradition, Donne's own letters in prose (§179) are consciously – often self-consciously – constructed, shaped, 'finished'.

Letters in verse became fashionable especially once Petrarch composed his celebrated 'metrical epistles'. The ensuing contributions by Donne may be described in the terms he used for his letters whether in prose or in verse, as the means 'by which we deliver over our affections, and assurances of friendship, and the best faculties of our souls' (§179: p. 23, in §547; see also below, p. 290, note on 3–14). Should Donne's occasional excess of flattery distress us, we would do well to heed his counsel: 'If you can thinke these flatteries, they are, / For then your judgement is below my praise' (below, p. 282, ll. 49–50). Alexander Pope numbered the poems among Donne's 'best things' (as reported by Joseph Spence, in §171: p. xvii).

The order of the verse letters is different in nearly every modern edition, in some cases because of a desire to gather poems addressed to the same individual close together, and in others because of an ambition to print them in their assumed chronological sequence. The present sequence follows that of the 1633 edition, which provides the text of thirty poems; there

follow the one poem added in 1635 (p. 311) and the six poems
first printed from 1896 to 1912.

It may be noted that as Donne wrote satires beyond his
Satyres (cf. p. 213), so he wrote verse letters beyond the ones
collected here – for example, the poem addressed to Edward
Tilman (below, p. 470).

THE STORME.
To Mr *Christopher Brooke*.

Thou which art I, ('tis nothing to be soe)
Thou which art still thy selfe, by these shalt know
Part of our passage; And, a hand, or eye
By *Hilliard* drawne, is worth an history,
By a worse painter made; and (without pride)　　　　　5
When by thy judgment they are dignifi'd,
My lines are such. 'Tis the preheminence
Of friendship onely to'impute excellence.
England to whom we'owe, what we be, and have,
Sad that her sonnes did seeke a forraine grave　　　　10
(For, Fates, or Fortunes drifts none can soothsay,
Honour and misery have one face and way.)

The Storme. Subtitled (acc. to 1635–69) 'from the Iland voyage with the Earle
　　of Essex' – i.e. the English expedition of over sixty ships to the Azores
　　(1597) to intercept the Spanish fleet transporting silver from the
　　Americas; but the storm here described damaged the fleet seriously.
　　Donne was present as a volunteer (§196).
　　Christopher Brooke, lawyer and sometimes poet, was one of Donne's
　　most intimate friends. He had been imprisoned for serving as best man at
　　Donne's clandestine marriage in 1601.
　　On the poem's 'rigorous classicism', consult §545.
　2.　*these*: i.e. the *lines* (cf. l. 7).
　4.　*Hilliard*: the famed English painter of miniatures (d. 1619).
　8.　On the symbol ', here and throughout, see above, p. 5.
　12.　*and way*: 'one way' (acc. to 1635–54).

From out her pregnant intrailes sigh'd a winde
Which at th'ayres middle marble roome did finde
Such strong resistance, that it selfe it threw   15
Downeward againe; and so when it did view
How in the port, our fleet deare time did leese,
Withering like prisoners, which lye but for fees,
Mildly it kist our sailes, and, fresh and sweet,
As, to a stomack sterv'd, whose insides meete,   20
Meate comes, it came; and swole our sailes, when wee
So joyd, as *Sara*'her swelling joy'd to see.
But 'twas but so kinde, as our countrimen,
Which bring friends one dayes way, and leave them then.
Then like two mighty Kings, which dwelling farre   25
Asunder, meet against a third to warre,
The South and West winds joyn'd, and, as they blew,
Waves like a rowling trench before them threw.
Sooner then you read this line, did the gale,
Like shot, not fear'd, till felt, our sailes assaile;   30
And what at first was call'd a gust, the same
Hath now a stormes, anon a tempests name.
Jonas, I pitty thee, and curse those men,
Who when the storm rag'd most, did wake thee then;
Sleepe is paines easiest salve, and doth fulfill   35
All offices of death, except to kill.
But when I wakt, I saw, that I saw not.
I, and the Sunne, which should teach mee'had forgot

---

13.   Winds were supposed to be caused by the earth's exhalations.
14.   *marble*: because the air's middle region was thought to be intensely cold.
17.   *leese*: lose.
18.   *Withering*: 'Waiting' (acc. to a MS).
      lye but for fees: prisoners remained in prison until they paid their jailer's fees.
21.   *swole*: swelled.
22.   Abraham's wife Sarah laughed joyfully on discovering she was pregnant with Isaac in her old age (Genesis 21.6–7).
29 (also 44).   *then*: than.
33–34.   Jonah was awakened during a storm and cast overboard by his shipmates (Jonah 1.5 ff.).
38.   *I*: 'aye' (a speculative emendation in §159).

East, West, day, night, and I could onely say,
If'the world had lasted, now it had been day.   40
Thousands our noyses were, yet wee'mongst all
Could none by his right name, but thunder call:
Lightning was all our light, and it rain'd more
Then if the Sunne had drunke the sea before;
Some coffin'd in their cabbins lye,'equally   45
Griev'd that they are not dead, and yet must dye.
And as sin-burd'ned soules from graves will creepe,
At the last day, some forth their cabbins peepe:
And tremblingly'aske what newes, and doe heare so,
Like jealous husbands, what they would not know.   50
Some sitting on the hatches, would seeme there,
With hideous gazing to feare away feare.
Then note they the ships sicknesses, the Mast
Shak'd with this ague, and the Hold and Wast
With a salt dropsie clog'd, and all our tacklings   55
Snapping, like too-high-stretched treble strings.
And from our totterd sailes, ragges drop downe so,
As from one hang'd in chaines, a yeare agoe.
Even our Ordinance plac'd for our defence,
Strive to breake loose, and scape away from thence.   60
Pumping hath tir'd our men, and what's the gaine?
Seas into seas throwne, we suck in againe;

39. *onely*: 'but' (acc. to most MSS).
40. *now*: 'yet' (acc. to 1635–54).
47. *graves* (plural acc. to most MSS, singular acc. to 1633–54).
48. *the last day*: the Last Judgement.
49. *tremblingly*: 'trembling' (acc. to 1635–69 and some MSS).
52. *feare away*: frighten away.
54. *this*: 'an' (acc. to 1635–69).
     ague: shivering fit.
     Wast: waist, the area amidships.
55. *salt dropsie*: an excess of sea-water.
56. *too-*: 'too-too-' (acc. to 1635–54).
57. *totterd*: 'tattred' (acc. to several MSS).
59. *Even*: 'Yea even' (acc. to 1635–69).
     Ordinance (used as a plural): ordnance, cannon.

Hearing hath deaf'd our saylers; and if they
Knew how to heare, there's none knowes what to say.
Compar'd to these stormes, death is but a qualme, 65
Hell somewhat lightsome, and the'Bermuda calme.
Darknesse, lights elder brother, his birth-right
Claims o'er this world, and to heaven hath chas'd light.
All things are one, and that one none can be,
Since all formes, uniforme deformity 70
Doth cover, so that wee, except God say
Another *Fiat*, shall have no more day.
So violent, yet long these furies bee,
That though thine absence sterve me,'I wish not thee.

65. *qualme*: a feeling of faintness or sickness (*ALC*).
66. *Bermuda* (or, acc. to 1635–54 and several MSS, 'Bermudas'): said to be ever tempestuous, 'still-vex'd' (in Shakespeare's explicit estimate in *The Tempest*, I, ii, 229, and in Marvell's implicit one in *Bermudas*).
67. *lights elder brother*: because darkness pre-existed the creation of light (Genesis 1.2–4).
      elder (acc. to most MSS): 'eldest' (acc. to 1633–69).
68. *Claims* (acc. to 1635–69 and the MSS): 'Claim'd' (acc. to 1633).
69. *none*: i.e. nothing.
70. *formes*: the Platonic Ideal images (§554)?
72. *Fiat*: 'Let it be done', the divine command to create light.
74. *I wish not thee*: I do not wish you here.

THE CALME.

Our storme is past, and that storms tyrannous rage,
A stupid calme, but nothing it, doth swage.
The fable is inverted, and farre more
A blocke afflicts, now, then a storke before.
Stormes chafe, and soon weare out themselves, or us;   5
In calmes, Heaven laughs to see us languish thus.
As steady'as I can wish, that my thoughts were,
Smooth as thy mistresse glasse, or what shines there,
The sea is now. And, as the Iles which wee
Seeke, when wee can move, our ships rooted bee.   10
As water did in stormes, now pitch runs out
As lead, when a fir'd Church becomes one spout.
And all our beauty, and our trimme, decayes,
Like courts removing, or like ended playes.
The fighting place now seamens ragges supply;   15
And all the tackling is a frippery.
No use of lanthornes; and in one place lay
Feathers and dust, to day and yesterday.
Earths hollownesses, which the worlds lungs are,
Have no more winde then the upper valt of aire.   20

The Calme. Pertaining to the episode 'in the same voyage' (acc. to a MS
  subtitle: see the headnote to the previous poem) when a part of the fleet
  was 'very much becalmed for a day or two' (§196). It is probable that this
  poem was also addressed to Christopher Brooke.
2.   *swage*: assuage.
3.   *the fable*: originally Aesop's – but much amended by Donne's time (§542)
     – told of the frogs' demand for a king other than the lethargic Log,
     whereupon Zeus sent King Stork who devoured them all.
4.   *blocke*: i.e. of wood; a log.
4 (also 20, 30, 52). *then*: than.
7.   On the symbol ', here and throughout, see above, p. 5.
8.   *glasse*: mirror.
9.   *Iles*: the Azores (see the headnote to the previous poem).
11. *pitch*: used to caulk the seams of ships.
12. *lead*: used to cover the roofs of churches.
15. *ragges*: clothing hung out to dry.
16. *frippery*: second-hand clothes shop.
17. *lanthornes*: hung on ships' sterns in order to keep the fleet together.
19. *hollownesses*: cf. previous poem, note on 13.
20. The air's upper region ('vault') was thought to be utterly calm.

We can nor lost friends, nor sought foes recover,
But meteorlike, save that wee move not, hover,
Onely the Calenture together drawes
Deare friends, which meet dead in great fishes jawes:
And on the hatches as on Altars lyes   25
Each one, his owne Priest, and owne Sacrifice.
Who live, that miracle do multiply
Where walkers in hot Ovens, doe not dye.
If in despite of these, wee swimme, that hath
No more refreshing, then our brimstone Bath,   30
But from the sea, into the ship we turne,
Like parboyl'd wretches, on the coales to burne.
Like *Bajazet* encag'd, the sheepheards scoffe,
Or like slacke sinew'd *Sampson*, his haire off,
Languish our ships. Now, as a Miriade   35
Of Ants, durst th'Emperours lov'd snake invade,
The crawling Gallies, Sea-goales, finny chips,
Might brave our Venices, now bed-ridde ships.
Whether a rotten state, and hope of gaine,
Or to disuse mee from the queasie paine   40
Of being belov'd, and loving, or the thirst
Of honour, or faire death, out pusht mee first,

---

21. *lost* ('left' acc. to several MSS and §171) *friends*: some ships had been
     separated from the main fleet.
23. *Calenture*: the tropical delirium which impelled sailors to leap into the
     sea.
24. *jawes*: 'mawes' (acc. to 1635–69).
27. *Who*: those who.
28. *walkers in hot Ovens*: see above, p. 225, note on 24.
29. *these*: the *great fishes* or sharks (24).
30. *our*: 'a' (acc. to 1635–69).
33. *Bajazet encag'd*: the Turkish emperor imprisoned in a cage by Tambur-
     laine – himself once a shepherd – as related in Marlowe's play.
34. *slacke sinew'd*: once his *haire* was shaved *off* (Judges 16.17 ff.).
36. Acc. to Suetonius' *Life of Tiberius*, *Ants* ate the Emperor's pet *snake*.
37. The galleys are slow (*crawling*) because propelled by oars, *gaoles* because
     rowed by chained prisoners, and *chips* because rather small, their oars
     protruding and acting like fins (§171).
38. *Venices* (acc. to 1633 and most MSS): i.e. motionless as cities rising out of
     the sea like Venice (§171); emended to 'Pinnaces' (acc. to 1635–54 and
     most MSS), i.e. light scouting boats.
40. *disuse mee*: free me from.

I lose my end: for here as well as I
A desperate may live, and a coward die.
Stagge, dogge, and all which from, or towards flies,   45
Is paid with life, or pray, or doing dyes.
Fate grudges us all, and doth subtly lay
A scourge,'gainst which wee all forget to pray,
He that at sea prayes for more winde, as well
Under the poles may begge cold, heat in hell.   50
What are wee then? How little more alas
Is man now, then before he was? he was
Nothing; for us, wee are for nothing fit;
Chance, or our selves still disproportion it.
Wee have no power, no will, no sense; I lye   55
I should not then thus feele this miserie.

To Sir *Henry Wotton*.

Sir, more then kisses, letters mingle Soules;
For, thus friends absent speake. This ease controules
The tediousnesse of my life: But for these
I could ideate nothing, which could please,
But I should wither in one day, and passe   5
To'a bottle'of Hay, that am a locke of Grasse.

The Calme.
44.   *A desperate*: one who, despaired of life, is careless of death.
45.   *from, or towards*: i.e. death.
46.   *pray*: prey.
47.   *grudges us all*: begrudges us all we desire (§171).
48.   *forget*: neglect.
55.   *power*: 'will' (acc. to some MSS).

To Sir Henry Wotton.   The recipient of three other verse letters (see pp. 264,
    294, 321), Wotton was a widely-respected lawyer, courtier, and dip-
    lomat, who served as ambassador to Venice (1604 ff.) and later Provost
    of Eton College (1624 ff.); a poet himself, he was the first to commend
    the emerging Milton (1638). The present poem may be part of a literary
    debate involving Bacon's 'The World' (§540).
  1.   Cf. Donne's remark in a prose letter: 'our Letters are our selves and in
       them absent friends meet' (§179: p. 240, in §547).
  1 (also 10, 38). *then*: than.
  4.   *ideate*: form an idea of (§171); 'invent' (acc. to 1669).
  6.   *bottle*: bundle.
       On the symbol ', here and throughout, see above, p. 5.

Life is a voyage, and in our lifes wayes
Countries, Courts, Towns are Rockes, or Remoraes;
They break or stop all ships, yet our state's such,
That though then pitch they staine worse, wee must touch. 10
If in the furnace of the even line,
Or under th'adverse icy poles thou pine,
Thou know'st two temperate Regions girded in,
Dwell there: But Oh, what refuge canst thou winne
Parch'd in the Court, and in the country frozen?   15
Shall cities built of both extremes be chosen?
Can dung and garlike be'a perfume? or can
A Scorpion, and Torpedo cure a man?
Cities are worst of all three; of all three
(O knottie riddle) each is worst equally.   20
Cities are Sepulchers; they who dwell there
Are carcases, as if no such there were.
And Courts are Theaters, where some men play
Princes, some slaves, all to one end, and of one clay.
The Country is a desert, where no good,   25
Gain'd, as habits, not borne is understood.
There men become beasts, and prone to more evils;
In cities blockes, and in a lewd court, devills.
As in the first Chaos confusedly
Each elements qualities were in the'other three;   30

8.   *Remoraes*: see above, p. 181, note on 58.
11. *the even line*: the equator.
     even (acc. to all MSS): 'raging' (acc. to 1633–54).
12. *adverse*: opposite to each other; also, hostile.
17 (also 18). *and*: 'or' (acc. to 1635–69 and several MSS).
18. *Torpedo*: the electric ray ('numbfish').
22. *there* (acc. to 1635–69 and most MSS): 'they' or 'then' (acc. to 1633 and various MSS).
24. *one end*: i.e. death.
     clay: 'day' (acc. to 1650–69).
25–26. *no good / Gain'd . . . understood*: 'the good / Gain'd inhabits not, borne, is not understood' (acc. to 1635–54 and some MSS).
27. *more*: 'all' (acc. to 1635–69) or 'mere' (acc. to a few MSS).
28. *blockes*: blockheads.
29. *Chaos*: from which the universe was created (see *Paradise Lost*, VII, 211 ff.).
30. *elements*: the traditional four (earth, water, air, fire).

So pride, lust, covetize, being severall
To these three places, yet all are in all,
And mingled thus, their issue incestuous.
Falshood is denizon'd. Virtue is barbarous.
Let no man say there, Virtues flintie wall   35
Shall locke vice in mee, I'll do none, but know all.
Men are spunges, which to poure out, receive,
Who know false play, rather then lose, deceive.
For in best understandings, sinne beganne,
Angels sinn'd first, then Devills, and then man.   40
Onely perchance beasts sinne not; wretched wee
Are beasts in all, but white integritie.
I thinke if men, which in these places live
Durst looke for themselves, and themselves retrive,
They would like strangers greet themselves, seeing then 45
Utopian youth, growne old Italian.
    Be thou thine owne home, and in thy selfe dwell;
Inne any where, continuance maketh hell,
And seeing the snaile, which every where doth rome,
Carrying his owne house still, still is at home.   50
Follow (for he is easie pac'd) this snaile,
Bee thine owne Palace, or the world's thy gaole.
And in the worlds sea, do not like corke sleepe
Upon the waters face; nor in the deepe
Sinke like a lead without a line: but as   55
Fishes glide, leaving no print where they passe,
Nor making sound; so, closely thy course goe,
Let men dispute, whether thou breathe, or no.

31. *covetize*: inordinate desire (§163).
33. *issue*: 'issue is' (acc. to 1635–69).
34. *denizon'd*: naturalized.
40–41. Also given in a MS as 'Anngells synd first, then Divells; & then
      man/onely peccantes; beasts syn not'.
44. *for* (acc. to the MSS): 'in' (acc. to 1633–69).
46. *Utopian*: idealistic.
     Italian: corrupt (cf. l. 66).
47. *thou*: 'then' (acc. to 1635–69 and the MSS).
48. *Inne*: dwell as at an inn.
52. *goale*: 'gaile' (acc. to 1635–69).

Onely'in this one thing, be no Galenist. To make
Courts hot ambitions wholesome, do not take   60
A dramme of Countries dulnesse; do not adde
Correctives, but as chymiques, purge the bad.
But, Sir, I advise not you, I rather doe
Say o'er those lessons, which I learn'd of you:
Whom, free from German schismes, and lightnesse   65
Of France, and faire Italies faithlesnesse,
Having from these suck'd all they had of worth,
And brought home that faith, which you carried forth,
I throughly love. But if my selfe, I'have wonne
To know my rules, I have, and you have   70

DONNE

59–62. In the classical medicine of Galen (2nd cent. A.D.), the defective
'humour' (hot, coild, moist, or dry) was corrected through drugs meant
to restore the balance; in the new 'chymique' medicine of Paracelsus
(d. 1541), diseases were purged through antagonistic remedies.
61. *dulnesse*: cf. *frozen* (l.15).
63 ff. In his response to Donne's poem, Wotton ended on an equally com-
plimentary note (§158):

> But this I doe not dedicate to thee,
>   As one that holds himself fitt to advise,
> Or that my lines to him should precepts be
>   That is less ill then I, and much more wise:
> Yet 'tis no harme mortality to preach,
>   For men doe often learne when they do teach.

65. *German*: 'Germanies' (acc. to 1635–69).
69. *throughly*: wholly.
70. Donne's punning on his name would later prove central to a very
different poem (below, p. 490).

To Sir *Henry Goodyere*.

Who makes the Past, a patterne for next yeare,
   Turnes no new leafe, but still the same things reads,
Seene things, he sees againe, heard things doth heare,
   And makes his life, but like a paire of beads.

A Palace, when'tis that, which it should be,   5
   Leaves growing, and stands such, or else decayes:
But hee which dwels there, is not so; for hee
   Strives to urge upward, and his fortune raise;

So had your body'her morning, hath her noone,
   And shall not better; her next change is night: 10
But her faire larger guest, to'whom Sun and Moone
   Are sparkes, and short liv'd, claimes another right.

The noble Soule by age growes lustier,
   Her appetite, and her digestion mend,
Wee must not sterve, nor hope to pamper her   15
   With womens milke, and pappe unto the end.

Provide you manlyer dyet; you have seene
   All libraries, which are Schools, Camps, and Courts;
But aske your Garners if you have not beene
   In harvests, too indulgent to your sports.   20

To Sir Henry Goodyere. Subtitled (acc. to a few MSS) 'moveing him to travell'.
   Goodyere or Goodere was responsible enough to have been a member
   of the Privy Council under James I. Yet his extravagance worried his
   intimate friend Donne, who voices his concern here (see especially
   ll. 17 ff.). It was said at the time that 'Goodere's rare match with only
   him was bless'd, / Who has outdonne and quite undonne the rest' (§157:
   II, 297).
      The poem's immediate occasion appears to have been Goodyere's
   promise to visit Donne's home at Mitcham in Surrey (1606 ff.); the letter
   was composed when Goodyere failed to come. See also their joint poem,
   below, p. 318.
  1. *Past*: 'Last' (acc. to 1669).
  4. *paire*: string.
  9. On the symbol ', here and throughout, see above, p. 5.
 11. *guest*: the soul.
 20. *sports*: diversions.

Would you redeeme it? then your selfe transplant
   A while from hence. Perchance outlandish ground
Beares no more wit, then ours, but yet more scant
   Are those diversions there, which here abound.

To be a stranger hath that benefit,   25
   Wee can beginnings, but not habits choke.
Goe, whither? hence; you get, if you forget;
   New faults, till they prescribe in us, are smoake.

Our Soule, whose country'is heaven, and God her father,
   Into this world, corruptions sinke, is sent,   30
Yet, so much in her travaile she doth gather,
   That she returnes home, wiser then she went;

It payes you well, if it teach you to spare,
   And make you 'asham'd, to make your hawks praise, yours,
Which when herselfe she lessens in the aire,
   You then first say, that high enough she toures.

However, keepe the lively tast you hold
   Of God, love him as now, but feare him more,
And in your afternoones thinke what you told
   And promis'd him, at morning prayer before.   40

Let falshood like a discord anger you,
   Else be not froward; But why doe I touch
Things, of which none is in your practise new,
   And Tables, or fruit-trenchers teach as much;

22. *outlandish*: foreign.
23 (also 32). *then*: than.
28. *prescribe*: claim title.
     in: 'to' (acc. to 1635–69).
33. *spare*: be temperate.
36. *toures*: towers, soars.
42. *Else be not froward*: do not otherwise be irascible (§166).
     touch: touch upon.
44. *Tables*: moralized emblems; 'Fables' (acc. to several MSS), i.e. moralized tales.
     -trenchers: platters, often decorated with moral maxims.

But thus I make you keepe your promise Sir,   45
   Riding I had you, though you still staid there,
And in these thoughts, although you never stirre,
   You came with mee to Micham, and are here.

To Mr *Rowland Woodward*.

Like one who'in her third widdowhood doth professe
Her selfe a Nunne, tyed to retirednesse,
So'affects my muse now, a chast fallownesse.

Since shee to few, yet to too many'hath showne
How love-song weeds, and Satyrique thornes are growne
Where seeds of better Arts, were early sown.

Though to use, and love Poëtrie, to mee,
Betroth'd to no'one Art, be no'adulterie;
Omissions of good, ill, as ill deeds bee.

For though to us it seeme, 'and be light and thinne,   10
Yet in those faithfull scales, where God throwes in
Mens workes, vanity weighs as much as sinne.

To Sir Henry Goodyere.
45.   *make*: 'made' (acc. to a few MSS).
      promise: see headnote.
48.   *with mee to*: 'to mee at' (acc. to a few MSS).
      Micham: see headnote.

To Mr Rowland Woodward. Entitled in a MS *A Letter of Doctor Dunne to one that
      desired some of his papers* (i.e. poems); but Donne declined for the reasons
      given. Woodward eludes us because of lack of biographical details; but he
      was evidently one of Donne's most intimate friends (see also the four
      other verse letters 'To Mr R.W.', pp. 290, 320, 322, 323).
  1.   On the symbol ', here and throughout, see above, p. 5.
       third widdowhood (cf. 5–6): most likely alluding to the *Songs and Sonets*
       ('love-song weeds'), the satires and elegies ('Satyrique thornes'), and the
       verse letters ('seeds of better Arts' [§163]).
  3.   *fallownesse*: a period of unproductiveness; 'holinesse' (acc. to a few MSS).
  5.   *love-song*: 'long loves' (acc. to 1635–54).
  9.   To omit to do good is as wrong as actively to do wrong.
 10.   *and be*: 'but' (acc. to 1635–69).
 11.   *faithfull*: accurate.
       scales: i.e. of Divine Justice.
 12.   *vanity*: the pursuit of *vaine outward things* (l. 35).

If our Soules have stain'd their first white, yet wee
May cloth them with faith, and deare honestie,
Which God Imputes, as native puritie.   15

There is no Vertue, but Religion:
Wise, valiant, sober, just, are names, which none
Want, which want not Vice-covering discretion.

Seeke wee then our selves in our selves; for as
Men force the Sunne with much more force to passe,   20
By gathering his beames with a christall glasse;

So wee, If wee into our selves will turne,
Blowing our sparkes of vertue, may outburne
The straw, which doth about our hearts sojourne

You know, Physitians, when they would infuse   25
Into any'oyle, the Soules of Simples, use
Places, where they may lie still warme, to chuse.

So workes retirednesse in us; to rome
Giddily and be every where, but at home,
Such freedome doth a banishment become.   30

14.   *honestie*: 'integritie' (acc. to some MSS).
15.   *Imputes*: in the theological sense of attribution by vicarious substitution.
17.   The cardinal virtues of prudence, fortitude, temperance, justice.
18.   *Want*: lack.
19.   *our selves in our selves*: cf. the maxim 'know thyself'.
21.   *christall*: magnifying.
23.   *our*: 'the' (acc. to a few MSS).
        outburne: burn away.
25.   *Physitians*: physicists, alchemists.
26.   *oyle*: the liquid form of any metal.
        Soule of Simples: the 'virtue' (essence etc.) of medicinal plants.
30.   *a banishment become*: become a banishment.

Wee are but farmers of our selves, yet may,
If we can stocke our selves, and thrive, uplay
Much, much deare treasure for the great rent day.

Manure thy selfe then, to thy selfe be'approv'd,
And with vaine outward things be no more mov'd,   35
But to know, that I love thee'and would be lov'd.

To Sir *Henry Wotton*.

Here's no more newes, then vertue,'I may as well
Tell you *Cales*, or *Saint Michaels* tale for newes, as tell
That vice doth here habitually dwell.

Yet, as to'get stomachs, we walke up and downe,
And toyle to sweeten rest, so, my God frowne,   5
If, but to loth both, I haunt Court, or Towne.

For here no one is from the'extremitie
Of vice, by any other reason free,
But that the next to'him, still, is worse then hee.

31. *farmers* (acc. to 1635–69): tenant farmers; 'termers' (acc. to 1633).
33. *deare*: 'good' (acc. to 1635–69).
      treasure: cf. 'lay up for yourselves treasures in heaven' (Matthew 6.20).
      great rent day: the Last Judgement.
35. *things*: 'shewes' (acc. to a MS).
36. *lov'd*: 'belov'd' (acc. to several MSS).

To Sir Henry Wotton. Subtitled in some MSS 'From [the] Court', dated in
      others 20 July 1598. On the letter's recipient, see above, headnote on
      p. 256.
 1.   *then*: than. On the symbol ', here and throughout, see above, p. 5.
 2.   Alluding to the expeditions of 1596 against Cadiz – *Cales* or 'Calis' (acc.
      to 1633: see the epigram above, p. 132) – and of 1597 against *St Michaels*
      isles or the Azores (see above, headnote on p. 250), which by now are
      alike stale news.
      tale for newes: 'tales' (acc. to 1635–54).
 4.   *stomachs*: appetites.
 9.   *then*: than.

In this worlds warfare, they whom rugged Fate,   10
(Gods Commissary,) doth so throughly hate,
As in'the Courts Squadron to marshall their state:

If they stand arm'd with seely honesty,
With wishing prayers, and neat integritie,
Like Indians 'gainst Spanish hosts they bee.   15

Suspitious boldnesse to this place belongs,
And to'have as many eares as all have tongues;
Tender to know, tough to acknowledge wrongs.

Beleeve mee Sir, in my youths giddiest dayes,
When to be like the Court, was a playes praise,   20
Playes were not so like Courts, as Courts'are like playes.

Then let us at these mimicke antiques jeast,
Whose deepest projects, and egregious gests
Are but dull Moralls of a game at Chests.

But now'tis incongruity to smile,   25
Therefore I end; and bid farewell a while,
At Court, though *From Court*, were the better stile.

11.   *Commisary*: deputy.
      throughly: thoroughly.
12.   *marshall their state*: assemble their panoply of power, follow their calling
      (§166).
13.   *seely*: simple.
14.   *wishing prayers*: 'wishes, prayers' (acc. to 1635–54) or 'wishing, prayers'
      (acc. to 1669).
      neat: pure.
15.   The innocent *Indians* of the Americas hosted by the cunning conquis-
      tadors.
20.   *playes*: 'players' (acc. to 1639–69).
21.   *are* (omitted acc. to 1635–69 and some MSS).
22.   *mimicke antiques*: posturing 'antics' or eccentrics (§171).
23.   *projects*: plots.
      gests: acts; 'guests' (acc. to 1669).
24.   *Moralls of a game at Chests*: representations of moral situations with
      analogies to the game of chess (§171).
27.   *At*, *From*: i.e. written at, and sent from; also, written at, although it were
      better to have been away from.

To the Countesse of Bedford.

MADAME,
Reason is our Soules left hand, Faith her right,
By these wee reach divinity, that's you;
Their loves, who have the blessings of your light,
Grew from their reason, mine from faire faith grew.

But as, although a squint lefthandednesse   5
Be'ungracious, yet we cannot want that hand,
So would I, not to encrease, but to expresse
My faith, as I beleeve, so understand.

Therefore I study you first in your Saints,
Those friends, whom your election glorifies,   10
Then in your deeds, accesses, and restraints,
And what you reade, and what your selfe devize.

But soone, the reasons why you'are lov'd by all,
Grow infinite, and so passe reasons reach,

To the Countesse of Bedford. Lucy, Countess of Bedford, was a central figure in
the period's social and intellectual life, herself a poet (see note on l. 12)
and patron of poets like Jonson, Chapman, Daniel, and Drayton. She
favoured Donne much, and stood godmother to his second daughter,
Lucy. In turn, he addressed more of his verse letters to her than to any
other individual (see pp. 268, 273, 277, 299, 301, 309), composed elegiac
poems on the deaths of her kinswomen Cecilia Bulstrode and Lady
Markham as well as of her brother John (pp. 378, 381, 385), and entitled
one of his *Songs and Sonets* after her estate at Twickenham Park (above,
p. 73). See further §534; cf. §548.
  3. *light*: 'sight' (acc. to many MSS).
  4. *faire*: 'farr' (acc. to several MSS).
  5. *squint lefthandednesse*: a perverse contrariness; also, a one-sided adherence
      to reason (§166).
  6. On the symbol ', here and throughout, see above, p. 5.
      want: do without.
 10. *election*: one's 'choice' (salvation) by God.
 11. *accesses, and restrains*: granting and withholding of favours (here as else-
      where the terminology is expressly theological).
 12. *devize*: write, since she was a poet herself.

Then backe againe to'implicite faith I fall,   15
And rest on what the Catholique voice doth teach;

That you are good: and not one Heretique
Denies it: if he did, yet you are so.
For, rockes, which high top'd and deep rooted sticke,
Waves wash, not undermine, nor overthrow.   20

In every thing there naturally growes
A *Balsamum* to keepe it fresh, and new,
If'twere not injur'd by extrinsique blowes:
Your birth and beauty are this Balme in you.

But you of learning and religion,   25
And vertue,'and such ingredients, have made
A methridate, whose operation
Keepes off, or cures what can be done or said.

Yet, this is not your physicke, but your food,
A dyet fit for you; for you are here   30
The first good Angell, since the worlds frame stood,
That ever did in womans shape appeare.

Since you are then Gods masterpeece, and so
His Factor for our loves; do as you doe,
Make your returne home gracious; and bestow   35
This life on that; so make one life of two.
    For so God helpe mee,'I would not misse you there
    For all the good which you can do me here.

---

16. *Catholique*: universal.
     voice (acc. to 1635–69 and most MSS): 'faith' (acc. to 1633 and a few
     MSS).
19. *top'd and*: 'to sense' (acc. to 1635–54) or 'do seem' (acc. to 1669) or 'to sun
     and' (acc. to a few MSS) or 'to some and' (ditto).
22. *Balsamum* (also 24: *Balme*): see above, p. 90, note 6.
27. *methridate*: an antidote against poison.
29. *physicke*: medicine.
34. *Factor*: agent.
35. *home*: i.e. to heaven.
     gracious: also in the theological sense, full of Grace.
36. *This* (acc. to 1635–69 and most MSS): 'Thy' (acc. to 1633).

To the Countesse of Bedford.

Madame,
You have refin'd mee, and to worthyest things
Vertue, Art, Beauty, Fortune, now I see
Rarenesse, or use, not nature value brings;
And such, as they are circumstanc'd, they bee.
   Two ills can ne're perplexe us, sinne to'excuse;   5
   But of two good things, we may leave and chuse.

Therefore at Court, which is not vertues clime,
Where a transcendent height, (as, lownesse mee)
Makes her not be, or not show: all my rime
Your vertues challenge, which there rarest bee;   10
   For, as darke texts need notes: there some must bee
   To usher vertue, and say, *This is shee*.

So in the country'is beauty; to this place
You are the season (Madame) you the day,
'Tis but a grave of spices, till your face   15
Exhale them, and a thick close bud display.
   Widow'd and reclus'd else, her sweets she'enshrines
   As China, when the Sunne at Brasill dines.

Out from your chariot, morning breaks at night,
And falsifies both computations so;   20
Since a new world doth rise here from your light,
We your new creatures, by new recknings goe.

To the Countesse of Bedford. See headnote to the previous poem.
  1. *refin'd*: transmuted, as in alchemy (§171).
  4. *circumstanc'd*: governed by circumstances.
  6. *and:* 'or' (acc. to 1669).
 11. *darke*: obscure.
      there: at Court (§229).
 13. On the symbol ', here and throughout, see above, p. 5.
      this place: her estate at Twickenham Park (cf. above, headnote on p. 73).
 16. *Exhale them*: cause them to exhale their spices.
 20. *both computations*: the natural cycle of twenty-four hours and the hours
      from sunrise to sunset (cf. 24: *artificiall day*).

This showes that you from nature lothly stray,
That suffer not an artificiall day.

In this you'have made the Court the Antipodes,   25
And will'd your Delegate, the vulgar Sunne,
To doe profane autumnall offices,
Whilst here to you, wee sacrificers runne;
   And whether Priests, or Organs, you wee'obey,
   We sound your influence, and your Dictates say.   30

Yet to that Deity which dwels in you,
Your vertuous Soule, I now not sacrifice;
These are *Petitions*, and not *Hymnes*; they sue
But that I may survay the edifice.
   In all Religions as much care hath bin   35
   Of Temples frames, and beauty,'as Rites within.

As all which goe to Rome, doe not thereby
Esteeme religions, and hold fast the best,
But serve discourse, and curiosity,
With that which doth religion but invest,   40
   And shunne th'entangling laborinths of Schooles,
   And make it wit, to thinke the wiser fooles:

So in this pilgrimage I would behold
You as you'are vertues temple, not as shee,
What walls of tender christall her enfold,   45
What eyes, hands, bosome, her pure Altars bee;
   And after this survay, oppose to all
   Bablers of Chappels, you th'Escuriall.

23. *lothly*: is loath to.
25. *Antipodes*: the direct opposite.
30. *say*: pronounce or expound as priests.
40. *but invest*: dress with outward observances only.
41. *Schooles*: medieval scholastic disputants (cf. l. 61).
48. *Bablers of Chappels*: those who chatter on about minor places of worship.
    Escuriall: the spacious and magnificent edifice built north of Madrid by
    Philip II (1563 ff.).

Yet not as consecrate, but merely'as faire;
On these I cast a lay and country eye.   50
Of past and future stories, which are rare
I finde you all record, and prophecie.
   Purge but the booke of Fate, that it admit
   No sad nor guilty legends, you are it.

If good and lovely were not one, of both   55
You were the transcript, and originall,
The Elements, the Parent, and the Growth,
And every peece of you, is both their All,
   So'intire are all your deeds, and you, that you
   Must do the same thinge still; you cannot two.   60

But these (as nice thinne Schoole divinity
Serves heresie to furder or represse)
Tast of Poëtique rage, or flattery,
And need not, where all hearts one truth professe;
   Oft from new proofes, and new phrase, new doubts grow,
   As strange attire aliens the men wee know.

Leaving then busie praise, and all appeale,
To higher Courts, senses decree is true,
The Mine, the Magazine, the Commonweale,
The story of beauty,'in Twicknam is, and you.   70
   Who hath seene one, would both; As, who had bin
   In Paradise, would seeke the Cherubin.

51. *stories*: histories (cf. l. 70).
52. *and*: 'all' (acc. to several MSS).
58. *both*: 'worth' (acc. to 1635–69).
60. *thinge* (singular acc. to the MSS, plural acc. to 1633–69).
61. *these*: i.e. verses; also, compliments.
     nice: foolish.
66. *aliens*: makes aliens of; 'alters' (acc. to 1635–54).
67. *busie*: elaborate.
69. *Magazine*: storehouse.
70. *Twicknam*: see note on 13.
72. *Cherubin*: see above, p. 243, note on 60–61.

To Sir *Edward Herbert*. at *Julyers*.

Man is a lumpe, where all beasts kneaded bee,
   Wisdome makes him an Arke where all agree;
The foole, in whom these beasts do live at jarre,
   Is sport to others, and a Theater,
Nor scapes hee so, but is himselfe their prey;   5
   All which was man in him, is eate away,
And now his beasts on one another feed,
   Yet couple'in anger, and new monsters breed;
How happy'is hee, which hath due place assign'd
   To'his beasts, and disaforested his minde!   10
Empail'd himselfe to keepe them out, not in;
   Can sow, and dares trust corne, where they have bin;
Can use his horse, goate, wolfe, and every beast,
   And is not Asse himselfe to all the rest.
Else, man not onely is the heard of swine,   15
   But he's those devills too, which did incline
Them to a headlong rage, and made them worse:
   For man can adde weight to heavens heaviest curse.
As Soules (they say) by our first touch, take in
   The poysonous tincture of Originall sinne,   20
So, to the punishments which God doth fling,
   Our apprehension contributes the sting.

To Sir Edward Herbert – i.e. the elder son of Mrs Magdalen Herbert (see below,
   headnote on p. 296) and brother of the poet (p. 316); poet himself,
   philosopher, soldier, and diplomat; created Lord Herbert of Chirbury in
   1629; and, as Donne's friend, competitor with him in 'obscurenesse' (cf.
   headnote on p. 373).

   The siege of Juliers in the Low Countries by the English, French, and
   Dutch (1610) heralded the advent of the Thirty Years' War. The poem is
   most likely in response to Herbert's *The State Progresse of Ill* (§544).

2. *Arke*: Noah's, wherein men and animals were at peace.
3. *at jarre*: in discord.
8. On the symbol ', here and throughout, see above, p. 5.
10. *disaforested*: in law, the transformation of a forest into a place fit for
    cultivation.
11. *Empail'd*: enclosed.
15–17. When Jesus healed a man by casting out the devils into a herd of swine,
     the devils ran into the sea (Matthew 8.30–34).
20. *poysonous tincture*: the opposite of the 'pure' tincture (above, p. 200, note
    on 66).

To us, as to his chickins, he doth cast
  Hemlocke, and wee as men, his hemlocke taste.
We do infuse to what he meant for meat,   25
  Corrosivenesse, or intense cold or heat.
For, God no such specifique poyson hath
  As kills we know not how; his fiercest wrath
Hath no antipathy, but may be good
  At lest for physicke, if not for our food.   30
Thus man, that might be'his pleasure, is his rod,
  And is his devill, that might be his God.
Since then our businesse is, to rectifie
  Nature, to what she was, wee'are led awry
By them, who man to us in little show;   35
  Greater then due, no forme we can bestow
On him; for Man into himselfe can draw
  All, All his faith can swallow,'or reason chaw.
All that is fill'd, and all that which doth fill,
  All the round world, to man is but a pill,   40
In all it workes not, but it is in all
  Poysonous, or purgative, or cordiall,
For, knowledge kindles Calentures in some,
  And is to others icy *Opium*.
As brave as true, is that profession than   45
  Which you doe use to make; that you know man.
This makes it credible, you have dwelt upon
  All worthy bookes; and now are such an one.
Actions are authors, and of those in you
  Your friends finde every day a mart of new.   50

---

24. *Hemlock*: a herb harmless to birds (*chickins*) but poison to man.
28. *we*: 'men' (acc. to 1635–69).
30. *lest*: least.
     physicke: medicine.
34. *what she was*: i.e. before the Fall of Man.
36. *then*: than.
38. *chaw*: chew.
43. *Calentures*: see above, p. 255, note on 23.
45. *brave*: excellent.
     than: then.
50. *mart*: market.

To the Countesse of Bedford.

T'have written then, when you writ, seem'd to mee
   Worst of spirituall vices, Simony,
And not t'have written then, seemes little lesse
   Then worst of civill vices, thanklessenesse.
In this, my debt I seem'd loath to confesse,   5
   In that, I seem'd to shunne beholdingnesse.
But 'tis not soe, *nothings*, as I am, may
   Pay all they have, and yet have all to pay.
Such borrow in their payments, and owe more
   By having leave to write so, then before.   10
Yet since rich mines in barren grounds are showne,
   May not I yeeld (not gold) but coale or stone?
Temples were not demolish'd, though prophane:
   Here *Peter Joves*, there *Paul* hath Dian's Fane.
So whether my hymnes you admit or chuse,   15
   In me you'have hallowed a Pagan Muse,
And denizend a stranger, who mistaught
   By blamers of the times they mard, hath sought
Vertues in corners, which now bravely doe
   Shine in the worlds best part, or all It; You.   20
I have been told, that vertue'in Courtiers hearts

To the Countesse of Bedford. On the letter's recipient, see above, headnote on
    p. 266.
2.   *Simony*: buying or selling of ecclesiastical preferment.
4 (also 10). *Then*: than.
5.   *debt* (acc. to 1669 and most MSS): 'doubt' (acc. to 1633–54).
7.   *nothings* (singular acc. to 1633, plural acc. to 1635–54).
14. St Peter's basilica in Rome is said to have been built on the site of a temple
    (*Fain*) to Jupiter; St Paul's cathedral in London, on that of a temple to
    Diana.
16. On the symbol ', here and throughout, see above, p. 5.
17. *denizend a stranger*: naturalized a foreigner.
18. *mard*: ruined through their very criticism.
19. *bravely*: excellently.
20. *or all It; You* (acc. to 1635–54): 'or all, in you' (acc. to 1633) or 'or all it,
    you' (acc. to most MSS).
21. *vertue*: its absence is hereafter said to affect adversely both soul and body,
    for the soul requires virtue's preserving power, the body its redemptive
    one (see ll. 57–58; §536).

Suffers an Ostracisme, and departs.
Profit, ease, fitnesse, plenty, bid it goe,
　But whither, only knowing you, I know;
Your (or you) vertue two vast uses serves,　　　　　　　25
　It ransomes one sex, and one Court preserves;
There's nothing but your worth, which being true,
　Is knowne to any other, not to you.
And you can never know it; To admit
　No knowledge of your worth, is some of it.　　　　　30
But since to you, your praises discords bee,
　Stoop, others ills to meditate with mee.
Oh! to confesse wee know not what we should,
　Is halfe excuse, wee know not what we would.
Lightnesse depresseth us, emptinesse fills,　　　　　　35
　We sweat and faint, yet still goe downe the hills;
As new Philosophy arrests the Sunne,
　And bids the passive earth about it runne,
So wee have dull'd our minde, it hath no ends;
　Onely the bodie's busie, and pretends;　　　　　　　40
As dead low earth ecclipses and controules
　The quick high Moone: so doth the body, Soules.
In none but us, are such mixt engines found,
　As hands of double office: For, the ground
We till with them; and them to heav'n wee raise;　　　45
　Who prayer-lesse labours, or, without this, prayes,
Doth but one halfe, that's none; He which said, *Plough*
　And looke not back, to looke up doth allow.

22.　*Ostracisme*: banishment.
23.　*fitnesse*: concern with fit points of etiquette.
25.　The parentheses are an emendation (acc. to some MSS).
26.　*ransomes one sex*: redeems the female sex.
30.　*praises*: 'Phrases' (acc. to a MS).
32.　The comma is an emendation.
37–38. The Copernican theory of the universe (see further below, p. 335, ll. 205 ff. and note).
40.　*pretends*: presumes (§171).
43.　*engines*: instruments.
47.　*He which said*: 'Jesus said unto him, No man, having put his hand to the plough, and looking back, is fit for the kingdom of God' (Luke 9.62).

Good seed degenerates, and oft obeys
  The soyles disease, and into cockle strayes.   50
Let the minds thoughts be but transplanted so,
  Into the body,'and bastardly they grow.
What hate could hurt our bodies like our love?
  Wee but no forraine tyrans could remove,
These not ingrav'd, but inborne dignities,   55
  Caskets of soules; Temples, and Palaces:
For, bodies shall from death redeemed bee,
  Soules but preserv'd, not naturally free;
As men to'our prisons, new soules to us are sent,
  Which learne vice there, and come in innocent.   60
First seeds of every creature are in us,
  What ere the world hath bad, or pretious,
Mans body can produce, hence hath it beene
  That stones, wormes, frogges, and snakes in man are
    seene:
But who ere saw, though nature can worke soe,   65
  That pearle, or gold, or corne in man did grow?
We'have added to the world Virginia,'and sent
  Two new starres lately to the firmament;
Why grudge wee us (not heaven) the dignity
  T'increase with ours, those faire soules company.   70

50. *cockle*: a weed.
51. *Let*: 'Let but' (acc. to 1669).
54. *tyrans*: tyrants.
55. *ingrav'd*: imposed from without.
58. *not*: 'borne' (acc. to 1635–69).
59. *new*: 'now' (ditto).
60. *vice* (ditto): 'it' (acc. to 1633).
61 ff. Physicians often claimed that creatures found in man included even
    serpents and scorpions (§192).
62. *pretious*: precious like *pearle, or gold, or corne* (66), not *bad* or useless like
    stones etc. (64).
67. *Virginia*: discovered, and named after Elizabeth I (the 'Virgin Queen'),
    late in the sixteenth century.
68. *new starres*: probably the ones in the northern constellation described in
    Kepler's *De stella nova* in 1606 (§209); but also alluding – 'almost cer-
    tainly' – to the deaths of Lady Markham and Cecilia Bulstrode (§196; see
    below, pp. 378, 381).
    firmament: see above, p. 65, note on 24.

But I must end this letter, though it doe
  Stand on two truths, neither is true to you.
Vertue hath some perversenesse; For she will
  Neither beleeve her good, nor others ill.
Even in you, vertues best paradise,   75
  Vertue hath some, but wise degrees of vice.
Too many vertues, or too much of one
  Begets in you unjust suspition.
And ignorance of vice, makes vertue lesse,
  Quenching compassion of our wretchednesse.   80
But these are riddles; Some aspersion
  Of vice becomes well some complexion.
Statesmen purge vice with vice, and may corrode
  The bad with bad, a spider with a toad:
For so, ill thralls not them, but they tame ill .   85
  And make her do much good against her will,
But in your Commonwealth or world in you
  Vice hath no office, or good worke to doe.
Take then no vitious purge, but be content
With cordiall vertue, your knowne nourishment.   90

72. *two truths*: the world's evil and the Countess' goodness.
81. *aspersion*: sprinkling.
82. *complexion*: temperament.
85. *thralls*: enslaves.
90. *cordiall*: restorative.

To the Countesse of Bedford.
On New-yeares day.

This twilight of two yeares, not past nor next,
    Some embleme is of mee, or I of this,
Who Meteor-like, of stuffe and forme perplext,
    Whose *what*, and *where*, in disputation is,
      If I should call mee *any thing*, should misse.   5

I summe the yeares, and mee, and finde mee not
    Debtor to th'old, nor Creditor to th'new,
That cannot say, My thankes I have forgot,
    Nor trust I this with hopes, and yet scarce true,
      This bravery is since these times shew'd mee you.   10

In recompence I would show future times
    What you were, and teach them to'urge towards such.
Verse embalmes vertue;'and Tombs, or Thrones of rimes,
    Preserve fraile transitory fame, as much
      As spice doth bodies from corrupt aires touch.   15

Mine are short-liv'd; the tincture of your name
    Creates in them, but dissipates as fast,
New spirits: for, strong agents with the same
    Force that doth warme and cherish, us doe wast;
      Kept hot with strong extracts, no bodies last: 20

To the Countesse of Bedford. Subtitled (acc. to several MSS) 'At New-yeares
    Tide'. On the letter's recipient, see above, headnote on p. 266.
  1. *two yeares*: the one ending, and the one beginning.
  3. *perplext*: confusedly intermixed.
10. *bravery*: bravado.
12. On the symbol ', here and throughout, see above, p. 5.
16. *Mine*: i.e. my verses.
    tincture: see above, p. 200, note on 66.
18. *strong agents*, like *strong extracts* such as vitriol (20), can destroy (*wast*) the
    new substances they have created (cf. §171).

So, my verse built of your just praise, might want
　　Reason and likelihood, the firmest Base,
And made of miracle, now faith is scant,
　　Will vanish soone, and so possesse no place,
　　And you, and it, too much grace might disgrace.　　25

When all (as truth commands assent) confesse
　　All truth of you, yet they will doubt how I
One corne of one low anthills dust, and lesse,
　　Should name, know, or expresse a thing so high,
　　And not an inch, measure infinity.　　30

I cannot tell them, nor my selfe, nor you,
　　But leave, lest truth b'endanger'd by my praise,
And turne to God, who knowes I thinke this true,
　　And useth oft, when such a heart mis-sayes,
　　To make it good, for, such a praiser prayes.　　35

Hee will best teach you, how you should lay out
　　His stock of *beauty*, *learning*, *favour*, *blood;*
He will perplex security with doubt,
　　And cleare those doubts; hide from you,'and shew you good,
　　And so increase your appetite and food;

Hee will teach you, that good and bad have not
　　One latitude in cloysters, and in Court;
Indifferent there the greatest space hath got;
　　Some pitty'is not good there, some vaine disport,
　　On this side, sinne with that place may comport.　　45

28.　*corne*: particle.
29.　The commas are emendations.
35.　*praises prayes* (acc. to 1635–69): 'prayer prayes' (acc. to 1633) or 'prayer praise' (acc. to some MSS).
37.　*favour*: charm.
38.　*perplex*: confound.
　　　security: overconfidence.
42.　*One latitude*: the same position.
43.　*Indifferent*: morally indifferent.
44.　*Some pitty'is not good*: to pity vice would be wrong if it led one to tolerate it (§166).
　　　disport: recreation.
45.　*comport*: agree with.

Yet he, as hee bounds seas, will fixe your houres,
  Which pleasure, and delight may not ingresse,
And though what none else lost, be truliest yours,
  Hee will make you, what you did not, possesse,
    By using others, not vice, but weakenesse.   50

He will make you speake truths, and credibly,
  And make you doubt, that others doe not so:
Hee will provide you keyes, and locks, to spie,
  And scape spies, to good ends, and hee will show
    What you may not acknowledge, what not know.   55

For your owne conscience, he gives innocence,
  But for your fame, a discreet warinesse,
And though to scape, then to revenge offence
  Be better, he showes both, and to represse
    Joy, when your state swells, *sadnesse* when'tis lesse.   60

From need of teares he will defend your soule,
  Or make a rebaptizing of one teare;
Hee cannot, (that's, he will not) dis-inroule
  Your name; and when with active joy we heare
    This private Ghospell, then'tis our New Yeare.   65

47. *Which* (acc. to 1635): 'With' (acc. to 1633).
     ingresse: intrude upon.
48. *what none else lost*: i.e. virtue, which they did not have, and so did not lose.
58. *then*: than.
60. *state*: financial position.
62. *rebaptizing*: regeneration through the sacrament of baptism as a result of penitence (cf. *teare*).
63. *dis-inroule*: remove from the Book of Life.
65. *Ghospell*: i.e. promise of salvation.

To the Countesse of Huntingdon.

MADAME,
Man to Gods image, *Eve*, to mans was made,
    Nor finde wee that God breath'd a soule in her,
Canons will not Church functions you invade,
    Nor lawes to civill office you preferre.

Who vagrant transitory Comets sees,   5
    Wonders, because they'are rare; But a new starre
Whose motion with the firmament agrees,
    Is miracle; for, there no new things are;

In woman so perchance milde innocence
    A seldome comet is, but active good   10
A miracle, which reason scapes, and sense;
    For, Art and Nature this in them withstood.

As such a starre, the *Magi* led to view
    The manger-cradled infant, God below.
By vertues beames by fame deriv'd from you,   15
    May apt soules, and the worst may, vertue know.

To the Countesse of Huntingdon – i.e. the youngest daughter of the Countess of
    Derby and wife of the 5th Earl of Huntingdon (1603 ff.); Donne knew
    her ever since her mother, widowed, had married Sir Thomas Egerton
    (1600) whom Donne was then serving as secretary (consult §558). See
    also below, p. 311.
1.   Widely believed, the claim is not in fact Biblical (cf. Genesis 1.26–27).
3.   *Church Canons* do not allow women to *invade Church functions*.
6 (also 31, 60). On the symbol ', see above, p. 5.
6–8. The *firmament* was said to be beyond change, devoid of *new things*,
    incorruptible (see above, p. 65, note on 24); therefore new stars – like
    those described by Kepler (above, p. 275, note on 68) – could only be
    'against nature', that is, a *miracle*.
10. *A seldome comet*: a rare wonder.
13. *the* (acc. to 1635): 'which' (acc. to 1633).

If the worlds age, and death be argued well
  By the Sunnes fall, which now towards earth doth bend,
Then we might feare that vertue, since she fell
  So low as woman, should be neare her end.   20

But she's not stoop'd, but rais'd; exil'd by men
  She fled to heaven, that's heavenly things, that's you;
She was in all men, thinly scatter'd then,
  But now amass'd, contracted in a few.

She guilded us: But you are gold, and Shee,   25
  Us she inform'd, but transubstantiates you,
Soft dispositions which ductile bee,
  Elixarlike, she makes not cleane, but new.

Though you a wifes and mothers name retaine,
  'Tis not a woman, for all are not soe,   30
But vertue having made you vertue,'is faine
  T'adhere in these names, her and you to show,

Else, being alike pure, wee should neither see,
  As, water being into ayre rarify'd,
Neither appeare, till in one cloud they bee,   35
  So, for our sakes you do low names abide;

Taught by great constellations, which being fram'd,
  Of the most starres, take low names, *Crab*, and *Bull*,
When single planets by the *Gods* are nam'd,
  You covet not great names, of great things full.   40

17. *the worlds age*: said in Donne's time to be nearing 6000 years (for the
    various estimates proposed, see §108).
18. Claimed as part of the 'evidence' for nature's decay (see further below,
    pp. 327 ff.).
23. *then*: i.e. before the Fall of Man.
25–26. The lines are punctuated variously in the editions.
25–28. The alchemical image refers to gold so refined that it may serve as the
    elixir (§218).
25. *guilded*: gilded.
26. *transubstantiates*: see above, p. 73, note on 6.
34–35. In alchemy the elements were said to be inter-convertible, there being a
    primary matter from which they all derived (§261).
38. *Crab, and Bull*: Cancer and Taurus.
39. *nam'd*: e.g. Venus, Mercury, etc.

So you, as woman, one doth comprehend,
    And in the vaile of kindred others see;
To some ye are reveal'd, as in a friend,
    And as a vertuous Prince farre off, to mee.

To whom, because from you all vertues flow,   45
    And 'tis not none, to dare contemplate you,
I, which doe so, as your true subject owe
    Some tribute for that, so these lines are due.

If you can thinke these flatteries, they are,
    For then your judgement is below my praise,   50
If they were so, oft, flatteries worke as farre,
    As Counsels, and as farre th'endeavour raise.

So my ill reaching you might there grow good,
    But I remaine a poyson'd fountaine still;
But not your beauty, vertue, knowledge, blood   55
    Are more above all flattery, then my will.

And if I flatter any, 'tis not you
    But my owne judgement, who did long agoe
Pronounce, that all these praises should be true,
    And vertue should your beauty, 'and birth outgrow.   60

Now that my prophesies are all fulfill'd,
    Rather then God should not be honour'd too,
And all these gifts confess'd, which hee instill'd,
    Your selfe were bound to say that which I doe.

41   *one*: her husband.
42   *vaile*: veil, disguise.
       others see: i.e. her relatives see her.
47   *doe so* (acc. to 1635–69): 'to you' (acc. to 1633).
53   *ill*: clumsy.
55   *But*: 'And' (acc. to 1635–69).
56   (also 62). *then*: than.
58   *long agoe*: Donne had met her many years earlier (see headnote).
59   *praises*: 'prayers' (acc. to a MS).

So I, but your Recorder am in this,   65
   Or mouth, or Speaker of the universe,
A ministeriall notary, for'tis
   Not I, but you and fame, that make this verse;

I was your Prophet in your yonger dayes,
And now your Chaplaine, God in you to praise.   70

To Mr *T. W.*

All haile sweet Poët, more full of more strong fire,
   Then hath or shall enkindle any spirit,
    I lov'd what nature gave thee, but this merit
Of wit and Art I love not but admire;
Who have before or shall write after thee,   5
Their workes, though toughly laboured, will bee
Like infancie or age to mans firme stay,
Or earely and late twilights to mid-day.

Men say, and truly, that they better be
Which be envyed then pittied: therefore I,   10
   Because I wish thee best, doe thee envie:
O wouldst thou, by like reason, pitty mee,

To the Countesse of Huntingdon.
66. *or Speaker*: 'and Speaker' (acc. to 1635–69).
67. *ministeriall notary*: a scribe of supernal authority.
69. *Prophet*: in that he foresaw.

To Mr T. W. (title acc. to most MSS; 'To Mr I. W.' acc. to 1633–69). The
    recipient of this and the next three letters is most likely – but not certainly
    – Thomas Woodward, brother of Rowland Woodward (see above,
    headnote on p. 262). We know only that he was a creditable poet (see his
    poem in §§158, 171).
2 (also 10). *Then*: than.
2. *any*: 'my dull' (acc. to 1635–69 and some MSS).
3. *this*: 'thy' (ditto).

But care not for mee: I, that ever was
In Natures, and in Fortunes gifts, (alas,
   Before thy grace got in the Muses Schoole)   15
   A monster and a begger, am a foole.

Oh how I grieve, that late borne modesty
   Hath got such root in easie waxen hearts,
   That men may not themselves, their owne good parts
Extoll, without suspect of surquedrie,   20
For, but thy selfe, no subject can be found
Worthy thy quill, nor any quill resound
   Thy worth but thine: how good it were to see
   A Poëm in thy praise, and writ by thee.

Now if this song be too'harsh for rime, yet, as   25
   The Painters bad god made a good devill,
   'Twill be good prose, although the verse be evill,
If thou forget the rime as thou dost passe.
Then write, that I may follow, and so bee
Thy debter, thy'eccho, thy foyle, thy zanee.   30
   I shall be thought, if mine like thine I shape,
   All the worlds Lyon, though I be thy Ape.

13. *ever*: 'never' (acc. to a few MSS).
13–16. The parentheses (acc. to 1633) are also placed in front of *But* and after
     Schoole (acc. to 1635–69) or in front of *Before* and after *begger* (acc. to the
     emendation in §158).
15. *Before*: 'But for' (acc. to 1635–69).
     Before thy grace: in contrast with your graciousness; also, in advance of
     your grace (in that Grace ever anticipates).
16. *am a*: 'am now' (acc. to several MSS).
18. *waxen*: impressed.
20. *suspect*: suspicion.
     surquedrie: arrogance.
23. *worth* (acc. to most MSS): 'worke' (acc. to 1633–54).
25 (also 30). On the symbol ', see above, p. 5.
26. *bad god made*: i.e. poorly painted god was inadvertently made to look.
29. *that I* (acc. to most MSS): 'then I' (acc. to 1633–54).
30. *zanee*: buffoon.

To Mr *T. W.*

Hast thee harsh verse as fast as thy lame measure
　Will give thee leave, to him; my pain, and pleasure.
I have given thee, and yet thou art too weake,
　Feete, and a reasoning soule and tongue to speake.
Plead for me, and so by thine and my labour　　　　　　5
　I am thy Creator, thou my Saviour.
Tell him, all questions, which men have defended
　Both of the place and paines of hell, are ended;
And 'tis decreed our hell is but privation
　Of him, at least in this earths habitation:　　　　　　10
And 'tis where I am, where in every street
　Infections follow, overtake, and meete:
Live I or die, by you my love is sent,
　And you'are my pawnes, or else my Testament.

To Mr *T. W.*

Pregnant again with th'old twins Hope, and Feare,
Oft have I askt for thee, both how and where
Thou wert, and what my hopes of letters were;

To Mr T. W. See the headnote to the previous poem. A number of these letters
　　are hereafter cast in sonnet-like forms and frequently as actual sonnets.
　4.　*Feete*: also in the sense of metrical units.
　5–6.　The lines occur in but one MS.
　8.　It was violently disputed where Hell in fact was, and whether its tor-
　　　ments were primarily physical or mental (as in 9: *privation* or absence of
　　　God).
12.　*Infections*: the plague was at the time rampant.
14.　On the symbol ', see above, p. 5.
　　　pawnes: pledges of love.
　　　Testament: testimony if he survives, Will if he does not.

To Mr T. W. On the letter's recipient, see above, headnote on p. 283.

As in the streets sly beggers narrowly
Watch motions of the givers hand and eye,   5
And evermore conceive some hope thereby.

And now thy Almes is given, thy letter'is read,
The body risen againe, the which was dead,
And thy poore starveling bountifully fed.

After this banquet my Soule doth say grace,   10
And praise thee for'it, and zealously imbrace
Thy love, though I thinke thy love in this case
    To be as gluttons, which say 'midst their meat,
    They love that best of which they most do eat.

To Mr *T. W.*

At once, from hence, my lines and I depart,
I to my soft still walks, they to my Heart;
I to the Nurse, they to the child of Art;

Yet as a firme house, though the Carpenter
Perish, doth stand: as an Embassadour   5
Lyes safe, how e'r his king be in danger:

So, though I languish, prest with Melancholy,
My verse, the strict Map of my misery,
Shall live to see that, for whose want I dye.

To Mr T. W.
5. *Watch*: 'Marke' (acc. to a MS).
       and (acc. to the MSS): 'or' (acc. to 1633–69).
6. *conceive*: cf. *Pregnant* (1).
7 (also 11). On the symbol ', see above, p. 5.
13. *meat*: food; also in the sacramental sense centred on the Eucharist.

To Mr T. W. In the 1633 edition the poem follows the preceding one without
       any break or title. On its recipient, see above, headnote on p. 283.
2. *my Heart*: i.e. the poem's recipient.
3. *Nurse . . . of Art*: leisure.
7. *prest*: oppressed.
9. *want*: lack.

Therefore I envie them, and doe repent,   10
That from unhappy mee, things happy'are sent;
Yet as a Picture, or bare Sacrament,
   Accept these lines, and if in them there be
   Merit of love bestow that love on mee.

To Mr *C. B.*

Thy friend, whom thy deserts to thee enchaine,
   Urg'd by this unexcusable occasion,
   Thee and the Saint of his affection
Leaving behinde, doth of both wants complaine;
And let the love I beare to both sustaine   5
   No blott nor maime by this division,
   Strong is this love which ties our hearts in one,
And strong that love pursu'd with amorous paine;
But though besides thy selfe I leave behind
   Heavens liberall and earths thrice-fairer Sunne,   10
   Going to where sterne winter aye doth wonne,
Yet, loves hot fires, which martyr my sad minde,
   Doe send forth scalding sighes, which have the Art
   To melt all Ice, but that which walls her heart.

To Mr T.W.
11. On the symbol ', see above, p. 5.
12. *Picture, Sacrament*: representation and sign of the narrator.

To Mr C. B. – i.e. Christopher Brooke (see above, headnote on p. 250). The
   poem draws on the Petrarchist tradition perhaps to an unmatched degree
   (§374).
2. *unexcusable*: 'inexcusable' (acc. to the MSS), i.e. unavoidable.
4. *both wants*: the lack of both the poem's recipient and his mistress (cf. l. 3).
10. *earths*: 'the' (acc. to 1635–54).
11. *sterne*: 'sterv'd' (acc. to 1635–69).
   wonne: 'dwell, or abide' (Bullokar).

To Mr *S. B*.

O thou which to search out the secret parts
   Of the India, or rather Paradise
   Of knowledge, hast with courage and advise
Lately launch'd into the vast Sea of Arts,
Disdaine not in thy constant travailing   5
   To doe as other Voyagers, and make
   Some turnes into lesse Creekes, and wisely take
Fresh water at the Heliconian spring;
I sing not, Siren like, to tempt; for I
   Am harsh, nor as those Scismatiques with you,   10
   Which draw all wits of good hope to their crew;
But seeing in you bright sparkes of Poetry,
   I, though I brought noe fuell, had desire
With these Articulate blasts to blow the fire.

To Mr S. B. – i.e. probably Christopher Brooke's younger brother Samuel
    (see above, headnote on p. 250), who officiated at Donne's clandestine
    marriage and was imprisoned; in time, he became Master of Trinity
    College, Cambridge (1629).
3. *advise*: judgement.
5. *travailing*: journeying; also, labouring.
8. *Heliconian spring*: the fountain Castalia in Mount Helicon, symbolizing
    poetic inspiration.
9. *Siren like*: see above, p. 181, note on 55.
10. *Scismatiques*: secessionists.
13. *I, though*: 'I thought' (acc. to 1650–54).
    had: 'but' (ditto).

To Mr *B. B.*

Is not thy sacred hunger of science
   Yet satisfy'd? Is not thy braines rich hive
   Fulfil'd with hony which thou dost derive
From the Arts spirits and their Quintessence?
Then weane thy selfe at last, and thee withdraw   5
   From Cambridge thy old nurse, and, as the rest,
   Here toughly chew, and sturdily digest
Th'immense vast volumes of our common law;
And begin soone, lest my griefe grieve thee too,
   Which is, that that which I should have begun   10
   In my youthes morning, now late must be done;
And I, as Giddy Travellers, must doe,
   Which stray or sleepe all day, and having lost
   Light and strength, darke and tir'd must then ride post.

If thou unto thy Muse be marryed,   15
   Embrace her ever, ever multiply,
   Be far from me that strange Adulterie
To tempt thee and procure her widowhed.
My Muse, (for I had one,) because I'am cold,
   Divorc'd her selfe, the cause being in me,   20
   That I can take no new in Bigamye,
Not my will only but power doth withhold.

To Mr B. B. Variously identified as Basil Brooke (not related to Christopher or
    Samuel Brooke: cf. headnote to the previous poem) or Beauprè Bell,
    'B.B.' in fact eludes every attempt at detection. Editors normally print
    the letter as a single poem; but constituted as it is of two sonnets, it can
    also be separated after l. 14 (cf. §171).
  1. *science*: knowledge.
  3. *Fulfill'd*: filled full (§166).
  4. *Quintessence*: as above, p. 79, note on 8.
  7. *digest*: 'disgest' (acc. to some MSS); cf. above, p. 220, note on 27.
 12. *Giddy*: foolish.
 13. *stray*: 'stay' (acc. to a MS).
 14. *ride post*: gallop furiously (§166).
 16. *ever, ever*: 'still: encrease and' (acc. to a MS).
 18. *widowhed* (ditto): 'widdowhood' (acc. to 1633–69).
 19. *Muse* (acc. to most MSS): 'nurse' (acc. to 1633–69).

Hence comes it, that these Rymes which never had
  Mother, want matter, and they only have
  A little forme, the which their Father gave;   25
They are prophane, imperfect, oh, too bad
  To be counted Children of Poetry
  Except confirm'd and Bishoped by thee.

To Mr *R. W.*

If, as mine is, thy life a slumber be,
  Seeme, when thou read'st these lines, to dreame of me,
Never did Morpheus nor his brother weare
  Shapes soe like those Shapes, whom they would appeare,
As this my letter is like me, for it
  Hath my name, words, hand, feet, heart, minde and wit;
It is my deed of gift of mee to thee,
  It is my Will, my selfe the Legacie.
So thy retyrings I love, yea envie,
  Bred in thee by a wise melancholy,   10
That I rejoyce, that unto where thou art,
  Though I stay here, I can thus send my heart,
As kindly'as any enamored Patient
  His Picture to his absent Love hath sent.

To Mr B. B.
28. *confirm'd*: approved; also, ritually *Bishoped* (confirmed by a bishop) on entering maturity.

To Mr R. W. – i.e. Rowland Woodward (see above, headnote on p. 262). The poem is also printed without breaks (acc. to 1635–69).
3–14. The lines are explicitly concerned with the function of letter-writing (§547).
3. The god of sleep *Morpheus* could assume the shapes of men; and *his brother* Phantasus, those of inanimate objects.
9. *retyrings*: the withdrawal of the contemplative man into a *wise melancholy* (10).
13 (also 28). On the symbol ', see above, p. 5.
13. *Patient*: sufferer.
15. *then*: than.

All newes I thinke sooner reach thee thcn mee;   15
  Havens are Heavens, and Ships wing'd Angels be,
The which both Gospell, and sterne threatnings bring;
  Guyanaes harvest is nip'd in the spring,
I feare; And with us (me thinkes) Fate deales so
  As with the Jewes guide God did; he did show   20
Him the rich land, but bar'd his entry in,
  Oh, slownes is our punishment and sinne;
Perchance, these Spanish businesse being done,
  Which as the Earth between the Moone and Sun
Eclipse the light which Guyana would give,   25
  Our discontinued hopes we shall retrive:
But if (as all th'All must) hopes smoake away,
  Is not Almightie Vertue 'an India?

If men be worlds, there is in every one
  Some thing to answere in some proportion   30
All the worlds riches: And in good men, this
  Vertue, our formes forme and our soules soule is.

16–18. With an eye always on the Spanish Empire in South America – espe-
    cially Guiana – the English fleet en route to the Azores was battered by a
    storm (see above, p. 250); it returned to such *Havens* as the harbour of
    Plymouth, giving up its role as an angel intent on disseminating the
    Gospell and warning the Spanish with *sterne threatnings*.
20. *the Jewes guide*: Moses, whose entry into the Promised Land was barred
    (21: *bar'd*) by God (Deuteronomy 3.27).
22. *Oh* (acc. to most MSS): 'Our' (acc. to 1633–69).
23. *businesse* (singular form with plural meaning).
27. *all th'All*: the totality of the created order which, like *hopes*, will be
    'smoked away' at the Last Judgement.
28. *India*: here, a mine of inestimable spiritual benefits.

To Mr *I. L.*

Of that short Roll of friends writ in my heart
   Which with thy name begins, since their depart,
Whether in the English Provinces they be,
   Or drinke of Po, Sequan, or Danubie,
There's none that sometimes greets us not, and yet   5
   Your Trent is Lethe', that past, us you forget.
You doe not duties of Societies,
   If from the'embrace of a lov'd wife you rise,
View your fat Beasts, stretch'd Barnes, and labour'd fields,
   Eate, play, ryde, take all joyes which all day yeelds,
And then againe to your embracements goe:
   Some houres on us your frends, and some bestow
Upon your Muse, else both wee shall repent,
   I that my love, she that her guifts on you are spent.

To Mr *I. L.*

Blest are your North parts, for all this long time
   My Sun is with you, cold and darke'is our Clime;
Heavens Sun, which staid so long from us this yeare,
   Staid in your North (I thinke) for she was there,

`To Mr I. L.` Also specified as 'T. L.' (acc. to a MS), but in either case not yet
   identified.
4. *Sequan*: the river Seine; cf. below, p. 405, l. 16 and note.
6. *Trent*: a river in north central England; the poem's recipient evidently
   hailed from the North.
   Lethe: the river of forgetfulness in Hades.
8. On the symbol ', see above, p. 5.
9. *stretch'd*: extensive; 'wretched' (acc. to a MS).

`To Mr I. L.` Also specified as 'I.P.' (acc. to 1633–69) and 'T.L.' (acc. to a MS).
   See the headnote to the previous poem.
1. *North parts*: see the previous poem, note on 6.
2. *Sun*: the narrator's mistress, who was staying with 'I.L.' (l. 4).
   On the symbol ', see above, p. 5.

And hether by kinde nature drawne from thence,   5
  Here rages, chafes, and threatens pestilence;
Yet I, as long as shee from hence doth staie,
  Thinke this no South, no Sommer, nor no day
With thee my kinde and unkinde heart is run,
  There sacrifice it to that beauteous Sun: 10
And since thou art in Paradise and need'st crave
  No joyes addition, helpe thy friend to save.
So may thy pastures with their flowery feasts,
  As suddenly as Lard, fat thy leane beasts;
So may thy woods oft poll'd, yet ever weare   15
  A greene, and when thee list, a golden haire;
So may all thy sheepe bring forth Twins; and so
  In chace and race may thy horse all out goe;
So may thy love and courage ne'r be cold;
  Thy Sonne ne'r Ward; Thy lov'd wife ne'r seem old;   20
But maist thou wish great things, and them attaine,
  As thou telst her and none but her my paine.

6. *chafes*: 'burnes' (acc. to a MS).
    pestilence: the plague.
11–12. The lines occur in but one MS.
12. *help thy friend to save*: help to save thy friend.
15. *poll'd*: have their branches cut off.
16. *when thee list*: when you wish it.
     thee: 'shee' (acc. to 1635–69).
     thee list: 'thou wilt' (acc. to a MS).
20. *ne'r Ward*: i.e. never need a guardian but have his father always.
     lov'd: 'fair' (acc. to one MS) or 'young' (acc. to another).
22. *her*: see note on 2.

To *E.* of *D.* with six holy Sonnets.

See Sir, how as the Suns hot Masculine flame
  Begets strange creatures on Niles durty slime,
  In me, your fatherly yet lusty Ryme
(For, these songs are their fruits) have wrought the same;
But though the ingendring force from whence they came   5
  Bee strong enough, and nature doe admit
  Seaven to be borne at once, I send as yet
But six, they say, the seaventh hath still some maime;
  I choose your judgement, which the same degree
  Doth with her sister, your invention, hold,   10
As fire these drossie Rymes to purifie,
  Or as Elixir, to change them to gold;
You are that Alchimist which alwaies had
Wit, whose one spark could make good things of bad.

To Sir *H. W.*
at his going Ambassador to *Venice.*

After those reverend papers, whose soule is
  Our good and great Kings lov'd hand and fear'd name,
By which to you he derives much of his,
  And (how he may) makes you almost the same,

To E. of D. – i.e. the Earl of Dorset. It is not known with certainty which six of
  the Holy Sonnets are referred to. Clearly a verse letter, the sonnet is
  nevertheless placed by all modern editors among the Divine Poems; but
  the 1633 edition disagrees.
1–2. See above, p. 230, note on 18–19.
8.   *maime*: defect.
12.   *Elixar*: see above, p. 86, note on 7.

To Sir H. W. – i.e. Henry Wotton (see above, headnote on p. 256), who was
  knighted by King James I on 8 July 1604 and sailed for Venice five days
  later.
1.   *papers*: the documents of Wotton's accreditation to the Venetian
  authorities; cf. his own *learned papers* (9) and Donne's *paper* or poem (17).
2.   *fear'd*: 'serv'd' (acc. to a MS).
3.   *derives*: imparts.

A Taper of his Torch, a copie writ   5
  From his Originall, and a faire beame
Of the same warme, and dazeling Sun, though it
  Must in another Sphere his vertue streame:

After those learned papers which your hand
  Hath stor'd with notes of use and pleasures too,   10
From which rich treasury you may command
  Fit matter whether you will write or doe:

After those loving papers, where friends send
  With glad griefe, to your Sea-ward steps, farewel,
Which thicken on you now, as prayers ascend   15
  To heaven in troupes at'a good mans passing bell:

Admit this honest paper, and allow
  It such an audience as your selfe would aske;
What you must say at Venice this meanes now,
  And hath for nature, what you have for taske.   20

To sweare much love, not to be chang'd before
  Honour alone will to your fortune fit;
Nor shall I then honour your fortune, more
  Then I have done your honour wanting it.

But'tis an easier load (though both oppresse)   25
  To want, then governe greatnesse, for wee are
In that, our owne and onely businesse,
  In this, wee must for others vices care;

---

5. *A Taper of his Torch*: as ambassador, Wotton serves King James; but both
    are 'tapers' (wicks) of a greater *Torch*, God (§555).
8. *Sphere*: see above, p. 80, note on 23.
11. *rich*: 'safe' (acc. to a MS).
13. *where*: 'which' (acc. to 1635–69).
16. On the symbol ', see above, p. 5.
24 (also 26). *Then*: than.
24. *honour wanting it*: 'noble-wanting-wit' (acc. to 1635–69).
26. *want*: lack.

'Tis therefore well your spirits now are plac'd
  In their last Furnace, in activity;   30
Which fits them (Schooles and Courts and warres o'rpast)
  To touch and test in any best degree.

For mee, (if there be such a thing as I)
  Fortune (if there be such a thing as shee)
Spies that I beare so well her tyranny,   35
  That she thinks nothing else so fit for mee;

But though she part us, to heare my oft prayers
  For your increase, God is as neere mee here;
And to send you what I shall begge, his staires
  In length and ease are alike every where.   40

To Mrs *M. H.*

Mad paper stay, and grudge not here to burne
  With all those sonnes whom my braine did create,
At lest lye hid with mee, till thou returne
  To rags againe, which is thy native state.

What though thou have enough unworthinesse   5
  To come unto great place as others doe,

To Sir H.W.
30. *last Furnace*: the final process in the refinement of substances until the
     production of the elixir (see above, p. 86, note on 7).
32. *test*: 'taste' (acc. to 1669).
38. *increase*: prosperity.
39. *staires*: as in Jacob's ladder to Heaven (Genesis 28.12).

To Mrs M. H. – i.e. Magdalen Herbert, mother of Sir Edward (see above,
    headnote on p. 271) and George Herbert (below, headnote on p. 316);
    widowed in 1596, she married in 1608 Sir John Danvers who was several
    years her junior. One of the period's great ladies, she was an intimate
    friend of Donne's (cf. §539). It is traditionally held that Elegy IX (above,
    p. 152) was also addressed to her; see further below, p. 317.
1. *paper*: the poem itself.
2. *sonnes*: both sons and suns.
    my: 'thy' (acc. to 1635–69).
3. *lest*: least.

That's much; emboldens, pulls, thrusts I confesse,
　But'tis not all; Though should'st be wicked too.

And, that thou canst not learne, or not of mee;
　Yet thou wilt goe? Goe, since thou goest to her　　　10
Who lacks but faults to be a Prince, for shee,
　Truth, whom they dare not pardon, dares preferre.

But when thou com'st to that perplexing eye
　Which equally claimes *love* and *reverence*,
Thou wilt not long dispute it, thou wilt die;　　　15
　And having little now, have then no sense.

Yet when her warme redeeming hand, which is
　A miracle; and made such to worke more,
Doth touch thee (saples leafe) thou grow'st by this
　Her creature; glorify'd more then before.　　　20

Then as a mother which delights to heare
　Her early child mis-speake halfe uttered words,
Or, because majesty doth never feare
　Ill or bold speech, she Audience affords.

And then, cold speechlesse wretch, thou diest againe,　　　25
　And wisely; what discourse is left for thee?
For, speech of ill, and her, though must abstaine,
　And is there any good which is not shee?

Yet maist thou praise her servants, though not her,
　And wit, and vertue,'and honour her attend,　　　30
And since they'are but her cloathes, thou shalt not erre
　If thou her shape and beauty'and grace commend.

7.　The line is punctuated variously in the MSS and the editions.
15.　*dispute*: argue about.
19.　*saples*: lifeless; 'sapp-lesse' (acc. to one MS) or 'shapeless' (acc. to another).
20.　*then*: than.
22.　*early*: young.
27.　*For*: 'From' (acc. to 1635–69).
30–32 (also 45). On the symbol ', see above, p. 5.

Who knowes thy destiny? when thou hast done,
   Perchance her Cabinet may harbour thee,
Whither all noble ambitious wits doe runne,   35
   A nest almost as full of Good as shee.

When thou are there, if any, whom wee know,
   Were sav'd before, and did that heaven partake,
When she revolves his papers, marke what show
   Of favour, she alone, to them doth make.   40

Marke, if to get them, she o'r skip the rest,
   Marke, if she read them twice, or kisse the name;
Marke, if she doe the same that they protest,
   Marke, if she marke whether her woman came.

Marke, if slight things be'objected, and o'r blowne,   45
   Marke, if her oathes against him be not still
Reserv'd, and that shee grieves she's not her owne,
   And chides the doctrine that denies Freewill.

I bid thee not doe this to be my spie;
   Nor to make my selfe her familiar;   50
But so much I doe love her choyce, that I
   Would faine love him that shall be lov'd of her.

33. *Who knowes*: 'We knowe' (acc. to a few MSS).
38. *sav'd*: preserved; also, made fit for heaven.
39. *his*: 'her' (acc. to a few MSS).
43. *protest*: stipulate (§171).
44. *whether*: 'whither' (acc. to 1635–69).
     woman: maid.
50. *familiar*: confidant.
51. *choyce*: the man she intends to marry, Sir John Danvers (§215).

To the Countesse of Bedford.

Honour is so sublime perfection,
And so refinde; that when God was alone
And creaturelesse at first, himselfe had none;

But as of the elements, these which wee tread,
Produce all things with which wee'are joy'd or fed,   5
And, those are barren both above our head:

So from low persons doth all honour flow;
Kings, whom they would have honoured, to us show,
And but *direct* our honour, not *bestow*.

For when from herbs the pure part must be wonne   10
From grosse, by Stilling, this is better done
By despis'd dung, then by the fire or Sunne.

Care not then, Madame,'how low your praysers lye;
In labourers balads oft more piety
Gods findes, then in *Te Deums* melodie.   15

And, ordinance rais'd on Towers so many mile
Send not their voice, nor last so long a while
As fires from th'earths low vaults in *Sicil* Isle.

Should I say I liv'd darker then were true,
Your radiation can all clouds subdue,   20
But one,'tis best light to contemplate you.

To the Countesse of Bedford. See above, headnote on p. 266.
  2. *sublime*: purified, in the alchemical sense prevalent in this poem.
  4. *elements*: the traditional four; *these* are earth and water, *those* (6) air and
    fire.
  5 (also 13). On the symbol ', see above, p. 5.
11. *Stilling*: distillation.
12. *dung*: regarded by alchemists as a source of reliably even heat.
    or: 'of' (acc. to 1635–54).
12 (also 15, 19). *then*: than.
13. *praysers* (acc. to most MSS): 'prayses' (acc. to 1633–69) or 'prayers' (acc.
    to a MS).
15. *Te Deums*: hymns of praise.
18. The volcanic Mount Etna in Sicily.
21. *But one*: except for God.

You, for whose body God made better clay,
Or tooke Soules stuffe such as shall late decay,
Or such as needs small change at the last day.

This, as an Amber drop enwraps a Bee,   25
Covering discovers your quicke Soule; that we
May in your through-shine front your hearts thoughts see.

You teach (though wee learne not) a thing unknowne
To our late times, the use of specular stone,
Through which all things within without were shown.   30

Of such were Temples; so and such you are;
Beeing and *seeming* is your equall care,
And *vertues* whole *summe* is but *know* and *dare*.

But as our Soules of growth and Soules of sense
Have birthright of our reasons Soule, yet hence   35
They fly not from that, nor seeke presidence:

Natures first lesson, so discretion,
Must not grudge zeale a place, nor yet keepe none,
Not banish it selfe, nor religion.

Discretion is a wisemans Soule, and so   40
Religion is a Christians, and you know
How these are one, her *yea*, is not her *no*.

<hr/>

26. *discovers*: uncovers, discloses.
     quicke: living; 'grosse' (acc. to a MS).
27. *through-shine*: translucent.
     front: countenance; 'face' (acc. to a few MSS).
     your hearts (acc. to most MSS): 'our hearts' (acc. to 1633–69).
29. *specular stone*: see above, p. 52, note on 6.
30. Because of the specular stone's translucent nature (§315).
31. *so and such*: 'so and of such' (acc. to several MSS).
34–35. Plants were said to have but the 'soul' of growth; animals, the 'soul' of
       sense too; and man, the 'soul' of reason in addition to the other two. Cf.
       below, p. 308, ll. 52–54, and p. 357, ll. 160–62.
36. *presidence*: 'precedence' (acc. to 1669).
40–42. These lines precede ll. 34–39 (acc. to 1635–69 and some MSS).
42. *her yea, is not her no*: i.e. discretion and religion are in complete accord.

Nor may we hope to sodder still and knit
These two, and dare to breake them; nor must wit
Be colleague to religion, but be it.   45

In those poor types of God (round circles) so
Religious tipes, the peecelesse centers flow,
And are in all the lines which alwayes goe.

If either ever wrought in you alone
Or principally, then religion   50
Wrought your ends, and your wayes discretion.

Goe thither stil, goe the same way you went,
Who so would change, do covet or repent;
Neither can reach you, great and innocent.

To the Countesse of *Bedford*.
Begun in France but never perfected.

Though I be *dead*, and buried, yet I have
    (Living in you,) Court enough in my grave,
As oft as there I thinke my selfe to bee,
    So many resurrections waken mee.
That thankfullnesse your favours have begot   5
    In mee, embalmes mee, that I doe not rot;
This season as 'tis Easter, as 'tis spring,
    Must both to growth and to confession bring

To the Countesse of Bedford.
43.   *sodder*: solder.
46.   *types*: emblems.
      round circles: assertive of perfection and therefore of God.
48.   *alwayes*: i.e. all ways.
50–51. *then* . . . etc.: ' 'twas Religion, / Yet you neglected not Discretion'
      (acc. to a MS).
51.   *wayes*: means.

To the Countesse of Bedford. See above, headnote on p. 266. This incomplete
      poem was written during Donne's stay in France in 1611–12.
  1.   *dead, and buried*: because absent from England.
  5.   *begot* (acc. to 1635): 'forgot' (acc. to 1633).

My thoughts dispos'd unto your influence, so,
  These verses bud, so these confessions grow;   10
First I confesse I have to others lent
  Your stock, and over prodigally spent
Your treasure, for since I had never knowne
  Vertue or beautie, but as they are growne
In you, I should not thinke or say they shine,   15
  (So as I have) in any other Mine;
Next I confesse this my confession,
  For, 'tis some fault thus much to touch upon
Your praise to you, where half rights seeme too much,
  And make your minds sincere complexion blush.   20
Next I confesse my'impenitence, for I
  Can scarce repent my first fault, since thereby
Remote low Spirits, which shall ne'r read you,
  May in lessc lessons finde enough to doe,
By studying copies, not Originals,   25
      Desunt cætera.

11 ff. The lines betray Donne's uneasiness lest he should be deprived of Lady Bedford's favour because he had overpraised Elizabeth Drury (see below, pp. 324 ff.); but his argument is 'more ingenious than convincing' (§196).
14. *or*: 'and' (acc. to 1650–69).
20. *complexion*: temperament.
21. On the symbol ', see above, p. 5.
24. *lesse*: inferior.
26. *Desunt cætera*: 'the rest is lacking'.

A Letter to the Lady *Carey*, and Mrs *Essex Riche*, From *Amyens*.

Madame,
Here, where by all, all Saints invoked are,
T'were too much Scisme to bee singulare,
And gainst a practise generall to war;

yett, turninge to Saints, should my'Humilitee
To other Saint, then yow, directed bee,   5
That were to make my Scisme Heresee.

nor would I bee a Convertite so cold
As not to tell ytt; If thys bee to bold,
Pardons are in thys Market cheaply sold.

where, because Fayth ys in too lowe degree,   10
I thought yt some Apostleship in mee,
To speak things which by Fayth alone I see:

A Letter . . . Written during Donne's stay in France (cf. headnote to the
    previous poem), the present verses were addressed to the first of the two
    ladies named. The daughters of Robert Lord Rich and his first wife
    Penelope Devereux (Sir Philip Sidney's 'Stella'), they were in all likeli-
    hood not known to Donne personally.
       Uniquely, the poem is the only one to survive in Donne's own
    handwriting. First announced by A. J. Smith (§553), then transcribed
    (faultily) by Helen Gardner and corrected by Nicolas Barker (§538), it is
    reproduced here without any of the variants whether of the editions or
    the MSS.
4. On the symbol ', here and throughout, see above, p. 5.
5. *then*: than.
6. *Heresee*: heresy.
7. *Convertite*: convert.
8. *to bold*: too bold.
9. The sale of pardons and indulgences was widespread in Catholic
    countries.
10. *Fayth*: the Protestant doctrine of justification (salvation) *by Fayth alone*
    (12), in opposition to the Catholic emphasis on the concurrent relevance
    of good works (cf. above, p. 106, note on 19–21).
11. *Apostleship*: mission.

That ys, of yow; who are a firmament
Of vertues, where no one ys growen, nor spent;
Thay'are your Materialls, not your Ornament.   15

Others, whom wee call vertuous, are not so
In theyr whole Substance, but theyr vertues grow
But in theyr Humors, and at Seasons show.

For when through tastles flatt Humilitee,
In Doe-bakd men, some Harmelesnes wee see,   20
Tis but hys Flegme that's vertuous, and not hee.

so ys the Blood sometymes; who ever ran
To Danger unimportund, hee was than
no better then a Sanguine vertuous man.

So Cloystrall Men who in pretence of fear,   25
All Contributions to thys Lyfe forbear,
Have vertu in Melancholy, and onely there.

spirituall Cholerique Critiqs, which in all
Religions, find faults, and forgive no fall,
Have, through thys Zeale, vertu, but in theyr Gall.   30

we'are thus but parcell-gilt; To Gold we'are growen,
when vertu ys our Soules Complexione;
who knowes hys vertues Name, or Place, hath none.

13.   *are*: 'is' (acc. to 1633).
13–14. *firmament . . . where no one ys growen, nor spent*: see above, p. 65, note
    on 24.
18.   *Humors*: the traditional four (see below, p. 336, note on 241), here
    specified as *Flegme* (21), *Blood* (22), *Melancholy* or black bile (27), and
    Cholerique or yellow bile (28).
20.   *Doe-bakd*: stodgy.
23.   *than*: then.
24.   *then*: than.
25.   *Cloystrall*: retiring.
28.   *spirituall*: concerned with spiritual matters.
30.   *thys*: 'their' (acc. to 1633).
31.   *parcell-gilt*: partly gilded.
32.   *Complexione*: temperament.

vertu ys but Aguishe, when tis Severall;
By'Occasion wak'd, and Circumstantiall;   35
True vertu ys Soule, allways in all deeds all.

Thys vertu, thinkinge to give Dignitee
To your Soule, found there no infirmitee;
for your Soule was as good vertu as shee.

shee therfore wrought upon that part of yow,   40
which ys scarse lesse then Soule, as shee could doe,
And soe hath made your Beauty vertue too;

Hence comes yt, that your Beauty wounds not harts
As others, with prophane and Sensuall darts,
But, as an Influence, vertuous thoughts imparts.   45

But if such frinds, by the'honor of your Sight
Grow capable of thys so great a light,
As to partake your vertues, and theyr might,

what must I thinke that Influence must doe,
where yt finds Simpathy, and Matter too,   50
vertu, and Beauty, of the same stuffe, as yow:

which ys, your noble worthy Sister; shee,
Of whom, if what in thys my extasye
And Revelation of yow both, I see,

I should write here, As in short Galleryes   55
The Master at the end large glasses tyes,
So to present the roome twice to our eyes,

---

34. *Aguishe*: fitful; 'anguish' (acc. to 1650–54).
     Severall: i.e. appears spasmodically, whether demanded by a given occa-
     sion or circumstance (35).
41. *then*: than.
53. *extasye*: the mystical state of one who obtains a *Revelation* (54).
56. *glasses*: mirrors.
57. *our*: 'your' (acc. to some MSS).

So I should give thys letter length, and say
That which I sayd of yow; There ys no way
from eyther, but by th'other, not to stray.   60

May therfore thys bee'inough to testify
My true Devotion, free from flattery.
He that beleevs himselfe, doth never ly.

To the Countesse of Salisbury.
August. 1614.

Faire, great, and good, since seeing you, wee see
What Heaven can doe, and what any Earth can be:
Since now your beauty shines, now when the Sunne
Growne stale, is to so low a value runne,
That his disshevel'd beames and scattered fires   5
Serve but for Ladies Periwigs and Tyres
In lovers Sonnets: you come to repaire
Gods booke of creatures, teaching what is faire.
Since now, when all is withered, shrunke, and dri'd,
All Vertues ebb'd out to a dead low tyde,   10
All the worlds frame being crumbled into sand,
Where every man thinks by himselfe to stand,
Integritie, friendship, and confidence,
(Ciments of greatnes) being vapor'd hence,
And narrow man being fill'd with little shares,   15
Court, Citie, Church, are all shops of small-wares,
All having blowne to sparkes their noble fire,
And drawne their sound gold-ingot into wyre;

To the Countesse of Salisbury – i.e. Lady Catherine Howard, wife of William
    Cecil, second Earl of Salisbury. Donne also wrote an epithalamion on the
    marriage of her sister (above, p. 197).
2. *and* (omitted acc. to 1635–54).
6. *Tyres*: attires, apparel.
8. *Gods booke of creatures*: the natural order, habitually contrasted to God's
    written book, the Bible (cf. Sir Thomas Browne, *Religio Medici*, I, 16).
9 ff. See further below, p. 335, ll. 212 ff.
15. *shares*: portions.

All trying by a love of littlenesse
To make abridgments, and to draw to lesse,   20
Even that nothing, which at first we were;
Since in these times, your greatnesse doth appeare,
And that we learne by it, that man to get
Towards him, that's infinite, must first be great.
Since in an age so ill, as none is fit   25
So much as to accuse, much lesse mend it,
(For who can judge, or witnesse of those times
Where all alike are guiltie of the crimes?)
Where he that would be good, is thought by all
A monster, or at best fantasticall: 30
Since now you durst be good, and that I doe
Discerne, by daring to contemplate you,
That there may be degrees of faire, great, good,
Through your light, largenesse, vertue understood:
If in this sacrifice of mine, be showne   35
Any small sparke of these, call it your owne.
And if things like these, have been said by mee
Of others; call not that Idolatrie.
For had God made man first, and man had seene
The third daies fruits, and flowers, and various greene,   40
He might have said the best that he could say
Of those faire creatures, which were made that day.
And when next day he had admir'd the birth
Of Sun, Moone, Stars, fairer then late-prais'd earth,
Hee might have said the best that he could say,   45
And not be chid for praising yesterday:
So though some things are not together true,
As, that another is worthiest, and, that you:

24. *him*: God.
29. *Where*: 'When' (acc. to a few MSS).
35. *sacrifice*: the offering that is the present poem.
38. *Idolatrie*: 'Adulterie' (acc. to a few MSS).
39 ff. *man*: created on the sixth 'day', while plants were made on the third, and
       the 'lights in the firmament' on the fourth (Genesis 1.11 ff.).
44. *then*: than.

Yet, to say so, doth not condemne a man,
If when he spoke them, they were both true than.   50
How faire a proofe of this, in our soule growes?
Wee first have soules of growth, and sense, and those,
When out last soule, our soule immortall came,
Were swallowed into it, and have no name.
Nor doth he injure those soules, which doth cast   55
The power and praise of both them, on the last;
No more doe I wrong any; I adore
The same things now, which I ador'd before,
The subject chang'd, and measure; the same thing
In a low constable, and in the King   60
I reverence; His power to work on mee;
So did I humbly reverence each degree
Of faire, great, good, but more, now I am come
From having found their *walkes*, to find their *home*.
And as I owe my first soules thankes, that they   65
For my last soule did fit and mould my clay,
So am I debtor unto them, whose worth,
Enabled me to profit, and take forth
This new great lesson, thus to study you;
Which none, not reading others, first, could doe.   70
Nor lacke I light to read this booke, though I
In a dark Cave, yea in a Grave doe lie;
For as your fellow Angells, so you doe
Illustrate them who come to study you.
The first whom we in Histories doe finde   75
To have profest all Arts, was one borne blinde:
He lackt those eyes beasts have as well as wee,
Not those, by which Angels are seene and see;
So, though I'am borne without those eyes to live,
Which fortune, who hath none her selfe, doth give,   80

50.   *than*: then.
52–54.   On the three 'souls', see above, p. 300, note on 34–35.
57.   *any; I*: 'any, if I' (acc. to 1635–69).
74.   *Illustrate*: enlighten.
76.   *one borne blind*: Homer.
77–78.   Both lines are omitted in some MSS.
79.   On the symbol ', see above, p. 5.

Which are, fit meanes to see bright courts and you,
Yet may I see you thus, as now I doe;
I shall by that, all goodnesse have discern'd,
And though I burne my librarie, be learn'd.

Elegie to the Lady Bedford.

You that are she and you, that's double shee,
    In her dead face, halfe of your selfe shall see;
Shee was the other part, for so they doe
    Which build them friendships, become one of two;
So two, that but themselves no third can fit,   5
    Which were to be so, when they were not yet
Twinnes, though their birth *Cusco*, and *Musco* take,
    As divers starres one Constellation make,
Pair'd like two eyes, have equall motion, so
    Both but one meanes to see, one way to goe;   10
Had you dy'd first, a carcasse shee had beene;
    And wee your rich Tombe in her face had seene;
She like the Soule is gone, and you here stay
    Not a live friend; but th'other halfe of clay;
And since you act that part, As men say, here   15
    Lies such a Prince, when but one part is there,
And do all honour and devotion due
    Unto the whole, so wee all reverence you;
For, such a friendship who would not adore
    In you, who are all what both was before,   20
Not all, as if some perished by this,
    But so, as all in you contracted is;

Elegie to the Lady Bedford. Written as a consolation to the Countess (see above,
    headnote on p. 266) on the death of someone close to her, the poem has
    been grouped under the Epicedes and Obsequies in several MSS and one
    modern edition (§163).
1. *she and you,*: 'she, and you' (acc. to 1633–39).
7. *Cusco, and Musco*: Cuzco in Peru, and Moscow.
8. *one Constellation*: such as Gemini, the *Twinnes* (7).

As of this all, though many parts decay,
　The pure which elemented them shall stay;
And though diffus'd, and spread in infinite,　　　　25
　Shall recollect, and in one All unite:
So madame, as her Soule to heaven is fled,
　Her flesh rests in the earth, as in the bed;
Her vertues do, as to their proper spheare,
　Returne to dwell with you, of whom they were;　　30
As perfect motions are all circular,
　So they to you, their sea, whence lesse streames are;
Shee was all spices, you all metalls; so
　In you two wee did both rich Indies know;
And as no fire, nor rust can spend or waste　　　　35
　One dramme of gold, but what was first shall last,
Though it bee forc'd in water, earth, salt, aire,
　Expans'd in infinite, none will impaire;
So, to your selfe you may additions take,
　But nothing can you lesse, or changed make.　　　40
Seeke not in seeking new, to seeme to doubt,
　That you can match her, or not be without;
But let some faithfull booke in her roome be,
　Yet but of *Judith* no such booke as shee.

23.　*all*: the created order.
25 (cf. 38). *in infinite*: infinitely.
26.　*recollect*: collect together yet again.
28.　*the bed*: 'a bed' (acc. to some MSS) or 'her bed' (acc. to another).
34.　*both rich Indies*: see above, p. 54, note on 17.
37.　*forc'd*: forcibly constricted (§166).
38.　*Expans'd in infinite*: cf. above, p. 98, l. 24.
41.　*new*: new friends.
42.　*without*: at a loss without her.
44.　*Judith*: celebrated in the apocryphal Book of Judith for 'beauty of face and
　　wisdom of words' (11.21).

To the Countesse of Huntingdon.

That unripe side of earth, that heavy clime
That gives us man up now, like *Adams* time
Before he ate; mans shape, that would yet bee
(Knew they not it, and fear'd beasts companie)
So naked at this day, as though man there   5
From Paradise so great a distance were,
As yet the newes could not arrived bee
Of *Adams* tasting the forbidden tree;
Depriv'd of that free state which they were in,
And wanting the reward, yet beare the sinne.   10
  But, as from extreme hights who downward looks,
Sees men at childrens shapes, Rivers at brookes,
And loseth younger formes; so, to your eye,
These (Madame) that without your distance lie,
Must either mist, or nothing seeme to be,   15
Who are at home but wits mere *Atomi*.
But, I who can behold them move, and stay,
Have found my selfe to you, just their midway;
And now must pitty them; for, as they doe
Seeme sick to me, just so must I to you.   20
Yet neither will I vexe your eyes to see
A sighing Ode, nor crosse-arm'd Elegie.

To the Countesse of Huntingdon. See above, headnote on p. 280. First printed in
    1635 and first admitted into the canon of Donne's poetry in 1929 (§159,
    cf. §171: App. D), the poem appears to be lacking several lines at the
    beginning.
  1. *heavy*: humid, tropical. The allusion is to the Americas, where the
      native Indians went naked like Adam before he *ate* (3) the fruit of *the
      forbidden tree* (8).
  9. *free state*: natural condition of freedom.
 10. *wanting the reward*: lacking the knowledge of our redemption by Christ.
 11. *downward*: 'inward' (acc. to a MS).
 13. *younger*: smaller.
 14. *without your distance*: outside the Countess's circle.
 16. *Atomi*: smallest particles, components (cf. above, p. 101, note on 47).
 18. *their midway*: halfway between them and her.
 21. *neither*: 'never' (acc. to a MS).
 22. *crosse-arm'd*: the conventional posture of the pining lover.

I come not to call pitty from your heart,
Like some white-liver'd dotard that would part
Else from his slipperie soule with a faint groane,   25
And faithfully, (without you smil'd) were gone.
I cannot feele the tempest of a frowne,
I may be rais'd by love, but not throwne down.
Though I can pittie those sigh twice a day,
I hate that thing whispers it selfe away.   30
Yet since all love is fever, who to trees
Doth talke, doth yet in loves cold ague freeze.
'Tis love, but, with such fatall weaknesse made,
That it destroyes it selfe with its owne shade.
Who first look'd sad, griev'd, pin'd, and shew'd his paine,
Was he that first taught women, to disdaine.
    As all things were one nothing, dull and weake,
Untill this raw disordered heape did breake,
And severall desires led parts away,
Water declin'd with earth, the ayre did stay,   40
Fire rose, and each from other but unty'd,
Themselves unprison'd were and purify'd:
So was love, first in vast confusion hid,
An unripe willingnesse which nothing did,
A thirst, an Appetite which had no ease,   45
That found a want, but knew not what would please.
What pretty innocence in those dayes mov'd!
Man ignorantly walk'd by her he lov'd;
Both sigh'd and enterchang'd a speaking eye,
Both trembled and were sick, both knew not why.   50
That naturall fearefulnesse that struck man dumbe,
Might well (those times consider'd) man become.
As all discoverers whose first assay
Findes but the place, after, the nearest way:
So passion is to womans love, about,   55
Nay, farther off, than when we first set out.

26. *faithfully*: 'finally' (acc. to several MSS).
    without: unless.
38. *heape*: Chaos, from which the universe was ordered into the four
    elements of *Water*, *earth*, *ayre*, *Fire* (40–41; cf. *Paradise Lost*, III, 708 ff.).
41. *but*: 'once' (acc. to a MS).

It is not love that sueth, or doth contend;
Love either conquers, or but meets a friend.
Man's better part consists of purer fire,
And findes it selfe allow'd, ere it desire.   60
Love is wise here, keepes home, gives reason sway,
And journeys not till it finde summer-way.
A weather-beaten Lover but once knowne,
Is sport for every girle to practise on.
Who strives through womans scornes, women to know, 65
Is lost, and seekes his shadow to outgoe;
It must be sicknesse, after one disdaine,
Though he be call'd aloud, to looke againe.
Let others sigh, and grieve; one cunning sleight
Shall freeze my Love to Christall in a night.   70
I can love first, and (if I winne) love still;
And cannot be remov'd, unlesse she will.
It is her fault if I unsure remaine,
Shee onely can untie, and binde againe.
The honesties of love with ease I doe,   75
But am no porter for a tedious woo.
   But (madame) I now thinke on you; and here
Where we are at our hights, you but appeare,
We are but clouds, you rise from our noone-ray,
But a foule shadow, not your breake of day.   80
You are at first hand all that's faire and right,
And others good reflects but backe your light.
You are a perfectnesse, so curious hit,
That youngest flatteries doe scandall it.
For, what is more doth what you are restraine,   85
And though beyond, is downe the hill againe.

---

59. *better part*: the rational faculty.
69. *sigh* (acc. to most MSS): 'sinne' (acc. to 1635–69).
79. The line is variously punctuated in the MSS; I follow the 1635 edition.
83. *curious hit*: exquisitely and accurately attained (§171).
84. *youngest*: least; 'the quaintest' (acc. to a MS).
    scandall: misrepresent.
85. *more*: i.e. more perfect (God).
    restraine: limit (§163).

We'have no next way to you, we crosse to it:
You are the straight line, thing prais'd, attribute;
Each good in you's a light; so many a shade
You make, and in them are your motions made.   90
These are your pictures to the life. From farre
We see you move, and here your *Zani's* are:
So that no fountaine good there is, doth grow
In you, but our dimme actions faintly shew.
  Then finde I, if mans noblest part be love,   95
Your purest luster must that shadow move.
The soule with body, is a heaven combin'd
With earth, and for mans ease, but nearer joyn'd.
Where thoughts the starres of soule we understand,
We guesse not their large natures, but command.   100
And love in you, that bountie is of light,
That gives to all, and yet hath infinite.
Whose heat doth force us thither to intend,
But soule we finde too earthly to ascend,
'Till slow accesse hath made it wholly pure,   105
Able immortall clearnesse to endure.
Who dare aspire this journey with a staine,
Hath waight will force him headlong backe againe.
No more can impure man retaine and move
In that pure region of a worthy love,   110
Then earthly substance can unforc'd aspire,
And leave his nature to converse with fire:

87. *next*: direct, short.
     crosse: go cross country.
88. *straight line*: i.e, rectitude.
     thing prais'd: virtue.
92. *Zani's*: clownish imitators (cf. above, p. 284, note on 30); 'fames' (acc. to a few MSS).
94. *shew*: appear.
98. *nearer*: 'never' (acc. to one MS) or 'ever' (acc. to another).
105. *wholly*: 'holy' (acc. to most MSS).
109. *retaine*: remain.
111. *Then*: than.
     unforc'd: unrefined.
112. *converse*: mingle.

Such may have eye, and hand; may sigh, may speak;
But like swoln bubles, when they are high'st they break.
   Though far removed Northerne fleets scarce finde   115
The Sunnes comfort; others thinke him too kinde.
There is an equall distance from her eye,
Men perish too farre off, and burne too nigh.
But as ayre takes the Sunne-beames equal bright
From the first Rayes, to his last opposite: 120
So able men, blest with a vertuous Love,
Remote or neare, or howsoe'r they move;
Their vertue breakes all clouds that might annoy,
There is no Emptinesse, but all is Joy.
He much profanes whom violent heats do move   125
To stile his wandring rage of passion, *Love*.
Love that imparts in every thing delight,
Is fain'd, which only tempts mans appetite.
Why love among the vertues is not knowne
Is, that love is them all contract in one.   130

119. *equall bright*: evenly–disseminated brightness.
125. *violent* (acc. to most MSS): 'valiant' (acc. to 1635–69).
128. The line reads variously in the MSS; it is also incomplete (acc. to 1635–39).
129. *vertues*: the four cardinal virtues (as above, p. 263, note on 17), here contracted or summed up in *love* (130).
130. *contract in* (acc. to some MSS): 'contracted' (acc. to 1635–39).

To Mr. George Herbert,
with my Seal,
of the Anchor and Christ

A sheafe of Snakes uſed heretofore to be
My Seal, The Crest of our poore Family.
Adopted in Gods Family, and so
Our old Coat lost, unto new armes I go.
The Crosse (my seal at Baptism) spred below,   5
Does, by that form, into an Anchor grow.
Crosses grow Anchors; Bear, as though shouldst do
Thy Crosse, and that Crosse grows an Anchor too.
But he that makes our Crosses Anchors thus,
Is Christ, who there is crucifi'd for us.   10
Yet may I, with this, my first Serpents hold,
God gives new blessings, and yet leaves the old;
The Serpent, may, as wise, my pattern be;
My poison, as he feeds on dust, that's me.
And as he rounds the Earth to murder sure,   15
My death he is, but on the Crosse, my cure.
Crucifie nature then, and then implore
All Grace from him, crucified there before;
When all is Crosse, and that Crosse Anchor grown,
This Seal's a Catechism, not a Seal alone.   20
Under that little Seal great gifts I send,

To Mr. George Herbert. Not in fact a poem by Donne but an anonymous
   translation of a Latin poem by him, it was first published in the 1650
   edition of his *Poems* and thus disseminated as if it were his. Izaak Walton's
   Life of Dr. John Donne (1640) quotes the translation together with Her-
   bert's response in order to demonstrate the 'happy friendship' between
   the two poets (see C. A. Patrides, *George Herbert: The Critical Heritage*
   [London, 1983], pp. 2 and 55–56).
1–2. The lines are printed in all early editions as a title, the poem proper
   beginning at l. 3.
11 ff. The serpent is at once the type of evil or death, of wisdom, and of Christ
   upon the Cross (§168).

Works, and prayers, pawns, and fruits of a friend.
And may that Saint which rides in our great Seal,
To you, who bear his name, great bounties deal.

To the Lady *Magdalen Herbert*, of St. *Mary Magdalen*.

Her of your name, whose fair inheritance
   Bethina was, and jointure *Magdalo*:
An active faith so highly did advance,
   That she once knew, more than the Church did know,
The *Resurrection*; so much good there is   5
   Deliver'd of her, that some Fathers be
Loth to believe one Woman could do this;
   But, think these *Magdalens* were two or three.
Increase their number, *Lady*, and their fame:
   To their *Devotion*, add your *Innocence*;   10
Take so much of th'example, as of the name;
   The latter half; and in some recompence
That they did harbour *Christ* himself, a Guest,
   Harbour these *Hymns*, to his dear name addrest.

To Mr George Herbert.
22. *Works*: emended by some editors – e.g. §§158, 159, 168 – to 'Wishes'.
24. *great bounties*: mistranslated from the accompanying Latin text, which
    reads 'regia . . . dona' (royal gifts) – an allusion to Herbert's aspirations
    after royal preferment (§421).

To the Lady Magdalen Herbert. On the letter's recipient, see above, headnote on
    p. 296. Although placed by all modern editors at the outset of the Divine
    Poems, the sonnet is self-evidently a verse letter. It was first published in
    Izaak Walton's *Life of Mr George Herbert* (1670).
2. Bethany and Magdala were Palestinian places associated in medieval
    legend with Mary Magdalen (Mark 15.40 ff.).
    jointure: who jointly held.
5. *Resurrection*: first witnessed by Mary Magdalen (Mark 16.9).
6. *Fathers*: of the Church.
8   *two or three*: it was debated whether the events associated with Mary
    Magdalen were in fact the experiences of more than one person.
13. *latter half*: the devout part of Mary Magdalen's life.
14. *these Hymns*: probably the seven sonnets comprising *La Corona* (below,
    pp. 429–34).

A Letter written by Sir H. G. and J. D.
alternis vicibus

[G:]   Since ev'ry Tree beginns to blossome now,
      Perfuminge and enamelinge each bow,
      Hartes should as well as they, some fruits allow.

[D:]   For since one old poore sunn serves all the rest,
      You sev'rall sunns that warme, and light each brest 5
      Doe by that influence all your thoughts digest.

[G:]   And that you two may soe your vertues move,
      On better matter then beames from above,
      Thus our twin'd souls send forth these buds of love.

[D:]   As in devotions men Joyne both their hands,   10
      Wee make ours doe one Act to seale the bands,
      By which we enthrall ourselves to your commands,

[G:]   And each for others faith and zeale stand bound:
      As safe as spirits are from any wound,
      Soe free from impure thoughts they shal be found. 15

[D:]   Admit our magique then by which wee doe
      Make you appeere to us, and us to you,
      Supplying all the Muses in you twoe.

[G:]   Wee doe consider noe flower that is sweet,
      But wee your breath in that exhaling meet,   20
      And as true types of you, them humbly greet.

[D:]   Heere in our Nightingales we heere you singe
      Who soe doe make the whole yeare through a springe,
      And save us from the feare of Autumns stinge.

A Letter written by Sir H. G. and J. D. – i.e. by Sir Henry Goodyere (see above,
    headnote on p. 260) and Donne 'in alternating turns'. The stanzas writ-
    ten by each are designated here by their initials. The poem was first
    printed by Chambers in 1896 (§157).
5 (cf. *you two* in 7). The letter was evidently addressed to two ladies.
8. *then*: than.
9. *twin'd*: both twined and twinned.
21. *types*: symbols; also, in the theological sense of prophetic representations.

[G:]   In Anchors calme face wee your smoothnes see,   25
        Your mindes unmingled, and as cleare as shee
        That keepes untoucht her first virginitie.

[D:]   Did all St. Edith nunns descend againe
        To honor Polesworth with their cloystred traine,
        Compar'd with you each would confesse some stayne.

[G:]   Or should wee more bleed out our thoughts in inke,
        Noe paper (though it woulde be glad to drinke
        Those drops) could comprehend what wee doe thinke.

[D:]   For t'were in us ambition to write
        Soe, that because wee two, you two unite,   35
        Our letter should as you, bee infinite.

To Mr *E. G.*

Even as lame things thirst their perfection, so
The slimy rimes bred in our vale below,
Bearing with them much of my love and hart,
Fly unto that Parnassus, where thou art.
There thou oreseest London: Here I have beene,   5
By staying in London, too much overseene.
Now pleasures dirth our City doth posses,

A Letter written by Sir H.G. and J.D.
25.   *Anchors*: the river Ancor – now Anker – passed through Goodyere's
      estate in *Polesworth* (29), Warwickshire.
28.   *St. Edith*: the Saxon founder of the Benedictine convent at Polesworth
      suppressed in 1538 and then sold to the Goodyere family.

To Mr E. G. – i.e. the minor poet Edward Guilpin of Suffolk. The poem was
    first printed by Gosse in 1899 (see below, p. 522).
 1.   *thirst*: thirst for.
 2.   *slimy . . . bred*: cf. above, p. 230, note on 18–19.
 4.   *Parnassus*: the mountain beloved of the Muses; here, Highgate, Guilpin's
      residence in London.
 6.   *overseene*: imprudent.
 7.   *dirth*: dearth.

Our Theatres are fill'd with emptines.
As lancke and thin is every street and way
As a woman deliver'd yesterday.   10
Nothing whereat to laugh my spleen espyes
But bearbaitings or Law exercise.
Therefore I'le leave it, and in the Country strive
Pleasure, now fled from London, to retrive.
Do thou so too: and fill not like a Bee   15
Thy thighs with hony, but as plenteously
As Russian Marchants, thy selfes whole vessel load,
And then at Winter retaile it here abroad.
Blesse us with Suffolks Sweets; and as it is
Thy garden, make thy hive and warehouse this.   20

To Mr *R. W.*

Zealously my Muse doth salute all thee,
Enquiring of that mistique trinitee
Whereof thou'and all to whom heavens do infuse
Like fyer, are made; thy body, mind, and Muse.
Dost thou recover sicknes, or prevent?   5
Or is thy Mind travail'd with discontent?
Or art thou parted from the world and mee,
In a good skorn of the worlds vanitee?
Or is thy devout Muse retyr'd to sing
Upon her tender Elegiaque string?   10
Our Minds part not, joyne then thy Muse with myne,
For myne is barren thus devorc'd from thyne.

To Mr E.G.
  8. *emptines*: because of the plague.
11. *spleen*: moroseness, dejection.
12. *bearbaiting*: a popular 'sport'.
     exercise: practice.
20. *this*: Highgate (see note on 4).

To Mr R. W. – i.e. Rowland Woodward (see above, headnote on p. 262). The
    poem was first printed by Gosse in 1899 (see below, p. 522).
  3. On the symbol ', see above, p. 5.
  6. *travail'd*: labouring.

Henrico Wottoni
in Hibernia belligeranti.

Went you to conquer? and have so much lost
your self, that what in you was best and most
Respective frendship should so quickly dye?
In publique gaine my share is not such, that I
Would loose your love for Ireland: better cheap   5
I pardon death (who though hee do not reap
yet gleanes hee many of our frends away)
then that your waking mind should bee a pray
to Letargies. Lett shotts and boggs, and skeines
with bodies deale, as fate bidds or restreynes   10
Ere sicknesses attach yong death is best
who payes before his death doth scape arest.
Lett not your soule (at first) with graces filld
And since and thorough crooked lymbecks, stild
In many schooles and courts, which quicken it,)   15
it self unto the Irish negligence submit.
I aske not labored letters which should weare
Long papers out: nor letters which should feare
dishonest cariage: or a seers Art
Nor such as from the brayne come, but the hart.   20

Henrico Wottoni . . . – which is to say, 'Henry Wotton fighting in Ireland' under
    Essex in 1599. On the letter's recipient see above, headnote on p. 256.
    The poem, first printed by Grierson in 1912 (§158), is here transcribed
    from the Burley manuscript (see p. 7).
  3. *Respective*: considerate.
  5. *loose*: lose.
  8. *then*: than.
      pray: prey.
  9. *Letargies*: lethargies.
      skeines: Irish daggers.
  11. *attach*: 'attack' (acc. to all modern editors).
      yong: early.
  14. *lymbecks*: see above, p. 91, note on 21.
      stild: distilled.
  15. *quicken*: enliven.
  16. *negligence*: dullness or indifference of spirit (§166).
  19. *cariage*: removal, theft.
      seers Art: the divining of their contents by powers of 'vision' (§171).

To Mr *R. W.*

Kindly I envy thy songs perfection
  Built of all th'elements as our bodyes are:
  That Litle of earth that is in it, is a faire
Delicious garden where all sweetes are sowne.
In it is cherishing fyer which dryes in mee   5
  Griefe which did drowne me: and halfe quench'd by it
  Are satirique fyres which urg'd me to have writt
In skorne of all: for now I admyre thee.
  And as Ayre doth fullfill the hollownes
  Of rotten walls; so it myne emptines,   10
Where tost and mov'd it did beget this sound
Which as a lame Eccho of thyne doth rebound.
  Oh, I was dead; but since thy song new Life did give,
I recreated, even by thy creature, live.

To Mr R. W. – i.e. Rowland Woodward (see above, headnote on p. 262). The
  poem was first printed by Grierson in 1912 (§158).
  2. *elements*: the traditional four, i.e. *earth* (3), *fyer* (5), water (cf. tears of
    Griefe, 6), and *Ayre* (9).
 10. *fullfill*: i.e. fill full.
 14. *recreated*: given pleasure; also, 're-created' (§163).
    creature: i.e. Woodward's *song* (l. 1).

To Mr *R. W.*

Muse not that by thy Mind thy body is led:
For by thy Mind, my Mind's distempered.
So thy Care lives long, for I bearing part
It eates not only thyne, but my swolne hart.
And when it gives us intermission   5
We take new harts for it to feede upon.
But as a Lay Mans Genius doth controule
Body and mind; the Muse beeing the Soules Soule
Of Poets, that methinks should ease our anguish,
Although our bodyes wither and minds languish.   10
Wright then, that my griefes which thine got may bee
Cur'd by thy charming soveraigne melodee.

To Mr R. W. See headnote to the previous poem.
  7. *Genius*: guardian angel.
 11. *Wright*: i.e. write.

The Anniversaries

The two *Anniversaries* and *A Funerall Elegie* are among the most substantial poems by Donne to have been published during his lifetime. They are certainly his most ambitious and, invariably, his most controversial too.

The First Anniversarie was on its initial appearance in 1611 entitled *An Anatomy of the World*; it gained its present title on its reappearance in 1612, in the same volume that included *Of the Progress of the Soule* – itself designated *The Second Anniversarie* – when Donne was evidently determined to relate the two poems closely. The term 'anniversary' can best be defined after the fashion of John Bullokar's dictionary, *An English Expositor* (1616), as 'A solemnitie kept every yeare at a set time'.

The verses prefixed to *The First Anniversarie*, 'To the Praise of the Dead, and the Anatomy', were in all likelihood written by Joseph Hall; those prefixed to *The Second Anniversarie*, 'The Harbinger to the Progres', were ascribed to Hall by Ben Jonson (in conversation with William Drummond of Hawthornden, in *Timber*). All these poems were jointly published again in 1621 and 1625, finally merging with Donne's other poems on the appearance of the first, posthumous edition of his *Poems* in 1633.

The subject of these poems is Elizabeth Drury, who died in December 1610 aged fourteen; but Donne had never met her and may not even have known her wealthy parents, who seem to have become his friends sometime after the publication of *The First Anniversarie*. One of the earliest critics of the poems was Jonson, who is reported to have said that 'Dones Anniversarie was profane and full of Blasphemies' and to have informed Donne that 'if it had been written of the Virgin Marie it had been something to which he answered that he described the idea of a Woman and not as she was' (*Timber*, as before).

Donne's defence would appear to rest thematically on the transformation of the young girl into a vaguely Platonic 'idea' – 'best, and first originall / Of all faire copies' (*First Ann.*, ll. 227–8) – and conceptually on the point also made by Sir Philip Sidney in his *Defence of Poesie* (1595): 'the skill of the artificer standeth in that *Idea* or foreconceit of the work, and not in the work itself' (§590). In the event, every reader must determine for himself whether the distance between the design and its execution is minimal or vast.

THE FIRST ANNIVERSARIE.

An Anatomy of the World.
Wherein, By occasion of the untimely death of Mistris Elizabeth Drury the frailty and the decay of his whole World is represented.

To The Praise of the Dead, and the Anatomy.
[by Joseph Hall?]

> Wel dy'de the world, that we might live to see
> This world of wit, in his Anatomee:
> No evill wants his good: so wilder heyres
> Bedew their fathers Toombs with forced teares,
> Whose state requites their los: whils thus we gain   5
> Well may wee walk in blacks, but not complaine.

To the Praise of the Dead. Joseph Hall, the poem's presumed author (see headnote, above, p. 324), was a satirist of considerable talent, an apologist of the Church of England, and eventually bishop of Exeter and later of Norwich. He agreed with Donne about 'the decay of this whole World', that is, the decreasing potency of the created order that to many suggested the imminence of history's end (see §107, with further references; and §589).
3. *wants*: is devoid of.
5. *state*: the estate to which the *heires* (3) succeeded (§170).

Yet, how can I consent the world is dead
While this Muse lives? which in his spirits stead
Seemes to informe a world: and bids it bee,
In spite of losse, or fraile mortalitee?   10
And thou the subject of this wel-borne thought,
Thrise noble maid, couldst not have found nor sought
A fitter time to yeeld to thy sad Fate,
Then whiles this spirit lives; that can relate
Thy worth so well to our last nephews eyne,   15
That they shall wonder both at his, and thine:
Admired match! where strives in mutuall grace
The cunning Pencill, and the comely face:
A taske, which thy faire goodnes made too much
For the bold pride of vulgar pens to tuch;   20
Enough is us to praise them that praise thee,
And say that but enough those praises bee,
Which had'st thou liv'd, had hid their fearefull head
From th'angry checkings of thy modest red:
Death bars reward and shame: when envy's gone,   25
And gaine; 'tis safe to give the dead their owne.
As then the wise Egyptians wont to lay
More on their Tombes, then houses: these of clay,
But those of brasse, or marble were; so wee
Give more unto thy Ghost, then unto thee.   30
Yet what we give to thee, thou gav'st to us,
And may'st but thanke thy selfe, for being thus:
Yet what thou gav'st, and wert, O happy maid,
Thy grace profest all due, where 'tis repayd.
So these high songs that to thee suited bine,   35
Serve but to sound thy makers praise, in thine,

8.   *this Muse*: i.e. Donne (cf. *this spirit* in l. 14).
12. *maid*: Elizabeth Drury (see headnote, above, p. 324).
15. *our nephews eyne*: the eyes of our descendants.
30. *then*: than.
32. *thus*: thus thanked.
35. *bine*: been.

Which thy deare soule as sweetly sings to him
Amid the Quire of Saints and Seraphim,
As any Angels tongue can sing of thee;
The subjects differ, tho the skill agree: 40
For as by infant-yeares men judge of age,
Thy early love, thy vertues, did presage
What an hie part thou bear'st in those best songs
Whereto no burden, nor no end belongs.
Sing on, thou Virgin soule, whose lossefull gaine   45
Thy love-sicke Parents have bewayl'd in vaine;
Never may thy name be in our songs forgot
Till we shall sing thy ditty, and thy note.

The First Anniversary.
An Anatomy of the World.

When that rich soule which to her Heaven is gone,   *The entrie*
Whom all they celebrate, who know they have one,   *into the*
(For who is sure he hath a soule, unlesse   *worke.*
It see, and Judge, and follow worthinesse,
And by Deedes praise it? He who doth not this,   5
May lodge an In-mate soule, but tis not his.)
When that Queene ended here her progresse time,
And, as t'her standing house, to heaven did clymbe,
Where, loth to make the Saints attend her long,
Shee's now a part both of the Quire, and Song,   10

To the Praise of the Dead.
38. *Seraphim*: traditionally, the highest order of angels; see above, p. 243,
     note on 60–61.
44. *burden*: wearisome load; also refrain.
48. *ditty*: words; *note*: music.

The First Anniversary.
  2. *celebrate*: praise; also commemorate (§585). *one*: i.e. soul.
  6. *In-mate*: guest, temporary lodger.
  7. *that Queene*: Elizabeth Drury's soul.
      progresse: royal journey.
  8. *standing house*: permanent residence.
  9. *attend*: wait for.

This world, in that great earth-quake languished;
For in a common Bath of teares it bled,
Which drew the strongest vitall spirits out:
But succour'd then with a perplexed doubt,
Whether the world did loose or gaine in this,   15
(Because since now no other way there is
But goodnes, to see her, whom all would see,
All must endevour to be good as shee,)
This great consumption to a fever turn'd,
And so the world had fits; it joy'd, it mourn'd.   20
And, as men thinke, that Agues physicke are,
And th'Ague being spent, give over care,
So thou, sicke world, mistak'st thy selfe to bee
Well, when alas, thou'rt in a Letargee.
Her death did wound, and tame thee than, and than   25
Thou mightst have better spar'd the Sunne, or Man;
That wound was deepe, but 'tis more misery,
That thou hast lost thy sense and memory.
T'was heavy then to heare thy voyce of mone,
But this is worse, that thou are speechlesse growne.   30
Thou hast forgot thy name, thou hadst; thou wast
Nothing but she, and her thou hast o'rpast.
For as a child kept from the Font, untill
A Prince, expected long, come to fulfill

11. *earth-quake*: the poem's numerous hyperboles are beginning to surface, here as elsewhere dependent on the analogy between the microcosm of man and the macrocosm of the world.
12–13. To bleed into a warm bath – here a bath of tears induced by our grief – is imperceptibly to be deprived of one's *vitall spirits*, the elements in the blood that were said to link body and soul.
21. *Agues physicke are*: fevers were said to be curative.
24. *in a Letargee*: at the point of death (§170).
25. *than . . . than*: then . . . then.
29. *heavy*: mournful.
    mone: moan.
31–32. On the paradox of nothing, see also ll. 145–46, 156–57, 171, etc. (§590).
32. *o'erpast*: outlived.
33. *the Font*: i.e. of baptism.

The Ceremonies, thou unnam'd hadst laid,   35
Had not her comming, thee her Palace made:
Her name defin'd thee, gave thee forme and frame,
And thou forgetst to celebrate thy name.
Some moneths she hath beene dead (but being dead,
Measures of times are all determined)   40
But long shee'ath beene away, long, long, yet none
Offers to tell us who it is that's gone.
But as in states doubtfull of future heyres,
When sickenes without remedy, empayres
The present Prince, they're loth it should be said,   45
The Prince doth languish, or the Prince is dead:
So mankind feeling now a generall thaw,
A strong example gone equall to law,
The Cyment which did faithfully compact
And glue all vertues, now resolv'd, and slack'd,   50
Thought it some blasphemy to say sh'was dead;
Or that our weakenes was discovered
In that confession; therefore spoke no more
Then tongues, the soule being gone, the losse deplore.
But though it be too late to succour thee,   55
Sicke world, yea dead, yea putrified, since shee
Thy'ntrinsique Balme, and thy preservative,
Can never be renew'd, thou never live,
I (since no man can make thee live) will trie,
What we may gaine by thy Anatomy.   60
Her death hath taught us dearely, that thou art
Corrupt and mortall in thy purest part.

35. *unnam'd*: without proper identity.
40. *determined*: ceased.
48. *gone equall to law*: tantamount to a law.
49. *compact*: hold together.
50. *resolv'd*: dissolved.
52 (also 64). *discovered*: displayed.
54. *Then*: than.
57. *Balme*: the vital essence assumed by Paracelsian medicine to exist in all created things and to operate as a preservative (§164).
59. *trie*: test.
60. *Anatomy*: dissection (cf. l. 66).

Let no man say, the world it selfe being dead,
'Tis labour lost to have discovered
The worlds infirmities, since there is none   65
Alive to study this dissectione;
For there's a kind of world remaining still,   *What life*
Though shee which did inanimate and fill   *the world*
The world, be gone, yet in this last long night,   *hath still.*
Her Ghost doth walke; that is, a glimmering light,   70
A faint weake love of vertue and of good
Reflects from her, on them which understood
Her worth; And though she have shut in all day,
The twi-light of her memory doth stay;
Which, from the carcasse of the old world, free,   75
Creates a new world; and new creatures be
Produc'd: The matter and the stuffe of this,
Her vertue, and the forme our practice is.
And though to be thus Elemented, arme
These Creatures, from hom-borne intrinsique harme,   80
(For all assum'd unto this Dignitee,
So many weedlesse Paradises bee,
Which of themselves produce no venemous sinne,
Except some forraine Serpent bring it in)
Yet, because outward stormes the strongest breake,   85
And strength it selfe by confidence growes weake,
This new world may be safer, being told
The dangers and diseases of the old: *The sicknesses*
For with due temper men do then forgoe,   *of the world.*
Or covet things, when they their true worth know.   90
There is no health; Physitians say that we   *Impossibility*
At best, enjoy, but a neutralitee.   *of health.*

---

73. *shut in all day*: enclosed within herself all light, thereby denying it to the
     world (§166).
75–77. The sun was thought to have the power to breed new life out of
     carcasses and mud (§170).
79. *Elemented*: constituted (cf. p. 115, note on 9–10).
81. *assum'd*: elevated.
84. The first of several explicit references to the Fall of Man: see also ll. 180,
     199, 272, 331, etc., as well as the notes on 389–90 and 409–12.
91–92. Thus in one of Donne's sermons: 'there is no health in *any*, so
     universall is sickness' (§192).

And can there be worse sicknesse, then to know
That we are never well, nor can be so?
We are borne ruinous: poore mothers crie, 95
That children come not right, nor orderly,
Except they headlong come, and fall upon
An ominous precipitation.
How witty's ruine? how importunate
Upon mankinde? It labour'd to frustrate 100
Even Gods purpose; and made woman, sent
For mans reliefe, cause of his languishment.
They were to good ends, and they are so still,
But accessory, and principall in ill.
For that first mariage was our funerall: 105
One woman at one blow, then kill'd us all,
And singly, one by one, they kill us now.
We doe delightfully our selves allow
To that consumption; and profusely blinde,
We kill our selves, to propagate our kinde. 110
And yet we doe not that; we are not men:
There is not now that mankinde, which was then
When as the Sunne, and man, did seeme to strive,
(Joynt tenants of the world) who should survive.   *Shortnesse*
When Stag, and Raven, and the long-liv'd tree,   *of life.*
Compar'd with man, dy'de in minoritee.
When, if a slow-pac'd starre had stolne away
From the observers marking, he might stay
Two or three hundred yeares to see't againe,
And then make up his observation plaine; 120

93.   *then*: than.
95.   *borne ruinous*: born with an inclination toward ruin; corruptible.
105.   *that first marriage*: Adam and Eve's.
106.   *kill'd*: also in the sexual sense; see above, p. 48, note on 16.
109.   *profusely*: wastefully.
110.   The act of coition was thought to diminish one's life (see above, p. 122, ll. 24-25).
112 ff.   The lines voice the widespread belief that men were once far longer lived and taller.
115.   The legend of the 'oldest animals' and the equally old oak- or yew-tree was widely credited (§561).
116.   *minoritee*: youth.
117-20.   On the period's astronomical activities, cf. below, note on 259-60.

When, as the age was long, the sise was great:
Mans growth confess'd, and recompenc'd the meat:
So spacious and large, that every soule
Did a faire Kingdome, and large Realme controule:
And when the very stature thus erect,   125
Did that soule a good way towards Heaven direct.
Where is this mankind now? who lives to age,
Fit to be made *Methusalem* his page?
Alas, we scarse live long enough to trie
Whether a new made clocke runne right, or lie.   130
Old Grandsires talke of yesterday with sorrow,
And for our children we reserve to morrow.
So short is life, that every peasant strives,
In a torne house, or field, to have three lives.
And as in lasting, so in length is man   135
Contracted to an inch, who was a span.   *Smalenesse*
For had a man at first, in Forrests stray'd,   *of stature.*
Or shipwrack'd in the Sea, one would have laid
A wager that an Elephant or Whale
That met him, would not hastily assaile   140
A thing so equall to him: now alas,
The Fayries, and the Pigmies well may passe
As credible; mankind decayes so soone,
We're scarse our Fathers shadowes cast at noone.
Onely death addes t'our length: nor are we growne   145
In stature to be men, till we are none.

122.   *meat*: food, its superior quality in the past *confess'd* (attested) by men's
       growth.
125–26. According to a commonplace also voiced by Donne, while animals
       grovel, man is 'of an erect, of an upright form, naturally built, and
       disposed to the contemplation of Heaven' (§108).
128.   Methuselah lived 969 years (Genesis 5.27).
134.   *three lives*: the conventional length of a lease was ninety-nine years
       (§164).
136.   *span*: nine inches.
144–45. *death addes t'our length*: stretched out when *none* (dead), we are in effect
       taller.

But this were light, did our lesse volume hold
All the old Text; or had we chang'd to gold
Their silver; or dispos'd into lesse glas,
Spirits of vertue, which then scattred was.　　　　　150
But 'tis not so: w'are not retir'd, but dampt;
And as our bodies, so our mindes are cramp't:
'Tis shrinking, not close-weaving, that hath thus,
In minde and body both bedwarfed us.
We seeme ambitious, Gods whole worke t'undoe;　　155
Of nothing he made us, and we strive too,
To bring our selves to nothing backe; and we
Do what we can, to do't so soone as hee.
With new diseases on our selves we warre,
And with new phisicke, a worse Engin farre.　　　160
Thus man, this worlds Vice-Emperor, in whom
All faculties, all graces are at home;
And if in other Creatures they appeare,
They're but mans ministers, and Legats there,
To worke on their rebellions, and reduce　　　　165
Them to Civility, and to mans use.
This man, whom God did wooe, and loth t'attend
Till man came up, did downe to man descend,
This man, so great, that all that is, is his,
Oh what a trifle, and poore thing he is!　　　　　170
If man were any thing, he's nothing now:
Helpe, or at least some time to wast, allow
T'his other wants, yet when he did depart
With her, whom we lament, he lost his hart.

147. *light*: of slight consequence.
148–50. An alchemical image.
151. *retir'd*: shrunk; *dampt*: extinguished.
159. *new diseases*: primarily syphilis, which first devastated Europe in the
        fifteenth century.
160. *new phisicke*: the new mineral drugs of the Paracelsians (§158).
        Engin: instrument.
161. *Vice-Emperor*: God's deputy on earth (Genesis 1.26 ff.).
164. *Legats*: delegates.
173–74. *depart / With her*: part with her.

She, of whom th'Auncients seem'd to prophesie,   175
When they call'd vertues by the name of shee;
She in whom vertue was so much refin'd,
That for Allay unto so pure a minde
Shee tooke the weaker Sex, she that could drive
The poysonous tincture, and the stayne of *Eve*,   180
Out of her thoughts, and deeds; and purifie
All, by a true religious Alchimy;
Shee, shee is dead; shee's dead: when thou knowest this,
Thou knowest how poore a trifling thing man is.
And learn'st thus much by our Anatomee,   185
The heart being perish'd, no part can be free.
And that except thou feed (not banquet) on
The supernaturall food, Religion,
Thy better Grouth growes withered, and scant;
Be more then man, or thou'rt lesse then an Ant.   190
Then, as mankinde, so is the worlds whole frame
Quite out of joynt, almost created lame:
For, before God had made up all the rest,
Corruption entred, and deprav'd the best:
It seis'd the Angels, and then first of all   195
The world did in her Cradle take a fall,
And turn'd her braines, and tooke a generall maime
Wronging each joynt of th'universall frame.
The noblest part, man, felt it first; and than
Both beasts and plants, curst in the curse of man.   200
So did the world from the first houre decay,   *Decay of nature*
The evening was beginning of the day,   *in other parts.*

176.   In Greek and Latin the names of virtues are feminine (§170).
177–82. The alchemical imagery is extended below, l. 415.
178.   *Allay*: alloy.
180.   *poysonous tincture*: see above, p. 271, note on 20.
187.   *banquet*: feed lightly (usually on a dessert).
190.   *then*: than.
195.   *It seis'd the Angels*: corruption first entered Heaven through the rebellion of Lucifer/Satan.
199.   *than*: then.
200.   *curst in the curse of man*: the Fall of Man directly affected the rest of the natural order (cf. Genesis 3.17–18).

And now the Springs and Sommers which we see,
Like sonnes of women after fifty bee.
And new Philosophy cals all in doubt,   205
The Element of fire is quite put out;
The Sun is lost, and th'earth, and no mans wit
Can well direct him, where to looke for it.
And freely men confesse, that this world's spent,
When in the Planets, and the Firmament   210
They seeke so many new; they see that this
Is crumbled out againe to his Atomis.
'Tis all in pieces, all cohærence gone;
All just supply, and all Relation:
Prince, Subject, Father, Sonne, are things forgot,   215
For every man alone thinkes he hath got
To be a Phœnix, and that there can bee
None of that kinde, of which he is, but hee.
This is the worlds condition now, and now
She that should all parts to reunion bow,   220
She that had all Magnetique force alone,
To draw, and fasten sundred parts in one;
She whom wise nature had invented then
When she observ'd that every sort of men

205. ff. *Philosophy*: i.e. natural philosophy (science), especially Copernicus's increasingly accepted theory that the universe is heliocentric (1543), here said to subvert everything (*all*) by displacing the *Sun* as much as by questioning the traditional order of the elements (*fire*, air water, earth). See also above, p. 274, ll. 37–38 and note.
210. *Firmament*: see above, p. 65, note on 24.
211. *many new*: i.e. planets and stars, as Galileo recently observed through a telescope (1610); but the allusion may also be to the much-debated possibility that there is a plurality of worlds.
212. *Atomis*: atoms, smallest particles (cf. above, p. 311, note on 16).
213. *cohærence*: cohesiveness, connectedness, order.
214. *just supply*: mutual support between the parts, fair distribution of goods; *Relation*; right relationship (§166).
217. The legendary *Phœnix* was deemed unique because only one was thought to exist at any one time.
220. *bow*: incline.
221. *Magnetique force*: one of the earliest allusions in poetry to William Gilbert's *De magnete* of 1600 (§209).

Did in their voyage in this worlds Sea stray,   225
And needed a new compasse for their way;
Shee that was best, and first originall
Of all faire copies; and the generall
Steward to Fate; shee whose rich eyes, and brest,
Guilt the West Indies, and perfum'd the East;   230
Whose having breath'd in this world, did bestow
Spice on those Isles, and bad them still smell so,
And that rich Indie which doth gold interre,
Is but as single money, coyn'd from her:
She to whom this world must it selfe refer,   235
As Suburbs, or the Microcosme of her,
Shee, shee is dead; shee's dead: when thou knowst this,
Thou knowst how lame a cripple this world is.
And learnst thus much by our Anatomy,
That this worlds generall sickenesse doth not lie   240
In any humour, or one certaine part;
But, as thou sawest it rotten at the hart,
Thou seest a Hectique fever hath got hold
Of the whole substance, not to be contrould,
And that thou hast but one way, not t'admit   245
The worlds infection, to be none of it.
For the worlds subtilst immateriall parts
Feele this consuming wound, and ages darts.

227–28. See above, p. 325.
229. *Fate*: the Divine Will.
230. *the West Indies* are *Guilt* (gilded) because a source of precious metals; the
      East Indies are *perfum'd* because a source of aromatic herbs and spices
      (see also above, p. 54, note on 17).
232. *those Isles*: the East Indies.
234. *single money*: small change.
235–36. *this world* [is] *the Microcosme of her*: an inversion of the common notion
      that man is the microcosm of the universe (§261).
241. *any humour*: any of the four 'humours' (blood, phlegm, black bile,
      yellow bile) which, according to the old physiology, determined one's
      health and disposition.
243. *Hectique*: consumptive.
247. *subtilst*: most attenuated.
248. *ages darts*: the darts of aging.

For the worlds beauty is decayd, or gone,
Beauty, that's colour, and proportion.   *Disformity*
We thinke the heavens enjoy their Spherical   *of parts.*
Their round proportion embracing all.
But yet their various and perplexed course,
Observ'd in divers ages doth enforce
Men to finde out so many Eccentrique parts,   255
Such divers downe-right lines, such overthwarts,
As disproportion that pure forme. It teares
The Firmament in eight and fortie sheeres,
And in those constellations there arise
New starres, and old do vanish from our eyes: 260
As though heav'n suffred earth-quakes, peace or war,
When new Townes rise, and olde demolish'd are.
They have empayld within a Zodiake
The free-borne Sunne, and keepe twelve signes awake
To watch his steps; the Goat and Crabbe controule,   265
And fright him backe, who els to eyther Pole,
(Did not these Tropiques fetter him) might runne:
For his course is not round; nor can the Sunne

251-57. The heavenly spheres' *course* (motions) and *pure forme* were tradition-
         ally said to be *Sphericall*, *round*; yet deviations (*Eccentrique parts*) had been
         postulated by ancient astronomers, and elliptical movements were to be
         posited by more recent astronomers like Kepler. The *disproportion* is
         attested even by charts of the celestial regions where *downe-right* (verti-
         cal) *lines* criss-cross *overthwarts* (horizontal) lines.
255.   *finde out*: invent (§81).
258.   *eight and fortie sheeres* (shares or perhaps shires, i.e. constellations): the
         division of the celestial regions according to the old astronomy (§209).
259-60. The 'new' stars included the impressive one observed by the Danish
         astronomer Tycho Brahe in the constellation of Cassiopeia (1572);
         many stars were also observed to disappear (§§209, 266). See also
         above, p. 275, note on 68.
263.   *empayld*: enclosed.
         Zodiake: 'An imaginarie winding circle in the heavens, under which the
         planets are still moved, and in which the twelve signes are placed'
         (Bullokar).
264-67. *twelve signs*: the divisions of the zodiac, inclusive of *the Goat and
         Crabbe* (i.e. Capricorn and Cancer) which the sun traverses at the winter
         and summer solstices respectively. As *Tropiques* or solstitial points,
         these two signs check the sun's movement toward the poles.

Perfit a Circle, or maintaine his way
One inche direct; but where he rose to day   270
He comes no more, but with a cousening line,
Steales by that point, and so is Serpentine:
And seeming weary with his reeling thus,
He meanes to sleepe, being now falne nearer us.
So, of the stares which boast that they do runne   275
In Circle still, none ends where he begunne.
All their proportion's lame, it sinks, it swels.
For of Meridians, and Parallels,
Man hath weav'd out a net, and this net throwne
Upon the Heavens, and now they are his owne.   280
Loth to goe up the hill, or labor thus
To goe to heaven, we make heaven come to us.
We spur, we raine the stars, and in their race
They're diversly content t'obey our pace.
But keepes the earth her round proportion still?   285
Doth not a Tenarif, or higher Hill
Rise so high like a Rocke, that one might thinke
The floating Moone would shipwracke there, and sink?
Seas are so deepe, that Whales being strooke to day,
Perchance to morrow, scarse at middle way   290
Of their wish'd journeys end, the bottom, dye.
And men, to sound depths, so much line untie,
As one might justly thinke, that there would rise
At end thereof, one of th'Antipodies:
If under all, a Vault infernall be,   295
(Which sure is spacious, except that we

269. *Perfit*: perfect.
274. *falne nearer us*: a frequently asserted theory.
271. *cousening*: cozening, deceiving.
275. *stares*: stars.
278. *Meridians, and Parallels*: the celestial longitude and latitude (cf. l. 256).
283. *raine*: rein, control.
286. *Tenarif*: the volcanic peak on Tenerife of the Canary Islands.
289. *strooke*: fatally harpooned (§163).
294. *Antipodies*: 'People under us that goe with their feete toward ours' (Bullokar).
295. *Vault infernall*: Hell, traditionally thought to be located at the earth's centre.
296. *except that*: unless.

Invent another torment, that there must
Millions into a strait hote roome be thrust)
Then solidnes, and roundnes have no place.
Are these but warts, and pock-holes in the face   300
Of th'earth? Thinke so: But yet confesse, in this
The worlds proportion disfigured is,
That those two legges whereon it doth relie,   *Disorder in*
Reward and punishment are bent awrie.   *the world.*
And, Oh, it can no more be questioned,   305
That beauties best, proportion, is dead,
Since even griefe it selfe, which now alone
Is left us, is without proportion.
Shee by whose lines proportion should bee
Examin'd, measure of all Symmetree,   310
Whom had that Ancient seen, who thought soules made
Of Harmony, he would at next have said
That Harmony was shee, and thence infer,
That soules were but Resultances from her,
And did from her into our bodies go,   315
As to our eyes, the formes from objects flow:
Shee, who if those great Doctors trucly said
That th'Arke to mans proportions was made,
Had beene a type for that, as that might be
A type of her in this, that contrary   320
Both Elements, and Passions liv'd at peace
In her, who caus'd all Civill warre to cease.
Shee, after whom, what forme soe're we see,
Is discord, and rude incongruitee,
Shee, shee is dead, she's dead; when thou knowst this,   325
Thou knowst how ugly a monster this world is:
And learnst thus much by our Anatomee,
That here is nothing to enamor thee:

298.   *strait*: narrow.
310.   *Examin'd*: verified.
311.   *that Ancient*: possibly Pythagoras.
312.   *at next*: immediately.
314.   *Resultances*: emanations.
317–18. A commonplace notion about Noah's Ark, endorsed by numerous
        Doctors or authorities (§4).

And that, not onely faults in inward parts,
Corruptions in our braines, or in our harts,   330
Poysoning the fountaines, whence our actions spring,
Endanger us: but that if every thing
Be not done fitly'and in proportion,
To satisfie wise, and good lookers on,
(Since most men be such as most thinke they bee)   335
They're lothsome too, by this Deformitee.
For good, and well, must in our actions meete:
Wicked is not much worse then indiscreet.
But beauties other second Element,
Colour, and lustre now, is as neere spent.   340
And had the world his just proportion,
Were it a ring still, yet the stone is gone.
As a compassionate Turcoyse which doth tell
By looking pale, the wearer is not well,
As gold fals sicke being stung with Mercury,   345
All the worlds parts of such complexion bee.
When nature was most busie, the first weeke,
Swadling the new-borne earth, God seemd to like,
That she should sport herselfe sometimes, and play,
To mingle and vary colours every day.   350
And then, as though she could not make inow,
Himselfe his various Rainbow did allow.

335.   Cf. Donne in a sermon: 'for the most part, most men are such, as most
       men take them to be' (§167).
337.   *well*: i.e. *fitly* (l. 333).
338.   *then*: than.
343–44.   Popularly believed of the turquoise.
345.   Wrought or stamped gold is covered with a ghostly luminosity if *stung*
       (rubbed) with quicksilver (§218).
346.   *complexion*: temperament.
347.   *the first weeke*: i.e. of history, when the world was created (Genesis 1).
347–50.   A commonplace notion, averred by the German astronomer Kepler
       among others: 'as the Creator played, so he also taught nature, as his
       image, to play; and to play the very same game that he played for her
       first' (*Tertius interveniens*, 1610).
351.   *inow*: enough.
352.   *various*: multicoloured; *Rainbow*: symbolic of God's new covenant with
       Noah (Genesis 9.11 ff.).

Sight is the noblest sense of any one,
Yet sight hath onely color to feed on,
And color is decayd: summers robe growes   355
Duskie, and like an oft dyed garment showes.
Our blushing redde, which us'd in cheekes to spred,
Is inward sunke, and onely our soules are redde.
Perchance the world might have recovered,
If she whom we lament had not beene dead: 360
But shee, in whom all white, and redde, and blue
(Beauties ingredients) voluntary grew,
As in an unvext Paradise; from whom
Did all things verdure, and their lustre come,
Whose composition was miraculous,   365
Being all colour, all Diaphanous,
(For Ayre, and Fire but thicke grosse bodies were,
And liveliest stones but drowsie, and pale to her,)
Shee, shee is dead; shee's dead: when thou knowst this,
Thou knowst how wan a Ghost this our world is: 370
And learnst thus much by our Anatomee,
That it should more affright, then pleasure thee.
And that, since all faire colour then did sinke,
Tis now but wicked vanity to thinke,
To color vitious deeds with good pretence, *Weaknesse in*
Or with bought colors to illude mens sense. *the want of*
Nor in ought more this worlds decay appeares, *correspondence of*
Then that her influence the heav'n forbeares, *heaven and earth.*
Or that the Elements doe not feele this,
The father, or the mother barren is.   380

353.   Of the senses, *sight* was ranked highest, and touch lowest.
357–58. The *blushing redde* intimates innocence; but the *redde* within our
        soules, guilt or sin.
363.   *unvext*: devoid of distress.
364.   *verdure*: the flesh green of new vegetation (§167).
365–66. *miraculous*: because at once *all color* and transparent.
372.   *then*: than.
376.   *with bought colors to illude*: with cosmetics to deceive (*ALC*).
378.   *Then*: than.
       influence: i.e. of the celestial bodies on the earth.
380.   *father*: the aggregate of celestial bodies; *mother*: the earth (§158).

The clouds conceive not raine, or doe not powre
In the due birth-time, downe the balmy showre.
Th'Ayre doth not motherly sit on the earth,
To hatch her seasons, and give all things birth.
Spring-times were common cradles, but are toombes;   385
And false-conceptions fill the general wombs.
Th'Ayre showes such Meteors, as none can see,
Not onely what they meane, but what they bee.
Earth such new wormes, as would have troubled much,
Th'Egyptian Mages to have made more such.   390
What Artist now dares boast that he can bring
Heaven hither, or constellate any thing,
So as the influence of those starres may bee
Imprisond in an Herbe, or Charme, or Tree,
And doe by touch, all which those starres could do?   395
The art is lost, and correspondence too.
For heaven gives little, and the earth takes lesse,
And man least knowes their trade, and purposes.
If this commerce twixt heaven and earth were not
Embarr'd, and all this trafique quite forgot,   400
Shee, for whose losse we have lamented thus,
Would worke more fully'and pow'rfully on us.
Since herbes, and roots, by dying, lose not all,
But they, yea Ashes too, are medicinall,

---

387.   *Meteors*: atmospheric phenomena in general, and comets in particular,
        were alike thought to portend disaster.
389.   *wormes*: serpents.
390.   *Mages*: the Egyptian magicians who transformed their rods into ser-
        pents (Exodus 7.10–12).
391.   *Artist*: astrologer.
392.   *constellate*: use the power of a favourable constellation for (§170).
393–94. See above, p. 71, ll. 33–36.
396.   *correspondence*: the close link – not simply analogical – between heaven
        and earth; cf. *commerce* (399), *trafique* (400).
400.   *Embarr'd*: stopped.
402.   On the symbol ', see above, p. 5.
404.   Medical writers often prescribed the ashes of certain herbs for specific
        diseases (§192).

Death could not quench her vertue so, but that   405
It would be (if not follow'd) wondred at:
And all the world would be one dying Swan,
To sing her funerall prayse, and vanish than.
But as some Serpents poyson hurteth not,
Except it be from the live Serpent shot,   410
So doth her vertue need her here, to fit
That unto us; she working more then it.
But she, in whom, to such maturity,
Vertue was growne, past growth, that it must die,
She from whose influence all Impressions came,   415
But, by Receivers impotencies, lame,
Who, though she could not transubstantiate
All states to gold, yet guilded every state,
So that some Princes have some temperance;
Some Counsaylors some purpose to advance   420
The common profite; and some people have
Some stay, no more then Kings should give, to crave;
Some women have some taciturnity;
Some Nunneries, some graines of chastity.
She that did thus much, and much more could doe,   425
But that our age was Iron, and rusty too,
Shee, shee is dead; shee's dead; when thou knowst this,
Thou knowst how drie a Cinder this world is.

407–8. Swans were believed to sing but once, just before their death.
408. *than*: then.
409–12. According to Numbers 21.8–9 and Renaissance medical lore, the
  serpent's poison also possessed healing properties; by extension, as
  Donne said in one of his sermons (X, 189), 'the groveling Serpent' or
  Satan is matched by 'the crucified Serpent' or Christ (§571).
412. *then*: than.
415. *influence*: i.e. as an elixir, purifying all other elements (§218).
417–18. *transubstantiate*: change the substance into *gold*, not merely have it
  guilded (i.e. gilded).
420. *Counsaylors*: lawyers.
422. *stay*: restraint.
  then: than.
426. The last of the legendary four ages of history – Gold, Silver,
  Bronze, and *Iron* – is here and elsewhere used as symbolic of history's
  degeneration.

And learnst thus much by our Anatomy,
That 'tis in vaine to dew, or mollifie   430
It with thy Teares, or Sweat, or Bloud: no thing
Is worth our travaile, griefe, or perishing,
But those rich joyes, which did possesse her hart,
Of which shee's now partaker, and a part.
But as in cutting up a man that's dead,   *Conclusion.*
The body will not last out to have read
On every part, and therefore men direct
Their speech to parts, that are of most effect;
So the worlds carcasse would not last, if I
Were punctuall in this Anatomy.   440
Nor smels it well to hearers, if one tell
Them their disease, who faine would think they're wel.
Here therefore be the end: And, blessed maid,
Of whom is meant what ever hath bcene said,
Or shall be spoken well by any tongue,   445
Whose name refines course lines, and makes prose song,
Accept this tribute, and his first yeares rent,
Who till his darke short tapers end be spent,
As oft as thy feast sees this widow'd earth,
Will yearely celebrate thy second birth,   450
That is, thy death. For though the soule of man
Be got when man is made, 'tis borne but than
When man doth die. Our body's as the wombe,
And as a mid-wife death directs it home.
And you her creatures, whom she workes upon   455

432. *travaile*: labour.
435–37. Anatomists dissected first those parts of cadavers likely to more
        immediate 'putrefactions or rottynges' (§192).
436. *read*: yielded instruction.
440. *punctuall*: detailed.
446. *course*: coarse.
447. *rent*: in a sermon Donne defined 'rents' as 'spiritual duties and Services'
        (§167).
448. *taper*: candle.
449. *feast*: saint's day.
450. *birth*: resurrection into Heaven.
452. *than*: then.

And have your last, and best concoction
From her example, and her vertue, if you
In reverence to her, doe thinke it due,
That no one should her prayses thus rehersc,
As matter fit for Chronicle, not verse,   460
Vouchsafe to call to minde, that God did make
A last, and lasting peece, a song. He spake
To *Moses* to deliver unto all,
That song: because hee knew they would let fall
The Law, the Prophets, and the History,   465
But keepe the song still in their memory.
Such an opinion (in due measure) made
Me this great Office boldly to invade.
Nor could incomprehensiblenesse deterre
Me, from thus trying to emprison her.   470
Which when I saw that a strict grave could do,
I saw not why verse might not doe so too.
Verse hath a middle nature: heaven keepes soules,
The grave keeps bodies, verse the fame enroules.

---

456.   *concoction*: purification (in alchemy).
460.   Cf. above, p. 58, ll. 31–32.
461–64. For the celebrated Song of Moses, see Deuteronomy 32.1–43.
465.   The Books of *the Law*, notably Leviticus and Deuteronomy; of *the
       Prophets* such as Isaiah and Ezekiel; and of *the History*, i.e. all 'historical'
       Books that chronicle events in the Near East.
467.   *in due measure*: with proper reverence; also, in verse (§170).

A Funerall Elegie.

Tis lost, to trust a Tombe with such a ghest,
 Or to confine her in a Marble chest.
Alas, what's Marble, Jeat, or Porphiry,
 Priz'd with the Chrysolite of eyther eye,
Or with those Pearles, and Rubies which shee was?   5
 Joyne the two Indies in one Tombe, 'tis glas;
And so is all to her materials,
 Though every inche were ten escurials.
Yet shee's demolish'd: Can we keepe her then
 In workes of hands, or of the wits of men?   10
Can these memorials, ragges of paper, give
 Life to that name, by which name they must live?
Sickly, alas, short–liv'd, aborted bee
 Those Carkas verses, whose soule is not shee.
And can shee, who no longer would be shee,   15
 Being such a Tabernacle, stoope to bee
In paper wrap't; Or, when she would not lie
 In such a house, dwell in an Elegie?
But 'tis no matter; we may well allow
 Verse to live so long as the world will now.   20
For her death wounded it. The world containes
 Princes for armes, and Counsailors for braines,
Lawyers for tongues. Divines for hearts, and more,
 The Rich for stomachs, and for backes the Pore;
The Officers for hands, Merchants for feet   25
 By which remote and distant Countries meet.
But those fine spirits, which doe tune and set
 This Organ, are those peeces which beget

A Funerall Elegie.
 1. *Tis lost*: it is labour lost.
 2. *chest*: tomb.
 4. *Chrysolite*: green gems such as topaz, regarded as symbolic of pure
  perfection (§166).
 6. *the two Indies*: see above, p. 54, note on 17.
 8. *escurials*: see above, p. 269, note on 48.
 27. *fine spirits*: exquisite individuals.
 28. *Organ*: the world at large.

Wonder and love; And these were shee; and shee
   Being spent, the world must needes decrepit bee.   30
For since death will proceed to triumph still,
   He can finde nothing, after her, to kill,
Except the world it selfe, so great as shee.
   Thus brave and confident may Nature bee,
Death cannot give her such another blow,   35
   Because shee cannot such another show.
But must we say shee's dead? May't not be said
   That as a sundred Clocke is peece-meale laid,
Not to be lost, but by the makers hand
   Repolish'd, without error then to stand,   40
Or as the Affrique Niger streame enwombs
   It selfe into the earth, and after comes,
(Having first made a naturall bridge, to passe
   For many leagues,) farre greater then it was,
May't not be said, that her grave shall restore   45
   Her, greater, purer, firmer, then before?
Heaven may say this, and joy in't; but can wee
   Who live, and lacke her, here this vantage see?
What is't to us, alas, if there have beene
   An Angell made a Throne, or Cherubin?   50
We lose by't: And as aged men are glad
   Being tastelesse growne, to joy in joyes they had,
So now the sicke starv'd world must feed upone
   This joy, that we had her, who now is gone.
Rejoyce then nature, and this world, that you   55
   Fearing the last fires hastning to subdue
Your force and vigor, ere it were neere gone,
   Wisely bestow'd, and layd it all on one.

---

40.   *Repolish'd*: reassembled and perfected (§166).
41–44. The River Niger was identified with the Upper Nile, flowing partly
      above the ground, partly below it (§170).
44 (also 46). *then*: than.
50.   *Throne*, *Cherubin*: angelic orders; see above, p. 243, note on 60–61.
52.   *tastelesse*: devoid of senses.
56.   *last fires*: the final conflagration expected to attend the Last Judgement.

One, whose cleare body was so pure, and thin,
   Because it neede disguise no thought within.   60
T'was but a through-light scarfe, her minde t'enroule,
   Or exhalation breath'd out from her soule.
One, whom all men who durst no more, admir'd;
   And whom, who ere had worth enough, desir'd;
As when a Temple's built, Saints emulate   65
   To which of them, it shall be consecrate.
But as when Heav'n lookes on us with new eyes,
   Those new starres ev'ry Artist exercise,
What place they should assigne to them they doubt,
   Argue, and agree not, till those starres go out: 70
So the world studied whose this peece should be,
   Till she can be no bodies else, nor shee:
But like a Lampe of Balsamum, desir'd
   Rather t'adorne, then last, shee soone expir'd;
Cloath'd in her Virgin white integrity;   75
   For mariage, though it doe not staine, doth dye.
To scape th'infirmities which waite upone
   Woman, shee went away, before sh'was one.
And the worlds busie noyse to overcome,
   Tooke so much death, as serv'd for *opium*.   80
For though she could not, nor could chuse to die,
   Shee'ath yeelded to too long an Extasie.
He which not knowing her sad History,
   Should come to reade the booke of destiny,

59. *thin*: fine.
61. *through-light*: translucent.
     enroule: enwrap.
65. *emulate*: view with each other (§170).
67. *new eyes*: i.e. *new starres*.
68–70. *new starres . . . go out*: see above, p. 337, note on 259–60.
68. *Artist*: astronomer (cf. above, p. 342, note on 391).
73. *Balsamum*: balsam or balm, an aromatic mixture said to possess curative
     powers.
74. *then*: than.
75. *white integrity*: cf. above, p. 258, l. 42.
80. *opium*: brief sleep (§170).
82. *Extasie*: mystic trance (§163).

How faire, and chast, humble, and high shee'ad beene,　85
　Much promis'd, much perform'd, at not fifteene,
And measuring future things, by things before,
　Should turne the leafe to reade, and reade no more,
Would thinke that eyther destiny mistooke,
　Or that some leafes were torne out of the booke.　90
But 'tis not so: Fate did but usher her
　To yeares of Reasons use, and then infer
Her destiny to her selfe; which liberty
　She tooke but for thus much, thus much to die.
Her modesty not suffering her to bee　95
　Fellow-Commissioner with destinee,
Shee did no more but die; if after her
　Any shall live, which dare true good prefer,
Every such person is her delegate,
　T'accomplish that which should have beene her fate.　100
They shall make up that booke, and shall have thankes
　Of fate and her, for filling up their blanks.
For future vertuous deeds are Legacies,
　Which from the gift of her example rise.
And 'tis in heav'n part of spirituall mirth,　105
　To see how well, the good play her, on earth.

86.　*not fifteene*: Elizabeth Drury died aged fourteen.
92.　*infer*: entrust.
94.　*thus much to die*: to die so far as this life is concerned (§158).
101.　*that booke*: 'the booke of destiny' (84 ff.).
106.　*play*: imitate.

THE SECOND ANNIVERSARIE.

Of the Progress of the Soule.
Wherein: By occasion of the Religious death of Mistris
Elizabeth Drury the incommodities of the Soule in this
life and her exaltation in the next, are contemplated.

The Harbinger to the Progres.
[by Joseph Hall]

Two soules move here, and mine (a third) must move
Paces of admiration, and of love;
Thy soule (Deare Virgin) whose this tribute is,
Mov'd from this mortall sphere to lively blisse;
And yet moves still, and still aspires to see   5
The worlds last day, thy glories full degree:
Like as those starres which thou ore-lookest farre,
Are in their place, and yet still moved are:
No soule (whiles with the luggage of this clay
It clogged is) can follow thee halfe way;   10
Or see thy flight; which doth our thoughts outgoe
So fast, that now the lightning moves but slow:
But now thou art as high in heaven flowne
As heav'ns from us; what soule besides thine owne
Can tell thy joyes, or say he can relate   15
Thy glorious Journals in that blessed state?
I envie thee (Rich soule) I envy thee,
Although I cannot yet thy glory see:
And thou (Great spirit) which her's follow'd hast
So fast, as none can follow thine so fast;   20

The Harbinger to the Progres. On Joseph Hall, the poem's presumed author, see
    above, headnote on p. 324. 'Harbinger' is one that precedes and
    announces someone's approach; 'progress' here as before (p. 327, note
    on 7) means royal journey.
16.   *Journals*: record of daily experiences.
19.   *thou*: i.e. Donne.

So far, as none can follow thine so farre
(And if this flesh did not the passage barre
Had'st raught her) let me wonder at thy flight
Which long agone had'st lost the vulgar sight
And now mak'st proud the better eyes, that thay   25
Can see thee less'ned in thine aery way;
So while thou mak'st her soules Hy progresse knowne
Thou mak'st a noble progresse of thine owne,
From this worlds carcasse having mounted hie
To that pure life of Immortalitie;   30
Since thine aspiring thoughts themselves so raise
That more may not beseeme a creatures praise,
Yet still thou vow'st her more; and every yeare
Mak'st a new progresse, while thou wandrest here;
Still upwards mount; and let thy makers praise   35
Honor thy Laura, and adorne thy laies.
And since thy Muse her head in heaven shrouds
Oh let her never stoope below the clouds:
And if those glorious sainted soules may know
Or what we doe, or what we sing below,   40
Those acts, those songs shall still content them best
Which praise those awful powers that make them blest.

23. *raught*: reached.
36. *Laura*: the lady so central to Petrach's poetry.

The Second Anniversary.
Of the Progres of the Soule.

Nothing could make mee sooner to confesse   *The entrance.*
That this world had an everlastingnesse,
Then to consider, that a yeare is runne,
Since both this lower worlds, and the Sunnes Sunne,
The Lustre, and the vigor of this All,   5
Did set; t'were Blasphemy, to say, did fall.
But as a ship which hath strooke saile, doth runne,
By force of that force which before, it wonne,
Or as sometimes in a beheaded man,
Though at those two Red seas, which freely ran,   10
One from the Trunke, another from the Head,
His soule be saild, to her eternall bed,
His eies will twinckle, and his tongue will roll,
As though he beckned, and cal'd backe his Soul,
He graspes his hands, and he puls up his feet,   15
And seemes to reach, and to step forth to meet
His soule; when all these motions which we saw,
Are but as Ice, which crackles at a thaw:
Or as a Lute, which in moist weather, rings
Her knell alone, by cracking of her strings.   20
So strugles this dead world, now shee is gone;
For there is motion in corruption.
As some Daies are, at the Creation nam'd,
Before the sunne, the which fram'd Daies, was fram'd,
So after this sunnes set, some show appeares,   25
And orderly vicisitude of yeares.

The Second Anniversary. The title *Of the Progres of the Soule* was its second use by
      Donne (cf. below, p. 402).
  2.   The world's eternity was rejected by nearly every Renaissance thinker.
  3.   *Then*: than.
  7.   *strooke*: lowered.
  8.   *wonne*: acquired.
19–20. The phenomenon was regarded as ominous (§170).
  22.   *motion in corruption*: as opposed to the eternal rest in the life beyond.
23–24. According to Genesis 1.16–19, the sun was not *fram'd* (created) until
      three *Daies* had passed.

Yet a new Deluge, and of Lethe flood,
Hath drown'd us all, All have forgot all good,
Forgetting her, the maine Reserve of all;
Yet in this Deluge, grosse and generall,⠀⠀⠀⠀⠀⠀⠀⠀⠀30
Thou seest mee strive for life; my life shalbe,
To bee hereafter prais'd, for praysing thee,
Immortal Mayd, who though thou wouldst refuse
The name of Mother, be unto my Muse,
A Father since her chast Ambition is,⠀⠀⠀⠀⠀⠀⠀⠀⠀35
Yearely to bring forth such a child as this.
These Hymes may worke on future wits, and so
May great Grand-children of thy praises grow.
And so, though not Revive, embalme, and spice
The world, which else would putrify with vice.⠀⠀⠀⠀40
For thus, Man may extend thy progeny,
Untill man doe but vanish, and not die.
These Hymns thy issue, may encrease so long,
As till Gods great Venite change the song.
Thirst for that time, O my insatiate soule,⠀⠀⠀⠀*A just*
And serve thy thirst, with Gods safe-sealing Bowle.⠀*disestimation*
Be thirsty still, and drinke still till thou goe;⠀⠀⠀*of this world.*
'Tis th'onely Health, to be Hydropique so.
Forget this rotten world; And unto thee,
Let thine owne times as an old story be,⠀⠀⠀⠀⠀⠀⠀50
Be not concern'd: study not why, nor whan;
Doe not so much, as not beleeve a man.

27.⠀*new Deluge*: another Noah's Flood.
⠀⠀⠀*Lethe*: as above, p. 292, note on 6.
29.⠀*Reserve*: store.
37.⠀*Hymes*: possibly a pun on 'hims', i.e. the male hymns which are to
⠀⠀⠀impregnate others (§167).
44.⠀*Venite*: 'come', i.e. God's call to man at the Last Judgement.
46.⠀*Bowle*: the chalice containing the Eucharist, *safe-sealing* in that it con-
⠀⠀⠀firms salvation through Grace.
47.⠀*goe*: forego the body.
48.⠀*Hydropique*: see above, p. 90, note on 6.
49.⠀*thee*: Donne addresses himself.

For though to erre, be worst, to try truths forth,
Is far more busines, then this world is worth.
The World is but a Carkas; thou are fed   55
By it, but as a worme, that carcas bred;
And why shouldst thou, poore worme, consider more,
When this world will grow better then before,
Then those thy fellow-wormes doe thinke upone
That carkasses last resurrectione.   60
Forget this world, and scarse thinke of it so,
As of old cloaths, cast off a yeare agoe.
To be thus stupid is Alacrity;
Men thus lethargique have best Memory.
Looke upward; that's towards her, whose happy state   65
We now lament not, but congratulate.
Shee, to whom all this world was but a stage,
Where all sat harkning how her youthfull age
Should be emploid, because in all, shee did,
Some Figure of the Golden times, was hid.   70
Who could not lacke, what ere this world could give,
Because shee was the forme, that made it live;
Nor could complaine, that this world was unfit,
To be staid in, then when shee was in it;
Shee that first tried indifferent desires   75
By vertue, and vertue by religious fires,
Shee to whose person Paradise adhear'd,
As Courts to Princes; shee whose eies enspheard
Star-light inough, t'have made the South controll,
(Had shee beene there) the Star-full Northern Pole,   80

53. *try*: test; *forth*: thoroughly.
54 (also 58, 59). *then*: than.
63. *stupid*: stupefied.
66. *congratulate*: rejoice with.
70. *the Golden times*: the Age of Gold (see above, p. 343, note on 426).
72. *the forme*: the world's soul (§158).
75. *tried*: tested.
     indifferent: morally neutral (§166).
78. *enspheard*: enclosed as in a sphere.
80. *Star-full*: 'we know', Donne wrote elsewhere, 'that there are more stars
     under the Northerne, then under the Southern Pole' (§170).

Shee, shee is gone; shee is gone; when thou knowest this,
What fragmentary rubbidge this world is
Thou knowest, and that it is not worth a thought;
He honors it too much that thinks it nought.
Thinke then, My soule, that death is but a Groome,   *Contemplation*
Which brings a Taper to the outward roome,   *of our state in*
Whence thou spiest first a little glimmering light,   *our death-bed.*
And after brings it nearer to thy sight:
For such approches doth Heaven make in death.
Thinke thy selfe laboring now with broken breath,   90
And thinke those broken and soft Notes to bee
Division, and thy happiest Harmonee.
Thinke thee laid on thy death bed, loose and slacke;
And thinke that but unbinding of a packe,
To take one precious thing, thy soule, from thence.   95
Thinke thy selfe parch'd with fevers violence,
Anger thine Ague more, by calling it
Thy Physicke; chide the slacknesse of the fit.
Thinke that thou hearst thy knell, and think no more,
But that, as Bels cal'd thee to Church before,   100
So this, to the Triumphant Church, cals thee.
Thinke Satans Sergeants round about thee bee,
And thinke that but for Legacies they thrust;
Give one thy Pride, to'another give thy Lust:
Given them those sinnes which they gave thee before,   105
And trust th'immaculate blood to wash thy score.
Thinke thy frinds weeping round, and thinke that thay
Weepe but because they goe not yet thy way.
Thinke that they close thine eyes, and thinke in this,
That they confesse much in the world, amisse,   110

82. *rubbidge*: rubbish.
85. *Groome*: servant.
92. *Division*: a melodic sequence composed of short notes; 'breaking' (cf. *broken* in 90 and 91) is the process of elaboration of the line of a particular melody (§56).
97. *Ague*: malarial fever.
98. *Physicke*: medicine.
      slacknesse: mildness.
102. *Satans Sergeants*: bailiffs, intent on arresting debtors (sinners).
103. *thrust*: gather about the death-bed.

Who dare not trust a dead mans eye with that,
Which they from God, and Angels cover not.
Thinke that they shroud thee up, and thinke from thence
They reinvest thee in white innocence.
Thinke that thy body rots, and (if so lowe,   115
Thy soule exalted so, thy thoughts can goe,)
Think thee a Prince, who of themselves create
Wormes which insensibly devoure their state.
Thinke that they bury thee, and thinke that rite
Laies thee to sleepe but a saint Lucies night.   120
Thinke these things cheerefully: and if thou bee
Drowsie or slacke, remember then that shee,
Shee whose Complexion was so even made,
That which of her Ingredients should invade
The other three, no Feare, no Art could guesse: 125
So far were all remov'd from more or lesse.
But as in Mithridate, or just perfumes,
Where all good things being met, no one presumes
To governe, or to triumph on the rest,
Onely because all were, no part was best.   130
And as, though all doe know, that quantities
Are made of lines, and lines from Points arise,
None can these lines or quantities unjoynt,
And say this is a line, or this a point,
So though the Elements and Humors were   135
In her, one could not say, this governes there.

114. *reinvest*: re-attire.
118. *Wormes*: parasites.
     insensibly: without their being aware of it (§170).
120. *saint Lucies night*: the longest night of the year (see above, p. 90).
123. *Complexion*: temperament.
     even: evenly balanced.
124. *Ingredients*: the four 'humours' (as above, p. 336, note on 241).
125. *Fear*: such as that of her parents; *Art*: of her doctors (§166).
127. *Mithridate*: see above, p. 267, note on 27.
     just: correctly blended.
130. *all were*: all the parts were best.
135. *Humors*: see above, p. 336, note on 241.

Whose even constitution might have wonne
Any disease to venter on the Sunne,
Rather then her: and make a spirit feare
That he to disuniting subject were.   140
To whose proportions if we would compare
Cubes, th'are unstable; Circles, Angulare;
Shee who was such a Chaine, as Fate emploies
To bring mankind, all Fortunes it enjoies,
So fast, so even wrought, as one would thinke,   145
No Accident, could threaten any linke,
Shee, shee embrac'd a sicknesse, gave it meat,
The purest Blood, and Breath, that ere it eat.
And hath taught us that though a good man hath
Title to Heaven, and plead it by his Faith,   150
And though he may pretend a conquest, since
Heaven was content to suffer violence,
Yea though he plead a long possession too,
(For they'are in Heaven on Earth, who Heavens workes do,)
Though he had right, and power, and Place before,   155
Yet Death must usher, and unlocke the doore.
Thinke further on thy selfe, my soule, and thinke;   *Incommodities*
How thou at first wast made but in a sinke;   *of the Soule*
Thinke that it argued some infermitee,   *in the Body.*
That those two soules, which then thou foundst in mee,   160
Thou fedst upon, and drewst into thee, both
My second soule of sence, and first of growth.

137. *wonne*: prevailed upon.
138. *venter*: venture.
       the Sunne: by definition not subject to change or *disease*.
139. *then*: than.
140. i.e. that he were subject to disuniting (division).
142. *unstable*: irregular.
143. *Chaine*: see below, p. 375, note on 71 ff.
147. *meat*: food.
151. *pretend*: claim by law.
152. Cf. Matthew 11.12: 'from the days of John the Baptist until now the
       kingdom of heaven suffereth violence' (§158).
154. On the symbol ', here and hereafter, see above, p. 5.
158. *sinke*: cesspool.
160–62. *two soules*: the one of *growth*, in plants, and the one of *sence*, in animals;
       the rational soul of man was said to subsume the other two.

Thinke but how poore thou wast, how obnoxious,
Whom a small lump of flesh could poison thus.
This curded milke, this poore unlittered whelpe   165
My body, could, beyond escape, or helpe,
Infect thee with originall sinne, and thou
Couldst neither then refuse, nor leave it now.
Thinke that no stubborne sullen Anchorit,
Which fixt to'a Pillar, or a Grave doth sit   170
Bedded and Bath'd in all his Ordures, dwels
So fowly'as our soules, in their first-built Cels.
Thinke in how poore a prison thou didst lie
After, enabled but to sucke, and crie.
Thinke, when t'was growne to most, t'was a poore Inne,   175
A Province Pack'd up in two yards of skinne,
And that usurped, or threatned with the rage
Of sicknesses, or their true mother, Age.
But thinke that Death hath now enfranchis'd thee,   *Her liberty*
Thou hast thy'expansion now and libertee;   *by death.*
Thinke that a rusty Peece, discharg'd, is flowen
In peeces, and the bullet is his owne,
And freely flies: This to thy soule allow,
Thinke thy sheell broke, thinke thy Soule hatch'd but now.
And thinke this slow-pac'd soule, which late did cleave, 185
To'a body,'and went by the bodies leave,
Twenty, perchance, or thirty mile a day,
Dispatches in a minute all the way,
Twixt Heaven, and Earth: shee staies not in the Ayre,
To looke what Meteors there themselves prepare;   190

163.   *obnoxious*: vulnerable.
165.   *curded milke*: cf. Job 10.9–10, 'thou hast made me as the clay . . . Hast
        thou not poured me out as milk, and curdled me like cheese?' (§167).
        unlittered: as yet unborn.
169.   *Anchorit*: see above, p. 153; note on 16.
173.   *prison*: the body; cf. *Tombe* (l. 252).
174.   *After*: after birth.
175.   *growne to most*: fully grown.
179.   *enfranchis'd*: liberated.
181.   *Peece*: firearm.
182.   *his owne*: its own master.
190.   *Meteors*: see above, p. 342, note on 387.

Shee carries no desire to know, nor sense,
Whether th'Ayrs middle Region be intense,
For th'Element of fire, shee doth not know,
Whether shee past by such a place or no;
She baits not at the Moone, nor cares to trie,   195
Whether in that new world, men live, and die.
Venus retards her not, to'enquire, how shee
Can, (being one Star) Hesper, and Vesper bee;
Hee that charm'd Argus eies, sweet Mercury.
Workes not on her, who now is growen all Ey;   200
Who, if shee meete the body of the Sunne,
Goes through, not staying till his course be runne;
Who finds in Mars his Campe, no corps of Guard;
Nor is by Jove, nor by his father barrd;
But ere shee can consider how shee went,   205
At once is at, and through the Firmament.
And as these stars were but so many beades
Strunge on one string, speed undistinguish'd leades
Her through those spheares, as through the beades, a string,
Whose quicke succession makes it still one thing: 210
As doth the Pith, which least our Bodies slacke,
Strings fast the little bones of necke, and backe;

192.   *intense*: dense.
195.   *baits*: pauses.
      trie: determine.
196.   It was often debated whether the moon was populated (see above, p. 335, note on 211).
197–98.   Donne explained in *Paradoxes and Problemes* that Venus is known as Hesperus 'because it is wholesomest in the Morning', and Vesper 'because it is pleasantest in the Evening' (cf. §568).
199.   The god *Mercury* used magic to close the hundred *eies* of *Argus*, and then slew him.
200.   *growen all Ey*: i.e. once the soul is freed from the body (cf. note on 173).
204.   *Jove* and *his father*: the spheres of Jupiter and Saturn.
206.   *the Firmament*: the sphere of the fixed stars (cf. above, p. 65, note on 24), the last of the regions traversed ever since l. 189.
208.   *undistinguish'd*: too fast to be distinguished.
209.   *spheares*: see above, p. 80, note on 23.
211.   *Pith*: spinal cord.
      least: lest.

So by the soule doth death string Heaven and Earth,
For when our soule enjoyes this her third birth,
(Creation gave her one, a second, grace,) 215
Heaven is as neare, and present to her face,
As colours are, and objects, in a roome
Where darknesse was before, when Tapers come.
This must, my soule, thy long-short Progresse bee;
To'advance these thoughts, remember then, that shee, 220
Shee, whose faire body no such prison was,
But that a soule might well be pleas'd to passe
An Age in her; shee whose rich beauty lent
Mintage to others beauties, for they went
But for so much, as they were like to her; 225
Shee, in whose body (if wee dare prefer
This low world, to so high a mark, as shee,)
The Westerne treasure, Esterne spiceree,
Europe, and Afrique, and the unknowen rest
Were easily found, or what in them was best; 230
And when w'have made this large Discoveree,
Of all in her some one part there will bee
Twenty such parts, whose plenty and riches is
Inough to make twenty such worlds as this;
Shee, whom had they knowne, who did first betroth 235
The Tutelar Angels, and assigned one, both
To Nations, Cities, and to Companies,
To Functions, Offices, and Dignities,
And to each severall man, to him, and him,
They would have given her one for every limme; 240
Shee, of whose soule, if we may say, t'was Gold,
Her body was th'Electrum, and did hold

---

214. *third birth*: presumably her resurrection into Heaven, earlier termed
      second birth (see p. 344, note on 450).
218. *Tapers*: candles.
219. *long-short*: i.e. long in space, short in time (§167).
224. *Mintage*: value (see above, p. 84, ll. 1–4).
226. *prefer*: promote.
228. See above, p. 54, note on 17.
236–40. The lines satirize the more extreme Roman Catholic views about
      guardian (*Tutelary*) angels.
242. *Electrum*: an alloy of gold and silver, less perfect than pure *Gold* (241).

Many degrees of that; we understood
Her by her sight, her pure and eloquent blood
Spoke in her cheekes, and so distinckly wrought,   245
That one might almost say, her bodie thought,
Shee, shee, thus richly, and largely hous'd, is gone:
And chides us slow-pac'd snailes, who crawle upon
Our prisons prison, earth, nor thinkes us well
Longer, then whil'st we beare our brittle shell.   250
But t'were but little to have chang'd our roome,   *Her ignorance in*
If, as we were in this our living Tombe   *this life and*
Oppress'd with ignorance, we still were so.   *knowledge in*
Poore soule in this thy flesh what do'st thou know.   *the next.*
Thou know'st thy selfe so little, as thou know'st not,   255
How thou did'st die, nor how thou wast begot.
Thou neither knowst, how thou at first camest in,
Nor how thou took'st the poyson of mans sin.
Nor dost thou, (though thou knowst, that thou art so)
By what way thou art made immortall, know.   260
Thou art too narrow, wretch, to comprehend
Even thy selfe: yea though thou wouldst but bend
To know thy body. Have not all soules thought
For many ages, that our body'is wrought
Of Ayre, and Fire, and other Elements?   265
And now they thinke of new ingredients.
And one soule thinkes one, and another way
Another thinkes, and ty's an even lay.
Knowst thou but how the stone doth enter in
The bladders Cave, and never breake the skin?   270

244. *sight*: appearance.
245. *wrought*: worked.
249. *Our prisons prison*: the prison of our bodies, which in turn are the prisons
      of our souls (see note on 173).
250. *then*: than.
256. *die*: incurred the penalty of death as a result of the Fall of Man.
262. *bend*: condescend.
265–66. The traditional four *Elements* (see above, p. 335, note on 205) were
      displaced by *new* ones, notably in Paracelsian medicine.
268. *ty's*: it is.
      lay: wager.

Knowst thou how blood, which to the hart doth flow,
Doth from one ventricle to th'other go?
And for the putrid stuffe, which thou dost spit,
Knowst thou how thy lungs have attracted it?
There are no passages so that there is   275
(For ought thou knowst) piercing of substances.
And of those many opinions which men raise
Of Nailes and Haires, dost thou know which to praise?
What hope have we to know our selves, when wee
Know not the least things, which for our use bee?   280
We see in Authors, too stiffe to recant,
A hundred controversies of an Ant.
And yet one watches, starves, freeses, and sweats,
To know but Catechismes and Alphabets
Of unconcerning things, matters of fact;   285
How others on our stage their parts did Act;
What Caesar did, yea, and what Cicero said.
Why grasse is greene, or why our blood is red,
Are mysteries which none have reach'd unto.
In this low forme, poore soule what wilt thou doe?   290
When wilt thou shake off this Pedantery,
Of being taught by sense, and Fantasy?
Thou look'st through spectacles; small things seeme great,
Below; But up unto the watch-towre get,

271–72. Much controverted at the time; William Harvey advanced his
          definitive proposals in 1628.
276.   *piercing of substances*: penetration of one substance by another, the Stoic
          doctrine opposed to Aristotle's theory of mixture of substances (§170).
277–78. It was much debated whether *Nailes and Haires* were skin, bones,
          organic substance, or waste matter (§170; cf. §192).
281–82. Cf. Donne's *Essays in Divinity:* 'There are marked an hundred differ-
          ences in mens Writings concerning an Ant' (§207).
281.   *stiffe*: intractable.
283.   *watches*: stays awake.
284.   *Catechismes and Alphabets*: i.e. the rudiments of knowledge (§170).
285.   *unconcerning*: trivial.
290.   *forme*: state.
292.   *Fantasy*: that part of the mind which receives and interprets sense
          impressions (§164).
293.   *spectacles*: artificial means of seeing like mirrors or telescopes (§170).
294.   *the watch-towre*: traditionally symbolic of the mind.

And see all things despoyld of fallacies: 295
Thou shalt not peepe through lattices of eies,
Nor heare through Laberinths of eares, nor learne
By circuit, or collections to discerne.
In Heaven thou straight know'st all, concerning it,
And what concernes it not, shall straight forget. 300
There thou (but in no other schoole) maist bee
Perchance, as learned, and as full, as shee,
Shee who all Libraries had throughly red
At home, in her owne thoughts, and practised
So much good as would make as many more: 305
Shee whose example they must all implore,
Who would or doe, or thinke well, and confesse
That aie the vertuous Actions they expresse,
Are but a new, and worse edition,
Of her some one thought, or one action: 310
Shee, who in th'Art of knowing Heaven, was growen
Here upon Earth, to such perfection,
That shee hath, ever since to Heaven shee came,
(In a far fairer print,) but read the same:
Shee, shee, not satisfied with all this waite, 315
(For so much knowledge, as would over-fraite
Another, did but Ballast her) is gone,
As well t'enjoy, as get perfectione.
And cals us after her, in that shee tooke,
(Taking herselfe) our best, and worthiest booke. 320
Returne not, my soule, from this extasee, *Of our company in this*
And meditation of what thou shalt bee, *life and in the next.*
To earthly thoughts, till it to thee appeare,
With whom thy conversation must be there.
With whom wilt thou Converse? what station 325
Canst thou choose out, free from infection,

298. *circuit:* circuitous processes; *collections:* inferences.
302. *full:* fully instructed.
308. *aie:* aye, always.
315. *waite:* weight.
321. *extasee:* as above, p. 348, note on 82.
324. *conversation:* association, society: cf. *Converse* (325).

That wil nor give thee theirs, nor drinke in thine?
Shalt thou not finde a spungy slack Divine
Drinke and sucke in th'Instructions of Great men,
And for the word of God, vent them agen?   330
Are there not some Courts, (And then, no things bee
So like as Courts) which, in this let us see,
That wits and tongues of Libellars are weake,
Because they doe more ill, then these can speake?
The poyson'is gone through all, poysons affect   335
Chiefly the cheefest parts, but some effect
In Nailes, and Haires, yea excrements, will show;
So will the poyson of sinne, in the most low.
Up, up, my drowsie soule, where thy new eare
Shall in the Angels songs no discord heare: 340
Where thou shalt see the blessed Mother-maid
Joy in not being that, which men have said.
Where shee'is exalted more for being good,
Then for her interest, of mother-hood.
Up to those Patriarckes, which did longer sit   345
Expecting Christ, then they'have enjoy'd him yet.
Up to those Prophets, which now gladly see
Their Prophecies growen to be Historee.
Up to th'Apostles, who did bravely runne
All the Sunnes course, with more light then the Sunne.   350
Up to those Martyrs, who did calmely bleed
Oyle to th'Apostles Lamps, dew to their seed.
Up to those Virgins, who thought that almost
They made joyntenants with the Holy Ghost,

---

330.   *vent*: discharge.
333–34. Courts do more ill than libellers can speak (§166).
334 (also 344, 346, 350). *then*: than.
339.   *new eare*: cf. the equally spiritual new eye (l. 200).
341.   *Mother-maid*: the Virgin Mary.
342.   *that*: i.e. free of original sin, as claimed (*said*) by many theologians.
344.   *her interest, of mother-hood*: her special claim in being Christ's mother.
345.   *Patriarckes*: i.e. of the Old Testament.
348.   The *Prophecies* of Christ's advent became historical fact.
350.   *All the Sunnes course*: i.e. everywhere, eventually bringing *more light* than
         does the sun.
354.   *joyntenants*: fellow-lodgers.

If they to any should his Temple give. 355
Up, up, for in that squadron there doth live
Shee, who hath carried thether, new degrees
(As to their number) to thcir dignitees.
Shee, who beeing to herselfe a state, enjoyd
All royalties which any state emploid, 360
For shee made wars, and triumph'd; reson still
Did not o'rthrow, but rectifie her will:
And shee made peace, for no peace is like this,
That beauty'and chastity together kisse:
Shee did high justice; for shee crucified 365
Every first motion of rebellious pride:
And shee gave pardons, and was liberall,
For, onely'herselfe except, shee pardond all:
Shee coynd, in this, that her impressions gave
To all our actions all the worth they have: 370
Shee gave protections; the thoughts of her brest
Satans rude Officers could nere arrest.
As these prerogatives being met in one,
Made her a soveraigne state, religion
Made her a Church; and these two made her all. 375
Shee who was all this All, and could not fall
To worse, by company; (for shee was still
More Antidote, then all the world was ill,)
Shee, she doth leave it, and by Death, survive
All this, in Heaven; whither who doth not strive 380
The more, because shee'is there, he doth not know
That accidentall joyes in Heaven doe grow.
But pause, My soule, and study ere thou fall
On accidentall joyes, th'essentiall.

Of essentiall joy in
this life and in the next.

355. *his Temple*: i.e. their bodies.
360. *royalties*: prerogatives of a sovereign.
369. *impressions*: a sovereign's 'stamped face' on coins (see above, p. 57, l. 7).
371. *protections*: immunities from arrest.
378. *then*: than.
382–84. *accidentall joyes*: non-essential joys; *essentiall*: i.e. the sight of God (see l. 441).

Still before Accessories doe abide   385
A triall, must the principall be tride.
And what essentiall joy can'st thou expect
Here upon earth? what permanent effect
Of transitory causes? Dost thou love
Beauty? (And beauty worthyest is to move)   390
Poore couse'ned cose'nor, that she, and that thou,
Which did begin to love, are neither now.
You are both fluid, chang'd since yesterday;
Next day repaires, (but ill) last daies decay.
Nor are, (Although the river keep the name)   395
Yesterdaies waters, and to daies the same.
So flowes her face, and thine eies, neither now
That saint, nor Pilgrime, which your loving vow
Concernd, remaines; but whil'st you thinke you bee
Constant, you'are howrely in inconstancee.   400
Honour may have pretence unto our love,
Because that God did live so long above
Without this Honour, and then lov'd it so,
That he at last made Creatures to bestow
Honour on him: not that he needed it,   405
But that, to his hands, man might grow more fit.
But since all honors from inferiors flow,
(For they doe give it; Princes doe but show
Whom they would have so honord) and that this
On such opinions, and capacities   410
Is built, as rise, and fall, to more and lesse,
Alas, tis but a casuall happinesse.
Hath ever any man to'himselfe assign'd
This or that happinesse, to'arrest his minde,

385–86. In law, the *triall* of the *principall* offender must precede that of the
        Accessories to the offence.
391. *couse'ned cose'nor*: deceived deceiver.
400. *inconstancee*: cf. above, p. 51, ll. 2–5.
401. *pretence unto*: claim upon.
412. *casuall*: accidental, subject to chance.
414. *arrest*: give rest to.

But that another man, which takes a worse, 415
Thinks him a foole for having tane that course?
They who did labour Babels tower t'erect,
Might have considerd, that for that effect,
All this whole solid Earth could not allow
Nor furnish forth Materials enow; 420
And that this Center, to raise such a place
Was far too little, to have beene the Base;
No more affoords this world, foundatione
To'erect true joye, were all the meanes in one.
But as the Heathen made them severall gods, 425
Of all Gods Benefits, and all his Rods,
(For as the Wine, and Corne, and Onions are
Gods unto them, so Agues bee, and war)
And as by changing that whole precious Gold
To such small Copper coynes, they lost the old, 430
And lost their onely God, who ever must
Be sought alone, and not in such a thrust,
So much mankind true happinesse mistakes;
No Joye enjoyes that man, that many makes.
Then, soule, to thy first pitch worke up againe; 435
Know that all lines which circles doe containe,
For once that they the center touch, do touch
Twice the circumference; and be thou such.
Double on Heaven, thy thoughts on Earth emploid;
All will not serve; Onely who have enjoyd 440

415. *a worse*: a worse course.
416. *tane*: taken.
417–22. The limitations of *Babels tower* (Genesis 11.1 ff.) were voiced quite
    often (§559).
418. *effect*: purpose.
420. *enow*: enough.
421. *this Center*: the earth.
426. *Rods*: chastisements.
432. *thrust*: crowd.
435. *pitch*: peak.
436. *lines* etc.: diameters (§170).
440. *All*: all one might do to think of Heaven.

The sight of God, in fulnesse, can thinke it;
For it is both the object, and the wit.
This is essentiall joy, where neither hee
Can suffer Diminution, nor wee;
Tis such a full, and such a filling good;   445
Had th'Angels once look'd on him, they had stood.
To fill the place of one of them, or more,
Shee whom we celebrate, is gone before.
Shee, who had Here so much essentiall joye,
As no chance could distract, much lesse destroy;   450
Who with Gods presence was acquainted so,
(Hearing, and speaking to him) as to know
His face, in any naturall Stone, or Tree,
Better then when in Images they bee:
Who kept, by diligent devotion,   455
Gods Image, in such reparation,
Within her heart, that what decay was growen,
Was her first Parents fault, and not her own:
Who being solicited to any Act,
Still heard God pleading his safe precontract;   460
Who by a faithfull confidence, was here
Betrothed to God, and now is married there,
Whose twilights were more cleare, then our mid day,
Who dreamt devoutlier, then most use to pray;
Who being heare fild with grace, yet strove to bee,   465
Both where more grace, and more capacitee

441.   *it*: the sight of God.
442.   God is both the *object* of knowledge and the source of the knowledge by
       which himself is known (§158).
443.   *essentiall joy*: see above, note on 382.
446.   *stood*: remained loyal.
450.   *distract*: undo.
454.   *then*: than.
456.   *reparation*: good repair.
458.   *her first Parents*: Adam and Eve's.
460.   *Still*: always.
       precontract: prior betrothal.
463 (also 464). *then*: than.
464.   *use*: are wont.

At once is given: shee to Heaven is gone,
Who made this world in some proportion
A heaven, and here, became unto us all,
Joye, (as our joyes admit) essentiall.   470
But could this low world joyes essentiall touch,   *Of accidentall*
Heavens accidentall joyes would passe them much.   *joyes in both*
How poore and lame, must then our casuall bee?   *places.*
If thy Prince will his subjects to call thee
My Lord, and this doe swell thee, thou art than,   475
By being a greater, growen to be lesse Man.
When no Physician of Redresse can speake,
A joyfull casuall violence may breake
A dangerous Apostem in thy brest;
And whilst thou joyest in this, the dangerous rest,   480
The bag may rise up, and so strangle thee.
What eie was casuall, may ever bee.
What should the Nature change? Or make the same
Certaine, which was but casuall, when it came?
All casuall joye doth loud and plainly say,   485
Onely by comming, that it can away.
Onely in Heaven joies strength is never spent;
And accidentall things are permanent.
Joy of a soules arrivall neere decaies;
For that soule ever joyes, and ever staies.   490
Joy that their last great Consummation
Approches in the resurrection;
When earthly bodies more celestiall
Shalbe, then Angels were, for they could fall;

470.   *as our joyes*: as far as our earthly joys.
472.   *accidentall joyes*: see above, note on 382.
473.   *casuall*: see above, note on 412.
475.   *swell thee*: i.e. with pride.
       than: then.
477.   *Redresse*: remedy.
479.   *Apostem*: abscess.
480.   *rest*: residue.
481.   *bag*: the sac containing the fluid (§170).
482.   *eie*: as above, note on 308.
494.   *then*: than.

This kind of joy doth every day admit   495
Degrees of grouth, but none of loosing it.
In this fresh joy, tis no small part, that shee,
Shee, in whose goodnesse, he that names degree,
Doth injure her; (Tis losse to be cald best,
There where the stuffe is not such as the rest)   500
Shee, who left such a body, as even shee
Onely in Heaven could learne, how it can bee
Made better; for shee rather was two soules,
Or like to full, on both sides written Rols,
Where eies might read upon the outward skin,   505
As strong Records for God, as mindes within.
Shee, who by making full perfection grow,
Peeces a Circle, and still keepes it so,
Long'd for, and longing for'it, to heaven is gone,
Where shee receives, and gives addition.   510
Here in a place, where mis–devotion frames   *Conclusion.*
A thousand praiers to saints, whose very names
The ancient Church knew not, Heaven knowes not yet,
And where, what lawes of poetry admit,
Lawes of religion, have at least the same,   515
Immortall Maid, I might invoque thy name.
Could any Saint provoke that appetite,
Thou here shouldst make mee a french convertite.
But thou wouldst not; nor wouldst thou be content,
To take this, for my second yeeres true Rent,   520
Did this Coine beare any other stampe, then his,
That gave thee power to doe, me, to say this.

498.   *degree*: rank in the angelic hierarchy (see above, p. 347, note on 50).
504.   *Rols*: rolls of parchment written *on both sides*.
508.   *Circle*: symbolic of perfection.
511.   *Here*: i.e. in Roman Catholic France, where Donne was with Elizabeth
       Drury's parents.
514.   *what lawes of poetry admit*: e.g. invocations of the Muses and of pagan
       deities.
518.   *convertite*: convert to Roman Catholicism.
520.   *Rent*: see above, p. 344, note on 447.
521.   *stampe*: see above, note on 369.
       then: than.

Since his will is, that to posteritee,
Thou shouldest for life, and death a patterne bee,
And that the world should notice have of this,   525
The purpose, and th'Autority is his;
Thou art the Proclamation; and I ame
The Trumpet, at whose voice the people came.

528. *Trumpet*: as prophets were considered to be trumpets of the Lord
(Judges 6.34, Ezekiel 33.3, etc.; §573).

Epicedes and Obsequies
Upon
The deaths of sundry Personages.

The poems in this section may be called 'elegies' not without some hesitation since by Donne's time the term had also assumed a rather particular meaning (see above p. 134). Their best designation is non-pastoral funeral elegies (§593), which is broad enough to encompass the tributes to Elizabeth Drury (above, pp. 324 ff.).

The commemorative poem on Prince Henry appears here first because, like the *Anniversaries*, it was first published quite far in advance of the *Poems* of 1633, in the memorial volume *Lachrymae Lachrymarum* edited by Joshua Sylvester in 1613. The remaining poems are reprinted from the 1633 edition, save that the last one – 'On Himselfe' – derives from the 1635 edition and is appended to this section in accordance with the practice of several modern editors (§§158, 159, 163, 164).

Elegie
On the untimely Death
of the incomparable Prince, Henry.

Look to me, *Faith;* and look to my *Faith,* GOD:
For, both my *Centres* feel This *Period*.
Of *Waight*, one *Centre;* one of *Greatness* is:

Elegie on . . . Henry – i.e. Prince Henry Frederick Stuart, James I's eldest son and heir apparent, who died of typhoid fever on 6 November 1612, aged eighteen. The outpouring of grief exceeded even that which followed the death of Elizabeth I less than a decade earlier. One of the most elaborate of the many poetic tributes then composed was by Sir Edward Herbert, whereupon Donne – so Jonson claimed to have been told – wrote this poem in order 'to match Sir Ed: Herbert in obscurenesse'. But whether the poem is devoid of feeling, 'the product of mere intellectual ingenuity' (§196), or 'one of the great funeral poems of the seventeenth century' (§595), must be left to the judgement of the individual reader.

And REASON is That *Centre;* FAITH is This.
For into our *Reason* flowe, and there doe end,   5
All that this naturall World doth comprehend;
Quotidian things, and Equi-distant hence,
Shut-in for Men in one *Circumference:*
But, for th'enormous *Greatnesses*, which are
So disproportion'd and so angulare,   10
As is GOD's *Essence, Place*, and *Providence*,
Where, How, When, What, Soules do, departed hence:
These *Things* (*Eccentrique* else) on Faith do strike;
Yet neither All, nor upon all alike:
For, *Reason,* put t'her best *Extension*,   15
Almost meetes *Faith*, and makes both *Centres* one:
And nothing ever came so neer to This,
As *Contemplation* of the PRINCE wee misse.
For, All that *Faith* could credit Mankinde *could*,
Reason still seconded that This PRINCE *would*.   20
If then, least Movings of the *Centre* make
(More then if whole Hell belcht) the World to shake,
What must This doo, *Centres* distracted so,
That Wee see not what to beleeve or knowe?
Was it not well believ'd, till now, that *Hee*,   25
Whose *Reputation* was an *Extasie*
On neighbour States; which knew not Why to wake
Till *Hee* discoverd what wayes *Hee* would take:
For *Whom* what *Princes* angled (when they tryed)
Mett a *Torpedo*, and were stupefied: 30

7.   *Quotidian things*: things that surround us in everyday experience (§170).
13. *Eccentrique*: not moving in a perfect circle.
21. *Movings of the Centre*: earthquakes.
22. *then*: than.
     World to shake: 'earth to quake' (acc. to a MS: §163).
26. *Extasie*: trance, apocalyptic of new dimensions.
28. *discoverd*: disclosed.
30. *Torpedo*: see above, p. 257, note on 18.

And Others studies, how *Hee* would be bent;
Was His great *Father's* greatest Instrument,
And activ'st spirit to convey and tye
This soule of *Peace* through CHRISTIANITIE?
Was it not well believ'd, that *Hee* would make   35
This *general Peace* th'eternall overtake?
And that *His* Times might have stretcht out so far
As to touch Those of which they *Emblems* are?
For, to confirm this just Belief, that Now
The *last Dayes* came, wee saw Heaven did allow   40
That but from *His* aspect and Exercise,
In *Peace*-full times, Rumors of *Warrs* should rise.
But *now* This *Faith* is *Heresie:* wee must
Still stay, and vexe our *Great-Grand-Mother*, DUST
Oh! Is GOD prodigall? Hath he spent his store   45
Of Plagues on us? and only now, when more
Would ease us much, doth he grudge Miserie,
And will not lett's enjoy our *Curse*, to *Dye?*
As, for the Earth throw'n lowest downe of all,
'Twere an *Ambition* to desire to fall: 50
So God, in our *desire* to *dye*, dooth know
Our Plot for *Ease*, in beeing *Wretched* so.
Therefore *Wee live:* though such a Life we have
As but so manie *Mandrakes* on his Grave.
      What had *His growth* and *generation* donne?   55
When what wee are, his *putrefaction*

---

31. *Others studies*: he was studied by others.
32. *Father*: James I, who aspired strenuously to be a peacemaker.
38. *Emblems*: i.e. of the eternal peace in Heaven.
40. *last Dayes*: the end of history, widely believed to be imminent; in conse-
      quence, the poem bristles with apocalyptic references.
42. *should*: 'did' (acc. to 1633 and many MSS).
44. *Dust*: cf. 'God formed man of the dust of the ground' (Genesis 2.7).
46. *Plagues*: like those inflicted on the Egyptians (Exodus 7 ff.).
54. *Mandrakes*: on their lore, see above, p. 50, note on 2.

Sustains in us, Earth, which *Griefs* animate?
Nor hath our World now other *soule* then That.
And could *Grief* gett so high as Heav'n, that *Quire*
Forgetting This, their new Joy, would desire   60
(With grief to see him) *Hee* had staid belowe,
To rectifie Our *Errors* They foreknowe.
   Is th'other *Centre*, REASON, faster, then?
Where should wee look for That, now w'are not Men?
For, if our *Reason* be our *Connexion*   65
With *Causes*, now to us there can be none.
For, as, if all the *Substances* were spent,
'Twere madnes to enquire of *Accident:*
So is't to looke for *Reason*, HEE being gone,
The only *subject* REASON wrought upon.   70
   If *Faith* have such a *chaine*, whose divers Links
Industrious Man discerneth, as he thinks,
When Miracle dooth joine, and to steal-in
A new link Man knowes not where to begin:
At a much deader Fault must *Reason* bee,   75
Death having broke-off such a Link as *Hee*.
But, now, for us with busie *Proofs* to come
That w'have no *Reason*, would prove we had some:
So would just *Lamentations*. Therefore Wee
May safelier say, that Wee are dead, then *Hee*.   80
So, if our *Griefs* wee doo not well declare,

---

58.   *then:* than.
62.   *foreknow:* i.e. the errors which they foreknow we will commit (§166).
63.   *faster:* more secure.
64.   *w'are not Men:* i.e. deprived of reason because of our grief.
65–66. *Connexion / With Causes:* link with the notion of causation (§170).
68–69. *Substances:* the basic natures of material things; *Accident:* their variable
          properties (§166).
71.   *Faith:* 'Fate' (acc. to 1633–69).
          chaine: an allusion to the golden chain of Homer (*Iliad*, VIII, 19–27),
          which by Donne's time was regarded as symbolic of Providence (§108).
73.   *joine:* 'come' (acc. to 1633–69).
          steal in: insert stealthily.
80.   *then:* than.

W'have double Excuse; *Hee* is not *dead*, We are.
Yet would not I dye yet; for though I bee
Too narrow, to think HIM, as *Hee* is HEE
(Our *Soule's* best Bayting and Mid-*period*   85
In her long *journey* of *Considering* GOD)
Yet (no Dishonor) I can reach Him *thus;*
As *Hee* embrac't the *Fires* of *Love* with us.
Oh! May I (*since* I live) but see or hear
That *Shee-Intelligence* which mov'd This *Sphear*,   90
I pardon Fate my Life. Who-e'r thou bee
Which hast the noble *Conscience*, Thou art *Shee.*
I conjure Thee by all the *Charmes Hee* spoke,
By th'*Oathes* which only you *Two* never broke,
By all the *Soules* you sigh'd; that if you see   95
These Lines, you wish I knew *Your Historie:*
So, much as *You Two mutual Heavens* were *here*,
I were an *Angel singing* what *You* were.

Elegie on the L.C.

Sorrow, who to this house scarce knew the way:
Is, Oh, heire of it, our All is his prey.
This strange chance claimes strange wonder, and to us
Nothing can be so strange, as to weepe thus.
'Tis well his lifes loud speaking workes deserve,   5
And give praise too, our cold tongues could not serve:

Elegie on . . . Henry.
84.   *as Hee is Hee*: as he really is in himself.
85.   *Bayting*: pause for refreshment.
88.   *the Fires of Love*: the lady in question has not been identified.
90.   *Intelligence, Sphear*: see above, p. 101, note on 52.
94.   *you Two*: the two lovers.

Elegie on the L.C. Untitled in the 1633 edition, where it was placed among the
    Elegies (VI); thus entitled from 1635. The poem may be an address to
    Lionel Cranfield, later Earl of Middlesex, on the death of his father in
    1595; in all likelihood, however, it is a tribute to the Lord Chamberlain,
    Henry Carey 1st Baron Hunsdon, who died in 1596.
6.   *serve*: 'sterve' (acc. to a MS).

'Tis well, hee kept teares from our eyes before,
That to fit this deepe ill, we might have store.
Oh, if a sweet briar, climbe up by'a tree,
If to a paradise that transplantcd bee,   10
Or fell'd, and burnt for holy sacrifice,
Yet, that must wither, which by it did rise,
As wee for him dead: though no familie
Ere rigg'd a soule for heavens discoverie
With whom more Venturers more boldly dare   15
Venture their states, with him in joy to share.
Wee lose what all friends lov'd, him; he gaines now
But life by death, which worst foes would allow,
If hee could have foes, in whose practise grew
All vertues, whose names subtile Schoolmen knew.   20
What ease, can hope that wee shall see'him, beget,
When wee must die first, and cannot dye yet?
His children are his pictures, Oh they bee
Pictures of him dead, senselesse, cold as he.
Here needs no marble Tombe, since hee is gone,   25
He, and about him, his, are turn'd to stone.

8.   *store*: plenty.
 9 (also 21). On the symbol ', see above, p. 5.
10.   *that*: that tree.
15.   *Venturers*: merchant venturers.
17.   *friends*: 'things' (acc. to some MSS).
16 (also 24). The full stop at line's end is an emendation.
20.   *Schoolmen*: medieval theologians.
22.   *die first*: i.e. in order to *see him* (21).
25.   *Tombe*: 'ston' (acc. to a MS).

Elegie on the Lady *Marckham*.

Man is the World, and death th'Ocean,
　To which God gives the lower parts of man.
This Sea invirons all, and though as yet
　God hath set markes, and bounds, twixt us and it,
Yet doth it rore, and gnaw, and still pretend,　　　　　5
　And breaks our bankes, when ere it takes a friend.
Then our land waters (teares of passion) vent;
　Our waters, then, above our firmament,
(Teares which our Soule doth for her sins let fall)
　Take all a brackish tast, and Funerall,　　　　　10
And even these teares, which should wash sin, are sin.
　We, after Gods *Noe*, drowne the world againe.
Nothing but man of all invenom'd things
　Doth worke upon itselfe, with inborne stings.
Teares are false Spectacles, we cannot see　　　　　15
　Through passions mist, what wee are, or what shee.
In her this sea of death hath made no breach,
　But as the tide doth wash the slimie beach,
And leaves embroder'd workes upon the sand,
　So is her flesh refin'd by deaths cold hand.　　　　　20

Elegie on the Lady Marckham – i.e. the widow of Sir Anthony Markham and first
　　cousin to Lucy, Countess of Bedford, in whose home at Twickenham
　　Park she died on 4 May 1609.
　5.　*pretend*: stretch forward, threaten (§170).
　7.　*vent*: flow out.
　8.　Ancient astronomers often supposed that there are *waters* beyond the
　　firmament, i.e. the sphere of the fixed stars (cf. above, p. 65, note on 24).
　10.　*brackish*: salty.
　12.　*Gods Noe*: God's promise to Noah never again to flood the earth (Genesis
　　9.11); cf. 'Wee after Gods mercy drowne our Soules againe' (acc. to a MS:
　　§158).
　　the: 'our' (acc. to most MSS).
　13–14.　'Man', said Donne in a sermon, 'hath a dram of poyson, originall-Sin,
　　. . . and he cannot choose but poyson himselfe' (§170).

As men of China,'after an ages stay,
  Do take up Porcelane, where they buried Clay;
So at this grave, her limbecke, which refines
  The Diamonds, Rubies, Saphires, Pearles, and Mincs,
Of which this flesh was, her soule shall inspire   25
  Flesh of such stuffe, as God, when his last fire
Annuls this world, to recompence it, shall,
  Make and name then, th'Elixar of this All.
They say, the sea, when it gaines, loseth too;
  If carnall Death (the yonger brother) doe   30
Usurpe the body,'our soule, which subject is
  To th'elder death, by sinne, is freed by this;
They perish both, when they attempt the just;
  For, graves our trophies are, and both deaths dust.
So, unobnoxious now, she'hath buried both;   35
  For, none to death sinnes, that to sinne is loth,
Nor doe they die, which are not loth to die;
  So hath she this, and that virginity.
Grace was in her extremely diligent,
  That kept her from sinne, yet made her repent.   40

21 (also 31, 35, 51). On the symbol ', see above, p. 5.
21–22. Cf. Sir Thomas Browne's report that, 'according to common belief',
    porcelain was 'made of Earth, which lieth in preparation about an
    hundred years under ground' (§158).
23.   *limbecke*: see above, p. 91, note on 21.
24.   *Mines*: precious metals (§170).
25.   *inspire*: infuse and animate (§166).
26.   *last fire*: see above, p. 347, note on 56.
28.   *then*: 'them' (acc. to 1649–69).
      Elixar: see above, p. 86, note on 7.
29.   A commonplace notion; cf. Spenser: 'whatsoever from one place doth
      fall, / Is with the tide unto an other brought' (*The Faerie Queene*, V, ii, 39;
      §593).
33.   *when they*: 'who' (acc. to a MS).
      attempt: try to subdue (§170).
34.   *both deaths dust*: also punctuated 'both, deaths dust' (acc. to 1633), 'both
      death's dust' (acc. to 1635–69), or 'both dead dust' (acc. to several MSS).
35.   *unobnoxious*: not exposed to harm.
36.   *to death*: i.e. mortally.
      to sinne: 'to death' (acc. to a MS).
38.   *this*: i.e. *not loth to die* (37) because assured of eternal life; *that*: i.e. *loth to*
      sinne (36). *virginity*: spiritual innocence.

Of what small spots pure white complaines! Alas,
  How little poyson cracks a christall glasse!
She sinn'd, but just enough to let us see
  That God's word must be true, All, sinners be.
Soe much did zeale her conscience rarefie,   45
  That, extreme truth lack'd little of a lye,
Making omissions, acts; laying the touch
  Of sinne, on things that sometimes may be such.
As *Moses* Cherubines, whose natures doe
  Surpasse all speed, by him are winged too: 50
So would her soule, already'in heaven, seeme then,
  To clyme by teares, the common staires of men.
How fit she was for God, I am content
  To speake, that Death his vaine haste may repent
How fit for us, how even and how sweet,   55
  How good in all her titles, and how meet,
To have reform'd this forward heresie,
  That women can no parts of friendship bee;
How Morall, how Divine shall not be told,
  Lest they that heare her vertues, thinke her old: 60
And lest we take Deaths part, and make him glad
  Of such a prey, and to his tryumph adde.

---

41. Cf. the proverbial 'A spot is most seen upon the finest cloth' (§170).
42. The fine crystal glass made in Venice was said to crack by 'the venome of some Spiders' (§170). *cracks*: 'breakes' (acc. to most MSS).
44. *All, sinners be*: see above, note on 13–14.
45. *rarefie*: 'rectifye' (acc. to some MSS) or 'ratifie' (acc. to one MS).
47. *acts*: 'artes' (acc. to a MS).
49. *Cherubines*: the winged cherubim on the Ark of the Covenant (Exodus 25.18–21); cf, above, p. 243, note on 60–61.
52. *teares*: penitential tears.
57. *forward*: presumptuous.
58. A commonplace thought in Renaissance writing (§164).

Elegie on M^ris *Boulstred*.

Death I recant, and say, unsaid by mee
  What ere hath slip'd, that might diminish thee.
Spirituall treason, atheisme 'tis, to say,
  That any can thy Summons disobey.
Th'earths face is but thy Table; there are set   5
  Plants, cattell, men, dishes for Death to eate.
In a rude hunger now hee millions drawes
  Into his bloody, or plaguy, or sterv'd jawes.
Now hee will seeme to spare, and doth more wast,
  Eating the best first, well preserv'd to last.   10
Now wantonly he spoiles, and eates us not,
  But breakes off friends, and lets us peecemeale rot.
Nor will this earth serve him; he sinkes the deepe
  Where harmlesse fish monastique silence keepe,
Who (were Death dead) by Roes of living sand,   15
  Might spunge that element, and make it land.
He rounds the aire, and breakes the hymnique notes
  In birds, Heavens choristers, organique throats,

Elegie on M^ris (Mistress, a title of courtesy even for unmarried women)
  Boulstred – i.e. Cecilia Bulstrode, who like Lady Markham (see previous
  poem) was related to Lucy, Countess of Bedford, and died at
  Twickenham Park in the same year, on 4 August 1609, aged twenty-five.
  Ben Jonson managed to write two very different poems about her, first
  the nasty *Epigram on the Court Pucell* (*Under-wood*, No. 51) and later an
  encomiastic elegy (§158).
1 ff. On Donne's attitude to death here – so different from that in Holy
  Sonnet X (below, p. 440) – see the Introduction, above, pp. 31 ff.
5. *there are set*: 'and the meate' (acc. to some MSS).
6. *dishes*: 'dished' (acc. to 1635–39 and several MSS).
8. *bloody*, *plaguy*, *sterv'd*: i.e. war, plague, famine – causes of death accord-
  ing to Revelation 6.8 (§170).
10. *first*: 'fruite' or 'fruites' (acc. to several MSS).
13. *sinkes*: sinks into.
15. *Roes*: cf. 'A female fishes sandie Roe' (below, p. 414, l. 223; §170); but
  'Rows' (acc. to 1669 and several MSS).
16. *spunge that element*: dry up that water.
17. *rounds*: encompasses.
18. *organique*: sounding like Church organs.

Which (if they did not dye) might seeme to bee
    A tenth ranke in the heavenly hierarchie.   20
O strong and long-liv'd death, how cam'st thou in?
    And how without Creation didst begin?
Thou hast, and shalt see dead, before thou dyest,
    All the foure Monarchies, and Antichrist.
How could I thinke thee nothing, that see now   25
    In all this All, nothing else is, but thou.
Our births and lives, vices, and vertues, bee
    Wastfull consumptions, and degrees of thee.
For, wee to live, our bellowes weare, and breath,
    Nor are wee mortall, dying, dead, but death.   30
And though thou beest, O mighty bird of prey,
    So much reclaim'd by God, that thou must lay
All that thou kill'st at his feet, yet doth hee
    Reserve but few, and leaves the most to thee.
And of those few, now thou hast overthrowne   35
    One whom thy blow, makes, not ours, nor thine own.
She was more stories high: hopelesse to come
    To her Soule, thou'hast offer'd at her lower roome.
Her Soule and body was a King and Court:
    But thou hast both of Captaine mist and fort.   40
As houses fall not, though the King remove,
    Bodies of Saints rest for their soules above.

---

20.   *the heavenly hierarchie*: Donne appears to accept the traditional nine orders
     of angels, much disputed in his time (§108); see also p. 347, note on 50.
24.   *foure Monarchies*: Babylon, Persia, Greece, and Rome (see §106).
     Antichrist: Christ's great opponent (Revelation 13.11 ff.).
27.   *lives* (acc. to 1635–60 and many MSS): 'life' (acc. to 1633 and many MSS).
29.   *bellowes*: lungs.
34.   *few*: the redeemed ones.
36.   *not ours, nor thine own*: i.e. but now God's.
37.   *more stories high*: i.e. beyond death's reach by reason of her virtue.
38 (also 47, 52, 60). On the symbol ', see above, p. 5.
38.   *offer'd at her lower roome*: made an attempt upon her *body* (39).
40.   *mist*: missed, failed to secure.
     Captaine . . . and fort: the commander (*King* or *Soule*) and his stronghold
     (*Court* or *body*).
41.   *As*: 'All' (acc. to a MS).
     King: 'Kings' (acc. to 1635–69).
     remove: depart.

Death gets 'twixt soules and bodies such a place
 As sinne insinuates 'twixt just men and grace,
Both worke a separation, no divorce.   45
 Her Soule is gone to usher up her corse,
Which shall be'almost another soule, for there
 Bodies are purer, then best Soules are here.
Because in her, her virtues did outgoe
 Her yeares, would'st thou, O emulous death, do so? 50
And kill her young to thy losse? must the cost
 Of beauty,'and wit, apt to doe harme, be lost?
What though thou found'st her proofe 'gainst sins of
  youth?
 Oh, every age a diverse sinne pursueth.
Thou should'st have stay'd, and taken better hold, 55
 Shortly ambitious; covetous, when old,
She might have prov'd: and such devotion
 Might once have stray'd to superstition.
If all her vertues must have growne, yet might
 Abundant virtue'have bred a proud delight.   60
Had she persever'd just, there would have bin
 Some that would sinne, mis-thinking she did sinne.
Such as would call her friendship, love, and faine
 To sociablenesse, a name profane,
Or sinne, by tempting, or, not daring that,   65
 By wishing, though they never told her what.
Thus might'st thou'have slain more soules, had'st thou
  not crost
 Thy selfe, and to triumph, thine army lost.
Yet though these wayes be lost, thou hast left one,

46. *corse*: corpse.
48. *then*: than.
50. *do so*: i.e. kill her young (51).
56. The semicolon is acc. to 1635–69.
58. *once*: some day.
61. *bin*: 'growne' (acc. to a MS).
62. *mis-thinking*: 'mistaking' (acc. to some MSS).
65. *sinne*: 'some' (acc. to a MS).
67. *crost*: thwarted.
68. *army*: 'Armor' (acc. to a MS).

Which is, immoderate griefe that she is gone.   70
But we may scape that sinne, yet weepe as much,
   Our teares are due, because we are not such.
Some teares, that knot of friends, her death must cost,
   Because the chaine is broke, but no linke lost.

To the Countesse of *Bedford*.

MADAME,

I *have learn'd by those lawes wherein I am a little conversant,
that hee which bestowes any cost upon the dead, obliges him
which is dead, but not the heire; I do not therefore send this
paper to your Ladyship, that you should thanke mee for it, or
thinke that I thanke you in it; your favours and benefits to mee
are so much above my merits, that they are even above my
gratitude, if that were to be judged by words which must
expresse it: But, Madame, since your noble brothers fortune
being yours, the evidences also concerning it are yours, so his
vertue being yours, the evidences concerning it, belong also to
you, of which by your acceptance this may be one peece, in
which quality I humbly present it, and as a testimony how
intirely your familie possesseth*
           Your Ladiships most humble,
            and thankfull servant
                      JOHN DONNE.

Elegie on . . . M^ris Boulstred.
74. *but* (acc. to 1633 and some MSS): 'though' (acc. to 1635–69, most MSS,
    and all modern editors).

Obsequies to the Lord Harrington, brother to the Lady Lucy, Countesse of Bedford.

Faire soule, which wast, not onely, as all soules bee,
Then when thou wast infused, harmony,
But did'st continue so; and now dost beare
A part in Gods great organ, this whole Spheare:
If looking up to God; or downe to us,   5
Thou finde that any way is pervious,
Twixt heav'n and earth, and that mans actions doe
Come to your knowledge, and affections too,
See, and with joy, mee to that good degree
Of goodnesse growne, that I can studie thee,   10
And, by these meditations refin'd,
Can unapparell and enlarge my minde,
And so can make by this soft extasie,
This place a map of heav'n, my selfe of thee.
Thou seest mee here at midnight, now all rest;   15
Times dead-low water; when all mindes devest
To morrows businesse, when the labourers have
Such rest in bed, that their last Church-yard grave,
Subject to change, will scarce be'a type of this,
Now when the clyent, whose last hearing is   20
To morrow, sleeps, when the condemned man,
(Who when hee opes his eyes, must shut them than

Obsequies to the Lord Harrington – i.e. John Harington, 2nd Baron of Exton,
   who died of smallpox on 27 February 1614, aged twenty-two. The
   brother of Lucy, Countess of Bedford, he was said to have been 'the
   most compleat yong gentleman of his age . . . for religion, learning,
   and courteous behaviour' (§170). The poem's title is borrowed from the
   MSS; that of the printed versions is oddly garbled.
   3.   *beare*: sing.
   4.   *Spheare*: the universe.
   6.   *pervious*: affording a passage, passable.
   7.   *mans*: 'mens' (acc. to 1635–69 and most MSS).
   11. *these*: 'those' (acc. to many MSS).
   12. *unapparell*: divest the flesh of clothing, i.e. its limitations.
   19. On the symbol ', here and throughout, see above, p. 5.
   22. *than*: then.

Againe by death,) although sad watch hee keepe,
Doth practice dying by a little sleepe,
Thou at this midnight seest mee, and as soone   25
As that Sunne rises to mee, midnight's noone,
All the world growes transparent, and I see
Through all, both Church and State, in seeing thee;
And I discerne by favour of this light,
My selfe, the hardest object of the sight.   30
God is the glasse; as thou when thou dost see
Him who sees all, seest all concerning thee,
So, yet unglorified, I comprehend
All, in these mirrors of thy wayes, and end;
Though God be our true glasse, through which we see   35
All, since the beeing of all things is hee,
Yet are the trunkes which doe to us derive
Things, in proportion fit by perspective,
Deeds of good men; for by their living here,
Vertues, indeed remote, seeme to be nere;   40
But where can I affirme, or where arrest
My thoughts on his deeds? which shall I call best?
For fluid vertue cannot be look'd on,
Nor can endure a contemplation;
As bodies change, and as I do not weare   45
Those Spirits, humors, blood I did last yeare,
And, as if on a streame I fixe mine eye,
That drop, which I looked on, is presently
Pusht with more waters from my sight, and gone,
So in this sea of vertues, can no one   50
Bee'insisted on; vertues, as rivers, passe,
Yet still remaines that vertuous man there was;

23. *sad*: sober.
31. *glasse*: mirror.
35. *our true*: 'truly our' (acc. to many MSS).
37–38. *trunkes . . . perspective*: telescopes (§170).
39. *living*: 'beeing' (acc. to 1635–69).
40. *nere*: i.e. 'neare' (acc. to 1635–69).
43. *fluid*: flowing through everything.
46. *humors*: as above, p. 336, note on 241.

And as if man feed on mans flesh, and so
Part of his body to another owe,
Yet at the last two perfect bodies rise,   55
Because God knowes where every Atome lyes;
So, if one knowledge were made of all those,
Who knew his minutes well, hee might dispose
His vertues into names, and ranks; but I
Should injure Nature, Vertue, and Destinie,   60
Should I divide and discontinue so,
Vertue, which did in one intirenesse grow.
For as, hee that would say, spirits are fram'd
Of all the purest parts that can be nam'd,
Honours not spirits halfe so much, as hee   65
Which sayes, they have no parts, but simple bee;
So is't of vertue; for a point and one
Are much entirer then a million.
And had Fate meant to have his vertues told,
It would have let him live to have beene old,   70
So then, that vertue in season, and then this,
We might have seene, and said, that now he is
Witty, now wise, now temperate, now just:
In good short lives, vertues are faine to thrust,
And to be sure betimes to get a place,   75
When they would exercise, lacke time, and space.
So was it in this person, forc'd to bee
For lack of time, his owne epitome.
So to exhibit in a few yeares as much,
As all the long breath'd Chronicles can touch;   80

55. *the last*: the Last Judgement, when there is to be a general resurrection of
    the dead.
57. *all those*: Harington's virtues.
61. *discontinue*: separate.
63. *would*: 'should' (acc. to 1635–69).
67. *a point and one*: a single indivisible whole (§166).
68. *entirer*: more complete.
    then: than.
69. *have*: 'have had' (acc. to 1635–69).
    told: enumerated.
74. *thrust*: throng.
76. *exercise*: 'encrease' (acc. to some MSS). *time*: 'room' (ditto).
80. *long breath'd*: long-winded (§170).

As when an Angell down from heav'n doth flye,
Our quick thought cannot keepe him company,
Wee cannot thinke, now hee is at the Sunne,
Now through the Moon, now he through th'aire doth run,
Yet when he's come, we know he did repaire   85
To all twixt Heav'n and Earth, Sunne, Moon, and Aire.
And as this Angell in an instant, knowes,
And yet wee know, this sodaine knowledge growes
By quick amassing severall formes of things,
Which he successively to order brings;   90
When they, whose slow-pac'd lame thoughts cannot goe
So fast as hee, thinke that he doth not so;
Just as a perfect reader doth not dwell,
On every syllable, nor stay to spell,
Yet without doubt, hee doth distinctly see   95
And lay together every A, and B;
So, in short liv'd good men, is'not understood
Each severall vertue, but the compound good.
For, they all vertues paths in that pace tread,
As Angells goe, and know, and as men read.   100
O why should then these men, these lumps of Balme
Sent hither, the worlds tempests to becalme,
Before by deeds they are diffus'd and spread,
And so make us alive, themselves be dead?
O Soule, O circle, why so quickly bee   105
Thy ends, thy birth and death clos'd up in thee?
Since one foot of thy compasse still was plac'd
In heav'n, the other might securely'have pac'd

85. *did repaire*: passed close to.
87–92. Angels apprehend by intuition; men, by discourse (cf. *Paradise Lost*,
       V, 486–90).
89. *formes*: 'shapes' (acc. to a MS).
93. *perfect*: skilled.
99. *pace*: speed.
101. *Balme*: see above, p. 329, note on 57.
102. *the*: 'this' (acc. to most MSS).
105–10. Cf. above, p. 98, ll. 25 ff.
107. *still*: ever.

In the most large extent, through every path,
Which the whole world, or man, the abridgment hath.   110
Thou knowst, that though the tropique circles have
(Yea and those small ones which the Poles engrave,)
All the same roundnesse, evennesse, and all
The endlesnesse of the equinoctiall;
Yet, when we come to measure distances,   115
How here, how there, the Sunne affected is,
When he doth faintly worke, and when prevaile,
Onely great circles, then, can be our scale:
So, though thy circle to thy selfe expresse
All, tending to thy endlesse happinesse,   120
And wee, by our good use of it may trye,
Both how to live well young, and how to die,
Yet, since we must be old, and age endures
His Torrid Zone at Court, and calentures
Of hot ambitions, irrelegions ice,   125
Zeales agues, and hydroptique avarice,
Infirmities which need the scale of truth,
As well as lust and ignorance of youth;
Why did'st thou not for these give medicines too,
And by thy doing tell us what to doe?   130
Though as small pocket-clocks, whose every wheele
Doth each mismotion and distemper feele,

---

110.   Man is the *abridgment* of *the whole world* in line with his usual designation
   as microcosm (cf. below, p. 437, l. 1).
111–12.   The *circles* running parallel to the equator are all equally circular, but
   diminish in size as they approach the *Poles* (§158).
114.   *equinoctiall*: the earth's equator.
117.   *When . . . when*: 'Where . . . where' (acc. to several MSS).
118.   *great circles*: meridians, circles of longitude which run through the poles,
   as distinguished from *the tropique circles* (see note on 111–12).
120.   *thy*: 'their' (acc. to some MSS).
124.   *Torrid Zone*: the equatorial region of intense heat.
   calentures: see above, p. 255, note on 23.
126.   *agues*: malarial fevers.
   hydroptique: see above, p. 90, note on 6.
127.   *scale*: yardstick.
130.   *tell*: 'set' (acc. to 1635–54 and some MSS).

Whose *hand* gets shaking palsies, and whose *string*
(His sinews) slackens, and whose *Soule*, the spring,
Expires, or languishes, whose pulse, the *flye*,   135
Either beates not, or beates unevenly,
Whose voice, the *Bell*, doth rattle, or grow dumbe,
Or idle,'as men, which to their last houres come,
If these clockes be not wound, or be wound still,
Or be not set, or set at every will;   140
So, youth is easiest to destruction,
If then wee follow all, or follow none;
Yet, as in great clocks, which in steeples chime,
Plac'd to informe whole towns, to'imploy their time,
An error doth more harme, being generall,   145
When, small clocks faults, only'on the wearer fall.
So worke the faults of age, on which the eye
Of children, servants, or the State relie.
Why wouldst not thou then, which hadst such a soule
A clock so true, as might the Sunne controule,   150
And daily hadst from him, who gave it thee,
Instructions, such as it could never be
Disordered, stay here, as a generall
And great Sun-dyall, to have set us All?
O why wouldst thou be any instrument   155
To this unnaturall course, or why consent
To this, not miracle, but Prodigie,
That when the ebbs, longer then flowings be,

---

133. *hand gets* (acc. to most MSS): 'hands get' (acc. to 1633–54).
135. *flye*: the winged portion of a clock's striking apparatus which regulates
      the speed of the stroke (§170); amended to 'flee' (acc. to 1635–69).
137. *rattle*: prattle.
138. *idle*: foolish.
139. *still*: continually.
150. *controule*: regulate.
155. *any*: 'an' (acc. to 1639–69).
157. *Prodigie*: an unnatural event, not divinely inspired (*miracle*).
158. *when*: 'where' (acc. to many MSS).
      the ebbs, longer then (i.e. than) *flowings be*: the tide takes longer to ebb than
      to reach the point of high water (§166).

Vertue, whose flood did with thy youth begin,
Should so much faster ebb out, then flow in? 160
Though her flood was blowne in, by thy first breath,
All is at once sunke in the whirlc-poole death.
Which word I would not name, but that I see
Death, else a desert, growne a Court by thee.
Now I grow sure, that if a man would have 165
Good companie, his entry is a grave.
Mee thinkes all Cities now, but Anthills bee,
Where, when the severall labourers I see,
For children, house, Provision, taking paine,
They'are all but Ants, carrying eggs, straw, and grain 170
And Church-yards are our cities, unto which
The most repaire, that are in goodnesse rich.
There is the best concourse, and confluence,
There are the holy suburbs, and from thence
Begins Gods City, New Jerusalem, 175
Which doth extend her utmost gates to them;
At that gate then Triumphant soule, dost thou
Begin thy Triumph; But since lawes allow
That at the Triumph day, the people may,
All that they will, 'gainst the Triumpher say, 180
Let me here use that freedome, and expresse
My griefe, though not to make thy Triumph lesse.
By law, to Triumphs none admitted bee,
Till they as Magistrates get victorie,
Though then to thy force, all youthes foes did yield, 185
Yet till fit time had brought thee to that field,
To which thy ranke in this state destin'd thee,
That there thy counsailes might get victorie,

159. *flood*: incoming tide.
160. *then*: than.
164. *growne*: 'is' (acc. to some MSS).
    Court: administrator of justice (§163).
165. *grow*: 'am' (acc. to some MSS).
170. *and*: 'or' (acc. to several MSS).
176. *utmost*: outermost.
178 ff. *Triumph*: the greatest honour bestowed in ancient Rome upon a
    victorious general (§170).
187. *destin'd*: 'defend' (acc. to a MS).

And so in that capacitie remove
All jealousies 'twixt Prince and subjects love,   190
Thou could'st no title, to this triumph have,
Thou didst intrude on death, usurp'dst a grave.
Then (though victoriously) thou hadst fought as yet
But with thine owne affections, with the heate
Of youths desires, and colds of ignorance,   195
But till thou should'st successefully advance
Thine armes 'gainst forraine enemies, which are
Both Envy, and acclamations popular,
(For, both these engines equally defeate,
Though by a divers Mine, those which are great,)   200
Till then thy War was but a civill War,
For which to Triumph, none admitted are;
No more are they, who though with good successe,
In a defensive war, their power expresse.
Before men triumph, the dominion   205
Must be *enlarg'd* and not *preserv'd* alone;
Why should'st thou then, whose battailes were to win
Thy selfe, from those straits nature put thee in,
And to deliver up to God that state,
Of which he gave thee the vicariate,   210
(Which is thy soule and body) as intire
As he, who takes endeavours, doth require,
But didst not stay, t'enlarge his kingdome too,
By making others, what thou didst, to doe;
Why shouldst thou Triumph now, when Heav'n no more
Hath got, by getting thee, then't had before?
For, Heav'n and thou, even when thou livedst here,
Of one another in possession were;

191. *could'st*: 'shouldst' (acc. to a MS).
193. *Then* (acc. to 1635–69): 'That' (acc. to 1633).
196. *successefully*: 'successively' (acc. to some MSS).
198. *acclamations* (plural acc. to most MSS, singular acc. to 1633–54).
199. *engines*: destructive weapons.
200. *a divers Mine*: different ways of undermining.
208. *straits*: the consequences of the Fall.
210. *vicariate*: responsibility as a deputy of God on earth (§170).
216. *then*: than.

But this from Triumph most disables thee,
That, that place which is conquered, must bee   220
Left safe from present warre, and likely doubt
Of imminent commotions to breake out.
And hath he left us so? or can it bee
His territory was no more then Hee?
No, we were all his charge, the Diocis   225
Of ev'ry exemplar man, the whole world is,
And he was joyned in commission
With Tutelar Angels, sent to every one.
But though this freedome to upbraid, and chide
Him who Triumph'd, were lawfull, it was ty'd   230
With this, that it might never reference have
Unto the Senate, who this triumph gave;
Men might at Pompey jeast, but they might not
At that authoritie, by which he got
Leave to Triumph, before, by age, he might;   235
So, though, triumphant soule, I dare to write,
Mov'd with a reverentiall anger, thus,
That thou so earely wouldst abandon us;
Yet I am farre from daring to dispute
With that great soveraigntie, whose absolute   240
Prerogative hath thus dispens'd with thee,
'Gainst natures lawes, which just impugners bee
Of early triumphs; And I (though with paine)
Lessen our losse, to magnifie thy gaine
Of triumph, when I say, It was more fit,   245
That all men should lacke thee, then thou lack it
Though then in our time, be not suffered
That testimonie of love, unto the dead,

---

224.   *then*: than; 'but' (acc. to several MSS).
228.   *Tutelar*: guardian (cf. above, p. 360, ll. 236–39).
231.   *reference*: 'reverence' (acc. to 1650–54).
233.   *Pompey*: because of his victories in Sicily and Africa, Pompey the Great
       was granted a 'triumph' (see note on 178) though aged only twenty-
       four.
241.   *with*: 'for' (acc. to several MSS).
243.   *early*: 'earthly' (ditto).
246.   *then*: than.

To die with them, and in their graves be hid,
As Saxon wives, and French soldurii did;   250
And though in no degree I can expresse
Griefe in great Alexanders great excesse,
Who at his friends death, made whole townes devest
Their walls and bullwarks which became them best:
Doe not, faire soule, this sacrifice refuse,   255
That in thy grave I doe interre my Muse,
Who, by my griefe, great as thy worth, being cast
Behind hand, yet hath spoke, and spoke her last.

250.   *soldurii*: soldiers who had vowed to share the fortunes of a chosen friend,
      including his death.
252–54. As reported in Plutarch's *Life of Alexander*.
256 ff. Donne's promise was not in fact kept.
257–58. *cast / Behind hand*: i.e. delayed.

An hymne to the Saints,
and to Marquesse Hamylton.
To Sir Robert Carr.

Sir,

I presume you rather try what you can doe in me, then what I
can doe in verse; you know my uttermost when it was best, and
even then I did best when I had least truth for my subjects. In
this present case there is so much truth as it defeats all Poetry.
Call therefore this paper by what name you will, and, if it bee
not worthy of him, nor of you, nor of mee, smother it, and bee
that the sacrifice. If you had commanded mee to have waited on
his body to Scotland and preached there, I would have embraced
the obligation with more alacrity; But, I thanke you that you
would command me that which I was loath to doe, for, even that
hath given a tincture of merit to the obedience of

Your poore friend and servant in Christ Jesus

J.D.

Whether that soule which now comes up to you
Fill any former ranke or make a new,
Whether it take a name nam'd there before,
Or be a name it selfe, and *order* more
Then was in heaven till now; (for may not hee   5
Bee so, if every severall Angell bee

An hymne to the Saints. Possibly the last poem Donne ever wrote, it was
    occasioned by the death of the Scottish peer James 2nd Marques Hamil-
    ton on 22 March 1625. Widely liked, the Marques was said to have been
    'the gallantest gentleman' in either Scotland or England; but Donne
    appears not to have known him personally.
        The prefatory letter to Carr was in 1633 placed after the poem, without
    the heading; it was shifted to its present position, naming Carr for the
    first time, from 1635. Sir Robert Ker or Carr, later Earl of Ancrum,
    requested the poem from Donne who responded willingly for the sake of
    his friend and patron but unwillingly because he was then in Orders.
1 (also 3). *Whether* (acc. to 1635): 'Whither' (acc. to 1633).
    you: the saints particularly, the angels generally.
2. *ranke* (also *order*, ll. 4 ff.): appertaining to the angelic hierarchy (see
    above, p. 382, note on 20).
5. *Then*: than.

A *kind* alone?) What ever order grow
Greater by him in heaven, wee doe not so;
One of your orders growes by his accesse;
But, by his losse grow all our *orders* lesse;   10
The name of *Father*, *Master*, *Friend*, the name
Of *Subject* and of *Prince*, in one are lame;
Faire mirth is dampt, and conversation black,
The *household* widdow'd, and the *garter* slack;
The *Chappell* wants an eare, *Councell* a tongue;   15
Story, a theame; and *Musicke* lacks a song;
Blest *order* that hath him! the losse of him
Gangred all *Orders* here; all lost a limbe.
Never made body such haste to confesse
What a soule was; All former comelinesse   20
Fled, in a minute, when the soule was gone,
And, having lost that beauty, would have none;
So fell our *Monasteries*, in one instant growne
Not to lesse houses, but, to heapes of stone;
So sent this body that faire forme it wore,   25
Unto the spheare of formes, and doth (before
His soule shall fill up his sepulchrall stone,)
Anticipate a Resurrection;
For, as in his fame, now, his soule is here,
So, in the forme thereof his bodie's there;   30
And if, faire soule, not with first *Innocents*
Thy station be, but with the *Pænitents*,

9. *accesse*: arrival in Heaven.
10. *all our orders*: all earthly dignities and ranks.
12. *are*: 'is' (acc. to 1635–69).
14. *garter*: Hamilton was made a Knight of the Garter in 1623.
18. *Gangred*: 'Gangreend' (acc. to 1635).
20–21. *All former comelinesse / Fled, in a minute*: it is reported that when Hamilton died his body 'swelled unmeasurablie' due to a tumour (§421).
23. *fell*: dissolved, by Henry VIII.
    one: 'an' (acc. to 1635–69).
25. *this*: 'his' (acc. to 1635–69).
26. *the spheare of formes*: a celestial region where the ideal forms of earthly bodies await the resurrection of the material bodies (§166).
27. *soule shall*: 'body' (acc. to a MS).
31. *Innocents*: those who died before maturing into wilful sin.

(And, who shall dare to aske then when I am
Dy'd scarlet in the blood of that pure Lambe,
Whether that colour, which is scarlet then,   35
Were black or white before in eyes of men?)
When thou rememb'rest what sins thou didst finde
Amongst those many friends now left behinde,
And seest such sinners as they are, with thee
Got thither by repentance, Let it bee   40
Thy wish to wish all there, to wish them cleane;
Wish *him* a *David, her* a *Magdalen*.

Elegie.

Language thou art too narrow, and too weake
    To ease us now; great sorrow cannot speake;
If we could sigh out accents, and weepe words,
    Griefe weares, and lessens, that tears breath affords.
Sad hearts, the lesse they seeme the more they are,   5
    (So guiltiest men stand mutest at the barre)
Not that they know not, feele not their estate,
    But extreme sense hath made them desperate;
Sorrow, to whom we owe all that we bee;
    Tyrant, in the fift and greatest Monarchy,   10

An hymne to the Saints.
42. *David, Magdalen*: initially sinners (see 2 Samuel 11 and Luke 7.37–50),
        later penitents (l. 32).

Elegie. Thus entitled in 1633; also entitled *Elegie XI. Death* (acc. to 1635–54,
        where it is placed among the *Elegies*) and *An Elegie upon the death of M^ris
        Boulstred* (acc. to several MSS). But the poem is obviously a funeral
        elegy, concerned rather with Sorrow than with Death; nor is its connec-
        tion with Cecilia Bulstrode (above, p. 381) beyond dispute.
 6. *barre*: court of law.
 7. *estate*: condition.
 8. *sense*: feeling (§170).
 9. Cf. 'I will greatly multiply thy sorrow and thy conception: in sorrow
        thou shalt bring forth children' (Genesis 3.16: §170).
10. *fift and greatest Monarchy*: Christ's kingdom on earth, expected to replace
        the four secular empires (see above, p. 382, note on 24).

Was't, that she did possesse all hearts before,
  Thou hast kil'd her, to make thy Empire more?
Knew'st thou some would, that knew her not, lament,
  As in a deluge perish th'innocent?
Was't not enough to have that palace wonne,   15
  But thou must raze it too, that was undone?
Had'st thou staid there, and look'd out at her eyes,
  All had ador'd thee that now from thee flies,
For they let out more light, then they tooke in,
  They told not when, but did the day beginne;   20
She was too Saphirine, and cleare to thee;
  Clay, flint, and jeat now thy fit dwellings be;
Alas, shee was too pure, but not too weake;
  Who e'r saw Christall Ordinance but would break?
And if wee be thy conquest, by her fall   25
  Th'hast lost thy end, for in her perish all;
Or if we live, we live but to rebell,
  They know her better now, that knew her well.
If we should vapour out, and pine, and die;
  Since, shee first went, that were not miserie;   30
Shee chang'd our world with hers; now she is gone,
  Mirth and prosperity is oppression;
For of all morall vertues she was all,
  The Ethicks speake of vertues Cardinall;

---

11. *she*: not yet identified.
15. *palace*: her body, already ruined by grief (*undone*), and now killed by it (*raze*).
19. *then*: than.
21. *Saphirine*: transparent like a sapphire; pure.
    to: 'for' (acc. to 1635–69).
24. *Christall Ordinance*: the alchemists' crystalline apparatus for very fine work.
26. *end*: purpose.
    for in her: 'in her we' (acc. to 1635–69).
34. *The Ethicks* [moral philosophy] *speake*: 'The ethenickes [i.e. pagans] spake' (acc. to a MS).
    vertues Cardinall: justice, prudence, temperance, and fortitude.

Her soule was Paradise; the Cherubin   35
  Set to keepe it was grace, that kept out sinne;
Shee had no more then let in death, for wee
  All reape consumption from one fruitfull tree;
God tooke her hence, lest some of us should love
  Her, like that plant, him and his lawes above,   40
And when wee teares, hee mercy shed in this,
  To raise our mindes to heaven where now she is;
Who if her vertues would have let her stay
  Wee'had had a Saint, have now a holiday;
Her heart was that strange bush, where, sacred fire,   45
  Religion, did not consume, but'inspire
Such piety, so chast use of Gods day,
  That what we turne to feast, she turn'd to pray,
And did prefigure here, in devout tast,
  The rest of her high Sabaoth, which shall last;   50
Angels did hand her up, who next God dwell,
  (For she was of that order whence most fell)
Her body left with us, lest some had said,
  Shee could not die, except they saw her dead;

35. *Cherubin*: the order of angels immediately below the Seraphim (see below, note on 52).
36. *keepe*: guard.
37. *then*: than. The line is also punctuated: 'She had no more; then let in death for we' (acc. to 1669).
38. *fruitfull tree*: the Tree of Knowledge in Eden, whose violation brought death into the world.
40. *that plant*: the *tree* (38).
     him: i.e. more than we *love God* (39).
41–42. *teares, hee mercy shed in this*, / *To*: 'see his mercy shewne in this / 'Twill' (acc. to a MS).
44. *holiday*: a saint's holy day.
45. *bush*: the burning bush (Exodus 3.2).
46. On the symbol ', see above, p. 5.
48. *what*: 'when' (acc. to a MS).
50. Cf. the last extant lines of *The Faerie Queene*: 'all shall rest eternally / With Him that is the God of Sabbaoth hight'.
52. *order*: the Seraphim, the highest order of angels, whose ranks yielded *most* of the fallen angels; see above, p. 243, note on 60–61.
53. *body*: 'bodie's' (acc. to 1635–69 and some MSS).
54. *except*: 'unlesse' (acc. to some MSS).

For from lesse vertue, and less beautiousnesse,   55
   The Gentiles fram'd them Gods and Goddesses.
The ravenous earth that now woes her to be
   Earth too, will be a *Lemnia*; and the tree
That wraps that christall in a wooden Tombe,
   Shall be tooke up spruce, fill'd with diamond;   60
And we her sad glad friends all beare a part
   Of griefe, for all would waste a Stoicks heart.

On himselfe.

MADAME,
   That I might make your Cabinet my tombe,
      And for my fame which I love next my soule,
Next to my soule provide the happiest roome,

   Admit to that place this last funerall Scrowle.
      Others by Wills give Legacies, but I   5
      Dying, of you doe beg a Legacie.

My Fortune and my choice this custome break,
When we are speechlesse grown, to make stones speak,

Elegie.
56. *fram'd*: 'fain'd' or 'form'd' (acc. to various MSS).
57. *woes*: woos, importunes.
58. *Lemnia*: 'Lemnian earth', a clay found in Lemnos and said to be an
     antidote (§158).
58–60. The ordinary wood of her coffin would also be transmuted (§170).
61. *all*: 'each' (acc. to some MSS).
62. *waste*: 'breake' (acc. to 1635–69 and several MSS).
     a Stoicks heart: Stoics claimed to be unaffected by passions.

On himselfe. First published in the 1635 edition, where two versions are
    provided (the one of ll. 1–16, the other of ll. 7–24). One MS designates
    the poem *Epitaph*; other MSS specify its recipient by adding *To the*
    Countesse of Bedford (see above, p. 266).
  1. *Cabinet*: private chamber.
  2. *fame*: reputation.
  5. *Others*: 'O then' (acc. to a MS).
     Wills: 'testament' (acc. to several MSS).

Though no stone tell thee what I was, yet thou
In my graves inside seest what thou art now,   10
Yet thou'art not yet so good, till death us lay
To ripe and mellow here, we are stubborne Clay.
Parents make us earth, and soules dignifie
Us to be glasse; here to grow gold we lie;
Whilst in our soules sinne bred and pamper'd is,   15
Our soules become wormeaten carkases;
So we our selves miraculously destroy.
Here bodies with less miracle enjoy
Such priviledges, enabled here to scale
Heaven, when the Trumpets ayre shall them exhale.   20
Heare this, and mend thy selfe, and thou mendst me,
By making me being dead, doe good for thee,
    And thinke me well compos'd, that I could now
    A last-sicke houre to syllables allow.

11. On the symbol ', see above, p. 5.
12. *here*: an emendation of 'there' (acc. to 1635, 1669) and 'thee' (acc. to
       1639–54).
13–14. An alchemical image, involving the refinement of base minerals until
       their eventual transmutation into gold (§218).
13. *earth*: dust (see above, p. 374, note on 44).
14. *glasse*: mirror to reflect the divine image in man.
20. *Trumpets ayre*: the trumpets' sound at the Last Judgement.
22. *for*: 'to' (acc. to most MSS).

INFINITATI SACRUM,
16. August 1601.

METEMPSYCOSIS.

Poêma Satyricon.

Metempsycosis [transmigration] is one of Donne's longest
poems (cf. the two *Anniversaries* and *The Lamentations of
Jeremy*). Its 'conceit', according to Ben Jonson, 'was that
[Donne] sought the soule of that apple which Eve pulled and
thereafter made it the soule of a bitch, then of a shee wolf, and
so of a woman; his generall purpose was to have brought in all
the bodies of the Hereticks from the soule of Cain, and at last
left [it] in the bodie of Calvin. Of this he never wrotte but one
sheet, and now, since he was made Doctor [of Divinity],
repenteth highlie and seeketh to destroy all his poems'. It has
also been claimed, however, that the soul's metempsychosis
through the scale of nature was eventually to have terminated
in Elizabeth I (see note on 61–62).

   In the event, the poem has generated many other theories
too. It has been described as an epic ('an Ovidian epic') no less
than as a mock-epic and an anti-epic; it has been specified as
comic, serious, and (inevitably) half-serious; and it has been
associated with the tradition of paradox (§600), of parody
(§606), and of satire, in the last case with reminders of its links
with Donne's earlier *Satyres* and of its express designation as
Poêma Satyricon. Although generally regarded as incomplete –
'a fragment not of whole cloth' (§605) – the poem has also been
claimed to be 'a complete work' (§601).

   Responses to the poem as a poem have also varied. Andrew
Marvell admired its 'witty fable'; Alexander Pope commended
it in the company of the satires and the verse letters as Donne's
'best' productions; and De Quincey praised its 'massy
diamonds'. But still other readers have inclined to agree with

Infinitati Sacrum . . . metempsycosis . . .
The title translates: *Sacred to Infinity . . . The Transmigration of the Soul. A Satiric
   Poem.*

Baron Hatherly who heard Coleridge read the poem and liked
its reference to destiny as 'Knot of all causes' (l. 35). 'The rest
of the poem', he added, 'seemed the effusion of a man very
drunk or very mad' (§210).

EPISTLE

Others at the Porches and entries of their Buildings set their
Armes; I, my picture; if any colours can deliver a minde so
plaine, and flat, and through-light as mine. Naturally at a new
Author, I doubt, and sticke, and doe not say quickly, good. I
censure much and taxe; And this liberty costs mee more than
others, by how much my owne things are worse than others.
Yet I would not be so rebellious against my selfe, as not to doe
it, since I love it; nor so unjust to others, to do it *sine talione*. As
long as I give them as good hold upon mee, they must pardon
mee my bitings. I forbid no reprehender, but him that like the
Trent Councell forbids not bookes, but Authors, damning
what ever such a name hath or shall write. None writes so ill,
that he gives not some thing exemplary, to follow, or flie.
Now when I beginne this booke, I have no purpose to come
into any mans debt; how my stocke will hold out I know not;
perchance waste, perchance increase in use; if I doe borrow any
thing of Antiquitie, besides that I make account that I pay it to
posterity, with as much and as good: You shall still finde mee
to acknowledge it, and to thanke not him onely that hath
digg'd out treasure for mee, but that hath lighted mee a candle
to the place. All which I will bid you remember, (for I will have
no such Readers as I can teach) is, that the Pithagorian doctrine
doth not onely carry one soule from man to man, nor man to
beast, but indifferently to plants also: and therefore you must
not grudge to finde the same soule in an Emperour, in a
Post-horse, and in a Mucheron, since no unreadinesse in the
soule, but an indisposition in the organs workes this. And
therefore though this soule could not move when it was a
Melon, yet it may remember, and now tell mee, at what
lascivious banquet it was serv'd. And though it could not

speake, when it was a spider, yet it can remember, and now tell me, who used it for poyson to attaine dignitie. How ever the bodies have dull'd her other faculties, her memory hath ever been her owne, which makes me so seriously deliver you by her relation all her passages from her first making when shee was that apple which Eve eate, to this time when shee is hee, whose life you shall finde in the end of this booke.

In the *Epistle*, 'through-light' means translucent, and 'sine talione', without retaliation; 'the Trent Council' refers to the Roman Catholic council convened to promote the Counter-Reformation (1545–63); 'the Pithagorian doctrine' is metempsychosis or the transmigration of the soul; 'a Mucheron' is a mushroom; and, in the penultimate line, 'shee is hee' is the reading of the 1633 edition, amended – without authority (§171) – to 'shee is shee' from 1635.

THE PROGRESSE OF THE SOULE.

First Song.

I.

I sing the progresse of a deathlesse soule,
Whom Fate, which God made, but doth not controule,
Plac'd in most shapes; all times before the law
Yoak'd us, and when, and since, in this I sing.
And the great world to his aged evening;   5
From infant morne, through manly noone I draw.
What the gold Chaldee, or silver Persian saw,
Greeke brasse, or Roman iron, is in this one;
A worke t'outweare *Seths* pillars, bricke and stone,
    And (holy writt excepted) made to yeeld to none.   10

II.

Thee, eye of heaven, this great Soule envies not,
By thy male force, is all wee have, begot,
In the first East, thou now beginst to shine,
Suck'st early balme, and Iland spices there,
And wilt anon in thy loose-rein'd careere   15
At Tagus, Po, Sene, Thames, and Danow dine.
And see at night thy Westerne land of Myne,

The Progresse of the Soule.
  1 ff. *I sing* etc.: the formula is characteristic of epic poetry, here reinforced
    by Donne's use of a modified Spenserian stanza.
  3–4. History was often divided into three periods: the one *before the law*
    given to Moses atop Mount Sinai; the one during the law; and the one
    since the law (i.e. the Christian era).
  5. *aged evening*: i.e. old age, in line with the belief in the world's decay best
    articulated in the two *Anniversaries* (above, pp. 324 ff.).
  7–8. The allusion is to the four ages of history (see above, p. 343, note on
    426), here reapportioned rather drastically.
  9. *Seths pillars*: the two pillars commemorating the astronomical dis-
    coveries of Seth, one of Adam's sons.
11–12. The *eye of heaven*, the sun, was thought to 'beget' all matter.
16. Rivers crossing – respectively – Lisbon, northwest Italy, Paris (the
    Seine), London, and central Europe to the Black Sea (the Danube).
17. *Westerne land of Myne*: the West Indies (see above, p. 54, note on 17).

Yet hast thou not more nations seene then shee,
That before thee, one day beganne to bee,
  And thy fraile light being quench'd, shall long, long
    out live thee.   20

III.

Nor, holy *Janus*, in whose soveraigne boate
The Church, and all the Monarchies did floate;
That swimming Colledge, and free Hospitall
Of all mankinde, that cage and vivarie
Of fowles, and beasts, in whose wombe, Destinie   25
us, and our latest nephewes did install
(From thence are all deriv'd, that fill this All,)
Did'st thou in that great stewardship embarke
So diverse shapes into that floating parke,
  As have beene moved, and inform'd by this heavenly
    sparke.   30

IV.

Great Destiny the Commissary of God,
That hast mark'd out a path and period
For every thing; who, where wee of-spring tooke,
Our wayes and ends seest at one instant; Thou
Knot of all causes, thou whose changelesse brow   35
Ne'r smiles nor frownes, O vouch thou safe to looke
And shew my story, in thy eternall booke:
That (if my prayer be fit) I may'understand

18. *then*: than.
21. *Janus*: the Roman god who could see both before and after, widely
     regarded as a 'type' of Noah (see §4).
24. *vivarie*: place artificially prepared for keeping animals and birds.
26. *nephewes*: descendants.
30. *inform'd*: given form and reason (§163).
31. *Commissary*: deputy; cf. above, p. 265, l. 11.
36. *vouch thou safe* (acc. to MSS): 'vouch safe thou' (acc. to 1633–69).
38. On the symbol ', here and throughout, see above, p. 5.

So much my selfe, as to know with what hand,
    How scant, or liberall this my lifes race is spand.   40

V.

To my sixe lustres almost now outwore,
Except thy booke owe mee so many more,
Except my legend be free from the letts
Of steepe ambition, sleepie povertie,
Spirit-quenching sicknesse, dull captivitie,   45
Distracting businesse, and from beauties nets,
And all that calls from this, and to others whets,
O let me not launch out, but let mee save
Th'expense of braine and spirit; that my grave
    His right and due, a whole unwasted man may have.   50

VI.

But if my dayes be long, and good enough,
In vaine this sea shall enlarge, or enrough
It selfe; for I will through the wave, and fome,
And shall, in sad lone wayes a lively spright,
Make my darke heavy Poëm light, and light.   55
For though through many streights, and lands I roame,
I launch at paradise, and I saile towards home;
The course I there began, shall here be staid,
Sailes hoised there, stroke here, and anchors laid
    In Thames, which were at Tigrys, and Euphrates waide.   60

40. *spand*: limited.
41. *sixe lustres*: thirty years, each lustrum being a five-year period.
43. *letts*: hindrances.
46. *nets*: entrapments.
52. *this sea*: the labour of writing this poem.
55. *light* as opposed to heavy, and *light* as opposed to dark.
54. *shall* (acc. to 1633): 'hold' (acc. to 1635–69).
57. *launch*: begin (§606).
57–60. The 'progresse' is here promised to terminate in London.
59. *hoised*: set.
60. *Tigrys, Euphrates*: rivers of Mesopotamia, the traditional site of Eden.
    waide: weighed, raised.

VII.

For the great soule which here amongst us now
Doth dwell, and moves that hand, and tongue, and brow,
Which, as the Moone the sea, moves us; to heare
Whose story, with long patience you will long;
(For 'tis the crowne, and last straine of my song)   65
This soule to whom *Luther* and *Mahomet* were
Prisons of flesh; this soule which oft did teare,
And mend the wracks of th'Empire, and late Rome,
And liv'd when every great change did come,
 Had first in paradise, a low, but fatall roome.   70

VIII.

Yet no low roome, nor then the greatest, lesse,
If (as devout and sharpe men fitly guesse)
That Crosse, our joy, and griefe, where nailes did tye
That All, which alwayes was all, every where,
Which could not sinne, and yet all sinnes did beare;   75
Which could not die, yet could not chuse but die;
Stood in the selfe same roome in Calvarie,
Where first grew the forbidden learned tree,
For on that tree hung in security
 This Soule, made by the Makers will from pulling free.   80

61–62. The allusion is often said to be to Elizabeth I (§§ 158, 159, 164, 166); but
  one must consider Jonson's choice of Calvin (above, p. 402) as well
  as the Epistle's identification of the soul's final host both as 'hee' (acc. to
  1633) and 'shee' (acc. to 1635–69). Donne had in any case been con-
  verted to Protestantism already, and there is no evidence that in 1601 he
  would have mounted such a massive attack on his sovereign. Among
  other possibilities, might the allusion be to Robert Cecil (§609) or to the
  poet himself?
68. *th'Empire*: the Roman Empire; *late Rome*: later (more recent) Rome.
69. *when*: 'where' (acc. to MSS).
70. *low*: because initially occupying a mere vegetable; *fatall*: destined to be
  plucked and to bring death into the world.
71. *then*: than.
74–76. The lines were later repeated in *La Corona*, below, p. 430, II, 2–4.
77–78. See below, p. 489, note on 21–22.
78. *learned*: because designated the tree of 'knowledge' of good and evil.

IX.

Prince of the orchard, faire as dawning morne,
Fenc'd with the law, and ripe as soone as borne
That apple grew, which this Soule did enlive
Till the then climing serpent, that now creeps
For that offence, for which all mankinde weepes, 85
Tooke it, and t'her whom the first man did wive
(Whom and her race, only forbiddings drive)
He gave it, she, t'her husband, both did eate;
So perished the eaters, and the meate:
 And wee (for treason taints the blood) thence die and sweat.

X.

Man all at once was there by woman slaine,
And one by one we'are here slaine o'er againe
By them. The mother poison'd the well-head,
The daughters here corrupt us, Rivolets,
No smalnesse scapes, no greatnesse breaks their nets, 95
She thrust us out, and by them we are led
Astray, from turning, to whence we are fled.
Were prisoners Judges, 'twould seeme rigorous,
Shee sinn'd, we beare, part of our paine is, thus
 To love them, whose fault to this painfull love yoak'd us.

XI.

So fast in us doth this corruption grow,
That now wee dare aske why wee should be so.
Would God (disputes the curious Rebell) make
A law, and would not have it kept? Or can
His creatures will, crosse his? Of every man 105

---

82. *borne*: created.
84–85. The serpent, said to have been erect before the Fall, was thereafter
  condemned to move on its belly (Genesis 3.14).
90. *sweat*: cf. 'in the sweat of thy face shalt thou eat bread' (Genesis 3.19).
91. *slaine*: also in the sexual sense (see above, p. 48, note on 16).
94. *Rivolets*: rivulets (the word, missing in 1633, was supplied from 1635).
99. *beare* (acc. to 1635–69): 'here' (acc. to 1633).
103. *curious*: ingeniously argumentative (§171).
105. *For one*: for the offence of one (Adam).

For one, will God (and be just) vengeance take?
Who sinn'd? t'was not forbidden to the snake
Nor her, who was not then made; nor is't writ
That Adam cropt, or knew the apple; yet
    The worme and she, and he, and wee endure for it.   110

XII.

But snatch mee heavenly Spirit from this vaine
Reckoning their vanities, lesse is their gaine
Then hazard still, to meditate on ill,
Though with good minde, their reasons, like those toyes
Of glassie bubbles, which the gamesome boyes   115
Stretch to so nice a thinnes through a quill
That they themselves breake, doe themselves spill,
Arguing is heretiques game, and Exercise
As wrastlers, perfects them; Not liberties
    Of speech, but silence; hands, not tongues, end heresies.   120

XIII.

Just in that instant when the serpents gripe,
Broke the slight veines, and tender conduit-pipe,
Through which this soule from the trees root did draw
Life, and growth to this apple, fled away
This loose soule, old, one and another day.   125
As lightning, which one scarce dares say, he saw,
'Tis so soone gone, (and better proofe the law
Of sense, then faith requires) swiftly she flew
To a darke and foggie Plot; Her, her fates threw
    There through th'earths pores, and in a Plant hous'd
    her anew.   130

113.   *Then*: than.
117.   *doe* (acc. to 1633 and MSS): 'and doe' (acc. to 1635–69).
119.   *As wrastlers*: as in the case of wrestlers.
121.   *the serpents gripe*: some accounts of the Fall claimed that the forbidden
    fruit was plucked, and handed to Eve, by Satan.
125.   *old, one and another day*: i.e. two days old.
128.   *then*: than.
129.   *foggie*: marshy.
130.   *a Plant*: i.e. eventually grown into a mandrake (ll. 141–70), which was
    thought to be an aphrodisiac (cf. 148–49: *in loves businesse . . . A dealer*)
    and a narcotic (167: *Poppie*); see further above, p. 50, note on 2.

XIV.

The plant thus abled, to it selfe did force
A place, where no place was; by natures course
As aire from water, water fleets away
From thicker bodies, by this root thronged so
His spungie confines gave him place to grow,   135
Just as in our streets, when the people stay
To see the Prince, and so fill up the way
That weesels scarce could passe, when she comes nere
They throng and cleave up, and a passage cleare,
   As if, for that time, their round bodies flatned were.   140

XV.

His right arme he thrust out towards the East,
West-ward his left; th'ends did themselves digest
Into ten lesser strings, these fingers were:
And as a slumberer stretching on his bed,
This way he this, and that way scattered   145
His other legge, which feet with toes upbeare;
Grew on his middle parts, the first day, haire,
To show, that in loves businesse hee should still
A dealer bee, and be us'd well, or ill:
   His apples kindle, his leaves, force of conception kill. 150

XVI.

A mouth, but dumbe, he hath; blinde eyes, deafe eares,
And to his shoulders dangle subtile haires;
A young *Colossus* there hee stands upright,
And as that ground by him were conquered
A leafie garland weares he on his head   155
Enchas'd with little fruits, so red and bright
That for them you would call your Loves lips white;

---

134. *thicker*: denser.
      thronged: squeezed.
137. *and so fill up* (acc. to 1635–69): 'and so fill'd' (acc. to 1633) or 'have so fill'd' (acc. to most modern editors).
142. *digest*: divide.
150. *kindle* (acc. to 1635–69): 'kinde' (acc. to 1633 and most MSS).
156. *Enchas'd*: inlaid, adorned.

So, of a lone unhaunted place possest,
Did this soules second Inne, built by the guest
   This living buried man, this quiet mandrake, rest.   160

XVII.

No lustfull woman came this plant to grieve,
But 'twas because there was none yet but Eve:
And she (with other purpose) kill'd it quite;
Her sinne had now brought in infirmities,
And so her cradled child, the moist red eyes   165
Had never shut, nor slept since it saw light,
Poppie she knew, she knew the mandrakes might;
And tore up both, and so coold her childs blood;
Unvirtuous weeds might long unvex'd have stood;
   But hee's short liv'd, that with his death can doe
      most good.   170

XVIII.

To an unfetterd soules quick nimble haste
Are falling stars, and hearts thoughts, but slow pac'd:
Thinner than burnt aire flies this soule, and she
Whom foure new comming, and foure parting Suns
Had found, and left the Mandrakes tenant, runnes   175
Thoughtlesse of change, when her firme destiny
Confin'd, and enjayld her, that seem'd so free,
Into a small blew shell, the which a poore
Warme bird orespread, and sat still evermore,
   Till her inclos'd child kickt, and pick'd it selfe a dore.

---

165. *child*: Cain, whose name was erroneously thought to mean 'constant weeping' (cf. *moist red eyes*).
169. *Unvirtuous*: without medicinal 'virtues'; *unvex'd*: untouched.
173. *burnt aire*: smoke.
175. *tenant*: tenancy.
180. *inclos'd* (acc. to 1635–69): 'uncloth'd' (acc. to 1633) or 'encloth'd' (acc. to some MSS).

XIX.

Outcrept a sparrow, this soules moving Inne,
On whose raw armes stiffe feathers now begin,
As childrens teeth through gummes, to breake with paine,
His flesh is jelly yet, and his bones threds,
All a new downy mantle overspreads,   185
A mouth he opes, which would as much containe
As his late house, and the first houre speaks plaine,
And chirps alowd for meat. Meat fit for men
His father steales for him, and so feeds then
   One, that within a moneth, will beate him from his hen. 190

XX.

In this worlds youth wise nature did make haste,
Things ripened sooner, and did longer last;
Already this hot cocke, in bush and tree
In field and tent oreflutters his next hen,
He asks her not, who did so last, nor when,   195
Nor if his sister, or his neece shee be;
Nor doth she pule for his inconstancie
If in her sight he change, nor doth refuse
The next that calls; both liberty doe use,
   Where store is of both kindes, both kindes may
      freely chuse.   200

XXI.

Men, till they tooke laws which made freedome lesse,
Their daughters, and their sisters did ingresse;
Till now unlawfull, therefore ill, 'twas not.
So jolly, that it can move, this soule is,
The body so free of his kindnesses,   205

185. *a new downy* (acc. to 1635–69 and most MSS): 'downy a new' (acc. to 1633).
193. *hot cocke*: the *sparrow* (181) was thought to be lecherous.
194. *next*: nearest.
197. *pule*: whine.
198. *change*: transfer his sexual allegiance (§166).
200. *store*: sexual opportunities.
202. *ingresse*: enter, copulate with.
203–05. The punctuation, erratic in all editions, is given as conjectured (§158).
204. *jolly*: sprightly, bold, lustful (§166).
205. *free of*: lavish with.

That selfe preserving it hath now forgot,
And slackneth so the soules, and bodies knot,
Which temperance streightens; freely on his she friends
He blood, and spirit, pith, and marrow spends,
   Ill steward of himself, himselfe in three yeares ends.   210

XXII.

Else might he long have liv'd; man did not know
Of gummie blood, which doth in holly grow,
How to make bird-lime, nor how to deceive
With faind calls, hid nets, or enwrapping snare
The free inhabitants of the Plyant aire.   215
Man to beget, and woman to conceive
Askt not of rootes, nor of cock-sparrowes, leave:
Yet chuseth hee, though none of these he feares,
Pleasantly three, than streightned twenty yeares
   To live, and to encrease his race, himselfe outweares. 220

XXIII.

This cole with overblowing quench'd and dead,
The Soule from her too active organs fled
T'a brooke. A female fishes sandie Roe
With the males jelly, newly lev'ned was,
For they had intertouch'd as they did passe,   225
And one of those small bodies, fitted so,
This soule inform'd, and abled it to rowe

---

208. *streightens*: tightens.
209. *spends* (also 220: *outweares*): cf. above, p. 122, ll. 24–25.
212–13. *gummie blood*: the sticky sap of the *holly* that yielded *bird-lime* to entrap small birds.
214. *hid* (acc. to some MSS): 'his' (acc. to 1633–69 and some MSS).
217. The *roots* of certain plants (e.g. the mandrake) and the dung of male *sparrowes* were regarded as aphrodisiacs.
219. *streightned*: confined.
220. *his race* (missing in 1633, supplied from 1635).
224. *lev'ned*: leavened, impregnated (§163).
225. *had* (missing in 1633, supplied from 1635).
     intertouch'd: see above, p. 88, note on 26.
227. *inform'd*: gave form to.

It selfe with finnie oares, which she did fit:
Her scales seem'd yet of parchment, and as yet
    Perchance a fish, but by no name you could call it.   230

XXIV.

When goodly, like a ship in her full trim,
A swan, so white that you may unto him
Compare all whitenesse, but himselfe to none,
Glided along, and as he glided watch'd,
And with his arched necke this poore fish catch'd.   235
It mov'd with state, as if to looke upon
Low things it scorn'd, and yet before that one
Could thinke he sought it, he had swallowed cleare
This, and much such, and unblam'd devour'd there
    All, but who too swift, too great, or well arm'd were. 240

XXV.

Now swome a prison in a prison put,
And now this Soule in double walls was shut,
Till melted with the Swans digestive fire,
She left her house the fish, and vapour'd forth;
Fate not affording bodies of more worth   245
For her as yet, bids her againe retire
T'another fish, to any new desire
Made a new prey; For, he that can to none
Resistance make, nor complaint, sure is gone.
    Weaknesse invites, but silence feasts oppression.   250

XXVI.

Pace with her native streame, this fish doth keepe,
And journeyes with her, towards the glassie deepe,
But oft retarded, once with a hidden net

---

228.   *finnie*: cf. above, p. 255, note on 37.
239.   *much*: many.
251.   *her* (acc. to most MSS): 'the' (acc. to 1633–69).

Though with greate windowes, for when Need first taught
These tricks to catch food, then they were not wrought   255
As now, with curious greedinesse to let
None scape, but few, and fit for use, to get,
As, in this trap a ravenous pike was tane,
Who, though himselfe distrest, would faine have slain
 This wretch; So hardly are ill habits left again.   260

XXVII.

Here by her smallnesse shee two deaths orepast,
Once innocence scap'd, and left the oppressor fast.
The net through-swome, she keepes the liquid path,
And whether she leape up sometimes to breath
And suck in aire, or finde it underneath,   265
Or working parts like mills or limbecks hath
To make the water thinne and airelike, faith
Cares not; but safe the Place she's come unto
Where fresh, with salt waves meet, and what to doe
 She knowes not, but betweene both makes a boord or two.

XXVIII.

So farre from hiding her guests, water is,
That she showes them in bigger quantities
Then they are. Thus doubtfull of her way,
For game and not for hunger a sea Pie
Spied through this traiterous spectacle, from high,   275

254. *windowes*: the net's openings.
256. *curious*: ingenious.
258. *tane*: taken.
260. *hardly*: with difficulty.
262. *Once*: for once.
266. *limbecks*: see above, p. 91, note on 21.
267–68. The manner in which fishes breathe is indifferent to *faith* (§158).
  thinne: less dense.
270. *makes a boord or two*: moves to and fro uncertainly (§171).
273. *Then*: than.
  Thus (acc. to 1633 and most MSS): 'Thus her' (acc. to 1635–69).
274. *sea Pie*: the sea-bird oyster-catcher.

The seely fish where it disputing lay,
And t'end her doubts and her, beares her away,
Exalted she'is, but to the exalters good,
As are by great ones, men which lowly stood.
   It's rais'd, to be the Raisers instrument and food.   280

XXIX.

Is any kinde subject to rape like fish?
Ill unto man, they neither doe, nor wish:
Fishers they kill not, nor with noise awake,
They doe not hunt, nor strive to make a prey
Of beasts, nor their yong sonnes to beare away;   285
Foules they pursue not, nor do undertake
To spoile the nests industrious birds do make;
Yet them all these unkinde kinds feed upon,
To kill them is an occupation,
   And lawes make fasts, and lents for their destruction.   290

XXX.

A sudden stiffe land-winde in that selfe houre
To sea-ward forc'd this bird, that did devour
The fish; he cares not, for with ease he flies,
Fat gluttonies best orator: at last
So long hee hath flowen, and hath flowen so fast   295
That leagues o'er-past at sea, now tir'd hee lyes,
And with his prey, that till then languisht, dies,
The soules no longer foes, two wayes did erre,
The fish I follow, and keepe no calender
   Of the other; he lives yet in some great officer.   300

276.   *seely*: foolish.
      disputing: arguing with itself.
291.   *self*: same.
296.   *leagues o'er-past* (acc. to 1633–69): 'leagues' (acc. to most MSS) or 'many
      leagues' (acc. to some MSS and most modern editors).
300.   *officer*: government official, now gluttony's best advocate (294).

XXXI.

Into an embrion fish, our Soule is throwne,
And in due time throwne out againe, and growne
To such vastnesse, as if unmanacled
From Greece, Morea were, and that by some
Earthquake unrooted, loose Morea swome,   305
Or seas from Africks body had severed
And torne the hopefull Promontories head,
This fish would seeme these, and, when all hopes faile,
A great ship overset, or without saile
  Hulling, might (when this was a whelp) be like this whale.

XXXII.

At every stroake his brazen finnes do take,
More circles in the broken sea they make
Then cannons voices, when the aire they teare:
His ribs are pillars, and his high arch'd roofe
Of barke that blunts best steele, is thunder-proofe: 315
Swimme in him swallowed Dolphins, without feare,
And feele no sides, as if his vast wombe were
Some inland sea, and ever as hee went
Hee spouted rivers up, as if he ment
  To joyne our seas, with seas above the firmament.   320

XXXIII.

He hunts not fish, but as an officer,
Stayes in his court, at his owne net, and there

302. *throwne out*: extended.
303–05. *Morea*, the Peloponnesus, is *loose* because *unmanacled* (separated) from
     mainland Greece by an isthmus.
307. *the hopefull Promontories head*: the tip of the Cape of Good Hope.
309. *overset*: capsized.
310. *Hulling*: floating along without sail (§166).
313. *Then*: than.
315. *barke*: outer skin.
320. *seas above the firmament*: see above, p. 378, note on 8.
321–22. *an officer . . . net*: 'a favourite / Lies still at Court, and is himselfe a
     nett' (acc. to a MS: §159).
322. *net*: i.e. with which to entrap petitioners (see note on 300).

All suitors of all sorts themselves enthrall;
So on his backe lyes this whale wantoning,
And in his gulfe-like throat, sucks every thing   325
That passeth neare. Fish chaseth fish, and all,
Flyer and follower, in this whirlepoole fall;
O might not states of more equality
Consist? and is it of necessity
   That thousand guiltlesse smals, to make one great, must
      die?

XXXIV.

Now drinkes he up seas, and he eates up flocks,
He justles Ilands, and he shakes firme rockes.
Now in a roomefull house this Soule doth float,
And like a Prince she sends her faculties
To all her limbes, distant as Provinces.   335
The Sunne hath twenty times both crab and goate
Parched, since first lanch'd forth this living boate,
'Tis greatest now, and to destruction
Nearest; There's no pause at perfection,
   Greatnesse a period hath, but hath no station.   340

XXXV.

Two little fishes whom hee never harm'd,
Nor fed on their kinde, two not throughly arm'd
With hope that they could kill him, nor could doe

---

327. *Flyer and follower*: pursued and pursuer (§166).
336. *times*: i.e. years.
     crab and goate: the summer and winter solstices (see below, p. 337, note
     on 264–67).
337. *this*: 'his' (acc. to 1635–69)
340. *station*: permanent resting-place.

Good to themselves by his death (they did not eate
His flesh, nor suck those oyles, which thence outstreat)   345
Conspir'd against him, and it might undoe
The plot of all, that the plotters were two,
But that they fishes were, and could not speake.
How shall a Tyran wise strong projects breake,
    If wreches can on them the common anger wreake?   350

XXXVI.

The flaile-finn'd Thresher, and steel-beak'd Sword-fish
Onely attempt to doe, what all doe wish.
The Thresher backs him, and to beate begins;
The sluggard Whale yeelds to oppression,
And t'hide himselfe from shame and danger, downe   355
Begins to sinke; the Swordfish upward spins,
And gores him with his beake; his staffe-like finnes,
So well the one, his sword the other plyes,
That now a scoffe, and prey, this tyran dyes,
    And (his owne dole) feeds with himselfe all companies.

XXXVII.

Who will revenge his death? or who will call
Those to account, that thought, and wrought his fall?
The heires of slaine kings, wee see are often so
Transported with the joy of what they get,
That they, revenge and obsequies forget,   365
Nor will against such men the people goe,
Because h'is now dead, to whom they should show

345.   *outstreat*: exude.
349.   *projects*: schemes.
351.   *Thresher*: 'thrasher', the fox-shark, which 'beats' (353) enemies with its
       long tail.
360.   *dole*: thing distributed.

Love in that act. Some kings by vice being growne
So needy of subjects love, that of their own
  They thinke they lose, if love be to the dead Prince shown.

XXXVIII.

This Soule, now free from prison, and passion,
Hath yet a little indignation
That so small hammers should so soone downe beat
So great a castle. And having for her house
Got the streight cloyster of a wreched mouse   375
(As basest men that have not what to eate,
Nor enjoy ought, doe farre more hate the great
Then they, who good repos'd estates possesse)
This Soule, late taught that great things might by lesse
  Be slaine, to gallant mischiefe doth herselfe addresse. 380

XXXIX.

Natures great master-peece, an Elephant,
The onely harmlesse great thing; the giant
Of beasts; who thought, no more had gone, to make one wise
But to be just, and thankfull, loth to offend,
(Yet nature hath given him no knees to bend)   385
Himselfe he up-props, on himselfe relies,
And foe to none, suspects no enemies,
Still sleeping stood; vex't not his fantasie
Blacke dreames, like an unbent bow, carelessly
  His sinewy Proboscis did remisly lie.   390

375. *streight cloyster*: narrow confine.
378. *Then*: than.
383. *who . . . wise* (acc. to 1633 and most MSS): 'who thought none had, to
       make him wise' (acc. to 1635–69).
385. The elephant was sometimes said not to have knees.
389–95. The ability of mice to kill the elephant by climbing up its proboscis (!)
       was a relatively recent notion (§603).

XL.

In which as in a gallery this mouse
Walk'd, and surveid the roomes of this vast house,
And to the braine, the soules bedchamber, went,
And gnaw'd the life cords there; Like a whole towne
Cleane undermin'd, the slaine beast tumbled downe,   395
With him the murtherer dies whom envy sent
To kill, not scape, (for, only hee that ment
To die, did ever kill a man of better roome,)
And thus he made his foe, his prey, and tombe:
   Who cares not to turn back, may any whither come.   400

XLI.

Next, hous'd this Soule a Wolves yet unborne whelp,
Till the best midwife, Nature, gave it helpe,
To issue. It could kill, as soone as goe:
Abel, as white, and milde as his sheepe were,
(Who in that trade, of Church, and kingdomes, there   405
Was the first type) was still infested soe,
With this wolfe, that it bred his losse and woe;
And yet his bitch, his sentinell attends
The flocke so neere, so well warnes and defends,
   That the wolfe, (hopelesse else) to corrupt her, intends.   410

XLII.

Hee tooke a course, which since, successfully,
Great men have often taken, to espie
The counsels, or to breake the plots of foes,
To Abels tent he stealeth in the darke,
On whose skirts the bitch slept; ere she could barke,   415

397–98. The helpful parentheses are conjectural (§158).
         ment: 'went' (acc. to some MSS).
398.   *roome*: rank.
400.   *any whither*: any place.
404.   *Abel*: the second son of Adam and Eve (Genesis 4.2 ff.), slain by his
         brother Cain (see note on 165).
405–06. In his *trade* of shepherd, Abel was an anticipatory *type* or figure of
         both pastors and kings.
406.   *still*: continually.

Attach'd her with streight gripes, yet hee call'd those,
Embracements of love; to loves worke he goes,
Where deeds move more than words; nor doth she show,
Nor much resist, nor needs hee streightcn so
   His prey, for, were shee loose, she would nor barke,
     nor goe.   420

XLIII.

Hee hath engag'd her; his, she wholy bides;
Who not her owne, none others secrets hides,
 ·If to the flocke he come, and Abell there,
She faines hoarse barkings, but she biteth not,
Her faith is quite, but not her love forgot.   425
At last a trap, of which some every where
·Abell had plac'd, ends all his losse, and feare,
By the Wolves death; and now just time it was
That a quick soule should give life to that masse
   Of blood in Abels bitch, and thither this did passe.   430

XLIV.

Some have their wives, their sisters some begot,
But in the lives of Emperours you shall not
Reade of a lust the which may equall this;
This wolfe begot himselfe, and finished
What he began alive, when hee was dead,   435
Sonne to himselfe, and father too, hee is
A ridling lust, for which Schoolemen would misse

416. *gripes*: grips.
418. *show*: show resistance.
419. *Nor*: 'Now' (acc. to some MSS).
     streighten: confine.
420. *loose*: free.
424. *faines*: feigns.
427. *ends all*: 'ended' or 'ends both' or 'end, both' (acc. to various MSS).
429. *quick*: living.
434. *begot himself*: i.e. his lust was passed to his offspring.
437. *Schoolemen*: medieval theologians.
     misse: unable to discover.

A proper name. The whelpe of both these lay
In Abels tent, and with soft Moaba,
   His sister, being yong, it us'd to sport and play.   440

XLV.

Hee soone for her too harsh, and churlish grew,
And Abell (the dam dead) would use this new
For the field, being of two kindes thus made,
He, as his dam, from sheepe drove wolves away,
And as his Sire, he made them his owne prey.   445
Five years he liv'd, and cosened with his trade,
Then hopelesse that his faults were hid, betraid
Himselfe by flight, and by all followed,
From dogges, a wolfe; from wolves, a dogge he fled;
   And, like a spie to both sides false, he perished.   450

XLVI.

It quickened next a toyfull Ape, and so
Gamesome it was, that it might freely goe
From tent to tent, and with the children play,
His organs now so like theirs hee doth finde,
That why he cannot laugh, and speake his minde,   455
He wonders. Much with all, most he doth stay
With Adams fift daughter *Siphatecia*,
Doth gaze on her, and, where she passeth, passe,
Gathers her fruits, and tumbles on the grasse,
   And wisest of that kinde, the first true lover was.   460

439 ff. Tradition provided Adam and Eve with many children besides Cain, Abel, and Seth (see §158). Donne mentions three daughters – *Moaba* (439), *Siphatecia* (457), and *Themech* (509) – as well as a son, *Tethlemite* (487).

443. *thus* (missing in 1633, supplied from 1635).

446. *cosened*: deceived.

451 ff. The ape in the guise of a human lover appears to have been a very popular motif (§602).

451. *quickned*: gave life to.
     toyfull: sportive.

XLVII.

He was the first that more desir'd to have
One then another; first that ere did crave
Love by mute signes, and had no power to speakc;
First that could make love faces, or could doe
The valters sombersalts, or us'd to wooe   465
With hoiting gambolls, his owne bones to breake
To make his mistresse merry; or to wreake
Her anger on himselfe. Sinnes against kinde
They easily doe, that can let feed their minde
  With outward beauty, beauty they in boyes and
    beasts do find.   470

XLVIII.

By this misled, too low things men have prov'd,
And too high; beasts and angels have beene lov'd;
This Ape, though else through-vaine, in this was wise,
He reach'd at things too high, but open way
There was, and he knew not she would say nay;   475
His toyes prevaile not, likelier meanes he tries,
He gazeth on her face with teare-shot eyes,
And up lifts subtly with his russet pawe
Her kidskinne apron without feare or awe
  Of Nature; Nature hath no gaole, though shee hath law. 480

XLIX.

First she was silly and knew not what he ment,
That vertue, by his touches, chaft and spent,
Succeeds an itchie warmth, that melts her quite,
She knew not first, now cares not what he doth,
And willing halfe and more, more then halfe loth,   485

462. *then*: than.
465. *The valters sombersalts*: the vaulter's somersaults.
466. *hoiting*: noisily mirthful.
468. *kinde*: nature.
471. *prov'd*: experienced.
473. *through*: thoroughly.
481. *silly*: innocent.
484. *now* (acc. to 1633): 'nor' (acc. to 1635–69).
485. *then*: than.   *loth* (a conjectural reading acc. to a MS and §158: 1633 reads 'Tooth', and 1635–69, 'wroth').

She neither puls nor pushes, but outright
Now cries, and now repents; when *Tethlemite*
Her brother, enterd, and a great stone threw
After the Ape, who, thus prevented, flew,
  This house thus batter'd downe, the Soule possest a new. 490

L.

And whether by this change she lose or win,
She comes out next, where the Ape would have gone in,
Adam and *Eve* had mingled bloods, and now
Like Chimiques equall fires, her temperate wombe
Had stew'd and form'd it: and part did become   495
A spungie liver, that did richly allow,
Like a free conduit, on a high hils brow,
Life keeping moisture unto every part;
Part hardned it selfe to a thicker heart,
  Whose busie furnaces lifes spirits do impart.   500

LI.

Another part became the well of sense,
The tender well-arm'd feeling braine, from whence,
Those sinowie strings which do our bodies tie,
Are raveld out; and fast there by one end,
Did this Soule limbes, these limbes a soule attend;   505
And now they joyn'd; keeping some quality
Of every past shape, she knew treachery,
Rapine, deceit, and lust, and ills enow
To be a woman. *Themech* she is now,
  Sister and wife to *Caine, Caine* that first did plow.   510

489. *prevented*: forestalled.
494. *Chimiques equall fires*: the even heat of the alchemists' fires, expected to
      produce the elixir (see above, p. 86, note on 7).
499. *thicker*: thicker than the liver.
505. *attend*: await.
508. *enow*: enough.

LII.

Who ere thou beest that read'st this sullen Writ,
Which just so much courts thee, as thou dost it,
Let me arrest thy thoughts; wonder with mee,
Why plowing, building, ruling and the rest,
Or most of those arts, whence our lives are blest,   515
By cursed *Cains* race invented be,
And blest *Seth* vext us with Astronomie,
Ther's nothing simply good, nor ill alone,
Of every quality comparison,
    The onely measure is, and judge, opinion.   520

---

517.   *Seth*: the son of Adam, intended to replace Abel (Genesis 4.25, 5.3).
      Astronomie: see p. 405, note on 9.

Divine Poëms

Of the thirty-eight *Divine Poëms* made available here, twenty-seven were provided by the 1633 edition and the rest by subsequent editions and one manuscript. Three other poems often included in this subdivision – a translation of a Latin poem to George Herbert and the sonnets to the Earl of Dorset and Magdalen Herbert – should more appropriately be numbered among the verse letters (see above, pp. 294, 316, 317).

Holy Sonnets, the single largest subdivision of the *Divine Poëms*, includes the seven sonnets comprising *La Corona* and the nineteen Holy Sonnets proper (also specified in some MSS as 'Divine Meditations' [pp. 434 ff.]). The latter group is normally constituted according to one of two basic schemes. The first, proposed by Grierson and duplicated by Hayward and Smith (§§ 158, 159, 166), clusters the sonnets in accordance with their arrangement in the 1635 edition, adding the three sonnets from the Westmoreland MS first printed by Gosse in 1899 (see below, p. 445); the second, proposed by Gardner and duplicated by Shawcross and Warnke (§§ 168, 163, 164), clusters the sonnets in three distinct groups of twelve, four, and three poems, which respectively include the sonnets in the 1633 edition, the sonnets added in the 1635 edition, and the sonnets in the Westmoreland MS. The present edition, applying the principles established earlier (pp. 2 ff.), avoids every subdivision in favour of a sequential – and strictly noncommittal – arrangement of the sonnets as given first in 1635 (I–XVI) and next in Westmoreland (XVII–XIX). In effect, the scheme coincides with Grierson's.

The numbering of the *Holy Sonnets* should be approached with studied caution lest one is tempted to detect an underlying design. The numerals prefixed in the present edition to all the sonnets are deployed solely for the sake of convenience and should under *no* circumstances be regarded as authoritative.

Our expectations notwithstanding, the *Divine Poëms* were not all written after Donne's ordination in 1615. On the contrary, it appears that several – or even, according to some scholars, most – were in fact penned before his ordination, however uncertain we may be about any single date of composition except those specified in the headnotes to the given poems.

HOLY SONNETS.

La Corona.

1.   *Deigne at my hands this crown of prayer and praise,*
     Weav'd in my low devout melancholie,
     Thou which of good, hast, yea art treasury,
     All changing unchang'd Antient of dayes,
     But doe not, with a vile crowne of fraile bayes,   5
     Reward my muses white sincerity,
     But what thy thorny crowne gain'd, that give mee,
     A crowne of Glory, which doth flower alwayes;

La Corona. Correctly translated in some MSS as *The Crowne*, the general title of the seven interlinked sonnets suggests a rosary of seven 'decades', by Catholics invariably addressed to the Virgin Mary, but here adapted into an address to Christ (§81). The seven sonnets may be the 'Hymns' which Donne sent to Magdalen Herbert (see above, p. 317).

Sonnet 1.
   1.   *this crown*: the seven sonnets (see headnote).
   2.   *low*: 'lone' (acc. to 1635–69 and some MSS).
   4.   *Antient of dayes*: the designation of God in Daniel 7.9.
   5.   *bayes*: laurel leaves, the traditional garland of poetic or military glory (§166).

The ends crowne our workes, but thou crown'st our ends,
For, at our end begins our endlesse rest,   10
The first last end, now zealously possest,
With a strong sober thirst, my soule attends.
'Tis time that heart and voice be lifted high,
Salvation to all that will is nigh.

Annunciation

2. *Salvation to all that will is nigh,*
That All, which alwayes is All every where,
Which cannot sinne, and yet all sinnes must beare,
Which cannot die, yet cannot chuse but die,
Loe, faithfull Virgin, yeelds himselfe to lye   5
In prison, in thy wombe; and though he there
Can take no sinne, nor thou give, yet he'will weare
Taken from thence, flesh, which deaths force may trie.
Ere by the spheares time was created, thou
Wast in his minde, who is thy Sonne, and Brother,   10
Whom thou conceiv'st, conceiv'd; yea thou art now
Thy Makers maker, and thy Fathers mother,
Thou'hast light in darke; and shutst in little roome,
Immensity cloysterd in thy deare wombe.

Sonnet 1.
11. *first last*: cf. 'I am . . . the first and the last' (Revelation 1.11).
    zealously: 'soberly' (acc. to a few MSS).
12. *attends*: awaits.

Sonnet 2.
2–4. The lines are repeated from *Metempsycosis*, above, p. 408, ll. 74–76.
2. *All*: Christ, often designated Pan (literally 'all').
7 (also 13). On the symbol ', see above, p. 5.
8. *trie*: put to the test.
9. *created*: 'begotten' (acc. to some MSS). Time was often thought to have
   been created before the celestial spheres.
13. *light*: God who is light.

NATIVITIE.

3.   *Immensitie cloysterd in thy deare wombe,*
    Now leaves his welbelov'd imprisonment,
    There he hath made himselfe to his intent
    Weake enough, now into our world to come;
    But Oh, for thee, for him, hath th' Inne no roome?   5
    Yet lay him in this stall, and from the Orient,
    Starres, and wisemen will travell to prevent
    Th'effect of *Herods* jealous generall doome;
    Seest thou, my Soule, with thy faiths eyes, how he
    Which fils all place, yet none holds him, doth lye?   10
    Was not his pity towards thee wondrous high,
    That would have need to be pittied by thee?
    Kisse him, and with him into Egypt goe,
    With his kinde mother, who partakes thy woe.

TEMPLE.

4.   *With his kinde mother who partakes thy woe,*
    Joseph turne backe; see where your child doth sit,
    Blowing, yea blowing out those sparks of wit,
    Which himselfe on the Doctors did bestow;
    The Word but lately could not speake, and loe   5
    It sodenly speakes wonders, whence comes it,
    That all which was, and all which should be writ,
    A shallow seeming child, should deeply know?

Sonnet 3.
  5. *th' Inne*: at which Mary and Joseph vainly tried to lodge (Luke 2.7).
  7. *prevent*: anticipate, precede.
  8. The line alludes to the Massacre of the Innocents (Matthew 2.16).
     jealous: 'dire and' (acc. to some MSS) or 'zealous' (ditto).
 13. The flight *into Egypt* is related in Matthew 2.13–15.

Sonnet 4.
  4. *Doctors*: the learned men with whom the boy Jesus conversed in the temple (Luke 2.42 ff.). The episode was usually interpreted as the first display of Christ's powers as both man and God (§652).
  5. *The Word*: the designation of the Son of God in John 1.1–14.

His Godhead was not soule to his manhood,
Nor had time mellowed him to this ripenesse,   10
But as for one which hath a long taske, 'tis good,
With the Sunne to beginne his businesse,
He in his ages morning thus began
By miracles exceeding power of man.

CRUCIFYING.

5. *By miracles exceeding power of man*,
    Hee faith in some, envie in some begat,
    For, what weake spirits admire, ambitious, hate;
    In both affections many to him ran,
    But Oh! the worst are most, they will and can,
    Alas, and do, unto the immaculate,   5
    Whose creature Fate is, now prescribe a Fate,
    Measuring selfe-lifes infinity to'a span,
    Nay to an inch. Loe, where condemned hee
    Beares his owne crosse, with paine, yet by and by   10
    When it beares him, he must beare more and die;
    Now thou art lifted up, draw mee to thee,
    And at thy death giving such liberall dole,
    Moyst, with one drop of thy blood, my dry soule.

RESURRECTION.

6. *Moyst with one drop of thy blood, my dry soule*,
    Shall (though she now be in extreme degree
    Too stony hard, and yet too fleshly,) bee
    Freed by that drop, from being starv'd, hard, or foule

Sonnet 5.
  2. On the symbol ', see above, p. 5.
  3. *weake*: 'meeke' (acc. to several MSS).
      weake spirits: cf. 'Blessed are the poor in spirit: for theirs is the kingdom of
      heaven' (Matthew 5.3).
  5. *the immaculate*: the sinless Christ (see below, p. 467, note on 249).
  8. *selfe-lifes*: Christ's; cf. below, p. 455, l. 17 (§655).
  13. *dole*: sustenance; also, pain (§166).

Sonnet 6.
  4. *starv'd*: withered.

And life, by this death abled, shall controule   5
Death, whom thy death slue; nor shall to mee
Feare of first or last death, bring miserie,
If in thy little booke my name thou enroule,
Flesh in that long sleep is not putrified,
But made that there, of which, and for which 'twas; 10
Nor can by other meanes be glorified.
May then sinnes sleep, and deaths soone from me passe,
That wak't from both, I againe risen may
Salute the last, and everlasting day.

ASCENSION.

7.   *Salute the last and everlasting day*,
     Joy at the uprising of this Sunne, and Sonne,
     Yee whose just teares, or tribulation
     Have purely washt, or burnt your drossie clay;
     Behold the Highest, parting hence away,   5
     Lightens the darke clouds, which hee treads upon,
     Nor doth hee by ascending, show alone,
     But first hee, and hee first enters the way.
     O strong Ramme, which hast batter'd heaven for mee,
     Mild lambe, which with thy blood, hast mark'd the path;

Sonnet 6.
   5.   *abled*: enabled, empowered.
   6.   *slue*: slew.
       shall: 'shall now' (acc. to several MSS).
   8.   *little*: 'life' (acc. to 1635–69 and some MSS).
   9.   *long*: 'last long' (acc. to some MSS).
  11.   *glorified*: 'purified' (acc. to a few MSS).

Sonnet 7.
   2.   *Sunne, Sonne*: the pun, widely used, predates the seventeenth century.
       See, for example, John Lydgate's elaborate analogy in his *Lyf of our Lady*,
       notably ll. 479–85; and for subsequent elaborations: Herbert's *Sunday*
       and Vaughan's *Son-days*.
   3.   *just*: 'true' (acc. to 1635–69 and some MSS).
  7–8.   The Son of God returns to Heaven leading the saved.

Bright torch, which shin'st, that I the way may see,
Oh, with thy owne blood quench thy owne just wrath,
And if thy holy Spirit, my Muse did raise,
Deigne at my hands this crown of prayer and praise.

Holy Sonnets
[*Divine Meditations*]

I

Thou hast made me, And shall thy worke decay?
Repaire me now, for now mine end doth haste,
I runne to death, and death meets me as fast,
And all my pleasures are like yesterday,
I dare not move my dimme eyes any way,   5
Despaire behind, and death before doth cast
Such terrour, and my feeble flesh doth waste
By sinne in it, which it t'wards hell doth weigh;
Onely thou art above, and when towards thee
By thy leave I can looke, I rise againe   10
But our old subtle foe so tempteth me,
That not one houre my selfe I can sustaine,
Thy Grace may wing me to prevent his art,
And thou like Adamant draw mine iron heart.

Sonnet 7.
11. *the way*: 'thy ways' (acc. to some MSS).
13. *raise*: exalt, celebrate.

Holy Sonnets: the title given by all early editions and most MSS. *Divine Meditations*: the additional title given by some MSS. On the symbol' used here, see above, p. 5.

Sonnet I. First printed, and placed 1st, in 1635.
5.   *dimme eyes*: a pun on 'demise' in the legal sense of transfer of an estate at the time of one's death (§656).
7.   *feeble*: 'feebled' (acc. to several MSS).
8.   *weigh*: carry; also, incline.
11. *foe*: Satan.
13. *prevent*: forestall, frustrate.
14. *Adamant*: the magnetic loadstone.
     draw: cf. the commonplace notion that love has 'an Adamantime power that is able to draw the hardest heart' (§107).

II

As due by many titles I resigne
My selfe to thee, O God, first I was made
By thee, and for thee, and when I was decay'd
Thy blood bought that, the which before was thine,
I am thy sonne, made with thy selfe to shine,   5
Thy servant, whose paines thou hast still repaid,
Thy sheepe, thine Image, and till I betray'd
My selfe, a temple of thy Spirit divine;
Why doth the devill then usurpe on mee?
Why doth he steale nay ravish that's thy right?   10
Except thou rise and for thine owne worke fight,
Oh I shall soone despaire, when I doe see
That thou lov'st mankind well, yet wilt'not chuse me,
And Satan hates mee, yet is loth to lose mee.

III

O might those sighes and teares returne againe
Into my breast and eyes, which I have spent,
That I might in this holy discontent
Mourne with some fruit, as I have mourn'd in vaine;
In mine Idolatry what showres of raine   5
Mine eyes did waste? what griefs my heart did rent?

Sonnet II. Placed 1st in 1633, 2nd in 1635.
  2. *titles*: legal rights.
  2. *God, first*: 'God. First' (acc. to 1635–69).
  3. *decay'd*: fell in the Fall of Adam.
  4. *bought*: redeemed.
  5. *sonne*: the usual pun on Son/sun; see above, p. 434, note on 7:2.
  6. *still*: always.
 10. *that's*: 'what's' (acc. to some MSS).
 12. *doe*: 'shall' (acc. to 1635–69 and a few MSS).

Sonnet III. First printed in 1635.
  5. *Idolatry*: profane love.
  6. *did rent*: tore asunder.

That sufferance was my sinne I now repent,
'Cause I did suffer I must suffer paine.
Th'hydroptique drunkard, and night-scouting thiefe,
The itchy Lecher, and selfe tickling proud   10
Have the remembrance of past joyes, for reliefe
Of comming ills. To (poore) me is allow'd
No ease; for, long, yet vehement griefe hath beene
Th'effect and cause, the punishment and sinne.

IV

Oh my black Soule! now thou art summoned
By sicknesse, deaths herald, and champion;
Thou art like a pilgrim, which abroad hath done
Treason, and durst not turne to whence hee is fled,
Or like a thief, which till deaths doome be read,   5
Wisheth himselfe delivered from prison;
But damn'd and hal'd to execution,
Wisheth that still he might be imprisoned;
Yet grace, if thou repent, thou canst not lacke;
But who shall give thee that grace to beginne?   10
Oh make thy selfe with holy mourning blacke,
And red with blushing, as thou art with sinne;
Or wash thee in Christs blood, which hath this might
That being red, it dyes red soules to white.

Sonnet III.
  7.   *sufferance*: suffering; also, tolerance (of *Idolatry*).
       sinne I now repent: 'sinne, now I repent;' (acc. to some MSS and all
       modern editors; but see §188).
  9.   *hydroptique*: see above, p. 90, note on 6.
       night-scouting: night-prowling.
  10. *proud*: proud man.

Sonnet IV. Placed 2nd in 1633, 4th in 1635.
  4.   *turne*: return.
  5.   *doome*: sentence.
       read: cf. 'red' (below).
  7.   *damn'd*: condemned.

V

I am a little world made cunningly
Of Elements, and an Angelike spright,
But black sinne hath betraid to endless night
My worlds both parts, and (oh) both parts must die.
You which beyond that heaven which was most high   5
Have found new sphears, and of new lands can write,
Powre new seas in mine eyes, that so I might
Drowne my world with my weeping earnestly,
Or wash it if it must be drown'd no more:
But oh it must be burnt; alas the fire   10
Of lust and envie have burnt it heretofore,
And made it fouler; Let their flames retire,
And burne me ô Lord, with a fiery zeale
Of thee and thy house, which doth in eating heale.

VI

This is my playes last scene, here heavens appoint
My pilgrimages last mile; and my race
Idly, yet quickly runne, hath this last pace,
My spans last inch, my minutes latest point,

Sonnet V. First printed in 1635.
1. *little world*: man was habitually said to be the microcosm or 'abridgment' of the universe (cf. above, p. 389, l. 110).
2. *Elements*: the traditional four (earth, water, air, fire).
    spright: spirit.
4. *both parts*: the soul (*spright*) and the elemental body.
    must die: a potentially dangerous notion, since the soul is immortal (see next sonnet, note on 7).
6. *new sphears, new lands*: the celestial regions observed telescopically by Galileo, but perhaps the suspected plurality of worlds too (§209); cf. above, p. 80, note on 23.
9. *drown'd no more*: as God promised Noah after the Flood, that 'neither shall there any more be a flood to destroy the earth' (Genesis 9.11).
10. *burnt*: by history's terminal fire (see below, p. 438, note on VII:5).
13–14. Cf. 'the zeal of thine house hath eaten me up' (Psalm 69.9).

Sonnet VI. Placed 3rd in 1633, 6th in 1635.
3. *Idly*: both lazily and foolishly (§657).
4. *spans*: life–span's.
    latest: 'last' (acc. to some MSS).

And gluttonous death, will instantly unjoynt   5
My body, and soule, and I shall sleepe a space,
But my'ever-waking part shall see that face,
Whose feare already shakes my every joynt:
Then, as my soule, to'heaven her first seate, takes flight,
And earth borne body, in the earth shall dwell,   10
So, fall my sinnes, that all may have their right,
To where they'are bred, and would presse me, to hell.
Impute me righteous, thus purg'd of evill,
For thus I leave the world, the flesh, the devill.

VII

At the round earths imagin'd corners, blow
Your trumpets, Angells, and arise, arise
From death, you numberlesse infinities
Of soules, and to your scattred bodies goe,
All whom the flood did, and fire shall o'erthrow,   5
All whom warre, dearth, age, agues, tyrannies,

Sonnet VI.
  6. *soule* (acc. to 1635–69 and most MSS): 'and soule' (acc. to 1633).
  7. *ever-waking part*: the immortal soul.
      that face: God's – or, on the contrary, Satan's (§675). The line also reads
      'Or presently, I know not, see that Face' (acc. to several MSS).
  8. *Whose feare*: the fear of whom.
 13. *Impute me righteous*: as Milton would later explain, '[Adam's] crime makes
      guilty all his sons, [Christ's] merit / Imputed shall absolve them who
      renounce / Their . . . deeds' (*Paradise Lost*, III, 290 ff.).
 14. *the devill*: 'and devill' (acc. to several MSS).

Sonnet VII. Placed 4th in 1633, 7th in 1635. See the discussion above, p. 32.
  1. Concerned as the poem is with the Last Judgement, echoes from the
      Book of Revelation are necessarily numerous, e.g.: 'I saw four angels
      standing on the four *corners* of the earth' (7.1).
  4. *scattred bodies*: at the Last Judgement the souls are to rejoin their resur-
      rected bodies wherever these may have been previously scattered; cf.
      above, p. 154, note on 41.
  5. *fire*: the universal conflagration at the end of history (2 Peter 3.10).
  6. *dearth* (acc. to a single MS): 'death' (acc. to 1633–69 and most MSS).
      agues: malarial fevers.

Despaire, law, chance, hath slaine, and you whose eyes,
Shall behold God, and never tast deaths woe,
But let them sleepe, Lord, and mee mourne a space,
For, if above all these, my sinnes abound,   10
'Tis late to aske abundance of thy grace,
When wee are there; here on this lowly ground,
Teach mee how to repent; for that's as good
As if thou'hadst seal'd my pardon, with thy blood.

VIII

If faithfull soules be alike glorifi'd
As Angels, then my fathers soul doth see,
And adds this even to full felicitie,
That valiantly I hels wide mouth o'rstride:
But if our mindes to these soules be descry'd   5
By circumstances, and by signes that be
Apparent in us not immediately,
How shall my mindes white truth by them be try'd?
They see idolatrous lovers weepe and mourne,
And vile blasphemous Conjurers to call   10
On Jesus name, and Pharisaicall
Dissemblers feigne devotion. Then turne
O pensive soule, to God, for he knowes best
Thy griefe, for he put it into my breast.

Sonnet VII.
  8. Cf. 'some . . . shall not taste of death, till they see the kingdom of God'
       (Luke 9.27).
  14. *seal'd*: the precise theological term attesting confirmation, witness the
       usual definition of a sacrament as 'a seale of saving graces' (§107).

Sonnet VIII. First printed in 1635.
  5–7. See above, p. 388, note on 87.
  5. *descry'd*: known.
  9. *idolatrous*: profane; self-regarding.
  10. *vile* (acc. to some MSS): 'vilde' (ditto) or, oddly enough, 'stile' (acc. to
       1635–69).
       Conjurers: magicians.
  14. *griefe*: pain, suffering. Cf. God's withholding of 'rest' in Herbert's *The
       Pulley*.

IX

If poysonous mineralls, and if that tree,
Whose fruit threw death on else immortall us
If lecherous goats, if serpents envious
Cannot be damn'd; Alas; why should I bee
Why should intent or reason, borne in mee,   5
Make sinnes, else equall, in mee more heinous
And mercy being easie, and glorious
To God, in his sterne wrath, why threatens hee?
But who am I, that dare dispute with thee?
O God, Oh! of thine onely worthy blood,   10
And my teares, make a heavenly Lethean flood
And drowne in it my sinnes blacke memorie;
That thou remember them, some claime as debt,
I thinke it mercy, if thou wilt forget.

X

Death be not proud, though some have called thee
Mighty and dreadfull, for, thou are not soe,
For, those, whom thou think'st, thou dost overthrow,
Die not, poore death, nor yet canst thou kill mee;
From rest and sleepe, which but thy pictures bee,   5
Much pleasure, then from thee, much more must flow,
And soonest our best men with thee doe goe,
Rest of their bones, and soules deliverie.

Sonnet IX. Sonnets IX through XVI were printed in the same sequence in both the 1633 and the 1635 editions.
 1–2. *that tree* etc.: cf. the opening lines of *Paradise Lost*; but there is no evidence that Milton 'must have known' Donne's sonnet (§263).
 10. *onely*: alone.
 11. *Lethean*: forgetful (from Lethe: as above, p. 292, note on 6).
 13. *them*: the speaker's own sins; *some*: those who maintain this view (§667).
  some claime: 'no more' (acc. to a few MSS).
  debt: the debt generally discharged by Christ.
 14. Cf. 'I will forgive their iniquity, and I will remember their sin no more' (Jeremiah 31.34).

Sonnet X.
 8. *bones*: 'bodyes' (acc. to some MSS).
  deliverie: deliverance, liberation.

Thou art slave to Fate, chance, kings, and desperate men,
And dost with poyson, warre, and sicknesse dwell,   10
And poppie, or charmes can make us sleepe as well,
And better then thy stroake; why swell'st thou then?
One short sleepe past, wee wake eternally,
And death shall be no more, death, thou shalt die.

XI

Spit in my face you Jewes, and pierce my side,
Buffet, and scoffe, scourge, and crucifie mee,
For I have sinn'd, and sinn'd, and onely hee,
Who could do no iniquitie, hath dyed:
But by my death can not be satisfied   5
My sinnes, which passe the Jewes impiety:
They kill'd once an inglorious man, but I
Crucifie him daily, being now glorified;
Oh let mee then, his strange love still admire:
Kings pardon, but he bore our punishment.   10
And *Jacob* came cloth'd in vile harsh attire
But to supplant, and with gainfull intent:
God cloth'd himselfe in vile mans flesh, that so
Hee might be weake enough to suffer woe.

Sonnet X.
10. *dost* (acc. to some MSS): 'doth' (acc. to 1633).
12. *better*: 'easier' (acc. to some MSS).
    then thy: than thy.
    swell'st: are puft up with pride.
13. *wake*: 'live' (acc. to some MSS).
14. Cf. 'The last enemy that shall be destroyed is death' (1 Corinthians 15.26).

Sonnet XI.
  3. *onely*: 'humbly' (acc. to a MS).
  5. *satisfied*: atoned for.
  6. *impiety*: 'iniquitye' (acc. to some MSS).
  7. *inglorious*: devoid of glory; obscure, humble.
  9. *admire*: marvel at; gaze with pleasure.
11–12. Jacob dressed up in animal skins in order to deceive his father Isaac and receive the blessing intended for Esau (Genesis 27.6 ff.).

XII

Why are wee by all creatures waited on?
Why doe the prodigall elements supply
Life and food to mee, being more pure then I,
Simple, and further from corruption?
Why brook'st thou, ignorant horse, subjection?   5
Why dost thou bull, and bore so seelily
Dissemble weaknesse, and by'one mans stroke die,
Whose whole kinde, you might swallow and feed upon?
Weaker I am, woe is mee, and worse then you,
You have not sinn'd, nor need be timorous,   10
But wonder at a greater wonder, for to us
Created nature doth these things subdue,
But their Creator, whom sin, nor nature tyed,
For us, his Creatures, and his foes, hath dyed.

XIII

What if this present were the worlds last night?
Marke in my heart, O Soule, where thou dost dwell,
The picture of Christ crucified, and tell
Whether his countenance can thee affright,
Teares in his eyes quench the amasing light,   5
Blood fills his frownes, which from his pierc'd head fell

Sonnet XII.
1.   *are wee*: 'am I' (acc. to a MS).
2.   *prodigall*: wasteful.
3 (also 9).   *then*: than.
4.   *Simple*: 'Simpler' (acc. to 1635–69 and several MSS).
6.   *bore*: boar.
     seelily: naïvely.
7.   *Dissemble*: feign.
9.   *Weaker I am*: 'Alas I'am weaker' (acc. to a MS).
10.   *timorous*: fearful.
11.   *greater number*: 'greater' (acc. to 1635–69).
13.   *tyed*: constricted.

Sonnet XIII.
1.   *last night*: i.e. the end of history at the Last Judgement.
2.   *Marke*: 'Looke' (acc. to a MS).
4.   *his*: 'that' (acc. to many MSS and all modern editors).
5.   *amasing*: terrifying.

And can that tongue adjudge thee unto hell,
Which pray'd forgivenesse for his foes fierce spight?
No, no; but as in my idolatrie
I said to all my profane mistresses,   10
Beauty, of pitty, foulnesse onely is
A signe of rigour: so I say to thee,
To wicked spirits are horrid shapes assign'd,
This beauteous forme assumes a pitious minde.

XIV

Batter my heart, three person'd God; for, you
As yet but knocke, breathe, shine, and seeke to mend;
That I may rise, and stand, o'erthrow mee,'and bend
Your force, to breake, blowe, burn and make me new.
I, like an usurpt towne, to'another due,   5
Labour to'admit you, but Oh, to no end,
Reason your viceroy in mee, mee should defend,
But is captiv'd, and proves weake or untrue,
Yet dearely'I love you,'and would be lov'd faine,
But am betroth'd unto your enemie,   10
Divorce mee,'untie, or breake that knot againe,
Take mee to you, imprison mee, for I
Except you'enthrall mee, never shall be free,
Nor ever chast, except you ravish mee.

Sonnet XIII.
8. *fierce*: 'ranck' (acc. to a MS).
   spight: spite, malice.
9. *idolatrie*: as above, p. 435, note on III:5.
11–12. Beauty is a sign of pity; ugliness, only a sign of strictness.
14. *assumes*: 'assures' (acc. to the MSS and all modern editors; but see §188).

Sonnet XIV. Man's relations with God have been set forth in terms of marriage
    or adultery ever since the great Hebrew prophets, beginning with Hosea.
    It was within such a context that Donne described adultery as 'every
    departing from that contract you made with God at your Baptisme'
    (*Sermons*, IX, 399; in §669).
1. *three person'd God*: the tripersonal Godhead of the Father, Son, and Holy
   Spirit.
9. *faine*: gladly.
13. *Except*: unless.
    enthrall: reduce to slavery; also, enchant.
14. *ravish*: violate; also, take away or remove spatially (§679); also, over-
    whelm with astonishment.

XV

Wilt thou love God, as he thee! then digest,
My Soule, this wholsome meditation,
How God the Spirit, by Angels waited on
In heaven, doth make his Temple in thy brest,
The Father having begot a Sonne most blest,   5
And still begetting, (for he ne'r begonne)
Hath deign'd to chuse thee by adoption,
Coheire to'his glory,'and Sabbaths endless rest;
And as a robb'd man, which by search doth finde
His stolne stuffe sold, must lose or buy'it againe: 10
The Sonne of glory came downe, and was slaine,
Us whom he'had made, and Satan stolne, to unbinde.
'Twas much, that man was made like God before,
But, that God should be made like man, much more.

XVI

Father, part of his double interest
Unto thy kingdome, thy Sonne gives to mee,
His joynture in the knottie Trinitie,
Hee keepes, and gives to me his deaths conquest.
This Lambe, whose death, with life the world hath blest, 5
Was from the worlds beginning slaine, and he

Sonnet XV.
    4. Cf. 'know not that ye are the temple of God, and that the Spirit of God dwelleth in you?' (1 Corinthians 3.16).
    6. *ne'r begonne*: 'never begun' yet *still begetting* since God is outside time, not bound to past, present, or future; cf. below, p. 453, note on 37–38.
    8. *Sabbaths endlesse rest*: see above, p. 399, note on 50.
    11. *Sonne*: also in the sense of 'Sunne' (the actual reading of 1635–69; cf. above, p. 433, note on 7:2).
    12. *Satan stolne*: whom Satan had stolen.
    14. *much more*: the redemption of man was commonly regarded as a divine activity far superior to the creation of the world.

Sonnet XVI.
    1. *double interest*: twofold claim.
    3. *joynture*: joint possession (cf. above, p. 82, note on 12).
    knottie: difficult to explain; also, closely interwoven.
    4. *deaths conquest*: conquest of death.
    5–6. Cf. 'the Lamb slain from the foundation of the world' (Revelation 13.8).

Hath made two Wills, which with the Legacie
Of his and thy kingdome, doe thy Sonnes invest,
Yet such are these laws, that men argue yet
Whether a man those statutes can fulfill;   10
None doth, but thy all-healing grace and spirit
Revive againe what law and letter kill.
Thy lawes abridgement, and thy last command
Is all but love; Oh let this last Will stand!

[XVII]

Since she whom I lov'd hath payd her last debt
To Nature, and to hers, and my good is dead,
And her Soule early into heaven ravished,
Wholly on heavenly things my mind is sett.
Here the admyring her my mind did whett   5
To seeke thee God; so streames do shew their head;
But thou I have found thee, and thou my thirst hast fed,
A holy thirsty dropsy melts mee yett.
But why should I begg more Love, when as thou
Dost wooe my soule for hers; offring all thine: 10

Sonnet XVI.
7. *two Wills*: the Old and New Testaments.
8. *invest*: grant the rights to.
9. *these*: 'those' or 'thy' (acc. to various MSS; see §188).
11. *thy*: omitted by a few MSS and some editors (§§ 158, 168; but see §188).
12. Cf. 'the letter killeth, but the spirit giveth life' (2 Corinthians 3.6).
    againe: 'and quicken' (acc. to some MSS).
    all but: nothing but.
    love: cf. 'A new commandment I give unto you, That ye love one
    another' (John 13.34).
14. *this*: 'that' or 'thy' (acc. to various MSS).

Sonnet XVII. The last three of the *Holy Sonnets* were initially printed by Gosse
    in 1899 from the Westmoreland MS (see below, p. 522); the numbering
    is conjectural.
1. Donne's wife Ann had died on 15 August 1617 at the age of thirty-three.
2. *hers*: her own nature as mortal.
6. *head*: source.
8. *dropsy*: immoderate thirst.

And dost not only feare least I allow
My Love to Saints and Angels things divine,
But in thy tender jealosy dost doubt
Least the World, Fleshe, yea Devill putt thee out.

[XVIII]

Show me deare Christ, thy Spouse, so bright and clear.
What! is it she, which on the other shore
Goes richly painted? or which rob'd and tore
Laments and mournes in Germany and here?
Sleepes she a thousand, then peepes up one yeare?   5
Is she selfe truth and errs? now new, now outwore?
Doth she, and did she, and shall she evermore
On one, on seaven, or on no hill appeare?
Dwells she with us, or like adventuring knights
First travaile we to seeke and then make Love?   10
Betray kind husband thy spouse to our sights,
And let myne amorous soule court thy mild Dove,
Who is most trew, and pleasing to thee, then
When she'is embrac'd and open to most men.

Sonnet XVII.
11 (also 14). *least*: lest.
13.   *jealosy*: zealousness.
        doubt: fear.

Sonnet XVIII. Cf. the search for the 'true religion' in *Satyre III*, ll. 43 ff.
(above, p. 226).
  1.   *Spouse*: the true Church, loyal to her 'bridegroom' Christ (Matthew
        25.1 ff.).
  2.   *the other shore*: Continental Europe.
  3.   *richly painted*: the Catholic Church.
  4.   Alluding to the Protestant Church inclusive of Lutheranism and Angli-
        canism.
  6.   *selfe truth*: truth itself.
  8.   The *one* hill alludes to Mount Moriah on which Solomon built his
        temple; *seaven* hills, to Catholic Rome; *no* hill, to Calvinist Geneva.
 10.   *travaile*: travel; also, labour.
 11.   *Betray*: disclose.
 14.   *open to most men*: possibly the boldest erotic image in Donne's sacred
        poetry.

[XIX]

Oh, to vex me, contraryes meet in one:
Inconstancy unnaturally hath begott
A constant habit; that when I would not
I change in vowes, and in devotione.
As humorous is my contritione   5
As my prophane Love, and as soone forgott:
As ridlingly distemperd, cold and hott,
As praying, as mute; as infinite, as none.
I durst not view heaven yesterday; and to day
In prayers, and flattering speaches I court God: 10
To morrow I quake with true feare of his rod.
So my devout fitts come and go away
Like a fantastique Ague: save that here
Those are my best dayes, when I shake with feare.

Sonnet XIX.
  5. *humorous*: appertaining to one's 'humours' or disposition (see above,
      p. 336, note on 241); mercurial, changeable (§207).
 13. *Ague*: fever attended by paroxysms.

The Crosse.

Since Christ embrac'd the Crosse it selfe, dare I
His image, th'image of his Crosse deny?
Would I have profit by the sacrifice,
And dare the chosen Altar to despise?
It bore all other sinnes, but is it fit   5
That it should beare the sinne of scorning it?
Who from the picture would avert his eye,
How would he flye his paines, who there did dye?
From mee, no Pulpit, nor misgrounded law,
Nor scandall taken, shall this Crosse withdraw,   10
It shall not, for it cannot; for, the losse
Of this Crosse, were to mee another Crosse.
Better were worse, for, no affliction,
No Crosse is so extreme, as to have none;
Who can blot out the Crosse, which th'instrument   15
Of God, dew'd on mee in the Sacrament?
Who can deny mee power, and liberty
To stretch mine armes, and mine owne Crosse to be?
Swimme, and at every stroake, thou art thy Crosse,
The Mast and yard make one, where seas do tosse.   20
Looke downe, thou spiest out Crosses in small things;
Looke up, thou seest birds rais'd on crossed wings;
All the Globes frame, and spheares, is nothing else
But the Meridians crossing Parallels.
Materiall Crosses then, good physicke bee,   25
But yet spirituall have chiefe dignity.

The Crosse. Not a meditation on the Passion, the poem is like many other
    emblem poems 'an analysis and didactic interpretation of an abstract
    symbolic figure' (§73).
  9–10. The reference is to the Puritans' refusal to use the Cross for devotional
    purposes.
16. *dew'd*: poured, bestowed.
20. *yard*: a spar slung from a mast and serving to support a sail.
23. *spheares*: see above, p. 80, note on 23.
25. *physicke*: medicine.
26. *But*: 'And' (acc. to some MSS).

These for extracted chimique medicine serve,
And cure much better, and as well preserve;
Then are you your own physicke, or need none,
When Still'd, or purg'd by tribulation.   30
For when that Crosse ungrudg'd, unto you stickes,
Then are you to your selfe, a Crucifixe.
As perchance, Carvers do not faces make:
But that away, which hid them there, do take.
Let Crosses, soe, take what hid Christ in thee,   35
And be his image, or not his, but hee.
But, as oft Alchimists doe coyners prove,
So may a selfe-dispising, get selfe-love.
And then as worst surfets, of best meates bee,
Soe is pride, issued from humility,   40
For, 'tis no child, but monster; therefore Crosse
Your joy in crosses, else, 'tis double losse,
And crosse thy senses, else, both they, and thou
Must perish soone, and to destruction bowe.
For if the'eye seeke good objects, and will take 45
No crosse from bad, wee cannot scape a snake.
So with harsh, hard, sowre, stinking, crosse the rest,
Make them indifferent; call nothing best.
But most the eye needs crossing, that can rome,
And move; To th'other th'objects must come home.   50
And crosse thy heart: for that in man alone
Pants downewards, and hath palpitation.

27. *extracted*: as in Paracelsian medicine, which sought to purge diseases through antagonistic remedies.
30. *Still'd*: distilled.
31. *ungrudg'd*: uncomplained of, welcomed (§166).
37. *coyners*: forgers of coins; alchemists were often said to prey on gullible people (§218).
41. *Crosse*: check, restrain.
44. *destruction*: 'corruption' (acc. to a MS).
45. *seeke*: 'see' (acc. to 1650–69). On the symbol ', see above, p. 5.
46. *a snake*: the satanic entrampment of mere appearances.
48. *indifferent; call*: 'indifferent; all,' (acc. to 1635–69).
50. *th'other th'objects*: 'th'others objects' (acc. to 1635–69).
52. *Pants*: 'Points' (acc. to several MSS and all modern editors; but see §188).

Crosse those dejections, when it downeward tends,
And when it to forbidden heights pretends.
And as the braine through bony walls doth vent   55
By sutures, which a Crosses forme present,
So when they braine workes, ere thou utter it,
Crosse and correct concupiscence of witt.
Be covetous of Crosses, let none fall.
Crosse no man else, but crosse thy selfe in all.   60
Then doth the Crosse of Christ worke faithfully
Within our hearts, when wee love harmlessly
The Crosses pictures much, and with more care
That Crosses children, which our Crosses are.

53. *dejections*: 'defections' (acc. to a MS) or 'detorsions', i.e. distortions (acc.
     to 1635–69).
     it: the heart.
56. *sutures*: seams (lines of union) between the bones of the skull (§163).
59. *fall*: evade you.
61. *faithfully* (acc. to 1633–69): 'fruitfully' (acc. to most MSS and all modern
     editors; but see §188).
63. *The*: 'That' (ditto).
     pictures: representations.

Resurrection, imperfect.

Sleep sleep old Sun, thou canst not have repast
As yet, the wound thou took'st on friday last;
Sleepe then, and rest; The world may beare thy stay,
A better Sun rose before thee to day,
Who, not content to'enlighten all that dwell   5
On the earths face, as thou, enlightned hell,
And made the darke fires languish in that vale,
As, at thy presence here, our fires grow pale.
Whose body having walk'd on earth, and now
Hasting to Heaven, would, that he might allow   10
Himselfe unto all stations, and fill all,
For these three daies become a minerall;
Hee was all gold when he lay downe, but rose
All tincture, and doth not alone dispose
Leaden and iron wills to good, but is   15
Of power to make even sinfull flesh like his.
Had one of those, whose credulous pietie
Thought, that a Soule one might discerne and see
Goe from a body,'at this sepulcher been,
And, issuing from the sheet, this body seen,   20
He would have justly thought this body a soule,
If, not of any man, yet of the whole.
                Desunt cætera.

Resurrection: 'imperfect' in that the poem is unfinished.
1. *repast*: recovered from.
2. Alluding to the eclipse during the Crucifixion (Matthew 27.45).
4. *Sun*: see above, p. 433, note on 7:2.
5 (also 19). On the symbol ', see above, p. 5.
6. *enlightned hell*: like Hell in ferocious fires, but unlike it in possessing light.
9–16. The alchemical image involves the transmutation or purification that
      follows death or reduction to the original elements (§218).
11. *all stations*: human experience generally; cf. the traditional Stations of the
      Cross.
12. *minerall*: earthly.
14. *tincture*: see above, p. 200, note on 66.
22. *of the whole*: i.e. the soul of the entire created order.
      Desunt cætera: 'the rest is lacking'.

The Annuntiation and Passion.

Tamely, fraile body,'abstaine to day; to day
My soule eates twice, Christ hither and away.
She sees him man, so like God made in this,
That of them both a circle embleme is,
Whose first and last concurre; this doubtfull day   5
Of feast or fast, Christ came, and went away;
Shee sees him nothing twice at once, who'is all;
Shee sees a Cedar plant it selfe, and fall,
Her Maker put to making, and the head
Of life, at once, not yet alive, yet dead;   10
She sees at once the virgin mother stay
Reclus'd at home, Publique at Golgotha.
Sad and rejoyc'd shee's seen at once, and seen
At almost fiftie, and at scarce fifteene.
At once a Sonne is promis'd her, and gone,   15
Gabriell gives Christ to her, He her to John;
Not fully a mother, Shee's in Orbitie,
At once receiver and the legacie;

The Annuntiation and Passion. The feast of the Annunciation, celebrated annu-
  ally on 25 March, coincided in 1608/9 with Good Friday.
 1 (also 7, 22, 27). For the symbol ', see above, p. 5.
 1. *Tamely*: submissively.
    body: 'flesh' (acc. to 1635–69 and several MSS).
 4. *circle*: symbolic of perfection.
 5. *first and last concurre*: see below, ll. 37–38.
 7. *nothing twice*: before his birth and after his death.
 8. *Cedar*: typifies the Godhead (§168).
 12. *Reclus'd*: secluded.
    Golgotha: the place of Crucifixion.
 14. The Virgin Mary was fifteen when Jesus was born, fifty when he was
    crucified.
 16. *He her to John*: as related in John 19.26.
 17. *Orbitie*: bereavement.

All this, and all betweene, this day hath showne,
Th'Abridgement of Christs story, which makes one   20
(As in plaine Maps, the furthest West is East)
Of the'Angels *Ave*,'and *Consummatum est*.
How well the Church, Gods Court of faculties
Deales, in some times, and seldome joyning these;
As by the selfe-fix'd Pole wee never doe   25
Direct our course, but the next starre thereto,
Which showes where the'other is, and which we say
(Because it strayes not farre) doth never stray;
So God by his Church, neerest to him, wee know
And stand firme, if wee by her motion goe;   30
His Spirit, as his fiery Pillar doth
Leade, and his Church, as cloud; to one end both:
This Church, by letting these daies joyne, hath shown
Death and conception in mankinde is one.
Or'twas in him the same humility,   35
That he would be a man, and leave to be:
Or as creation he hath made, as God,
With the last judgement, but one period,
His imitating Spouse would joyne in one
Manhoods extremes: He shall come, he is gone: 40

21. *plaine*: flat; see below, p. 488, note on 13–14.
22. *Ave*: 'Hail', Gabriel's first word to Mary announcing the Incarnation (Luke 1.28).
      Consummatum est: 'It is finished', Christ's last words on the Cross (John 19.30).
23. *Court of faculties*: the learned who administer the Church.
25. *the selfe-fix'd Pole*: the fixed North Pole itself.
26. *next starre*: the North Star, which guides sailors even though it is not the actual North Pole.
31–32. God appeared to the Israelites 'in a pillar of fire' and 'in a cloud' (Exodus 13.21 and 19.9).
33. *these* (acc. to most MSS): 'those' (acc. to 1633–69).
      daies: 'feastes' (acc. to 1635–69).
34. *is*: 'are' (ditto).
37–38. The creation and the Last Judgement, said Donne, 'are not a minute asunder in respect of eternity, which hath no minutes' (*Sermons*, VI, 331; §168).
39. *Spouse*: the Church.

Or as though one blood drop, which thence did fall,
Accepted, would have serv'd, he yet shed all;
So though the least of his paines, deeds, or words,
Would busie a life, she all this day affords;
This treasure then, in grosse, my Soule uplay   45
And in my life retaile it every day.

Goodfriday, 1613. Riding Westward.

Let mans Soule be a Spheare, and then, in this,
The intelligence that moves, devotion is,
And as the other Spheares, by being growne
Subject to forraigne motion, lose their owne,
And being by others hurried every day,   5
Scarce in a yeare their naturall forme obey:
Pleasure or businesse, so, our Soules admit
For their first mover, and are whirld by it.
Hence is't, that I am carryed towards the West
This day, when my Soules forme bends towards the East. 10

The Annunciation and Passion
44.   *busie*: 'buy' (acc. to a MS).
      she: 'he' (ditto).
45.   *grosse*: bulk.
      uplay: lay up, store.
46.   *my*: 'thy' (acc. to a MS).

Goodfriday, 1613. Also subtitled in some MSS 'Riding to Sir Edward Harbert
      family in Montgomery (see also above, headnotes on pp. 110 and 271).
      The ride toward the West is ultimately a ride toward the East: 'the
      furthest West is East', as Donne said in another poem (above, p. 453,
      l. 21; cf. p. 488, ll. 13–14: 'West and East / In all flatt Mapps . . . are
      one').
1–2. See above, p. 101, note on 52.
3–6. In Ptolemaic astronomy the lower celestial spheres 'lose their owne'
      eastward motion because, on a diurnal basis, they are affected by the
      'forraigne' motion of the higher spheres; but on an annual basis they
      regain their motion from west to east (§294).
4.   *motion*: 'motions' (acc. to most MSS; but see §188).
6.   *forme*: guiding principle; 'course' (acc. to a MS).

There I should see a Sunne, by rising set,
And by that setting endlesse day beget;
But that Christ on this Crosse, did rise and fall,
Sinne had eternally benighted all.
Yet dare I'almost be glad, I do not see   15
That spectacle of too much weight for mee.
Who sees Gods face, that is selfe life, must dye;
What a death were it then to see God dye?
It made his owne Lieutenant Nature shrinke,
It made his footstoole crack, and the Sunne winke.   20
Could I behold those hands which span the Poles,
And tune all spheares at once peirc'd with those holes?
Could I behold that endlesse height which is
Zenith to us, and our Antipodes,
Humbled below us? or that blood which is   25
The seat of all our Soules, if not of his,
Made durt of dust, or that flesh which was worne
By God, for his apparell, rag'd, and torne?
If on these things I durst not looke, durst I
Upon his miserable mother cast mine eye,   30

11. *Sunne*: also in the sense of 'Son' (cf. above, p. 433, note on 7:2).
13. *But that*: save that.
     this: 'his' (acc. to 1635–69).
15 (also 34). For the symbol ', see above, p. 5.
17. Cf. 'Thou canst not see my face: for there shall no man see me, and live' (Exodus 33.20).
     selfe life: cf. above, p. 432, note on V:8.
19–20. According to some of Donne's other metaphors, nature is 'Gods immediate commissioner', 'foreman', and 'Vicegerent' (§107: Ch. III). Her protest over the Crucifixion took the form of an earthquake and an eclipse (Matthew 27.45 and 51); cf. above, p. 451, l. 2.
20. *footstoole*: cf. 'Thus saith the Lord, The heaven is my throne, and the earth is my footstool' (Isaiah 66.1).
22. *tune*: 'turne' (acc. to many MSS and §§ 158, 625; but see §§ 159, 188).
24. The highest point to us as well as to the people who live on the other side of the globe (§166).
25. *Antipodes*: cf. above, p. 338, note on 294.
30. *Upon his miserable*: 'On his distressed' (acc. to 1635–69).

Who was Gods partner here, and furnish'd thus
Halfe of that Sacrifice, which ransom'd us?
Though these things, as I ride, be from mine eye,
They'are present yet unto my memory,
For that looks towards them; and thou look'st towards mee,
O Saviour, as thou hang'st upon the tree;
I turne my backe to thee, but to receive
Corrections, till thy mercies bid thee leave.
O thinke mee worth thine anger, punish mee,
Burne off my rusts, and my deformity,   40
Restore thine Image, so much, by thy grace,
That thou may'st know mee, and I'll turne my face.

The Litanie.

I.
The FATHER.

    Father of Heaven, and him, by whom
It, and us for it, and all else, for us
    Thou madest, and govern'st ever, come
And re-create mee, now growne ruinous:
        My heart is by dejection, clay,   5
        And by selfe-murder, red.
From this red earth, O Father, purge away
All vicious tinctures, that new fashioned
I may rise up from death, before I'm dead.

Goodfriday, 1613.
32.   *Halfe of that Sacrifice*: one of the most explicit statements of Mariolatry in
      Donne's poetry; cf. the next poem, note on 39.
      ransom'd: the precise theological term for 'redeemed'.
36.   *the tree*: the Cross.
38.   *Corrections*: correcting punishments (§166).
      leave: cease.
40.   *rusts*: 'rust' (acc. to 1635–69).

The Litanie. 'Since my imprisonment in my bed', Donne wrote to his friend
      Henry Goodyer in 1609 or 1610, 'I have made a meditation in verse
      which I call a Litany; the word you know imports no other then
      supplication' (§179: p. 32).
  7. *red earth*: the presumed meaning of 'Adam'.
  8. *vicious tinctures*: see above, p. 271, note on 20.

II.
The SONNE.

O Sonne of God, who seeing two things,   10
Sinne, and death crept in, which were never made,
   By bearing one, tryed'st with what stings
The other could thine heritage invade;
      O be thou nail'd unto my heart,
        And crucified againe,   15
Part not from it, though it from thee would part,
But let it be by applying so thy paine,
Drown'd in thy blood, and in thy passion slaine.

III.
The HOLY GHOST.

O Holy Ghost, whose temple I
Am, but of mudde walls, and condensed dust,   20
   And being sacrilegiously
Halfe wasted with youths fires, of pride and lust,
      Must with new stormes be weatherbeat;
        Double in my heart thy flame,
Which let devout sad teares intend; and let   25
(Though this glasse lanthorne, flesh, do suffer maime)
Fire, Sacrifice, Priest, Altar be the same.

IV.
The TRINITY.

O Blessed glorious Trinity,
Bones to Philosophy, but milke to faith,
   Which, as wise serpents, diversly   30
Most slipperinesse, yet most entanglings hath,

---

12. *tryed'st*: proved.
20. *mudde . . . dust*: see above, note on 7.
25. *intend*: intensify.
26. *glasse lanthorne*: 'darke lanterne' (acc. to a MS: §§ 619, 641).
29. *Bones to*: the foundation of – or, conversely, incomprehensible to.
30. *serpents*: proverbially emblematic of wisdom.

    As you distinguish'd undistinct
     By power, love, knowledge bee,
Give mee a such selfe different instinct
Of these let all mee elemented bee,   35
Of power, to love, to know, you unnumbred three.

V.
The Virgin MARY.

  For that faire blessed Mother-maid,
Whose flesh redeem'd us; That she-Cherubin,
  Which unlock'd Paradise, and made
One claime for innocence, and disseiz'd sinne,   40
      Whose wombe was a strange heav'n for there
      God cloath'd himselfe, and grew,
Our zealous thankes wee poure. As her deeds were
Our helpes, so are her prayers; nor can she sue
In vaine, who hath such title unto you.   45

VI.
The Angels.

  And since this life our nonage is,
And wee in Wardship to thine Angels be,
  Native in heavens faire Palaces,
Where we shall be but denizen'd by thee,
      As th'earth conceiving by the Sunne,   50
      Yeelds faire diversitie,
Yet never knowes which course that light doth run,

---

32. *undistinct*: not separable, hence *unnumbred* (36).
33. Attributes of the Father, the Son, and the Holy Spirit, respectively.
34. *a such*: 'such' (acc. to 1635–69).
35. *elemented*: composed.
39. *unlock'd Paradise*: in crediting Mary with a share in mankind's redemption, Donne ventures a theological position suspect to many Protestants (§207).
40. *disseiz'd*: dispossessed; 'diseased' (acc. to some MSS).
45. *titles*: just claims.
46. *nonage*: infancy.
49. *denizen'd*: naturalized.

So let mee study, that mine actions bee
Worthy their sight, though blinde in how they see.

VII.
The Patriarches.

And let thy Patriarches Desire   55
(Those great Grandfathers of thy Church, which saw
  More in the cloud, then wee in fire,
Whom Nature clear'd more, then us Grace and Law,
    And now in Heaven still pray, that wee
      May use our new helpes right,)   60
Be sanctified and fructifie in mee;
Let not my minde be blinder by more light
Nor Faith by Reason added, lose her sight.

VIII.
The Prophets.

Thy Eagle-sighted Prophets too,
Which were thy Churches Organs, and did sound   65
  That harmony, which made of two
One law, and did unite, but not confound;
    Those heavenly Poëts which did see
      Thy will, and it expresse
In rythmique feet, in common pray for mee,   70
That I by them excuse not my excesse
In seeking secrets, or Poëtiquenesse.

56. *great Grandfathers*: the Hebrew Patriarchs (Abraham, Isaac, *et al*.) fathered the Apostles who in turn fathered the early Christian theologians known as Church Fathers.
57. *cloud, fire*: God's appearance in both is attested often (cf. above, p. 453, note on 31–32).
    then (also 58): than.
58. *clear'd*: enlightened.
    grace and law: the dispensations under the New and Old Testaments respectively, merged into *One law* (67).
61. *sanctified*: 'satisfy'd' (acc. to 1635–69 and most MSS; but see §188).
63. *by*: 'to' (acc. to a MS: §641).
66. *two*: the Old and New Testaments.

IX.
The Apostles.

And thy illustrious Zodiacke
Of twelve Apostles, which ingirt this All,
   (From whom whosoever do not take   75
Their light, to darke deep pits, throw downe, and fall,)
       As through their prayers, thou'hast let mee know
       That their bookes are divine;
May they pray still, and be heard, that I goe
Th'old broad way in applying; O decline   80
Mee, when my comment would make thy word mine.

X.
The Martyrs.

And since thou so desirously
Did'st long to die, that long before thou could'st,
   And long since thou no more couldst dye,
Thou in thy scatter'd mystique body wouldst   85
       In Abel dye, and ever since
       In thine, let their blood come
To begge for us, a discreet patience
Of death, or of worse life: for Oh, to some
Not to be Martyrs, is a martyrdome.   90

XI.
The Confessors.

Therefore with thee triumpheth there
A Virgin Squadron of white Confessors,
   Whose bloods betroth'd, not marryed were;
Tender'd, not taken by those Ravishers:

74. *ingirt*: engirt, encompass, in that they journeyed far.
75. *whosoever*: 'whoever' (acc. to several MSS).
77. On the symbol ', here and throughout, see above, p. 5.
78. *bookes*: 'workes' (acc. to several MSS).
80. *decline*: humble.
85. *mystique body*: the Church.
86. *Abel*: the first martyr (Genesis 4.2–8) and hence a 'type' of Christ.
92. *white*: innocent.
     Confessors: confessors of the faith but not martyrs.
94. *Tender'd*: offered.

They know, and pray, that wee may know,   95
    In every Christian
Hourly tempestuous persecutions grow,
Tentations martyr us alive; A man
Is to himselfe a Dioclesian.

XII.
The Virgins.

The cold white snowie Nunnery,   100
Which, as thy mother, their high Abbesse, sent
    Their bodies backe againe to thee,
As thou hadst lent them, cleane and innocent,
        Though they have not obtain'd of thee,
            That or thy Church, or I,   105
Should keep, as they, our first integrity;
Divorce thou sinne in us, or bid it die,
And call chast widowhead Virginitie.

XIII.
The Doctors.

Thy sacred Academie above
Of Doctors, whose paines have unclasp'd, and taught   110
    Both bookes of life to us (for love
To know thy Scriptures tells us, we are wrought
        In thy other booke) pray for us there
            That what they have misdone
Or mis-said, wee to that may not adhere,   115
Their zeale may be our sinne. Lord let us runne
Meane waies, and call them stars, but not the Sunne.

98. *Tentations*: temptations.
99. The Roman emperor Diocletian persecuted Christians in A.D.
     303–305.
110. *Doctors*: the great theologians, notably Saints Gregory the Great,
     Ambrose, Augustine, and Jerome.
111. *Both bookes*: the Old and New Testaments, aligned with the *other booke*
     (113) which is God's register of the elect.
112. *wrought*: 'wrote' (acc. to 1635–69), i.e. written down in.
117. *Meane waies*: middle courses.

XIV.

And whil'st this universall Quire,
That Church in triumph, this in warfare here,
   Warm'd with one all-partaking fire   120
Of love, that none be lost, which cost thee deare,
     Prayes ceaslesly,'and thou hearken too
     (Since to be gratious
Our taske is treble, to pray, beare, and doe)
Heare this prayer Lord, O Lord deliver us   125
From trusting in those prayers, though powr'd out thus.

XV.

From being anxious, or secure,
Dead clods of sadnesse, or light squibs of mirth,
   From thinking, that great courts immure
All, or no happinesse, or that this earth   130
     Is only for our prison fram'd,
     Or that thou art covetous
To them thou lovest, or that they are maim'd
From reaching this worlds sweet, who seek thee thus,
With all their might, Good Lord deliver us.   135

XVI.

From needing danger, to bee good,
From owing thee yesterdaies teares to day,
   From trusting so much to thy blood,
That in that hope, wee wound our soule away,

119. *That*: the Church in Heaven; *this*: the Church on earth.
126. *trusting in those prayers*: relying solely on the Church's prayers to the
     neglect of our own.
     powr'd: poured.
127. *secure*: over-confident (§250).
128. *clods*: 'clouds' (acc. to 1635–69 and some MSS).
     squibs: fire-crackers (as above, p. 90, note on 4).
129. *immure*: confine, wall in.
133. *maim'd*: incapacitated.

From bribing thee with Almes, to excuse   140
  Some sinne more burdenous,
From light affecting, in religion, newes,
From thinking us all soule, neglecting thus
Our mutuall duties, Lord deliver us.

XVII.

From tempting Satan to tempt us,   145
By our connivence, or slack companie,
  From measuring ill by vitious,
Neglecting to choake sins spawne, Vanitie,
    From indiscreet humilitie,
      Which might be scandalous,   150
And cast reproach on Christianitie,
From being spies, or to spies pervious,
From thirst, or scorne of fame, deliver us.

XVIII.

Deliver us for thy descent
Into the Virgin, whose wombe was a place   155
  Of midle kind; and thou being sent
To'ungratious us, staid'st at her full of grace,
      And through thy poore birth, where first thou
        Glorifiedst Povertie,
And yet soone after riches didst allow,   160
By accepting Kings gifts in the Epiphanie,
Deliver, and make us, to both waies free.

142. *newes*: innovations.
147. *by vitious*: in the light rather of vices than of virtues.
152. *Spies*: cf. 'false brethren . . . who came in privily to spy out our liberty
       which we have in Christ' (Galatians 2.4; §163).
       pervious: accessible.
153. *thirst*: thirst for.
       fame (acc. to 1635): 'flame' (acc. to 1633) or 'fame good Lord' (acc. to
       some MSS).
154. *for*: 'through' (acc. to 1635–69 and some MSS).
156. *midle kind*: between the divine and the human.
157. *ungracious*: devoid of God's Grace.

XIX.

And through that bitter agonie,
Which is still the agonie of pious wits,
   Disputing what distorted thee,   165
And interrupted evennesse, with fits,
      And through thy free confession
      Though thereby they were then
Made blind, so that thou might'st from them have gone,
Good Lord deliver us, and teach us when   170
Wee may not, and we may blinde unjust men.

XX.

Through thy submitting all, to blowes
Thy face, thy clothes to spoile; thy fame to scorne,
   All waies, which rage, or Justice knowes,
And by which thou could'st shew, that thou wast born,   175
      And through thy gallant humblenesse
      Which thou in death did'st shew,
Dying before thy soule they could expresse,
Deliver us from death, by dying so,
To this world, ere this world doe bid us goe.   180

XXI.

When senses, which thy souldiers are,
Wee arme against thee, and they fight for sinne,
   When want, sent but to tame, doth warre
And worke despaire a breach to enter in,
      When plenty, Gods image, and seale   185
      Makes us Idolatrous,
And love it, not him, whom it should reveale,
When wee are mov'd to seeme religious
Only to vent wit, Lord deliver us.

---

163.   *through* (acc. to 1635): 'though' (acc. to 1633).
166.   *evennesse*: steadiness, both Christ's and the world's.
167.   *free confession*: Christ's acknowledgment of his identity, whereupon the
      arresting soldiers were struck *blind* (l. 169; see John 18.4–6).
173.   *clothes*: 'robes' (acc. to 1635–69 and some MSS).
178.   *expresse*: press out.
185.   *seale*: guarantee of divine favour; cf. above, p. 439, note on VII:14.

XXII.

In Churches, when the'infirmitie   190
Of him which speakes, diminishes the Word,
   When Magistrates doe mis-apply
To us, as we judge, lay or ghostly sword,
      When plague, which is thine Angell, raignes,
        Or wars, thy Champions, swaie,   195
When Heresie, thy second deluge, gaines;
In th'houre of death, the'Eve of last judgement day,
Deliver us from the sinister way.

XXIII.

Heare us, O heare us Lord; to thee
A sinner is more musique, when he prayes,   200
   Then spheares, or Angels praises bee,
In Panegyrique Allelujaes,
      Heare us, for till thou heare us, Lord
        We know not what to say.
Thine eare to'our sighes, teares, thoughts gives voice and word.
O Thou who Satan heard'st in Jobs sicke day,
Heare thy selfe now, for thou in us dost pray.

XXIV.

That wee may change to evennesse
This intermitting aguish Pietie,
   That snatching cramps of wickednesse   210
And Apoplexies of fast sin, may die;
      That musique of thy promises,
      Not threats in Thunder may

---

193. *lay or ghostly sword*: secular or spiritual authority.
194. *thine Angell*: cf. 'the Lord sent a pestilence upon Israel' etc. (2 Samuel
     24.15; §163).
196. *When*: 'Where' (acc. to many MSS).
     second deluge: second after Noah's Flood.
201. *Then*: than.
     spheares . . . praises: as emitted through the music of the Spheres.
206. *Jobs sicke day*: as related in Job 2.2–7.
208. *evennesse*: unremitting devotion; 'enemies' (acc. to a MS).
209. *aguish*: feverish; 'anguish' (acc. to some MSS).
211. *fast*: tenacious.

Awaken us to our just offices,
What in thy booke, thou dost, or creatures say,   215
That we may heare, Lord heare us, when wee pray.

XXV.

That our eares sicknesse wee may cure,
And rectifie those Labyrinths aright,
    That wee by harkning, not procure
Our praise, nor others dispraise so invite,   220
        That wee get not a slipperinesse,
        And senslesly decline,
From hearing bold wits jeast at Kings excesse,
To'admit the like of majestie divine,
That we may locke our eares, Lord open thine.   225

XXVI.

That living law, the Magistrate,
Which to give us, and make us physicke, doth
    Our vices often aggravate,
That Preachers taxing sinne, before her growth,
        That Satan, and invenom'd men   230
        Which well, if we starve, dine,
When they doe most accuse us, may see then
Us, to amendment, heare them; thee decline;
That we may open our eares, Lord lock thine.

XXVII.

That learning, thine Ambassador,   235
From thine allegeance wee never tempt,
    That beauty, paradises flower
For physicke made, from poyson be exempt,

215.   *thy booke*: the Bible.
222.   *senslesly*: without being aware of it (§166).
227.   *physicke*: corrective medicine.
230.   *invenom'd*: poisoned by the serpentine Satan.
231.   *well*: 'will' (acc. to 1635–69).
233.   *heare them*: 'hearken' (acc. to some MSS).
234.   *lock*: 'stop' (ditto).
238.   *physicke*: healing.

That wit, borne apt, high good to doe,
    By dwelling lazily   240
On Natures nothing, be not nothing too,
That our affections kill us not, nor dye,
Heare us, weake ecchoes, O thou eare, and cry.

XXVIII.

    Sonne of God heare us, and since thou
By taking our blood, owest it us againe,   245
    Gaine to thy self, or us allow;
And let not both us and thy selfe be slaine;
        O Lambe of God, which took'st our sinne
          Which could not stick to thee,
O let it not returne to us againe,   250
But Patient and Physition being free,
As sinne is nothing, let it no where be.

Upon the translation of the Psalmes
by Sir *Philip Sydney*,
and the Countesse of Pembroke his Sister.

Eternall God, (for whom who ever dare
Seeke new expressions, doe the Circle square,
And thrust into strait corners of poore wit
Thee, who art cornerlesse and infinite)

The Litanie.
241. *Natures nothing*: nature's inconsequential trifles.
243. *ecchoes*: 'wretches' (acc. to some MSS).
      cry: 'eye' (ditto).
245. *taking our blood*: assuming our human nature.
249. Jesus was necessarily without sin (cf. 2 Corinthians 5.21).
252. *sinne is nothing*: the widely credited theory that evil is but the absence of good and so, in itself, 'nothing'.

Upon the translation etc. First printed in 1635, the poem addresses itself to the Sidney Psalter which in Donne's time circulated widely in manuscript and was finally published in 1823.
  1–4. Any attempt to change a circle into a square involves reducing the infinite to the finite (§52).

I would but blesse thy Name, not name thee now;   5
(And thy gifts are as infinite as thou:)
Fixe we our prayses therefore on this one,
That, as thy blessed Spirit fell upon
These Psalmes first Author in a cloven tongue;
(For 'twas a double power by which he sung   10
The highest matter in the noblest forme;)
So thou hast cleft that spirit, to performe
That worke againe, and shed it, here, upon
Two, by their bloods, and by thy Spirit one;
A Brother and a Sister, made by thee   15
The Organ, where thou art the Harmony.
Two that make one *John Baptists* holy voyce,
And who that Psalme, *Now let the Iles rejoyce*,
Have both translated, and apply'd it too,
But told us what, and taught us how to doe.   20
They shew us Ilanders our joy, our King,
They tell us *why*, and teach us *how* to sing.
Make all this All, three Quires, heaven, earth, and sphears;
The first, Heaven, hath a song, but no man heares,
The Spheares have Musick, but they have no tongue,   25
Their harmony is rather danc'd than sung;
But our third Quire, to which the first gives eare,
(For, Angels learne by what the Church does here)
This Quire hath all. The Organist is hee
Who hath tun'd God and Man, the Organ we: 30
The songs are these, which heavens high holy Muse
Whisper'd to *David*, *David* to the Jewes:
And *Davids* Successors, in holy zeale,
In formes of joy and art doe re-reveale
To us so sweetly and sincerely too,   35
That I must not rejoyce as I would doe

---

9. *Author*: traditionally said to be David (see further ll. 31–32 but, for a
    reservation, l. 48).
    cloven: double, i.e. divine and human.
17. *voyce*: i.e. preparatory to the reception of Christ.
18. *that Psalme*: Psalm 97.
23. *sphears*: see above, p. 80, note on 23.

When I behold that these Psalmes are become
So well attyr'd abroad, so ill at home,
So well in Chambers, in thy Church so ill,
As I can scarce call that reform'd, untill   40
This be reform'd; Would a whole State present
A lesser gift than some one man hath sent?
And shall our Church, unto our Spouse and King
More hoarse, more harsh than any other, sing?
For *that* we pray, we praise thy name for *this*,   45
Which, by this *Moses* and this *Miriam*, is
Already done; and as those Psalmes we call
(Though some have other Authors) *Davids* all:
So though some have, some may some Psalmes translate,
We thy Sydnean Psalmes shall celebrate,   50
And, till we come th'Extemporall song to sing,
(Learn'd the first hower, that we see the King,
Who hath translated those translators) may
These their sweet learned labours, all the way
Be as our tuning, that, when hence we part,   55
We may fall in with them, and sing our part.

38. *abroad*: notably in the metrical versions of the Psalms by Clement Marot
     and in Lutheran psalmody generally.
39. *Chambers*: music rooms (§163).
40. *that*: the Church of England, claimed to have been *reform'd* of the errors of
     the Church of Rome.
46. The Song of Moses (Exodus 15.1 ff.) was taken up by his sister Miriam
     (15.21).
51. *Extemporall*: beyond time, celestial.
52. *the King*: God.
53. *translated*: removed to Heaven.

To Mr *Tilman* after he had taken orders.

Thou, whose diviner soule hath caus'd thee now
To put thy hand unto the holy Plough,
Making Lay-scornings of the Ministry,
Not an impediment, but victory;
What bringst thou home with thee? how is thy mind   5
Affected since the vintage? Dost thou finde
New thoughts and stirrings in thee? and as Steele
Toucht with a Loadstone, dost new motions feele?
Or, as a Ship after much paine and care,
For Iron and Cloth brings home rich Indian ware,   10
Hast thou thus traffiqu'd, but with farre more gaine
Of noble goods, and with lesse time and paine?
Thou art the same materials, as before,
Onely the stampe is changed; but no more.
And as new crowned Kings alter the face,   15
But not the monies substance; so hath grace
Chang'd onely Gods old Image by Creation,
To Christs new stampe, at this thy Coronation;
Or, as we paint Angels with wings, because
They beare Gods message, and proclaime his lawes,   20
Since thou must doe the like, and so must move,
Art thou new feather'd with cœlestiall love?

To Mr Tilman etc. First printed in 1635, the poem was written after Edward
Tilman, who had versified several 'motives not to take orders' (printed in
§189), reversed himself and was ordained deacon in December 1618. On
the relations between the two men, see §§168 (App. D) and 639.
  3. *Lay-scornings*: the scorn with which some of the gentry regarded the
clerical profession is reiterated below, ll. 26 ff.
  6. *vintage*: maturity; 'voyage' (acc. to a MS: §641).
  8. *Loadstone* (lodestone): magnet.
  11. *more gaine*: 'againe' (acc. to a MS).
  17. *old Image*: the image initially imprinted on man (Genesis 1.27).
  18. *stampe*: 'birth' (acc. to a MS).
  20. *message*: 'image' (ditto).

Deare, tell me where thy purchase lies, and shew
What thy advantage is above, below.
But if thy gainings doe surmount expression,   25
Why doth the foolish world scorne that profession,
Whose joyes passe speech? Why do they think unfit
That Gentry should joyne families with it?
As if their day were onely to be spent
In dressing, Mistressing and complement;   30
Alas poore joyes, but poorer men, whose trust
Seemes richly placed in sublimed dust;
(For, such are cloathes and beauty, which though gay,
Are, at the best, but of sublimed clay)
Let then the world thy calling disrespect,   35
But goe thou on, and pitty their neglect.
What function is so noble, as to bee
Embassadour to God and destinie?
To open life, to give kingdomes to more
Than Kings give dignities; to keepe heavens doore?   40
Maries prerogative was to beare Christ, so
'Tis preachers to convey him, for they doe
As Angels out of clouds, from Pulpits speake,
And blesse the poore beneath, the lame, the weake.
If then th'Astronomers, whereas they spie   45
A new-found Starre, their Opticks magnifie,

23. *purchase*: gain.
24. Demonstrate to us here on earth the advantage you have gained in
     Heaven.
29–30. The lines are borrowed from Herbert's *The Church porch*, ll. 79–80:
     'Flie idlenesse, which yet thou canst not flie / By dressing, mistressing,
     and complement' (§421).
30. *Mistressing*: 'undressinge' (acc. to a MS) or 'mis-dressing' (ditto).
32. *sublimed*: 'refined' (ditto).
34. *of*: 'as' (ditto).
40. *dignities*: honours and titles.
     keepe: guard.
42. *convey*: express.
46. *Opticks*: telescopes.

How brave are those, who with their Engine, can
Bring man to heaven, and heaven againe to man?
These are thy titles and preheminences,
In whom must meet Gods graces, mens offences,   50
And so the heavens which beget all things here,
And the earth our mother, which these things doth beare,
Both these in thee, are in thy Calling knit,
And make thee now a blest Hermaphrodite.

A Hymne to Christ, at the Authors
last going into Germany.

In what torne ship soever I embarke,
That ship shall be my embleme of thy Arke;
What sea soever swallow mee, that flood
Shall be to mee an embleme of thy bloode;
Though thou with clouds of anger do disguise   5
Thy face; yet through that maske I know those eyes,
   Which, though they turne away sometimes,
       They never will despise.

To Mr Tilman.
47.   *brave*: excellent.
      Engine: instrument.
48.   *againe*: omitted in some MSS.
54.   *Hermaphrodite*: one who combines opposites (cf. above, p. 210, note on
      30).

   A Hymne to Christ etc. Donne journeyed to Germany in May 1619 as chaplain
      to the Earl of Doncaster's diplomatic mission. The MSS and two modern
      editions (§§163, 168) merge the last two lines of each stanza into a single
      line.
   2.   *Arke*: symbolic of Divine Providence, with specific reference to Noah's
        ark during the Flood (Genesis 6.14 ff.).
   3.   *mee*: 'mee up' (acc. to some MSS).

I sacrifice this Iland unto thee,
And all whom I lov'd there, and who lov'd mee;   10
When I have put our seas twixt them and mee,
Put thou thy sea betwixt my sinnes and thee.
As the trees sap doth seeke the root below
In winter, in my winter now I goe,
   Where none but thee, th'Eternall root   15
     Of true Love I may know.

Nor thou nor thy religion dost controule,
The amorousnesse of an harmonious Soule,
But thou would'st have that love thy selfe: As thou
Art jealous, Lord, so I am jealous now,   20
Thou lov'st not, till from loving more, thou free
My soule: Who ever gives, takes libertie:
   O, if thou car'st not whom I love
     Alas, thou lov'st not mee.

Seale then this bill of my Divorce to All,   25
On whom those fainter beames of love did fall;
Marry those loves, which in youth scattered bee
On Fame, Wit, Hopes (false mistresses) to thee.
Churches are best for Prayer, that have least light:
To see God only, I goe out of sight: 30
   And to scape stormy dayes, I chuse
     An Everlasting night.

9. *Iland*: England.
10. *lov'd . . . lov'd*: 'love . . . love' (acc. to 1635–69).
     there: 'here' (ditto).
11. *our*: 'this' (ditto).
     seas: 'flood' (ditto).
12. *sea*: 'blood' (ditto).
15. *thee, th'Eternall root*: 'thy eternal work' (acc. to some MSS).
17. *controule*: censure, restrain.
20. *jealous*: full of zeal, fervent.
25. *Seale*: as above, p. 439, note on VII:14.
28. *Fame*: 'face' (acc. to 1635–69).
     Hopes: i.e. of advancement.
29. Possibly an allusion to the *Utopia* of his martyred kinsman Sir Thomas
     More, in which churches excluded light because darkness was believed to
     intensify religious faith (§207).

The Lamentations of *Jeremy*,
for the most part according to *Tremelius*.

CHAP. I

1 How sits this citie, late most populous,
  Thus solitary, and like a widdow thus!
Amplest of Nations, Queene of Provinces
  She was, who now thus tributary is!

2 Still in the night shee weepes, and her teares fall   5
  Downe by her cheeks along, and none of all
Her lovers comfort her; Perfidiously
  Her friends have dealt, and now are enemie.

3 Unto great bondage, and afflictions
  Juda is captive led; Those nations   10
With whom shee dwells, no place of rest afford,
  In streights shee meets her Persecutors sword.

4 Emptie are the gates of Sion, and her waies
  Mourne, because none come to her solemne dayes.
Her Priests doe groane, her maides are comfortlesse,   15
  And shee's unto her selfe a bitternesse.

5 Her foes are growne her head, and live at Peace,
  Because when her transgressions did increase,
The Lord strooke her with sadnesse: Th'enemie
  Doth drive her children to captivitie.   20

The Lamentations of Jeremy. One of Donne's longest poems (cf. *Metempsycosis*
  and the two *Anniversaries*), his free translation of the Lamentations
  attributed to the prophet Jeremiah depends on two Latin versions: St
  Jerome's Vulgate, formally in use by the Catholic Church, and espe-
  cially the translation of the Old Testament by the great Biblical scholars
  Immanuel Tremellius and Franciscus Junius (1575 ff.), which may be
  regarded as Protestantism's authorized Latin version (§421). So far as
  English versions are concerned, Donne's phrasing was affected by the
  Geneva Bible of 1560 (§638) and the Authorized Version of 1611.
  1. *this citie*: Jerusalem, capital of the southern kingdom of Judah, which fell
    to Nebuchadnezzar of Babylon in 586 B.C.

6 From Sions daughter is all beauty gone,
  Like Harts, which seeke for Pasture, and find none,
Her Princes are, and now before the foe
  Which still pursues them, without strength they go.

7 Now in her daies of Teares, Jerusalem   25
  (Her men slaine by the foe, none succouring them)
Remembers what of old, shee esteemed most,
  Whiles her foes laugh at her, for what she hath lost.

8 Jerusalem hath sinn'd, therefore is shee
  Remov'd, as women in uncleannesse bee;   30
Who honor'd, scorne her, for her foulnesse they
  Have seene, her selfe doth groane, and turne away.

9 Her foulnesse in her skirts was seene, yet she
  Remembered not her end; Miraculously
Therefore she fell, none comforting: Behold   35
  O Lord my affliction, for the Foe growes bold.

10 Upon all things where her delight hath beene,
  The foe hath stretch'd his hand, for shee hath seene
Heathen, whom thou command'st, should not doe so,
  Into her holy Sanctuary goe.   40

11 And all her people groane, and seeke for bread;
  And they have given, only to be fed,
All precious things, wherein their pleasure lay:
  How cheape I'am growne, O Lord, behold, and weigh.

12 All this concernes not you, who passe by mee,   45
  O see, and marke if any sorrow bee
Like to my sorrow, which Jehova hath
  Done to mee in the day of his fierce wrath?

---

25. *her*: 'their' (acc. to 1633–69 and some MSS).
40. *the Sanctuary*: the Great Temple in Jerusalem (see 2 Chronicles 36.19).
44. On the symbol ', here and throughout, see above, p. 5.

13 That fire, which by himselfe is governed
  He hath cast from heaven on my bones, and spred   50
A net before my feet, and mee o'rthrowne,
  And made me languish all the day alone.

14 His hand hath of my sinnes framed a yoake
  Which wreath'd, and cast upon my neck, hath broke
My strength. The Lord unto those enemies   55
  Hath given mee, from whom I cannot rise.

15 He under foot hath troden in my sight
  My strong men; He did company invite
To breake my young men, he the winepresse hath
  Trod upon Juda's daughter in his wrath.   60

16 For these things doe I weepe, mine eye, mine eye
  Casts water out; For he which should be nigh
To comfort mee, is now departed farre,
  The foe prevailes, forlone my children are.

17 There's none, though *Sion* do stretch out her hand   65
  To comfort her, it is the Lords command
That *Jacobs* foes girt him. *Jerusalem*
  Is as an uncleane woman amongst them.

18 But yet the Lord is just, and righteous still,
  I have rebell'd against his holy will;   70
O heare all people, and my sorrow see,
  My maides, my young men in captivitie.

19 I called for my *lovers* then, but they
  Deceiv'd mee, and my Priests, and Elders lay
Dead in the citie; for they sought for meat   75
  Which should refresh their soules, they could not get.

56. *whom* (acc. to 1635–69 and most MSS): 'whence' (acc. to 1633).
58. *invite*: 'accite' i.e. summon (acc. to 1635–69 and some MSS).
76. *they could not*: 'and none could' (ditto).

20 Because I am in streights, *Jehova* see
  My heart o'rturn'd, my bowells muddy bee,
Because I have rebell'd so much, as fast
  The sword without, as death within, doth wast.   80

21 Of all which heare I mourne, none comforts mee,
  My foes have heard my griefe, and glad they be,
That thou hast done it; But thy promis'd day
  Will come, when, as I suffer, so shall they.

22 Let all their wickednesse appeare to thee,   85
  Doe unto them, as thou hast done to mee,
For all my sinnes: The sighs which I have had
  Are very many, and my heart is sad.

CHAP. II

1 How over Sions daughter hath God hung
  His wraths thicke cloud! and from heaven hath flung   90
To earth the beauty of *Israel*, and hath
  Forgot his foot-stoole in the day of wrath!

2 The Lord unsparingly hath swallowed
  All Jacobs dwellings, and demolished
To ground the strengths of *Juda*, and prophan'd   95
  The Princes of the Kingdome, and the land.

3 In heat of wrath, the horne of *Israel* hee
  Hath cleane cut off, and lest the enemie
Be hindred, his right hand he doth retire,
  But is towards *Jacob*, All-devouring fire.   100

4 Like to an enemie he bent his bow,
  His right hand was in posture of a foe,
To kill what *Sions* daughter did desire,
  'Gainst whom his wrath, he poured forth, like fire.

78. *o'rturn'd* (acc. to 1635): 'return'd' (acc. to 1633).
80. *wast*: waste.
81. *heare I*: 'heare me' (acc. to a MS) or 'here I' (acc. to 1639–69).
92. *foot-stoole*: see above p. 455, note on 20.
98. *horne*: military power (§166).

5 For like an enemie *Jehova* is,   105
    Devouring *Israel*, and his Palaces,
Destroying holds, giving additions
    To *Juda's* daughters lamentations.

6 Like to a garden hedge he hath cast downe
    The place where, was his congregation,   110
And *Sions* feasts and sabbaths are forgot;
    Her Kings, her Priest, his wrath regardeth not.

7 The Lord forsakes his Altar, and detests
    His Sanctuary, and in the foes hand rests
His Palace, and the walls, in which their cries   115
    Are heard, as in the true solemnities.

8 The Lord hath cast a line, so to confound
    And levell *Sions* walls unto the ground.
He drawes not back his hand, which doth oreturne
    The wall, and Rampart, which together mourne.   120

9 Their gates are sunke into the ground, and hee
    Hath broke the barres; their King and Princes bee
Amongst the heathen, without law, nor there
    Unto their Prophets doth the Lord appeare.

10 There *Sions Elders* on the ground are plac'd,   125
    And silence keepe; Dust on their heads they cast,
In sackcloth have they girt themselves, and low
    The Virgins towards ground, their heads do throw.

11 My bowells are growne muddy, and mine eyes
    Are faint with weeping: and my liver lies   130
Pour'd out upon the ground, for miserie
    That sucking children in the streets doe die.

12 When they had cryed unto their Mothers, where
    Shall we have bread, and drinke? they fainted there
And in the streets like wounded persons lay   135
    Till 'twixt their mothers breasts they went away.

107.   *holds*: strongholds.
122.   *barres*: defensive barriers.

13 *Daughter Jerusalem*, Oh what may bee
   A witnesse, or comparison for thee?
Sion, to ease thee, what shall I name like thee?
   Thy breach is like the sea, what help can bee?   140

14 For thee vaine foolish things thy Prophets sought,
   Thee, thine iniquities they have not taught,
Which might disturne thy bondage: but for thee
   False burthens, and false causes they would see.

15 The passengers doe clap their hands, and hisse   145
   And wag their head at thee, and say, Is this
That citie, which so many men did call
   Joy of the earth, and perfectest of all?

16 Thy foes doe gape upon thee, and they hisse,
   And gnash their teeth, and say, Devoure wee this,   150
For this is certainly the day which wee
   Expected, and which now we finde, and see.

17 The Lord hath done that which he purposed,
   Fulfill'd his word of old determined;
He hath throwne downe, and not spar'd, and thy foe   155
   Made glad above thee, and advanc'd him so.

18 But now, their hearts against the Lord do call,
   Therefore, O walls of *Sion*, let teares fall
Downe like a river, day and night; take thee
   No rest, but let thine eye incessant be.   160

19 Arise, cry in the night, poure, for thy sinnes,
   Thy heart, like water, when the watch begins;
Lift up thy hands to God, lest children dye,
   Which, faint for hunger, in the streets doe lye.

143.   *disturne*: avert.
145.   *passengers*: passers by (§166).
157.   *against*: 'unto' (acc. to 1635–69).
161.   *poure, for*: 'poure out' (ditto).

20 Behold O Lord, consider unto whom   165
   Thou hast done this; what, shall the women come
To eate their children of a spanne? shall thy
   Prophet and Priest be slaine in Sanctuary?

21 On ground in streets, the yong and old do lye,
   My virgins and yong men by sword do dye;   170
Them in the day of thy wrath thou hast slaine,
   Nothing did thee from killing them containe.

22 As to a solemne feast, all whom I fear'd
   Thou call'st about mee; when his wrath appear'd,
None did remaine or scape, for those which I   175
   Brought up, did perish by mine enemie.

CHAP. III

1 I am the man which have affliction seene,
   Under the rod of Gods wrath having beene,
2 He hath led mee to darknesse, not to light,
   3 And against mee all day, his hand doth fight.   180

4 Hee hath broke my bones, worne out my flesh and
      skinne,
   5 Built up against mee; and hath girt mee in
With hemlocke, and with labour; 6 and set mee
   In darke, as they who dead for ever bee.

7 Hee hath hedg'd me lest I scape, and added more   185
   To my steele fetters, heavier then before,
8 When I crie out, he out shuts my prayer: 9 And hath
   Stop'd with hewn stone my way, and turn'd my path.

10 And like a Lion hid in secrecie,
   Or Beare which lyes in wait, he was to mee.   190
11 He stops my way, teares me, made desolate,
   12 And hee makes mee the marke he shooteth at.

166. *this*: 'thus' (acc. to a MS).
167. *of a spanne*: young (§166).
174. *his*: 'thy' (acc. to 1635–69).
182. *girt*: 'hemd' (acc. to some MSS).
186. *then*: than.

13 Hee made the children of his quiver passe
   Into my reines, 14 I with my people was
All the day long, a song and mockery.   195
   15 Hee hath fill'd mee with bitternesse, and he

Hath made me drunke with wormewood. 16 He hath burst
   My teeth with stones, and covered mee with dust;
17 And thus my Soule farre off from peace was set,
   And my prosperity I did forget.   200

18 My strength, my hope (unto my selfe I said)
   Which from the Lord should come, is perished.
19 But when my mournings I do thinke upon,
   My wormwood, hemlocke, and affliction,

20 My Soule is humbled in remembring this;   205
   21 My heart considers, therefore, hope there is.
22 'Tis Gods great mercy we'are not utterly
   Consum'd, for his compassions do not die;

23 For every morning they renewed bee,
   For great, O Lord, is thy fidelity.   210
24 The Lord is, saith my Soule, my portion,
   And therfore in him will I hope alone.

25 The Lord is good to them, who on him relie,
   And to the Soule that seeks him earnestly.
26 It is both good to trust, and to attend   215
   (The Lords salvation) unto the end:

27   'Tis good for one his yoake in youth to beare;
   28 He sits alone, and doth all speech forebeare,
Because he hath borne it. 29 And his mouth he layes
   Deepe in the dust, yet then in hope he stayes.   220

30 He gives his checkes to whosoever will
   Strike him, and so he is reproched still.
31 For, not for ever doth the Lord forsake,
   32 But when he'hath strucke with sadnes, hee doth take

Compassion, as his mercy'is infinite;   225
  33 Nor is it with his heart, that he doth smite,
34 That underfoot the prisoners stamped bee,
  35 That a mans right the Judge himselfe doth see

To be wrung from him, 36 That he subverted is
  In his just cause; the Lord allowes not this: 230
37 Who then will say, that ought doth come to passe,
  But that which by the Lord commanded was?

38 Both good and evill from his mouth proceeds;
  39 Why then grieves any man for his misdeeds?
40 Turne wee to God, by trying out our wayes;   235
  41 To him in heaven, our hands with hearts upraise.

42 Wee have rebell'd, and falne away from thee,
  Thou pardon'st not. 43 Usest no clemencie;
Pursuest us, kill'st us, coverest us with wrath,
  44 Cover'st thy selfe with clouds, that our prayer hath

No power to passe. 45 And thou hast made us fall
  As refuse, and off-scouring to them all.
46 All our foes gape at us. 47 Feare and a snare
  With ruine, and with waste, upon us are.

48 With watry rivers doth mine eye oreflow   245
  For ruine of my peoples daughter so;
49 Mine eye doth drop downe teares incessantly,
  50 Until the Lord looke downe from heaven to see.

51 And for my city daughters sake, mine eye
  Doth breake mine heart. 52 Causles mine enemy,   250
Like a bird chac'd me. 53 In a dungeon
  They have shut my life, and cast on me a stone.

54 Waters flow'd o'r my head, then thought I, I am
  Destroy'd; 55 I called Lord, upon thy name
Out of the pit. 56 And thou my voice didst heare;   255
  Oh from my sigh, and crye, stop not thine eare.

256. *sigh*: 'sight' (acc. to 1649–69).

57 Then when I call'd upon thee, thou drew'st nere
  Unto mee, and said'st unto mee, do you feare.
58 Thou Lord my Soules cause handled hast, and thou
  Rescud'st my life. 59 O Lord do thou judge now,   260

Thou heardst my wrong. 60 Their vengeance all they
    have wrought;
  61 How they reproach'd, thou hast heard, and what
    they thought,
62 What their lips uttered, which against me rose,
  And what was ever whisper'd by my foes.

63 I am their song, whether they rise or sit,   265
  64 Give them rewards Lord, for their working fit,
65 Sorrow of heart, thy curse. 66 And with thy might
  Follow, and from under heaven destroy them quite.

Chap. IV

1 How is the gold become so dimme? How is
  Purest and finest gold thus chang'd to this?   270
The stones which were stones of the Sanctuary,
  Scattered in corners of each street do lye.

2 The pretious sonnes of Sion, which should bee
  Valued at purest gold, how do wee see
Low rated now, as earthen Pitchers, stand,   275
  Which are the worke of a poore Potters hand.

3 Even the Sea-calfes draw their brests, and give
  Sucke to their young; my peoples daughters live
By reason of the foes great cruelnesse,
  As do the Owles in the vast Wildernesse.   280

4 And when the sucking child doth strive to draw,
  His tongue for thirst cleaves to his upper jaw.
And when for bread the little children crye,
  There is no man that doth them satisfie.

5 They which before were delicately fed,   285
  Now in the streets forlorne have perished,
And they which ever were in scarlet cloath'd,
  Sit and embrace the dunghills which they loath'd.

6 The daughters of my people have sinned more,
  Then did the towne of *Sodome* sinne before;   290
Which being at once destroy'd, there did remaine
  No hands amongst them, to vexe them againe.

7 But heretofore purer her Nazarite
  Was then the snow, and milke was not so white;
As carbuncles did their pure bodies shine,   295
  And all their polish'dnesse was Saphirine.

8 They are darker now then blacknes, none can know
  Them by the face, as through the streets they goe,
For now their skin doth cleave unto their bone,
  And withered, is like to dry wood growne.   300

9 Better by sword then famine 'tis to dye;
  And better through pierc'd, then through penury.
10 Women by nature pitifull have eate
  Their children drest with their owne hand for meat.

11 *Jehova* here fully accomplish'd hath   305
  His indignation, and powr'd forth his wrath,
Kindled a fire in *Sion*, which hath power
  To eate, and her foundations to devour.

12 Nor would the Kings of the earth, nor all which live
  In the inhabitable world beleeve,   310
That any adversary, any foe
  Into *Jerusalem* should enter so;

---

290 (also 294, 297, 301, 302). *Then*: than.
293.   *Nazarite*: a religious devotee like Samson (Judges 13.5, cf. Numbers 6.2–3) or the Rechabites (Jeremiah 35).
296.   *Saphirine* (acc. to 1635–69): 'Seraphine' (acc. to 1633).
302.   *through penury*: 'by penury' (ditto).

13 For the Priests sins, and Prophets, which have shed
    Blood in the streets, and the just murthered:
14 Which when those men, whom they made blinde,
        did stray   315
    Thorough the streets, defiled by the way

With blood, the which impossible it was
    Their garments should scape touching, as they passe,
15 Would cry aloud, depart defiled men,
    Depart, depart, and touch us not, and then   320

They fled, and strayd, and with the *Gentiles* were,
    Yet told their friends, they should not long dwell there;
16 For this they are scattered by Jehovahs face
    Who never will regard them more; No grace

Unto their old men shall the foe afford,
    Nor, that they are Priests, redeeme them from the sword.
17 And wee as yet, for all these miseries
    Desiring our vaine helpe, consume our eyes:

And such a nation as cannot save,
    We in desire and speculation have.   330
18 They hunt our steps, that in the streets wee feare
    To goe: our end is now approached neere,

Our dayes accomplish'd are, this the last day.
    19 Eagles of heaven are not so swift as they
Which follow us, o'r mountaine tops they flye   335
    At us, and for us in the desart lye.

20 The annointed Lord, breath of our nostrils, hee
    Of whom we said, under his shadow, wee
Shall with more ease under the Heathen dwell,
    Into the pit which these men digged, fell.   340

337.   *The anointed Lord*: the King of Judah.

21 Rejoyce O *Edoms daughter*, joyfull bee
   Thou which inhabitst *Huz*, for unto thee
This cup shall passe, and thou with drunkennesse
   Shalt fill thy selfe, and shew thy nakednesse.

22 And then thy sinnes O *Sion*, shall be spent,   345
   The Lord will not leave thee in banishment.
Thy sinnes O *Edoms daughter*, hee will see,
   And for them, pay thee with captivitie.

Chap. V

1 Remember, O Lord, what is fallen on us,
   See, and marke how we are reproached thus,   350
2 For unto strangers our possession
   Is turn'd, our houses unto Aliens gone,

3 Our mothers are become as widowes, wee
   As Orphans all, and without father be;
4 Waters which are our owne, wee drunke, and pay,   355
   And upon our owne wood a price they lay.

5 Our persecutors on our necks do sit,
   They make us travaile, and not intermit,
6 We stretch our hands unto th'*Egyptians*
   To get us bread; and to the *Assyrians*.   360

7 Our Fathers did these sinnes, and are no more,
   But wee do beare the sinnes they did before.
8 They are but servants, which do rule us thus,
   Yet from their hands none would deliver us.

9 With danger of our life our bread wee gat;   365
   For in the wildernesse, the sword did wait.
10 The tempests of this famine wee liv'd in,
   Black as an Oven colour'd had our skinne:

342.   *Huz*: Uz, the territory southeast of Palestine, the land of Job.
368.   *Oven* (acc. to 1635): 'Ocean' (acc. to 1633).

11 In *Judaes* cities they the maids abus'd
   By force, and so women in *Sion* us'd.   370
12 The Princes with their hands they hung; no grace
   Nor honour gave they to the Elders face.

13 Unto the mill our yong men carried are,
   And children fell under the wood they bare.
14 Elders, the gates; youth did their songs forbeare,   375
15 Gone was our joy; our dancings, mournings were.

16 Now is the crowne falne from our head; and woe
   Be unto us, because we'have sinned so.
17 For this our hearts do languish, and for this
   Over our eyes a cloudy dimnesse is.   380

18 Because mount *Sion* desolate doth lye,
   And foxes there do goe at libertie:
19 But thou O Lord art ever, and thy throne
   From generation, to generation.

20 Why should'st thou forget us eternally?   385
   Or leave us thus long in this misery?
21 Restore us Lord to thee, that so we may
   Returne, and as of old, renew our day.

22 For oughtest thou, O Lord, despise us thus
   And to be utterly enrag'd at us?   390

Hymne to God my God, in my sicknesse.

Since I am comming to that Holy roome,
   Where, with thy Quire of Saints for evermore,
I shall be made thy Musique; As I come
   I tune the Instrument here at the dore,
   And what I·must doe then, thinke here before.   5

Whilst my Physitians by their love are growne
   Cosmographers, and I their Mapp, who lie
Flat on this bed, that by them may be showne
   That this is my South-west discoverie
   Per fretum febris, by these streights to die,   10

I joy, that in these straits, I see my West;
   For, those theire currants yeeld returne to none,
What shall my West hurt me? As West and East
   In all flatt Maps (and I am one) are one,
   So death doth touch the Resurrection.   15

Is the Pacifique Sea my home? Or are
   The Easterne riches? Is *Jerusalem?*

Hyme to God my God. Although dated by Isaak Walton a few days before
    Donne's death in 1631, the poem was most likely written during Donne's
    grave illness in 1623 (cf. below, headnote on p. 490) and first printed in
    1635.
  1–5. Anticipating its return to God, the soul is to be tuned for participation in
    the divine melodies of *musica mundana* (§52).
  4. *Instrument*: also in the specialized sense of a minister of the Gospel (§383).
  5. *here*: 'now' (acc. to most MSS).
  10. *Per fretum febris*: 'through the strait [*also* raging] of fever', analogous to
    the *South-west* journey through the Straits of Magellan (cf. l. 18).
    streights: also in the sense of sufferings.
  11–15. The sun (Son) in setting in the *West* suggests *death*, in rising in the *East*
    avers life (*Resurrection*).
  12. *those*: 'theire' (acc. to a MS and all modern editors; but see §188).
  13–14 'In a flat Map', Donne wrote, 'there goes no more, to make West
    East . . . but to paste that flat Map upon a round body, and then West and
    East are all one' (*Sermons*, VI, 59; §207).
  16–17. Images of serenity.

Anyan, and *Magellan*, and *Gibraltare*,
  All streights, and none but streights are wayes to them,
  Whether where *Japhet* dwelt, or *Cham*, or *Sem*.   20

We thinke that *Paradise* and *Calvarie*,
  Christs Crosse, and *Adams* tree, stood in one place;
Looke Lord, and finde both *Adams* met in me;
  As the first *Adams* sweat surrounds my face,
  May the last *Adams* blood my soule embrace.   25

So, in his purple wrapp'd receive mee Lord,
  By these his thornes give me his other Crowne;
And as to others soules I preach'd thy word,
  Be this my Text, my Sermon to mine owne,
  Therfore that he may raise the Lord throws down.   30

18.   *Anyan*: not an actual physical location such as the Bering Straits but the presumed northwest passage from the Atlantic to the Pacific (§637).
20.   The descendants of Noah's sons were said to have populated the three continents which at the time were thought to comprise the habitable world: in Japhet's case, Europe; in Ham's, Africa; in Shem's, Asia (§383; see also §4).
21–22. In accordance with a widespread if but implicit belief (§620, but also §§612 and 168: App. F), reiterated above, p. 408, ll. 77–78.
23.   *both Adams*: the *first* (24) and the second or *last*, i.e. Christ (25).
24.   *surrounds*: in the sense that sweat pours from the hair and runs *round* the face (§290).
26.   *purple*: Christ's redeeming blood; also, his royal cloak.

A Hymne to God the Father.

I.

Wilt thou forgive that sinne where I begunne,
  Which was my sin, though it were done before?
Wilt thou forgive that sinne, through which I runne,
  And do run still: though still I do deplore?
    When thou hast done, thou hast not done,   5
        For, I have more.

II.

Wilt thou forgive that sinne which I have wonne
  Others to sinne? and, made my sinne their doore?
Wilt thou forgive that sinne which I did shunne
  A yeare, or two: but wallowed in, a score?   10
    When thou hast done, thou hast not done,
        For I have more.

III.

I have a sinne of feare, that when I have spunne
  My last thred, I shall perish on the shore;

A Hymne to God the Father. Most likely written after Donne's grave illness in
    1623 (cf. headnote to the previous poem), the hymn survives in two
    versions: the one printed ever since 1633 (above), and another entitled in
    some MSS *To Christ* or *Christo Salvatori* (reprinted in §§158, 166, and
    heavily relied on for the texts in §§163, 168). For the musical setting by
    John Hilton – commissioned by Donne – see §§169, 190; the version with
    music by Johann Sebastian Bach forms part of the English Hymnal, No.
    515 (see §163).
       The poem's refrains are informed by two puns personal to Donne, the
    obvious one on his name (Donne/done), and the less obvious one on the
    maiden name of his wife Ann (More/more). See further §§630, 635.
1–2. Alluding to original sin.
2. *was*: 'is' (acc. to most MSS).
3. *that sinne*: 'those sinnes' (acc. to most MSS).
4. *run*: 'them' (ditto).
7. *which I have*: 'by which I' or 'by which I have' (acc. to various MSS).
8. *my sinne*: 'my sins' (acc. to 1639–69).

But sweare by thy selfe, that at my death thy sonne   15
     Shall shine as he shines now, and heretofore;
          And, having done that, Thou haste done,
                    I feare no more.

Translated out of Gazæus

God grant thee thine own wish, and grant thee mine,
Thou, who dost, best friend, in best things outshine;
May thy soul, ever chearfull, nere know cares,
Nor thy life, ever lively, know gray haires.
Nor thy hand, ever open, know base holds,   5
Nor thy purse, ever plump, know pleits, or folds.
Nor thy tongue, ever true, know a false thing,
Nor thy word, ever mild, know quarrelling.
Nor thy works, ever equall, know disguise,
Nor thy fame, ever pure, know contumelies.   10
Nor thy prayers, know low objects, still Divine;
God grant thee thine own wish, and grant thee mine.

A Hymne to God the Father.
15.   *But sweare*: 'Sweare' (acc. to most MSS).
       sonne: 'Sunne' (ditto); see above, p. 433, note on 7:2.
17.   *haste*: hast.
18.   *feare*: 'have' (acc. to most MSS).

Translated out of Gazæus. First published in the 1650 edition, which further
       specifies the title of the poem as *Vota amico facta* ('Prayers composed by a
       friend') and provides the reference in the Belgian Jesuit Angelin Gazet's
       collection of poems and songs to St Hilary, *Pia Hilaria variaque carmina*
       (1618).
 9.   *equall*: just; *disguise*: falsity (§163).
10.   *contumelies*: insulting reproaches.

Appendix I
The Arrangement of the Poems in the 1633 Edition

Donne's poems are in the present volume grouped under the subdivisions and in the order provided by the second edition of 1635 (see above, p. 2). The arrangement of the poems in the first edition of 1633 may seem to be, and perhaps is, rather too haphazard; yet it is an arrangement one should not dismiss altogether since a major intent may have been to demonstrate the variety and range of Donne's poetic achievement. The placing of *Metempsycosis* at the very outset of the 1633 edition is not the only surprise in that underestimated collection.

Metempsycosis
La Corona
Holy Sonnets II, IV, VI, VII, IX–XVI
Epigrams
Elegies I–V
Elegie on the L.C.
Elegies VI–VII
The Storme
The Calme
To Sir Henry Wotton: Sir, more then kisses
The Crosse
Elegie on the Lady Marckham
Elegie on M^ris Boulstred
[Verse Letters: the sequence as given above, pp. 260–309]
An Epithalamion . . . on the Lady Elizabeth
Ecclogue. 1613
Epithalamion made at Lincolnes Inne
Obsequies to the Lord Harrington
Elegies VIII–X
Elegie on . . . Prince Henry
Resurrection, imperfect
An hymne to the Saints, and to Marquesse Hamylton
Sapho to Philænis
The Annuntiation and Passion
Goodfriday, 1613. Riding Westward

The Litanie
[Songs and Sonets: the sequences as given above, pp. 89–98 and
      48–87; The Flea; The Curse]
The First Anniversarie
A Funerall Elegie
The Second Anniversarie
[Songs and Sonets: the sequence as given above, pp. 99–120]
Elegie: Language thou art too narrow
Elegie to the Lady Bedford
Elegie XV
[Songs and Sonets: The Paradox]
A Hymne to Christ, at the Authors last going into Germany
The Lamentations of Jeremy
Satyres I–V
A Hymne to God the Father
(Select letters in prose)
(Elegiac poems on Donne)

Appendix II
Poems attributed to Donne

Poems attributed to Donne range from a two-line epigram ('Faustus
keepes his sister and a whore, / Faustus keepes his sister and no more')
whose authenticity has been urged by John T. Shawcross (*ANQ*, 5
[1967], 104–05, and §163), to an elegy of fifty-four lines ('When my
harte was my owne . . .') whose attribution to Donne has been
ventured with 'no doubt' by E. K. Chambers (*RES*, 7 [1931], 69–71,
and reprinted as an elegy by Bennett [§160] but as one of the *Songs and
Sonets* by Shawcross [§163]). For the most thorough list of attributed
poems, the reader is referred to Grierson (§158: I, 401–32).

   Most of the 'dubia' listed by Gardner (§169: p. 92–108) are included
in the present edition as authentic.

Appendix III
Poems on Donne

The most substantial cluster of poems on Donne are the twelve 'Elegies upon the Author' appended to the first edition of his poems in 1633 (pp. 373–406) and the supplementary tributes published in subsequent editions. Reprinted by Donne's editors either in part (e.g. §163: pp. 3–9) or in their entirety (e.g. §158: I, 371–95; §170: pp. 81–107), they are detailed most fully in A. J. Smith's *John Donne: The Critical Heritage* (§753: especially pp. 67–68, 84–103, 110–14). Only two of these poems are made available here, but they are the most noteworthy, written as they are by the considerable poets Henry King and Thomas Carew. I have added the two 'epigrams' by Ben Jonson which, scarcely 'commemorative' since they were written c. 1610, appeared first in Jonson's *Works* of 1616 and next in the editions of Donne's poems from 1650 to 1669. For a modern effort, see §203.

Coleridge, remarking on the impressive commemorative poems written during the Renaissance, concluded that 'These on Donne are more than usually excellent, their chief, and, indeed, almost only fault, being want of smoothness, flow, and perspicuity, from too great compression of thought – too many thoughts, and, often, too much thought in each'. He added: 'There are occasions, in which a regret expresses itself, not only in the most manly but likewise in the most natural way, by intellectual effort and activity, in proof of intellectual admiration. This is one; and with this feeling should these poems be read' (§210).

Henry King:
'To the Memorie of My Ever Desired Friend Dr. Donne'

To have liv'd eminent, in a degree
Beyond our lofty'st flights, that is, like Thee,
Or t' have had too much merit, is not safe;
For, such excesses finde no Epitaph.
At common graves we have Poetique eyes   5
Can melt themselves in easie Elegies,

Each quill can drop his tributary verse,
And pin it, like the Hatchments, to the Hearse:
But at Thine, Poeme, or Inscription
(Rich soule of wit, and language) we have none.   10
Indeed a silence does that tombe befit,
Where is no Herald left to blazon it.
Widow'd invention justly doth forbeare
To come abroad, knowing Thou art not here,
Late her great Patron: Whose Prerogative   15
Maintain'd, and cloth'd her so, as none alive
Must now presume, to keepe her at thy rate,
Though he the Indies for her dowre estate.
Or else that awfull fire, which once did burne
In thy cleare Braine, now falne into thy Urne   20
Lives there, to fright rude Empiricks from thence,
Which might prophane thee by their Ignorance.
Who ever writes of Thee, and in a stile
Unworthy such a Theme, does but revile
Thy precious Dust, and wake a learned Spirit   25
Which may revenge his Rapes upon thy Merit.
For, all a low pitch't phansie can devise,
Will prove, at best, but Hallow'd Injuries.
     Thou, like the dying Swanne, didst lately sing
Thy Mournfull Dirge, in audience of the King;   30
When pale lookes, and faint accents of thy breath,
Presented so, to life, that peece of death,
That it was fear'd, and prophesi'd by all,
Thou thither cam'st to preach thy Funerall.
O! had'st Thou in an Elegiacke Knell   35
Rung out unto the world thine owne farewell,
And in thy High Victorious Numbers beate
The solemne measure of thy griev'd Retreat;
Thou might'st the Poets Service now have mist
As well, as then thou did'st prevent the Priest;   40
And never to the world beholding bee
So much, as for an Epitaph for thee.
     I doe not like the office. Nor is 't fit
Thou, who did'st lend our Age such summes on wit,
Should'st now re-borrow from her bankrupt Mine,   45
That Ore to Bury Thee, which once was Thine,
Rather still leave us in thy debt; And know
(Exalted Soule) more glory 't is to owe

Unto thy Hearse, what we can never pay,
Then, with embased Coine those Rites defray.   50
   Commit we then Thee to Thy selfe: Nor blame
Our drooping loves, which thus to thy owne Fame
Leave Thee Executour. Since, but thine owne,
No pen could doe Thee Justice, nor Bayes Crowne
Thy vast desert; Save that, wee nothing can   55
Depute, to be thy Ashes Guardian.
   So Jewellers no Art, or Metall trust
   To forme the Diamond, but the Diamonds dust.

Thomas Carew:
'An Elegie upon the death of the Deane of Pauls, Dr. John Donne'

Can we not force from widdowed Poetry,
Now thou art dead (Great DONNE) one Elegie
To crowne thy Hearse? Why yet dare we not trust
Though with unkneaded dowe-bak't prose thy dust,
Such as the uncisor'd Churchman from the flower   5
Of fading Rhetorique, short liv'd as his houre,
Dry as the sand that measures it, should lay
Upon thy Ashes, on the funerall day?
Have we no voice, no tune? Did'st thou dispense
Through all our language, both the words and sense?   10
'Tis a sad truth: The Pulpit may her plaine,
And sober Christian precepts still retaine,
Doctrines it may, and wholesome Uses frame,
Grave Homilies, and Lectures, But the flame
Of thy brave Soule, that shot such heat and light,   15
As burnt our earth, and made our darknesse bright,
Committed holy Rapes upon our Will,
Did through the eye the melting heart distill;
And the deepe knowledge of darke truths so teach,
As sense might judge, what phansie could not reach;   20
Must be desir'd for ever. So the fire,
That fills with spirit and heat the Delphique quire,
Which kindled first by thy Promethean breath,
Glow'd here a while, lies quench't now in thy death;
The Muses garden with Pedantique weedes   25
O'rspred, was purg'd by thee; The lazie seeds

Of servile imitation throwne away;
And fresh invention planted, Thou didst pay
The debts of our penurious bankrupt age;
Licentious thefts, that make poëtique rage   30
A Mimique fury, when out soules must bee
Possest, or with Anacreons Extasie,
Or Pindars, not their owne; The subtle cheat
Of she Exchanges, and the jugling feat
Of two-edg'd words, or whatsoever wrong   35
By ours was done the Greeke, or Latine tongue,
Thou hast redeem'd, and open'd Us a Mine
Of rich and pregnant phansie, drawne a line
Of masculine expression, which had good
Old Orpheus seene, Or all the ancient Brood   40
Our superstitious fooles admire, and hold
Their lead more precious, then thy burnish't Gold,
Thou hadst beene their Exchequer, and no more
They each in others dust, had rak'd for Ore.
Thou shalt yield no precedence, but of time,   45
And the blinde fate of language, whose tun'd chime
More charmes the outward sense; Yet thou maist claime
From so great disadvantage greater fame,
Since to the awe of thy imperious wit
Our stubborne language bends, made only fit   50
With her tough-thick-rib'd hoopes to gird about
Thy Giant phansie, which had prov'd too stout
For their soft melting Phrases. As in time
They had the start, so did they cull the prime
Buds of invention many a hundred yeare,   55
And left the rifled fields, besides the feare
To touch their Harvest, yet from those bare lands
Of what is purely thine, thy only hands
(And that thy smallest worke) have gleaned more
Then all those times, and tongues could reape before;   60
But thou art gone, and thy strict lawes will be
Too hard for Libertines in Poetrie.
They will repeale the goodly exil'd traine
Of gods and goddesses, which in thy just raigne
Were banish'd nobler Poems, now, with these   65
The silenc'd tales o'th'Metamorphoses
Shall stuffe their lines, and swell the windy Page,
Till Verse refin'd by thee, in this last Age,

Turne ballad rime, Or those old Idolls bee
Ador'd againe, with new apostasie;   70
Oh, pardon mee, that breake with untun'd verse
The reverend silence that attends thy herse,
Whose awfull solemne murmures were to thee
More then these faint lines, A loud Elegie,
That did proclaime in a dumbe cloquence   75
The death of all the Arts, whose influence
Growne feeble, in these panting numbers lies
Gasping short winded Accents, and so dies:
So doth the swiftly turning wheele not stand
In th'instant we withdraw the moving hand,   80
But some small time maintaine a faint weake course
By vertue of the first impulsive force:
And so whil'st I cast on thy funerall pile
Thy crowne of Bayes, Oh, let it crack a while,
And spit disdaine, till the devouring flashes   85
Suck all the moysture up, then turne to ashes.
I will not draw the envy to engrosse
All thy perfections, or weepe all our losse;
Those are too numerous for an Elegie,
And this too great, to be express'd by mee.   90
Though every pen should share a distinct part,
Yet art thou Theme enough to tyre all Art;
Let others carve the rest, it shall, suffice
I on thy Tombe this Epitaph incise.

    Here lies a King, that rul'd as hee thought fit   95
    The universall Monarchy of wit;
    Here lie two Flamens, and both those, the best,
    Apollo's first, at last, the true Gods Priest.

Ben Jonson:
'To John Donne'

(I)

Donne, the delight of Phœbus, and each *Muse*,
  Who, to thy one, all other braines refuse;
Whose every worke, of thy most earely wit,
  Came forth example, and remaines so, yet:
Longer a knowing, then most wits doe live.   5
  And which no affection praise enough can give!
To it, thy language, letters, arts, best life,
  Which might with halfe mankind maintayne a strife.
All which I meant to praise, and, yet, I would;
  But leave, because I cannot as I should!   10

(II)

Who shall doubt, Donne, where I a *Poet* bee,
  When I dare send my *Epigrammes* to thee?
That so alone canst judge, so alone dost make:
  And, in thy censures, evenly, dost take
As free simplicitie, to dis-avow,   5
  As thou hast best authoritie, t'allow.
Reade all I send: and, if I find but one
  Mark'd by thy hand, and with the better stone,
My title's seal'd. Those that for claps doe write,
  Let pui'nees, porters, players praise delight,   10
And, till they burst, their backs, like asses load:
  A man should seeke great glorie, and not broad.

To John Donne (II).
  8. *the better stone*: i.e. the white stone with which the ancient Romans
     observed happy days.
 10. *pui'nees*: inferiors.

Appendix IV
Pope's Versions of Donne's Satyres II and IV

The 'tagging' of poems – as Milton described Dryden's efforts freely to adapt *Paradise Lost* – is uncommon enough to be of interest in itself. But when the efforts are mounted by a poet like Pope in positive reappraisal of a poet like Donne, the result may fairly be regarded as a measure of the differences between two radically different attitudes to poetry.

Pope 'versified' two of Donne's *Satyres*, the second and the fourth, in 1713; they were published in 1733–35, in each case preceded by the same quotation from Horace: 'why shouldn't we inquire as we read Lucilius' writings / whether it was the harshness of his own nature or that of his circumstances / which prevented his verses from being more finished and more smoothly flowing?' (*Satires*, I, x, 56–59; trans. Niall Rudd, 1973).

The Second Satire of Dr. John Donne, Dean of St. Paul's, Versifyed

Yes; thank my stars! as early as I knew
This Town, I had the sense to hate it too:
Yet here, as ev'n in Hell, there must be still
One Giant-Vice, so excellently ill,
That all beside one pities, not abhors;   5
As who knows Sapho, smiles at other whores.
  I grant that Poetry's a crying sin;
It brought (no doubt) th' *Excise* and *Army* in:
Catch'd like the plague, or love, the Lord knows how,
But that the cure is starving, all allow.   10
Yet like the Papists is the Poets state,
Poor and disarm'd, and hardly worth your hate.
  Here a lean Bard, whose wit could never give
Himself a dinner, makes an Actor live:

The Thief condemn'd, in law already dead,   15
So prompts, and saves a Rogue who cannot read.
Thus as the pipes of some carv'd Organ move,
The gilded Puppets dance and mount above,
Heav'd by the breath th' inspiring Bellows blow;
Th' inspiring Bellows lie and pant below.   20
   One sings the Fair; but Songs no longer move,
No Rat is rhym'd to death, nor Maid to love:
In Love's, in Nature's spite, the siege they hold,
And scorn the Flesh, the Dev'l, and all but Gold.
   These write to Lords, some mean reward to get,   25
As needy Beggars sing at doors for meat.
Those write because all write, and so have still
Excuse for writing, and for writing ill.
   Wretched indeed! but far more wretched yet
Is he who makes his meal on others wit.   30
'Tis chang'd no doubt from what it was before,
His rank digestion makes it wit no more:
Sense, past thro' him, no longer is the same,
For food digested takes another name.
   I pass o'er all those Confessors and Martyrs   35
Who live like S—tt—n, or who die like Chartres,
Out-cant old Esdras, or out-drink his Heir,
Out-usure Jews, or Irishmen out-swear;
Wicked as Pages, who in early years
Act Sins which Prisca's Confessor scarce hears: 40
Ev'n those I pardon, for whose sinful sake
Schoolmen new tencments in Hell must make;
Of whose strange crimes no Canonist can tell
In what Commandment's large contents they dwell.
   One, one man only breeds my just offence;   45
Whom Crimes gave wealth, and wealth gave impudence:
Time, that at last matures a Clap to Pox,
Whose gentle progress makes a Calf an Ox,
And brings all natural events to pass,
Hath made him an Attorney of an Ass.   50
No young Divine, new-benefic'd, can be
More pert, more proud, more positive than he.
What further could I wish the Fop to do,
But turn a Wit, and scribble verses too?
Pierce the soft lab'rinth of a Lady's ear   55
With rhymes of this *per Cent.* and that *per Year?*

Or court a Wife, spread out his wily parts,
Like nets or lime-twigs, for rich Widows hearts?
Call himself Barrister to ev'ry wench,
And wooe in language of the Pleas and Bench?   60
Language, which Boreas might to Auster hold,
More rough than forty Germans when they scold.
    Curs'd be the Wretch! so venal and so vain;
Paltry and proud, as drabs in Drury-lane.
'Tis such a bounty as was never known,   65
If Peter deigns to help you to your *own:*
What thanks, what praise, if Peter but supplies!
And what a solemn face if he denies!
Grave, as when Pris'ners shake the head, and swear
'Twas only Suretyship that brought 'em there.   70
His *Office* keeps your Parchment-Fates entire,
He starves with cold to save them from the Fire;
For you, he walks the streets thro' rain or dust,
For not in Chariots Peter puts his trust;
For you he sweats and labours at the Laws,   75
Takes God to witness he affects your Cause,
And lyes to every Lord in every thing,
Like a King's Favourite—or like a King.
    These are the talents that adorn them all,
From wicked Waters ev'n to godly –   80
Not more of Simony beneath black Gowns,
Nor more of Bastardy in heirs to Crowns.
In shillings and in pence at first they deal,
And steal so little, few perceive they steal;
Till like the Sea, they compass all the land,   85
From Scots to Wight, from Mount to Dover strand.
And when rank Widows purchase luscious nights,
Or when a Duke to Jansen punts at White's,
Or City heir in mortgage melts away,
Satan himself feels far less joy than they.   90
Piecemeal they win this Acre first, then that,
Glean on, and gather up the whole Estate:
Then strongly fencing ill-got wealth by law,
Indentures, Cov'nants, Articles they draw;
Large as the Fields themselves, and larger far   95
Than Civil Codes, with all their glosses, are:
So vast, our new Divines, we must confess,
Are Fathers of the Church for writing less.

But let them write for You, each Rogue impairs
The Deeds, and dextrously omits, *ses Heires:*   100
No Commentator can more slily pass
O'er a learn'd, unintelligible place;
Or, in Quotation, shrewd Divines leave out
Those words, that would against them clear the doubt.
  So Luther thought the Paternoster long,   105
When doom'd to say his Beads and Evensong:
But having cast his Cowle, and left those laws,
Adds to Christ's prayer, the *Pow'r and Glory* clause.
  The Lands are bought; but where are to be found
Those ancient Woods, that shaded all the ground?   110
We see no new-built Palaces aspire,
No Kitchens emulate the Vestal Fire.
Where are those Troops of poor, that throng'd of yore
The good old Landlord's hospitable door?
Well, I could wish, that still in lordly domes   115
Some beasts were kill'd, tho' not whole hecatombs,
That both Extremes were banish'd from their walls,
Carthusian Fasts, and fulsome Bacchanals;
And all mankind might that just mean observe,
In which none e'er could surfeit, none could starve.   120
These, as good works 'tis true we all allow;
But oh! these works are not in fashion now:
Like rich old Wardrobes, things extremely rare,
Extremely fine, but what no man will wear.
  Thus much I've said, I trust without offence;   125
Let no Court-Sycophant pervert my sense,
Nor sly Informer watch these words to draw
Within the reach of Treason, or the Law.

The Fourth Satire of Dr. John Donne, Dean of St. Paul's, Versified

Well, if it be my time to quit the Stage,
Adieu to all the Follies of the Age!
I die in Charity with Fool and Knave,
Secure of Peace at least beyond the Grave.
I've had my *Purgatory* here betimes,   5
And paid for all my Satires, all my Rhymes:

The Poet's Hell, its Tortures, Fiends and Flames,
To this were Trifles, Toys, and empty Names.
    With foolish *Pride* my Heart was never fir'd,
Nor the vain Itch *t'admire*, or *be admir'd*;   10
I hop'd for no *Commission* from his Grace;
I bought no *Benefice*, I begg'd no *Place*;
Had no *new Verses*, or *new Suit* to show;
Yet went to Court! – the Dev'l wou'd have it so.
But, as the Fool, that in reforming Days   15
Wou'd go to Mass in jest, (as Story says)
Could not but think, to pay his *Fine* was odd,
Since 'twas no form'd Design of serving God:
So was I punish'd, as if full as *proud*,
As prone to *Ill*, as negligent of *Good*,   20
As deep in *Debt*, without a thought to pay,   ⎫
As *vain*, as *idle*, and as *false*, as they   ⎬
Who *live* at *Court*, for going once that Way!   ⎭
    Scarce was I enter'd, when behold! there came
A Thing which *Adam* had been pos'd to name;   25
Noah had refus'd it lodging in his Ark,
Where all the Race of *Reptiles* might embark:
A verier Monster than on *Africk's* Shore
The Sun e're got, or slimy *Nilus* bore,
Or *Sloane*, or *Woodward*'s wondrous Shelves contain;   30
Nay, all that lying Travellers can feign.
The Watch would hardly let him pass at noon,
At night, wou'd swear him dropt out of the moon,
One whom the mob, when next we find or make
A Popish plot, shall for a Jesuit take;   35
And the wise Justice starting from his chair
Cry, by your Priesthood tell me what you are?
    Such was the Wight: Th' apparel on his back
Tho' coarse was rev'rend, and tho' bare, was black.
The suit, if by the fashion one might guess,   40
Was velvet in the youth of good Queen *Bess*,
But mere tuff-taffety what now remained;
So Time, that changes all things, had ordain'd!
Our sons shall see it leisurely decay,
First turn plain rash, then vanish quite away.   45
    This Thing has *travell'd*, speaks each language too,
And knows what's fit for ev'ry State to do;
Of whose best Phrase and courtly Accent join'd,
He forms one Tongue exotic and refin'd.

Talkers, I've learn'd to bear; *Motteux* I knew,   50
Henley himself I've heard, nay *Budgel* too:
The Doctor's Wormwood Style, the Hash of Tongues,
A Pedant makes; the Storm of *Gonson*'s Lungs,
The whole Artill'ry of the Terms of War,
And (all those Plagues in one) the bawling Bar;   55
These I cou'd bear; but not a Rogue so civil,
Whose Tongue can complement you to the Devil.
A Tongue that can cheat Widows, cancel Scores,
Make *Scots* speak Treason, cozen subtlest Whores,
With Royal Favourites in Flatt'ry vie,   60
And *Oldmixon* and *Burnet* both out-lie.
   He spies me out. I whisper, gracious God!
What Sin of mine cou'd merit such a Rod?
That all the Shot of Dulness now must be
From this thy Blunderbuss discharg'd on me!   65
'Permit (he cries) no stranger to your fame
To crave your sentiment, if —'s your name.
What *Speech* esteem you most?' – 'The *King*'s,' said I,
'But the best *Words*?' – 'O Sir, the *Dictionary*.'
'You miss my aim; I mean the most acute   70
And perfect *Speaker*?' – '*Onslow*, past dispute.'
'But Sir, of Writers?' – '*Swift*, for closer Style,
And *Ho—y* for a Period of a Mile.'
'Why yes, 'tis granted, these indeed may pass
Good common Linguists, and so *Panurge* was: 75
Nay troth, th'*Apostles*, (tho' perhaps too rough)
Had once a pretty Gift of Tongues enough.
Yet these were all *poor Gentlemen*! I dare
Affirm, 'twas *Travel* made them what they were.'
   Thus others Talents having nicely shown,   80
He came by sure Transition to his own:
Till I cry'd out, 'You prove yourself so able,
Pity! you was not Druggerman at *Babel*:
For had they found a Linguist half so good,
I make no question but the *Tow*'r had stood.'   85
   'Obliging Sir! for Courts you sure were made:
Why then for ever buried in the shade?
Spirits like you, believe me, shou'd be seen,
The King would smile on you – at least the Queen?'
'Ah gentle Sir! you Courtiers so cajol us –   90
But *Tully* has it, *Nunquam minus solus*:

But as for *Courts*, forgive me if I say,
No Lessons now are taught the *Spartan* way:
Tho' in his Pictures Lust be full display'd,
Few are the Converts *Aretine* has made;   95
And tho' the Court show *Vice* exceeding clear,
None shou'd, by my Advice, learn *Virtue* there.'
    At this, entranc'd, he lifts his Hands and Eyes,
Squeaks like a high-stretch'd Lutestring, and replies:
'Oh 'tis the sweetest of all earthly things   100
To gaze on Princes, and to talk of Kings!'
'Then happy Man who shows the Tombs!' said I,
'He dwells amidst the Royal Family;
He, ev'ry Day, from *King* to *King* can walk,
Of all our *Harries*, all our *Edwards* talk,   105
And get by speaking Truth of Monarchs dead,
What few can of the living, *Ease* and *Bread*.'
'Lord! Sir, a meer *Mechanick*! strangely low,
And coarse of Phrase – your *English* all are so.
How elegant your *Frenchman?*' – 'Mine, d'ye mean?   110
I have but one, I hope the Fellow's clean.'
'Oh! Sir, politely so! nay, let me dye,
Your only wearing is your *Padua-soy*.'
'Not Sir, my only – I have better still,
And this, you see, is but my Dishabille –'   115
Wild to get loose, his Patience I provoke,
Mistake, confound, object, at all he spoke.
But as coarse Iron, sharpen'd, mangles more,
And Itch most hurts, when anger'd to a Sore;
So when you plague a Fool, 'tis still the Curse,   120
You only make the Matter worse and worse.
    He past it o'er; affects an easy Smile
At all my Peevishness, and turns his Style.
He asks, 'What *News?*' I tell him of new Plays,
New Eunuchs, Harlequins, and Operas.   125
He hears; and as a Still, with Simples in it,
Between each Drop it gives, stays half a Minute;
Loth to enrich me with too quick Replies,
By little, and by little, drops his Lies.
Meer *Household Trash*! of Birth-Nights, Balls and Shows,   130
More than ten *Holingsheds*, or *Halls*, or *Stows*.
When the *Queen* frown'd, or smil'd, he knows; and what
A subtle Minister may make of that?

Who sins with whom? who got his Pension *Rug*,
Or quicken'd a Reversion by a *Drug?*   135
Whose Place is *quarter'd out*, three Parts in four,
And whether to a Bishop, or a Whore?
Who, having lost his Credit, pawn'd his Rent,
Is therefore fit to have a *Government?*
Who in the *Secret*, deals in Stocks secure,   140
And cheats th'unknowing Widow, and the Poor?
Who makes a *Trust*, or *Charity*, a Job,
And gets an Act of Parliament to rob?
Why *Turnpikes* rise, and now no Cit, nor Clown
Can *gratis* see the *Country*, or the *Town?*   145
Shortly no Lad shall *chuck*, or Lady *vole*,
But some excising Courtier will have Toll.
He tells what Strumpet Places sells for Life,
What 'Squire his Lands, what Citizen his Wife?
And last (which proves him wiser still than all)   150
What Lady's Face is not a whited Wall?
As one of *Woodward*'s Patients, sick and sore,
I puke, I nauseate, — yet he thrusts in more;
Trims *Europe*'s Balance, tops the Statesman's part,
And talks *Gazettes* and *Post-Boys* o'er by heart.   155
Like a big Wife at sight of loathsome Meat,
Ready to cast, I yawn, I sigh, and sweat:
Then as a licens'd Spy, whom nothing can
Silence, or hurt, he libels the *Great Man*;
Swears every *Place entail'd* for Years to come,   160
In *sure Succession* to the Day of Doom:
He names the *Price* for ev'ry *Office* paid,
And says our *Wars thrive ill*, because *delay'd*;
Nay hints, 'tis by Connivance of the Court,
That *Spain* robs on, and *Dunkirk*'s still a Port.   165
Not more Amazement seiz'd on *Circe*'s Guests,
To see themselves fall endlong into Beasts,
Than mine, to find a Subject staid and wise,
Already half turn'd Traytor by surprize.
I fear'd th'Infection slide from him to me,   170
As in the Pox, some give it, to get free;
And quick to swallow me, methought I saw
One of our Giant *Statutes* ope its Jaw!
In that nice Moment, as another Lye
Stood just a-tilt, the *Minister* came by.   175

Away he flies. He bows, and bows again;
And close as *Umbra* joins the dirty Train.
Not *Fannius* self more impudently near.
When half his Nose is in his Patron's Ear.
I quak'd at heart; and still afraid to see   180
All the Court fill'd stranger things than he,
Ran out as fast, as one that pays his Bail,
And dreads more Actions, hurries from a Jail.

Bear me, some God! oh quickly bear me hence
To wholesome Solitude, the Nurse of Sense: 185
Where Contemplation prunes her ruffled Wings,
And the free Soul looks down to pity Kings.
There sober Thought pursu'd th'amusing theme
Till Fancy colour'd it, and form'd a Dream.
A *Vision* Hermits can to Hell transport,   190
And force ev'n me to see the Damn'd at Court.
Not *Dante* dreaming all th' Infernal State,
Beheld such Scenes of *Envy*, *Sin*, and *Hate*.
Base Fear becomes the Guilty, not the Free;
Suits Tyrants, Plunderers, but suits not me.   195
Shall I, the Terror of this sinful Town,
Care, if a livery'd Lord or smile or frown?
Who cannot flatter, and detest who can,
Tremble before a *noble Serving-Man?*
O my fair Mistress, *Truth*! Shall I quit thee,   200
For huffing, braggart, puft *Nobility?*
Thou, who since Yesterday, hast roll'd o'er all
The busy, idle Blockheads of the Ball,
Hast thou, O *Sun*! beheld an emptier sort,
Than such as swell this Bladder of a Court?   205
Now pox on those who shew a *Court in Wax*!
It ought to bring all Courtiers on their backs.
Such painted Puppets, such a varnish'd Race
Of hollow Gewgaws, only Dress and Face,
Such waxen Noses, stately, staring things,   210
No wonder some Folks bow, and think them *Kings*.
See! where the *British* Youth, engag'd no more
At *Fig*'s at *White*'s, with *Felons*, or a *Whore*,
Pay their last Duty to the *Court*, and come
All fresh and fragrant, to the *Drawing-Room*:   215
In Hues as gay, and Odours as divine,
As the fair Fields they sold to look so fine.

'That's *Velvet* for a *King*!' the Flattr'er swears;
'Tis true, for ten days hence 'twill be *King Lear*'s.
Our Court may justly to our Stage give Rules,   220
That helps it both to *Fool's-Coats* and to *Fools*.
And why not Players strut in Courtiers Cloaths?
For these are Actors too, as well as those:
Wants reach all States; they beg but better drest,
And all is *splendid Poverty* at best.   225
  Painted for sight, and essenc'd for the smell,
Like Frigates fraught with Spice and Cochine'l,
Sail in the *Ladies*: How each Pyrate eyes
So weak a Vessel, and so rich a Prize!
Top-gallant he, and she in all her Trim,   230
He boarding her, she striking sail to him.
'Dear *Countess*! you have Charms all Hearts to hit!'
And '*sweet Sir Fopling*! you have so much wit!'
Such Wits and Beauties are not prais'd for nought,
For both the Beauty and the Wit are *bought*.   235
'Twou'd burst ev'n *Heraclitus* with the Spleen,
To see those Anticks, *Fopling* and *Courtin*:
The *Presence* seems, with things so richly odd,
The Mosque of *Mahound*, or some queer *Pa-god*.
See them survey their Limbs by *Durer*'s Rules,   240
Of all Beau-kind the best proportion'd Fools!
Adjust their Cloaths, and to Confession draw
Those venial sins, an Atom, or a Straw:
But oh! what Terrors must distract the Soul,
Convicted of that mortal Crime, a Hole!   245
Or should one Pound of Powder less bespread
Those Monkey-Tails that wag behind their Head!
Thus finish'd and corrected to a hair,
They march, to prate their Hour before the Fair,
So first to preach a white-glov'd Chaplain goes,   250
With Band of Lily, and with Cheek of Rose,
Sweeter than *Sharon*, in immaculate trim,
Neatness itself impertinent in him.
Let but the Ladies smile, and they are blest;
Prodigious! how the Things *Protest, Protest*:   255
Peace, Fools! or *Gonson* will for Papists seize you,
If once he catch you at your *Jesu! Jesu!*
  Nature made ev'ry Fop to plague his Brother,
Just as one Beauty mortifies another.

But here's the *Captain*, that will plague them both,   260
Whose Air cries Arm! whose very Look's an Oath:
Tho' his Soul's Bullet, and his Body Buff!
Damn him, he's honest, Sir, – and that's enuff.
He spits fore-right; his haughty Chest before,
Like batt'ring Rams, beats open ev'ry Door;   265
And with a Face as red, and as awry,
As *Herod*'s Hang-dogs in old Tapestry,
Scarecrow to Boys, the breeding Woman's curse;
Has yet a strange Ambition to *look worse*:
Confounds the Civil, keeps the Rude in awe,   270
Jests like a licens'd Fool, commands like Law.
Frighted, I quit the Room, but leave it so,
As Men from Jayls to Execution go;
For hung with *Deadly Sins* I see the Wall,
And lin'd with *Giants*, deadlier than 'em all: 275
Each Man an *Ascapart*, of Strength to toss
For Quoits, both *Temple-Bar* and *Charing-Cross*.
Scar'd at the grizly Forms, I sweat, I fly,
And shake all o'er, like a discover'd Spy.
Courts are too much for Wits so weak as mine;   280
Charge them with Heav'n's Artill'ry, bold *Divine*!
From such alone the Great Rebukes endure,
Whose *Satyr*'s *sacred*, and whose Rage *secure*.
'Tis mine to wash a few slight Stains; but theirs
To deluge Sin, and drown a Court in Tears.   285
Howe'er, what's now *Apocrypha*, my Wit,
In time to come, may pass for *Holy Writ*.

Bibliography

Contents

Abbreviations

CP	*Concerning Poetry*
CQ	*Critical Quarterly*
CR	*Critical Review* (Melbourne)
ditto	'as before'
EIC	*Essays in Criticism*
ELH	*A Journal of English Literary History*
ELN	*English Language Notes*
ELR	*English Literary Renaissance*
ES	*English Studies*
ESEA	*Essays and Studies* by Members of the English Association
Ex	*Explicator*
FK	Frank Kermode (ed.), *Discussions of John Donne* (Boston, 1962)
FKM	Frank Kermode (ed.), *The Metaphysical Poets: Key Essays . . .* (Greenwich, Conn., 1969)
GAS	Gary A. Stringer (ed.), *New Essays on Donne* (Salzburg, 1977)
HG	Helen Gardner (ed.), *John Donne: A Collection of Critical Essays* (Englewood Cliffs, N.J., 1962)
HLQ	*Huntington Library Quarterly*
ibid.	*ibidem*: 'in the same place'
i.e.	*id est*: 'that is to say'
JDJ	*John Donne Journal*
JEGP	*Journal of English and Germanic Philology*
JHI	*Journal of the History of Ideas*
JL	Julian Lovelock (ed.), *Donne: 'Songs and Sonnets' – A Casebook* (1973)
JRR	John R. Roberts (ed.), *Essential Articles for the Study of John Donne's Poetry* (Hamden, Conn., 1975)
KR	*Kenyon Review*
LL	*Language and Literature*
LS	*Language and Style*
LWU	*Literatur in Wissenschaft und Unterricht*
MLN	*Modern Language Notes*
MLQ	*Modern Language Quarterly*
MLR	*Modern Language Review*
MP	*Modern Philology*
MS/MSS	manuscript(s)
MWP	Margaret W. Pepperdene (ed.), *That Subtile Wreath* (Atlanta, 1973) [quatercentenary essays]
NQ	*Notes and Queries*
NS	*Die neueren Sprachen*

OED	*The Oxford English Dictionary*
PAF	Peter A. Fiore (ed.), *Just so much Honor* (University Park, Pa., 1972) [quatercentenary essays]
PBSA	*Papers of the Bibliographical Society of America*
PLL	*Papers on Language and Literature*
PQ	*Philological Quarterly*
PMLA	*Publications of the Modern Language Association*
QJS	*Quarterly Journal of Speech*
RES	*Review of English Studies*
RLC	*Revue de littérature comparée*
RLMC	*Rivista di letterature moderne e comparate*
RR	*Renaissance and Reformation*
SAQ	*South Atlantic Quarterly*
SCN	*Seventeenth Century News*
SEL	*Studies in English Literature*
Sermons	*The Sermons of John Donne*: see §181
SP	*Studies in Philology*
SR	*Sewanee Review*
TLS	*Times Literary Supplement* (London)
TS	Theodore Spencer (ed.), *A Garland for John Donne* (Cambridge, Mass., 1931)
TSE	*Tulane Studies in English*
TSL	*Tennessee Studies in Literature*
TSLL	*Texas Studies in Literature and Language*
UTQ	*University of Toronto Quarterly*
WRK	William R. Keast (ed.), *Seventeenth-Century English Poetry: Modern Essays in Criticism* (1962)
XUS	*Xavier University Studies*

The place of publication is given only if it is other than London or New York (see 'A Note on Abbreviations', above, p. 1).

For the symbol ', see above, p. 5.

A Bibliographical Note

There are detailed bibliographies in C. S. Lewis (§75); Douglas Bush (§15); *The New Cambridge Bibliography of English Literature*, ed. George Watson, Vol. I (1974); and especially *The Age of Milton* (§109), which includes bibliographies of both primary sources ('An Introduction to *The Short-Title Catalogue*') and secondary sources.

Annual bibliographies include: The English Association's *The Year's Work in English Studies* (1919 ff.); the Modern Humanities Research Association's *Annual Bibliography of English Language and Literature* (1920 ff.); *PMLA* (1922 ff.); and *SP* (1922 ff.).

On Donne in particular, see below, pp. 521 ff.; and on poets related to him: the bibliography in *The English Poems of George Herbert*, ed. C. A. Patrides (Everyman's University Library, London and Totowa, N.J., 1974), pp. 214–38, and the fuller bibliographies by John R. Roberts on Herbert (1978) and Crashaw (1985).

Background Studies

§1. Addleshaw, G. W. O.: *High Church Tradition: A Study in the Liturgical Thought of the Seventeenth Century* (1941).

§2. Addleshaw, G. W. O., and Frederick Etchells: *The Architectural Setting of Anglican Worship* (1948).

§3. Akrigg, G. P. V.: *Jacobean Pageant; or the Court of James I* (1962).

§4. Allen, Don C.: *The Legend of Noah: Renaissance Rationalism in Art, Science and Letters* (Urbana, 1949).

§5. Ashley, Maurice: *The Golden Century: Europe 1598–1715* (1969).

§6. Ashton, Trevor (ed.): *Crisis in Europe 1560–1660* (1965).

§7. Atkins, J. W. H.: *English Literary Criticism: The Renascence*, 2nd ed. (1951).

§8. Baker, Herschel: *The Dignity of Man* (Cambridge, Mass., 1947, repr. as *The Image of Man*, 1961), and *The Wars of Truth* (1952). Companion volumes on the climax and decay of Renaissance Christian humanism.

§9. Baroway, Israel: 'The Bible as Poetry in the English Renaissance: An Introduction', *JEGP*, 32 (1933), 447–80; and three related studies in *ELH*: 2 (1935), 66–91; 8 (1941), 119–42; and 17 (1950), 115–35.

§10. Beardslee, John W. (ed. and trans.): *Reformed Dogmatics* (1965). Primary sources. Cf. §53.

§11. Benevolo, Leonardo: *The Architecture of the Renaissance*, trans. Judith Landry (1977).

§12. Bennett, H. S.: *English Books and Readers 1558 to 1603* and *1603 to 1640* (Cambridge, 1965 and 1970).

§13. Bradbury, Malcolm, and David Palmer (eds.): *Metaphysical Poetry* (1970; Bloomington, 1971).

§14.   Burtt, Edwin A.: *The Metaphysical Foundations of Modern Physical Science*, 2nd rev. ed. (1932).

§15.   Bush, Douglas: *English Literature in the Earlier Seventeenth Century*, 2nd rev. ed. (Oxford, 1962); with extensive bibliographies.

§16.   Bush, Douglas: *Prefaces to Renaissance Literature* (Cambridge, Mass., 1965).

§17.   Bush, Douglas: *The Renaissance and English Humanism* (Toronto, 1939).

§18.   Butler, Christopher: *Number Symbolism* (1970).

§19.   Campbell, Lily B.: *Divine Poetry and Drama in Sixteenth Century England* (Cambridge, 1959).

§20.   Cassirer, Ernst: *The Platonic Renaissance in England*, trans. J. P. Pettegrove (1953).

§21.   Chandos, John (ed.): *In God's Name: Examples of Preaching in England . . . 1534–1662* (1971).

§22.   Charlton, Kenneth: *Education in Renaissance England* (1965).

§23.   Christianson, Paul K.: *Reformers and Babylon: Apocalyptic Visions in England from the Reformation to the Outbreak of the Civil War* (Toronto, 1977).

§24.   Cochrane, Eric (ed.): *The Late Italian Renaissance 1525–1630* (1970).

§25.   Cohen, J. M.: *The Baroque Lyric* (1963).

§26.   Coleman, D. C.: *The Economy of England, 1450–1750* (1977). Also, *Industry in Tudor and Stuart England* (1975).

§27.   Colie, Rosalie L.: *Paradoxia Epidemica: The Renaissance Tradition of Paradox* (Princeton, 1966).

§28.   Colie, Rosalie L.: *The Resources of Kind: Genre-Theory in the Renaissance* (Berkeley, 1973).

§29.   Collinson, Patrick: *The Elizabethan Puritan Movement* (1967).

§30.   Cruttwell, Patrick: *The Shakespearean Moment and its Place in the Poetry of the Seventeenth Century* (1954).

§31.   Curtis, Mark H.: *Oxford and Cambridge in Transition, 1558–1642* (Oxford, 1959).

§32.   Daiches, David: *The King James Version of the English Bible* (Chicago, 1941).

§33.   Davies, Godfrey: *The Early Stuarts 1603–1660*, 2nd ed. (Oxford, 1959).

§34.   Denonain, Jean-Jacques: *Thèmes et formes de la poésie 'métaphysique'* (Paris, 1956).

§35.   Dickens, A. G.: *The English Reformation* (1964).

§36.   Ellrodt, Robert: *L'Inspiration personelle et l'esprit du temps chez les poètes métaphysique anglais* (Paris, 1960), 2 vols. (in 3).

§37.   Elton, G. R.: *England under the Tudors*, 2nd ed. (1974).

§38.   Firth, Katherine R.: *The Apocalyptic Tradition in Reformation Britain 1530–1645* (Oxford, 1979).

§39.   Freeman, Rosemary: *English Emblem Books* (1948).

§40.   Fussner, F. Smith: *The Historical Revolution: English Historical Writing and Thought 1580–1640* (1962).

§41.   Garin, Eugenio: *Italian Humanism*, trans. Peter Munz (1965).

§42.   George, Charles H. and Katherine: *The Protestant Mind of the English Reformation* (Princeton, 1961).

§43.   Grierson, H. J. C.: *Cross-Currents in English Literature of the Seventeenth Century* (1961).

§44.   Halewood, William H.: *The Poetry of Grace: Reformation Themes and Structures in English Seventeenth-Century Poetry* (New Haven, 1970).

§45.   Hall, Marie Boas: *The Scientific Renaissance 1450–1630* (1962).

§46.   Hamilton, K. G.: *The Two Harmonies: Poetry and Prose in the Seventeenth Century* (Oxford, 1963).

§47.   Hardison, O. B., Jr.: *The Enduring Monument: A Study of the Idea Praise in Renaissance Literary Theory and Practice* (Chapel Hill, 1962).

§48.   Harris, Victor: *All Coherence Gone* (Chicago, 1949). On the widespread belief in nature's decay; with a discussion of Donne, pp. 123–29.

§49.   Harrison, A. W.: *Arminianism* (1937).

§50.   Hathaway, Baxter: *Marvels and Commonplaces: Renaissance Literary Criticism* (1968).

§51.   Heninger, S. K., Jr.: *A Handbook of Renaissance Meteorology* (Durham, N.C., 1960).

§52.   Heninger, S. K., Jr.: *Touches of Sweet Harmony: Pythagorean Cosmology and Renaissance Poetics* (San Marino, Calif., 1974). Also: *The Cosmological Glass: Renaissance Diagrams of the Universe* (San Marino, Calif., 1977).

§53.   Heppe, Heinrich (ed.): *Reformed Dogmatics*, trans. G. T. Thomson (1960). Primary sources. Cf. §10.

§54.   Hill, Christopher: *Society and Puritanism in Pre-Revolutionary England* (1964).

§55.   Holden, William P.: *Anti-Puritan Satire, 1572–1642* (New Haven, 1954).

§56.   Hollander, John: *The Untuning of the Sky: Ideas of Music in English Poetry 1500–1700* (Princeton, 1961).

§57.   Howell, Wilbur S.: *Logic and Rhetoric in England, 1500–1700* (Princeton, 1956).

§58. Hughes, Philip: *Rome and the Counter-Reformation in England* (1942).

§59. Johnson, Francis R.: *Astronomical Thought in Renaissance England* (Baltimore, 1937).

§60. Johnson, Paula: *Form and Transformation in Music and Poetry in the English Renaissance* (New Haven, 1972).

§61. Joseph, B. L.: *Shakespeare's Eden: The Commonwealth of England 1558–1629* (1971).

§62. Kamen, Henry: *The Iron Century: Social Change in Europe 1550–1660* (1971).

§63. Kernan, Alvin: *The Cankered Muse: Satire of the English Renaissance* (New Haven, 1959).

§64. Knappen, M. M.: *Tudor Puritanism* (Chicago, 1939).

§65. Knights, L. C.: *Drama and Society in the Age of Jonson* (1937), and 'On the Social Background of Metaphysical Poetry', *Scrutiny*, 13 (1945), 37–52.

§66. Kocher, Paul H.: *Science and Religion in Elizabethan England* (San Marino, Calif., 1953).

§67. Koenigsberger, H. G.: *The Habsburgs and Europe, 1516–1660* (Ithaca, N.Y., 1971).

§68. Koenigsberger, H. G., and George L. Mosse: *Europe in the Sixteenth Century* (1968).

§69. Koyré, Alexandre: *From the Closed World to the Infinite Universe* (Baltimore, 1957).

§70. Kristeller, Paul O., and Philip P. Wiener (eds.): *Renaissance Essays* (1968).

§71. Kuhn, Thomas S.: *The Copernican Revolution* (Cambridge, Mass., 1957).

§72. Levy, F. J.: *Tudor Historical Thought* (San Marino, Calif., 1967).

§73. Lewalski, Barbara K.: *Protestant Poetics and the Seventeenth-Century Religious Lyric* (Princeton, 1979).

§74. Lewis, C. S.: *The Discarded Image: An Introduction to Medieval and Renaissance Literature* (Cambridge, 1964).

§75. Lewis, C. S.: *English Literature in the Sixteenth Century excluding Drama* (Oxford, 1954); with extensive bibliographies.

§76. Lockyer, Roger: *Tudor and Stuart Britain 1471–1714* (1964).

§77. Long, Kenneth R.: *The Music of the English Church* (1971). With eight chapters on developments in the sixteenth and early seventeenth centuries.

§78. Lovejoy, Arthur O.: *The Great Chain of Being: A Study of the History of an Idea* (Cambridge, Mass., 1936).

§79. McAdoo, H. R.: *The Spirit of Anglicanism: A Survey of Anglican Theological Method in the Seventeenth Century* (1965).

§80.   Maclure, Millar: *The Paul's Cross Sermons, 1534–1642* (Toronto, 1958).

§81.   Martz, Louis L.: *The Poetry of Meditation: A Study in English Religious Literature of the Seventeenth Century*, rev. ed. (New Haven, 1962). Cf. §§259–60, 577–78.

§82.   Mazzaro, Jerome: *Transformations in the Renaissance English Lyric* (Ithaca, N.Y., 1970).

§83.   Mazzeo, Joseph A.: 'A Critique of Some Modern Theories of Metaphysical Poetry', in *ALC*, pp. 134–43; *FK*, pp. 118–25; *FKM*, pp. 158–71; *WRK*, pp. 63–74.

§84.   Mazzeo, Joseph A.: *Renaissance and Revolution: Backgrounds to Seventeenth-Century English Literature* (1965).

§85.   Mazzeo, Joseph A.: *Renaissance and Seventeenth-Century Studies* (1964).

§86.   Mercer, Eric: *English Art 1553–1625* (Oxford, 1962).

§87.   Miles, Josephine: *The Primary Language of Poetry in the 1640s* (Berkeley, 1948), being Part I of *The Continuity of Poetic Language* (Berkeley, 1951). Cf. §262.

§88.   Miner, Earl: *The Metaphysical Mode from Donne to Cowley* (Princeton, 1969).

§89.   Minta, Stephen: *Love Poetry in Sixteenth Century France: A Study in Themes and Traditions* (Manchester, 1977).

§90.   Minta, Stephen: *Petrarch and Petrarchism: The English and French Traditions* (Manchester, 1980).

§91.   Miriam Joseph, Sister, C.S.C.: *Rhetoric in Shakespeare's Time: Literary Theory of Renaissance Europe* (1962), abridged from her *Shakespeare's Use of the Arts of Language* (1947).

§92.   Mitchell, W. Fraser: *English Pulpit Oratory from Andrewes to Tillotson* (1932).

§93.   More, Paul E., and Frank L. Cross (eds.): *Anglicanism: The Thought and Practice of the Church of England, illustrated from the Religious Literature of the Seventeenth Century* (1935).

§94.   Morris, Christopher: *Political Thought in England: Tyndale to Hooker* (1953).

§95.   Mulder, John R.: *The Temple of the Mind: Education and Literary Taste in Seventeenth-Century England* (1969).

§96.   Neale, Sir John: *The Elizabethan House of Commons* (1949), and *Elizabeth I and her Parliaments* (1953).

§97.   Nelson, John C.: *Renaissance Theory of Love: The Context of Giordano Bruno's 'Eroici furori'* (1958).

§98.   Nicolson, Marjorie H.: *The Breaking of the Circle: Studies in the*

Effect of the 'New Science' upon Seventeenth-Century Poetry, rev. ed. (1960).

§99. Notestein, Wallace: 'The English Woman, 1580 to 1650', in *Studies in Social History*, ed. J. H. Plumb (1955), Ch. III.

§100. O'Connell, Marvin R.: *The Counter-Reformation, 1560–1610* (1974).

§101. Ogg, David: *Europe in the Seventeenth Century*, 9th ed. (1971).

§102. Ong, Walter J.: 'Wit and Mystery: A Revaluation of Mediaeval Latin Hymnody', *Speculum*, 22 (1947), 310–41.

§103. Ortiz, A. D.: *The Golden Age of Spain, 1516–1659* (1971).

§104. Parker, Derek: *John Donne and his World* (1975).

§105. Patrides, C. A.: *'The Grand Design of God': The Literary Form of the Christian View of History* (1972).

§106. Patrides, C. A.: *Milton and the Christian Tradition* (Oxford, 1966; repr. Hamden, Conn., 1979). On theological patterns of the sixteenth and seventeenth centuries.

§107. Patrides, C. A.: *Premises and Motifs in Renaissance Thought and Literature* (Princeton, 1982).

§108. Patrides, C. A., and Raymond B. Waddington (eds.): *The Age of Milton: Backgrounds to Seventeenth-Century Literature* (Manchester and New York, 1980). Eleven comprehensive essays, with detailed bibliographies.

§109. Patrides, C. A., and Joseph Wittreich (eds.): *The Apocalypse in English Renaissance Thought and Literature* (Manchester and Ithaca, N.Y., 1984).

§110. Pattison, Bruce: *Music and Poetry of the English Renaissance* (1948).

§111. Pennington, D. H.: *Seventeenth Century Europe* (1970).

§112. Penrose, Boies: *Travel and Discovery in the Renaissance 1420–1620* (Cambridge, Mass., 1952).

§113. Peterson, Douglas L.: *The English Lyric from Wyatt to Donne: A History of the Plain and Eloquent Styles* (Princeton, 1967).

§114. Powell, Chilton L.: *English Domestic Relations 1487–1653* (1917).

§115. Powicke, Sir Maurice: *The Reformation in England* (1941).

§116. Praz, Mario: *Studies in Seventeenth-Century Imagery*, 2nd rev. ed. (Rome, 1964).

§117. Quinn, David B.: *Raleigh and the British Empire* (1947).

§118. Raab, Felix: *The English Face of Machiavelli: A Changing Interpretation, 1500–1700* (1964).

§119. Reese, Gustave: *Music in the Renaissance*, rev. ed. (1959).

§120. Rice, Eugene F.: *The Renaissance Idea of Wisdom* (Cambridge, Mass. 1958).

§121. Richmond, H. M.: *The School of Love: The Evolution of the Stuart Love Lyric* (Princeton, 1964).

§122. Robb, Nesca: *Neoplatonism of the Italian Renaissance* (1935).

§123. Rowse, A. L.: *The Elizabethan Age*, a trilogy: *The England of Elizabeth: The Structure of Society* (1950); *The Elizabethan Renaissance: The Life of Society* (1971); and *The Elizabethan Renaissance: The Cultural Achievement* (1972).

§124. Russell, Conrad: *The Crisis of Parliaments: English History 1509–1660* (Oxford, 1971).

§125. Ruthveen, K. K.: *The Conceit* ('The Critical Idiom', 4; 1969).

§126. Rye, William B.: *England as seen by Foreigners in the Days of Elizabeth and James I* (1865). Still the best collection of primary sources.

§127. Shumaker, Wayne: *The Occult Sciences in the Renaissance* (Berkeley, 1972).

§128. Siegel, Paul N.: 'The Petrarchan Sonneteers and Neoplatonic Love', *SP*, 42 (1945), 165–82.

§129. Simon, Joan: *Education and Society in Renaissance England* (Cambridge, 1966).

§130. Smart, Alastair: *The Renaissance and Mannerism in Italy*, and *The Renaissance and Mannerism outside Italy* (1972).

§131. Spitzer, Leo: *Classical and Christian Ideas of World Harmony*, ed. A. G. Hatcher (Baltimore, 1963).

§132. Stone, Lawrence (ed.): *Social Change and Revolution in England 1540–1640* (1965). Also: *The Causes of the English Revolution* 1529–1642 (1972).

§133. Strong, Roy: *The English Icon: Elizabethan and Jacobean Portraiture* (1969). Also his collection of *Tudor and Jacobean Portraits* (1969), 2 vols.

§134. Sypher, Wylie: *Four Stages of Renaissance Style: Transformations in Art and Literature 1400–1700* (1955).

§135. Ten Harmsel, Henrietta (ed.): *Jacobus Revius: Dutch Metaphysical Poet* (Detroit, 1968). Texts with translations.

§136. Trevor-Roper, H. R. (ed.): *The Age of Expansion: Europe and the World, 1559–1660* (1968).

§137. Tuve, Rosemond: *Elizabethan and Metaphysical Imagery* (Chicago, 1947).

§138. Walton, Geoffrey: *Metaphysical to Augustan: Studies in Tone and Sensibility in the Seventeenth Century* (1955).

§139. Warnke, Frank J.: *Versions of Baroque: European Literature in the Seventeenth Century* (New Haven, 1972). Also: 'Marino and the English Metaphysicals', *Studies in the Renaissance*, 2 (1956), 160–75.

§140. Warnke, Frank J. (ed.): *European Metaphysical Poetry* (New Haven, 1961). Texts with translations.

§141. Whale, J. S.: *The Protestant Tradition* (Cambridge, 1955).

§142. Whiffen, Marcus: *An Introduction to Elizabethan and Jacobean Architecture* (1952).

§143. Wiener, Philip P. (ed.): *Dictionary of the History of Ideas* (1973), 3 vols. A wide-ranging collection of authoritative studies.

§144. Wiley, Margaret L.: *The Subtle Knot: Creative Scepticism in Seventeenth-Century England* (1952).

§145. Wilkins, Ernest H.: 'A General Survey of Renaissance Petrarchism', in his *Studies in the Life and Works of Petrarch* (Cambridge, Mass., 1955), Ch. XII; with further references.

§146. Willey, Basil: *The Seventeenth Century Background* (1934).

§147. Williamson, George: *The Senecan Amble: A Study in Prose Form from Bacon to Collier* (1951).

§148. Williamson, George: *Seventeenth Century Contexts* (1960). Also: *The Proper Wit of Poetry* (1961).

§149. Wilson, F. P.: *Elizabethan and Jacobean* (Oxford, 1945). An excellent introduction to the period of transition.

§150. Wright, Louis B.: *Middle-Class Culture in Elizabethan England* (Chapel Hill, 1935).

§151. Wright, Louise B., and Virginia A. Lamar (eds.): *Life and Letters in Tudor and Stuart England* (Ithaca, N.Y., 1962).

§152. Yates, Frances A.: *Giordano Bruno and the Hermetic Tradition* (1964). Also: *The Occult Philosophy in the Elizabethan Age* (1979).

Studies of Donne

The definitive bibliographies of Donne are three:

§153. Keynes, Sir Geoffrey: *A Bibliography of Dr. John Donne*, 3rd rev. ed. (Cambridge, 1958).

§154. Roberts, John R.: *John Donne: An Annotated Bibliography of Modern Criticism 1912–1967* (Columbia, Mo., 1973).

§155. Roberts, John R.: *John Donne: An Annotated Bibliography of Modern Criticism 1968–1978* (Columbia, Mo., 1982).

For a shorter bibliography, see W. Milgate, 'Donne, 1572–1631', in *English Poetry: Select Bibliographical Guides*, ed. A. E. Dyson (1971), Ch. III.

There is but one concordance to Donne's poetry, very much in need of revision: Homer C. Combs and Zay R. Sullens, *A Concordance to the English Poems of John Donne* (Chicago, 1940).

The earliest biography of Donne is also a masterpiece in its own right: Izaak Walton's *Life* (§313; cf. §746). Of subsequent biographies, mention should certainly be made of Edmund Gosse's *The Life and Letters of John Donne* (1899), 2 vols., for it is still useful in parts, however obsolete its judgements may now seem to us. Of modern biographies, some are scarcely worth one's attention, such as Mary Clive's *Jack and the Doctor* (1966); others are more substantial if still rather 'popular' accounts, such as Evelyn Hardy's *Donne: A Spirit in Conflict* (1942) and especially Edward Le Comte's *Grace to a Witty Sinner: A Life of John Donne* (1965). The definitive modern biography is by R. C. Bald (§196), who has additionally untangled the relations between *Donne and the Drurys* (Cambridge, 1959).

Editions of Donne's poetry and prose include the following:

POETRY: COLLECTIONS

§156.　*Poems* (Menston, Yorkshire, 1969). A facsimile of the first edition of 1633.

§157.　*Poems*, ed. E. K. Chambers (1896), 2 vols.

§158.　*Poems*, ed. Herbert J. C. Grierson (Oxford, 1912), 2 vols.

§159.　*Complete Poetry and Selected Prose*, ed. John Hayward (1929).

§160.　*Complete Poems*, ed. Roger E. Bennett (Chicago, 1942).

§161.　*Poetry and Prose*, ed. W. H. Garrod (Oxford, 1946).

§162.　*Complete Poetry and Selected Prose*, ed. Charles M. Coffin (1952).

§163.　*Complete Poetry*, ed. John T. Shawcross (1967).

§164.　*Poetry and Prose*, ed. Frank J. Warnke (1967).

§165.　*Poems*, ed. Frank Kermode (Cambridge, 1968; repr. 1970).

§166.　*Complete English Poems*, ed. A. J. Smith (Harmondsworth, Middx. 1971).

POETRY: INDIVIDUAL COLLECTIONS

§167.　*The Anniversaries*, ed. Frank Manley (Baltimore, 1963).

§168.　*The Divine Poems*, ed. Helen Gardner (Oxford, 1952; 2nd ed., 1978).

§169.　*The Elegies and The Songs and Sonnets*, ed. Helen Gardner (Oxford, 1965).

§170. *The Epithalamions, Anniversaries and Epicedes*, ed. W. Milgate (1978).

§171. *The Satires, Epigrams and Verse Letters*, ed. W. Milgate (Oxford, 1967).

§172. *The Songs and Sonets*, ed. Theodore Redpath, 2nd ed. (1983). See also *ALC*.

POETRY: SELECTIONS

§173. *Metaphysical Lyrics and Poems of the Seventeenth Century*, ed. Herbert J. C. Grierson (Oxford, 1921).

§174. *The Metaphysical Poets*, ed. Helen Gardner (1957).

§175. *Selected Poetry*, ed. Marius Bewley (1966).

PROSE

§176. *Devotions upon Emergent Occasions*, ed. John Sparrow (Cambridge, 1923); ed. Anthony Raspa (Montreal, 1975); ed. Elizabeth Savage (Salzburg, 1975), 2 vols.

§177. *Essays in Divinity*, ed. Evelyn M. Simpson (Oxford, 1952).

§178. *Ignatius his Conclave*, ed. T. S. Healy (1970).

§179. *Letters to Severall Persons of Honour* (Delmar, N.Y., 1977). A facsimile of the first edition of 1651.

§180. *Paradoxes and Problems*, ed. Helen Peters (Oxford, 1980).

§181. *Sermons*, ed. George R. Potter and Evelyn M. Simpson (Berkeley, 1953–62), 10 vols.

§182. *Selected Prose*, chosen by Evelyn Simpson, ed. Helen Gardner and Timothy Healy (Oxford, 1967).

The text of Donne's poems is studied in all the major editions listed above. Other relevant studies include:

§183. Redpath, Theodore: 'Some Textual Problems in Donne's *Songs and Sonets*', *ESEA* (1979), Ch. V.

§184. Roberts, Mark: 'If it were Donne when 'tis Done', *EIC*, 16 (1966), 309–29. See also 17 (1967), 258–77. Further: 'Problems in Editing Donne's *Songs and Sonnets*', in *Editing Poetry*, ed. A. H. de Quehen (1981), pp. 15–45.

§185. Shawcross, John T.: 'The Text of John Donne and the Inadequacy of All Solutions', *JDJ*, 1 (1982), 55–67. Also, 'A Text of John Donne's Poems: Unsatisfactory Compromise', *JDJ*, 2 (1983), 1–19.

§186. Simpson, Evelyn M.: 'A Note on Donne's Punctuation', *RES*, 4 (1928), 295–300. See also §641.

§187. Whitlock, Baird W.: 'A Note on Two Donne Manuscripts', *Renaissance News*, 18 (1965), 9–11.

§188.   Williamson, George: 'Textual Difficulties in Donne's Poetry', in §148: Ch. IV.
§189.   Wood, H. Harvey: 'A Seventeenth-Century Manuscript of Poems by Donne and Others', *ESEA*, 16 (1930), 179–90.
Consult also: Ernest W. Sullivan, 'Replicar Editing of John Donne's Text', *JDJ*, 2 (1983), 21–29, and C. A. Patrides, 'John Donne Methodized', *MP*, 83 (1985).

A major effort now in preparation and likely to take many years is *The Variorum Edition of the Poetry of John Donne*. Another ambitious enterprise, the *John Donne Journal* (ed. M. Thomas Hester and R. V. Young), was begun in 1982.

Musical settings of Donne's poems are also relevant in that some of them – for example, Benjamin Britten's setting of 'At the round earths imagin'd corners' – are themselves imaginative commentaries on the poems set. In addition to the settings provided by some editors (§§163, 169, etc.), see:

§190.   Souris, André (ed.): *Poèmes de Donne, Herbert et Crashaw mis en musique par leurs contemporains* (Paris, 1961).

Translations include the French effort by Jean Fuzier and Yves Denis, *Poèmes de John Donne* (Paris, 1962).

1. General Studies

§191.   Aers, David, and Gunther Kress: 'Vexatious Contraries: A Reading of Donne's Poetry', in *Literature, Language and Society in England*, by Aers *et al.* (Dublin, 1981), Ch. III.
§192.   Allen, Don C.: 'John Donne's Knowledge of Renaissance Medicine', in *JRR*, pp. 93–106.
§193.   Altizer, Alma B.: 'John Donne', in her *Self and Symbolism in the Poetry of Michelangelo, John Donne, and Agrippa d'Aubigné* (The Hague, 1973), Ch. III.
§194.   Alvarez, A.: 'Donne and the Understander', in his *The School of Donne* (1961), Ch. I.
§195.   Andreasen, N. J. C.: *John Donne: Conservative Revolutionary* (Princeton, 1967).
§196.   Bald, R. C.: *John Donne: A Life*, ed. W. Milgate (Oxford, 1970). The definitive modern biography.
§197.   Beall, Chandler B.: 'A Quaint Conceit from Guarini to Dryden', *MLN*, 64 (1949), 61–68.
§198.   Bennett, Joan: 'John Donne' and 'Donne's Technical Originality', in her *Five Metaphysical Poets*, 3rd ed. (Cam-

bridge, 1964), Ch. II–III. See also §253.

§199. Bethel, S. L.: 'The Nature of Metaphysical Wit', in *FK*, pp. 136–49.

§200. Bewley, Marius: 'The Mask of John Donne', in his *Masks and Mirrors* (1970), pp. 3–49.

§201. Bozanich, Robert: 'Donne and Ecclesiastes', *PMLA*, 90 (1975), 270–76.

§202. Bredvold, Louis I.: 'The Religious Thought of Donne in Relation to Some Renaissance Traditions', *University of Michigan Publications in Language and Literature*, 1 (1925), 193–232. Also: 'The Naturalism of Donne in Relation to Some Renaissance Traditions', *JEGP*, 22 (1923), 471–502; abridged in *FK*, pp. 48–55.

§203. Brodsky, Joseph: 'Elegy for John Donne', trans. George L. Kline, *Russian Review*, 24 (1965), 341–53. A translation of Brodsky's Russian poem.

§204. Bullough, Geoffrey: 'Donne the Man of Law', in *PAF*, pp. 57–94.

§205. Cardenal, Luis C. B.: *El manierismo inglés: John Donne* (Granada, 1978).

§206. Carey, John: 'Donne and Coins', in *English Renaissance Studies presented to Dame Helen Gardner* (Oxford, 1980), pp. 151–63.

§207. Carey, John: *John Donne: Life, Mind and Art* (1981).

§208. Cathcart, Dwight: *Doubting Conscience: Donne and the Poetry of Moral Argument* (Ann Arbor, 1975).

§209. Coffin, Charles M.: *John Donne and the New Philosophy* (1937).

§210. Coleridge, Samuel Taylor: 'John Donne', in *Coleridge on the Seventeenth Century*, ed. Roberta F. Brinkley (Durham, N.C., 1955), pp. 519–30.

§211. Colie, Rosalie L.: 'John Donne and the Paradoxes of Incarnation', in §27: Ch. III.

§212. Cousins, A. D.: 'The Coming of Mannerism: The Later Ralegh and the Early Donne', *ELR*, 9 (1979), 86–107.

§213. Crawshaw, Eluned: 'Hermetic Elements in Donne's Poetic Vision', in *AJS*, Ch. XII.

§214. Crofts, J. E. V.: 'John Donne: A Reconsideration', in *HG*, pp. 77–89.

§215. Datta, Kitty: 'Love and Asceticism in Donne's Poetry: The Divine Analogy', *CQ*, 19 (1977), ii, 5–25.

§216. Davis, Kay: 'Unpublished Coleridge Marginalia in a Volume of John Donne's Poetry', *NQ*, n.s., 10 (1963), 187–89.

§217. Doggett, Frank A.: 'Donne's Platonism', *SR*, 42 (1934), 274–92.

§218. Duncan, Edgar H.: 'Donne's Alchemical Figures', in *FK*, pp. 73–89.

§219. Durand, Laura G.: 'Sponde and Donne: Lens and Prism', *CL*, 21 (1969), 319–36.

§220. Eliot, T. S.: 'The Metaphysical Poets' (1921), in his *Selected Essays 1917–1932* (1932), pp. 241–50. Also in *ALC*, pp. 123–30; *FK*, pp. 42–47; *FKM*, pp. 126–35; *WRK*, pp. 22–30.

§221. Empson, William: 'Donne and the Rhetorical Tradition', *KR*, 11 (1949), 571–81; repr. in *Elizabethan Poetry*, ed. Paul J. Alpers (1967), pp. 63–77. Also: 'Rescuing Donne', in *PAF*, pp. 95–148.

§222. Esch, Arno: 'John Donnes religiöse Dichtung', in his *Englische religiöse Lyrik des 17. Jahrhunderts* (Tübingen, 1955), Ch. II.

§223. Everett, Barbara: 'Donne: A London Poet', *Proceedings of the British Academy*, 58 (1972), 245–73.

§224. Fowler, Alastair: *Triumphal Forms: Structural Patterns in Elizabethan Poetry* (Cambridge, 1970), pp. 71–74, 107–08, 158, 160, etc. On numerological patterns in Donne.

§225. Freitag, Hans-Heinrich: *John Donne: Zentrale Motive und Themen in seiner Liebeslyrik* (Bonn, 1975).

§226. Gardner, Helen: 'The Metaphysical Poets', in *WRK*, pp. 50–62; from §174.

§227. Gardner, Helen: 'The Titles of Donne's Poems', in *Friendship's Garland*, ed. Vittorio Gabrieli (Rome, 1966), I, 189–207.

§228. Geraldine, Sister M.: 'John Donne and the Mindes Indeavours', *SEL*, 5 (1965), 115–31.

§229. Gransden, K. W.: *John Donne* (1954).

§230. Grierson, H. J. C.: 'Donne's Love Poetry', in *HG*, pp. 23–35; from §158. Also: 'Metaphysical Poetry', in *ALC*, pp. 112–22, and *WRK*, pp. 3–21; from §173.

§231. Grierson, H. J. C.: 'John Donne and the "Via Media"', *MLR*, 43 (1948), 305–14.

§232. Häublein, Ernst: 'King Imagery in the Poetry of John Donne', *Anglia*, 97 (1979), 94–115.

§233. Hagopian, John V.: 'Some Cruxes in Donne's Poetry', *NQ*, n.s., 4 (1957), 500–02.

§234.   Harding, D. W.: 'Donne's Anticipation of Experience', in his
         Experience into Words (1963), Ch. I.

§235.   Harris, Victor: 'John Donne and the Theatre', *PQ*, 41 (1962),
         257–69.

§236.   Hoover, L. Elaine: *John Donne and Francisco de Quevedo: Poets
         of Love and Death* (Chapel Hill, 1978).

§237.   Hughes, Richard E.: *The Progress of the Soul: The Interior
         Career of John Donne* (1968).

§238.   Jackson, Robert S.: *John Donne's Christian Vocation* (Evanston,
         1970).

§239.   Johnson, Beatrice: 'Classical Allusions in the Poetry of
         Donne', in *JRR*, pp. 85–92.

§240.   Johnson, Samuel: 'The Life of Cowley', in *Lives of the English
         Poets* (Everyman ed., 1925), I, 1–53.

§241.   Jonas, Leah: 'John Donne', in *The Divine Science: The Aesthetic
         of Some Representative Seventeenth-Century English Poets*
         (1940), Ch. X.

§242.   Kawasaki, Toshihiko: 'Donne's Microcosm', in *Seven-
         teenth-Century Imagery*, ed. Earl Miner (Berkeley, 1971),
         Ch. II.

§243.   Keeble, N. H.: 'The Love Poetry of John Donne', *LL*, 1
         (1972), iii, 7–19.

§244.   Kermode, Frank: 'John Donne', in his *Shakespeare, Spenser,
         Donne* (1971), Ch. V.

§245.   Knights, L. C.: 'All or Nothing: A Theme in John Donne', in
         William Empson: the Man and his Work, ed. Roma Gill
         (1974), Ch. XI.

§246.   Kremen, Kathryn R.: 'The First Resurrection in Donne's
         Religious Prose and Poetry', in her *The Imagination of the
         Resurrection* (Lewisburg, Pa., 1972), Ch. II.

§247.   Leavis, F. R.: 'The Line of Wit', in his *Revaluation* (1936), Ch.
         I; also in *WRK*, pp. 31–49.

§248.   Le Comte, Edward: 'Jack Donne: From Rake to Husband', in
         PAF, pp. 9–32.

§249.   Lederer, Josef: 'John Donne and the Emblematic Practice', in
         JRR, pp. 107–21.

§250.   Leishman, J. B.: *The Monarch of Wit*, 5th rev. ed. (1962). Ch. I
         repr. in *HG*, pp. 109–22, and *WRK*, pp. 75–91.

§251.   Lerner, Laurence: 'The Truest Poetry is the Most Feigning',
         in his *The Truest Poetry* (1960), Ch. IX.

§252.   Lewalski, Barbara K., *et al.*: exchanges on Donne's 'per-
         sonae', in *Southern Quarterly*, 14 (1976), 173–213.

§253. Lewis, C. S.: 'Donne and Love Poetry in the Seventeenth Century', in *Seventeenth-Century Studies presented to Sir Herbert Grierson* (Oxford, 1938), pp. 64–84; with John Bennett's 'Reply', pp. 85–104. Both also in *ALC*, pp. 144–77; *JL*, pp. 113–55; and *WRK*, pp. 92–131.

§254. Louthain, Doniphan: *The Poetry of John Donne: A Study in Explication* (1951).

§255. McCanles, Michael: 'Paradox in Donne', in *JRR*, pp. 220–35.

§256. McFarland, Ronald E.: 'Figures of Repetition in John Donne's Poetry', *Style*, 11 (1977), 391–406.

§257. McGrath, Lynette: 'John Donne's Apology for Poetry', *SEL*, 20 (1980), 73–89.

§258. Mahood, M. M.: 'Donne: The Progress of the Soul', in her *Poetry and Humanism* (1950), Ch. IV.

§259. Martz, Louis L.: 'John Donne: The Meditative Voice' and 'John Donne: A Valediction', in his *The Poem of the Mind* (1966), Ch. I–II. Cf. §81.

§260. Martz, Louis L.: 'John Donne: Love's Philosophy', in his *The Wit of Love* (Notre Dame, Ind., 1969), Ch. I. Also in *JL*, pp. 169–84.

§261. Mazzeo, Joseph A.: 'Notes on John Donne's Alchemical Imagery', in §85: Ch. IV.

§262. Miles, Josephine: 'Ifs, And, and Buts for the Reader of Donne', in her *Poetry and Change* (Berkeley, 1974), Ch. IV. Also in *PAF*, pp. 273–91. Cf. §§87, 742.

§263. Moloney, Michael F.: *John Donne: his Flight from Mediaevalism* (Urbana, 1944).

§264. Moloney, Michael F.: 'Donne's Metrical Practice', in *JL*, pp. 207–17, and *JRR*, pp. 171–77.

§265. Nelly, Una: *The Poet Donne: A Study in his Dialectal Method* (Cork, 1969).

§266. Nicolson, Marjorie H.: 'The "New Astronomy" and English Literary Imagination', in her *Science and Imagination* (Ithaca, N.Y., 1956), Ch. II.

§267. Norford, Don P.: 'Microcosm and Macrocosm in Seventeenth-Century Literature', *JHI*, 38 (1977), 409–28.

§268. Nye, Robert: 'The Body is his Book: The Poetry of John Donne', *CQ*, 14 (1972), 345–60.

§269. Oras, Ants: 'Shakespeare, Ben Jonson, and Donne', in his *Pause Patterns in Elizabethan and Jacobean Drama: An Experiment in Prosody* (Gainesville, Fla., 1960), Ch. III.

§270. Partridge, A. C.: *John Donne: Language and Style* (1978).

§271. Payne, F. W.: *John Donne and his Poetry* (1926).

§272. Perry, T. Anthony: *Erotic Spirituality: The Integrative Tradition from Leone Ebreo to John Donne* (University, Ala., 1980).

§273. Peterson, Douglas L.: 'John Donne', in §113: Ch. VIII.

§274. Power, Helen W.: 'The Speaker as Creator: The Voice in Donne's Poems', *XUS*, 11 (1972), i, 21–28.

§275. Praz, Mario: *John Donne* (Turin, 1958); revised from the first part of his *Secentismo e marinismo in Inghilterra* (Florence, 1925). Also: 'Donne's Relation to the Poetry of his Time', in *HG*, pp. 61–76; revised from *TS*, Ch. III.

§276. Ramsay, Mary P.: 'Donne's Relation to Philosophy', in *TS*, Ch. V. Also her *Les Doctrines médiévales chez Donne* (1917).

§277. Ransom, John Crowe: 'Poetry: A Note in Ontology', in his *The World's Body* (1938), pp. 111–42.

§278. Rees, David: 'Marino and Donne', in *Essays in Honour of John Humphreys Whitfield* (1975), pp. 181–97.

§279. Richards, Michael R.: 'The Romantic Critics and John Donne', *BR*, 25 (1980), ii, 40–51.

§280. Richmond, H. M.: 'Donne's Master: The Young Shakespeare', *Criticism*, 15 (1973), 126–44.

§281. Rickey, Mary E.: *Utmost Art: Complexity in the Verse of George Herbert* (Lexington, 1966), pp. 185–87. A list of classical allusions in Donne's poetry.

§282. Ringler, Richard N.: 'Donne's Specular Stone', *MLR*, 60 (1965), 333–39.

§283. Roberts, D. H.: '"Just Such Disparitie": The Real and the Representation in Donne's Poetry', *South Atlantic Bulletin*, 41 (1976), iv, 99–108.

§284. Roberts, Donald R.: 'The Death Wish of John Donne', *PMLA*, 62 (1947), 958–76.

§285. Roberts, John R.: 'John Donne's Poetry: An Assessment of Modern Criticism', *JDJ*, 1 (1982), 55–67.

§286. Rockett, William: 'Donne's Libertine Rhetoric', *ES*, 52 (1971), 507–18.

§287. Roston, Murray: *The Soul of Wit: A Study of John Donne* (Oxford, 1974).

§288. Ruffo–Fiore, Silvia: *Donne's Petrarchism: A Comparative View* (Florence, 1979).

§289. Rugoff, Milton A.: *Donne's Imagery: A Study in Creative Sources* (1939).

§290. Sanders, Wilbur: *John Donne's Poetry* (Cambridge, 1971).

§291. Selden, Raman: 'John Donne's "Incarnational Conviction"', *CQ*, 17 (1975), 55–73.

§292. Shaw, Robert B.: *The Call of God: The Theme of Vocation in the Poetry of Donne and Herbert* (Cambridge, Mass., 1981).

§293. Sherwood, Terry G.: *Fulfilling the Circle: A Study of John Donne's Thought* (Toronto, 1983).

§294. Sicherman, Carol M.: 'Donne's Discoveries', *SEL*, 11 (1971), 69–88.

§295. Sicherman, Carol M.: 'The Mocking Voices of Donne and Marvell', *BR*, 17 (1969), ii, 32–46.

§296. Simon, Irène: *Some Problems of Donne Criticism* ('Langues Vivantes', No. 40: Brussels, 1952).

§297. Skelton, Robin: 'The Poetry of John Donne', in *Elizabethan Poetry*, ed. John Russell Brown and Bernard Harris, Stratford-upon-Avon Studies, 2 (1960), Ch. X.

§298. Slights, Camille W.: 'John Donne as Casuist', in her *The Casuistical Tradition* (Princeton, 1981), Ch. IV.

§299. Sloan, Thomas O.: 'The Rhetoric in the Poetry of John Donne', in *JRR*, pp. 189–98.

§300. Sloane, Mary C.: *The Visual in Metaphysical Poetry* (Atlantic Highlands, N.J., 1980).

§301. Smalling, Michael: 'Donne's Medieval Aesthetics and his Use of Morally Distant *Personae*', in *GAS*, pp. 74–109.

§302. Smith, A. J.: 'The Metaphysic of Love', in *FK*, pp. 150–60. Also: 'The Dismissal of Love: or, Was Donne a Neoplatonic Lover?' in *AJS*, Ch. V, and 'No Man is a Contradiction', *JDJ*, 1 (1982), 21–38.

§303. Smith, A. J.: 'The Poetry of John Donne', in *English Poetry and Prose, 1540–1674*, ed. Christopher Ricks (1970), Ch. VII.

§304. Smith, James: 'On Metaphysical Poetry', *Scrutiny*, 2 (1933), 222–39.

§305. Spencer, Theodore: 'Donne and his Age', in *TS*, Ch. VIII.

§306. Stampfer, Judah: *John Donne and the Metaphysical Gesture* (1970).

§307. Stein, Arnold: 'Donne's Obscurity and the Elizabethan Tradition', *ELH*, 13 (1946), 98–118.

§308. Stein, Arnold: 'Meter and Meaning in Donne's Verse', in *JRR*, pp. 161–70.

§309. Stein, Arnold: 'Structures of Sound in Donne's Verse', *KR*, 13 (1951), 20–36 and 256–78. See further 18 (1956), 439–60. Also §449.

§310. Summers, Claude J., and Ted-Larry Pebworth (eds.): *The Eagle and the Dove: Reassessing John Donne* (Columbia, Mo., 1985).

§311. Tomlinson, T. B.: 'Donne and his Critics', *CR*, 13 (1970), 84–100.

§312. Waller, G. F.: 'John Donne's Changing Attitudes to Time', *SEL*, 14 (1974), 79–89.

§313. Walton, Izaak: *Life of Dr John Donne* (1640, revised thereafter), in *Lives* (1675; reprinted frequently).

§314. Wanamaker, Melisa C.: 'John Donne: Yoking of Opposites', in her *Discordia concors: The Wit of Metaphysical Poetry* (Port Washington, N.Y., 1975), Ch. II.

§315. Wendell, John P.: 'Two Cruxes in the Poetry of Donne', *MLN*, 63 (1948), 471–81.

§316. White, Helen C.: 'The Conversions of John Donne', in her *The Metaphysical Poets* (1936), Ch. IV.

§317. Wiley, Margaret L.: 'John Donne and the Poetry of Scepticism', in §144: Ch. IV.

§318. Williamson, George: 'Strong Lines', in §148: Ch. V. Also in *FK*, pp. 58–63.

§319. Williamson, George: 'The Two Worlds of Donne' and 'John Donne, 1572–1631', in his *Six Metaphysical Poets: A Reader's Guide* (1967; English ed.: *A Reader's Guide to the Metaphysical Poets*, 1968), Ch. III–IV.

§320. Winny, James: *A Preface to Donne* (1982).

§321. Woodhouse, A. S. P.: 'The Seventeenth Century: Donne and his Successors', in his *The Poet and his Faith* (Chicago, 1965), Ch. III.

§322. Zunder, William: *The Poetry of John Donne: Literature and Culture at the Turn of the Century* (1982).

2. On *Songs and Sonets*

§323. Ahrends, Günter: 'Discordia concors: John Donne's "Nocturnall upon S. Lucies Day" ', *NS*, 20 (1971), 68–85.

§324. Allen, D. C.: 'Donne's Specular Stone', *MLN*, 61 (1946), 63–64.

§325. Allen, D. C.: 'Donne on the Mandrake', *MLN*, 74 (1959), 393–97.

§326. Alphonse, Sister Mary, O. P.: 'Donne's "Loves Growth" ', *Ex*, 25 (1967), 43.

§327. Armitage, C. M.: 'Donne's Poems in Huntington Manuscript 198: New Light on "The Funerall" ', *SP*, 63 (1966), 697–707.

§328. Bauer, Robert J.: 'The Great Prince in Donne's "The Extasie" ', *TSL*, 14 (1969), 93–102.

§329. Beale, Walter H.: 'On Rhetoric and Poetry: John Donne's "The Prohibition" Revisited', *QJS*, 62 (1976), 376–86. Cf. §442.

§330. Bell, Ilona: 'The Role of the Lady in Donne's *Songs and Sonnets*', *SEL*, 23 (1983), 113–29.

§331. Brodsky, Claudia: 'Donne: The Imaging of the Logical Conceit', *ELH*, 49 (1982), 829–48.

§332. Brooks, Cleanth: *The Well-Wrought Urn: Studies in the Structure of Poetry* (1947), pp. 10–17. Condensed in *FK*, pp. 64–72, and *HG*, pp. 100–8. On 'The Canonization'.

§333. Brower, Reuben A.: *The Fields of Light: An Experiment in Critical Reading* (1951), pp. 7–83. On 'The Extasie'.

§334. Brown, Nancy P.: 'A Note on the Imagery of Donne's "Loves Growth" ', *MLR*, 48 (1953), 324–27.

§335. Brumble, H. David, III: 'John Donne's "The Flea": Some Implications of the Encyclopedic and Poetic Flea Traditions', *CQ*, 15 (1973), 147–54.

§336. Chambers, A. B.: 'Glorified Bodies and the "Valediction forbidding Mourning" ', *JDJ*, 1 (1982), 1–20.

§337. Chambers, A. B.: 'The Fly in Donne's "Canonization" ', *JEGP*, 65 (1966), 252–59.

§338. Cirillo, Albert R.: 'The Fair Hermaphrodite: Love-Union in the Poetry of Donne and Spenser', *SEL*, 9 (1969), 81–95.

§339. Clair, John A.: 'Donne's "The Canonization" ', *PMLA*, 80 (1965), 300–2.

§340. Cognard, Roger A.: 'Donne's "The Dampe" ', *Ex*, 36 (1978), ii, 19–20.

§341. Collmer, Robert G.: 'Another Look at "The Apparition" ', *CP*, 7 (1974), i, 34–40.

§342. Cross, K. Gustav: ' "Balm" in Donne and Shakespeare: Ironic Intention in "The Extasie" ', *MLN*, 71 (1956), 480–82. On the poem's l. 6.

§343. Cruttwell, Patrick: 'The Love Poetry of John Donne: Pedantique Weedes or Fresh Invention?' in §13: Ch. I.

§344. Cunnar, Eugene R.: 'Donne's "Valediction: Forbidding Mourning" and the Golden Compasses of Alchemical Creation', in *Literature and the Occult*, ed. Luanne Frank (Arlington, Texas, 1977), pp. 77–110.

§345. Daiches, David: 'A Reading of "The Good-Morrow" ', in *PAF*, pp. 177–88.

§346. Davies, Hugh S.: 'Text or Context?' *Review of English Literature* (Leeds), 6 (1965), i, 93–107. On 'Aire and Angels'. See further: i, 108–10; ii, 102; iii, 106.

§347. Dean, John: 'The Two Arguments of Donne's "Air and Angels" ', *Massachusetts Studies in English*, 3 (1972), 84–90.

§348. Divine, Jay D.: 'Compass and Circle in Donne's "A Valediction: Forbidding Mourning" ', *PLL*, 9 (1973), 78–80.

§349. Doebler, Bettie A.: 'Donne's Incarnate Venus', *SAQ*, 71 (1972), 504–12.

§350. Dolan, Kathleen H.: '*Materia in potentia*: The Paradox of the Quintessence in Donne's "A Nocturnall upon S. Lucies Day" ', *Renascence*, 32 (1979), 13–10.

§351. Dunlap, Rhodes: 'Donne as Navigator', *TLS*, 28 December 1946 (p. 643).

§352. Durr, R. A.: 'Donne's "The Primrose" ', in *ALC*, pp. 212–16.

§353. Dyson, A. E., and Julian Lovelock: 'Contracted thus: "The Sun Rising" ', in *JL*, pp. 185–92.

§354. Edgecombe, Rodney: 'An Enquiry into the Syntax of Donne's "The Good-Morrow" and "The Sunne Rising" ', *English Studies in Africa*, 25 (1982), 29–38.

§355. Empson, William: 'A Valediction of Weeping', in his *Seven Types of Ambiguity*, 3rd ed. (1953), pp. 139–48; also in *HG*, pp. 52–60.

§356. Evans, G. Blakemore: 'Two Notes on Donne', *MLR*, 57 (1962), 60–62.

§357. Ferry, Anne: 'Donne', in her *All in War with Time: Love Poetry of Shakespeare, Donne, Jonson, Marvell* (Cambridge, Mass., 1975), Ch. II.

§358. Fietz, Lothar: 'John Donne: "The Sunne Rising": Eine Beschreibung der thematischen und rhetorischen Textstruktur und ihrer strategischen Funktion', *LWU*, 13 (1980), 151–69.

§359. Flinker, Noam: 'Donne's "The Undertaking" ', *Ex*, 36 (1978), iii, 17–18.

§360. Fluchère, Henri: 'Fragments d'un *Donne*: Réflexions sur *Songs and Sonnets*', *RLC*, 50 (1976), 32–48.

§361. Françon, Marcel: 'Un motif de la poésie amoureuse au XVIe siècle', *PMLA*, 56 (1941), 307–36. See also §469.

§362. Freccero, John: 'Donne's "Valediction: Forbidding Mourning" ', in *JRR*, pp. 279–304.

§363.   French, Roberts W.: 'Donne's "Dissolution": What does a poem mean, and is it any good?' *CEA Critic*, 38 (1976), ii, 11–15 and 46.

§364.   Gallant, Gerald, and A. L. Clements: 'Harmonized Voices in Donne's *Songs and Sonets*: "The Dampe" ', *SEL*, 15 (1975), 71–82.

§365.   Gardner, Helen: 'The Argument about "The Ecstasy" ', in *JL*, pp. 218–48, and *JRR*, pp. 239–58. See also §169: App. D.

§366.   Gardner, Helen: *The Business of Criticism* (Oxford, 1959), pp. 62–75. On 'Aire and Angels'.

§367.   Gardner, Helen: ' "A Nocturnall upon St. Lucy's Day" ', in *Poetic Traditions of the English Renaissance*, ed. Maynard Mack and George deF. Lord (New Haven, 1982), pp. 181–201.

§368.   Gérard, Albert: 'John Donne et le maniérisme: La structure scolastique de "The Extasie" ', in *Approches de l'art: Mélanges d'esthétique et de sciences de l'art offerts à Arsène Soreil* (Brussels, 1973), pp. 171–83.

§369.   Gransden, K. W.: ' "Lente cvrrite, noctis eqvi": Chaucer, *Troilus and Criseyde* 3.1422–70, Donne, "The Sun Rising", and Ovid, *Amores* 1.13', in *Creative Imagination and Latin Literature*, ed. David West and Tony Woodman (Cambridge, 1979), Ch. IX.

§370.   Graziani, René: 'John Donne's "The Extasie" and Ecstasy', *RES*, n.s., 19 (1968), 121–36.

§371.   Grunes, Dennis: 'John Donne's "The Good Morrow" ', *American Imago*, 33 (1976), 261–65.

§372.   Guss, Donald L.: *John Donne, Petrarchist: Italianate Conceits and Love Theory in 'The Songs and Sonets'* (Detroit, 1966).

§373.   Haefner, Gerhard: 'John Donne: "The Canonization" – Eine Interpretation', *NS*, 18 (1969), 169–75.

§374.   Hamilton, R. W.: 'John Donne's Petrarchist Poems', *Renaissance and Modern Studies*, 23 (1979), 45–62.

§375.   Hardy, Barbara: 'Thinking and Feeling in the *Songs and Sonnets*', in *AJS*, Ch. IV.

§376.   Harrison, James: 'Syntax in Donne's "The Dreame" ', *Humanities Ass'n Review* (Canada), 25 (1974), 141–45.

§377.   Hayes, Thomas W.: 'Alchemical Imagery in John Donne's "A Nocturnall upon S. Lucies Day" ', *Ambix*, 24 (1977), i, 55–62.

§378.   Hedetoft, Ulf: 'The Contracted Universe of *Songs and Sonets*: A Dialectical Analysis', *LL*, 2 (1974), iii, 32–54.

§379. Hogan, Patrick G., Jr.: 'The Iconographic Background of the First Verse of Donne's "A Valediction Forbidding Mourning" ', in *GAS*, pp. 26–44.

§380. Hotson, Leslie, *et al*.: 'A Crux in Donne', *TLS*, 16 April (p. 249), 6 May (p. 297), and 10 June (p. 381) 1949. On 'Farewell to Love', ll. 18–20.

§381. Hughes, Merritt Y.: 'Some of Donne's "Ecstasies" ', in *JRR*, pp. 259–70.

§382. Hughes, Merritt Y.: 'John Donne's "Nocturnall upon S. Lucies Day": A Suggested Resolution', *Cithara*, 4 (1965), 60–68.

§383. Hunt, Clay: *Donne's Poetry: Essays in Literary Analysis* (New Haven, 1954). Primarily on 'The good-morrow' and 'The Canonization'.

§384. Jahn, J. D.: 'The Eschatological Scene of Donne's "A Valediction: Forbidding Mourning" ', *College Literature*, 5 (1978), 34–47.

§385. Jones, R. T.: 'John Donne's *Songs and Sonets*: The Poetic Value of Argument', *Theoria*, 51 (1978), 33–42.

§386. Kelly, T. J.: 'Donne's "Firme Substantiall Love" ', *CR*, 13 (1970), 101–10.

§387. Kronenfeld, Judy Z.: 'The Asymmetrical Arrangement of Donne's "Love's Growth" as an Emblem of its Meaning', *CP*, 9 (1976), ii, 53–58.

§388. Labriola, Albert C.: 'Donne's "The Canonization": its Theological Context and its Religious Imagery', *HLQ*, 36 (1973), 327–39.

§389. Le Comte, Edward: 'Donne's "The Canonization", line 13', *SCN*, 35 (1977), 6.

§390. Legouis, Pierre: *Donne the Craftsman* (Paris, 1928).

§391. Levine, George R.: 'Satiric Intent and Baroque Design in Donne's "Go and Catch a Falling Star" ', *NS*, 20 (1971), 384–87.

§392. Levine, Jay A.: " 'The Dissolution": Donne's Twofold Elegy', *ELH*, 28 (1961), 301–15.

§393. Lewalski, Barbara K.: 'A Donnean Perspective on "The Extasie" ', *ELN*, 10 (1973), 258–62.

§394. McCanles, Michael: 'Distinguish in Order to Unite: Donne's "The Extasie" ', *SEL*, 6 (1966), 59–75.

§395. MacColl, Alan: 'A Note on Donne's "Loves Growth" ', *ES*, 56 (1975), 314–15. On ll. 15–18.

§396. McLaughlin, Elizabeth: ' "The Extasie": Deceptive or Authentic?' *BR*, 18 (1971), iii, 55–78.

§397.   Madison, Arthur L.: 'Explication of John Donne's "The Flea" ', *NQ*, n.s., 4 (1957), 60–61.

§398.   Manley, Frank: 'Formal Wit in the *Songs and Sonnets*', in *MWP*, pp. 5–27.

§399.   Manley, Francis: 'Chaucer's Rosary and Donne's Bracelet: Ambiguous Coral', *MLN*, 74 (1959), 385–88. On 'The Token', l. 10.

§400.   Mann, Lindsay A.: 'Radical Consistency: A Reading of Donne's "Communitie" ', *UTQ*, 50 (1981), 284–99.

§401.   Mann, Lindsay A.: ' "The Extasie" and 'A Valediction: Forbidding Mourning": Body and Soul in Donne', in *Familiar Colloquy*, ed. Patricia Bruckmann (Toronto, 1978), pp. 68–80.

§402.   Marotti, Arthur F.: 'Donne and "The Extasie" ', in *The Rhetoric of Renaissance Poetry from Wyatt to Milton*, ed. Thomas O. Sloan and Raymond B. Waddington (Berkeley, 1974), Ch. VII.

§403.   Marotti, Arthur F.: 'Donne's "Loves Progress", ll. 37–38, and Renaissance Bawdry', *ELN*, 6 (1968), 24–25.

§404.   Matchett, William H.: 'Donne's "Peece of Chronicle" ', *RES*, n.s., 18 (1967), 290–92. Cf. Fernand Corin, *ES*, 50 (1969), 89–93.

§405.   Mauch, Katherine: 'Angel Imagery and Neoplatonic Love in Donne's "Air and Angels" ', *SCN*, 35 (1977), 106–11.

§406.   Milgate, Wesley: ' "Aire and Angels" and the Discrimination of Experience', in *PAF*, pp. 149–76.

§407.   Miller, C. William, and Dan S. Norton: 'Donne's "The Apparition" ', *Ex*, 4 (1946), 24.

§408.   Miller, Clarence H.: 'Donne's "A Nocturnall upon S. Lucies Day" and the Nocturns of Matins', in *JRR*, pp. 305–10.

§409.   Mills, Lloyd L.: 'The Literary Character of Donne's References to Specular Stone', *Humanities Ass'n Bulletin* (Canada), 23 (1972), i, 37–41.

§410.   Mitchell, Charles: 'Donne's "The Extasie": Love's Sublime Knot', *SEL*, 8 (1968), 91–101.

§411.   Molella, Lynne: 'Donne's "A Lecture upon the Shadow" ', *Thoth*, 3 (1962), 69–77.

§412.   Morillo, Marvin: 'Donne's Compasses: Circles and Right Lines', *ELN*, 3 (1966), 173–76.

§413.   Morillo, Marvin: 'Donne's "Farewell to Love": The Force of Shutting Up', *TSE*, 13 (1963), 33–40.

§414.   Morillo, Marvin: 'Donne's "Nocturnall": A Textual Note', *ELN*, 16 (1979), 278–81.

§415. Morillo, Marvin: 'Donne's "The Relique" as Satire', *TSE*, 21 (1974), 47–55.

§416. Morris, William E.: 'Donne's Use of Enallage in "The good-morrow" ', *ANQ*, 11 (1972), 19–20.

§417. Murray, W. A.: 'Donne and Paracelsus: An Essay in Interpretation', in *JRR*, pp. 122–28. On 'Loves Alchemy' and 'A Nocturnall'.

§418. Murray, W. A.: 'Donne's Gold-Leaf and his Compasses', *MLN*, 73 (1958), 329–30. On 'A Valediction forbidding mourning', l. 24.

§419. Nelson, Lowry, Jr.; 'Poems of Donne', in his *Baroque Lyric Poetry* (New Haven, 1961), Ch. X.

§420. Nitchie, George W.: 'Donne in Love: Some Reflections on "Loves Alchymie" ', *Southern Review*, 15 (1979), 16–21.

§421. Novarr, David: ' "The Extasie": Donne's Address on the States of Union', and 'Contextual Study and Donne's "A Valediction: Forbidding Mourning" ', in his *The Disinterred Muse: Donne's Texts and Contexts* (Ithaca, N.Y., 1980), Ch. I–II.

§422. Otten, Charlotte F.: 'Donne's Manna in "The Primrose" ', *ELN*, 13 (1976), 260–62.

§423. Parish, John E.: 'The Parley in "The Extasie" ', *XUS*, 4 (1965), 188–92.

§424. Perrine, Laurence: 'On Donne's "The Apparition" ', *CP*, 9 (1976), i, 21–24.

§425. Peter, Harry W.: 'Donne's "Nocturnall" and the *Nigredo*', *Thoth*, 9 (1968), 48–57.

§426. Pinka, Patricia G.: *The Dialogue of One: The 'Songs and Sonnets'* (University, Ala., 1982).

§427. Pritchard, E. F.: 'Donne's "Aire and Angels" ', *Ex*, 41 (1982), 17–20.

§428. Prosky, Murray: 'Donne's "Aire and Angels" ', *Ex*, 27 (1968), 27.

§429. Rajan, Tilottama: ' "Nothing Sooner Broke": Donne's *Songs and Sonets* as Self-Consuming Artifact', *ELH*, 49 (1982), 805–28.

§430. Rauber, D. F.: 'Donne's "Farewell to Love": A Crux Revisited', *CP*, 3 (1970), ii, 51–63.

§431. Richards, Bernard: 'Donne's "Twickenham Garden" and the *fons amatoria*', *RES*, n.s., 33 (1982), 180–83.

§432. Rickey, Mary E.: 'Donne's "The Relique", 27–28', *Ex*, 22 (1964), 58.

§433. Riemer, A. P.: 'A Pattern for Love: The Structure of Donne's "The Canonization" ', *Sydney Studies in English*, 3 (1977), 19–31. On the numerological structure.

§434. Rooney, William J.: ' "The Canonization": The Language of Paradox Reconsidered', in *JRR*, pp. 271–78. Cf. §332.

§435. Sanders, Wilbur: (as above, §290), Ch. III–V.

§436. Schaar, C.: ' "Balme" in Donne's "Extasie" ', *ES*, 53 (1972), 224–25. On l. 6.

§437. Selden, R.: 'Donne's "The Dampe", ll. 22–24', *MLR*, 64 (1969), 726–27.

§438. Seng, Peter J.: 'Donne's Compass Image', *NQ*, 203 (1958), 214–15.

§439. Serpieri, Alessandro: 'Sull'uso del modello comunicativo nella poesia di John Donne: "The Funerall" e "The Relique" ', *Strumenti critici*, 9 (1975), 275–308.

§440. Sharp, Robert L.: 'Donne's "Good-Morrow" and Cordiform Maps', *MLN*, 69 (1954), 493–95.

§441. Sleight, Richard: 'John Donne: "A Nocturnall . . ." ', in *Interpretations*, ed. John Wain, 2nd ed, (1972), pp. 31–58.

§442. Sloan, Thomas O.: 'A Rhetorical Analysis of John Donne's "The Prohibition" ', *QJS*, 48 (1962), 38–45.

§443. Smith, A. J.: 'Donne in his Time: A Reading of "The Extasie" ', *RLMC*, 10 (1957), 260–75.

§444. Smith, A. J.: *John Donne: The 'Songs and Sonets'* (1965).

§445. Smith, A. J.: 'The Metaphysic of Love', *RES*, n.s., 9 (1958), 362–75. On the background of 'The Extasie'.

§446. Smith, A. J.: 'New Bearings in Donne: "Air and Angels" ', in *HG*, pp. 171–79.

§447. Spenko, James L.: 'Circular Form in Two Donne Lyrics', *ELN*, 13 (1975), 103–07. On 'The Undertaking' and 'A Nocturnall'.

§448. Spitzer, Leo: 'Three Poems on Ecstasy: John Donne, St. John of the Cross, Richard Wagner', in his *Essays on English and American Literature*, ed. Anna Hatcher (Princeton, 1962), Ch. IX.

§449. Stein, Arnold: *John Donne's Lyrics: The Eloquence of Action* (Minneapolis, 1962).

§450. Stewart, Jack F.: 'Irony in Donne's "The Funeral" ', and 'Image and Idea in Donne's "The Good-Morrow" ', *Discourse*, 12 (1969), 193–99 and 465–76.

§451. Stringer, Gary A.: 'Donne's "The Primrose": Manna and Numerological Dalliance', *Explorations in Renaissance Culture*, 1 (1974), 23–29.

§452. Stringer, Gary A.: 'Learning "Hard and Deepe": Biblical Allusion in Donne's "A Valediction: Of my Name"', *South Central Bulletin*, 33 (1973), 227–31.

§453. Swinden, Patrick: 'John Donne: "Air and Angels"', *CQ*, 21 (1979), i, 51–54.

§454. Tate, Allen: 'The Point of Dying: Donne's "Virtuous Men"', in his *Essays of Four Decades* (Chicago, 1969; 1970), pp. 247–52. On 'A Valediction: forbidding mourning'.

§455. Thomason, T. Katharine: 'Plotinian Metaphysics and Donne's "Extasie"', *SEL*, 22 (1982), 91–106.

§456. Traci, Philip: 'The Supposed New Rhetoric of Donne's *Songs and Sonets*', *Discourse*, 11 (1968), 98–107.

§457. Traister, Barbara: 'Donne's "Loves Growth"', *Ex*, 34 (1976), 60.

§458. Tuve, Rosemond: 'Imagery and Logic: Ramus and Metaphysical Poetics', *JHI*, 3 (1942), 365–400. With a discussion of 'A Valediction of weeping'.

§459. Unger, Leonard: *Donne's Poetry and Modern Criticism* (1950).

§460. Van Doren, Mark: *Introduction to Poetry* (1951), pp. 26–31. On 'A Lecture upon the Shadow'.

§461. Vickers, Brian: 'The *Songs and Sonnets* and the Rhetoric of Hyperbole', in *AJS*, Ch. VI.

§462. Walker, Julia M.: '"The Extasie" as an Alchemical Process', *ELN*, 20 (1982), 1–8.

§463. Warren, Austin: 'Donne's "Extasie"', *SP*, 55 (1958), 472–80.

§464. Welch, Dennis M.: 'The Meaning of Nothingness in Donne's "Nocturnall upon S. Lucies Day"', *BR*, 22 (1976), i, 48–56.

§465. Wertenbaker, Thomas J., Jr.: 'Donne's "A Jeat Ring Sent"', *Ex*, 35 (1977), iv, 27–28.

§466. Wiggins, Peter De Sa: '"Aire and Angels": Incarnations of Love', *ELR*, 12 (1982), 87–101.

§467. Williamson, George: 'Donne's "Farewell to Love"', *MP*, 36 (1939), 301–03.

§468. Williamson, George: 'The Convention of "The Extasie"', in §148: Ch. III. Also in *WRK*, pp. 132–43.

§469. Wilson, David B.: '*La Puce de Madame Desroches* and John Donne's "The Flea"', *Neuphilologische Mitteilungen*, 72 (1971), 297–301. On the collection of French poems (1583) relevant to Donne's. Cf. §361.

§470. Wilson, G. R., Jr.: 'The Interplay of Perception and Reflection: Mirror Imagery in Donne's Poetry', *SEL*, 9 (1969), 107–21.

§471.   Wilson, Scott W.: 'Process and Product: Reconstructing Donne's Personae', *SEL*, 20 (1980), 91–103.

3. On the epigrams

§472.   Hester, M. Thomas: '*Genera mixta* in Donne's "Sir John Wingfield" ', *ELN*, 16 (1979), 202–06.

4. On the elegies

§473.   Allen, D. C.: 'A Note on Donne's Elegy VIII', *MLN*, 68 (1953), 238–39.

§474.   Armstrong, Alan: 'The Apprenticeship of John Donne: Ovid and the *Elegies*', *ELH*, 44 (1977), 419–42.

§475.   Bennett, J. A. W.: 'Donne, "Elegy", XVI, 31', *NQ*, n.s., 13 (1966), 254.

§476.   Bowers, Fredson T.: 'An Interpretation of Donne's Tenth Elegy', *MLN*, 54 (1939), 280–82.

§477.   Brilli, Attilio: 'Gli *Amores* ovidiana e la poesia di J. Donne', *Studi urbinati di storia, filosofia e letteratura*, 38 (1964), 100–39.

§478.   Brock, D. Heyward: 'Jonson and Donne: Structural Finger-printing and the Attribution of Elegies 38–41', *PBSA*, 72 (1978), 519–27.

§479.   Bryan, R. A.: 'A Sidelight on Donne's 17th Century Literary Reputation', *SCN*, 1954, p. 21.

§480.   Deitz, Jonathan E.: 'Donne's "To his Mistress Going to Bed", 33–38', 32 (1974), 36.

§481.   Duncan-Jones, E. E.: 'The Barren Plane-Tree in Donne's "The Autumnall" [ll. 29–32]', *NQ*, n.s., 7 (1960), 53.

§482.   French, Roberts W.: 'Donne's Elegy XVIII, 38', *Ex*, 34 (1975), 5.

§483.   Gill, Roma: '*Musa Iocosa Mea*: Thoughts on the *Elegies*', in *AJS*, Ch. III.

§484.   Gregory, E. R., Jr.: 'The Balance of Parts: Imagistic Unity in Donne's "Elegie XIX" ', *University Review* (Kansas City, Mo.), 35 (1968), 51–54.

§485.   Greller, Mary A.: 'Donne's "The Autumnall": An Analysis', *LWU*, 9 (1976), 1–8.

§486.   Howarth, R. G.: 'References to John Donne', *NQ*, n.s., 5 (1958), 43.

§487.   Hurley, C. Harold: ' "Covering" in Donne's Elegy XIX', *CP*, 11 (1978), ii, 67–69.

§488. LaBranche, A.: '"Blanda Elegeia": The Background to Donne's *Elegies*', in *JRR*, pp. 399–410.

§489. Lewis, E. Glyn: 'An Interpretation of Donne's "Elegie 'The Dream'"', *MLR*, 29 (1943), 436–40.

§490. Miller, Henry K.: 'The Paradoxical Encomium with Special Reference to its Vogue in England', *MP*, 53 (1956), 145–78.

§491. Palmer, D. J.: 'The Verse Epistle', in §13: Ch. III.

§492. Peacock, A. J.: 'Donne's Elegies and Roman Love Elegy', *Hermathena*, 119 (1975), 20–29.

§493. Reisner, Thomas A.: 'The Rope in Donne's "Elegie XIV" [ll. 64–65]', *NQ*, n.s., 24 (1977), 527–28.

§494. Rockett, William: 'John Donne: The Ethical Argument of Elegy III', *SEL*, 15 (1975), 57–69.

§495. Schwartz, Elias: 'Donne's Elegie X', *Ex*, 19 (1961), 67.

§496. Simpson, Evelyn: 'Jonson and Donne: A Problem of Authorship', *RES*, 15 (1939), 274–82. Cf. §478.

§497. Ure, Peter: 'The "Deformed Mistress" Theme and the Platonic Convention', *NQ*, 193 (1948), 269–70.

§498. Wiggins, Peter De Sa: 'The Love Quadrangle: Tibullus 1.6 and Donne's "lay Ideot"', *PLL*, 16 (1980), 142–50.

§499. Wilder, Malcolm L.: 'Did Jonson write "The Expostulation" attributed to Donne?' *MLR*, 21 (1926), 431–35. Attributes it to Jonson. Cf. §478.

5. On *Sapho and Philænis*

§500. Allen, D. C.: 'Donne's "Sapho to Philænis"', *ELN*, 1 (1964), 188–91.

6. On the epithalamions

§501. Allen, D. C.: 'Donne's Phoenix', *MLN*, 62 (1947), 340–42. On 'An Epithalamion, or Marriage Song', ll. 18–22.

§502. Halio, Jay L.: '"Perfection" and Elizabethan Ideas of Conception', *ELN*, 1 (1964), 179–82.

§503. McGowan, Margaret M.: '"As Through a Looking-glass": Donne's Epithalamia and their Courtly Context', in *AJS*, Ch. VII.

§504. Novarr, David: 'Donne's "Epithalamion made at Lincoln's Inn": Context and Date', in §421: Ch. III.

§505. Ousby, Heather D.: 'Donne's "Epithalamion made at Lincolnes Inne": An Alternative Interpretation', *SEL*, 16 (1976), 131–43. Cf. §504.

7. On the *Satyres*

§506.   Andreasen, N. J. C.: 'Theme and Structure in Donne's *Satyres*', in *JRR*, pp. 411–23.

§507.   Atkins, Sidney H.: 'Mr. Banks and his Horse', *NQ*, 167 (1934), 39–44. On *Sat.* I, ll. 79–82.

§508.   Bellette, A. F.: 'The Originality of Donne's *Satires*', *UTQ*, 44 (1975), 130–40.

§509.   Cobb, Lucille S.: 'Donne's Satyre II, 71–72', *Ex*, 14 (1956), 40; also Vernon Hall, Jr., 15 (1957), 24, and Thomas O. Malbott, 16 (1957), 19.

§510.   Dubrow, Heather: ' "No man is an island": Donne's Satires and Satiric Traditions', *SEL*, 19 (1979), 71–83.

§511.   Eddy, Yvonne S., and Daniel P. Jaeckle: 'Donne's *Satyre I*: The Influence of Persius's *Satire III*', *SEL*, 21 (1981), 111–22.

§512.   Elliott, Emory B., Jr.: 'The Narrative and Allusive Unity of Donne's *Satyres*', *JEGP*, 75 (1976), 105–16.

§513.   Geraldine, Sister M.: 'Donne's *Notitia*: The Evidence of the Satires', *UTQ*, 36 (1966), 24–36.

§514.   Hamilton, R. W.: 'Donne and Castiglione', *NQ*, n.s., 26 (1979), 404–5.

§515.   Hester, M. Thomas: ' "Carelesse Phrygius": Donne's Separatist Sectarian', in *A Fair Day in the Affections*, ed. Jack D. Durant and M. Thomas Hester (Raleigh, N.C., 1980), pp. 87–99.

§516.   Hester, M. Thomas: *'Kinde Pitty and Brave Scorn'*: *John Donne's 'Satyres'* (Durham, N.C., 1982). Encompasses six essays published before but now revised.

§517.   Hutchison, Alexander N.: 'Constant Company: John Donne and his Satiric Personae', *Discourse*, 13 (1970), 354–63.

§518.   Koch, Walter A.: 'Linguistic Analysis of a Satire', *Linguistics*, 33 (1967), 68–81. On *Sat.* II.

§519.   Lauritsen, John R.: 'Donne's *Satyres*: The Drama of Self-Discovery', *SEL*, 16 (1976), 117–30.

§520.   Lein, Clayton D.: 'Theme and Structure in Donne's *Satyre II*', *CL*, 32 (1980), 130–50.

§521.   Miller, Clarence H., and Caryl K. Berrey: 'The Structure of Integrity: The Cardinal Virtues in Donne's *Satyre III*', *Costerus*, n.s., 1 (1974), 27–45.

§522.   Moore, Thomas V.: 'Donne's Use of Uncertainty as a Vital Force in *Satyre III*', *MP*, 67 (1969), 41–49.

§523.   Newton, Richard C.: 'Donne the Satirist', *TSLL*, 16 (1974), 427–45.

§524. Parker, Barbara L., and J. Max Patrick: 'Two Hollow Men: The Pretentious Wooer and the Wayward Bridegroom of Donne's *Satyre I*', *SCN*, 33 (1975), 10–14.

§525. Sellin, Paul R.: 'The Proper Dating of John Donne's *Satyre III*', *HLQ*, 43 (1980), 275–312. Dates it in 1620.

§526. Shawcross, John T.: ' "All Attest his Writs Canonical": The Texts, Meaning and Evaluation of Donne's Satires', in *PAF*, pp. 245–72.

§527. Simpson, Evelyn M.: 'Notes on Donne', *RES*, 20 (1944), 224–27.

§528. Sloan, Thomas O.: 'The Persona as Rhetor: An Interpretation of Donne's *Satyre III*', in *JRR*, pp. 424–38.

§529. Smith, Hallett: *Elizabethan Poetry: A Study in Conventions, Meaning, and Expression* (Cambridge, Mass., 1952), pp. 223–27. On Donne's satires generally.

§530. Zivley, Sherry: 'Imagery in John Donne's *Satyres*', *SEL*, 6 (1966), 87–95.

8. On the verse letters

§531. Aers, David, and Gunther Kress: ' "Darke Texts Needs Notes": Versions of Self in Donne's Verse Epistles', in §191: Ch. II.

§532. Bauer, Robert J.: 'Donne's Letter to Herbert [of Cherbury] Re-examined', in *GAS*, pp. 60–73.

§533. Bennett, R. E.: 'John Donne and Everard Gilpin', *RES*, 15 (1939), 66–72. See further P. J. Finkelpearl, *RES*, n.s., 14 (1963), 164–67.

§534. Byard, Margaret M.: 'The Trade of Courtiership: The Countess of Bedford and the Bedford Memorials – A Family History from 1585 to 1607', *History Today*, January 1979, pp. 20–28. On the recipient of six of Donne's verse letters.

§535. Cameron, Allen B.: 'Donne's Deliberative Verse Epistles', *ELR*, 6 (1976), 369–403.

§536. Collins, Dan S.: 'Donne's "To the Countess of Bedford" (T'have written then)', *Ex*, 31 (1972), 19.

§537. Gale, Steven H.: 'John Donne's "The Calme" ', *Horizontes*, 44 (1979), 59–64.

§538. Gardner, Helen: *John Donne's Holograph of 'A Letter to the Lady Carey and Mrs Essex Riche'* (1972). A facsimile of the unique holograph, with a transcription which, faulty as it is, has been corrected by Nicolas Barker in *Book Collector*, 22 (1973), 487–93.

§539.   Garrod, H. W.: 'Donne and Mrs Herbert', *RES*, 21 (1945), 161–73. On the recipient of 'To Mrs M.H.'.

§540.   Grierson, H. J. C.: 'Bacon's Poem "The World": its Date and Relation to Certain Other Poems', in his *Essays and Addresses* (1940), Ch. XI.

§541.   Harrison, Robert: 'Donne's "To the Countess of Huntingdon" ("Man to Gods image . . .")', *Ex*, 25 (1966), 33.

§542.   Jacobsen, Eric: 'The Fable is Inverted or Donne's Aesop', *Classica et mediaevalia*, 13 (1952), 1–37. On the fable used in 'The Calme', ll. 1–4.

§543.   Jordan, John: 'The Early Verse-Letters of John Donne', *University Review* (Dublin), 2, x (1962), 3–24.

§544.   Kester, Don A.: 'Donne and Herbert of Cherbury: An Exchange of Verses', *MLQ*, 8 (1947), 430–34.

§545.   Lein, Clayton D.: 'Donne's "The Storme": The Poem and the Tradition', *ELR*, 4 (1974), 137–63.

§546.   Levine, Jay A.: 'The Status of the Verse Epistle before Pope', *SP*, 59 (1962), 658–84.

§547.   Maurer, Margaret: 'John Donne's Verse Letters', *MLQ*, 37 (1976), 234–59.

§548.   Maurer, Margaret: 'The Real Presence of Lucy Russell, Countess of Bedford, and the Terms of John Donne's "Honour is so sublime perfection" ', *ELH*, 47 (1980), 205–34.

§549.   Mizejewski, Linda: 'Darkness and Disproportion: A Study of Donne's "Storme" and "Calme" ', *JEGP*, 76 (1977), 217–30.

§550.   Nellist, B. F.: 'Donne's "Storm" and "Calm" and the Descriptive Tradition', *MLR*, 59 (1964), 511–15.

§551.   Pebworth, T.-L., and C. J. Summers: '. . . The Exchange of Verse Letters between Donne and Henry Wotton', *MP*, 81 (1984), 361–77.

§552   Sackton, Alexander: 'Donne and the Privacy of Verse', *SEL*, 7 (1967), 67–82.

§553   Smith, A. J.: 'A John Donne Poem in Holograph', *TLS*, 7 January 1972 (p. 19). Donne's own draft of 'A Letter to the Lady Carey . . .'. See also *TLS*, 21 January (pp. 68–69) and 24 March (p. 337) 1972.

§554   Stapleton, Laurence: 'The Theme of Virtue in Donne's Verse Epistles', in *JRR*, pp. 451–61.

§555   Storhoff, Gary: 'Metaphors of Despair in Donne's "The Storme" and "The Calme" ', *CP*, 9 (1976), ii, 41–45.

§556.   Thomson, Patricia: 'Donne and the Poetry of Patronage: The Verse Letters', in *AJS*, Ch. XI.

§557. Tourney, Leonard D.: 'Donne, the Countess of Bedford, and the Petrarchan Manner', in *GAS*, pp. 45–59.

§558. Yoklavich, John: 'Donne and the Countess of Huntingdon', *PQ*, 43 (1964), 283–88.

9. On the *Anniversaries*

§559. Allen, D. C.: 'John Donne and the Tower of Babel', *MLN*, 64 (1949), 481–83. On the 2nd Anniv., ll. 417–22.

§560. Anselment, Raymond A.: ' "Ascensio mendax, descensio crudelis": The Image of Babel in the *Anniversaries*', *ELH*, 38 (1971), 188–205.

§561. Bath, Michael: 'Donne's *Anatomy of the World* and the Legend of the Oldest Animals', *RES*, 32 (1981), 302–8.

§562. Bellette, Antony F.: 'Art and Imitation in Donne's *Anniversaries*', *SEL*, 15 (1975), 83–96.

§563. Colie, Rosalie L.: ' "All in Peeces": Problems of Interpretation in Donne's Anniversary Poems', in *PAF*, pp. 189–218. Also: 'John Donne's Anniversary Poems and the Paradoxes of Epistemology', in §27: pp. 412–29.

§564. Demaray, John G.: 'Donne's Three Steps to Death', *The Personalist*, 46 (1965), 366–81.

§565. Elliott, Emory B., Jr.: 'Persona and Parody in Donne's *The Anniversaries*', *QJS*, 58 (1972), 48–57.

§566. Fox, Ruth A.: 'Donne's *Anniversaries* and the Art of Living', *ELH*, 38 (1971), 528–41.

§567. Gilman, Ernest B.: *The Curious Perspective: Literary and Pictorial Wit in the Seventeenth Century* (New Haven, 1978), pp. 179–88.

§568. Goldberg, Jonathan: 'Hesper-Vesper: Aspects of Venus in a Seventeenth-Century Trope', *SEL*, 15 (1975), 37–55. On the 2nd Anniv., ll. 198–99.

§569. Hardison, O. B., Jr.: 'The Idea of Elizabeth Drury', in §47: Ch. VII.

§570. Hughes, Richard E.: 'The Woman in Donne's *Anniversaries*', *ELH*, 34 (1967), 307–26.

§571. Kreps, Barbara I.: 'The Serpent and Christian Paradox in Donne's *First Anniversary*', *RLMC*, 24 (1971), 198–207.

§572. Lebans, W. M.: 'Donne's *Anniversaries* and the Tradition of Funeral Elegy', *ELH*, 39 (1972), 545–59.

§573. Lewalski, Barbara K.: *Donne's 'Anniversaries' and the Poetry of Praise: The Creation of a Symbolic Mode* (Princeton, 1973).

§574. Love, Harold: 'The Argument of Donne's *First Anniversary*', in *JRR*, pp. 355–62.

§575. Low, Anthony: 'The "Turning Wheele": Carew, Jonson, Donne and the First Law of Motion', *JDJ*, 1 (1982), 69–80.

§576. Mahony, Patrick: 'The *Anniversaries*: Donne's Rhetorical Approach to Evil', in *JRR*, pp. 363–67. Also: 'The Heroic Couplet in Donne's *Anniversaries*', *Style*, 4 (1970), 107–17, and 'The Structure of Donne's *Anniversaries* as Companion Poems', *Genre*, 5 (1972), 235–56.

§577. Martz, Louis L.: 'John Donne in Meditation: The *Anniversaries*', in §81: Ch. VI. Also in *WRK*, pp. 144–77; abridged in *HG*, pp. 152–70; an earlier version in *FK*, pp. 90–105.

§578. Martz, Louis L.: 'Donne's *Anniversaries* Revisited', in *MWP*, pp. 29–55; with bibliography.

§579. Maud, Ralph: 'Donne's *First Anniversary*', *Boston University Studies in English*, 2 (1956), 218–25.

§580. Morris, June: 'A Study of Humor in Donne's *Anniversaries*', *English Miscellany*, 28–29 (1979–80), 157–70.

§581. Nicolson, Marjorie H.: 'The Death of a World', in §98: Ch. III.

§582. Parrish, Paul A.: 'Donne's "A Funerall Elegie" ', *PLL*, 11 (1975), 83–87.

§583. Parrish, Paul A.: 'Donne's *The First Anniversarie*', *Ex*, 33 (1975), 64.

§584. Parrish, Paul A.: 'Poet, Audience, and the Word: An Approach to the *Anniversaries*', in *GAS*, pp. 110–39.

§585. Quinn, Dennis: 'Donne's *Anniversaries* as Celebration', in *JRR*, pp. 368–73.

§586. Rowland, Daniel B.: 'John Donne: Mannerist Style in the Meditative Genre', in his *Mannerism – Style and Mood* (New Haven, 1964), Ch. III.

§587. Sicherman, Carol M.: 'Donne's Timeless *Anniversaries*', in *JRR*, pp. 374–86.

§588. Stanwood, P. G.: ' "Essential Joye" in Donne's *Anniversaries*', in *JRR*, pp. 387–96.

§589. Tourney, Leonard D.: 'Joseph Hall and the *Anniversaries*', *PLL*, 13 (1977), 25–34.

§590. Voss, A. E.: 'The Structure of Donne's *Anniversaries*', *English Studies in Africa*, 12 (1969), 1–30.

§591. Williamson, George: 'The Design of Donne's *Anniversaries*', in his *Milton and Others* (Chicago, 1964; 1965), Ch. IX. Cf. §81.

10. On the epicedes and obsequies

§592. Kolin, Philip C.: 'Donne's 'Obsequies to the Lord Harrington'': Theme, Structure, and Image', *Southern Quarterly*, 13 (1974), 65–85.

§593. Lebans, W. M.: 'The Influence of the Classics in Donne's *Epicedes and Obsequies*', *RES*, n.s., 23 (1972), 127–37.

§594. Pottle, Frederick A.: 'Two Notes on Ben Jonson's *Staple of News*', *MLN*, 40 (1925), 223–26. On Donne's elegy on Prince Henry, l. 1.

§595. Tourney, Leonard D.: 'Convention and Wit in Donne's "Elegie" on Prince Henry', *SP*, 71 (1974), 473–83.

§596. Wallerstein, Ruth: 'The Death of Prince Henry', in her *Studies in Seventeenth-Century Poetic* (Madison, 1950), Ch. II. On the occasion's numerous elegies, including Donne's.

§597. Williamson, J. W.: *The Myth of the Conqueror: Prince Henry Stuart* (1978). On the context of Donne's elegy.

§598. Wilson, Elkin C.: 'Elegiac', in his *Prince Henry and English Literature* (Ithaca, N.Y., 1946), Ch. III. On the occasion's numerous elegies, including Donne's.

11. On *Metempsycosis*

§599. Bryan, Robert A.: '*Translatio* Concepts in Donne's *The Progress of the Soul*', in *All These to Teach: Essays in Honor of C. A. Robertson* (Gainesville, Fla., 1965), pp. 120–29.

§600. Corthell, Ronald J.: 'Donne's *Metempsychosis*: An "Alarum to Truth" ', *SEL*, 21 (1981), 97–110.

§601. Gardner, Helen: 'The *Metempsychosis* of John Donne', *TLS*, 29 December 1972 (pp. 1587–88).

§602. Janson, H. W.: *Apes and Ape Lore in the Middle Ages and the Renaissance* (1952), pp. 272–75. On the poem's 'toyfull Ape' (ll. 451 ff.).

§603. Milgate, Wesley: 'A Difficult Allusion in Donne [*Metemps*., ll. 388–95] and Spenser', *NQ*, n.s., 13 (1966), 12–14.

§604. Mueller, Janel M.: 'Donne's Epic Venture in the *Metempsychosis*', *MP*, 70 (1972), 109–37.

§605. Murray, W. A.: 'What was the Soul of the Apple?' in *JRR*, pp. 462–74.

§606. Snyder, Susan: 'Donne and DuBartas: *The Progress of the Soule* as Parody', *SP*, 70 (1973), 392–407.

§607. Tepper, Michael: 'John Donne's Fragment Epic: *The Progresse of the Soule*', *ELN*, 13 (1976), 262–66.

§608. Thomas, John A.: 'John Donne's *The Progresse of the Soule*: A

Re-Evaluation', *Bulletin of the Rocky Mountain Modern Language Association*, 25 (1971), 112–21.

§609.   van Wyk Smith, M.: 'John Donne's *Metempsychosis*', *RES*, n.s., 24 (1973), 17–25 and 141–52.

§610.   Wentersdorf, Karl P.: 'Symbol and Meaning in Donne's *Metempsychosis*', *SEL*, 22 (1982), 69–90.

§611.   Williamson, George: 'Donne's Satirical *Progress of the Soule*', *ELH*, 36 (1969), 250–64.

12. On the divine poems: general studies

§612.   Allen, Don C.: 'John Donne's "Paradise and Calvarie" ', *MLN*, 60 (1945), 398–400. Cf. §620.

§613.   Anderson, Donald K., Jr.: 'Donne's "Hymne to God my God, in my Sicknesse" and the T-in-O Maps', *SAQ*, 71 (1972), 465–72.

§614   Archer, Stanley: 'The Archetypal Journey Motif in Donne's Divine Poems', in *GAS*, pp. 173–91.

§615.   Asals, Heather: 'David's Successors: Forms of Joy and Art', *Proceedings of the Patristic, Medieval and Renaissance Conference*, 2 (1977), 31–37.

§616.   Campbell, Harry M.: 'Donne's "Hymn to God, my God, in my Sickness" ', *College English*, 5 (1944), 192–96.

§617.   Chambers, A. B.: ' "Goodfriday, 1613. Riding Westward": The Poem and the Tradition', in *JRR*, pp. 333–48.

§618.   Clark, Ira: 'Explicating the Heart and Dramatizing the Poet: Seventeenth-Century Innovations by English Emblematists and Donne', in his *Christ Revealed* (Gainesville, Fla., 1982), Ch. III.

§619.   Elmen, Paul: 'John Donne's Dark Lantern', *PBSA*, 49 (1955), 181–86. On 'A Litanie', l. 26.

§620.   Esch, Arno: ' "Paradise and Calvary": Zu Donnes "Hymne to God, my God, in my Sicknesse", V.21–22', *Anglia*, 78 (1960), 74–77.

§621.   Evans, Gillian R.: 'John Donne and the Augustinian Paradox of Sin', *RES*, n.s., 33 (1982), 1–22.

§622.   Friedman, Donald M.: 'Memory and the Art of Salvation in Donne's Good Friday Poem', *ELR*, 3 (1973), 418–42.

§623.   Gardner, Helen: 'The Religious Poetry of John Donne', in *FKM*, pp. 203–21, and *HG*, pp. 123–36; abridged in *ALC*, pp. 217–26; from §168.

§624.   Goldberg, Jonathan S.: 'Donne's Journey East: Aspects of a Seventeenth-Century Trope', *SP*, 68 (1971), 470–83. Mainly on 'Goodfriday, 1613'.

§625. Grierson, H. J. C.: 'Donne and Lucretius', *TLS*, 5 December 1929 (p. 1032).

§626. Hazo, Samuel: 'Donne's Divine Letter', in *Essays and Studies in Language and Literature*, ed. Herbert H. Petit (Pittsburgh, 1964), pp. 38–43. On 'The Crosse'.

§627. Herbold, Anthony: ' "Seeking Secrets or Poëtiquenesse": Donne's Dialectics in the Divine Poems', *Moderna Språk* (Stockholm), 59 (1965), 277–94.

§628. Hunt, Clay: 'Hymn to God, my God, in my Sickness' ", in §383: Ch. IV.

§629. Klinck, Dennis: 'John Donne's "Knottie Trinitie" ', *Renascence*, 33 (1981), 240–55. See also Lucio P. Ruotolo, *JHI*, 27 (1966), 445–46.

§630. Leigh, David J.: 'Donne's "A Hymne to God the Father": New Dimensions', *SP*, 75 (1978), 84–92.

§631. Lewalski, Barbara K.: 'John Donne: Writing after a Copy of a Metaphorical God', in §73: Ch. VIII.

§632. Low, Anthony: 'John Donne: Liturgy, Meditation, and Song', in his *Love's Architecture: Devotional Modes in Seventeenth-Century English Poetry* (1978), Ch. III.

§633. Malpezzi, Frances M.: 'Christian Poetics in Donne's "Upon the Translation of the Psalmes" ', *Renascence*, 32 (1980), 221–28.

§634. Maxwell, Herbert: 'John Donne's "All Tincture" ', *NQ*, 168 (1935), 104. On 'Resurrection imperfect', l. 15.

§635. Morris, Harry: 'John Donne's Terrifying Pun', *PLL*, 9 (1973), 128–37. On 'More-more'.

§636. Novarr, David: 'Two Flamens: The Poems of Dr. Donne', in §421: Ch. V.

§637. Owens, Robert R.: 'Donne's South-West Discoverie', *NQ*, n.s., 24 (1977), 142–43, and 'The Myth of Arian', *JHI*, 36 (1975), 135–38. Annotations of the 'Hymne to God my God'.

§638. Pollock, John J.: 'Donne's *Lamentations of Jeremy* and the Geneva Bible', *ES*, 55 (1974), 513–15.

§639. Pollock, John J.: 'The "Everlasting Night" in Donne's "Hymne to Christ" ', *ES*, 59 (1978), 119–20.

§640. Pritchard, Allan: 'Donne's Mr. Tilman', *RES*, n.s., 24 (1973), 38–42.

§641. Simpson, Evelyn M.: 'The Text of Donne's *Divine Poems*', *ESEA*, 26 (1940), 88–105.

§642. Smith, A. J.: 'Two Notes on Donne', *MLR*, 51 (1956), 405–7. Cf. Helen Gardner, *ibid.*, 52 (1957), 564–65.

§643. White, Helen C.: 'The Divine Poetry of John Donne', in §316: Ch. V.

13. On the *Holy Sonnets*

§644. Archer, Stanley: 'Meditation and the Structure of Donne's *Holy Sonnets*', in *ALC*, pp. 237–46. Cf. §§81 and 168.

§645. Asals, Heather: 'John Donne and the Grammar of Redemption', *English Studies in Canada*, 5 (1979), 125–39.

§646. Bellette, Anthony F.: ' "Little Worlds Made Cunningly": Significant Form in Donne's *Holy Sonnets* and "Goodfriday, 1613" ', *SP*, 72 (1975), 322–47.

§647. Blanch, Robert J.: 'Fear and Despair in Donne's *Holy Sonnets*', *American Benedictine Review*, 25 (1974), 476–84.

§648. Bloomer, Peggy A.: 'A Re-Examination of Donne's *La Corona*', *Essays in Arts and Sciences* (University of New Haven), 7 (1978), 37–44.

§649. Bond, Ronald B.: 'John Donne and the Problem of "Knowing Faith" ', *Mosaic*, 14 (1981), i, 25–35.

§650. Brower, Reuben: in §333: pp. 24–27, 67–70. On Sonnets VII and XVIII.

§651. Chambers, A. B.: '*La Corona*: Philosophic, Sacred, and Poetic Uses of Time', in *GAS*, pp. 140–72.

§652. Chambers, A. B.: 'The Meaning of "Temple" in Donne's *La Corona*', in *JRR*, pp. 349–52.

§653. Clements, Arthur L.: 'The Paradox of Three-in-One', in *ALC*, pp. 251–55. On Sonnet XIV.

§654. Cornelius, David K.: 'Donne's Holy Sonnet XIV', *Ex*, 24 (1965), 25.

§655. Daniels, Edgar F.: 'Donne's "Crucifying", 8', *Ex*, 30 (1971), 25.

§656. Dubinski, R. R.: 'Donne's *La Corona* and Christ's Mediatorial Office', *RR*, 4 (1980), 203–8.

§657. French, A. L.: 'The Psychopathology of Donne's Holy Sonnets', *CR*, 13 (1970), 111–24.

§658. Gardner, Helen: 'The Interpretation of Donne's Sonnet on the Church', in §168: App. C.

§659. Grant, Patricia: 'Augustinian Spirituality and the *Holy Sonnets* of John Donne', in her *The Transformation of Sin* (Montreal, and Amherst, Mass., 1974), Ch. II.

§660. Gregory, Michael: 'A Theory for Stylistics Exemplified: Donne's Holy Sonnet XIV', *LS*, 7 (1974), 108–18.

§661. Grenander, M. E.: 'Holy Sonnets VIII and XVII', in *JRR*, pp. 324–32.

§662. Handscombe, Richard: 'Donne's Holy Sonnet VI [i.e., X]: A Problem of Plainness', *LS*, 13 (1980), ii, 98–108.

§663. Heist, William W.: 'Donne on Divine Grace: Holy Sonnet XIV', *Papers of the Michigan Academy of Science, Arts, and Letters*, 53 (1968), 311–20.

§664. Höltgen, K. J.: 'Eine Emblemfolge in Donnes Holy Sonnet XIV', *Archiv für das Studium der neueren Sprachen und Literaturen*, 200 (1963), 347–52.

§665. Jackson, Robert S.: 'Donne's Sonnet on Christ's Spouse [XVIII]', in §238: Ch. VIII.

§666. Kerrigan, William: 'The Fearful Accommodations of John Donne', *ELR*, 4 (1974), 337–63. On Sonnets XIV and XVIII.

§667. Linville, Susan: 'Donne's Holy Sonnet IX', *Ex*, 36 (1978), iv, 21–22.

§668. Maurer, Margaret: 'The Circular Argument of Donne's *La Corona*', *SEL*, 22 (1982), 51–68.

§669. Mueller, William R.: 'Donne's Adulterous Female Town', *MLN*, 76 (1961), 312–14. On Sonnet XIV.

§670. Nania, John, and P. J. Klemp: 'John Donne's *La Corona*: A Second Structure', *RR*, n.s., 2 (1978), 49–54.

§671. Nelson, T. G. A.: 'Death, Dung, the Devil, and Worldly Delights: A Metaphysical Conceit in Harington, Donne, and Herbert', *SP*, 76 (1979), 272–87.

§672. O'Connel, Patrick F.: 'The Successive Arrangements of Donne's *Holy Sonnets*', *PQ*, 60 (1981), 323–42.

§673. Parish, John E.: 'The Sonnet's Unity', in *ALC*, pp. 255–59. On Sonnet XIV.

§674. Peterson, Douglas L.: 'John Donne's *Holy Sonnets* and the Anglican Doctrine of Contrition', in *JRR*, pp. 313–23.

§675. Pitts, Arthur W., Jr.: 'Donne's Holy Sonnet VI', *Ex*, 29 (1971), 39. Cf. 31 (1972), 12.

§676. Pollock, John J.: 'Another Donne Pun', *ANQ*, 16 (1978), 83. On Holy Sonnet I, l. 5.

§677. Ricks, Don M.: 'The Westmoreland Manuscript and the Order of Donne's *Holy Sonnets*', *SP*, 63 (1966), 187–95.

§678. Stachniewski, John: 'John Donne: The Despair of the *Holy Sonnets*', *ELH*, 48 (1981), 677–705.

§679. Steele, Thomas J.: 'Donne's Holy Sonnet XIV', *Ex*, 29 (1971), 74.

§680. Steig, Michael: 'Donne's Divine Rapist: Unconscious Fantasy in Holy Sonnet XIV', *University of Hartford Studies in Literature*, 4 (1972), 52–58.

§681. Stull, William L.: ' "Why are not Sonnets made of thee?": A New Context for the *Holy Sonnets* of Donne, Herbert, and Milton', *MP*, 80 (1982), 129–35.

§682. Wall, John N., Jr.: 'Donne's Wit of Redemption: The Drama of Prayer in the *Holy Sonnets*', *SP*, 73 (1976), 189–203.

§683. Zitner, S. P.: 'Rhetoric and Doctrine in Donne's Holy Sonnet IV [i.e., VII]', *RR*, n.s., 3 (1979), 66–76.

14. On the prose works

The ensuing list is necessarily limited, intended solely to guide readers interested in advancing from Donne's poetry to his prose.

§684. Bennett, Roger E.: 'Donne's *Letters to Severall Persons of Honour*', *PMLA*, 56 (1941), 120–40. Also: 'Donne's Letters from the Continent in 1611–12', *PQ*, 19 (1940), 66–78.

§685. Carey, John: 'John Donne's Newsless Letters', *ESEA*, n.s., 34 (1981), 45–61.

§686. Carrithers, Gale H., Jr.: *Donne at Sermons* (Albany, N.Y., 1972).

§687. Chamberlin, John S.: *Increase and Multiply: Arts-of-Discourse Procedure in the Preaching of Donne* (Chapel Hill, 1976).

§688. Coffin, Charles M.: 'Donne's Divinity', *KR*, 16 (1954), 292–98.

§689. Coleridge, Samuel Taylor: 'John Donne', in §210: pp. 163–205, 428–31.

§690. Corthell, Ronald J.: ' "Frendships Sacraments": John Donne's Familiar Letters', *SP*, 78 (1981), 409–25.

§691. Cox, Gerald H., III: 'Donne's *Devotions*: A Meditative Sequence on Repentance', *Harvard Theological Review*, 66 (1973), 331–51.

§692. Doebler, Bettie A.: *The Quickening Seed: Death in the Sermons of John Donne* (Salzburg, 1974).

§693. Harding, D. W.: 'The *Devotions* Now', in *AJS*, Ch. XIV.

§694. Heatherington, Madelon E.: ' "Decency" and "Zeal" in the Sermons of John Donne', *TSLL*, 9 (1967), 307–16.

§695. Henricksen, Bruce: 'Donne's Orthodoxy', *TSLL*, 14 (1972), 5–16, and 'The Unity of Reason and Faith in Donne's Sermons', *PLL*, 11 (1975), 18–30.

§696. Hickey, Robert L.: 'Donne's Art of Preaching', *TSL*, 1 (1956), 65–74.

§697. Husain, Itrat: *The Dogmatic and Mystical Theology of John Donne* (1938).

§698. Korkowski, Eugene: 'Donne's *Ignatius* and Menippean Satire', *SP*, 72 (1975), 419–38.

§699. Mahood, M. M.: 'Donne: The Baroque Preacher', in §258: Ch. V.

§700. Mueller, Janel M.: 'The Exigencies of Experience: Dean Donne's *Devotions upon Emergent Occasions*', *JEGP*, 67 (1968), 1–19.

§701. Mueller, William R.: *John Donne, Preacher* (Princeton, 1962).

§702. Ornstein, Robert: 'Donne, Montaigne, and Natural Law', in *JRR*, pp. 129–41.

§703. Patrides, C. A.: 'The Epistolary Art of the Renaissance: The Biblical Dimension', *PQ*, 60 (1981), 357–67.

§704. Patterson, Annabel: 'Misinterpretable Donne: The Testimony of the Letters', *JDJ*, 1 (1982), 39–53.

§705. Potter, George R.: 'John Donne: Poet to Priest', in *Five Gayley Lectures 1947–1954*, ed. L. B. Bennion and G. R. Potter (Berkeley, 1954), pp. 105–26.

§706. Quinn, Dennis: 'Donne's Christian Eloquence', *ELH*, 27 (1960), 276–97, and 'John Donne's Principles of Christian Exegesis', *JEGP*, 61 (1962), 313–29.

§707. Schleiner, Winfried: *The Imagery of John Donne's Sermons* (Providence, R.I., 1970).

§708. Simpson, Evelyn: *A Study of the Prose Works of John Donne* (Oxford, 1924). Also: 'The Literary Value of Donne's Sermons', in *HG*, pp. 137–51, from §181; and 'Donne's Paradoxes and Problems', in *TS*, Ch. II.

§709. Smith, Don N.: 'The Artistry of John Donne's *Devotions*', *University of Dayton Review*, 10 (1973), i, 3–12.

§710. Stapleton, Laurence: 'John Donne: The Moment of the Sermons', in her *The Elected Circle* (Princeton, 1973), Ch. I.

§711. Stein, Arnold: 'Handling Death: John Donne in Public Meditation', *ELH*, 48 (1981), 496–515.

§712. Sullivan, Ernest W., III: 'The Problem of Text in Familiar Letters', *PBSA*, 75 (1981), 115–26. On Donne's letters.

§713. Warren, Austin: 'The Very Reverend Dr. Donne', *KR*, 16 (1954), 268–77.

§714. Webber, Joan: *Contrary Music: The Prose Style of John Donne* (Madison, 1963).

§715. Williamson, George: 'The Libertine Donne', in §148: Ch. II.

15. On Donne's reputation and influence

On the commemorative and other poems on Donne (see above, Appendix III, pp. 494 ff.), consult Smith (§753) and Sidney Gottlieb's '*Elegies upon the Author*: Defining, Defending, and Surviving Donne', *JDJ*, 2 (1983), 23–28.

§716.   Adams, Robert M.: 'Metaphysical Poets, Ancient and Modern', in his *Strains of Discord* (Ithaca, N.Y., 1958), pp. 105–20. Compares Donne and T. S. Eliot.

§717.   Bachrach, A. G. H.: 'Constantijn Huygens's Acquaintance with Donne', in *Neederlandica manuscripta*, ed. J. P. Gumbert and M. J. M. de Haan (Amsterdam, 1976), pp. 111–17.

§718.   Bald, R. C.: *Donne's Influence in English Literature* (Morpeth, N.S.W., 1932).

§719.   Bollier, E. P.: 'T. S. Eliot and John Donne: A Problem in Criticism', *TSL*, 9 (1959), 103–18.

§720.   Brooks, Cleanth: *Modern Poetry and the Tradition* (Chapel Hill, 1939).

§721.   Bross, Addison C.: 'Alexander Pope's Revisions of John Donne's *Satyres*', *XUS*, 5 (1966), 133–52.

§722.   Bryan, Robert A.: 'John Donne's Poems in Seventeenth-Century Commonplace Books', *ES*, 43 (1962), 170–74.

§723.   Colie, Rosalie L.: 'Constantijn Huygens and the Metaphysical Mode', *Germanic Review*, 34 (1959), 59–73.

§724.   Collmer, Robert G.: 'Donne and Borges', *RLC*, 43 (1969), 219–32.

§725.   Duncan, Joseph E.: *The Revival of Metaphysical Poetry: The History of a Style, 1800 to the Present* (Minneapolis, 1959).

§726.   Eldredge, Frances: 'Further Allusions and Debts to John Donne', *ELH*, 19 (1952), 214–28.

§727.   Eliot, T. S.: 'Donne in our Time', in *TS*, Ch. I.

§728.   Erskine-Hill, Howard: 'Courtiers out of Horace: Donne's *Satyre IV* and Pope's *Fourth Satire of Dr John Donne . . . Versifyed*', in *AJS*, Ch. X.

§729.   Gardner, Helen: 'Musical Settings of Donne's Poems', in §169: App. B.

§730.   Granqvist, Raoul: *The Reputation of John Donne 1779–1873* (Uppsala, 1975).

§731.   Heuer, Hermann: 'Browning und Donne (Hintergründe einer Wortenlehnung)', *Englische Studien*, 72 (1938), 227–44.

§732.   Höltgen, K. J.: 'Unpublished Early Verses "On D^r. Donnes Anatomy" ', *RES*, n.s., 22 (1971), 302–6.

§733.   Hughes, Merritt Y.: 'Kidnapping Donne', in *JRR*, pp. 37–57.

§734.   Jack, Ian: 'Pope and "the Weighty Bullion of Dr. Donne's Satires" ', *PMLA*, 62 (1951), 1009–22.

§735.   Johnson, H. A. T.: ' "Despite Time's Derision": Donne, Hardy, and the 1913 Poems', *The Thomas Hardy Yearbook*, 7 (1977), 7–20.

§736. Keast, William R.: 'Johnson's Criticism of the Metaphysical Poets', in *JRR*, pp. 11–19.

§737. Kermode, Frank: ' "Dissociation of Sensibility": Modern Symbolist Readings of Literary History', in his *Romantic Image* (1957), Ch. VIII; also in *JRR*, pp. 66–82.

§738. Leach, Elsie: 'T. S. Eliot and the School of Donne', *Costerus*, 3 (1972), 163–80.

§739. Long, Ada, and Hugh Maclean: ' "Deare Ben", "Great Donne", and "my Celia": The Wit of Carew's Poetry', *SEL*, 18 (1978), 75–94. Examines *inter alia* Carew's elegy on Donne.

§740. MacColl, Alan: 'The Circulation of Donne's Poems in Manuscript', in *AJS*, Ch. II.

§741. Meurs, J. C. van: 'John Donne in the Twentieth Century', *Levende Talen* (Groningen), 1970, pp. 545–55.

§742. Miles, Josephine: 'The Language of the Donne Tradition', in her *Eras and Modes in English Poetry*, 2nd rev. ed. (Berkeley, 1964), Ch. II. Also: 'Twentieth-Century Donne', in §262: Ch. X.

§743. Milgate, Wesley: 'The Early References to John Donne', *NQ*, 195 (1950), 229–31, 246–47, 290–92, 381–83.

§744. Morris, Brian: ' "Not, Siren-like, to Tempt": Donne and the Composers', in *AJS*, Ch. VIII.

§745. Nethercot, Arthur H.: three studies of the reputation of the 'metaphysical' poets from the seventeenth to the early nineteenth centuries: *JEGP*, 23 (1924), 173–98; *PQ*, 4 (1925), 161–79; and *SP*, 22 (1925), 81–132. Also: 'The Term "Metaphysical Poetry" before Johnson', *MLN*, 37 (1922), 11–17, and 'The Reputation of John Donne as Metrist', *SR*, 30 (1922), 463–74.

§746. Novarr, David: *The Making of Walton's 'Lives'* (Ithaca, N.Y., 1958), Part I. The best account of Walton's oft-revised *Life* of Donne (1640–75): §313.

§747. O'Connor, William van: 'The Influence of the Metaphysicals', in his *Sense and Sensibility in Modern Poetry* (Chicago, 1948), Ch. VI.

§748. Richards, Michael R.: 'The Romantic Critics and John Donne', in *Romanticism, Modernism, Postmodernism*, ed. Harry R. Garvin, being *BR*, 25 (1980), ii, 40–51.

§749. Shafer, Aileen: 'Eliot Re-Donne: The Prufrockian Spheres', *Yeats Eliot Review*, 5 (1978), ii, 39–43.

§750. Sharp, Robert L.: *From Donne to Dryden: The Revolt against Metaphysical Poetry* (Chapel Hill, 1940).

§751. Sharrock, Roger: 'Wit, Passion, and Ideal Love: Reflections on the Cycle of Donne's Reputation', in *PAF*, pp. 33–56.

§752. Smith, A. J.: 'Donne's Reputation', in *AJS*, Ch. I.

§753. Smith, A. J. (ed.): *John Donne: The Critical Heritage* (1975).

§754. Sparrow, John: 'George Herbert and John Donne among the Moravians', in Martha W. England and John Sparrow, *Hymns Unbidden: Donne . . . and the Hymnographers* (1966), pp. 1–28.

§755. Summers, Joseph H.: *The Heirs of Donne and Jonson* (1970).

§756. Tillotson, Kathleen: 'Donne's Poetry in the Nineteenth Century', in *JRR*, pp. 20–33.

§757. Williams, Aubrey L.: 'What Pope did to Donne', in *A Provision of Human Nature*, ed. Donald Kay (University, Ala., 1977), pp. 111–19.

§758. Williamson, George: *The Donne Tradition: A Study in English Poetry from Donne to the Death of Cowley* (Cambridge, Mass., 1930). Also: 'Donne and the Poetry of Today', in *TS*, Ch. VII.

Index of Titles

Index of First Lines